ON THE RAILS
AROUND
BRITAIN
AND IRELAND

Day trips and holidays by train

Edited by Neil Wenborn

A Thomas Cook Touring Handbook

Published by Thomas Cook Publishing
The Thomas Cook Group Ltd
PO Box 227, Peterborough PE3 8BQ
United Kingdom

ISBN 0 906273 54 4

British Library Cataloguing in Publication Data. A
catalogue record for this book is available from
the British Library.

Managing Editor: Stephen York
Project Editor: Giovanna Battiston
Map and Timetable Editor: Bernard Horton
Additional rail text: David Gunning
Additional rail research: Hester Woodliffe
Cover design by Greene Moore Lowenhoff
Cover illustration by Michael Benallack-Hart
Text typeset in Frutiger using Advent 3B2
Maps and diagrams created using GST
  Designworks
Printed in Great Britain by Bell & Bain Ltd,
  Glasgow

The Writing Team

Book Editor: **Neil Wenborn**
England, Scotland and Wales:
Written by **Katy Carter, Ruth Wallis**
Tourist Information supplied by
**The British Tourist Authority, Information
Services Unit**
Researched for the British Tourist Authority by
Mary Lammer and Elizabeth Oliphant
Northern Ireland and the Republic of Ireland:
Researched and written by
Ruth and Eric Bailey

Acknowledgements
The authors and publishers would like to thank
the following people and organisations for their
assistance during the preparation of this book:
Tegwen Jackson, British Rail International,
London; Cyril Ferris, Irish Rail; Derek Town-
send, Thomas Cook Holidays, David Taylor,
Robert Gordon University, Aberdeen; and last
but not least Lynn Sugars, Julie Burton and
colleagues at the British Tourist Authority, as
well as the staff of all the Tourist Information
Centres of England, Scotland and Wales who
contributed information in our research.

CONTENTS

Routes and Cities – Britain

To find a town not shown here, look it up in the Index, pp. 349–351. Routes are listed in the direction in which they are described in the book and, where necessary as a reminder, again in the reverse direction, in *italic* type. For example, the route from Birmingham to Bristol is also shown under BRISTOL as *Bristol to Birmingham.*

CONTENTS

Routes and Cities – Ireland

Reference Section

INTRODUCTION

Despite the cutbacks that have taken place since the Second World War, Britain still possesses one of the richest and densest rail networks in the world. A small country, with hundreds of miles of track, it can boast that virtually everything the tourist or holidaymaker might want to see is either on or within easy reach of a rail route. For the independent traveller, rail remains one of the best ways of seeing the beautiful and varied countryside and the many fascinating and historic sights that Britain and Ireland have to offer. Whether you are a backpacker on a tight budget or a mature holidaymaker looking for a way of covering large distances in comfort, this book is designed to help you plan your trip and to provide you with the information you need to make it a smooth and memorable one.

The book is built around a series of rail routes designed to connect and give access to hundreds of towns and other places of interest. It provides practical information to help ensure that you remain in control of your own holiday, including details of rail and other public transport services, together with advice and information on tourist offices, sightseeing, getting around, accommodation, entertainment and a great deal more.

On the Rails Around Britain and Ireland has been exhaustively researched to provide you with the essential planning aid and travelling companion for your trip. However, things do change, and we would be most grateful if you could use the Reader Survey on p. 347 to notify us of any errors you may find – for which we apologise in advance – or with suggestions as to how we might increase the usefulness of the next edition. In the meantime, we hope the book will help you to get the most out of your holiday in Great Britain and Ireland.

HOW TO USE THIS BOOK

ROUTES AND CITIES

The book describes 40 **recommended routes**, chosen to provide a practical yet flexible framework for making the most of a rail-based holiday. The routes are designed to take you through as many interesting places as possible, thus giving you the opportunity to stop off for a visit (of hours or days) or to pass straight through.

The book also gives detailed descriptions of 28 **key cities**, chosen for their tourist convenience as railheads and centres of public transport networks, as well as for their intrinsic interest. Every route begins in a key city, and most also end in one. Some key cities, such as London, Birmingham and Manchester, form the starting-point of a number of routes, thus enabling you to use one city as a base for exploration of a number of different areas if you so choose. A chapter is devoted to each route and each key city, and the chapters are arranged alphabetically. Routes beginning in the same key city thus follow the chapter devoted to that city.

In addition to the key cities, more than 150 **smaller cities and towns** are described along the lines of the routes on which they lie, together with a wide range of places of interest. To avoid repetition, each route and each place is described once only, but every route can be taken in either direction – for example, the London to York route can easily be followed by those travelling from York to London.

WITHIN EACH ROUTE

 Fast Track

This describes the quickest and most direct journey between the beginning and end of each route – not necessarily in the same direction as the On Track.

 On Track

This introduces the full route, with recommended stops, and details of train frequencies, approximate schedules and journey times between them. Details are deliberately general so that they will not date too fast but they will give you a clear idea of how convenient any section of the journey will be.

ETT tables at the beginning of the **TRAINS** section refer to the appropriate table numbers in the *Thomas Cook European Timetable* (or the *Thomas Cook Timetable of Britain, France and Benelux*, which gives the same numbers). These tables will give you specific and up-to-date information on train times.

The route diagrams sum up the train information in an at-a-glance graphic form. White arrows show Side Tracks, black arrows show interconnected routes.

Recommended Stops

Recommended stops along each route are described in varying detail, depending on the nature of the place concerned. They represent the places of greatest interest along the route, but are not intended as comprehensive guides to tourist attractions in the area. Nor, obviously, do you have to stop at every town we mention; by consulting the timetable and local information, you may be able to find faster trains which will take you from town A to town C without stopping in town B.

Side Tracks from . . .

You will frequently find this heading after one or more of the stops on a recommended route. It is used to indicate a town, or occasionally a smaller place of interest, which is accessible by rail or other public transport from the stop concerned and which you may wish to visit. Side tracks sometimes start from places along a route that are not intrinsically of tourist interest (for example railway junctions), and such places are therefore not described in detail.

THE REST OF THE BOOK

Travel Essentials (p. 16) is an alphabetical section of general advice for the traveller about such matters as accommodation; **Travelling by Train** (p. 28) takes a more detailed look at how the British and Irish rail network works, with information on everything from sleeping cars to rail passes and how to buy them. The **Themed Itineraries** (p. 36) are designed to show the potential of the recommended routes to help you explore Great Britain and Ireland.

The quickest way to find information on any place, large or small, and on general topics, is to look it up in the **Index** (pp. 349–651). The easiest way to look up a route is to consult the **Rail Route Maps** overleaf. Alternatively, the **Contents** list (p. 3) contains an alphabetical listing of all the key cities and the routes from and to them. Information is also given on **Through Routes** (p. 10) for those wishing to travel quickly between major cities, and on the main gateway airports and their public transport connections (**Airport Connections**, p. 11). For those wishing to travel between Britain and Ireland by ferry or to take trips onto the Continent of Europe, details of **Sea Crossings** are given on pp. 12–13. Finally, at the end of the book you can find further information on **Private Railways in Britain and Ireland** (p. 339) and on **Special Trains** (p. 341).

Abbreviations used in the book			
Ave	Avenue	Blvd	Boulevard
BR	British Rail	hr(s)	hour(s)
min(s)	minute(s)	Rd	Road
Sq.	Square	St	Street
tel:	telephone		

Jan, Feb are January, February, etc.
Sun, Mon are Sunday, Monday, etc

TIC	Tourist Information Centre.

Abbreviations used within the TIC details are:

AR	Advance reservations taken
BABA	Book a Bed Ahead scheme
DP	Disabled persons (services)
GT	Guided tours booked
SHS	Sympathetic Hearing Scheme

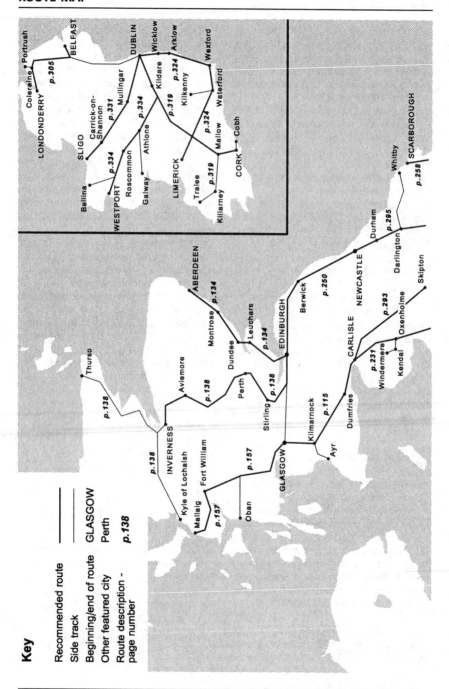

Key

Recommended route ——

Side track

Beginning/end of route **GLASGOW**

Other featured city Perth

Route description - **p.138**
page number

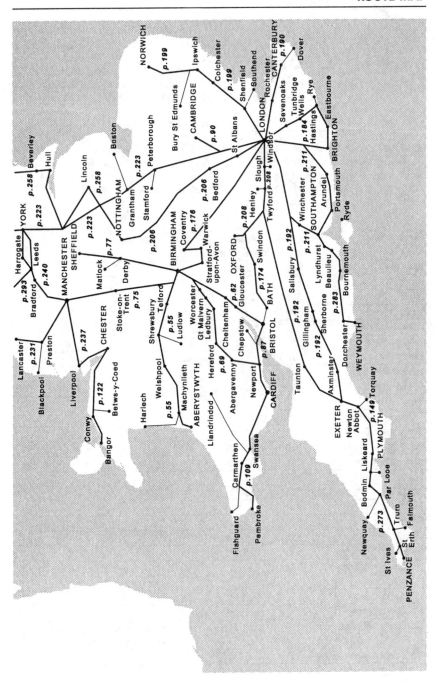

THROUGH ROUTES

The following table shows a selection of possible longer 'through routes', as an aid to journey planning, with approximate summer frequencies and journey times. All these through routes may also be taken in the reverse direction to that shown but number of trains per day may differ. Not all trains run on Saturdays. Sunday services may differ considerably.

Some travellers wish to make their way as quickly as possible to a chosen city to begin their more leisurely travel from that point. This will often mean going through two or more consecutive routes in this book without stopping.

Always consult the latest issue of the Thomas Cook European Timetable (ETT), or the Thomas Cook Timetable of Britain, France and Benelux (see p. 5), which give up-to-date schedules for these and many other long-distance trains.

Through route	ETT table number	Approx journey time	Trains per day	Notes
London–Cardiff	530	2 hrs	19	
London–Edinburgh	570	4–4½ hrs	15	
London–Glasgow	550	5–6 hrs	7	
London–Leeds	570	2–2½ hrs	18	
London–Liverpool	550	2 hr 45 mins	14	
London–Manchester	550	2½ hrs	16	
London–Newcastle	570	3 hrs	23	
London–Plymouth	510	3½ hrs	12	
Belfast–Dublin	630	2–2½ hrs	6	
Birmingham–Edinburgh	550	5 hrs	7	
Birmingham–Newcastle	520	3½ hrs	7	
Birmingham–Plymouth	520	4 hrs	9	
Birmingham–Southampton	520	3 hrs	8	
Birmingham–York	520	2½ hrs	11	
Bristol–Newcastle	520	5 hrs	6	
Bristol–Plymouth	510	2¼ hrs	14	
Bristol–Southampton	532	2 hrs	17	
Bristol–York	520	4 hrs	8	
Cardiff–Manchester	535	3¼ hrs	11	
Cardiff–Southampton	532	2½ hrs	16	
Edinburgh–Manchester	550	4 hrs	4	Other services are available by changing trains at Preston
Edinburgh–York	570	2½ hrs	18	
Manchester–York	551	1½ hrs	32	
Manchester–Southampton	520	5 hrs	4	Other services are available by changing trains at Birmingham
Manchester–Newcastle	551	3 hrs	9	

AIRPORT CONNECTIONS

The following are brief details of bus/train services to and from principal airports in the UK and the Irish Republic. Frequency where shown applies between 0630 and 1800. Outside these hours and usually all day on Sundays the frequency may be reduced.

Rail information for England and Scotland is subject to change due to the on-going privatisation of British Rail. At press date neither the operators of the services nor a contact telephone number can be stated with certainty.

BELFAST INTERNATIONAL

Airbus 300 from city centre (Europa Centre, Glengall Street Stand 20), calling at Oxford Street Bus Station, Stand 22) and Belfast Central Rail Station. Journey time: 30–40 mins. Frequency: half-hourly. Operator: Ulsterbus *tel: (01232) 352201.* Fare: £3.50.

BIRMINGHAM INTERNATIONAL

Frequent weekday train service from Birmingham New Street to adjacent rail station. Journey time: 10–15 mins. Fare: £1.95. Long distance services from many parts of the country.

Also bus service 900 from St Martin's Circus, Queensway (close to New Street Station). Journey time: 30 mins. Frequency: 20 mins. Operator: West Midlands Travel: *tel: (0121) 200 2700.* Fare: £1.17 (£0.82 off-peak).

DUBLIN

Airlink bus from Dublin Heuston Station, calling at Busaras (bus station) stand 14. Journey time: 40 mins from Heuston, 30 mins from Busaras.

Frequency: 20–30 mins. Operator: Dublin Bus *tel: (353 1) 703 3022.* Fare: IR£ 2.50/2.80.

GLASGOW

Bus service 500 from Buchanan Bus Station. Journey time: 25 mins. Frequency: every 20 mins. Operator: Scottish City Link *tel: (0141) 332 9191.* Fare: £2.00 single, £3.50 return.

LONDON GATWICK

Gatwick Express train service from London Victoria to adjacent rail station. Journey time: 30 mins (45 in evenings and at night). Frequency: 15 mins. Fare: £8.90 single, £16.90 return.

LONDON HEATHROW

Frequent Piccadilly Line underground train from Central London direct to airport terminal building. Journey time: 1 hr from Kings Cross. Operator: London Underground Limited (0171) 222 1234. Fare: £3.10 single, £6.20 return.

LONDON STANSTED

Direct train service from London Liverpool Street and Tottenham Hale to airport terminal building. Journey time: 30 mins. Frequency: half-hourly. Fare: £10.80 single, £21.60 return.

MANCHESTER

Frequent train service from Manchester Piccadilly station direct to airport terminal building. Journey time: 15–20 mins. Fare: £2.30 single, £4.60 return. Also through services from many north-west and north-east stations.

SHANNON

Bus service from Limerick Bus station. Numbers vary as most are longer distance services from many parts of Ireland. Journey time: 35 mins. Frequency: twice per hour at irregular intervals. Operator: Bus Éireann *tel: (061) 313333.*

SEA CROSSINGS

SEA CROSSINGS

These pages list ferries operating between Britain and Ireland, and between Britain and Ireland and France and the Low Countries, at the time of going to press. Frequencies and journey times from port to port are those of the summer season. Ferries within Britain, e.g. to the Scottish Islands, are described in the appropriate route chapters.

UK–IRELAND

From . . . To	No. of Sailings	Journey Time	Operating Company	Tel. for further details
CAIRNRYAN to . . .				
Larne	5 per day	2¼ hrs	P. & O. European Ferries	tel: (01304) 203388
FISHGUARD to . . .				
Rosslare	2 per day	3½ hrs	Stena Sealink	tel: (01233) 647047
Rosslare (catamaran)	4 per day	2 hrs	Stena Sealink	tel: (01233) 647047
HOLYHEAD to . . .				
Dublin	2 per day	4 hrs	Irish Ferries	tel: (0151) 227 3131
Dun Laoghaire	4 per day	3½ hrs	Stena Sealink	tel: (01233) 647047
Dun Laoghaire (catamaran)	4 per day	2 hrs	Stena Sealink	tel: (01233) 647047
PEMBROKE to . . .				
Rosslare	2 per day	4¼ hrs	Irish Ferries	tel: (0151) 227 3131
STRANRAER to . . .				
Larne	6 per day	2½ hrs	Stena Sealink	tel: (01233) 647047
Belfast	4 per day	1½ hrs	Hoverspeed	tel: (01304) 240241
SWANSEA to . . .				
Cork	1 per day	10 hrs	Swansea Cork Ferries	tel: (01792) 456116

UK–FRANCE

Since the opening of the Channel Tunnel in November 1994 (see p. 14) there has been a thorough reorganisation of the ferry services linking Britain and Ireland to Europe. On short routes, companies have introduced bigger and faster ships to increase car-carrying capacity to compete with Le Shuttle; for longer routes, they have gone into the 'mini cruise' aspects of sea travel, concentrating on quality and convenience. The next few years could see further changes.

From . . . To	No. of Sailings	Journey Time	Operating Company	Tel. for further details
PLYMOUTH to . . .				
Roscoff	1 per day	6 hrs	Brittany Ferries	tel: (01752) 221321
PORTSMOUTH to . . .				
St Malo	1 per day	9 hrs	Brittany Ferries	tel: (01752) 221321

From . . . To	No. of Sailings	Journey Time	Operating Company	Tel. for further details
PORTSMOUTH to . . .				
Ouistreham	2 per day	6 hrs	Brittany Ferries	*tel: (01752) 221321*
Le Havre	3 per day	6 hrs	P&O European Ferries	*tel: (01304) 203388*
Cherbourg	4 per day	5 hrs	P&O European Ferries	*tel: (01304) 203388*
POOLE to . . .				
St Malo	4 per week	8 hrs	Brittany Ferries	*tel: (01752) 221321*
Cherbourg	2 per day	4¼ hrs	Truckline	*tel: (01752 221321*
CORK to . . .				
Roscoff	2 per week	14 hrs	Brittany Ferries	*tel: (01752) 221321*
St Malo	1 per week	18 hrs	Brittany Ferries	*tel: (01752) 221321*
Cherbourg	1 per week	20 hrs	Irish Ferries	*tel: (01) 855 2222*
Le Havre	1 per week	20 hrs	Irish Ferries	*tel: (01) 855 2222*
DOVER to . . .				
Calais (catamaran)	12 per day	35 mins	Hoverspeed	*tel: (01304) 240241*
Calais	25 per day	75 mins	P&O European Ferries	*tel: (01304) 203388*
Calais	25 per day	1½ hrs	Stena Sealink	*tel: (01233) 647047*
FOLKESTONE to . . .				
Boulogne	6 per day	55 mins	Hoverspeed	*tel: (01304) 240241*
ROSSLARE to . . .				
Cherbourg	2 per week	17 hrs	Irish Ferries	*tel: (01) 855 2222*
Le Havre	3 per week	21 hrs	Irish Ferries	*tel: (01) 855 2222*
RAMSGATE to . . .				
Dunkerque	5 per day	2½ hrs	Sally Ferries	*tel: (01843) 595522*
NEWHAVEN to . . .				
Dieppe (ship)	4 per day	4 hrs	Stena Sealink	*tel: (01233) 647047*
Dieppe (catarmaran)	4 per day	2 hrs	Stena Sealink	*tel: (01233) 647047*
SOUTHAMPTON to . . .				
Cherbourg	2 per day	5 hrs	Stena Sealink	*tel: (01233) 647047*

UK–BELGIUM/NETHERLANDS

From . . . To	No. of Sailings	Journey Time	Operating Company	Tel. for further details
HULL to . . .				
Rotterdam Europoort	daily	13 hrs	North Sea Ferries	*tel: (01482) 377177*
Zeebrugge	daily	13 hrs	North Sea Ferries	*tel: (01482) 377177*
RAMSGATE to . . .				
Oostende (ship)	5 per day	4 hrs	Oostende Lines	*tel: (01843) 595522*
Oostende (jetfoil)	5 per day	1½ hrs	Oostende Lines	*tel: (01843) 595522*
FELIXSTOWE to . . .				
Zeebrugge	2 per day	5½ hrs	P. & O. European Ferries	*tel: (01304) 203388*
HARWICH to . . .				
Hoek van Holland	2 per day	7 hrs	Stena Sealink	*tel: (01233) 647047*

The Channel Tunnel

The idea of a cross-Channel tunnel was first proposed as long ago as 1802, but it was 1881 before anybody made a serious attempt to build one. The British stopped this, and later efforts, for fear of military invasion, and the project only got the green light in 1985. This extraordinary feat of engineering actually consists of three tunnels (one in each direction for trains, and one in the centre for services and safety), each one 50 km long. Opened by Queen Elizabeth II and President Mitterand on 6 May 1994, Eurostar rail services began in Autumn 1994 and the shuttle car-carrying service started at Christmas of the same year.

Le Shuttle

Running from Cheriton, near Folkestone, to Coquelles, at Calais, this is the car transporter service, with trains eventually leaving every 15 mins throughout the day. The aim is a maximum journey time of 1 hr from terminal to terminal, including waiting, loading and unloading. Both UK and French customs and immigration are passed before boarding. The carriages have toilet facilities and room to stand and walk about, but no refreshments or seats – passengers remain in or near their car for the duration of the crossing. Book in advance or on arrival at the terminal.

Passenger Services

Eurostar day trains concentrate on two routes. **London (Waterloo)–Paris (Nord)** takes 3 hrs (2 hrs 30 mins when the British rail link to the channel opens around the year 2000). **London (Waterloo)–Lille (Europe)–Brussels (Midi/Zuid)** takes 3 hrs 15 mins (2 hrs 40 mins after the completion of the new Belgian high-speed link; 2 hrs 10 mins by 2000). Additional trains will run at peak demand periods. Connections can be made at Brussels for trains to Amsterdam, Germany etc. and at Lille for TGVs to the rest of France.

The service is on new trains with first- and standard-class accommodation. All seats have personal foot rests, reading lights and magazine racks. All first-class seats recline. There are also family compartments with foldaway tables and baby-changing facilities. First-class tickets include a full meal (served at your seat), and in the rest of the train there will be two bar-buffet coaches and a trolley service. Passengers clear customs before boarding and immigration checks are carried out on board. There are no duty-free sales.

Beyond London and Overnight

It will not be possible to catch a train from outside London to go through the tunnel before 1996. Until then, special connecting services are being introduced between the various UK regions and London Waterloo (as well as the usual Inter-City trains to other London stations). When finally in place, **Beyond London day services** will run south from Edinburgh, via Newcastle and York (amongst other stops); and from Manchester, via Birmingham (and several other stops) to Brussels, Lille and Paris, and vice versa. **Overnight services from London** will include trains to Amsterdam (via Rotterdam, The Hague); Dortmund (via Cologne, Dusseldorf); and Frankfurt (via Bonn, Koblenz). **Beyond London overnight services** will include trains from Glasgow to Paris and Brussels, Swansea to Paris and Plymouth to Brussels (the last two interconnecting in Bristol).

Overnight trains will be made up of reclining seats, deluxe sleepers with en-suite shower and toilet, and standard sleepers, with en-suite toilet. All cabins will have a private basin, tea and coffee-making facilities. There will be a light refreshment service.

A new international tickets and reservation system, based at Lille Europe, will be connected by computer to allow ticketing through many travel agents and most UK stations, for the Eurostar and most other major European routes.

TRAVEL ESSENTIALS

The following is an alphabetical listing of helpful hints for overseas visitors planning a holiday around Britain and Ireland by rail.

Accommodation

Finding a Room

Generally, tourist accommodation is plentiful, and you should be able to choose whatever suits your budget, from top-class hotels to the simplest bed-and-breakfast (b. & b.). Boards advertising the latter are to be seen everywhere. This very British institution consists of rooms offered by private individuals in their own homes. Though quality varies, it can be amazingly good value, particularly as you travel further away from London, while the welcome tends to be much more personal and informal than a hotel. Similar accommodation is offered in guest-houses, farmhouses and inns; with all these types of rooms, evening meals may also be available.

If you haven't prebooked, your best starting point on arrival at your destination will normally be the Tourist Information Centre (TIC); details of the whereabouts of these offices are given throughout the text. These almost always have either free or inexpensive listings of accommodation on offer, and for a small fee they will book a room for you within your stated price range. Remember that prices are often quoted per person, even for a double room. Many TICS have particular busy times of day – check in the text for details. However, it is a good idea to make advance bookings, especially for your first few nights, or if you are heading for the major tourist destinations. Be warned that in July and August there will be long queues to book accommodation at TICs, particularly those in London, Edinburgh, Cambridge and Stratford,

Background

These small islands offer an exhilarating diversity of landscape, architecture, and culture, which can make even a short trip an extraordinarily rich experience. To begin with some simple political facts, there are five separate countries: England, Scotland, Wales, and Northern Ireland – which together make up the United Kingdom – and the Republic of Ireland (Southern Ireland, Eire), which broke away from Britain politically in 1921. Though English is the predominant language, Welsh is widely spoken in Wales (road-signs are bilingual) and Gaelic in parts of Scotland and Ireland; even where English is spoken, each part of Britain has its own dialect, so that a trained ear can instantly 'place' the speaker as soon as he or she begins to talk. There are political tensions: the legacy of the centuries-old Irish problem have so far proved intractable to politicians, and there are strong Welsh and Scottish nationalist movements. But for the visitor, these simply add to the perception of a land of startling contrasts; and rail travellers can, by and large, be assured of a friendly welcome wherever they go.

and unless you arrive before 1400 you are unlikely to find a bed. Prebooking is best done, if you are coming from outside the country, when you purchase your ticket. There are also many published listings, including guides published by the Irish Tourist Board and Regional Tourist Boards in Britain or you can obtain listings from relevant TICs in advance and book direct. Many TICs offer the invaluable 'book-a-bed-ahead' service (indicated in the text by BABA), whereby for a small fee they will reserve you a room at your next port of call, subject to there being a vacancy within your price range. This can take much of the anxiety out of late afternoon arrivals, and will give you more time to explore.

Hotel chains are well represented in Britain,

Hotel Chains

The following abbreviations have been used in this book to denote the chain to which a hotel belongs.

Andrew Weir	*AW*	Granada	*Gr*	Minotels	*Mn*
Best Western	*BW*	Great Southern Hotels	*GS*	MinOtels Ireland Hotels	*MO*
Business and Leisure Ireland	*BL*	Hatton Group	*HG*	Moat House	*MH*
Butterfly	*BU*	Hilton	*Hn*	Mount Charlotte Thistle	*MC*
Campanile	*Ca*	Holiday Inn	*Ho*	Novotel	*No*
Choice	*Ch*	Holidays Ireland Hotels	*HH*	Premier Lodge	*PL*
Coast and Country Hotels	*CC*	Hostelling International		Principal	*Pr*
Consort	*Co*	(see below)	*HI*	Ramada	*Ra*
Copthorne	*Cp*	Ibis	*Ib*	Resort	*Re*
De Vere	*DV*	Inter-Continental	*IC*	Ryan Hotel Group	*RH*
Doyle Hotel Groupe	*DH*	Jarvis	*Ja*	Scandic Crown	*SC*
Fitzpatrick Hotel Group	*Fk*	Jurys Hotel Group	*Ju*	Sheraton	*Sh*
Forte Crest	*FC*	Lyric	*Ly*	Stakis	*St*
Forte Grand	*FG*	Manor House Hotels	*MN*	Swallow	*Sw*
Forte Post House	*FP*	Marriott	*Ma*	Travel Inns	*TI*
Friendly	*Fr*	Metropole	*Mp*	Travelodge	*Tl*

and though they are more expensive may suit many travellers by offering the security of consistent standards as well as central reservations. We have indicated in the text which chains are represented in the major destinations by means of initials under the 'Accommodation' heading, e.g. *FP, MH* means that the town has Forte Post House and Moat House properties (the initials used are explained in the box opposite). Further details can be obtained from the chain's central reservation phone number in your country, or through a travel agent.

Hostelling International (HI)

For those on a tight budget, whatever their age, taking out membership of HI (the new name of the International Youth Hostel Federation) is highly recommended. Those who recall barrack-like dormitories endured on long-ago school trips need not quake: many hostels have been refurbished and, though still predominantly aimed at young, single travellers, the HI imposes no age limit and caters for families. Some (usually the more remote) still do impose curfews and chores, but kitchen and laundry facilities can be excellent; some large hostels offer hot evening meals, and besides camping, the accommodation is usually the cheapest available. There are 400 or so hostels in Britain and Ireland affiliated to HI – look for the HI initials on the YHA (Youth Hostel Association) symbol. Membership for those over/under 18 is: A$40/free (Australia); C$25/12 (Canada); NZ$24 plus $10 joining fee (New Zealand); £9/3 (UK); $25/12 (USA). A directory *Budget Accommodation You Can Trust* (£6.99), which lists addresses, contact numbers, locations and facilities of all member associations is available on joining or from bookshops.

Though hostels in quieter places tend to close in the daytime, in large cities they remain open 24 hours. Booking well in advance is sensible, almost essential in summer. If you haven't prebooked, check on arrival how long you can stay, as some hostels impose a three-day limit at peak times. For information, to join, and to book accommodation: Australia *tel: (02) 261 1111*; Canada *tel: (0800) 663 5777*; New Zealand *tel: (09) 379 4224*; UK *tel: (0171) 836 1036*; USA *tel: (0202) 783 6161*.

In Ireland, holiday hostel accommodation is offered by several other organisations, none of which requires membership: further details are available from the Irish Tourist Board. There are also independent hostels in Scotland; the Scottish Tourist Board produces a *Youth Accommodation* guide.

Wherever accommodation details are given

in this book, the nearest hostels have been included with their locations. There may also be hostels in towns we have covered in less detail, so it's worth checking in the handbook.

Camping

If you are prepared to carry your own equipment, this is the cheapest option; camp sites are plentiful in both Britain and Ireland, and the local TIC supplies lists. The main drawback for rail travellers is that campsites tend to be some way out of town; details are given in the text under 'Accommodation'. For more information on camping in Britain in general, the British Tourist Authority publishes a free booklet *Camping and Caravanning in Britain*, and the Irish Tourist Board also publishes a listing.

Self-Catering

In Britain there is a great range of self-catering facilities, from the most luxurious to the primitive. There is plenty of accommodation both in towns (convenient for rail travellers), and in more rural locations. Advance booking is the norm for this type of accommodation, and is usually by the week (though short breaks are sometimes available). TICs have listings and there are many published guides.

Larger Groups

If you are travelling in a group, Budget Select is a non-commission agency which can book a variety of budget accommodation in Britain and Ireland, including accommodation in university halls of residence during student vacations: *22a Fishergate, York YO1 4AB; tel: (01904) 610070.* You can also write direct to the British Universities Accommodation Consortium, *PO Box 956, University Park, Nottingham NG7 2RD; tel. (01602) 504571.*

Bicycles

Cycling in the larger cities may be hair-raising (especially if you are not used to driving on the left), but there are many quieter, rural areas where bicycles offer one of the best methods of exploring locally. Many books about touring by bike are available and TICs usually have information about bike rental, good touring routes, and special cycle paths. The Cyclists' Touring Club (*tel: (01483) 417217*) can provide information, including a list of rental firms; for the Republic of Ireland, the Irish Tourist Board has a list of locations of Raleigh 'Rent-a-Bike' dealers.

The more adventurous can hire a bike from one destination and take it on the train (British Rail allows bikes to be carried in the guard's van of most trains for a fee of £3 per single journey). Numbers are restricted due to limited luggage space, so it is wise to obtain a free reservation in advance. Bikes can be taken free on all ferries from Britain and Ireland. *The Rail Traveller's Guide to Biking by Train* is available at larger

---

Building Styles

Britain and Ireland have a legacy of historic buildings and monuments second to none. Here are some brief definitions of some of the terms used in this book to describe periods and styles of building. Many published guides will provide more detail.

Anglo-Saxon: dating from the period after the Roman occupation of Britain until the Norman Conquest (c. AD650–1066).

Classical/Baroque: style of the 17th and 18th centuries, characterised by formal symmetry and inspired by the architecture of ancient Greece and Rome.

Edwardian: early 20th-century period, recognisable by its revival of vernacular or countryside styles.

Georgian: a development of Classical style, characterised by elegance and symmetry (1760–1840).

Gothic: architecture of the later Middle Ages, c.1180–1500, characterised by larger, higher and lighter buildings than the preceding Norman style, and by pointed arches. Loosely divided into three phases, successively more elaborate in character: Early English (1190–1300), Decorated (1280–1377), and Perpendicular (1370–1500).

---

stations. If you choose to combine bike and rail travel in this way, you will, of course, have to travel very light; and even if just hiring a bike for one day, invest in something waterproof, and don't be fooled by morning sunshine into leaving it behind.

Buses

Buses offer an excellent means of reaching areas that the railways do not, though in many parts of the countryside services are very poor, and not to be relied upon. Since bus services were 'deregulated' in the 1980s, many towns and cities have a bewildering array of different buses, both double and single decker, which may or may not operate from a central bus station. Only some display their destinations clearly. The text of this book gives details of bus numbers and companies operating to the attractions listed, but you would do best to check the service you require, and where to catch it, at the TIC. Most buses are 'driver only': you pay the driver when you board (try to have plenty of change), and press a button to ring the bell when you want the bus to halt at the next stop.

There is also an efficient network of inter-city coaches, run mainly by National Express *tel: (0171) 730 0202* in Britain; and by Bus Eireann in the Republic of Ireland *tel: (01) 836 6222* (see bus routes in Ireland p. 338).

Children

Travelling with young children by train has several advantages over car travel, especially on long distance journeys: they have more space and freedom to do what they like (within reasonable limits), while you do not have to develop Houdini-like qualities retrieving vital toys from the floor behind you without removing your seat belt. It can also be a nightmare, principally getting on and off without leaving either children or baggage behind, and keeping them occupied. Seasoned travellers, while travelling as light as possible, will have a survival pack full of age-appropriate activities, including a few surprise items, to stave off the ominous signs of boredom, as well as a carefully rationed supply of snacks. Older children might be interested in keeping a travel diary, and collecting tickets and other memorabilia in a scrapbook. Up to two children under five can travel free with any fare-paying passenger, while children aged 5–15 travel at half the full price; family railcards are available to reduce the cost if you are doing plenty of travelling.

Many tourist destinations in Britain, as well as seaside resorts, are finally acknowledging the existence of young children, something at which the British are traditionally very bad, and providing children's menus, high chairs, nappy changing facilities, and the like. Children are not allowed in the bar area of pubs, though many pubs now actively encourage their presence with family restaurants and indoor and outdoor playgrounds. Many hotels offer baby-sitting services, but check that what is on offer is acceptable to you – it may only mean listening in occasionally on the hotel telephone. There are several guidebooks available from bookshops recommending attractions, restaurants and hotels where children are welcome, and local guides are often available from newsagents. Most attractions offer substantial discounts (usually 50%) for children.

Climate

The British climate is temperate: no one should expect more than the occasional searingly hot day, but equally there are rarely extremes of cold. It is also notoriously fickle, which at least has the advantage that if you awake to rain, there is a sporting chance of a fine afternoon! It is wetter than most of Europe, with prevailing westerly winds bringing considerably more rain to the north and west than to the south and east. Generally, it is noticeably warmer the further south you go, with June–Sept being the warmest months: the temperature in the south is generally between 60 and 75 degrees °F (15–24 degrees °C) in August, 5 degrees cooler in Scotland, and cool all the time in highland areas. Whenever you are travelling, especially if heading north, pack something warm as well as rainproof footwear and clothing. Daylight hours are longest in May and June; in November–January it gets dark around 1600–1700. Spring

---

Bicycles–Buses–Children–Climate

and autumn are probably the most rewarding seasons to travel, especially to see the major cities and national parks, if you are not tied to school holidays.

Clothing

Travel as light as you can: however light your bag may seem at home as you add another T-shirt, it will seem infinitely heavier when you are dragging it on and off trains. As well as a warm cover-up and rainproof outer wear, you may find yourself investing in the standard British accoutrements of Wellington boots and fold-up umbrella. Despite the generally mild climate, it is easy to get sunburnt in Britain, the unpredict-ability of the weather almost makes it more likely than if you are heading for the Mediterra-nean expecting sun, so the fair skinned and children should be especially careful to cover up as well as use high-protection-factor sunscreen. Bring scarf, hat, gloves and plenty of layers in winter. There is no need for formal clothes, even for evening wear, unless you are planning on formal dining or reserving the best seats at the Royal Opera House.

Currency

The pound sterling (£) is divided into 100 pence (p). There are 1p, 2p, 5p, 10p, 20p, 50p and £1 coins (in a confusing variety of sizes and weights), and £5, £10, £20 and £50 notes. Scottish notes (which include a £1 note) comprise the same units of currency but look different from English notes and are not always acceptable outside Scotland. Channel Islands, Isle of Man and Northern Irish currency is also different and far less acceptable outside these regions. The Irish punt (£) is worth slightly less than its British counterpart: though the coins and notes are issued in the same denomina-tions, they are not interchangeable.

The usual rules for travellers apply: do not carry too much cash, take most of your money in traveller's cheques (preferably in £ sterling) or Eurocheques, and use a credit card for extras and emergencies: the major cards are very widely accepted, though smaller establishments like b&bs often do not accept them. Commis-sion rates tend to be high in exchange bureaux,

particularly in London, and in post offices, so shop around. Banks are open on weekdays in England and Wales 0930–1530, and many also open on Saturday mornings: in Scotland and Ireland many close for an hour around 1230, while in Ireland they usually open shorter hours, generally 1000–1500.

The Thomas Cook offices listed throughout this book will cash any type of Eurocheque/travellers' cheque and will replace Thomas Cook travellers' cheques if yours are lost or stolen. Thomas Cook travellers' cheques refund (for lost or stolen travellers' cheques) *tel: 0800 622 101*.

Customs

Importing narcotics and offensive weapons is prohibited, so do not be tempted, or offer to carry anything for anyone else. If you have to take a prescribed drug on a regular basis, carry a prescription or doctor's letter to prove that it is legitimate. Britain also prohibits the import of horror comics, fireworks, meat and poultry, plants, fruit and vegetables, while animals are subject to six months in quarantine. Similar rules apply when returning home, and other rules apply to US, Canadian and Australian citizens sending gifts home, so check with the relevant customs department. There are no limits on the amount of currency you may bring into either Britain or Ireland.

Customs Allowances

The UK and Irish customs allowances for tobacco, alcohol and perfume are those set throughout the EU, and apply to anyone aged 17 or over. To all intents and purposes, there are no restrictions between EU countries for goods bought in ordinary shops, but you might be questioned if carrying excessive amounts as to whether it is all for your personal use. Allowances are:
800 cigarettes, 200 cigars, 400 cigarillos and 1 kg tobacco.
+ 90 litres wine (max. 60 litres sparkling).
+ 10 litres alcohol over 22% volume (e.g. most spirits).
+ 20 litres alcohol under 22% volume (e.g. port and sherry).
+ 110 litres beer.

The allowances for goods bought outside the EU and/or in EU duty-free shops are: 200 cigarettes, 50 cigars, 100 cigarillos and 250 g tobacco.

+ 2 litres still table wine.
+ 1 litres spirits or 2 litres sparkling wine.
+ 50g/60 ml perfume.
+ 0.5 l/250 ml toilet water.

For further information on UK customs *tel: (0181) 750 1603*; for Irish customs *tel: (01) 679 2777*.

Allowances When Returning Home

Australia: goods to the value of A$400 (half for those under 18) plus 250 cigarettes or 250 g tobacco and 1 litre alcohol.

Canada: goods to the value of C$300, provided you have been away for over a week and have not already used up part of your allowance that year. You are also allowed 50 cigars plus 200 cigarettes and 1 kg tobacco (if over 16) and 40 oz/1 litre alcohol.

New Zealand: goods to the value of NZ$700. Anyone over 17 may also take 200 cigarettes or 250 g tobacco or 50 cigars or a combination of tobacco products not exceeding 250 g in all plus 4.5 litres of beer or wine and 1.125 litres spirits.

USA: goods to the value of US$400 as long as you have been out of the country for at least 48 hours and only use your allowance once every 30 days. Anyone over 21 is also allowed 1 litre alcohol plus 100 (non-Cuban) cigars and 100 cigarettes.

Disabled Travellers

Britain and Ireland are increasingly well provided with facilities for disabled visitors, even though they sometimes fall short of what is advertised. Experienced travellers with disabilities will already know that planning is the key to ensure both that you have accommodation and that you can travel when and where you want.

Travel

The Holiday Care Service, *2 Old Bank Chambers, Station Road, Hourly, Surrey RH6 9HW; tel: (01293) 774535* publishes *Accessible Travel* (£8.95 direct, £9.95 from bookshops) which includes invaluable guidance on travelling by

rail. British Rail has a Disabled Liaison Officer *tel: (0171) 928 5151*, who can offer advice, and leaflets are available from main stations. British Rail has a reputation for being accommodating to disabled travellers, but the break-up of the service into constituent parts, underfunding and a decrease in manpower are not good news for the disabled traveller. As usual, you should make your arrangements well in advance to avoid frustration.

Accommodation

Help in finding accommodation is again provided by the Holiday Care Service, while RADAR (the Royal Association for Disability and Rehabilitation), *12 City Forum, 250 City Rd, London EC1V 8AF tel: (0171) 250 3222* publishes annually *Holidays in the British Isles: A Guide for Disabled People*. The English Tourist Board grades all its approved accommodation, from hotels to self-catering, according to suitability, so TICs will be able to help on a local basis. Some hotel chains at the higher end of the market have bedrooms adapted for wheelchair users. In the Republic of Ireland, the National Rehabilitation Board has a county-by-county fact sheet: write to the *Access Dept, 25 Clyde Rd, Dublin 4*.

Visitor Attractions and Facilities

RADAR publishes a number of useful guides on access to visitor attractions, while you can write to the British Tourist Authority or Irish Tourist Board for free access guides. The National Trust and English Heritage also publish booklets about access to their properties, including facilities for the visually and hearing impaired – these are available from all staffed sites. Again, TICs have information on access to local sites. A small number of sites offer the Sympathetic Hearing Scheme; the main text indicates which TICs offer this service. Tourist Information Centres accessible to disabled persons are indicated throughout this book by the initials DP.

Toilets for wheelchair users are increasingly being provided at museums and other tourist attractions, but they are by no means universal; a booklet, listing toilets and a special key to them, is available from RADAR.

Visiting Historic Places

For the avid stately home, castle and garden visitor, joining one of the national organisations responsible for running historic places can be a bargain, even if you are only on a short stay in Britain; once you join, you obtain free entry to all the other properties of that organisation.

The best way to join is probably at one of the properties themselves, in which case the cost of your first visit will be deducted from the membership fee. Alternatively, you can join by post, or at many TICs (addresses of TICs are given throughout this guide). All the organisations offer various discounts, for joint membership, young people, senior citizens, families, etc. The 'Sightseeing' sections in this book will tell you which organisations are responsible for particular properties: the initials NT denote National Trust (NTS for National Trust for Scotland); EH, English Heritage; Cadw, Welsh Historic Properties; HS, Historic Scotland; OPW, Office of Public Works (Republic of Ireland).

The **National Trust**, an independent charity, runs mainly historic houses (generally well furnished) and many gardens, as well as vast tracts of coast and countryside; most of its money goes on the land and buildings it protects. The adult annual subscription of £24 gives free access to these and to **National Trust for Scotland** properties (there is also a reverse arrangement). **English Heritage**, the government's official adviser on conservation matters and the main national body responsible for building conservation, manages many castles and abbeys, prehistoric and Roman remains. Though often ruinous, their sites tend to be more peaceful and remote, though they include such prime attractions as Stonehenge and Dover Castle. Annual membership costs £17.50. If you are concentrating on Wales or Scotland, **Cadw** and **Historic Scotland** are the equivalents of English Heritage and have some superb properties; membership is £15 and £16 respectively, and there are reciprocal admission arrangements between all three bodies. In the Irish Republic, a **National Heritage Card** (£10) gives free admission to national parks and the historic properties and gardens run by the Office of Public Works.

Discounts

At most tourist attractions and on public transport there are reductions for senior citizens, students and children. Students and senior citizens should carry proof of status; no student should be without the International Student Identity Card (ISIC), which allows many discounts as well as providing accident insurance – ask at your local student travel office. Many attractions offer a discounted family ticket. The 'Travelling by Train' section (see pp. 28–35) gives details of the numerous rail passes available that can make savings if you are travelling in a particular area or within a given period of time.

Membership of one of the national organisations which manage historic properties may be worthwhile if you are planning to visit a number (see box above).

Driving

Even if you are not planning to hire a car, remember that the British and Irish drive on the left. To hire a car you need to be over 21 or 25 (according to agency) and have two years' driving experience. TICs can provide details of agencies and you can book with the main companies via a travel agent in advance; some companies have offices at stations or offer a delivery service. Non-EU nationals will need an International Driving Permit; although US and Canadian licence holders can drive without it for up to three months, it is recommended anyway. A Green Card (International Insurance Certificate) is also required; car rental agencies will often include one in the package.

Electricity

Britain and Ireland use 230V (unlike the rest of

Europe, which uses 220V), so bring an adapter.

Food and Drink

Usual eating hours are: breakfast 0730–0900, lunch 1200–1400, afternoon tea 1600–1700, and dinner 1930–2130.

The stereotype of British food is of roast meat, heavy puddings, fish and chips, and cream tea in the afternoon. All these are readily available, and highly recommended (not on a daily basis though, if you value your cholesterol level). Most hotels and b&bs will offer you a full English breakfast: this is a wonderful institution, consisting of fried eggs, bacon, sausage, grilled tomatoes and fried bread, followed by toast and marmalade. If you can stomach this before 0900, you may decide to waive lunch.

Such is the ethnic mix in Britain that, particularly in bigger towns and cities, there is an enormous range of food available. At the budget end, most towns will have Chinese, Indian, and Greek restaurants and/or take-aways, plus burger bars, pizza parlours and fish and chip takeaways, of varying quality. You can also buy good quality sandwiches and other takeaway food from larger supermarkets.

Pubs usually serve a good range, from the ubiquitous ploughman's lunch (bread, cheese and pickle) to three-course meals. They are your best bet if you are seeking more traditional British fare at a reasonable price.

Vegetarians are better provided for in Britain than in most of Europe: contact the Vegetarian Society *tel: (0161) 928 0793* for a listing. There are many widely available published guides to eating establishments, from cheap eats to gourmet.

Tea, usually served with milk, and coffee (specify black or white), is served everywhere. Spirits are expensive in Britain due to heavy taxation, but naturally carbonated beer (heavier and more bitter than most European or American beer) is a speciality. Be prepared for the fact that this is not served chilled. There are many different breweries, and some pubs ('free houses') serve a wide range for the connoisseur. Cider, a fermented apple juice, is another very English drink worth sampling. Wine bars on the whole serve better wine than pubs, and cocktail bars are also popular. Many drinking places have a happy hour (usually early evening), when drinks are served at half price. Note that pub hours are usually 1100–2300 Mon–Sat (though some close in the afternoon), and 1200–2230 on Sunday.

Tips on British English

A few phrases which have different meanings in British and US English.

bank holiday	(public) holiday
bill	check
biscuit	cookie/cracker
car	automobile
car park	parking lot
carriage	railroad car
chemist	pharmacy/drugstore
chips	french fries
coach	long-distance bus/railroad car
crisps	potato chips
first floor	second floor (and so on)
flat	apartment
fortnight	two weeks
gents	men's restroom
ground floor	first floor
ladies	women's restroom
lift	elevator
loo	restroom
nappy	diaper
note (bank)	bill
pavement	sidewalk
petrol	gasoline
phone box	telephone booth
platform	track
public holiday	holiday
pudding	dessert
quid	pound sterling
return ticket	roundtrip ticket
rubber	eraser
serviette	napkin
single ticket	one-way ticket
subway	underground walkway
sweets	candy
timetable	schedule
traffic lights	stop light
Tube	London subway

Food and Drink–British English

Landscape

Where should you head for to see the kind of scenery that appeals to you? Despite its density of population, Britain has an extraordinary variety of countryside, from the domestic to the wild. Some of the best of English and Welsh scenery is to be found in the National Parks: for mountain scenery, the highest peaks are to be found in spectacular Snowdonia, the Lake District offers a magical combination of lakes, mountains and woodland, while the Peak District and the less visited Brecon Beacons are also dramatically beautiful. The wildest and most remote landscapes are to be found in Ireland and in Scotland, where in many areas of the north and west it seems unimaginable that such remoteness can exist on the same island as south-eastern England. In southern England, Dartmoor offers the largest expanse of open country, and the Cotswolds and Dorset more domesticated, hilly landscapes in which buildings seem in perfect harmony with their surroundings. Britain's irregular shape and diverse geology have resulted in an amazingly varied coastline: Dover's white cliffs are a symbol of this island nation, but for dramatic coastal scenery, the Cornish, Pembrokeshire, north Norfolk and Northumberland coasts are incomparable.

Guided Walks

An excellent way of getting your bearings in a new town or city is to take a guided walk. Accredited tour guides are known as Blue Badge Guides, and details of the tours they offer can be obtained from TICs; in larger cities you can choose from a multitude of themes and routes.

Health

You do not need any vaccinations before visiting the UK and Ireland. The climate may be mild, but don't forget a sunscreen. If you are likely to have casual sex, take precautions against sexually transmitted diseases including AIDS (condoms are widely available in pharmacies, pubs and supermarkets). It is safe to drink tap water, but wash all fresh food.

You are entitled to care at the Accident and Emergency Department of any public hospital, but for an overnight or longer stay you may be required to pay (see 'Insurance' below), if your country does not have a reciprocal agreement. If you are visiting from another EU country, it is recommended that you take an E111 form with you. If you are on regular medication, it makes sense to keep a note with you of what you use.

Hitchhiking

Hitching is always tempting to budget travellers. Britain may seem a relatively safe country to have a go, but even so you are still at the mercy of whoever stops to pick you up: even if the driver is sane, he or she may be drunk or simply a bad driver. Women on their own are not safe. If you must hitch, don't go alone, and don't get into any vehicle if you are in any doubt about its occupants, or if they outnumber you. Hitchhiking on motorways (freeways) is illegal, but you are allowed to hitch in motorway service areas.

Insurance

If you are a visitor to Britain or Ireland, check that you have insurance to cover your health as well as your belongings (you might save unnecessary additional expense by checking whether your policies at home provide some level of cover while travelling). Your insurance should also give cover in case of cancellation or the need for an emergency flight home.

Luggage

The easiest way to carry luggage if you are doing plenty of travelling is in a backpack. Otherwise, choose a lightweight, soft-sided zippable bag, with a shoulder strap, which will be easier to carry than a conventional suitcase and more amenable to cramming into luggage compartments. If choosing a backpack, take some time over it and spend as much as you can afford. A strong frame, padded shoulder straps and a hip strap are essential, and quality and fit here can make a massive difference to your comfort.

Most major stations have left luggage offices and many will let you register your bags and send them ahead to your destination.

Opening Hours

Banks in the UK are open Mon–Fri 0900–1630; many also open on Saturday morning. In Ireland, hours are 1000–1230 and 1330–1500 Mon–Fri. All shops are typically open Mon–Sat 0900–1730; in smaller towns and rural areas they may close at lunchtime one day a week, while many areas and most supermarkets have at least one late-night opening (usually until 2000). Sunday opening is increasingly common in Britain for supermarkets and small food shops; in Edinburgh everything stays open on Sundays. Museums tend to be open Mon–Sat 0900/1000–1730/1800 and either Sunday morning or afternoon; parks and gardens usually close at dusk in winter, from 1600 onwards. Many tourist attractions are closed on Mondays except in high season, and a number (such as the majority of National Trust houses) close for a period in winter. All published times given in the text are subject to change, and you should phone in advance to avoid a wasted trip.

Passports and Visas

All overseas visitors to the United Kingdom must carry a valid passport, with the exclusion of nationals of EU countries that issue national identity cards. Nationals of Austria, Liechtenstein, Monaco and Switzerland who are visiting for up to six months for purposes other than employment may use a national identity card instead of a passport. Visas are required by all except visitors from Commonwealth countries (with the exclusion of Bangladesh, India, Ghana, Nigeria, Pakistan, and Sri Lanka); EU countries that issue national identity cards; and certain other nations including the USA, Japan, Austria, Finland, Iceland, Sweden and Switzerland. For full details, check with the British Consulate.

All visitors to the Republic of Ireland must carry a valid passport except people born in the United Kingdom who are travelling direct from there and holder's of EC national identity cards.

Citizens from the USA, Canada, Australia and New Zealand need a passport and can stay up to three months without a visa.

Postage

There is an excellent network of post offices and sub post offices, which often double up as the local newsagent or stationer; opening hours are usually Mon–Fri 0900–1700, and Sat 0900–1230. Smaller offices shut for lunch and on Wednesday afternoons. Many other newsagents, stores and hotels also sell books of stamps. Red post boxes are easily found and

Public Holidays

Dates are correct for 1995; most will change by a day or so in 1996. Note that dates written in numbers are usually day-month-year, not month-day-year as in North America; so 12-5-95 in Britain is May 12th 1995, not December 5th.

England and Wales

New Year (2 January); Good Friday (14 April); Easter Monday (17 April); 8 May; Spring Bank Holiday (29 May); Summer Bank Holiday (28 August); Christmas Day (25 December); Boxing Day (26 December).

Scotland

New Year (2 and 3 January); Good Friday; 1 and 8 May; Spring Bank Holiday; Summer Bank Holiday (7 August) Christmas Day; Boxing Day.

Northern Ireland

New Year; St Patrick's Day (17 March); Good Friday; Easter Monday; 8 May; Spring Bank Holiday; 12 July; Summer Bank Holiday (28 August); Christmas Day; Boxing Day.

Republic of Ireland

New Year's Day; St. Patrick's Day; Good Friday; Easter Monday; 1 May; 5 June; 7 August; 30 October; Christmas Day; St Stephen's Day (26 December).

should have post times displayed on them. First-class letters (more expensive in the Irish Republic than in Britain) should arrive next day, second class (cheaper) one or more days later.

If you wish to receive mail, ask those writing to you to label their letters with 'Poste Restante', and the name of the town: to collect them, go to the main post office there.

Security

Whatever the public perception, Britain and Ireland are still among the safest places to travel in Europe. Rural areas are generally far safer than conurbations: however, you should take sensible precautions wherever you are. Try not to give the impression that you are worth stealing from: keep valuables, travel documents and cash safely inside a money belt. If you carry a handbag or shoulder bag wear it slung across your body, and keep it between your feet in restaurants. Despite the abatement of the Irish terrorist threat in 1994, you should still avoid leaving any bags or suitcases unattended, not only because they might be stolen but because you might cause a security alert (you can always use the station's left luggage facility). If you are sleeping in a public place, such as in a dormitory or on a train, put your small valuables at the bottom of your sleeping bag, and padlock your luggage to your seat in sleeping cars.

Mugging is uncommon in rural areas and unlikely in the most frequented parts of towns and cities, particularly if you take the precautions outlined above. Women should try to avoid walking alone at night, and dress so as not to attract undue attention. TICs will be able to advise you on any areas of towns and cities that are best avoided by lone women. There are still some trains which have small, non-corridor compartments – avoid these if you are travelling alone, and be wary also of large but unoccupied carriages. This applies also to London Underground trains which are generally very safe in the busier, central area, but less so on the outer reaches of some lines where the trains are less well used.

If you are unlucky, you must report any incident to the local police. Keep a note (separate from your valuables) of the numbers of your travellers' cheques, credit cards and insurance documents, together with a photocopy of the important page(s) of your passport, to help you if you do run into trouble. Have a note of these numbers at home as well. In an emergency, you can dial 999 (for Police, Fire Brigade or Ambulance) free from any phone box.

Smoking

Smoking is banned in many public places in the UK, including most public transport; where it is allowed, it is usually in restricted areas. The same applies to many restaurants, shops and (indoor) shopping centres. The majority of pubs and bars, however, still allow unrestricted smoking.

Taxis

There are taxi ranks at most stations and elsewhere in towns, the TIC will tell you where. The solid, box-like black cabs found in large towns and cities can be hailed anywhere if the orange light is shown, and they charge standard, metered fares; if you are using a minicab service, check what the fare will be in advance.

Telephones

British public telephone boxes were once all bright red, but in most towns and cities they are now a far less obvious silver-grey. They are usually to be found near shops, on street corners, or at stations, where you may find rows of booths. They either run on a mix of coins (10p–£1) or on phone cards, which are available in various denominations and can be bought at newsagents and Thomas Cook bureaux de change. It makes sense to arm yourself with one of these early in your travels, to avoid the not uncommon predicament of finding that the only phone box available to you when you need to make an urgent call is a phonecard one. When making a call, the card or cash has to be inserted before you dial. If you are using cash, try to use low-value coins, as unused coins will be returned at the end of your call. A small number also run on credit cards. When making telephone calls, both the length of the call and the time of day affect the cost. There are two time bands: the cheapest is Mon–Fri 1800–0800 and all weekend; the more expensive is Mon–Fri 0800–1800.

To make an international call from the UK and the Irish Republic, dial 00 followed by the country code (1 for USA, Canada and Caribbean, 62 for Australia, 64 for New Zealand, 27 for South Africa, 31 for the Netherlands, 33 for France, 43 for Germany, 32 for Belgium) and then the phone number, leaving out the initial 0 of the area code if there is one.

To call a UK number from your own country, dial your country's international access code, followed by 44 (for the Irish Republic 353), and then the number; remember to leave out the initial 0 of the area code. British and Irish area codes are always given in brackets in this book.

For UK domestic enquiries, *tel: 192*, Irish Republic *tel: 1190*; for international enquiries *tel: 153*. In an emergency, to call Police, Fire Brigade, Ambulance or Coastguard, *tel: 999* (these calls are free).

Toilets/WCs

Public facilities in Britain and Ireland vary considerably in quality and ease of finding. Signposting varies: you may see signs for 'Toilets', 'WCs', 'Ladies' and 'Gentlemen', or simply male and female figures (though some toilets are unisex). If you can't find a public one, head for a large department store if you are in a town; pub, restaurant and hotel toilets are, of course, for customers only. Most railway stations have toilets; in the main London termini there is a small charge for the privilege.

Useful Reading

The *Thomas Cook Rail Timetable of Britain, France and Benelux Summer Special 95* (see p. 5), which is published in May each year, costs £7.95 and has summer timings for most rail services and many shipping services in Britain, France and Benelux. It is essential both for pre-planning and for making on-the-spot decisions about independent rail travel. A useful companion is the *Thomas Cook Visitor's Rail Map of Great Britain and Ireland* (see p. 5), which costs £4.95. All of these publications are available by

phoning *01733 268943*, or from many bookshops and branches of Thomas Cook travel agency. In North America, contact the Forsyth Travel Library Inc. *9154 West 57th St, PO Box 2975, Shawnee Mission, Kansas 66201; tel: (800) 367 7984* (toll-free).

There are so many other guides to Britain available that it would be invidious to name particular books. Head for a bookshop and make your choice, by region or by interest, and remember that a surprising amount of material is available free from tourist information centres.

Useful Addresses

British Tourist Authority, *Thames Tower, Black's Rd, London W6 9EZ tel: (0181) 846 9000; 551 Fifth Ave (7th floor), New York, NY10176 tel: (212) 986 2200.* **Irish Tourist Board**, *150 New Bond St, London W1Y 0AQ tel: (0171) 493 3201; 757 Third Ave (19th floor), New York, NY10017 tel: (212) 418 0800.* **Cadw (Welsh Historic Monuments)**, *Brunel House, 2 Fitzalan Rd, Cardiff CF2 1UY tel: (01222) 465511.* **English Heritage**, *23 Savile Row, London W1X 1AB tel: (0171) 973 3000.* **Historic Scotland**, *20 Brandon St, Edinburgh EH3 5RA tel: (0131) 224 3101.* **National Trust**, *36 Queen Anne's Gate, London SW1 9AS tel: (0171) 222 9251.*

VAT

Value added tax (sales tax) is automatically added to many goods and services in the UK at a rate of 17.5%; in Eire the rate varies between 8% and 35%. On large purchases, you can reclaim your VAT: ask the shop to fill in a tax refund form, which you give to customs to certify on leaving Britain or Eire (within three months of purchase). If you post this back to the shop, you will receive a refund.

What to Take

Few parts of Britain and Ireland are so remote that you will be unable to buy anything which suddenly seems essential or which you have forgotten. But consider bringing a travel electricity adapter and a money belt; and, if you plan to sleep on long train journeys, an inflatable pillow is highly recommended.

TRAVELLING
by
TRAIN

This section covers all the essential facts a tourist needs to plan an independent rail journey around Britain and Ireland.

BRITAIN

Twenty-five Train Operating Units (TOUs) provide rail services, currently under the control of the British Railways Board (British Rail – BR). Railway infrastructure (including stations) is the property of Railtrack. Under UK Government plans, Railtrack and the TOUs will eventually be privatised. International services via the Channel Tunnel are operated by European Passenger Services.

Trains

Trains in Britain fall into three main types: high-speed InterCity services; long-distance cross-country services and local or suburban services.

All InterCity trains offer both first- and standard-class travel; standard class is the norm for local and cross-country services. As a rule, in Britain standard class is perfectly OK for all but the most ardent comfort-seeker.

First class coaches usually have a yellow stripe along the top of the windows and large figure '1's on the side of the coach, on the door or on the windows. Non-smoking coaches are distinguished by signs, usually of a cigarette with a red cross, or one red band over it. Trains can be completely non-smoking, although some have one or two smoking carriages – these may be positioned at the ends of the train.

British railway stations have raised platforms allowing access to the train without the need to climb steps.

Overnight Trains

The small size of Britain and the speed of day trains mean that there is little requirement for sleeping-car services. Provision of these services (and their operator) was under review at the time of going to press and will be subject to confirmation from June 1995. It is expected however, that the London to Fort William, London to Carlisle and Plymouth to Edinburgh and Glasgow services will be discontinued leaving only the London to Edinburgh and Glasgow and London to Aberdeen and Inverness services, which will most likely run as combined trains south of Scotland, dividing and joining en route.

Sleeping cars cost £25 per berth in standard class, and £30 per berth in first class. The advantage of using such services is that the traveller can cover large distances as he or she rests and means that precious holiday time will not be wasted in transit. If your chosen train arrives at your destination in early morning, you are often allowed to stay in your berth until around 0730–0800. Sleepers can usually be reserved up to three months in advance; early booking is recommended as space is limited.

Sleeping cars have bedroom-style compartments with washing facilities (usually just a wash-basin) and full bedding. WCs are located at one or both ends of the coach. An attendant travels with each car, or pair of cars, and serves drinks or light refreshments in the evening (extra charge), and a complimentary newspaper and continental breakfast in the morning. In standard class only tea/coffee and biscuits are complimentary. First-class sleeping compartments have one berth and standard-class compartments have two berths. Berths should be claimed on boarding the train as they may be resold 15 minutes after train departure.

Timetables

Most large stations have electronic departure boards or large paper timetables which list the route, the time of departure and the relevant platform.

You should have little problem finding your

train at main stations; smaller stations may be unstaffed. Where announcements are made, listen carefully for any change of platform or other information affecting your service – if in doubt ask a member of staff.

At larger stations each platform may have one or more television screens giving arrival and departure times, platform numbers and details of any delays. Two trains may sometimes share one platform, which will be divided into an 'a' and a 'b' section. InterCity and long-distance cross-country services often have paper notices attached to the carriage windows stating the principal stops and ultimate destination.

Some trains may split en route with carriages heading off to different destinations so be careful to join the correct part. If unsure, ask the guard or driver.

Advance Reservations

Seats on all InterCity trains can be booked in advance and it is usually worthwhile to do this, especially on Fridays, summer Saturdays and around public holidays (such as Christmas and Easter), when trains on popular routes can fill up a long way ahead and you could spend hours standing in a crowded corridor. On some very busy trains seat reservations are considered essential and are provided free of charge; first-class seat reservations are free to full-fare ticket holders and cost £2 for passengers travelling on discounted tickets. Standard-class seats cost £1 to reserve (up to 4 seats for one fee for passengers travelling together). If you are travelling during the summer period without a reservation, board your train as early as possible.

It is obligatory to make an advance reservation for sleeping accommodation. This can usually be made at major stations. In the USA, advance reservations and sleeping cars can be booked from Forsyth Travel Library Inc; *tel: (800) 367 7984* (toll-free). Berths may be bought from the sleeping-car attendant if there are any left when the train departs – don't expect to find many of these though.

Reserved seats have labels attached to their head-rests indicating between which stations they are reserved; they can be used at any other point on the route.

Meals on Trains

Most InterCity trains in Britain have restaurant cars serving full meals (usually Mondays–Fridays only) at set times and/or buffet cars selling drinks and snacks. Buffet cars are open for long periods but not necessarily for the entire duration of the journey. On some services full meals may only be available to first-class passengers and may be served at their seat. If you are travelling first class, you must state whether or not you require a meal when you make your seat reservation. All catering cars have a red band above the windows and doors.

There is an increasing tendency, on some services, for refreshments to be served aircraft-style from a trolley wheeled through the train.

InterCity Pullman trains have a restaurant car and in addition offer full-meals to passengers at their seats, which must be reserved in advance. Light refreshments are also available; tea, coffee and seat reservations are complimentary.

In general, always take emergency rations – something to eat and drink – as these items are usually quite expensive on trains. If you need to save money, take a picnic.

Luggage

You are allowed to carry up to three pieces of luggage (two suitcases and an item of hand luggage) on train journeys. Excess or bulky luggage can be stored in the guards van at extra cost (only if it is not so heavy that it cannot be carried by any one person though). Bicycles can be carried on most InterCity and some cross-country trains subject to available space (prior reservation is compulsory and numbers are strictly limited; charges are set by individual Train Operating Units).

Some major stations have left luggage offices or lockers, where, for a small charge, luggage can be stored for short periods. It is advisable to check in advance whether the station you are travelling to has this facility.

Tickets

Always buy your ticket before travelling, unless you board at an unstaffed station (unstaffed stations may have self-service ticket machines or

Permit to Travel machines), or you could face heavy penalties or even criminal prosecution if caught out by the numerous ticket checks. Always check what discounts are available, especially if you are prepared to travel outside peak periods (rush hours, Fridays and summer Saturdays), before purchasing a ticket.

At weekends, when first-class accommodation is under-used, standard-class passengers can upgrade to special 'Weekend First' carriages for a modest extra charge. These upgrades can be purchased from stations or from the senior conductor on the train. Children under 5 travel free and those aged 6–14 travel at reduced rates.

There are a number of rail tickets that are designed to save you money for point to point journeys, which are purchased as and when required. They can be used by anyone but are only available for purchase in Britain from principal British Rail stations or from selected agents.

The following tickets may not be available on certain services – check in advance.

APEX

APEX tickets must be booked at least seven days in advance and the return journey must be booked at the same time as the outward journey. Bookings are limited and include a free compulsory seat reservation in both directions of travel. APEX tickets are valid for standard class only and for trips of 150 miles or more.

SuperApex Return

These offer a further discount off the price of an APEX ticket and must be booked 14 days in advance.

SuperAdvance Return

These tickets operate in a similar manner to APEX tickets. They are available in limited numbers, on peak-time trains, and must be booked by 1200 hours prior to the date of travel. Their fare is equal to that of the SuperSaver Return but they are valid for travel on Fridays and summer Saturdays.

Saver Return

Saver-Return tickets can be used on any day of the week with less restriction on time or availability than with the following SuperSaver Return.

SuperSaver Return

These tickets can be used on off-peak days but are not usually valid for travel much before 1030, nor on any Friday or summer Saturday. Travel in rush hours is also usually prohibited.

Cheap Day Return

Available at off-peak times for a limited number of local journeys.

Rail Cards

There are several rail cards which are not in themselves tickets, but which are designed to give certain categories of travellers a reduction on the normal rail fare.

The Young Person's Railcard

For people aged 16–25 years and students aged 26 or over, the Young Persons Railcard offers a 34% discount on certain fares and lasts for 12 months. The price is currently £16. Proof of age or student status is necessary for purchase of this card.

The Family Railcard

This offers a discount for adults and children travelling together, although people using the card do not need to be related. Discounts are offered on certain fares and accompanying children can travel for £2.

The Senior Railcard

Offers a discount (usually 34%) on certain fares to people aged 60 or over. Lasts for 12 months and is valid in both first and standard class.

Rail Passes

The passes described below allow freedom of travel for a limited period of time without the need to buy any other tickets. A large range of regional rail passes are available, and those listed below are a guide as to the type of pass that may be used for exploring Britain by train. Enquire at your local station for further details.

Rail Rovers

Rail Rover tickets offer you the chance to tour and explore either particular regions of Britain or the whole country, at affordable prices. Children under 5 travel free and 5–15 year olds, as well as holders of certain rail cards, are entitled to a 34% discount.

Rail Rovers are readily available at most major rail stations and can also be bought at local stations provided you give three days notice. They can also be obtained from some 'Rail Appointed Travel Agents': look for the sign in your local travel agent's window. Alternatively, you can use the booking form on the back of the Rail Rovers' leaflet to order one in advance. Refer to the information numbers listed below for each particular area. There are three types of Rail Rover ticket to choose from:

Regional Rover: ideal for exploring particular areas of the country. They offer 7-days travel (8 days with the ScotRail Rover) in one of 7 regions around Britain.

Flexi Rovers: ideal for those who don't wish to travel every day. Depending on the area you choose, Flexi Rovers allow you 3-days travel in any 7-day period, 4 days in any 8-day period, or 12 days in any 15-day period.

All-Line Rail Rover: this rail pass gives you the freedom to travel anywhere on the British rail network and is available as a 7-day or 14-day ticket in either first or standard class.

The seven regions offering Rail Rover passes can be contacted on the following telephone numbers: Scotland, tel: (0131) 556 2451; north-east, tel: (0113) 244 8133; north-west coast and peaks, tel: (0161) 832 8353; central and eastern England, tel: (0121) 643 2711; Wales, tel: (01222) 228000; south-west (Cornwall and Devon), tel: (01752) 221300; East Anglia; tel: (01603) 632055.

Rail Passes Available Outside Britain

BritRail Products

BritRail Passes offer overseas visitors the opportunity to enjoy the freedom of rail travel throughout Great Britain, providing exciting, comfortable and affordable ways to explore England, Scotland and Wales. In addition to rail travel, some BritRail products include added-value offers, details of which are available at the time of purchase.

There are several different types of passes, which are outlined in more detail below. BritRail products are only available from the country in which you are normally resident; they are not available in the UK.

Countries Where BritRail Products are Sold

Only the USA and Canada offer the full range of BritRail products; most of the other countries listed below only stock a selection. The 'pass-by-pass' listing which follows highlights the countries in which each is currently available, but either your local BritRail office, authorised agency (see addresses below) or a local travel agent will be able to confirm these availability details. At present, BritRail passes can be bought in: the USA, Canada, Argentina, Brazil, Mexico, Australia, New Zealand, South Africa, Zimbabwe, Hong Kong, Japan, India, Argentina, Dubai, Israel, Korea, Saudi Arabia, Singapore, Taiwan, Thailand, Austria, Belgium*, Cyprus, Denmark*, Republic of Ireland*, Finland, France*, Germany*, Greece, Italy*, Malta, the Netherlands*, Norway, Portugal, Spain, Sweden and Switzerland*.

*Countries marked with an asterisk have British Rail International Europe offices, which you can contact for any further details that you may require.

Information and Booking

USA and Canada: The Forsyth Travel Library Inc., 9154 West 57th St, PO Box 2975, Shawnee Mission, Kansas 66201; tel: (800) 367 7984 (toll free). BritRail Travel International Inc., 1500 Broadway, New York, NY 10036; tel: (212) 575 2667.

Australia: Thomas Cook Pty Ltd, Level 8, 321 Kent Street, Sydney; tel: (2) 248 6100, fax: (2) 248 6200.

New Zealand: Thomas Cook (NZ) Ltd, 96–98 Anzac Avenue, PO Box 24, Auckland 1; tel: (9)

Rail Passes–Rail Passes Available Outside Britain

379 6800, fax: (9) 303 0266.

South Africa: World Travel Agency (Pty) Ltd, 8th floor, Everite House, 20 De Korte Street, Braamfontein, 2001 Johannesburg; tel: (11) 403 2606, fax: (11) 403 1037.

Hong Kong: Westminster Travel Ltd, 16th floor, Oriental Centre, 67 Chatham Road, Tsimshatsui, Kowloon; tel: 3695051, fax: 7233746.

Singapore: Diners World Travel, 7500-E Beach Road, #02-201, The Plaza, Singapore 0719; tel: 292 5544, fax: 295 1481.

Japan: Travel Plaza International Inc., 7th floor NV Tomioka Building, 2-1-9 Tomioka, Koto-Ku, Tokyo, Japan 135; tel: (3) 3820 8032, fax: (3) 3820 7790. Ohshu Express Limited, Wako Building, 4F, 1-12-16, Jinnan, Shibuya-Ku, Tokyo, Japan 150; tel: (3) 3780 5514, fax: (3) 3780 1290.

For all other countries, further information about purchasing a BritRail Pass can be obtained from either British Rail International offices (see countries marked with an asterisk above), from authorised agencies or from your local travel agent.

Once you have purchased a BritRail pass, it must be validated upon your arrival in the UK. Tickets can be validated at selected major British Rail stations throughout the UK or at the BritRail Welcome Centre situated on Platform 2, Victoria Station, London, where special Welcome Packs containing discount coupons and city maps can also be obtained.

Alternatively, BritRail Passes purchased in North America may be issued via an airline-type ticketing system, whereby a 'coupon' is bought, rather than an actual ticket. Once in the UK, these coupons must be exchanged for a ticket and then validated as normal, either at selected British Rail stations or at the BritRail Welcome Centre.

Prices

Prices for the different types of BritRail passes vary according to both the class (first being more expensive than standard), and to the age-group (adult, senior, youth and child). There are generally no youth prices available for first-class passes and in addition, several of the passes only

offer adult and child prices, with no reductions for senior citizens or under 25 year olds. Many local trains in England, Scotland and Wales have standard-class accommodation only, but this is allowed for in the first-class price.

Due to the extremely wide range of prices, those quoted below in the pass-by-pass section refer to the USA only. See the Forsyth Travel Library advertisement on pp. 343–345 for a wider range of prices. Prices are in US$ and are valid for 1995 adult standard-class fares. You can use these prices as a rough indication of the cost of other options, and the likely cost in other countries, where passes are priced in local currencies. In some countries however, notably Korea, Israel, and Saudi Arabia, BritRail passes are sold in US$. In all cases your local BRI office or travel agent can give prices for the complete range of passes that are available in your country.

BritRail Pass

This pass offers unlimited travel on the British Rail network (England, Scotland and Wales) for a period of consecutive days. The pass is particularly suitable if you wish to travel extensively in Britain, and it offers total flexibility and great value for money. Passes are available for 4 days (US$155), 8 days (US$230), 15 days (US$355), 22 days (US$445) or 1 month (US$520).

The BritRail Pass is available in all the countries listed on p. 31.

BritRail Flexipass

The Flexipass differs from the BritRail Pass in that it allows you to travel on a specific number of days within the period of one month. This pass is ideal for those wishing to stop over and explore a particular location before resuming their travels.

Available for any 4 days in a month (US$195), any 8 days in a month (US$275) or any 15 days in a month (US$405). A special youth fare of US$319 (ages 16–25) is available in all the countries listed above except Europe and offers 15 days travel in 2 months.

England/Wales Pass

This pass offers unlimited travel on the British Rail network in England (as far north as Berwick and Carlisle) and throughout Wales. It is available for travel on any 4 days out of 1 month (US$155).

Available in the USA, Canada, Australia, Hong Kong, New Zealand, Singapore, South Africa, Taiwan, Japan, Israel and Zimbabwe.

Freedom of Scotland Travelpass

This pass provides unlimited travel in Scotland, including travel to and from Berwick and Carlisle, transportation on Caledonian Mac-Brayne ferries, Strathclyde PTE, and the Glasgow Underground.

Available for consecutive periods of 8 (US$159), 15 (US$220) or 22 days (US$269). It is also possible to buy a Flexipass which is valid for any 8 days out of a 15-day period (US$185).

The Freedom of Scotland Travelpass can be bought in the following countries: the USA, Canada, Australia, Japan, New Zealand, South Africa and Europe.

Britrail/Drive Pass

This combines a BritRail Flexipass with Hertz car rental, offering the speed of the train for longer journeys and the freedom of a car to explore local areas.

Available only in North America; Forsyth Travel Library (see pp. 343–345) can provide details on prices and validity.

London Visitor Travelcard

This allows unlimited travel on London's public buses and the Underground for a period of consecutive days. Prices range from $25–$49, depending on the duration of the pass.

Available in North America and in the European countries listed on p. 31.

London Extra

This gives all the benefits of the London Visitor Travelcard plus a Rail Flexipass that covers a large section of Southern England. Prices range from $85–$175 depending on the duration of the pass, with special rates for children.

Available in North America; not available in Europe (except Ireland and Spain) or in Saudi Arabia, Argentina, Mexico, Thailand and Dubai.

BritFrance Railpass

This offers unlimited travel on both the BritRail and French Rail networks for any 5 days within a 1 month period (US$259) or for any 10 days in 1 month (US$399). Transportation between Britain and France is not included in this pass. Available only in the USA and Canada.

BritGerman Railpass

This allows unlimited travel on the BritRail and German Rail networks. Passes are for first class travel only and are available for any 5 days within 1 month (US$359) or any 10 days in 1 month (US$569). Only available in the USA and Canada.

Inter-Rail Pass

The Inter-Rail pass can be bought by anyone who will be under 26 on the first day for which it is valid, provided that they can prove that they have lived for at least six months in Europe and that they hold a valid passport. It can be purchased up to two months before travel begins. The current cost is £249 for a month and you can buy two consecutive passes for longer journeys. You will not get free travel in the country where you buy the pass, but you may get some discount.

At present, an Inter-Rail pass gives you unlimited second-class rail travel for a month on the national railways of most countries in Europe including the Republic of Ireland. In the UK, Inter-Rail provides a discount of 34% on rail travel in Great Britain and Northern Ireland, plus a discount on the rail portion of tickets between London and the Continental ports, plus 30% or 50% discount (depending on the company) on most of the ferries to Ireland and Europe.

Zonal Inter-Rail Passes

These regional variations on the Inter-Rail Pass are for those under 26. The same rules about eligibility apply. For zonal passes, Europe has been divided into seven geographical zones including zone 1: the United Kingdom and the

---

Republic of Ireland. Passes are available for 1 zone (15 days only; £179); 2 zones (1 month; £209); and 3 zones (1 month; £229).

Inter-Rail 26+ Pass

This is the same as the Inter-Rail Pass, except that it is for people over 26 and does not cover travel in Belgium, France, Italy, Portugal, Spain or Switzerland. The current cost is £269 for a month or £209 for 15 days.

IRELAND

Services in Northern Ireland are provided by the state-owned Northern Ireland Railway Co. Ltd (NIR). NIR operates lines from Belfast to Londonderry (with a branch from Coleraine to Portrush), Larne and Bangor, as well as – jointly with larnród Éireann – the Belfast to Dublin line.

In the Republic of Ireland, larnród Éireann (IÉ) – literally, Irish Rail – is the state railway, providing InterCity trains to most parts of the country as well as a few cross-country services. IÉ also operates the Dublin Area Rapid Transport (DART) system of electric trains and other suburban services into and out of the capital.

Trains

In Northern Ireland many railway lines were closed in the 1960s and only those from Belfast to Dublin, Londonderry, Larne and Bangor and between Coleraine and Portrush remain. Services between Belfast and Dublin have first-class carriages – all others are standard class only.

In the Republic of Ireland first-class travel is available on all lines except those between Dublin and Rosslare and Rosslare and Limerick via Tipperary. Some services on the Belfast–Dublin line are operated by Irish Rail and only accept Irish currency.

First-class carriages on trains in both Northern Ireland and the Republic have the figure '1' near the door and no-smoking carriages have the same crossed-out cigarette symbol found on British trains.

Dublin Heuston–Cork main line trains have an enhanced type of first-class service known as CityGold available three times daily (twice on

Suns). This is principally for business people; it includes a full-meal-at-seat service, complimentary coffee and newspapers. Seat-back headphones provide national radio programmes and telephone/fax services are also available.

An express bus service operated by Bus Éireann serves places inaccessible by rail; see p. 338 for more details.

Timetables

Stations in Eire range from modern buildings with a variety of timetable information to small, unstaffed halts where information may be very limited.

Advance Reservations

Advance reservations can only be made if you are holding a first-class ticket and main-line services tend to be very busy at all times – be sure to turn up for your train in good time.

Meals on Trains

In Northern Ireland a trolley service is provided on services to/from Londonderry and a restaurant and/or buffet car on express trains to/from Dublin. In the Republic of Ireland, many trains have a restaurant and/or buffet car serving full meals and light snacks.

Luggage

Left luggage facilities are available at only a few principal stations in the Republic; there are none at stations in Northern Ireland. There are lockers at some stations in the Republic – check which before you travel.

Tickets

Single, day- and monthly-return tickets are available in Northern Ireland; the first two and the outward portion of the monthly ticket are valid on the day of issue only. A 7-day rail runabout ticket is available April–Oct for all lines within Northern Ireland and cross-border services as far as Dundalk. On the Belfast–Dublin line day returns are not available for first-class travel but singles and monthly-return tickets are.

Irish Rail standard- and first-class fares are quite expensive, especially on the Dublin–Cork route where the 'CityGold' (see under 'Trains' on this page) is available on principal services. Tickets for travel on other lines may be a little less than their UK equivalents with the exception of the super-standard class (equivalent to UK first class), for which a single journey supplement of £5.00 (up to 150kms) and £7.50 (over 150kms) is charged.

Special day-saver and monthly-saver return fares from and to many destinations are available on InterCity services along with discounted family tickets for two adults and up to four children and rambler tickets.

If you are under 26, ask for a **Faircard**, which offers discounts of up to 50% on InterCity travel; discounts are available to over 26 year olds with the **Weekender** card. Both discount cards are valid for one year – you will need a photograph to obtain either.

Rail Passes

Irish Explorer tickets (run by Irish Rail) offer the freedom to travel Ireland by train and bus. There are several types of tickets and passes available, as detailed below. All prices quoted refer to standard-class accommodation.

Emerald Card

This card covers all of Ireland, including Northern Ireland, and offers you the freedom of the entire bus and rail network. Emerald Cards are available for 15 days travel out of 30 consecutive days (IR£180 adult; IR£90 child) or for 8 days travel out of 30 consecutive days (IR£105 adult; IR£53 child).

Irish Rover

This covers all of Ireland and is valid on the rail network only. A pass providing 5 days travel out of 15 consecutive days costs IR£70 for adults and IR£35 for children.

Irish Explorer (Rail only)

This rail pass covers the Republic of Ireland and is valid for 5 days travel out of 15 consecutive days (IR£60 adult; IR£30 child).

Irish Explorer (Rail/Bus)

This ticket allows 8 days travel out of 15 consecutive days (IR£85 adult; IR£42 child) throughout the Republic of Ireland.

Rail Passes Available Outside Ireland

BritIreland Railpass

This provides unlimited travel in England, Scotland, Wales, Northern Ireland and the Republic of Ireland, and includes a round trip Stena Sealink ferry service between Britain and Ireland via one of three routes. Passes are available for any 5 days in 1 month (US$289), or for any 10 days in 1 month (US$419).

Currently available in: the USA, Canada, Australia, Hong Kong, Japan, New Zealand, Singapore, South Africa, Taiwan and Zimbabwe. In North America only, BritRail also offer a number of unescorted tours for the independent traveller. Air-inclusive or land-only packages are available and range from theme-based tours such as the 'Cathedrals and Churches Tour' to tours of the London area. For further details contact either the Forsyth Travel Library (see pp. 343–345) or your local travel agent.

Eurail Pass

The Eurail pass, which can only be purchased by people living outside Europe, cannot be used in mainland Britain but is valid for travel around the Republic of Ireland and mainland Europe. Eurail passes should be purchased before leaving for Europe, as they are considerably more expensive to buy once you've arrived.

There are several versions of the basic Eurail Pass, valid for 15 days, 21 days, 1 month, 2 months or 3 months. Prices range from US$498 for 15 days to US$1398 for 3 months.

There are many other types of Eurail Pass; to find out more details you can contact either Forsyth Travel Library in the USA (see pp. 343–345), or your local Eurail Aid Office.

Inter-Rail Passes

For details of all Inter-Rail passes, which are valid for travel in Northern Ireland and the Republic of Ireland, see p. 33.

THEMED ITINERARIES

This chapter consists of a series of ideas for planning your own rail itineraries, using the recommended routes to take in sights associated with particular aspects of Britain's life, history or landscape. They take key cities and recommended routes and identify the sights connected with the theme of the itinerary to be found in those chapters. These itineraries are intended both as guides for planning journeys which you can follow or adapt to your tastes as you choose, and also as a source of ideas for developing your own themed itineraries along similar lines.

PLANNING AN ITINERARY

Themes can make a trip more fun but to make sure tours are practical, here are some tips.

1. Work out train times with the detailed leaflets available free at most rail stations, or take an up-to-date copy of the *Thomas Cook European Timetable* or *Timetable of Britain, France and Benelux* (see p. 5). Do pay attention to table footnotes, as they may refer to days when train services are not operating to the usual time. Ask the staff at the rail station to double-check anything you do not understand, or just to reassure yourself. A copy of the *Thomas Cook Visitor's Rail Map of Great Britain and Ireland* will also help when planning a tour.
2. If the place you are planning to visit is very small and you have luggage with you, check beforehand if there is somewhere to leave your bags.
3. Allow plenty of time for your visit to the attraction or town. This may be quite a distance from the rail station, so do not plan quick change-overs. Stay longer to look around

or build time for a meal or coffee break into your stay. Double-check the opening times of a museum or gallery which you definitely want to see so that you don't miss the whole point of your visit.

4. Pre-book accommodation if you plan to arrive fairly late in the evening or after the tourist office is closed.
5. Try to pick places with frequent train services. If you are a real enthusiast about the theme you have chosen, an obscure place that is a real gem might be worth all the waiting around, otherwise it might be interesting to fit in a couple of other more accessible locations.
6. Be flexible. If you discover that real gem, stay longer to explore it and discard something else planned for another day.
7. Allow plenty of time to get back to your departure point, whether it's an airport, station or ferry port.

1. ROUND-BRITAIN ROUTE

The following itinerary links many of the recommended routes in this book, in whole or in part, to provide a round-Britain super-route, enabling you to see as much of the country as possible in a series of journeys which make up one circular itinerary beginning and ending in London. Suggested day trips from London are added at the end. The time the itinerary will take depends entirely on much sightseeing you plan to do between journeys.

Some sections of the itinerary use train connections not forming part of our book but easily looked up in one of the Thomas Cook timetables (*ETT* or *Britain, France and Benelux*) – the relevant table numbers are given below. Using the timetables, in conjunction with our Route Maps on pp. 8–9, the Through Routes on p. 10, and the recommended routes throughout this book, will reveal many ways of modifying this grand tour to take in the sights important to you.

London to York (pp. 223–225)
York to Newcastle (pp. 295–300)
Newcastle to Edinburgh (pp. 250–251)
Edinburgh to Aberdeen (pp. 134–137)

---

2. ROYAL BRITAIN

The history of Great Britain is inextricably linked with the history of its kings and queens, and many of the most famous features of Britain's heritage have royal connections – some legendary, some genuine, some firmly rooted in the past, others continuing to the present day. The following route and city chapters take in some of the most celebrated as well as some of the less well known.

London (pp. 160–173)

As the official home of the royal family and the seat of British government for centuries, London has a wide range of sights associated with the monarchy, including Buckingham Palace, Westminster Abbey, the Tower of London and the Banqueting House, Whitehall . Just out of town are Hampton Court, Eltham Palace and the Queen's House, Greenwich . The capital is also an excellent base from which to visit other places with royal connections.

London to Brighton (pp. 184–189)

Battle; Queen Elizabeth's oak at Northiam

Brighton (pp. 79–82)

The Royal Pavilion.

London to Southampton
(pp. 211–222)

Henry VIII's flagship, the Mary Rose; Osborne House, Isle of Wight; Charles I's one-time prison, Carisbrooke Castle, Isle of Wight; Broadlands.

London to Oxford (pp. 208–210)

Windsor Castle.

Cambridge (pp. 90–94)

Sandringham.

Edinburgh (pp. 126–133)

As the capital of Scotland and seat of the Scottish monarchy until the Union with England in 1603, Edinburgh also has its royal attractions, prime among which is **Holyrood House.**

Edinburgh to Aberdeen (pp. 134–137)

Glamis Castle

---

3. LITERARY TOUR OF BRITAIN

Britain has a particularly rich literary heritage, stretching from Geoffrey Chaucer, whose Canterbury pilgrims never reached their destination in the unfinished 'Canterbury Tales', through Shakespeare – who has a heritage industry all to himself – right through to the present day. The following itineraries take in a wide range of places associated with some of the world-f amous figures of literary Britain.

London (pp. 160–173)

London has one of the greatest concentrations of literary attractions in the world, from the various houses lived in by Charles Dickens, for whom London was almost a symbol of human life, through the Bloomsbury of Virginia Woolf and her associates, to Dr Johnson's house in Gough Square and John Keats' in Hampstead. Karl Marx wrote *Das Kapital* in the British Museum Reading Room and is buried in Highgate Cemetery. Horace Walpole built himself an extraordinary Gothic fantasy of a house at Strawberry Hill, Twickenham. Other literary figures to have made London their home include Oscar Wilde, Thomas Carlyle, Robert and Elizabeth Barrett Browning, George Eliot and Samuel Pepys. The city is also a good starting point for literary tours to the south and west and to the Midlands.

London to Brighton (pp. 184–189)

The Sackville-Wests' Knole House; Sir Philip Sidney's birthplace, Penshurst Place; Rudyard Kipling's house, Bateman's; Henry James' Lamb House in Rye; Virginia Woolf's Monk's House; Vanessa Bell and Duncan Grant's Charleston Farmhouse, Lewes.

London to Canterbury (pp. 190–191)

Dickens' Centre, Rochester.

Southampton to Weymouth
(pp. 283–288)

Lawrence of Arabia's house, Cloud's Hill; gateway to Thomas Hardy's Wessex; Hardy's Birthplace at Lower Bockhampton; Hardy's house, Max Gate, Dorchester.

London to Birmingham (pp. 176–183)

The Shakespeare properties in and around Stratford-upon-Avon.

Nottingham (pp. 256–257)

D H Lawrence Birthplace Museum, Eastwood; Lord Byron's home, Newstead Abbey.

Manchester to Carlisle (pp. 231–236)

The Lake District, one-time haunt of the Romantic Lake Poets, Wordsworth and Coleridge, is easily accessible from Manchester. The area also has associations with the perennially popular children's author, Beatrix Potter. places descibed include: Windermere; Wordsworth's Dove Cottage, Grasmere; Rydal Mount, Ambleside; Beatrix Potter's Hill Top, Near Sawrey.

Manchester to York (pp.240–244)

The Brontë Museum, Haworth

Carlisle to Glasgow (pp. 115–117)

Burns' House and Burns Centre, Dumfries; Burns' Cottage and Museum, Alloway.

---

3. HISTORIC HOUSES AND GARDENS

Britain boasts an enormous number of historic houses, ranging from palaces to relatively modest country seats, many of which are also famous for their gardens. This itinerary lists routes and cities close to a wide selection of some of the country's most celebrated houses and gardens. The array of places worth visiting is so wide that we have included under the appropriate route or city some houses and gardens which you may want to visit even though they are not covered in our text; handbooks of organisations such as the National Trust and English Heritage will alert you to many architectural and horticultural gems which we had no space to describe.

London (pp. 160–173)

The capital has more than its share of famous addresses and is also home to some of Britain's most renowned gardens. London's historic houses include Buckingham Palace, Hampton Court, Kenwood House, Chiswick House and Osterley Park, while Polesden Lacy is a short journey to the south. Kew and Syon Park are among the jewels in Britain's horticultural crown; on the fringe of London, Wisley Royal Horticultural Society Gardens and Capel Manor Institute of Horticultural and Field Studies will also repay a visit.

London to Brighton (pp. 184–189)

Hever Castle; Knole House; Chartwell; Ightham Mote; Emmetts Garden; Penshurst Place; Scotney Castle Garden; Sissinghurst Castle Garden; Royal Pavilion; Sheffield Park Garden; Leonardslee Gardens; Nymans; Wakehurst Place Garden.

London to Canterbury (pp. 190–191)

Leeds Castle.

London to Southampton
(pp. 211–222)

Petworth House; Goodwood House; Osborne

House; Broadlands; Beaulieu; Kingston Lacy.

London to Exeter (pp. 192–198)

Wilton House; Longleat House; Stourhead; Montacute House; Tintinhull House and Garden. Knightshayes Court; Castle Drogo.

Exeter to Plymouth (pp. 149–151)

Saltram House; Cotehele House; Buckland Abbey.

Plymouth to Penzance (pp. 272–279)

Lanhydrock; Trelissick Gardens; Trewithen House Garden; Glendurgan Garden.

London to Norwich (pp. 199–205)

Helmingham Hall Gardens; Felbrigg Hall; Blickling Hall: Somerleyton Hall.

Cambridge (pp. 90–98)

Ickworth; Melford Hall; Kentwell Hall; Bressingham Gardens; Oxburgh Hall; Sandringham House; Houghton Hall; Holkham Hall.

London to Oxford (pp. 208–210)

Cliveden; Hughenden Manor; West Wycombe Park; Windsor Castle; Savile Garden.

Oxford (pp. 265–269)

University Botanical Gardens; Blenheim Palace.

London to Birmingham (pp. 176–183)

Stowe Gardens; Althorp House; Arbury Hall; Charlecote Park; Hagley Hall

London to Nottingham (pp. 206–207)

Hatfield House; Luton Hoo; Knebworth House; Wrest Park House and Gardens.; Woburn Abbey Boughton House; Rockingham Castle; Deene Park; Hardwick Hall.

Nottingham (pp. 256–257)

Belvoir Castle; The Dukeries (a collection of stately homes north of Nottingham in the Sherwood Forest area, including Clumber Park).

London to York (pp. 223–225)

Burghley House; Belton House.

Birmingham to Bristol (pp. 62–68)

Sudeley Castle; Hidcote Manor Garden; Westonbirt Arboretum; Westbury Court Garden; Dyrham Park; Bowood House and Gardens; Lacock Abbey.

Birmingham to Aberystwyth (pp. 55–61)

Attingham Park; Powis Castle.

Birmingham to Manchester (pp. 75–76)

Shugborough; Little Moreton Hall; Tatton Park.

Birmingham to Sheffield (pp. 77–78)

Calke Abbey; Kedleston Hall; Chatsworth; Haddon Hall; Lyme Park

Manchester to York (pp. 240–244)

Harewood House.

York (pp. 289–292)

Castle Howard

Newcastle to Edinburgh (pp. 250–251)

Bamburgh Castle; Dunstanburgh Castle

Edinburgh (pp. 126–133)

Edinburgh Royal Botanical Gardens; Dalmeny House; Hopetoun House.

Edinburgh to Aberdeen (pp. 134–137)

Glamis Castle; Dundee University Botanical Gardens.

Carlisle to Glasgow (pp. 115–117)

Threave Gardens; Drumlanrig Castle; Culzean Castle Garden and Country Park.

Edinburgh to Inverness (pp. 138–)

Blair Castle; Scone Palace; Eilean Donan Castle.

---

4 . SCENIC BRITAIN

For a small country, Britain boasts a wide variety of countryside and natural features, from the green rolling hills so often thought of as the archetypal English landscape to the rugged gran-

---

Historic Houses and Gardens–Scenic Britain

deur of the Scottish Highlands. The following routes give access to some of these natural wonders of the British Isles.

Norwich (pp. 252–255)

The Norfolk Broads

London to Southampton (pp. 211–222)

The Needles; Alum Bay; the New Forest.

Southampton to Weymouth (pp. 283–288)

The Blue Pool Chesil Beach; Portland Bill.

London to Exeter (pp. 192–198)

Quantock Hills; Blackdown Hills; Exmoor; Salisbury Plain;

Exeter to Plymouth (pp. 149–151)

Dartmoor

Plymouth to Penzance (pp. 272–279)

Lizard Point; Land's End; Cornwall Coastal Path; St Michael's Mount

Birmingham to Aberystwyth (pp. 55–61)

The Wrekin; the Shropshire Hills; Devil's Bridge Falls

Birmingham to Bristol (pp. 62–68)

The Cotswolds; Glastonbury Tor; Cheddar Gorge; Wookey Hole Caves; the Mendip Hills.

Birmingham to Cardiff (pp. 69–74)

The Malvern Hills; Brecon Beacons; Sugar Loaf Mountain; Forest of Dean; Symonds Yat.

Birmingham to Sheffield (pp. 77–78)

Heights of Abraham; Peak District Blue John Cavern and Mine; Pool's Caves; Peak Cavern; Speedwell Cavern

Cardiff to Pembroke (pp. 109–113)

The Mumbles; Gower Peninsula; the Elan Valley Cenarth Falls; Pembrokeshire Coastal Path

Chester to Bangor (pp. 122–125)

Snowdonia National Park; Snowdon; Lake Bala.

Manchester to Carlisle (pp. 231–236)

The Lake District, including Scafell Pike, Coniston Water, Windermere.

York to Carlisle (pp. 293–294)

Yorkshire Dales, including Malham Cove, Malham Tarn and Gordale Scar, Wensleydale, the Buttertubs and Aysgarth Falls

York to Newcastle (pp. 295–300)

North Yorkshire Moors Railway; Swaledale; Cuddy Crags, Kielder Water.

Travelling by train in Scotland can in itself be an exhilarating way of exploring some of the most spectacular countryside in Europe. The following routes additionally provide jumping-off points for specific attractions.

Edinburgh to Inverness (pp. 138–144)

Cairngorm Mountains; Loch Ness; Speyside; North-west Highlands; Isle of Skye.

Glasgow (pp. 152–156)

From Glasgow it is a short trip to **Loch Lomond**, famed in song for its 'bonny banks' .

Glasgow to Oban (pp. 157–159)

Ben Nevis; Isle of Mull.

Belfast to Londonderry (pp.305–308)

Giant's Causeway.

Dublin to Cork (pp. 319–323)

Killarney; Ring of Kerry.

Dublin to Limerick (pp. 324–330)

Wicklow Hills.

Dublin to Westport (pp. 334–337)

Galway Bay.

ABERDEEN

Aberdeen is often called the 'Granite City', as most of its magnificent buildings glisten with locally quarried sparkling granite. Aberdeen is also famous for its fabulous floral displays – in parks, gardens and along roadsides. Scotland's third largest city, historic Aberdeen is a place of contrasts: the harbour, busy with colourful fishing boats and oil supply ships; Old Aberdeen, with its picturesque cottages; and the seaside resort's clean, sandy beach.

Tourist Information

TIC: *St Nicholas House, Broad St, Aberdeen AB9 1DE; tel: (01224) 632727; fax (01224) 620415.* Open Mon–Fri 0900–1700; Sat 1000–1400 (Oct–May). Mon–Sat 0900–1800, Sun 1000–1600 (Jun and Sep), Mon–Fri 0900–2000, Sat 0900–1800, Sun 1000–1800 (Jul and Aug). DP, SHS services available, local bed-booking and BABA at 10% of first night's stay. Guided tours booked in summer season. Theatre tickets, day bus passes, Great British Heritage Pass (BTA) and NTS Tourer tickets sold. *Grampian, Highlands and Aberdeen* guide (including accommodation listings) available free of charge.

Arriving and Departing

Airport

Aberdeen Airport, *Dyce; tel: (01224) 722331* Regular bus service no. 27 between the airport and city centre *(Guild St)*, Mon–Fri 0550–2135, Sat 0550–2102, Sun 1010–2125. Journey time 40 minutes.

Station

Aberdeen Station, *Guild St; tel: (01224) 594222* is in the town centre. The station has a **Hertz Rent-a-Car** desk and a taxi rank outside.

Getting Around

Most attractions are within walkable distance. A free town map is available from the TIC and transport maps can be obtained from either the TIC or from Grampian Transport *tel: (01224) 637047*, cost £0.25.

Buses

Grampian Transport, *tel: (01224) 633333* and **Bluebird Northern**, *tel: (01224) 212266* are the main bus companies serving the area. Services are very good in the town centre and fairly good also to outlying districts with frequent buses up to 2300 Mon–Sat and to 2230 Sun with night buses on Sat up to 0200 hours. There is a **City Ride Day Pass** costing £3.50.

Taxis

The main taxi rank is in *Back Wynd, Hadden St*, and there are a number of taxi ranks in the city centre. Taxis can be hailed in the street.

Staying in Aberdeen

Accommodation

There is a large selection of accommodation of most types in the city centre, with cheaper accommodation to be found in the areas of Mannofield (3 miles west), Kincorth (4 miles south) and Old Aberdeen (2 miles north). Generally it is easy to find accommodation on arrival in the city except during the **Offshore Europe** exhibition, which takes place for three days every second year in early September (1995, 1997 etc). It must also be noted that many smaller establishments are closed over Christmas and New Year.

Hotel chains in Aberdeen include *Ja, MC, MH*.

There is an accommodation finding agency, **Munro's Tourist Agency**, *130 Union St, Aberdeen; tel: (01224) 648422, fax (01224) 624450*. The youth hostel is **King George VI Memorial Hostel**, *8 Queen's Rd; tel :(01224) 646988*. Open from 1400 daily. Grampian Bus no. 15 from the city centre passes nearby.

There are two campsites within a reasonable distance. **Hazlehead Camping and Caravan**

Park, *Beach Leisure Centre; tel: (01224) 647647* is 3 miles west of the city centre and Grampian Bus 15 goes to Hazlehead Park, which is nearby. **Craighill Caravan Park**, *Stonehaven Rd; tel: (01224) 873529* is 4 miles south; take Grampian Bus 25 to Kincorth, then walk ¼ mile to the park.

Eating and Drinking

The TIC has a free list of restaurant and eating places, *Eating out in Aberdeen*. **The Courtyard on the Lane**, *1 Alford Ln; tel: (01224) 213795* includes vegetarian food on the menu and **The Lemon Tree**, *5 West North St; tel: (01224) 642230* is a vegetarian and vegan restaurant. **Ashvale Fish and Chip Restaurant** *44-48 Great Western Rd; tel: (01224) 596981* and **Silver Darling** *Pocra Quay, North Pier; tel (01224) 576229* are both recommended fish restaurants.

Communications

The main post office is at *St Nicholas Centre*, open Mon–Fri 0900–1730, Sat 0900-1900.

Entertainment and Events

What's on in Aberdeen is a listing available free from the TIC and a local publication, also free, entitled *57 North* has a listing of entertainment and events. **His Majesty's Theatre**, *Rosemount Viaduct; tel: (01224) 637788* is one of the main theatres in the area and is considered a favourite amongst visiting actors. **Aberdeen Exhibition and Conference Centre**, *Bridge of Don; tel: (01224) 824824* is a major conference and concert venue.

Aberdeen International Football Festival, at *Seaton Park* every July, is a major event in Aberdeen's calendar. Bus nos 1, 2, 3 and 4 go to the venue from the city centre. **The Scottish Connection Festival** at Easter every year is also a popular event.

Shopping

A free leaflet *Shopping in Aberdeen* is available from the TIC. The main shopping areas are *St Nicholas St*, Bon Accord Shopping Centre in *George St* and the Trinity Shopping Centre in *Union St*.

Sightseeing

The 'Granite City' of Aberdeen has a wealth of fine architecture; the **Central Library, St Mark's Church** and **His Majesty's Theatre** are a trio known locally as 'Education, Salvation and Damnation' **Marischal College**, founded in the 16th century, is the second largest granite building in the world.

St Andrew's, one of Aberdeen's magnificent cathedrals, has links with the American Episcopacy; the Seabury memorial commemorates the consecration of the first bishop of the USA. **Provost Ross's House**, dating from 1593, now houses the **Maritime Museum**, telling the story of Aberdeen's seafaring history, from fishing to North Sea oil. **Provost Skene's House** is also a museum and has furnished period rooms depicting lifestyles of the 17th and 18th centuries. After learning all about the past, catch up with the latest in science and technology at the **Satrosphere**, an interactive exhibition with 'hands on' displays.

In Old Aberdeen, **Kings College Visitor Centre** looks at the history of one of Britain's oldest universities. Out of town is **Storybook Glen**, a 28-acre landscaped park with models of nursery rhyme characters.

Grampian Transport, *tel: (01224) 637047*, **McIntyres Coaches**, *tel: (01224) 493112* and **Bluebird Northern** *tel: (01224) 212266* offer guided bus tours of the city and area and guided walks can be booked through **Bon Accord Tours**, *tel: (01224) 733704*.

Churches and Cathedrals

St Andrew's Cathedral, *King St; tel: (01224) 640290*. Open Mon–Sat 1000–1600 (May–Sep), Fri 1000–1200 (all year). Admission free. **St Mary's Cathedral**, *Huntly St; tel: (01224) 640160*. Open daily 0800–1600. Admission free

Art Galleries and Museums

Satrosphere, *19 Justice Mill Ln; tel :(01224) 213232*. Open Mon and Wed–Fri 1000-1600, Sat 1000–1700, Sun 1330–1700. Admission £3 **Aberdeen Maritime Museum**, *Shiprow; tel: (01224) 585788*. Open Mon–Sat 1000-1700. Admission free. **James Dun's House**, *Schoolhill;*

tel: (01224) 646333. Open Mon–Sat 1000–1700. Admission free.

Provost Skene's House, *Guest Row (off Broad St); tel: (01224) 641086.* Open Mon–Sat 1000–1700. Admission free. **Aberdeen Art Gallery**, *Schoolhill; tel: (01224) 646333.* Open Mon–Sat 1000–1700, Thu 1000–2000, Sun 1400–1700. Admission free.

Out of Town

Garden

Cruickshank Botanic Gardens, *Chanonry, Old Aberdeen; tel: (01224) 272704.* Open Mon–Fri 0900–1630 (all year), Sat and Sun 1400–1700 (May–Sept). Admission free. Two miles from the city centre, via Grampian Bus nos 17 and 20.

Museums

King's College Visitor Centre, *High St, Old Aberdeen; tel: (01224) 273701.* Open Mon–Sat 1000–1700, Sun 1200–1700. Admission free. Two miles north west of the city, via Grampian Bus no. 20 from Littlejohn Street.

Castles

Haddo House, *Tarves; tel: (01651) 851440.* Open daily 1330–1730 (May, June and Sept), also 1st weekend in Oct), daily 1100–1730 (July and Aug). Admission £3.50. 16 miles north west of Aberdeen, no public transport. **Castle Fraser**, *Sauchen, by Kennay; tel: (01330) 833463.* Open daily 1330–1730 (May, June and Sept), daily 1100–1730 (July and Aug). Admission £4.00. Eight miles north-west, no public transport.

Theme Parks and Attractions

Storybook Glen, *Maryculter; tel: (01224) 732941.* Open daily 1000–1800 (Mar–Oct), Sat and Sun 1100–1600 (Nov–Feb). Admission £3. Six miles west of the city. Bluebird Northern *tel: (01224) 212266* run a bus service in the summer, otherwise no public transport. **Crombie Woollen Mill**, *Grandholm Mills, Woodside; tel: (01224) 483201.* Open Mon–Sat 0900–1630. Admission free. Three miles north west of the city, by Grampian bus no. 25.

BATH

One of Britain's oldest cities, the elegant spa town of Bath is the gateway to the West Country and a World Heritage City. The Romans discovered the natural hot springs here and created an important settlement called Aquae Sulis in AD 44. However, Bath's heyday was the 18th century, when it became the place to be seen; it remained a fashionable resort into the 19th century, and is still a popular city for visitors from near and far.

Tourist Information

TIC: The Colonnades, Bath St BA1 1SW; tel: (01225) 462831. Open from mid-Sept to mid-June Mon–Sat 0930–1700, closed Sun, mid-Jun–mid-Sep Mon–Sat 0930–1800, Sun 1000–1600. DP service offered: local bed-booking service available up to closing time, deposit 10% of first night's accommodation, deductible from final bill, tel: (01225) 460722. BABA (latest 1630) £2 booking fee – be prepared to queue for accommodation bookings in summer season. Guided tours booked, Great British Heritage Pass and Longleat passport tickets sold in summer season. Bath Official Guide is £0.75, Bath Accommodation Guide is free.

Arriving and Departing

The Bath Spa, Dorchester St; tel: (0117) 9294255 is ¼ mile from the city centre. **Guide Friday,** Station Forecourt; tel: (01225) 444102 operate an accommodation-finding service and **Hertz Rent-a-Car** have a car-hire desk there. Taxis can be hailed outside the station.

Getting Around

Most attractions are within walking distance of the town centre and a town map is available for £0.25 from the TIC. Minibus transport services covering the city centre are very good, but are less frequent to outlying areas of the town.

Badgerline is the main local bus operator, Bus Station, Manvers St; tel: (01225) 464446. They operate a frequent service within the city limits, including evenings. Services to outlying villages are less frequent. They have a 'Day Rambler' ticket that can be used on any services in and around Bath, price £4.50 adult, £3.30 child and senior citizens; also a weekly 'Maxi Rover' Card at £19.60. The 'Bath City Rover' is for services inside the city and costs £8.70 weekly (no concessions).

The main taxi rank is on Orange Gve, tel: (01225) 447777 and the TIC can provide details of other registered taxi companies.

Staying in Bath

Accommodation

It is always advisable to book accommodation in advance and particularly over Easter, the peak summer season, Christmas and Bank Holiday weekends. The **Bath International Festival** in May/June means that accommodation is booked well in advance for this period. There is a wide range of hotels and guest-houses in the city, although the smaller ones are situated on the outskirts, usually a short walk or bus ride from the centre. Hotel chains in Bath include: BW, FC, Hn and MH.

A **Youth Hostel,** Bathwick Hill; tel (01225) 465674, is open daily from 0730–2230 and is on the bus route No 18. There is also a **YMCA** at Broad Street Pl; tel: (01225) 460471, open 24 hours a day. Several buses pass the door and it is only a 3-min walk to the city centre, 10 mins from the bus station. Nearest campsites are **Newbridge Caravan Park,** Brassmill Ln; tel: (01225) 428778, ½ mile west of the city centre, on main A4 road, and **Newton Mill Touring Centre,** Newton St Loe; tel: (01225) 333909, about 3 miles west of the centre, off the A4/A39 roads – take bus No. 9 from the city centre. A list of camping and caravan parks is available free from the TIC.

Eating and Drinking

There is a good selection of restaurants and pubs offering food of all nationalities, and many restaurants have vegetarian menus. The TIC has

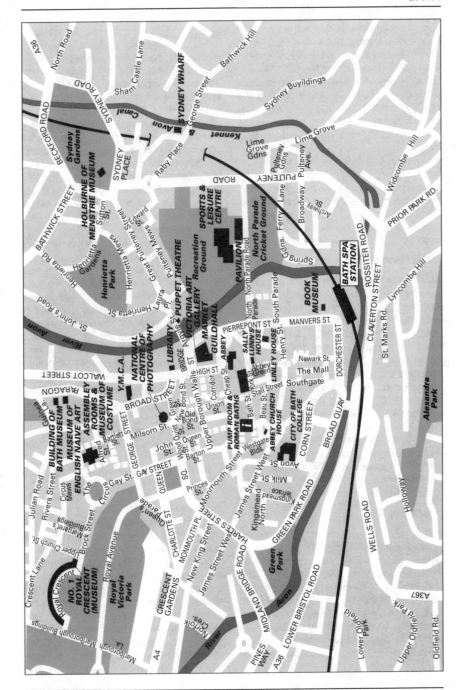

a list of restaurants in Bath, available free. **Sally Lunn's Refreshment House and Museum**, *4 North Parade Passage*, is the oldest house in Bath, c1482. Excavations in the Cellar Museum show remains of Roman, Saxon and medieval buildings. In 1680 Sally Lunn worked in this building, creating the legendary **Sally Lunn Bun**. Other local delicacies are **Bath Olivers**, (a biscuit for eating with cheese) and the **Bath Bun.**

Communications and Money

The main post office is on *New Bond Street*, open Mon–Fri 0900–1730, Sat 0900–1300. Post restante facilities are available. **Thomas Cook** bureaux de change can be found at *20 New Bond St.*

Entertainment and Events

An entertainment list, *This Month in Bath*, is available free from the TIC and the *Bath Chronicle* has an list of events and venues. The main entertainment venue is the **Theatre Royal Bath**, *Sawclose; tel: (01225) 448844* which offers a top-class selection of drama, comedy, opera, ballet and pantomime. They also give backstage tours of this historic theatre. There is a selection of nightlife venues with live music and discos at many pubs and clubs, including **Joe Bananas**, *Barton St*, open until 0200 every night. The TIC has a free list, *Nightlife in Bath*.

The main event is the **Bath International Festival**, which takes place annually in May and June at various venues and is a celebration of music and the arts. There are also regular antiques fairs held in different venues.

Shopping

Bath is noted for antiques and other specialist shops. The main shopping areas are *Milson St*, *Stall St* and *Union St* for major stores and small boutiques and shops. *Northumberland Place* and *The Corridor* are pedestrianised streets with small shops, while *Barlett St* and *Walcot St* specialise in antiques. There is an **Antique Market** every Wed 0630–1430 at *Guinea Lane* and the **Paragon Antiques Market** is on Weds from 0630–1530 in *3 Bladud Buildings, Paragon*.

Sightseeing

Bath is the best-preserved Georgian city in Britain and has some superb architectural features, like the unique shop-lined **Pulteney Bridge** (designed by Robert Adam in 1771), which spans the river Avon and has shops on either side. To the north of the city are many interesting streets such as **The Circus** and the graceful **Royal Crescent; No 1 Royal Crescent** is a restored and furnished Georgian residence that appears as it might have done in the 18th century. The picturesque streets around the centre of Bath are a hive of activity where shoppers and tourists are entertained by lively street entertainers and musicians.

Bath is famous for its **Roman Baths**, a complex of ancient swimming pools, saunas and baths which are some of the best-preserved Roman remains anywhere in England. The baths were built around a natural hot spring which rises at 46.5°C. The adjoining 18th-century **Pump Room** has a hot spa water pump and present day visitors can still taste the waters here. Overlooking the Roman Baths is **Bath Abbey** which dates from the late 15th century but has been altered and restored several times since. The fascinating **Museum of Costume**, situated in the 18th-century **Assembly Rooms**, shows the development of British fashion over the last 400 years; with 200 dressed figures and thousands of other items it is one of the finest collections in the world.

Bath makes an ideal touring base being surrounded by pleasant countryside dotted with attractions, all just a short drive away. The **American Museum** at Claverton recreates 17th-19th century American homes and includes displays of textiles and folk art. Picturesque **Lacock** is an unspoilt medieval village and the setting for **Lacock Abbey** (founded in 1232), with its house, cloisters and lovely grounds. At the gates of the Abbey is the **Fox Talbot Museum of Photography**, commemorating William Henry Fox Talbot, the father of modern photography. The area boasts many fine country houses, such as 18th-century **Bowood House and Gardens**, with its collection of family heirlooms and splendid landscaped parkland.

In the region south of Bath are **Iford Manor Gardens** (beautiful riverside Italianate gardens) and **Longleat**, home of the Marquess of Bath, which provides an ideal family day out. Amongst its attractions are a splendid fine art collection and an excellent safari park containing many rare and endangered species.

There are various sightseeing tours covering all aspects of interest in Bath. **City Tour** is a 45-minute hop-on and -off tour of the city on a red open-top bus showing the principal places of interest with a trained guide. Tours start from *Terrace Walk* and frequency is posted at the bus stops. For detailed timetable information *tel: (01225) 424157*, tickets are £4 adult and are valid all day. **Badgerline/Guide Friday** *tel: (01225) 464446/444102*, run a coach tour of the city, approximately 1¼ hours, daily in the summer and Mon–Fri from Oct–Mar. Tours start from the *Bus Station* or *Terrace Walk*. A free walking tour of Bath lasts 2 hrs and includes the main points of historical and architectural interest. The walk starts by the 'Free Walking Tours Here' notice in the *Abbey Church Yard; tel: (01225) 461111 ext. 2786* for further information. There is also **Ghost Walks of Bath** from The Garrick Head (next door to the Theatre Royal) at 2000 Mon–Fri (May–Oct), Fri only (Nov–Apr), price £3 adults. Canal and river trips are also available during the day and punts and canoes can be hired.

Art Galleries and Museums

Museum of Costume and Assembly Rooms, *Bennett Street; tel: (01225) 461111 ext 2785* open Mon–Sat 0930–1800, Sun 1000-1800 Mar–Oct, Mon–Sat 1000–1700, Sun 1100–1700 Nov–Feb. Admission £3.20. **Building of Bath Museum,** *The Paragon; tel: (01225) 333895*, open Tue–Sun 1030–1700; closed mid-Dec–Feb. Admission £2. **No 1 Royal Crescent,** *1 Royal Cres; tel: (01225) 428126*, open Tue–Sun 1030–1700 Mar–Oct; closed Mon except Bank Holiday Mons and Bath Festival Mon, Tue–Sun 1030–1600 Nov–Feb. Admission £3.50. **Beckford's Tower and Museum,** *Lansdown; Tel: (01225) 422212*, open Sat, Sun and Bank Holiday 1400–1700 Apr–Oct. Admission £1.50. **Bath Postal Mu-**

seum, *8 Broad St; tel: (01225) 460333*, open Mon–Sat all year 1100–1700, Sun 1400–1700 Mar-Dec. Admission £2. **Holburne Museum and Crafts Study Centre,** *Great Pulteney St; tel: (01225) 466669*, open Mon–Sat and Bank Holiday 1100–1700, Sun 1430–1800, Apr–mid Dec (closed Mon Nov–Dec). Admission £3.50. **Victoria Art Gallery,** *Bridge St; tel: (01225) 461111 ext 2772*, open Mon–Fri 10–1730, Sat 1000–1700. Admission free.

Historic Buildings

Bath Abbey, *tel: (01225) 422462*, Mon–Sat 0900–1800 (1630 in winter), Sun 1315–1430 and 1630–1730. Admission £1 Abbey, £2 vaults. **Roman Baths and Pump Room,** *Abbey Churchyard; tel: (01225) 461111 ext 2785*, open daily 0900–1800 Mar–Oct (also Aug 2000–2200) Mon–Sat 0900–1700, Sun 1000–1700 Nov–Feb. Admission £5.

Out of Town

Museums

The American Museum, *Claverton; tel: (01225) 460503*, open Tue–Sun end Mar–early Nov 1400-1700 and Easter Mon 1100-1700. Admission £5. Take bus no. 18 from bus station, alight at The Avenue, walk 10 mins to museum. **Fox Talbot Museum of Photography,** *Lacock, near Chippenham; tel: (01249) 730549*, open daily end Mar–Oct 1100–1730. Admission £2.30. On A350, 3 miles south of Chippenham. Badgerline buses 234, 237, 264, 267 from Bath stop at in Lacock village. On the same visit, **Lacock Abbey,** *tel: (01249) 730227*, open Tue–Sun end Mar–Oct 1300–1730. Admission £4.20.

Stately Homes and Gardens

Bowood House and Gardens, *Calne; tel: (01249) 812102*, open daily end Mar–Oct 1100–1800. Admission £4.70 (rhododendron gardens only, £2.50). On A4 between Calne and Chippenham, bus X55 from Chippenham rail station. **Dyrham Park,** *Dyrham, Chippenham; tel: (01272) 372501*, open daily 1200–1730. Admission £5. Eight miles north of Bath on A43, two miles south of M4 junction 18. **Longleat,**

Warminster; tel: (01985) 844400, open daily mid Mar–Oct 1000–1800. Admission £10 Passport to all attraction, £4 house only. Bus from Bath stops at gate, then a 2-mile walk down the drive. **Iford Manor Gardens** (7 miles southeast), *Bradford-on-Avon; tel: (01225) 863146*, open Sun Apr and Oct 1400–1700; Tue–Thu, Sat, Sun and Bank Holiday Mon May–Sep. Admission £2. Two-mile walk from Bradford-on-Avon station.

 ## Connection: Bristol

There are very frequent services from Bath Spa to Bristol Temple Meads Mon to Sat (less on Suns), taking from 15 to 20 mins.

–––––––––––––––––––

 ## Side Tracks from Bath

WELLS

TIC: *Town Hall, Market Pl, Wells, Somerset BA5 2RB; tel: (01749) 672552.* Open Mon–Sun 0930–1730 (Apr–Oct), 1000–1600 (Nov–Mar). DP Services offered: local bed-booking service (10% commission charged and latest booking closing time), BABA (10% commission charged and latest booking closing time), guided tours booked. Tickets booked for local attractions. *Wells Information and Accommodation Pack* is £0.50.

Bus: there are no direct rail services from Bath to Wells; instead, take the hourly Badgerline bus *(tel: (01225) 464446)* which costs £2.40 and takes 1 hr for the journey.

Getting Around

The majority of attractions are within a walkable distance of the town centre. Town and transport maps are available free of charge from the TIC. **BadgerLine Buses** is the main operator for local buses *tel: (01749 673084)*. Public transport is generally good to all areas of Wells but is infrequent at the weekends and on Bank Holidays. The main taxi rank is on *Saddler St, tel: (01749) 670200.*

Staying in Wells

There is generally no problem in finding accommodation on arrival, except during weekends July–Aug, when it is advisable to book in advance. There are a few hotels and guesthouses and a good selection of cheaper accommodation, both in the town centre and in the outskirts. The only hotel chain in Wells is *Re*. **The Youth Hostel**, *The Chalet, Ivythorn Hill, Street; tel: (01458) 42961* can be reached by bus nos 376 or 163. Campsites: take bus 172 for **Hampstead Park**, *Wookey Hole; tel: (01749) 673022* and **Ebbarlands**, *Wookey Hole; tel: (01749) 672550*, both 1½ miles west of Wells.

Sightseeing

Wells lies at the foot of the Mendip Hills and is perhaps best known for being the smallest city in England. Dating from the 12th century, **Wells Cathedral** can be seen from a distance, its early English Gothic architecture standing out against the surrounding countryside. As you come closer, approaching through one of the medieval gateways, you are faced with the superb West Front that still carries 293 pieces of medieval sculpture extending across the whole facade – an array of figures unique in Europe.

Wells is also known for its **Literary Festival**, held in **Bishop's Palace**, where speakers from previous years have included novelists Joanna Trollope and Penelope Lively.

Wells Cathedral, *tel: (01749) 674483.* Open 0700–dusk. Admission £2.50. **Bishop's Palace**, *The Henderson Rooms, The Palace; tel: (01749) 678691.* Open Tues, Thur and Bank Holiday Mon 1000–1800, Sun 1400–1800 (Apr–Oct) and daily 1000–1800 throughout August. Admission £1.50. **Wells Museum**, *8 Cathedral Green; tel: (01749) 673477.* Open daily 1000–1730 (14 Apr–Jun, Sept–Oct), daily 1000–2030 (July–Aug) and Wed–Sun 1100–1600 (Nov–13 Apr). Admission £0.80.

GLASTONBURY

TIC: *The Tribunal, 9 High Street, Glastonbury, Somerset BA6 9DP; tel: (01458) 832954.* Open Sun–Thu 1000–1700, Fri–Sat 1000–1730 (Apr–Sep), Sun–Thu 1000–1600, Fri–Sat 1000–1630 (Oct–Mar). Local bed-booking service, BABA.

Glastonbury and District Accommodation and Services Guide is free, *Glastonbury Guide* costs £1.50.

Bus: there is a half-hourly Badgerline bus service from Wells to Glastonbury, which takes approximately 16 mins and costs £1.50. If you are not planning to spend more than a day in Glastonbury or Wells, the Day Rambler ticket (see p. 44) is good value.

Getting Around

The attractions in town are all within walking distance of the centre. Free town and transport maps are available from the TIC. The main bus operator is **Badgerline**, *tel: (01749) 673084*. Services are very patchy, so it is best to contact the bus company for further information. The main taxi rank is at the **Town Hall**, *Magdalene St*. For details of registered taxi companies contact the TIC.

Staying in Glastonbury

The majority of accommodation consists of b. & b.s and several guest-houses. Accommodation is cheaper on the edge of the town centre. It is generally easy to book, except for the second Saturday in November (Glastonbury Carnival). The TIC has details of youth hostels and campsites in the area – the nearest youth hostel is **Street Youth Hostel**, *Ivythorn Hill St; tel: (01458) 42961*. The nearest campsites are **The Old Oaks Touring Park**, *Wick Farm, Wick; tel: (01458) 831437*, 2 miles from the centre and **Ashwell Farmhouse**, *Ashwell Ln; tel: (01458) 832313*, 1 mile from the centre; take the Shepton Mallet bus and Tor bus in summer.

Sightseeing

Apart from being a shrine of religion, history and legend, Glastonbury is the ideal base from which to explore the many beauties of central Somerset. **Glastonbury Abbey** is the first Christian sanctuary in the British Isles, so ancient that only legend can recall its origin. It is said to have been founded in the first century and to be the burial place of King Arthur. Not to be missed are the 'Miracle Plays' held in the Abbey grounds in July. The impressive **Glastonbury Tor**, some 525 ft above sea level, rewards energetic climbers with panoramic views and St Michael's Tower remains a landmark for many miles around.

Situated some 7 miles north are the **Wookey Hole Caves**. Formed in limestone of the Mendip Hills by the River Axe, and lived in by man more than 2000 years ago, they are shrouded in legend. Also situated in the Mendips is **Cheddar Gorge**, one of the greatest natural fissures in the country, noted for a series of caves with limestone rock formations and collections of prehistoric weapons. Bus tours can be arranged by **Avalon Coaches**, *Northload St; tel: (01458) 832293*, and guides are available from **Gothic Image Bookshop**, *High St*, and **Robert Baulch**, *tel: (01458) 43164*.

Glastonbury Abbey, *Magdalene St; tel: (01458) 832267*. Open 0900–1800 (Jun–Sep), 0930–1630 (Oct–May). Admission £2.00. **Somerset Rural Life Museum**, *Chilkwell St; tel: (01458) 831197*. Open daily in summer, Mon–Sat in the winter. Admission £1.50. **Glastonbury Lake Village Museum**, *The Tribunal, 9 High St; tel: (01458) 832954*. Open Sun–Thu 1000–1700, Fri–Sat 1000–1730 (Apr–Sep), Sun–Thu 1000–1600, Fri–Sat 1000–1630 (Oct–Mar). Admission £1.50.

Chalice Well Gardens, *Chilkwell St; tel: (01458) 831154*. Open daily 1000–1800 (Jun–Sep), 1300–1600 (Oct–May). Admission 60p. **Glastonbury Tor**, *Wellhouse Ln*. Open any time day and night. Admission free.

Out of Town

Cheddar Showcaves, *The Gorge, Cheddar; tel: (01934) 742343*. Open daily 1000–1730 (Jun–Sep), 1030–1630 (Oct–May). Admission £5.00. Take bus 126. **Wookey Hole Caves**, *Wookey Hole, Wells; tel: (01749) 672243*. Open 0930–1730 (Jun–Sep), 1030–1630 (Oct–May). Admission £6.00. Take bus from Wells town centre. **Montacute House**, *Montacute; tel: (01935) 823289*. Admission £4.70. Take bus no. 681. **Fleet Air Arm Museum**, *Royal Naval Air Station, Yeovilton, Yeovil; tel: (01935) 840565*. Open daily 1000–1730 (Apr–Oct), 1000–1630 (Nov–Mar). Admission £5.50. Take the train from Bath to Yeovil Pen Mill. (Approx 22 miles south).

Glastonbury

BIRMINGHAM

Britain's second city after London, sprawling Birmingham cannot claim to be the most attractive of conurbations – it has been extensively rebuilt since World War II and is renowned more as a business and conference centre than as a tourist venue. Despite this, it has a thriving cultural life, has built up a number of excellent visitor attractions, and makes an good accommodation base for sightseeing in the Midlands.

Tourist Information

TIC: 2 City Arcade, Birmingham, West Midlands B2 5TX; tel: (0121) 643 2514 or (0121) 780 5321. Open Mon–Sat 0930–1730, closed Bank Holidays. DP SHS Services offered: local bed-booking service and BABA (latest 1700), advance reservations handled. Busy for accommodation bookings during major events at the **National Exhibition Centre**. The Pocket Guide to Birmingham is free and includes an accommodation list.

TIC: Exhibition Centre, Birmingham; tel: (0121) 780 4321. Open Mon–Thur 0845–1700, Fri 0845–1645. Open weekends during major exhibitions. DP Services offered: local bed-booking services, BABA.

Information Desk, Birmingham Airport, Birmingham; tel: (0121) 767 7145. Open 24 hours. DP Services offered: accommodation lists available, with courtesy telephones for bookings.

Arriving and Departing

Airport

Birmingham International Airport, 9 miles east of centre; tel: (0121) 767 5511. Rail connections from **Birmingham International Station** at the airport into **Birmingham New Street Station** in the city centre run every 15 mins,

journey time 15 mins, fare: £1.95. There are also direct rail connections to other major cities. **West Midlands Travel** bus service 900 goes to St Martin's Queensway in the centre every 20 mins, journey time 40 mins, fare: £1.17 (£0.82 off-peak). A taxi into the centre costs about £12. Airport facilities include a tourist information desk (see above) car hire, taxis and bureau de change.

Station

The main railway stations are **Birmingham International Station** at the airport (see above) and **Birmingham New Street Station**, New St; tel: (0121) 643 2711 in the city centre, where a taxi rank and car hire service are available. **Snow Hill** is mainly for local services.

Buses

National Express services tel: (0121) 622 4373 operate from Digbeth High St, just south-east of the centre.

Getting Around

Although Birmingham and its satellite towns stretch for miles in all directions, most attractions are within walking distance of the centre. Town and transport maps are available free from the TIC. For general transport information call the **Centro Hotline**, tel: (0121) 200 2700.

Buses

The majority of local bus services are operated from the **Midland Red Bus Station**, behind Birmingham New Street Station. Services are frequent both within the city and to the suburbs, and an hourly night service operates on main routes.

Taxis

Main taxi ranks can be found on New St, Corporation St and Colmore Row; for a black cab tel: (0121) 236 8888.

Staying in Birmingham

Accommodation

It is usually easy to book on arrival, except during major events at the **National Exhibition**

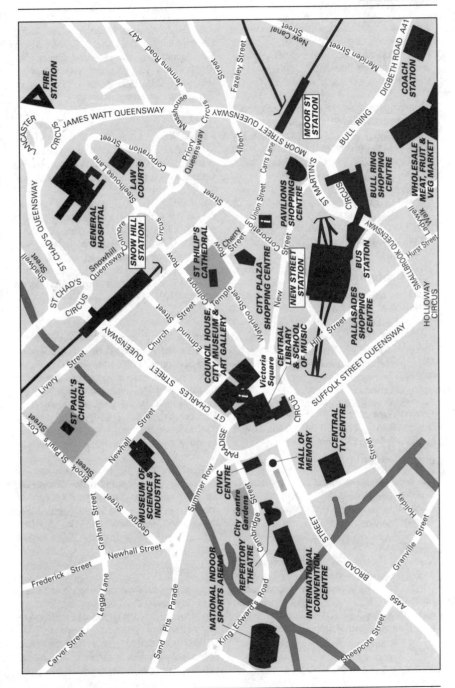

Centre, when it is advisable to book in advance. There is a good range of hotel, guest-house and b.&b. accommodation, with cheaper establishments located just outside the centre.

Hotel chains in Birmingham include *Ca, Cp, FH, Fr, Ho, MC, MH, Nv, Sw.* For budget accommodation there is a summer youth hostel, **IH Cambrian Halls**, *Brindley Drive, off Cambridge St; tel; (0121) 233 3044,* open early July to early Sept. For other times of year *tel; (01789) 297093.* For campsite information contact the TIC.

Eating and Drinking

A free list of restaurants is available from the TICs. There is a large choice of international cuisine in all price ranges. Birmingham is well known for its many Balti restaurants (Kashmiri cooking) to the south of the city, in *Sparkbrook, Bamsall Heath* and *Moseley,* and its lively Chinatown around *Hurst St.* There is one vegan restaurant, at *54 Allison St.*

Communications

The main post office is on *Victoria Sq,* open Mon–Fri 0910–1710, Sat 0900–1200, and has post restante facilities.

Money

Thomas Cook bureaux de change in the city centre: *99 New St* and *50 Corporation St,* and at Midland Bank, *130 New St.*

Entertainment

Free events listings and *What's On* magazine are available from the TICs. Birmingham has lots of entertainment to offer, a sample of which is listed below.

Theatre, Opera and Ballet

Alexandra Theatre, *Suffolk St, Queensway; tel: (0121) 643 1231* (home to the D'Oyly Carte Opera Company). **Birmingham Hippodrome**, *Hurst St; tel: (0121) 622 7486* (home to the Birmingham Royal Ballet). **Birmingham Repertory Theatre**, *Broad St; tel: (0121) 236 4555.*

Music

Birmingham Town Hall, *Victoria Sq; tel: (0121)* *236 2392.* **National Indoor Arena**, *King Edward's Rd; tel: (0121) 200 2202.* **NEC Arena Birmingham**, *National Exhibition Centre; tel: (0121) 780 4133.* **Symphony Hall**, *Broad St; tel: (0121) 236 1555* (home of the City of Birmingham Symphony Orchestra).

Sport

National Indoor Arena, *King Edward's Rd; tel: (0131) 200 3202* (home to the Gladiators). **Warwickshire County Cricket Club**, *County Ground, Edgbaston; tel: (0121) 446 4422.*

Nightclubs

Bakers The Club, *161/163 Broad St; tel: (0121) 633 3839.* **Bobby Browns The Club**, *52 Gas St; tel: (0121) 643 2573.* **Hot Spot Cabaret Bar**, *11 Exeter St, off Holloway Head; tel: (0121) 622 1742.* **Liberty's**, *184 Hagley Rd, Edgbaston; tel: (0121) 454 4444.* **Ronnie Scott's Club**, *Broad St; tel: (0121) 643 4525.*

Shopping

There are various shopping centres to explore, including the **Arcadian Centre**, *Hurst St*; **Bull Ring Shopping Centre**, *Bull Ring*; **City Plaza**, *Cannon St*; **Pallasades Shopping Centre**, *The Pallasades* and **The Pavilions**, *High St.*

Pay a visit to the **Jewellery Quarter** in Hockley (bus 101), the historic jewellery manufacturing district of the city which has been the centre of the British jewellery industry for almost 200 years.

There are also the following markets for bargain hunters: **Bull Ring Centre Market Hall**, *Bull Ring*, open Mon–Sat; **Rag Market** *Edgbaston St*, open Tues, Fri and Sat, with an antiques market on Mon; **Row and Flea Markets** *(adjacent to Rag Market)*, open Tues, Fri and Sat.

Sightseeing

Birmingham has a number of good art collections and museums. Notable for fine and decorative art is the **Birmingham Museum and Art Gallery**, which has the world's finest Pre-Raphaelite collection; away from the centre, **Aston Hall** is a fine Jacobean house with 27 period rooms open to the public.

Birmingham's important contribution to science and engineering is celebrated at the **Museum of Science and Industry**, which houses the world's oldest working steam engine. The **Jewellery Discovery Centre** gives a glimpse of working life in one of the city's traditional industries; and **Cadbury World** is devoted to the development of another of Birmingham's industries: chocolate (with free samples to aid the understanding!).

Edgbaston, a suburb 3 miles from the centre, is the place to head for a quieter atmosphere. Here, the **Barber Institute of Fine Art** houses the university's superb art collection; the **Botanical Gardens and Glasshouses**, containing many exotic species, provide a haven from the traffic-laden streets; and the **Birmingham Nature Centre** has otters, beavers, foxes, reptiles and wildfowl in enclosures designed to replicate their natural habitats.

For a trip around Birmingham's extensive old waterways network – which gives a whole new perspective on the city's many flyovers – contact **Brummagem Boats**, *Sherborne Street Wharf; tel: (0121) 455 6163*, departing at 1130, 1400 and 1600 (Easter–Oct).

Guide Friday, *tel: (0121) 6432514*, offer sightseeing bus tours starting from *Waterloo St*, from £6.

Churches and Cathedrals

St Chad's Cathedral, *St Chad's Queensway; tel: (0121) 236 2251*. Open daily 0910–1830. Admission free. **St Martin's in the Bull Ring**, *Bull Ring; tel: (90121) 643 5428*. Open Mon–Sat 1000–1600. Admission free. **St Paul's Church**, *St Paul's Square; tel: (0121) 236 7858*. Open Mon, Wed, Fri 1200–1430, Sun for services. Admission free. **St Philip's Cathedral**, *Colmore Row; tel: (0121) 236 6323*. Open daily 0630–1900. Admission free.

Historic Buildings

Aston Hall, *Trinity Rd, Aston; tel; (0121) 327 2333*. Open daily 1400–1700 (end Mar to end Oct). Admission free. Bus no. 7, then 5-min walk. Three miles north of centre. **Perrott's Folly**, *Waterworks Rd*. Open Sun and Bank Holiday Mons 1400–1700 (Easter to end Sept).

Admission £1.50. Bus 9, 128 or 129, 2 miles west.

Museums and Art Galleries

Barber Institute of Fine Arts, *University of Birmingham, Edgbaston Park Rd, Edgbaston; tel: (0121) 472 0962*. Open Mon–Fri 1000–1700, Sat 1000–1300. Admission free. **Birmingham Museum and Art Gallery**, *Chamberlain Sq; tel: (0121) 235 2834*. Open Mon–Sat 1100–1700, Sun 1100–1730. Admission free.

Birmingham Shakespeare Memorial Room, *Chamberlain Sq; tel: (0121) 235 3382*. Open Mon–Sat 0900–1700 (by prior arrangement). Admission free. **The Ikon Gallery**, *58–72 John Bright St; tel: (0121) 643 0708*. Open Tues–Sat 1100–1800 (Thur 1100–2000). Admission free. **Jewellery Quarter Discovery Centre**, *77–79 Vyse Street, Hockley; tel: (0121) 554 3598*. Open Mon–Fri 1000–1600, Sat 1100–1700. Admission £2.

Museum of Science and Industry, *Newhall St; tel: (0121) 235 1661*. Open Mon–Sat 1100–1700, Sun 1100–1730. Admission free. **Railway Museum**, *670 Warwick Rd, Tyseley; tel: (0121) 707 4696*. Open daily 1000–1700 (dusk in winter). Admission free. **Royal Birmingham Society of Artists**, *69a New St; tel: (0121) 643 3768*. Open for exhibitions, Mon–Sat 1030–1700. Admission varies according to exhibition.

Nature

Birmingham Nature Centre, *Pershore Rd, Edgbaston; tel: (0121) 472 7775*. Open daily 1000–1630 (end Mar to end Oct). Admission free. Bus 45 or 47, 3 miles south. **Botanical Gardens and Glasshouses**, *Westbourne Rd, Edgbaston; tel: (0121) 454 1860*. Open Mon–Sat 0900–2000, Sun 1000–2000 (dusk if earlier). Admission £2.90. Bus no. 10, 21, 22, 23 or 29, 3 miles south-west.

Out of Town

Cadbury World, *Lineen Rd, Bournville; tel: (0121) 451 4180* for opening times. It is advisable to book tickets in advance, *tel: (0121) 451 4159*. Admission £4.75. Bus no. 83, 84 or 85, 5 miles south.

Sightseeing–Out of Town   **53**

Connection: Stratford upon Avon

Trains leave Snow Hill and Moor St stations for Stratford upon Avon (see p. 180) every hour (services restricted on Suns). See ETT table 524.

 Side Track from Birmingham

KIDDERMINSTER

TIC: *Station Approach, Comberton Hill, Kidderminster, Worcestershire DY10 1QX; tel: (01562) 829400.* Open daily 1100–1630, 1 May to 30 Sept. DP SHS Services offered: local bed-booking service, advance reservations handled, BABA (latest 1600). The free guide *Discover Worcestershire's Wyre Forest* includes an accommodation list.

Arriving and Departing

Trains leave every half hour from Birmingham New Street for Kidderminster, taking about 30 mins. **Kidderminster Station,** *Comberton Hill; tel: (0121) 643 2711* is just to the west of the town centre, and has a taxi rank.

Getting Around

There is a free transport map *Kidderminster by Bus* available from the TIC. Most bus services are operated by **Midland Red West**, from *Midland Red Bus Depot, New Rd; tel: (01905) 763888.* There are good regular services within Kidderminster and to various surrounding towns, with reduced services after 1900, and no services on Sun. There is a daily Rover Ticket covering all Midland Red services for £3.50. There is a taxi rank at *Bridge St*, and further details of registered companies are available from the TIC.

Staying in Kidderminster

There are just six hotels, one guesthouse and one b.&b., and it is advisable to book in advance when there are gala weekends on at the Severn Valley Railway (see below).

There are two campsites quite close by:

Wolverley Camping and Caravan Park, *Brown Westhead Park, Wolverley; tel: (01562) 850909.* Take bus 6 or 6a to Sion Hill, then a ½-mile walk (2 miles north-east of town). **Shorthill Caravan, Camping and Leisure Park,** *Worcester Rd South, Crossway Green, Hartlebury; tel: (01299) 266458.* Take bus 303 or 304 (5 miles south).

Sightseeing

Kidderminster was once the leading centre of carpet manufacture in the world, and a variety of mills and chimneys remain along the attractive canal as a monument to its industrial heritage. But the real reason for stopping off at this otherwise unremarkable town is for a 16-mile wallow in nostalgia on the **Severn Valley Railway,** which runs from the old station alongside BR. One of Britain's finest steam railways, this takes you on a picturesque riverside trip via pretty Georgian **Bewdley** to cliffside **Bridgnorth,** whose two halves are linked by funicular railway.

Near Kidderminster, the moated, Elizabethan **Harvington Hall** boasts plenty of priestholes – hiding places for Catholics on the run in Tudor England – to stir the imagination.

Severn Valley Railway – see Private Railways on p. 339.

Out of Town

Harvington Hall, *Mustow Green; tel: (01562) 777267.* Open daily 1130–1730 (Mar–Oct). Admission donation requested. Take bus 133 to Mustow Green (3 miles south-east).

Hereford and Worcester County Museum, *Hartlebury Castle, Hartlebury; tel: (01299) 250416.* Open Mon–Thurs 1000–1700, Fri and Sun 1400–1700; closed Sat. Admission £1.50. Bus 305 to Hartlebury (4 miles south).

West Midland Safari and Leisure Park, *Spring Grove, Bewdley; tel: (01299) 4022114.* Open daily 1000–1700 (Apr–Oct). Admission £3.99. Take bus 2a, 192 or 292 to Bewdley (2 miles west). A car is needed for touring the animal enclosures.

BIRMINGHAM
to
ABERYSTWYTH

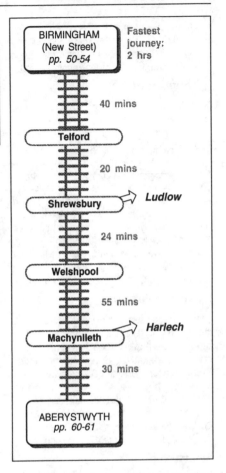

BIRMINGHAM
(New Street)
pp. 50-54

Fastest journey: 2 hrs

40 mins

Telford

20 mins

Shrewsbury → *Ludlow*

24 mins

Welshpool

55 mins

Machynlleth → *Harlech*

30 mins

ABERYSTWYTH
pp. 60-61

This itinerary takes you to the birthplace of England's Industrial Revolution and the once-troubled border country of the Marches, before cutting a scenic path through the heart of Wales to the seaside resort and university town of Aberystwyth. Skirting the natural splendours of Snowdonia, it also takes in the man-made grandeur of Powis and Harlech castles.

TRAINS

ETT table: 542

 Fast Track

A through train runs between Birmingham New Street station and Aberystwyth approximately every 2 hours (Sunday services are sparser and a change of train at Wolverhampton may be necessary). The journey takes 3 hrs.

〰 On Track

Birmingham–Telford–Shrewsbury

A train every 20–30 mins (hourly from late morning on Suns) connects Birmingham New Street with Shrewsbury, calling at Telford Central en route. A change of train at Wolverhampton is sometimes necessary. Birmingham to Telford takes 40 mins, Telford to Shrewsbury takes 20 mins.

Shrewsbury–Welshpool–Machynlleth–Aberystwyth

A train serves this route every two hours. Shrewsbury to Welshpool takes 24 mins, Welshpool to Machynlleth takes 55 mins and Machynlleth to Aberystwyth takes 30 mins.

TELFORD

TIC: *The Telford Centre, Management Suite, Telford, Shropshire TF3 4BX; tel: (01952) 291370.* Open Mon–Thur 0845–1715, Fri 0845–2000, Sat 0900–1700. DP Services offered: local bed-booking service (latest 30 mins before closing). The brochure *Ironbridge Gorge, Telford & The Wrekin*, including an accommodation listing, is available free. There is also a TIC, at *The Wharfage, Ironbridge; tel: (01952) 432166.* Open Mon–Fri 0900–1715, Sat, Sun 1000–1800 (earlier closing in winter). **Station**: Telford Central Station, *Euston Way; tel: (0345) 056785* is just ½ mile from the town centre and has a taxi rank. National Express, *tel: (0121) 622 4373* operates coach services into Telford's town centre bus station from *Coach Central* (along the side of the Telford Centre).

Getting Around

Telford's attractions are not within walking distance of the centre, so arm yourself with a transport and town map, which are available free from the TIC (main Telford map costs £3).

Local buses operate mainly from the bus station on *Coach Central; tel: (0345) 056785*. The service is good in the town centre, but rather patchy to outlying areas, with limited evening and Sunday services. In high season and on Bank Holidays there is a bus service called **Park and Ride** linking the sites which belong to **Ironbridge Gorge Museum**; daily rover ticket costs £0.30. There is a taxi rank at the Telford Centre and the TIC has details of taxi companies.

Staying in Telford

There is a good selection of hotels, guesthouses and b. & b.s in Telford and Ironbridge, so it is usually not difficult to book on arrival. Hotel chains include *MH* and *Ho.* For **Ironbridge Youth Hostel**, *Paradise, Coalbrookdale*, near *Ironbridge* (5 miles south-west of Telford Centre), *tel: (01952) 433281*, take bus no. 99. The nearest campsite is the **Severn Gorge Caravan Park** (2 miles south), *Bridgnorth Rd, Tweedale; tel: (01952) 684789*; bus no. 2/12.

Sightseeing

This new town, a burgeoning business centre, is the jumping-off point for Britain's best industrial heritage museum. The nearby gorge of the River Severn witnessed a key event in Britain's industrial revolution: here Abraham Darby discovered how to mass-produce iron, and built the world's first **Iron Bridge** in 1779. This is now the focal point of the **Ironbridge Gorge Museum**, which comprises seven sites spread over nearly 6 square miles, preserving an impressive amount of the valley's industrial past. You need at least a day to take it all in, but if time is limited make the beautiful bridge itself and **Blists Hill**, a 'living' Victorian village, your priorities.

Out of Town

The **Aerospace Museum** has one of the largest collections of its kind in the UK, from bombers to airliners, and is located at *Cosford, Shifnal; tel: (01902) 374112*. Open 1000–1700, last entry 1600. Admission £4. Train to Cosford, 8 miles east. **Ironbridge Gorge Museum**, *Ironbridge; tel: (01952) 433522 (432166* at weekends). Open daily 1000–1700 (–1800 July and Aug); some sites close in winter. For bus connections between the sites, see **Park and Ride** above. Passport ticket to all sites: £8 (individual site tickets: **Tar Tunnel** £0.80; **Museum of the River** and **Rosehill House** £2; **Coalport, Jackfield Tile Museum** and **Museum of Iron** £3; **Blists Hill** £6). Take bus no. 99 from Telford Centre to Ironbridge, 5 miles south-west. **Weston Park** (*Weston-under-Lizard*, near *Shifnal; tel: (01952) 76207*) is a 17th-century mansion, with notable pictures, furniture and tapestries, set in 1000 acres of landscaped parkland containing five gardens and good children's attractions. Open various dates Easter–Sept, daily in August. Park 1100–1700, house 1300–1630. Admission £4.50 (house, park and gardens), £3 (park and gardens only); 5–6 miles east; no public transport link.

SHREWSBURY

TIC: *The Music Hall, The Square, Shrewsbury, Shropshire SY1 1LH; tel: (01743) 350761*. Open Mon–Sat 0930–1715 (Oct–Apr), Mon–Sat 0930–1800 (May–Sept), Sun 1000–1600 (June–Sept); Easter and late May Bank Holidays 1000–1600. DP SHS Services offered: local bed-booking service and BABA (latest 30 mins before closing), advance reservations handled, guided tours booked. YHA membership, coach and events tickets sold. *Shrewsbury Town and Countryside* includes an accommodation list and is available free.

Station: Shrewsbury Station, *Castle St; tel: (01743) 364041* is central and has a taxi rank.

Getting Around

Most attractions are within easy walking distance of the centre. Free town and transport maps are available from the TIC. There are several local bus companies, operating mainly from the bus station on *Raven Meadows; tel: (0345) 056785*. Services are good in the town centre, but patchy to outlying areas, with reduced services in the evenings and on Suns.

Staying in Shrewsbury

There is a good range of hotels, pubs, b.&b. and guesthouse accommodation, with cheaper establishments located on the edge of the town centre. It is generally easy to book on arrival, except during the **West Midlands Agriculture Show** in May, and the **Shrewsbury Flower Show** in Aug. Hotel chains in Shrewsbury include *Co, FH, MH*. There is budget accommodation at **Shrewsbury Youth Hostel**, *The Woodlands, Abbey Foregate; tel: (01743) 360179*. The nearest campsite is **Severn House** (4 miles north-west), *Monford Bridge; tel: (01743) 850229*; take bus D70.

Sightseeing

Although currently being promoted for its associations with the fictional medieval detective Brother Cadfael, Ellis Peters' famous monk-sleuth, Shrewsbury is a genuinely historic town with a lovely setting on a loop of the River Severn. A plethora of well-cared-for half-timbered buildings, especially in the lanes around the *High St*, includes **Abbot's House** (*Butcher Row*, 1450) and **Ireland's Mansion** (*High St*, 1575). Sixteenth-century **Rowley's House** is a museum which has finds excavated from the nearby Roman city of **Wroxeter**, while **Clive House Museum** was once the home of Clive of India (Shrewsbury's MP in the 1760s). The much altered **Castle**, originally Norman, has a refurbished regimental museum. Across *English Bridge*, the restored church of **Shrewsbury Abbey** survives and has some interesting monuments; and the **Quarry**, Shrewsbury's riverside park, has a striking sunken flower garden as its centrepiece. Guided walks of the town (May–Oct) leave the TIC daily at 1430 (price £1.60).

Among many nearby attractions, **Hodnet Hall Gardens** offers 60 acres of tranquil pools, planting and trees; and **Much Wenlock** is an unspoilt market town with a substantial **priory** enhanced by some unusual topiary. Elegant, neo-classical **Attingham Park** has an impressive picture collection and a landscaped deer park through which there are attractive woodland walks. The TIC organises bus tours of the surrounding area July–Sept (price: £4.50–£7).

Clive House Museum, *College Hill; tel: (01743) 354811*. Open Tues–Sat 1000–1700, Sun 1100–1600. Admission £1. **Quarry Park and The Dingle** (Percy Thrower Gardens), *The Quarry; tel: (01743) 231456*. Open from 0800 until 30 mins before dusk. Admission free (except for **Flower Show** in Aug). **Rowley's House Museum**, *Barker St; tel: (01743) 361196*. Open Tues–Sat 1000–1700, Sun 1100–1600. Admission £1.20. **St Mary's Church**, *St Mary's St*. Open Mon, Wed, Sat 1000–1200, Tues, Fri 1015–1215. Admission free. **Shrewsbury Abbey**, *Abbey Foregate; tel: (01743) 232723*. Open 0930–1700 (Easter–Oct), 1100–1400 (Nov–Easter). Admission free. **Shrewsbury Castle**; *tel: (01743) 350761 (TIC)*. Due to open early 1995, 1000–1600. **Shrewsbury Quest Museum**, *Abbey Foregate; tel: (01743) 243324*. Open Mon–Sat 1000–1700, Sun 1200–1700. Admission £3.50.

Out of Town

Attingham Park (NT), *near Shrewsbury; tel: (01743) 709203*. Open Sat–Wed 1330–1700 (late Mar to late Sept), Sat, Sun 1330–1700 (Oct). Bank Holiday Mons 1100–1700. Last admission 1630. Admission £3.30. Take bus X96. Four miles south-east. **Hodnet Hall Gardens**, *Hodnet, Market Drayton; tel: (01630) 685202*. Open Mon–Sat 1400–1700, Sun and Bank Holiday Mons 1200–1730 (Apr–Sept). Admission £2.60. Take bus X64 to *Hodnet*, 12 miles north-east. **Stokesay Castle** – see under Ludlow. **Wenlock Priory** (ET), *Much Wenlock; tel: (01952) 727466*. Open daily 1000–1800 (Apr–Oct), Wed–Sun 1000–1600 (Nov–Mar). Admission £1.80. Take bus 436 or 437 to *Much Wenlock*, 10 miles south-east. **Wroxeter Roman City** (ET), *Wroxeter; tel: (01743) 761330*. Open daily 1000–1800 (Apr–Oct), Wed–Sun 1000–1600 (Nov–Mar). Admission £1.80. Bus no. X96; 6 miles south-east.

Side Track from Shrewsbury

LUDLOW

TIC: *Castle St, Ludlow, Shropshire SY8 1AS; tel: (01584) 875053.* Open Mon–Fri 1000–1700, Sat 1000–1600 (Jan–Mar and Nov–Dec); Mon–Sat 1000–1700, Sun 1030–1700 (Apr–Oct). DP Services offered: local bed-booking service and BABA (latest 30 mins before closing) advance reservations handled. Tickets booked for local coach day trips. *Ludlow Town Guide* £0.95, *Discover South Shropshire* free, including accommodation listing. Accommodation booking (busiest on Bank Holiday Sats) *tel: (01584) 875053.*

Station: Ludlow Station, *Station Rd; tel: (01584) 877090* (½ mile north-east of town centre). There is no taxi rank. Hourly trains (less frequent on Suns) run from Shrewsbury, taking about 30 mins.

Getting Around

The attractions in Ludlow are all within walking distance of the town centre. For general transport enquiries *tel: (01345) 056785.* There is an hourly bus service in town and two good, regular routes to outlying towns and some villages. Other routes are variable. There are few services after 1800, and only one route operates on Suns. The main bus company is **Midland Red West**, *tel: (01905) 763888.* To book taxis **Annette's Taxis**, *tel: (01584) 878787;* **Ludlow Travel**, *tel: (01584) 876000.*

Staying in Ludlow

There is a moderate choice of accommodation in the town, with five hotels, four b.&b., three guesthouses and five pubs offering rooms. There is, however, more on offer in the surrounding area. It is generally easy to book on arrival, except during Bank Holiday weekends and the **Ludlow Festival**, which takes place in the last week of June and first week of July.

Ludlow Youth Hostel, *Ludford Bridge; tel: (01584) 872472* is within walking distance of the centre. Open 14 Jan, Fri and Sat (Feb, Nov, Dec), Mon–Sat (Apr–Aug), Tues–Sat (Mar, Sept, Oct); closed from 18 Dec. Ludlow also has a campsite at **North Farm**, *Whitcliffe; tel: (01584) 872026.* One mile west of town.

Sightseeing

The loveliest border town on the English side of the Marches, Ludlow today exudes serenity and charm; only its impressive 11th-century **castle** with its massive red sandstone keep, little round Norman chapel and medieval and Tudor additions is a reminder of more turbulent times. This market town boasts nearly 500 listed buildings and preserves its Norman street pattern almost intact, making it rewarding to stroll around. *Broad St* is particularly impressive with its many Tudor timber-framed and elegant 17th–19th-century brick buildings. Guided walking tours are led by members of **Ludlow Historical Research Group**, *tel: (01584) 875079.* Tours start at 1430 by the cannon at the castle entrance and run Sat, Sun (Easter to late Sept), also Wed, Thurs (late July and Aug) and daily during **Ludlow Festival** (last week June, first week July). Price: £1.

The fine late-medieval church of **St Laurence** is well worth a visit; the ashes of Shropshire's poet A. E. Housman (1859–1936) are buried in the churchyard. Out of town, don't miss the extraordinarily picturesque **Stokesay Castle**, a rare 13th-century fortified manor house with an archetypally quaint half-timbered gatehouse; it lies in an idyllic agricultural landscape at the end of Wenlock Edge. For a complete contrast, **Berrington Hall** is a formal late 18th-century house, with delicate interiors and fine furniture; nearby **Croft Castle** has a medieval exterior, Georgian interior and some ancient trees in its grounds. **Acton Scott Historic Working Farm** gives a vivid introduction to traditional methods of farming and rural life.

Castle Lodge, *Castle Square; tel: (01584) 878098.* Open daily 1100–1700. Admission £1. **Dinham House**, *Dinham; tel: (01584) 874240.* Open daily 1000–1700. Admission for exhibitions only. **Ludlow Castle**; *tel: (01584) 873355.* Open 1030–1600 (Feb–Apr, Oct and Nov), 1030–1700 (May–Sept); closed Dec and Jan. Last admission 30 mins before closing. Admission £2. **Ludlow Museum**, *Castle St; tel: (01584) 873857*. Open Mon–Sat 1030–1300, 1400–1700 (Apr–Sept), also Sun 1030–1700 in Jul and Aug. Admission £0.50. **St Laurence's Church**; *tel: (01584) 872073*. Open all year, stewards on duty 1000–1700 (Easter to Oct). Admission free, donations welcome.

Out of Town

Acton Scott Historic Working Farm (13½ miles north of Ludlow), near *Church Stretton; tel: (01694) 781306*. Open Tues–Sat 1000–1700 (Apr–Oct), Sun and Bank Holidays 1000–1800. Admission £2.75. Take bus 435 to Church Stretton, then a ½-mile walk. **Berrington Hall** (NT), *Ashton, near Leominster; tel: (01568) 615721*. Open Wed–Sun and Bank Holiday Mons 1330–1730 (Apr–Sept), Wed–Sun 1330–1630 (Oct); grounds open from 1230. Admission £3.50. Take bus no. 192 towards Leominster, get off at Berrington Hall (10 miles south). **Croft Castle** (NT), *Leominster; tel: (01568) 780246*. Open Easter Sat–Mon 1400–1800; Sat, Sun 1400–1700 (Apr and Oct); Wed–Sun and Bank Holiday Mons 1400–1800. Admission £3. Take bus 192 towards Leominster, get off at Gorbett Bank, then 2½-mile walk (8 miles south). Admission £3. **Stokesay Castle** (ET), *Stokesay, near Craven Arms; tel: (01588) 672544*. Open daily 1000–1800 (Apr–Oct), Wed–Sun 1000–1600 (Nov–Mar). Admission £2.30. Bus 435 to *Craven Arms*, 7 miles north.

- - - - - - - - - - - - - - - - - - -

WELSHPOOL

TIC: *The Flash Leisure Centre, Welshpool, Powys SY21 7DH; tel: (01938) 552043/554038*. Open daily 0900–1800. DP Services offered: local bed-booking service, advance reservations handled, BABA. National Trust membership and local theatre and events tickets sold. *Montgomeryshire Guide*, with accommodation list, is free. **Station**: Welshpool Station, *Severn Rd; tel: (01743) 364041*, is ½ mile south of the centre, and has a taxi rank.

Getting Around

Welshpool's attractions are walkable from the centre, and free town and transport maps are available from the TIC. The main bus company is **Crosville**, *tel: (01691) 652402*. Services operate from the centre of town, but are very limited, both in frequency and coverage. There is a taxi rank on *Broad St*, or contact one of the following companies: **Mount Taxis** *tel: (01938) 554976*; **Ron's Taxis** *tel: (01938) 553522*; **Steve's Taxis** *tel: (01831) 304904*; **Stonebridge Taxis** *tel: (01938) 555119*.

Staying in Welshpool

There are three hotels, including one in the *Co* hotel chain, and a reasonable range of guesthouse and b.&b. accommodation. It is usually easy to book on arrival. The closest campsites are: **Severn**, *Cilcewydd, Forden; tel: (01938) 580238*, 1½ miles south (not on a bus route), and **Maes yr Afon** (4 miles west), *Berriew; tel: (01686) 640587*, bus D75.

Sightseeing

The Georgian architecture and pleasant walks along the attractive canal make this small market town worth lingering over. Just outside town and dominating it lies **Powis Castle**, medieval stronghold turned stately home: latterly the home of the Clive family (noted for Clive of India, the 18th-century soldier-statesman), it has one of the finest country-house collections in Wales and magnificent terraced gardens. The **Welshpool and Llanfair Light Railway** offers an 8-mile trip on a narrow-gauge steam train through some splendid countryside.

Montgomery Canal Cruises, *Severn St Wharf; tel: (01938) 553271* run daily from 1100 (Apr–Oct), price: £2.25, and the trip lasts one hour. **Powysland Museum and Montgomery Canal Centre**, *The Canal Wharf; tel: (01938) 554656*. Open Mon, Tues, Thur, Fri 1100–1300 and 1400–1700, Sat, Sun 1000–1300 and 1400–1700 (Easter–Sept); Sat 1400–1700 (Oct–Easter). Admission free. **Welshpool and Llanfair Light Railway**, *The Station, Llanfair Caereinion; tel: (01938) 810441*. Open on specific days, call for details. Admission £6.

Out of Town

Powis Castle (NT), near *Welshpool; tel: (01938)*

554336. Open Wed–Sun (Apr–June, Sept and Oct), Tues–Sun (July and Aug), and Bank Holiday Mons: Garden 1100–1800, Castle and Clive Museum 1200–1700. Last admission 30 mins before closing. Admission £5.80 (all-inclusive), £3.80 (garden only). Bus D75. Two miles south.

 ## Side Tracks from Machynlleth

HARLECH

TIC: *Gwyddfor House, High Street, Harlech, Gwynedd LL46 2YA; tel: (01766) 780658.* Open daily 1000–1800 (Easter–Oct). Services offered: local bed-booking service (latest 1750), BABA (latest 1730). *Harlech and District* brochure is free and includes an accommodation list.
Station: Harlech Station, *A496; tel: (01743) 364041* is quarter of a mile south of the town centre. There is no taxi rank; for taxi details see below. There are between four and eight trains from Machynlleth to Harlech depending largely on the day of the week and the time of the year. Journey time is anything from 1 hour 15 mins to 2 hrs depending on the number (and length) of intermediate stops.

Getting Around

The TIC has free town and transport maps. **Harlech Castle**, towering above the railway station, is the town's main attraction and is walkable from the town centre. For general transport enquiries *tel: (01286) 679535.* Local bus services are limited and there are no evening or Sun services. There is no town taxi rank. For taxis contact **Morfa Garage** *tel: (01766) 780288* or **Parry's** *tel: (01766) 780392.*

Staying in Harlech

There is a small range of hotel, guesthouse and b. & b. accommodation, and it is generally easy to book on arrival, except during Aug. The closest youth hostel is **Plas Newydd Youth Hostel**, *Llanbedr; tel: (01341) 23287.* Open Tues–Sat (Mar, Apr, Sept and Oct), Tues–Sun and Bank Holiday Mons (May and June), daily (July and Aug). Take bus 38 to *Llanbedr*, 3 miles south. The closest campsite is **Min Y Don** (1

mile west), *Beach Rd; tel: (01766) 780286.* Take bus no. 38.

Sightseeing

This little town of steep, narrow streets boasts probably the most famous of Edward I's 'iron ring' of castles, built to contain the Welsh in the 13th century. **Harlech Castle**, built 1283–90 by a vast workforce, is memorable not only for its strength (though the Welsh leader Owain Glyndwr captured it in 1404) but for the views from its battlements of Snowdonia, the Lleyn Peninsula, and the sea which once lapped at the rocks below.

Maes Artro is a tourist village based on a wartime RAF camp, converted to house a variety of lisplays, including an original air raid shelter. The tiny **Llanfair Slate Caverns** are less crowded than their Snowdonian counterparts. The TIC has information on guided bus tours and walking tours around the area. **Harlech Castle** (Cadw); *(01766) 780552.* Open 0930–1830 (late Mar to late Oct), 0930–1600 (late Oct to late Mar). Admission £2.90.

Out of Town

Ffestiniog Railway – see 'Private Railways', pp. 339–340. **Llanfair Slate Caverns**, *Llanfair; tel: (01766) 780247.* Open daily 1000–1700 (Easter to mid-Oct). Admission £2.30. Take bus 38 to *Llanfair*, 1½ miles south. **Maes Artro Village**, *Llanbedr; tel: (01341) 23467.* Open daily 1000–1730 (Easter to end Sept). Admission £2.50. Take bus 38 to *Llanbedr*, 3 miles south. **Portmeirion** (see Chester–Bangor route, pp. 122–125) is accessible from Harlech by rail – take the train to Minffordd station.

ABERYSTWYTH

TIC: *Terrace Road, Aberystwyth, Dyfed SY23 2AG; tel: (01970) 612125.* Open daily 1000–1700 (closed Sun Oct–May). DP Services offered: local bed-booking service, BABA, guided tours booked. *Ceredigion West Wales* and an accommodation guide are available free.
Station: Aberystwyth Station, *Alexander Rd; tel: (01654) 702311* is central and has a taxi rank.

Getting Around

The attractions in town are all within walking distance of the centre. Free town maps and transport details are available from the TIC. The main bus operator is **Crosville Wales** *tel: (01970) 617951/615426*. Services are quite good within the town but less frequent to outlying areas, with reduced services in the evenings and on Sun. A one-day **Crosville Rover** ticket costs £4.70 and covers all the Crosville services. Some places are only accessible by **Post Bus**; for information contact **Royal Mail** *tel: (01970) 612500*. The main taxi rank is at the station. For details of registered taxi companies contact the TIC.

Staying in Aberystwyth

There is a good range of accommodation available, particularly mid-range hotels and guesthouses. Cheaper accommodation is located mainly in outlying villages. It is generally easy to book on arrival, except during July and Aug (due to university graduation, the **Ian Rush Soccer Tournament** and school holidays).

The closest budget accommodation is **Borth Youth Hostel** (7 miles north), *Morlais, Borth; tel: (01970) 871498*, open from 1700. The TIC has details of campsites in the area; the nearest is **Aberystwyth Holiday Village** (½ mile south of the centre), *Penparcau Rd; tel: (01970) 624211*.

Sightseeing

The largest town on the west coast of Wales, Aberystwyth is both a seaside resort (with a Victorian air) and a university town. Edward I's **Castle** offers a good viewpoint, and at the other end of the promenade the **Electric Cliff Railway** takes you to the summit of Constitution Hill: from here there are views to Snowdonia, and the **Great Aberystwyth Camera Obscura** offers an unusual means of viewing the town. North of town lies the **National Library of Wales**, which as well as books and manuscripts houses fine prints, watercolours and drawings relating to Wales.

If you have time for only one excursion from here, take the narrow-gauge **Vale of Rheidol Steam Railway**, which climb for 12 miles up the Rheidol valley to the spectacular gorges and waterfalls spanned by three bridges at **Devil's Bridge**, one of Wales' most popular beauty spots. Thirteenth-century **Cilgerran Castle** is another stirring sight, with its massive stone towers perched on a crag above the steep gorge of the River Teifi. **Borth Animalarium** (zoo) has a wide range of animals on display.

Aberystwyth Arts Centre, *Penglais Hill; tel: (01970) 622887*. Open Mon–Sat 1000–2000, Sun 1400–1700 (closed mid-May to end June for university exams). Admission varies according to event. **Aberystwyth Castle**; *tel: (01970) 612125* (TIC). Open at all times. Admission free. **Aberystwyth Electric Cliff Railway**; *tel: (01970) 617642*. Operates every 10–15 mins, daily 1000–1800 (Easter to end Oct). Return fare £1.85. **Aberystwyth Yesterday** (permanent exhibition), above the station, *Alexander Rd; tel: (01970) 617119*. Open daily 1000–1700 (Apr to end Oct), 1400–1600 (Nov–Mar). **The Ceredigion Museum**, *Terrace Rd; tel: (01970) 634212*. Open 1000–1700 Mon–Sat (and Sun in Aug). Admission free. **The Great Aberystwyth Camera Obscura**; *tel: (01970) 617642*. Open daily 1000–1800. Admission free. **National Library of Wales**, *Penglais Hill; tel: (01970) 623816*. Open Mon–Fri 0930–1800, Sat 0930–1700. Admission: free. **Vale of Rheidol Narrow Gauge Steam Railway** runs from Aberystwyth to Devil's Bridge, *tel: (01970) 622882*. Departures twice daily (four times daily Mon–Thur in Aug), most days (Apr–Oct). Return fare: £9.90.

Out of Town

Cilgerran Castle (Cadw), *Cilgerran; tel: (01239) 615136*. Open daily 0930–1830 (Apr to end Oct), Mon–Sat 0930–1600, Sun 1400–1600 (end Oct to Mar). Admission £1.50. Take bus 550 to *Cardigan*, then bus 430 to *Cilgerran*. Thirty miles south-west of Aberystwyth. **Devil's Bridge Falls** (12 miles south-east), *Devil's Bridge; tel: (01970) 85233*. Open all year (entry by coin-operated turnstiles), attendant on duty 1000–1700 (Easter to end Sept). Admission £1.50. Take Post Bus or Vale of Rheidol Narrow Gauge Railway (see above).

_ _ _ _ _ _ _ _ _ _ _ _ _ _ _ _ _ _ _ _

BIRMINGHAM to BRISTOL

Striking out from the Midlands to the premier city of the West Country, this route encompasses the 18th-century elegance of Cheltenham and the historic cathedral city of Gloucester. It also provides a jumping-off point for the picture-book green hills and honey-coloured stone towns and villages of the Cotswolds, one of England's archetypal landscapes.

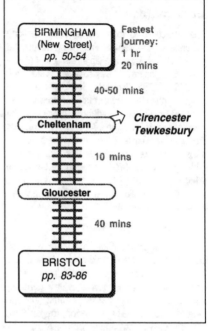

TRAINS

ETT tables: 520

Fast Track

Up to 15 trains run daily from Birmingham New Street to Bristol Temple Meads (less on Sun). Journey time is 1 hr 20 mins–1 hr 40 mins (20 mins longer if the train calls at Gloucester).

ᎦᎦᎦ On Track

Birmingham–Cheltenham–Gloucester

Most Inter–City services running Birmingham–Bristol call at Cheltenham Spa (some also detour via Gloucester where the train must reverse direction). Birmingham–Cheltenham takes 40–50 mins and Cheltenham–Gloucester 10 mins.

Gloucester–Bristol

17 trains (weekdays), 5–8 (Suns) run from Gloucester to Bristol Temple Meads. Most are local trains (a few are InterCity expresses). The journey takes 45 mins to 1 hr.

CHELTENHAM

TIC: *77 Promenade, Cheltenham, Gloucestershire GL50 1PP; tel: (01242) 522878/264136.* Open Mon–Fri 0930–1800, Sat 0930–1700 (June–Oct), Sun 1000–1600 (July and Aug); Mon–Sat 0930–1700 (Nov–May), Bank Holidays 1000–1600. Services offered: local bed-booking service, advance reservations handled, BABA, guided tours booked. Tickets sold for National Express, theatre, events and coach tours; membership sold for HI and Ramblers Association. *Cheltenham Spa, Centre for the Cotswolds* is free and includes an accommodation listing.
Station: Cheltenham Spa Station, *Queens Rd; tel: (01452) 529501* is one mile south-west of town. The Metro bus from *Gloucester Rd* at the rear of the station takes you into town in 5 mins, or it is a 15-min walk. There is a taxi rank.
Bus Station: coaches run by National Express *tel: (01242) 584111* operate from Royal Well Bus Station, just off *Royal Well Rd*.

Getting Around

With the exception of the racecourse and Pump Room, attractions are walkable from the centre. The TIC has free town and transport maps.

Shopmobility, *Car Park Level 1, Beechwood Place; tel: (01242) 255333.* Open Mon–Sat 0930–1630. Offers scooters, powered chairs or wheelchairs to people with mobility problems, for free use in the town centre.

Local buses (Cheltenham and Gloucester Omnibus Company) operate out of Royal Well Bus Station *tel: (01242) 511655.* The service is good in the town centre and to many of the Cotswold Villages, but reduced after 1800.

There are taxi ranks on the *High St, Royal Well Rd* and *The Promenade.* Taxis can be hailed in the street, or *tel: (01242) 580580/242777.*

Staying in Cheltenham

Accommodation is plentiful in Cheltenham, with a particularly large choice of smaller hotels, guesthouse and b. & b. accommodation. It is generally easy to book on arrival, except during the **Cheltenham Gold Cup** (National Hunt Festival) in March. Hotel chains in Cheltenham include *BW, FH, Ly, MC.* For youth hostel accommodation there is the **YMCA**, *Victoria Walk; tel: (01242) 524024,* in the town centre, and **Cleeve Youth Hostel**, *Cleeve Hill; tel: (01242) 672025* (take bus C11 – 10 mins). The nearest campsites are: **Cheltenham Caravan Clubsite** (1 mile north), *Cheltenham Racecourse, Prestbury Park; tel: (01241) 523102* (take bus D or E); **Beggars Roost Caravan and Camping Park** (1½ miles north), *Bamfurlong Lane, Staverton; tel: (01452) 712705* (take bus 94).

There is a very good range of eating places, with many of the more expensive restaurants to be found in the *Montpellier* area. There is a vegetarian restaurant (**Peppers**, *317 High St*), about four gourmet restaurants and 15 cheaper eating places.

Cheltenham has a few very good shopping areas: *The Promenade, Regent Arcade* (with its interesting Fishing Wish Clock), *Regent St,* the *High St, Beechwood Place* and particularly the area of *Montpellier and Suffolk,* where you will also find many antique shops.

The main post office is on the *High St.* Open Mon–Fri 0900–1700, Sat 0900–1300.

Entertainment and Events

The TIC can provide events listings free of charge, including the *Cheltenham and Gloucester Bulletin.* The main theatre venue is **Everyman Theatre**, *Regent St; tel: (01242) 572573,* and for concerts and other entertainment, there is the **Town Hall and Pittville Pump Room**, *Imperial Sq; tel: (01242) 227979.* There are also various nightclubs and some restaurants also have live music regularly. For spectator sports, there is horseracing at **Cheltenham Racecourse** (1 mile north), *Prestbury; tel: (01242) 513014,* bus D or E.

The most important events in Cheltenham are the **Cheltenham Gold Cup** (National Hunt Festival) in March, at *Cheltenham Racecourse;* the **Festival of Music**, every year in July; and the **Festival of Literature** in Oct–Nov, both at various venues in the town centre.

Sightseeing

Cheltenham developed as a fashionable spa in the 18th century, after George III gave it his stamp of approval. It boasts an exceptionally harmonious and elegant appearance, with its many fine Regency buildings laid out in spacious crescents, squares and terraces, all built of mellifluous golden Cotswold stone. For such a well-preserved place, it is surprisingly free of tourist trappings. If time is short, head for the *Promenade* and *Montpellier Walk,* with its slightly incongruous colonnade of female statues. For guided walks and bus tours of the town's main attractions, contact the TIC.

The spa waters may be sampled at the town hall or the **Pittville Pump Room**, which also happens to be perhaps Cheltenham's finest building, with its Greek revival colonnade and dome. It now houses a museum of costume and jewellery, from Regency times to the Swinging Sixties. **Cheltenham Art Gallery and Museum** has a good Arts and Crafts collection, as well as displays on Cheltenham's history. The **Holst Birthplace Museum**, in the Regency house where the composer of *The Planets* was born in 1874, explores his life and music, and has been well restored to reveal the workings of domestic life from Regency to Edwardian times. At Cheltenham's prestigious racecourse, the **Hall of Fame** recounts the history of steeplechasing.

The TIC has details of bus excursions around the Cotswolds, for which Cheltenham makes a good touring centre. Chief among local attractions is the charming **Sudeley Castle**, the inspiration for P. G. Wodehouse's fictional castle Blandings and the home of Queen Katherine Parr after the death of Henry VIII; it lies against the dramatic backdrop of the Cotswolds escarpment. Nearby **Hailes Abbey** is a graceful ruin in a peaceful woodland setting, with some fine medieval sculptures in its museum. **Painswick Rococo Gardens** is a unique survival of an 18th-century garden, with buildings, woodland walks and formal vistas. Near the classic Cotswold village of Broadway lies Tudor **Snowshill Manor**, renowned for its unusual crafts collection which includes musical instruments, bicycles and Japanese armour.

Art Gallery and Museum, *Clarence St; tel: (01242) 237431.* Open Mon–Sat 1000–1720; closed Bank Holidays. Admission: free. **Holst Birthplace Museum**, *4 Clarence Rd; tel: (01242) 524846.* Open Tues–Sat 1000–1620; closed Bank Holidays. Admission: free. **Pittville Pump Room Museum** (1½ miles north), *Pittville Park; tel: (01242) 523852.* Open Tues–Sat 1000–1420, Sun and Bank Holidays 1100–1420 (June–Sept). Admission: £1. Bus D or E.

Out of Town

Chedworth Roman Villa (see Cirencester p. 65). **Painswick Rococo Garden** (10 miles southwest), *The Stables, Painswick House, Painswick; tel: (01452) 813204.* Open Wed–Sun 1100–1700 (Feb to mid–Dec). Admission: £2.50. Stroud Valley bus 46, 46b and X43 (40 mins). **Sudeley Castle and Gardens** (8 miles northeast), *Winchcombe; tel: (01242) 602308.* Open daily 1100–1700 (Apr–Oct). Admission: £4.90. Castleways/Marchants bus M (20 mins). **Hailes Abbey** (English Heritage), *Hailes, near Winchcombe; tel: (01242) 602398.* Open daily 1000–1800 (Apr–Sept), Tues–Sun 1000–1600 (Oct–Mar). Admission: £1.90. Take Castleways bus C11 to *Winchcombe*, then 2-mile walk. Ten miles north-east. **Snowshill Manor** (National Trust), *Snowshill, near Broadway; tel: (01386) 852410.* Open Wed–Mon 1300–1800 (May–Sept and Easter weekend), Sat, Sun 1300–1700

(Apr and Oct). Last admission 30 mins before closing. Admission: £4.20. Take Castleways bus C11 to *Broadway*, then a taxi (3 miles south). Approximately 18 miles north-east.

 ## Side Tracks from Cheltenham

CIRENCESTER

TIC: *Corn Hall, Market Place, Cirencester, Gloucestershire GL7 2NW; tel: (01285) 654180/655526.* Open Mon 0945–1630, Tues–Sat 0930–1630 (Jan–Mar), Mon 0945–1700, Tues–Sat 0930–1700 (Apr–Dec). Services offered: local bed-booking service (latest 15 mins before closing), advance reservations handled, BABA (latest 30 mins before closing). National Trust membership and tickets for local events sold. *Cirencester Mini Guide* (price on application), *Accommodation in the Cotswolds* (£0.25).

Station: the nearest station is **Kemble Station**, *Kemble; tel: (01452) 529501*, which is four miles south-west of Cirencester (bus A1) and has a taxi rank. There are 12 trains on weekdays, 7 on Suns from Cheltenham Spa to Kemble, taking 40–50 mins.

Bus Station: There are about five bus services daily from *Clarence St* in Cheltenham to Cirencester. The service (no. 51), which is operated by Stryde Valley Buses, takes 40 mins. Cirencester is well served by National Express coaches, *tel: (01242) 584111*, which operate from *Market Place*.

Getting Around

Most attractions are within a walkable area of the centre, and a free transport map is available from the TIC. There is reasonable bus coverage in town, but it is patchy to outlying areas, with no local services after 1845 or on Suns. For visiting outlying attractions a car is recommended, as public transport facilities are poor. For general transport enquiries *tel: (01452) 425543*. Most local bus services are operated from *Market Place* by a number of companies, including **Stroud Valley Bus Company** *tel: (01453) 763421*, **Thames Down Transport** *tel:*

(01793) 523700 and **Harvey's Coaches** *tel: (01285) 720221.* A daily 'Explorer Ticket' covers all services for £3. The main taxi rank is on *Market Place.*

Staying in Cirencester

There is a small number of hotels, including the *Ja* and *Mn* chains, and a range of guesthouses, b. & b.s and pubs. It is generally easy to book on arrival, except during the **International Air Tattoo** – one of the largest flying displays in the country – at *Fairford* in late July.

For budget accommodation there is **Duntisbourne Abbots Youth Hostel,** *Duntisbourne Abbots; tel: (01285) 821682,* bus 52 (Mon and Fri only). The closest campsites are **Mayfield Touring Park** (2 miles north), *Cheltenham Rd, Perrotts Brook; tel: (01285) 831301* (bus 51) and **Ermin Farm** (2 miles south), *Cricklade Rd; tel: (01285) 860270* (bus 51).

Sightseeing

Cirencester, which is a typical example of a Cotswold town, was once also an important Roman town and has impressive Roman artefacts in the **Corinium Museum** and remains of an amphitheatre. The finest building in this attractive town is the large, 15th-century **Parish Church,** which has a magnificent interior and tower. The 40-ft yew hedge in front of **Cirencester Park**'s Mansion House is reputed to be the highest in Europe. Guided walks are available May–Sept (£1).

Though public transport in the surrounding area is meagre, you can reach **Barnsley House Garden,** which includes a splendid *potager ornée* (decorative vegetable garden). **Chedworth Roman Villa,** built for a wealthy landowner, has the remains of two bath houses and some fine mosaics. For tours of the area, the TIC operates **Cotswold Scenic Bus Tours** (£7.50).

Cirencester Amphitheatre, off *Cotswold Ave.* Grassed over remains, open at all times. Admission: free. **Corinium Museum,** *Park St; tel: (01285) 655611.* Open Mon–Sat 1000–1700, Sun 1400–1700 (closed Mons Nov–Mar). Admission: £1.25. **St John the Baptist Parish Church,** *Market Place; tel: (01285) 653142.*

Open daily Mon–Sat 0930–1700, Sun 1415–1730. Admission: free. (Note 12th-century Norman Arch in the Abbey Grounds behind the church.)

Out of Town

Barnsley House Garden (3 miles north), *Barnsley; tel: (01285) 740281.* Open Mon, Wed, Thur, Sat 1000–1800. Admission: £2. Bus 75, H20 or M31. **Chedworth Roman Villa** (National Trust), *Yanworth; tel: (01242) 890256.* Open Tues–Sun and Bank Holiday Mons 1000–1730 (Mar–Oct), Wed–Sun 1100–1600 (Nov). Admission: £2.60. Ten miles north, no public transport. **Sudeley Castle** (see Cheltenham p. 64). **Wildfowl and Wetlands Centre,** *Slimbridge* (see Gloucester p. 68).

TEWKESBURY

TIC: *The Museum, 64 Barton St, Tewkesbury, Gloucestershire GL20 5PX; tel: (01684) 295027/272277.* Open Mon–Sat 0900–1700, Sun and Bank Holidays 1000–1600 (Easter to end Sept). SHS Services offered: local bed-booking service, advance reservations handled, BABA, National Express tickets sold. *Visitor Guide to Tewkesbury and Winchcombe* is free and includes an accommodation listing.

Station: Tewkesbury station is currently closed; the nearest stations are in *Cheltenham* (9 miles south-east) and *Gloucester* (12 miles south-west). From *Cheltenham* take bus 41 (Mon–Sat only) from *Clarence St,* near the bus station (25 mins). From *Gloucester,* take Swanbrook bus S51a from the bus station, *Market Parade* (25 mins). Ashchurch (for Tewkesbury) Station should re-open in 1995 or 1996. For enquiries *tel: (01452) 529501.*

Getting Around

The majority of Tewkesbury's attractions are in walking distance of the centre. Free town and transport maps are available from the TIC. There are various companies operating local services, including **Swanbrook Coaches** *tel: (01242) 574444,* **Cheltenham and District** *tel: (01242) 522021,* **Midland Red West** *tel: (01905) 763888* and **Warners Bus Company** *tel:*

(01684) 292108. Services within the town are good, and they are reasonable to Gloucester, Cheltenham and Worcester, but very patchy to surrounding villages. There are no buses after 1900 or on Sun. **Tewkesbury Town Taxis** *tel: (01684) 294122* operate from the *High St.* Other taxi companies include **Abbey Taxis** *tel: (01684) 292028* and **Avonside Taxis** *tel: (01684) 293916*.

Staying in Tewkesbury

There is a small choice of accommodation in the town, mainly b.&b., and a range of guesthouse and b.&b. establishments in the surrounding villages. It is generally easy to book on arrival, except during the Cheltenham Gold Cup in March. The nearest youth hostel is in Cheltenham (see p. 63). There are a number of campsites around Tewkesbury, ask for details at the TIC. The closest is in the town itself: **Abbey Caravan Club Site**, *Gander Lane; tel: (01684) 294035*.

Sightseeing

This attractive town lies at the confluence of the Rivers Severn and Avon, on the very edge of the Cotswolds; its many fine medieval and later buildings are of timber, not Cotswold stone. The main attraction is **Tewkesbury Abbey**, one of the largest abbey churches to survive Henry VIII's Dissolution, when it was bought by the townspeople. It is one of the country's finest examples of Romanesque architecture.

Tewkesbury was the site of an important battle during the Wars of the Roses: **Tewkesbury Town Museum** has models of both town and battle. **John Moore Museum**, housed in a 15th-century timber-framed building, has a natural history collection designed with children in mind. Guided town walks in the summer are run by **Cotswold and Gloucestershire Tourist Guides** *tel: (01242) 226554*, price £1.50. The TIC has the *Battle Trail Walk* and *Tewkesbury's Alleyways* leaflets, for themed walks around the town. For boat trips on the rivers *Severn* and *Avon* which meet at Tewkesbury, price £3.50, from *Tolsey Quay*, contact **The Pride of Avon** *tel: (01684) 275906*. The TIC has bus tours of the surrounding area

including the *Cotswolds* and the *Forest of Dean*, price £7.50.

Tewkesbury Abbey, *Church St; tel: (01684) 850959*. Open Mon–Sat 0730–1730 (–1700 in winter), Sun 0730–1800. Admission: free, donations welcomed. **Tewkesbury Town Museum**, *64 Barton St; tel: (01684) 295027*. Open daily 1000–1300 and 1400–1630 (Easter–Oct). Admission: £0.50.

GLOUCESTER

TIC: *St Michael's Tower, The Cross, Gloucester GL1 1PD; tel: (01452) 421188/504273*. Open Mon–Sat 1000–1700. DP, SHS Services offered: local bed-booking service (1630 latest), AR (next day only), BABA (1630 latest), GT (in summer), theatre and coach tickets booked, YHA membership sold. Busiest times of day for accommodation bookings are 1200–1400 and 1600 onwards. The *Gloucester Travel Guide*, including information on where to stay, is available free of charge. **Tourist Information Point**, *Llanthony Warehouse, The Docks*. Open daily 1000–1800 (summer), 1000–1700 (winter). D, SHS. No accommodation booking service available.

Station: Gloucester Station, *Bruton Way; tel: (01452) 529501* is within walking distance of the city centre, an important rail junction with direct rail services to London, Edinburgh, Bristol, the West Country, the Midlands and Wales. There is a taxi rank at the station.

Bus Station: Gloucester Coach and Bus Station, *Market Parade*, just opposite the station; *(01452) 527516*, is also within easy walking distance of the centre, with good National Express coach links to most of the country, and various companies offering local bus transport.

Getting Around

The majority of attractions in Gloucester are within a walkable area of the centre, and free town and transport maps are available from the TIC. The public transport coverage is good in the town centre and on popular routes, but rather patchy on some rural routes. Evening services are more limited and on Suns there are few services beyond the city centre. **Shopmobility**,

Herbert Warehouse, The Docks; (01452) 396898, is a Gloucester City Council service offering battery-powered scooters and wheelchairs to people with mobility problems, for use in the city centre. A number of companies run local services from the bus station. The main operator is Stagecoach Gloucester Citybus *tel: (01452) 527516*, who also offer a Rovercard for their bus services (£6 for 7 days). The main taxi rank is on *The Oxbode*, and further taxi ranks can be found at the rail and bus stations. There are approximately eight registered taxi companies (telephone numbers available from TIC) and taxis can also be hailed in the street.

Staying in Gloucester

There is a wide range of accommodation available which is generally easy to book on arrival, except during the following events: Cheltenham Gold Cup (Mar); Three Choirs Festival (Aug every third year) and Fairford International Air Tattoo (major aviation display, July). Hotel chains include *FP, HG, Ja, Ly, RH, TI*. In addition to the many hotels, there is a good range of cheaper guesthouse and b.&b. accommodation, and also farmhouse accommodation within a few miles of the city.

The nearest youth hostel (13 miles from the centre) is **Slimbridge YHA**, *Shepherd's Patch, Slimbridge; tel: (01453) 890275*. The 91 bus from Gloucester stops at the Slimbridge crossroads, approximately 1½ miles from Slimbridge. The closest campsites are **Red Lion Camping and Caravan Site**, *Wainlode Hill, Norton; tel: (01452) 730251*, 4 miles north of Gloucester (Midland Red bus 373 goes four times a day to Norton, about 1 mile away); **Gables Farm Camping and Caravan Site**, *Moreton Valence; tel: (01452) 720331*, 7½ miles south of Gloucester (the 91 bus goes there hourly).

Gloucester has a number of historic inns, offering a good atmosphere, real ales and in many instances excellent food, while outside the city are various more expensive restaurants offering excellent cuisine, for example **Kingshead House** in the village of *Birdlip*, 8 miles from Gloucester *(tel: (01452) 862299)*, and **Greenway Hotel**, *Shurdington Road*, 9 miles from Gloucester *(tel: (01242) 862352)*; for both

it is best to go there by taxi. For vegetarian and vegan food try **Down to Earth**, *11 The Forum, Eastgate Shopping Centre*. Don't forget to eat some Double Gloucester cheese or Gloucester sausage, for which the city is well known!

The main post office can be found in *King's Square*, open Mon–Fri 0900–1730, Sat 0900–1230. Post restante facilities are available.

Entertainment and Events

Free entertainment listings, *Events in Gloucester* and the *Cheltenham and Gloucester Bulletin*, are available from the TIC; another listing is the *Gloucester Citizen*, £0.27 from newsagents. The **Guildhall Arts Centre**, *Eastgate St; tel: (01452) 50589*, functions as the main theatre, cinema and music venue. As well as a good variety of lively nightclubs (try **Crackers** in *Bruton Way*, **King of Clubs** in *Quay St* and **Fifth Avenue** at *The Leisure Centre, Bruton Way*), Gloucester has one of the largest dry-ski complexes in the south west. **Gloucester Ski Centre**, *Robinswood Hill; tel: (01452) 414300*, open Mon–Fri 1000–2000, Sat, Sun 1000–1800, closed Aug. Take bus number 1 from *Clarence St* to *Matson Lane* (approximately 20 mins).

Gloucester, Hereford and Worcester take turns in hosting the **Three Choirs Festival** in Aug, a festival of choral and sacred music. This will be held in Gloucester in 1995, in the Cathedral. The festival has a major impact on visitor numbers, making accommodation hard to find.

The **Gloucester Festival** is an annual festival, taking place in the last week of July and first week of Aug and including many sporting and cultural events at a variety of locations around the city. In the traditional **Cooper's Hill Cheese Roll** on the late May Bank Holiday, local athletes compete annually in chasing cheeses down the Cooper's Hill slope, 3 miles south west of the city. This event is free, and can be reached by taking a bus to *Cross Hands Roundabout* and then the Cheltenham to Stroud bus to the slope.

Shopping

You can get a free shopping guide from the TIC. *North, South, East* and *Westgate Streets* are pedestrianised shopping areas with branches of most chain stores. Gloucester Docks also has an interesting shopping centre, including the **Gloucester Antiques Centre**, a converted warehouse with 67 antique shops. **Prinknash Abbey Pottery**, *Prinknash Abbey*, is also worth a visit. The pottery shop is open 0900–1730 daily except Good Friday and 25, 26 Dec; four miles east of city centre, take a bus to *Cross Hands Roundabout* and then the Cheltenham to Stroud bus.

Sightseeing

Gloucester's **cathedral** alone makes it worth a visit: its amazing riches include a vast east window with 14th-century stained glass; the earliest surviving fan vaulting in the cloister; and the painted tombs of Edward II and Robert, Duke of Normandy. Even the monks' washroom is exquisite. Gloucester has a small historic heart centred on the cathedral precinct and *Westgate St*, where there is a **Folk Museum** housed in a group of Tudor and Jacobean half-timbered houses and **Llanthony Priory**, with its distinctive medieval buildings, is worth a detour. It also has a great number of interesting churches (obtain a trail from the TIC), while **Blackfriars** is a rare survival of a Dominican priory. The **House of the Tailor of Gloucester** was the inspiration for Beatrix Potter's famous story. Gloucester Civic Trust (*tel: (01452) 301903*) offer many walking tours including excellent city walks starting from the TIC at 1430 every Sun and Wed, June–Sept, and daily during school summer holidays. No charge is made, but donations are welcomed.

As well as being a cathedral city, surprisingly Gloucester was once a flourishing inland port, linked by canal to the River Severn. The **Docks** have been revitalised, and the 19th-century warehouses now house some unusual museums, including the **National Waterways Museum** and the **Robert Opie Collection**, which takes a nostalgic look at changing fashions in advertising and packaging. Tours of the Docks are organised by the National Waterways Museum (*tel: (01452) 318054*), price £2. Out of town, **Berkeley Castle**, the scene of Edward II's brutal murder, is a beautiful

Norman fortress turned stately home, with park and terraced Elizabethan gardens; while en route at Slimbridge is the **Wildfowl and Wetlands Trust**, Sir Peter Scott's world-renowned collection of water birds – both captive and wild – in beautiful surroundings. The TIC organises scenic guided bus tours of the Cotswolds and Gloucestershire during the summer, departing from Barclays Bank, *Southgate St*, price £7.50.

Gloucester Cathedral, *Westgate St; tel: (01452) 528095*. Open 0800–1700 (–1800 summer), closed during some events. Admission: free. **Blackfriars Priory** (EH), *Southgate St; tel: (01452) 527688*. Open Mon–Fri 1000–1500. Admission: free. **City Museum and Art Gallery**, *Brunswick Rd; tel: (01452) 524131*. Open Mon–Sat 1000–1700, July–Sept Sun 1000–1600. Closed 1 Jan, Good Friday, 25 Dec. Admission: free. **Gloucester Folk Museum**, *99103 Westgate St; tel: (01452) 526467*. Open Mon–Sat 1000–1700, July–Sept Sun 1000–1600. Admission: free. **House of the Tailor of Gloucester**, *9 College Court; tel: (01452) 422586*. Open Mon–Sat 0930–1730. Admission: free. **National Waterways Museum**, *Llanthony Warehouse, The Docks; tel: (01452) 318054*. Open daily 1000–1800 (–1700 in winter); closed 25 Dec. Admission: £3.95. **Robert Opie Collection Museum of Advertising and Packaging**, *Albert Warehouse, The Docks; tel: (01452) 302309*. Open 1000–1800 (–1700 in winter), Mon May–Sept and Bank Holidays except 25, 26 Dec. Admission: £2.75.

Out of Town

Berkeley Castle (16 miles south west of city), *Berkeley; tel: (01453) 810332*. Open Tues–Sun 1400–1700 (Apr); Tues–Sat 1100–1700, Sun 1400–1700 (May–Sept and Bank Holidays); Sun 1400–1630 (Oct). Admission: £3.70. Take Badgerline 308 bus. **Wildfowl and Wetlands Centre**, *Slimbridge; tel: (01453) 890333*. Open daily 0930–1700 (summer), 0930–1600 (winter). Admission: £4.50. Take Badgerline bus to Cambridge, 12½ miles south, then 1½ mile walk.

BIRMINGHAM
to
CARDIFF

This route takes you from Birmingham into Wales via the cathedral city of Worcester and the Victorian spa town of Malvern, set amid some of Britain's most ancient hills. On its way to the Welsh capital, it skirts the strange and rugged beauty of the Brecon Beacons National Park, which can be explored from Abergavenny.

TRAINS

ETT tables: 520 (direct), 528/535 (On Track).

➡ Fast Track

The hourly, direct service (Sun services do not start until early afternoon) from Birmingham New Street to Cardiff Central via Gloucester takes 2–2½ hrs. The On Track route below is much longer.

∿ On Track

Birmingham–Worcester

Trains run approximately half-hourly from Birmingham New Street to Worcester Foregate Street, taking 50 mins. Sun services are hourly.

Worcester–Gt Malvern

Two to three trains per hour run Worcester Foregate Street–Great Malvern, taking 15 mins. Sunday service is hourly (in winter starting midday).

Gt Malvern–Ledbury–Hereford

A service runs approximately every hour from Great Malvern to Hereford calling at Ledbury en route. Great Malvern to Ledbury takes 11 mins, Ledbury to Hereford 15 mins.

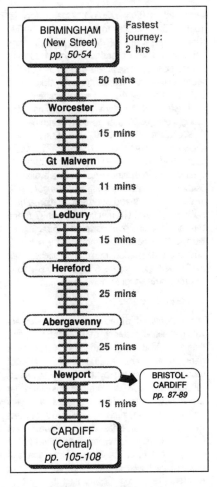

BIRMINGHAM (New Street) *pp. 50-54* — Fastest journey: 2 hrs

50 mins

Worcester

15 mins

Gt Malvern

11 mins

Ledbury

15 mins

Hereford

25 mins

Abergavenny

25 mins

Newport → BRISTOL-CARDIFF *pp. 87-89*

15 mins

CARDIFF (Central) *pp. 105-108*

Hereford–Abergavenny–Newport

An hourly service (more on Suns) runs between Hereford, Abergavenny and Newport. Hereford to Abergavenny takes 25 mins, Abergavenny to Newport 25 mins.

Newport–Cardiff

The frequent service from Newport to Cardiff Central takes less than 15 mins.

WORCESTER

TIC: *The Guildhall, High St, Worcester WR1*

2EY; tel: (01905) 726311. Open Mon–Sat 1030–1730 (mid-Mar to end Oct), 1030–1600 (Nov to mid-Mar). DP Services offered: local bed-booking service and BABA (latest 30 mins before closing, busiest late afternoon). Guided tours booked, HI membership sold, tickets sold for day trips, events and entertainment. *The Worcester Visitor*, including an accommodation listing, costs £0.60 (free to postal enquiries).

Worcester City DIAL, *54 Friary Walk, Crowngate Centre; tel: (01905) 27790.* Open Tues, Wed, Fri 0900–1500, Thur 0900–1300. Disablement Information Advice Line available.

Station: Foregate Street Station, *Foregate St*, is in the city centre and Shrub Hill Station, *Shrub Hill* is ½ mile east (10-min walk or bus 27 to the centre). For train enquiries *tel: (01452) 529501.* Both stations have a taxi rank.

Bus Station: National Express coaches, *tel: (0121) 622 4373*, operate from the bus station at *Crowngate, Angel Place*.

Getting Around

The majority of attractions in the town are within walking distance of the centre. A free map is available from the TIC. For general transport enquiries *tel: (0345) 125436.* Most services are operated by **Midland Red West**, *tel: (01905) 763888*, from the bus station at *Crowngate, Angel Place*. Services are very frequent in town, running until 2330, but less frequent to rural areas. A daily **Rover** ticket (£3.50) covers all of Worcester's services. The main taxi rank is at *The Cross, High St*, and taxis can also be hailed in the street. For details of registered taxi companies, contact the TIC.

Staying in Worcester

There are a reasonable number of hotels to choose from, and a good choice of b. & b. and guesthouse accommodation, with cheaper accommodation mainly outside the town. It is generally easy to find accommodation on arrival, except during the Three Choirs Festival (held in August every three years, next in 1996). The nearest youth hostel is in Great Malvern (see p. 72). The TIC has details of campsites, the closest being: **Millhouse** (3 miles north), *Hawford; tel: (01905) 451283* (take bus 303) and **Lenchford**

Meadow Park, *Shrawley; tel: (01905) 620246*, take bus 293 (6 miles north-west).

There is a fair range of eating places, both in the city centre and on the outskirts, with a small choice of gourmet restaurants. **King Charles Restaurant**, *King Charles House, 29 New St; tel: (01905) 22449*, is situated in a beautiful, listed building – the house from which King Charles II escaped his enemies after the Battle of Worcester in 1651.

Worcester is well endowed with pretty, pedestrianised shopping areas like *Crown Passage, Reindeer Court, Friar Street* and *The Hopmarket*. The **Royal Worcester Porcelain Factory** (*Severn St*) has bestware and factory seconds shops.

The main post office is on *Foregate St*. Open Mon–Fri 0900–1730, Sat 0900–1230.

Entertainment and Events

The TIC displays a poster around town called 'Where and When', which is a guide to what is currently on. *Worcester Evening News* (£0.25 from newsagents) also has entertainment listings. There is the **Swan Theatre**, *The Moors; tel: (01905) 27322*, for drama; the **Countess of Huntingdon's Hall**, *Deansway; tel: (01905) 611427*, for live music; and the **Northwick Theatre**, *Ombersley Rd; tel: (01905) 755141*, for cabaret, as well as five nightclubs, and many pubs and winebars. The **Worcester Races**, *The Racecourse, Pitchcroft; tel: (01905) 25364*, are held throughout the year; the TIC has a fixture list. The **Three Choirs Festival** takes place in *Worcester Cathedral* (every third year in Aug – next 1996).

Sightseeing

Worcester is dominated by the outline of the graceful **cathedral**, with its 14th-century tower; notable inside are the beautiful 11th-century crypt and a number of fine monuments, including King John's tomb with its Purbeck marble effigy. Worcester's old buildings can easily be seen on foot: they include **Greyfriars**, a well-restored, half-timbered Franciscan friary of 1480, with a lovely peaceful garden; the 14th-century **Edgar Tower** (College Precinct); **King Charles House** (*New St*), which dates from

1577 and now houses a restaurant; and the ornate **Guildhall** of 1722. Guided walks are run by **Faithful City Guides** tel: (01905) 451894, bookable from the TIC, where they start (price £2). In summer there are also river trips on the Severn operated by **Bickerline** tel: (01531) 670679, starting at South Quay (price £2.50).

Worcester was strongly Royalist during the 17th-century civil wars; the story of that conflict, focusing on Charles' defeat at Worcester in 1651, is traced at the **Commandery**, which was the Royalist headquarters. The town is also famous for its distinctive and brilliantly coloured porcelain: a tour of the **Royal Worcester Porcelain Factory** reveals how it is manufactured, and the **Dyson Perrins Museum** has a collection of fine pieces. The **Tudor House Museum** explores Worcester's social history.

Worcester is full of connections with the composer Sir Edward Elgar; ask for the Elgar Route leaflet from the TIC. At nearby Broadheath, **Elgar's Birthplace Museum** houses a collection of musical scores, photos and memorabilia in the cottage where this quintessentially English composer was born in 1857. In complete contrast to this humble abode, the shell of **Witley Court**, a vast Victorian Italianate mansion, is redolent with the atmosphere of high society house parties; the equally lavish parish church nearby was Witley Court's private chapel.

City Museum and Art Gallery, Foregate St; tel: (01905) 25371. Open Mon–Wed and Fri 0930–1800, Sat 0930–1700. Admission free. **Greyfriars** (NT), Friar St; tei: (01905) 23571. Open Wed, Thur and Bank Holiday Mons 1400–1730 (Apr–Oct). Admission £2. **The Guildhall**, High Street; tel: (01905) 23471. Open Mon–Sat 0900–1700. Admission free. **The Commandery, Civil War Centre**, Sidbury; tel: (01905) 355071. Open Mon–Sat (1000–1700), Sun 1330–1730. Admission £3.10. **Royal Worcester Porcelain Factory/Dyson Perrins Museum**, Severn St; tel: (01905) 23221. Museum open Mon–Fri 0930–1700, Sat 1000–1700; factory tours Mon–Fri except Bank Holidays and factory holidays. Admission museum £1.50, factory tour £3.

Tudor House Museum, Friar St; tel: (01905)

20904. Open Mon–Wed, Fri and Sat 1030–1730. Admission £1.50. **Worcester Cathedral**, College Green; tel: (01905) 28854. Open 0800–1800. Admission free (donations welcomed).

Out of Town

Elgar's Birthplace (3 miles west), Crown East Lane, Lower Broadheath; tel: (01905) 333224. Open daily except Wed 1030–1800 (May–Sept), 1330–1630 (Oct to mid-Jan and mid-Feb to Apr); closed mid-Jan to mid-Feb. Admission £3. Take bus 419 or 420 (Midland Red West), then 30-min walk. **Spetchley Park Gardens**, 3 miles east (30 acres of gardens, with rare trees, shrubs and plants), Spetchley; tel: (01905) 65213. Open Tues–Fri and Bank Holiday Mons 1100–1700, Sun 1400–1700 (Apr–Sept). Admission £2.10. Take bus 350 (Dudley Coaches). **Witley Court** (ET), Great Witley; tel: (01299) 896636. Open daily 1000–1800 (Apr–Oct), Wed–Sun 1000–1600 (Nov–Mar). Admission £1.25. Take 758 bus (Yarronton Brothers), then a 1-mile walk (10 miles north-west of town).

GREAT MALVERN

TIC: Grange Rd, Malvern, Worcestershire WR14 3HB; tel: (01684) 892289. Open daily 1000–1700 (Easter–Oct), Mon–Sat 1000–1700 (Nov–Easter). DP SHS Services offered: local bed-booking service, BABA, advance reservations handled. The Malverns, including an accommodation listing, is free.

Station: Great Malvern Station, Avenue Rd; tel: (01452) 529501 is ½ mile east of the town centre, and has a taxi rank.

Getting Around

Most of Malvern's attractions are within walking distance of the centre. Town and transport maps are available free from the TIC. Buses run frequently within the town centre, and every two hours to outlying areas until 1800 (except Worcester, until 2245). Most services are operated by **Midland Red West** from the bus depot at Worcester. Day **Rover** tickets (£3.50) are available for Midland Red West Services. For local bus information tel: (0345) 125436. The main taxi rank is outside the Post Office, on

Abbey Rd. Further details of registered taxi companies are available from the TIC.

Staying in Great Malvern

There is a fair range of hotels, and a good number of cheaper b.&b. and guesthouse accommodation, mostly in Malvern Link, Malvern Wells, West Malvern, Little Malvern and North Malvern. Hotel chains in Malvern include *DV, BW*. **Malvern Youth Hostel** is at *Hatherley, Peachfield Rd; tel: (01684) 573300*, open from 1700. The nearest campsites are about 5–6 miles away, but are not accessible by public transport: **Riverside**, *Clevelode; tel: (01684) 310475*; **Camping and Caravan Club of Great Britain**, *Site 2, Hanley Swan; tel: (01684) 310280*; **Eastnor Deer Park**, *Eastnor Castle, Eastnor, Ledbury; tel: (01531) 632302*.

Sightseeing

Great Malvern is the largest of the five towns known as the Malverns, which lie beneath the 9-mile range of the Malvern Hills; the hills and countryside around the town are very popular with walkers. The TIC has details of local bus tours and guided walks.

The town developed in the 18th century after the beneficial effects of Malvern spring waters were discovered: sample them at **St Ann's Well**, on the hill slope below the 1395-ft **Worcestershire Beacon** (a fine viewpoint). **Great Malvern Priory** is a beautiful Norman building with superb 15th-century stained glass. The **Museum**, housed in one of the surviving abbey buildings, traces the town's history. Like Worcester, Great Malvern has many connections with the composer **Sir Edward Elgar**; ask the TIC for a copy of the *Elgar Route* leaflet that has all the details. Out of town, **Little Malvern Priory** retains its tower and east end which has some interesting 15th-century stained glass depicting Edward IV and his family.

Great Malvern Priory, *Church St; tel: (01684) 561020*. Open 0900–1800. Admission free. **Malvern Museum**, *Abbey Rd; tel: (01684) 567811*. Open 1000–1700. Admission £0.50. **St Ann's Well**, *Rose Bank Gardens, Belle Vue Terrace* (with a climb of 95 steps), open from 1000–1800. Admission free.

LEDBURY

TIC: *Church La, Ledbury, Herefordshire HR8 1DH; tel: (01531) 636147*. Open 1000–1300 and 1400–1700 (closed Sun Nov–Mar). DP SHS Services offered: local bed-booking service (latest 1645), advance reservations handled, BABA (latest 1630), guided tours booked. *Ledbury Town Guide* costs £1, and *The Malverns* accommodation listing is free.

Station: Ledbury Station, *The Homend; tel: (01452) 529501*, ½ mile north of centre.

Getting Around

Most of the town's attractions are within walking distance of the centre. The TIC can provide free town and transport maps. There are a number of local bus companies, and most services run from the **Market House** or **The Memorial** on the *High St*. Services are good within Ledbury and to many nearby towns. There are no buses on Suns or after 2000. For bus enquiries *tel: (0345) 125436*. There is no taxi rank in Ledbury. For taxis, contact: **Ledbury Taxis** *tel: (01531) 633596* or **Martin Powell** *tel: (01531) 635249*.

Staying in Ledbury

There is a small range of hotels, and a bigger range of guesthouse and b.&b. accommodation in the town and surrounding area. There are also four pubs with rooms in the centre. It is generally easy to book on arrival, except during the **National Mountain Bike Rally** at *Eastnor* in July. The closest budget accommodation is **Malvern Hills Youth Hostel**, *18 Peachfield Rd, Malvern Wells; tel: (01684) 569131*, open Thur–Mon (Mar), daily (Apr–Oct), Fri, Sat (Nov–Dec). Take bus 675 to *Malvern Wells*, (approximately 40 mins). The closest campsites are **Keepers Cottage**, *Falcon La; tel: (01531) 670269*, 1½ miles south-west, and **Eastnor Deer Park**, *Eastnor; tel: (01531) 632302*, 2 miles east (not on bus route).

Sightseeing

A small market town of great charm, Ledbury has many well-preserved black-and-white timbered houses. Guided walks start from the timbered **Market House** (1650) on the *High St, tel: (01531) 634229,* price: £2.30. Cobbled *Church Lane,* often used for film sets, is particularly picturesque; it leads to the large Norman and Perpendicular **Church of St Michael and All Angels,** with its unusual detached tower. The **Painted Room,** only recently discovered, has a series of 16th-century frescoes. Near Newent, the **National Birds of Prey Centre** has an exceptional collection of hunting birds and offers frequent displays. **Church of St Michael and All Angels,** *Church La.* Open 1000–1800 (summer), enquire at TIC for winter opening hours.

Out of Town

National Birds of Prey Centre (10 miles south) near *Newent; tel: (01531) 820286.* Open daily 1030–1730 or dusk if earlier (Feb–Nov). Admission £3.75. Take Tudor Coaches service 677, Tues and Fri only.

HEREFORD

TIC: *1 King St, Hereford HR4 9BW; tel: (01432) 268430.* Open daily 0900–1700; closed Sun (Oct–Apr). DP Services offered: local bed-booking (booking fee £1.50), BABA (booking fee £2.50) (latest bookings 1630), advance reservations handled, guided tours booked, YHA membership sold. *Places to Visit* and an accommodation list are available free.
Station: Hereford Station, *Barrs Court; tel: (01452) 529501* is ½ mile from the centre, and has a taxi rank.

Getting Around

Free town and transport maps are available from the TIC. Local bus services, run by Midland Red *tel: (01905) 763888,* operate from **Hopper Bus Station**, *Bewell St.* Services in town are good, but patchy to outlying areas and are reduced at weekends and in the evenings. The main taxi rank is on *Widemarsh St.*

Staying in Hereford

It is generally easy to find accommodation on arrival, except during summer Bank Holidays, and the **Three Choirs Festival**, which takes place in Hereford once every three years (next in 1997). Hotel chains in Hereford include *MH, FH.*

There is a reasonable range of places to stay, with rather more choice of smaller, b. & b. and guesthouse establishments than hotels, and a few inns with rooms outside the town. The TIC can provide campsite information. The closest is: **Hereford Racecourse Campsite** (2 miles), *Roman Rd; tel: (01432) 272364.*

Sightseeing

This ancient county town has some pleasant streets to roam, around *Broad St* and *High Town.* The TIC has information on guided walks conducted by **Hereford Guild of Guides**, and on bus tours of the area. The much altered 12th-century **cathedral** has two great treasures: the *Mappa Mundi,* a world map drawn in 1289, and the medieval chained library, where nearly 1,500 rare books are chained to the bookcases.

Hereford is renowned for its cider-making: Bulmers have been making cider there for 100 years, and there are tours of the **Cider Mill** *tel: (01432) 352000.* The **Cider Museum** explains cider-making through the ages. The town is surrounded by lush countryside: the climb to **Dinmore Manor**, once a monastery, is well worthwhile for a happy mix of real and mock medieval, and for the superb views over its gardens and surrounding hills.

Cider Museum and King Offa Distillery, *Pomona Pl; tel: (01432) 354207.* Open daily 1000–1730 (Apr–Oct), Mon–Sat 1300–1700 (Nov–Mar). Admission £1.95. **Hereford Cathedral**; *tel: (01432) 356250.* Mappa Mundi open 1000–1515 (–1615 in summer); Chained Library open 1030–1230 and 1400–1600 (Easter–Oct), reduced opening hours in winter. Admission to Cathedral: free (charge for Mappa Mundi £2.60; Chained Library £0.60). **Hereford City Museum and Art Gallery**, *Broad St; tel: (01432) 268121.* Open Tues–Fri 1000–1800 (–1700 Thur), Sat 1000–1700 (–1600 winter), and Bank Holiday Suns and Mons. Admission free.

Out of Town

Dinmore Manor (6 miles north); *tel: (01432) 830322.* Open daily 0930–1730. Admission £2. Bus 292 towards Leominster, then 2-mile walk.

ABERGAVENNY

TIC: (Brecon Beacons National Park Information Centre is also located here) *Swan Meadow, Monmouth Rd, Abergavenny, Gwent NP7 5HH; tel: (01873) 857588.* Open daily 1000–1800 (Easter–Oct). DP Services offered: local bed-booking service and BABA (latest 1730), advance reservations handled. *Browsing Around Abergavenny* and *Abergavenny Where to Stay* are available free of charge.

Station: Abergavenny Station, *Station Rd; tel: (01222) 228000* is half a mile east of the town centre (bus 20 or 21), and taxis are usually waiting to meet trains.

Getting Around

The town's attractions are within walking distance of the centre, and a free town map and transport timetables are available from the TIC. Most local services are operated from *Swan Meadow, Monmouth Rd*, by **Red and White** *tel: (01633) 266336* and **Phil Anslow** *tel: (01495) 792323.* Services are good within the town, and to Newport and Cardiff. Hardly any buses run after 2000 or on Sun. For taxis contact **Lewis's** *tel: (01873) 854140;* **Park Taxis** *tel: (01873) 858416* or **Carlton Taxis** *tel: (01873) 850716.*

Staying in Abergavenny

There is a small number of hotels, including the *FH and MC* chains, and a good choice of guesthouse and b. & b. accommodation. Cheaper places can be found within the town and in farmhouse accommodation in the surrounding area. It is generally easy to book on arrival. The nearest youth hostel is **Abergavenny Youth Hostel**, *Capel-y-Ffin; tel: (01873) 890650,* which is 16 miles north and not accessible by public transport. The closest campsites are **Pyscodlyn Farm** (2 miles north-west), *Llanwenarth Citra; tel: (01873) 853271* (bus 21) and **Clydach Gorge** (4 miles south-west); *tel: (01495) 350555* (bus X4).

Sightseeing

A busy market town on the River Usk, Abergavenny proclaims itself the 'Gateway to Wales'. There are remains of the **Castle** walls, towers and gateway, and the **Museum** displays traditional furnishings and crafts.

Lying on the fringe of the Brecon Beacons National Park, Abergavenny makes a superb base for walking the hills, which rise all around. The extinct volcano, **Sugar Loaf Mountain** (1950 ft), lies 2½ miles north. Elegant, 15th-century **Raglan Castle**, with its hexagonal towers, is the most complete of local fortresses, while the imposing, moated **White Castle** was probably built by Henry II in the 12th century. There are lovely views of the Black Mountains from the graceful ruined church at **Llanthony Priory**. Just south of here lies the once thriving South Wales coalfield: at the excellent **Big Pit Mining Museum**, ex-miners guide visitors down the 300-ft shaft of a colliery that closed in 1980.

Abergavenny Castle and Museum, *Castle St; tel: (01873) 854282.* Open Mon–Sat 1100–1300 and 1400–1700, Sun 1400–1700 (Mar–Oct); Mon–Sat 1100–1300 and 1400–1600 (Nov–Feb). Admission £1.

Out of Town

Big Pit Mining Museum, *Blaenafon; tel: (01495) 790311.* Open daily 0930–1700 (Mar–Oct), underground tours 1000–1530. Also open some days during winter; telephone for details. Admission £4.95. Take Edmund's bus to *Blaenafon* (Tues and Fri), otherwise X4 to *Brynmawr* and change to Phil Anslow bus to *Blaenafon*, 8 miles south-west.

Llanthony Priory (Cadw), *Llanthony Valley.* Always open. Admission free. Ten miles north, not accessible by public transport. **Raglan Castle** (Cadw), *Raglan; tel: (01291) 690228.* Open daily 0930–1830 (Easter–Oct); Mon–Sat 0930–1600, Sun 1100–1600 (Nov–Easter). Admission £2. Phil Anslow bus to *Raglan*, then ½-mile walk. Ten miles south-east.

NEWPORT

For details of Newport, see Bristol–Cardiff route, pp. 87–89.

BIRMINGHAM to MANCHESTER

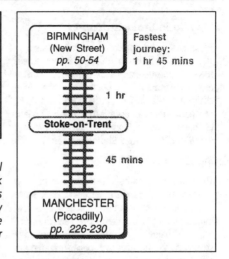

Connecting two of Britain's former industrial giants – Birmingham, the hub of the Black Country, and Manchester, once the world's cotton capital and still Britain's third largest city – this itinerary passes through the heart of the Potteries. It also gives access to the popular Alton Towers theme park.

TRAINS

ETT tables: 550

Fast Track

Hourly express trains run from Birmingham New Street to Manchester Piccadilly taking about 1 hr 45 mins. The service is much reduced on Suns.

On Track

Most services call at Stoke-on-Trent. Birmingham–Stoke takes 1 hour and Stoke–Manchester 45 mins. Several additional express trains run on the Stoke–Manchester section.

STOKE-ON-TRENT

TIC: *Quadrant Rd, Hanley, Stoke-on-Trent, Staffordshire ST1 1RZ; tel: (01782) 284600,* for accommodation bookings *tel: (01782) 284222.* Open Mon–Sat 0915–1715. DP Services offered: local bed-booking and BABA (latest 1630), advance reservations handled. Tickets booked for factory tours, National Express, some events and theatre bookings. *The China Experience* and an accommodation listing are available free.
Station: *Station Rd; tel: (01782) 411411.* Two miles south of the centre; linked by buses 45, 46 and 47. There is a taxi rank at the station.

Getting Around

Stoke-on-Trent comprises six separate towns, known as the **Potteries**. From north to south these are *Tunstall, Burslem, Hanley, Stoke-upon-Trent, Fenton* and *Longton*. Hanley is the city centre and main shopping area. The city's attractions are spread throughout its six towns, which are well linked by frequent bus services (bus no. 24). For general transport enquiries *tel: (01782) 747000.*

The China Link is a special bus service (with distinctive blue-and-white liveries) connecting the many factory shops and attractions, ceramic museums and visitor centres in the Potteries. It runs daily, on the hour, from 1000–1600, starting from outside Stoke-on-Trent Station. Other pick-up points are **Gladstone Pottery Museum**, *Longton*; **Minton Museum**, *Stoke-on-Trent*; **Potteries Shopping Centre**, *Hanley*; **Royal Doulton**, *Burslem*, and the **Wedgwood Visitor Centre**, *Barlaston*. Single journeys cost from £0.50, a **Day Rover** costs £4. Services run Apr–Nov. (The TIC has a free leaflet with details.)

Most buses are run by the **PMT Bus Company**, from **Hanley Bus Station**, *Lichfield St, Hanley; tel: (01782) 747000.* There is a limited Sun service, particularly to outlying areas.

Staying in Stoke-on-Trent

There is a good choice of accommodation in and around Stoke-on-Trent including hotels, b. & b.s, guesthouses and farmhouses: it is recommended that you book in advance. Hotel chains in Stoke-on-Trent include *FP, Gr, MH, Pr, St*. The nearest campsite is **Trentham Gardens** (3 miles south), *Stone Rd, Trentham; tel: (01782) 657341*. Take Stafford bus no. 260.

Sightseeing

The Stoke area has been the centre of pottery-making in Britain since before the Romans came. Its many pottery factories, shops, museums and visitor centres, a few of which are listed below, are scattered throughout the six towns: the TIC's *China Experience* leaflet has full details. A good place to start is the **City Museum and Art Gallery** for its huge collection of ceramics, especially Staffordshire pottery; you can also tour the individual factories of the world-famous names (such as **Royal Doulton**, **Royal Grafton** and **Spode**). Traditional skills are demonstrated at the **Wedgwood Visitor Centre**, and the **Gladstone Pottery Museum** has been preserved as a working Victorian pottery, retaining its giant bottle kiln – once a common feature of the Staffordshire landscape.

When pottery threatens to overwhelm you, one of the biggest visitor attractions in the country awaits at **Alton Towers**, Britain's most famous theme park – a blend of stomach-churning rides and fantasy experiences aimed at families, and set in parkland surrounding a ruined country house.

For a more restful experience, **Biddulph Grange Garden** is a fascinating survival of an unusual Victorian garden, divided into smaller plots which comprise a miniature 'world tour' of gardening.

Pottery Factory Visits

Royal Doulton, *Nile St, Burslem; tel: (01782) 292434).* Tours by arrangement Mon–Fri 1030–1400. **Royal Grafton China**, *Marlborough Rd, Longton; tel: (01782) 599667).* Tours by arrangement Mon–Fri. **Spode**, *Spode Works, Church St, Stoke-upon-Trent; tel: (01782)*

744011. Tours by arrangement Mon–Thur 1000–1400, Fri 1000.

Pottery Museums and Visitor Centres

City Museum and Art Gallery, *Bethesda St, Hanley; tel: (01782) 202173.* Open Mon–Sat 1000–1700, Sun 1400–1700. Admission: free. **Etruria Industrial Museum**, *Lower Bedford St, Etruria (west of Hanley); tel: (01782) 287557.* Open Wed–Sun 1000–1600. **Gladstone Working Pottery Museum**, *Uttoxeter Rd, Longton; tel: (01782) 319232.* Open Mon–Sat 1000–1700 (closed Mon except Bank Holidays Nov–Feb); last entry 1600. Admission: £3. **Minton Museum**, *London Rd, Stoke-upon-Trent; tel: (01782) 292292.* Open Mon–Fri 0930–1300 and 1345–1630; closed factory holidays. **Sir Henry Doulton Gallery**, *Nile St, Burslem; tel: (01782) 292292.* Open 0900–1615; closed some factory holidays. **Wedgwood Visitor Centre**, *Barlaston; tel: (01782) 204218.* Open Mon–Fri 0900–1700; Sat, Sun 1000–1700 (Easter–Oct), Sat only 1000–1600 (Oct–Easter). 6 miles south of Stoke-on-Trent, but connected by **China Link** bus service (see above).

Out of Town

Alton Towers, *Alton; tel: (01538) 702200.* Open daily from 0900–1800, later in high season (Mar–Nov); rides open 1000. Admission £15. Transfer bus once daily (0925) from Stoke-on-Trent railway station, included in admission charge (16 miles east). **Biddulph Grange Garden** (NT), *Biddulph; tel: (01782) 517999.* Open Wed–Fri 1200–1800, Sat, Sun and Bank Holiday Mons 1100–1800 (Apr–Oct); Sat, Sun 1200–1600 (Nov to mid-Dec). Admission £3.90. Bus 6a or 6b from Stop E on *Piccadilly, Hanley* (7 miles north). **Foxfield Steam Railway**, *Blythe Bridge; tel: weekends only (01782) 396210.* Open Sun and Bank Holiday Mons 1130–1600. Tickets: £3 for 5-mile round trip. Hourly train from Stoke to Blythe Bridge, then ½-mile walk (6 miles east of Stoke). **Shugborough** (NT), *Shugborough; tel: (01889) 881388.* Open daily 1100–1700 (Apr–Oct). Admission: House, Museum and Farm £3.50 each; all inclusive ticket £7.50. Bus 825 from the station to *Shugborough Farm*, then 2-mile walk. Six miles east.

BIRMINGHAM
to
SHEFFIELD

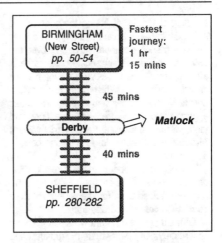

This route between Birmingham and the former steel- and cutlery-manufacturing capital of the North of England serves as a springboard for the celebrated beauties of the Derbyshire Dales and the Peak District.

TRAINS

ETT tables: 520

 Fast Track

There is an approximately hourly service (Suns from midday) from Birmingham New Street, taking 1 hr 15 – 1 hr 30 mins.

 On Track

Birmingham–Derby

Two trains an hour (less on Suns) run Birmingham New Street–Derby, taking about 45 mins.

Derby–Sheffield

Two expresses each hour run Derby–Sheffield (irregular service on Suns), taking 40 mins.

- -
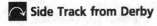 **Side Track from Derby**

MATLOCK

TIC: *The Pavilion, Matlock Bath, Derbyshire DE4 3NR; tel: (01629) 55082.* Open daily 0930–1730 (Mar–Oct); Wed–Mon 1000–1600, Sat 0930–1630 (Nov–Feb). DP SHS Services offered: local bed-booking service and BABA (latest 1 hour before closing), guided tours booked. *Illustrated Guide to Matlock* is £0.40, and a free accommodation guide is available.

Station: Matlock Bath Station *tel: (01332) 25700* is central. There are hourly services from Derby to Matlock (much reduced on Sun); the journey takes about 30 mins.

Getting Around

Matlock Bath is approximately one mile south of *Matlock*; there are train and bus services (R1 and R32) connecting the two. Town maps and transport maps are available from the TIC. Most attractions are within a walkable distance of Matlock Bath centre. The **Derbyshire Wayfarer** ticket allows one day's travel on all buses and trains in Derbyshire for £6.70. For bus information *tel: (01298) 23098.* Local services are reasonable in Matlock, but irregular to outlying areas. **Matlock Taxis** *tel: (01629) 584195* operate the taxi service at the station.

Staying in Matlock

There is a reasonable range of b.&b. and guesthouse accommodation but very few hotels. It is generally easy to find accommodation on arrival. For budget accommodation try **Matlock Youth Hostel**, *40 Bank Rd, Matlock; tel: (01629) 582983.* The closest campsite is **Wayside Farm** (2 miles north-east), *Matlock Moor; tel: (01629) 582967;* bus no. 17 or 64.

Sightseeing

A popular inland resort, Matlock Bath is famous for its spa water – there is a pump for free sampling at the TIC. It lies on the edge of the Peak District National Park in a dramatic gorge; the **Heights of Abraham**, towering over the town, can be reached by sedate cable car, and offer caverns and walks as well as superb views at the top. The **Whistletop Countryside Centre**, in the former station buildings, offers a good introduction to Derbyshire flora and fauna, while the excellent **Peak District Mining Musuem** tells the story of lead mining back to Roman times.

Matlock is a good base for exploring the beautiful dales of the southern Peak – the TIC can book guided tours for you with **Derbyshire Tourist Guides** tel: (01629) 650213.

Of the three great historic houses in the area, choose between **Chatsworth**, the grandest and most famous, **Hardwick Hall**, a fine Elizabethan mansion, and **Haddon Hall**, one of the most atmospheric of medieval manor houses.

Arkwright's Mill at nearby Cromford, dating to 1771, was the world's first water-powered cotton mill. **Middleton Top Engine House** boasts a steam engine of 1829 which, until 1963, hauled wagons up the steep Middleton incline on the Cromford and High Peak Railway; the visitor centre tells the story of this historic railway and makes a good walking base. The marvellous **National Tramway Museum** at Crich has working examples from far and wide.

Matlock Bath

Heights of Abraham Country Park and Caverns, *Matlock Bath; tel: (01629) 582365.* Open daily 1000–1700 (Easter–Oct). Call for winter opening hours. Admission £5.30. **Gulliver's Kingdom** (theme park), *Matlock Bath; tel: (01629) 57100.* Open daily 1030–1700 (end Mar to mid-Sept); closed some Fridays. Admission £4.50. **Matlock Bath Aquarium and Hologram Gallery**, *110 North Parade; tel: (01629) 583624.* Open daily 1000–1730 (Easter–Sept), Sat, Sun 1000–1730 (Oct–Easter). Admission £1.20. **Peak District Mining Museum**, *Matlock Bath Rd; tel: (01629) 583834.* Open daily 1100–1600. Admission £2 (museum), £2 (mine) or £3 (joint ticket). **Riber Castle Wildlife Park**, *Matlock; tel: (01629) 582073.* Open daily 1000–1700 (–1500 winter).

Admission £3.80. **Whistlestop Countryside Centre**, *Old Railway Station; tel: (01629) 580958.* Open daily 1000–1700 (Apr–Oct); Sat, Sun 1200–1600 (Nov–Mar). Admission free.

Out of Town

Arkwright's Cromford Mill (1 mile south), *Cromford; tel: (01629) 824297.* Open daily 0900–1700. Admission £1.50. Take bus R1 or R32. **Chatsworth** (10 miles north), near *Bakewell; tel: (01246) 582204.* Open daily 1100–1630 (late Mar to Oct). Admission £5.50. Take bus R1 or R32 to *Bakewell*, then bus 170 to the park, then 1½-mile walk. **Crooked Spire Church of St Mary and All Saints** (10 miles north), *Chesterfield; tel: (01246) 206506.* Open Mon–Sat 0900–1700, Sun during services only. Telephone for tower opening times. Admission free to church, small charge for tower. Take bus 17 or 64.

Haddon Hall, *Bakewell; tel: (01629) 812855.* Open Tues–Sat 1100–1800 (Apr–Sept), Sun (Apr–June and Sept) and Bank Holiday Mons. Last admission: 1715. Admission £4; bus R1 or R32, 6½ miles north. **Hardwick Hall** (NT), near *Chesterfield; tel: (01246) 850430.* Open Wed, Thur, Sat, Sun and Bank Holiday Mons 1230–1700 (or sunset if earlier), garden 1230–1730 (Apr–Oct). Admission £5.50; bus 17 or 64 to *Chesterfield*, 48, 63 or X2 to *Glapwell*, then 1½-mile walk (12 miles east). **Middleton Top Engine House**, *Wirksworth; tel: (01629) 823204.* Open (static) Sun 1030–1700 and (working) first Sat of month (Easter–Oct). Admission £0.35 (static), £0.60 (working). Take bus 412 or R32 to *Rise End*, then ½-mile walk. Four miles south.

National Stone Centre, *Porter Lane, Wirksworth; tel: (01629) 824833.* Open daily 1000–1700 (Easter to end Oct), 1000–1600 (Nov–Mar). Admission free except for exhibitions and tours. Take bus 412 or R32 to *Steeple Grange*, then ½-mile walk; 4 miles south. **National Tramway Museum**, *Crich; tel: (01773) 852565.* Open Mon–Fri 1000–1730, Sat, Sun and Bank Holidays 1000–1830 (Apr–Oct). Closed on some Fridays, open some winter weekends; call for details. Admission £4.50; bus 135, 140, 254, 901 or B1. Six miles south-east.

BRIGHTON

'London-by-the-Sea', Brighton began to develop as a seaside town after a local doctor had extolled the curative virtues of seabathing, introducing the taste for seaside holidays. It became hugely fashionable as a result of the patronage of the Prince Regent, later George IV: Georgian and Regency terraces sprang up everywhere after Brighton's royal admirer had built the exotic Royal Pavilion. Today, Brighton's combination of elegant buildings, exclusive shops and typical seaside amusements give it a unique, raffish charm; it deserves at least a day's exploration.

Tourist Information

TIC: *10 Bartholomew Sq, Brighton BN1 1JS; tel: (01273) 323755/326450*. Open Mon–Fri 0900–1700 (Sept–May); Sat 1000–1700, Sun 1000–1600 (Sept–mid-July); Mon–Fri 0900–1800 (June–July); Sat–Sun 1000–1800 (mid-July–August). DP SHS Services offered: local bed-booking service (£1.00 booking fee plus 10% deposit on first night stay, latest 1630 except Sun) – afternoons are busiest times for bookings especially during major conferences and bank holidays; BABA (£2.50 booking fee plus 10% deposit on first night stay, latest booking one hour before closing). Guided tours booked, tickets for National Express, local coach tours, Guide Friday and local concert venues sold.

A booklet, *Brighton and Hove The Big Difference*, including accommodation listings, is free.

Arriving and Departing

Station: *Queens Rd, tel: (01273) 206755*, is ½ mile north of the seafront and many buses connect it to the town centre. There is an accommodation agency at the station, a courtesy phone for car hire and a taxi rank.

Getting Around

The majority of attractions are within walking distance of the town centre except for **Preston Manor** and **Brighton Marina**. A free town map and a free transport map is available from the TIC. The transport map is also available from the local bus offices.

Buses

There are two main bus companies operating in Brighton and Hove: **Brighton & Hove Bus & Coach Co.** *tel: (01273) 886200*, whose central station is at *Conway St, Hove* and **Brighton Blue Buses** *tel: (01273) 674881*, which operates from *Lewes Road, Brighton*. Other services are provided as part of the County Council's 'Rider' network, *tel: (01273) 482123/478007*. Most buses pass through *The Old Steyne* in the town centre. Daily and weekly 'Saver' tickets from Brighton & Hove Buses cost £2.30 for a daily ticket; a similar 'Diamond' ticket for Brighton Blue Bus Service costs £1.80. A weekly travel card covering all services costs £12.50.

Taxis

The main taxi ranks are at *East Street, Queens Sq, St Peters Place* and the station; taxis can also be hailed in the street. The three main registered taxi companies are: **Brighton Streamline Taxis**, *tel: (01273) 747474*, **Southern Taxis Brighton Ltd**, *tel: (01273) 205205*, and **Brighton & Hove Radio Cabs**, *tel: (01273) 204066*.

Staying in Brighton

Accommodation

Thomas Cook has a hotel reservation desk on the main concourse of Queen's Rd railway station for travellers arriving by train.

There is a good choice of accommodation in the town and most price ranges are catered for. Cheaper accommodation is mostly located near the seafront in the town centre. There is no accommodation in pubs or inns in the town but a wide choice is available in the outlying villages. It is generally easy to find accommodation on arrival except during major conferences, bank holidays and summer Sats. If you have made a reservation, it is advisable to arrive before 2000 as small hotels are reluctant to hold rooms any later.

Hotel chains in Brighton include *FH, DV, Ja, Mp, MH*.

Brighton Youth Hostel is at *Patcham Pl, London Rd;* tel: *(01273) 556196*, open daily from 1000 (closed Jan). Take bus 107, 770 or 773 from *Marlborough Place* in the town centre. **Brighton Backpackers** is an independant hostel at *7576 Middle St;* tel: *(01723) 777717*, open daily from 1000.

There are no campsites in Brighton, the closest are: **Downsview Caravan Park**, *Bramlands Lane, Woodmancote,* near *Henfield;* tel: *(01273) 492801;* **New Barn Farm**, *New Barn Lane, Henfield;* tel *(01273) 494105;* **Farmhouse Campsite**, *Tottington Drive, Small Dole, Henfield;* tel: *(01273) 493157* (all 8 miles northwest on the 107 bus from *Old Steyne* to *Henfield*); and **Hampden Vale Caravan Centre**, *South Heighton, Newhaven;* tel *(01273) 713530*, 8 miles east along the coast, take the train or bus 712 from the station to Newhaven.

Eating and Drinking

There are a large number of restaurants in the town centre, especially in *The Lanes* and *Preston St.*

Communications

The main post office is on *Ship St.* Open Mon–Fri 0900–1730, Sat 0900–1230. Post Restante facility available.

Money

Thomas Cook bureaux de change are located at *58 North St* and *138 London Rd*, as well as at Midland Bank, *153 North St.*

Entertainment

Details of current entertainment can be found in the TIC's publications *Brighton Scene* (price £0.30), *What's On* (price: £0.30) and *Punter* (price £0.70); all are available from newsagents and the TIC.

Brighton has two major entertainment venues: **Brighton Centre** on the seafront, *Kings Rd;* tel: *(01273) 202881;* and **The**

Dome concert hall, next to the Royal Pavilion *Church St;* tel *(01273) 709709*. It also offers over 35 pubs with live music, 25 discos and two pubs with theatres.

Events

The **Brighton Festival**, an annual international arts festival, takes place in May at venues all over town.

The **London to Brighton Veteran Car Run** is an annual event, the final stage of which takes place along the seafront the first Sunday in November.

The TIC's publications *Brighton Scene* and *Annual Diary of Events* (price £0.30 each) list all the events in town.

Shopping

The main department stores and high street shops are in *Churchill Sq. and Western Rd. The Lanes* are good for antiques, gifts and high class boutiques, *North Laine* for arts and crafts and specialist shops. There is also the **Upper Gardner Street Market** (Flea Market) in the middle of the town centre, open Sat 0700–1300, and **Brighton Station Market** (general and car boot), Sun 0900–1400.

Brighton is famous for Brighton Rock, which can be purchased from all souvenir shops and the TIC.

Sightseeing

A stroll down Brighton's broad **Promenade**, which backs the pebbly beach, is a must, or you could take a ride on the historic **Volk's Electric Railway**, which runs along the seafront. Likewise, no visitor to Brighton can miss the 100-year old **Palace Pier**, alive with flashy amusements as well as a museum of slot machines; the earlier West Pier, built in 1866, is now a sad, derelict ghost. The **Sealife Centre** specialises in British marine life, and boasts the longest underwater tunnel display in Europe.

Behind the seafront, white stucco terraces abound, with **Kemp Town** just to the east, centred around *Lewes Crescent*, a fine example of early 19th-century planning. But the magnetic attraction is the **Royal Pavilion**, George IV's bizarre confection of a seaside palace and a

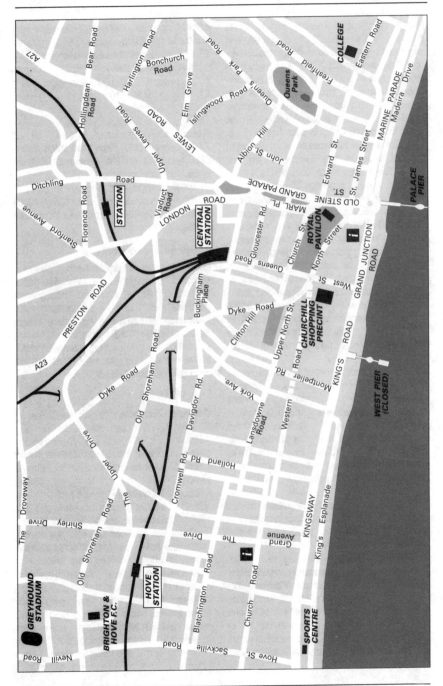

fitting monument to Regency high living. Its mass of Indian-inspired onion domes and minarets on the outside were contributed by John Nash between 1815 and 1822, while the recently restored interior, famed for its elaborate Chinoiserie and rich decor, is one of the most extraordinary in Europe. Particularly breathtaking is the opulent music room, while even the Great Kitchen has cast-iron palm trees.

Brighton's famous **Lanes** are what survives of the old village before George IV and the fashionable hordes descended: only 3 ft wide in places, these 17th-century alleyways south of *North St* are renowned for their antique shops, boutiques and cafés. The **Brighton Museum and Art Gallery**, built as the Prince Regent's stables and riding school, has interesting collections of musical instruments, pottery, paintings and some excellent Art Nouveau and Art Deco furniture. The **Booth Museum of Natural History** boasts its original bird collection as well as many other specimens and a magnificent assortment of animal skeletons. Just out of the centre, **Preston Manor** is a brilliantly presented Georgian manor house, allowing an insight into the 'upstairs' and 'downstairs' life of a genteel Edwardian home.

Outside Brighton, **Leonardslee Gardens**, on the edge of ancient St Leonard's Forest, is one of the loveliest woodland gardens in England, particularly impressive for its rhododendrons and azaleas in spring and for its striking autumn colours. There are also wallaby and deer parks. **Charleston Farmhouse** was the country home of Vanessa Bell and Duncan Grant, and became a focal point for the early 20th-century intellectual and artistic élite known as the Bloomsbury Group; the decor, furniture and ceramics preserved in the house are the legacy of their collective creative talents.

There are various sightseeing tours which give an excellent introduction to Brighton, details of which are available from the TIC. Fishing trips are available from Brighton Pier, organised by Fred Cox, *tel: (0181) 647 8414*; guided walks can be arranged at the TIC by *Brighton Blue Badge Guides*, price £3.

Sealife Centre, *Marine Parade; tel: (01273)*

604234, open daily 1000–1800 (longer during summer). Admission: adults £4.50; children £3.25 (these prices are subject to change).

Volk's Electric Railway operates Easter to end Sept from 1100–1700. Admission: adults £1; children £0.50.

Historic Buildings

Preston Manor, *Preston Rd*, tel: *(01273) 713239*, open daily 1000–1700, Mon 1300–1700, Sun 1400–1700. Admission: £2.60. Bus 5 or 5a, 1½ miles north.

Royal Pavilion, *Old Steyne*; tel: *(01273) 603005*, in town centre. Open daily 1000–1700, Sun 1400–1700, closed Wed. Admission: £3.75.

Museums and Galleries

Booth Museum of Natural History, *Dyke Rd*; tel: *(01273) 552586*, open Mon–Sat 1000–1700, Sun 1400–1700, closed Thurs. Admission: free. Bus 10 or 11, 1½ miles northwest.

Brighton Museum and Art Gallery, *Church St*; tel: *(01273) 603005*, open daily 1000–1700, Sun 1400–1700, closed Wed. Admission: free.

Palace Pier, *King's Rd*, tel: *(01273) 609361*, open daily all year. Admission: free.

Out of Town

Charleston Farmhouse (15 miles east), *Firle, tel: (01323) 811265*, open April–Oct, Wed–Sun. Admission: £3.75. Take bus no. 30, operated by Eastbourne Buses, *tel: (01323) 416416*; service takes 25–30 mins and runs in the summer season only.

Drusilla's Zoo Park (20 miles east), *Alfriston*, tel: *(01323) 870234*, open all year from 1000–1600. Admission: £3.95 (adults); £3.35 (children) Bus no. 30 from Brighton, operated by Eastbourne Buses (*tel: (01323) 416416*), takes approx. 30 mins.

Leonardslee Gardens (15 miles north-west), *Lower Beeding*, tel: *(01403) 891212*, open daily April–end-Oct 1000–1800. Admission: £4. Take Horesham bus no. 107, run by Stagecoach Buses (*tel: (01903) 237661*), which takes approx. 1 hr and stops at entrance.

BRISTOL

According to former Poet Laureate John Betjeman, Bristol is 'the most beautiful, interesting and distinguished city in England'. Beautiful parks and gardens lead onto interesting alleys and lanes, whilst distinguished Georgian houses climb the hills of Bristol culminating in Brunel's masterpiece, the Clifton Suspension Bridge. Part of Bristol's unique appeal stems from its many maritime features – John Cabot set sail from here in 1497 for North America.

Tourist Information

TIC: St. Nicholas Church, St. Nicholas St, Bristol BS1 1UE; tel: (0117) 926 0767 fax: (0117) 929 7703. Open Mon–Sun 0930–1730 and Bank Holidays. The TIC is accessible to DP: local bed-booking service (latest 30 mins before closing); 10% deposit to be paid in advance, BABA 10% of first night as a deposit (latest 30 mins before closing). An Official Visitors Guide is available at £1.50, however it does not have accommodation listings. There is a free accommodation listing available, Where to Stay.

Arriving and Departing

Bristol Temple Meads Station, Temple Gate; tel: (0117) 929 4255 is in the centre and **Bristol Parkway,** Stoke Gifford, which is 6 miles north-east of Bristol. All telephone enquiries can be made to Bristol Temple Meads. **Hertz,** tel: (0177) 977 9777 is represented here.

Getting Around

Most of the attractions in the town are within a walkable area of the centre. Free town and transport maps are available from the TIC. The area is well served by trains, buses, coaches and the Water-Bus operates in the city centre only. General bus enquiries from Marlborough St; tel: (0117) 955 8433. Bus services are good everywhere within the city and outskirts.

Tickets/passes which cover the whole town are the **Day Rider, Bus Card Plus, City Ten** and **Rover Card**.

Taxi ranks can be found at the train station and around the city centre.

Staying in Bristol

Accommodation

There is a good range of accommodation ranging from large independents to b. & b. establishments. It is always a good idea to book in advance. Most cheaper accommodation is located around the town centre. There is a youth hostel at **Hayman House,** 64 Prince St; tel: (0117) 922 1659. The TIC is able to provide information on campsites surrounding Bristol. The closest are: **Baltic Wharf Campsite,** Cumberland Rd; tel: (0117) 926 8030. Stay is limited to 21 days – take summer bus no 511 from Bristol City Centre; **Boars Head Campsite,** Boars Head Public House, Main Rd; tel: (01454) 632278, 7 miles west, no access by public transport; **Salthouse Farm Holiday and Caravan Site,** Severn Beach; tel:(01454) 632374 – take Badgerline bus 624 from Bristol bus station; and **Brook Lodge Farm Caravan and Camping Park,** Cowslip Green; tel: (01934) 862311 – Badgerline buses 120 and 121 go from Bristol bus station (services are every 2 hrs).

Eating and Drinking

The TIC provides a list of local restaurants and there are a good number of excellent ones around the centre (which are likely to be more expensive) and outlying areas. There are a larger number of restaurants around **Park St** and **Clifton.** The **Broadmead Shopping Area** has cheaper restaurants, where good Greek, French, Italian, Mexican, Spanish and Oriental food is available. Vegetarians are also catered for.

Communications

Galleries is the main post office and is at 13 Castle Gallery. Open Mon–Sat, 0900–1730.

Entertainment and Events

An entertainments list, Great Western City Events, which is released monthly, is available free from the TIC. There is also a twice-monthly *Bristol Entertainments Bulletin* available from the TIC. **Colston Hall,** *Colston St,* is a popular concert venue and bookings can be made on *tel: (0117) 922 3682.* **Bristol Hippodrome,** *Colston Ave,* is a great venue for those with a taste for the arts: Box office is open Mon–Sat, 1000–2000, bookings *tel: (0117) 929 9444.* Theatre: **Bristol Old Vic** *tel: (0117) 987 7877.* Sport: **Gloucestershire County Cricket Club,** *Nevil Rd; tel: (0117) 924 5216.*

A free events listing is available from the TIC. Main events include: **International Balloon Fiesta,** *Ashton Court Estate; tel: (0117) 926 0767),* which takes place annually in August; **Ashton Court Festival,** *Ashton Court Estate; tel: (0117) 942 0140,* is a pop and folk music event, taking place annually in July.

Shopping

The TIC can provide a free shopping guide. The main shopping areas in the city are the **Broadmead and Galleries Centre, Park St, Queens St** and **Gloucester Rd.** Bristol has two markets: **St. Nicholas Glass Arcade and Covered Market,** *St. Nicholas St.* Open Mon–Sat, for books, records, crafts and food; **Corn Exchange,** *Corn St.* Open Mon–Sat for clothing, crafts, furniture, antiques and bric-a-brac. Sunday markets are also held at **Bristol Wholesale Fruit Centre, Bristol City Football Ground** and **Eastville Stadium.** See also **Bristol Blue Glass Ltd,** *Glassworks, 1 Colston Yard, Colston St.* Open Mon–Sat, 1000–1800.

Sightseeing

Part of Bristol's unique appeal stems from its many maritime features. Within a relatively small area, the visitor can marvel at the **Avon Gorge,** visit the **SS Great Britain,** stroll around the **Maritime Heritage Centre** or just sit and watch the world go by, near to where John Cabot set sail for the New World in 1497. Bristol is surrounded by some of the most beautiful countryside in Britain, making the city a natural base for a touring holiday. **The Maritime Walk,** along the south side of **Bristol's Historic Harbour,** takes in some of the city's most famous landmarks and ends with a return trip

by harbour ferry. It is possible to walk around the harbour, or use a ferry to visit specific attractions. The walk itself will take approximately 1–1½ hours and refreshments can be obtained en route. The ferry service is subject to seasonal changes; *tel: (0117) 927 3416.* Boat trips are operated by **Waverley and Balmoral;** *tel: (01446) 720656.* Guided walks and guides can be arranged through the TIC. A sightseeing bus departs from the centre (Apr–Sept), bus station, route 511.

Art Galleries and Museums

City Museum and Art Gallery, *Queen's Rd, Clifton; tel: (0117) 922 3571.* Open Daily 1000–1700. Admission: £2. **Bristol Industrial Museum,** *Princes Wharf, Wapping Rd; tel: (0117) 925 1470.* Open Tues–Sun and Bank Holidays 1000–1700. Admission: free.

Harvey's Wine Cellar Museum, *12 Denmark St; tel: (0117) 927 5036.* Open Mon–Sat 1000–1300, 1400–1700.

Maritime Heritage Centre, *Wapping Wharf, Gas Ferry Road; tel: (0117) 926 0680.* Open daily 1000–1800. Admission: free.

Historic Buildings

Bristol Cathedral, *College Green; tel (0117) 926 4879.* Open daily 0800–1800. Admission: free. **John Wesley's Chapel,** *36 The Horsefair; tel: (0117) 926 4740.* Open Mon–Sat 1000–1300 and 1400–1600 (closed Wed winter and Bank Holidays). **St Mary Redcliffe Church,** *Redcliffe Way; tel: (0117) 929 1487.* Admission: free.

The Georgian House, *7 Great George St; tel: (0117) 921 1362.* Open Tues–Sat and Bank Holidays 1000–1300, 1400–1700. Admission: £1. **The Red Lodge,** *Park Row; tel: (0117) 921 1360.* Open Tues–Sat and Bank Holidays 1000–1300, 1400–1700. Admission: £1.

Permanent Exhibition

The Matthew, *Redcliffe Wharf; tel (0117) 922 1996.* Open daily 1000–1700. Admission: £1. Hands-on science centre

The Exploratory, *Bristol Old Station, Temple Meads; tel (0117) 922 5944.* Open daily 1000–1700. Admission: £4.75.

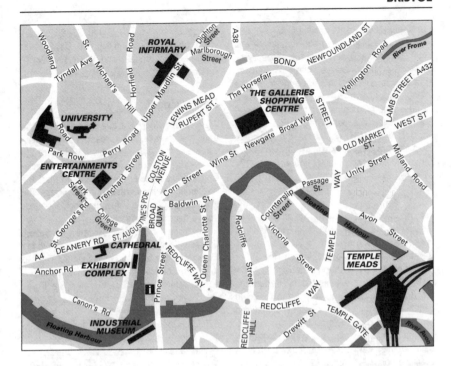

Out of Town

Architectural Interest

Clifton Suspension Bridge, tel: (0117) 973 2122. Open all year. Two–three miles north-west. Bus no. 8.

Historic Buildings

Ashton Court Estate, Ashton Court, Long Ashton; tel: (0117) 963 3221. Open all year but for guided tours it is advisable to check in advance.

    Berkeley Castle – see Gloucester p. 66.

Zoo

Bristol Zoo and Gardens, Clifton; tel: (0117) 973 8951. Open daily, except Christmas Day, 0900–1700. Admission: £5.50. Four miles north. Take bus 8/9, 508/509, 582/583.

Scenic Views

Clifton Observatory, Clifton Downs; tel: (0117) 974 1242. Open Summer, 1100–1800;

winter, 1100–1600. Admission: camera £0.75, cave £0.75.

Museums

Blaise Castle House Museum, Henbury Rd, Henbury; tel: (0117) 950 6789. Open Tues–Sun and Bank Holidays 1000–1300, 1400–1700. Admission: free. 5 miles north.

Ships

SS Great Britain, Wapping Wharf, Gas Ferry Rd; tel: (0117) 926 0680. Open Summer 1000–1800, winter 1000–1700. Admission: £2.90. 1½ miles. Bus 511.

- - - - - - - - - - - - - - - - - -

 Side Track from Bristol

WESTON-SUPER-MARE

TIC: Beach Lawns, Weston-super-Mare, Avon BS23 1AT; tel: (01934) 626838/634512. Open Mon–Sat 0930–1700 (mid-Oct to Mar); Mon–

Sun 0930–1800 (Apr to mid-Oct). DP SHS Services offered: local bed-booking service and BABA (£2 and £3 booking fee respectively, latest one hour before closing). Theatre, attraction and boat trip tickets sold. The *Weston-super-Mare Guide* is available free and includes accommodation listings.

Station: Weston-super-Mare Station, *Station Rd; tel: (01934) 621131* is in the centre of town and has a taxi rank. Trains run from Bristol Temple Meads, twice hourly, journey time 18–27 mins (fewer trains on Suns).

Getting Around

The majority of attractions are in the town centre with the exception of the **International Helicopter Museum** which is 2½ miles out. A free transport map is available from the TIC or from the **Badgerline** shop in the *High St*.

Most services are operated by **Badgerline** *tel: (01934) 621201* and are good in the town centre and to major towns nearby. A reduced service operates on most routes in the evening and on Sun and during the winter season. A daily 'Golden Rail' ticket for senior citizens is available after 0900 (price £2.80) and a variety of 'Rovercards' is also on offer. Taxi ranks are located on the *Seafront*, in *Alexander Parade* and at the *Station*.

Staying in Weston-super-Mare

There is a reasonable range of hotels, guesthouses and b. & b. accommodation in Weston-super-Mare including a hotel in the *FH* chain. The majority of accommodation in pubs and inns is located in the outlying suburbs and villages. It is generally easy to find accommodation on arrival except over Bank Holiday weekends.

There are a number of campsites within easy reach of the town, of which the closest are **Airport View**, *Moor Lane, Worle; tel: (01934) 622168*, 2 miles east on bus route 4; **Country View**, *Sand Rd, Sand Bay; tel: (01934) 627595*, 3 miles north on bus route 1; **Manor Farm**,

Grange Road; tel: (01934) 823288, 2 miles south on bus routes 5, 2 and 83 (stop is opposite the hospital); and **West End Farm**, *Locking; tel: (01934) 822529*, 3 miles east on bus route 126.

Sightseeing

Weston-super-Mare is a busy resort with all the traditional features of a seaside town: piers, gardens and a wide sandy beach. Many of the town's attractions are situated on the two-mile-long **Marine Parade**: visit the **Grand Pier**, the fascinating **Sealife Centre**, and **Tropicana**. The town's **Woodspring Museum** includes finds from a nearby Iron Age camp.

Bus tours of the area operated by **Bakers Coaches** and boat trips from **Waverley Excursions** can be booked at the TIC. The bus routes to Cheddar and Wells and to Sand Bay are particularly scenic. Don't miss the illuminated carnival in November.

Grand Pier, *Marine Parade; tel: (01934) 620238*. Open daily 1000 to dusk (Easter to Oct). Admission: free.

Heritage Centre, *6–3 Wadham St; tel: (01934) 412144*. Open Mon–Sat 1000–1700. Admission: £1.

International Helicopter Museum, *Locking Rd; tel: (01934) 635227*. Open daily 1000–1800 (Mar–Oct), 1000–1600 (Oct–Mar). **Sealife Centre,** *Marine Parade*. Opening Summer 1995 (check with TIC for opening hours).

Tropicana, *Marine Parade; tel: (01934) 626581*. Open daily 1000–1800 (May–Sept). Admission: £4.

Woodspring Museum, *Burlingham St; tel: (01934) 621028*. Open Tue–Sun and Bank Hol Mon 1000–1700. Admission: £1.60.

Out of Town

Clevedon Court, (NT) *Tickenham Rd, Clevedon; tel: (01275) 872257*. Open Wed, Thurs, Sun and Bank Hol Mon, 1430–1700. Admission: £3.30. Take bus no. X24, X25 or 823, 12 miles northwest.

BRISTOL to CARDIFF

This route provides a fast-track gateway to Wales, crossing the Severn estuary to connect the busy trading port of Bristol with the Welsh capital. Newport, once a major steelmaking centre, provides a good base for visiting the Roman Baths and Amphitheatre at Caerleon – an important Roman garrison and the most impressive Roman remains in Wales. A side-track to Chepstow brings you to the beauty of the Wye Valley and the romantic ruins of Tintern Abbey.

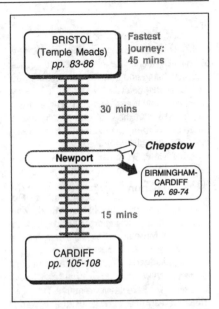

TRAINS

ETT table: 532

 Fast Track

Two trains per hour at irregular intervals (less frequently on Suns) run from Bristol Temple Meads to Cardiff Central, taking about 45 mins.

 On Track

Bristol–Newport–Cardiff

All trains from Bristol Temple Meads to Cardiff Central call at Newport. Bristol–Newport takes 30 mins, Newport–Cardiff 15 mins.

NEWPORT

TIC: *John Frost Sq, Newport, Gwent NP9 1PA; tel: (01633) 842962.* Open Mon–Fri 0930–1700, Sat 0930–1600. DP Services offered: local bed-booking service (latest 5 mins before closing), advance reservations handled, BABA (latest 15 mins before closing). *Newport Guide* (including accommodation listing) and *Street Plan*, £0.50 each.

Station: Newport Station, *Queensway; tel: (01222) 228000,* is central and has a taxi rank.

Getting Around

Except for **Tredegar House**, Newport's attractions are within walking distance of the centre; free town and transport maps are available from the TIC. There is good bus and train coverage of the town and surrounding area. The main bus companies are **Newport Transport**, *tel: (01633) 263600,* for services in the town and **Red and White Bus Company**, *tel: (01633) 266336,* for the outlying areas. Most services depart from the bus station on *Kingsway.* The main taxi ranks are at the station, and on *Upper Dock St.*

Staying in Newport

There is a reasonable range of hotels and a good choice of b.&b. and guest-house accommodation, with cheaper options in the centre and suburbs. It is generally easy to book on arrival. Hotel chains include *Hn, St.* The closest youth hostel is in Cardiff (see p. 105). The nearest campsite is at **Tredegar House and Park** (2 miles west), *Newport; tel: (01633) 816650* (bus 15a or 15c).

Sightseeing

A busy port, Newport is the commercial centre of Gwent, where new electronic and service industries have sprung up as the steel industry has declined; before the decline of heavy industry in the Welsh valleys it was a major steel port, and in the mid 19th century was a centre of Chartism, the electoral reform movement. Occasional free guided walks are organised by **Newport Museum** (contact details below). Look out for Newport's public art, amongst others, the **Steel Wave** on *Town Reach Promenade*, **Old Green Murals**, *Old Green Crossing* and the **Chartist Mural**, *John Frost Square*. The **Transporter Bridge**, built to carry cars and passengers by 'aerial ferry' across the Usk, is one of only two such bridges remaining in Britain. Currently closed, it should re-open in 1996 after funds have been found for repairs. Seventeenth-century **Tredegar House** reveals the lifestyle of the powerful Morgan family and their servants; it has a 90-acre landscaped park with many attractions.

Three miles up the Usk at **Caerleon** are the most impressive Roman remains in Wales, including particularly well-preserved baths and an amphitheatre; the **Caerleon Museum** illustrates the history of Roman Caerleon and its garrison. **Penhow Castle**, a small border fortress, is the oldest lived-in castle in Wales; each of its rooms represents life in different eras.

Newport Museum and Art Gallery, *John Frost Sq; tel: (01633) 840064.* Open Mon–Thur 0930–1700, Fri, Sat 0930–1600. Admission free. **Tredegar House and Park** (2 miles west), *Newport; tel: (01633) 815880.* House open 1130–1600 Wed–Sun (Easter to end Sept), daily (Aug), Sat, Sun (Oct), Bank Holiday Mons and following Tues. Park open daily all year 0900–dusk. Admission £3.50; bus 15a or 15c.

Out of Town

Big Pit Mining Museum, see Abergavenny, p. 74. **Caerleon Museum**, *High St, Caerleon; tel: (01633) 423134.* Open Mon–Sat 1000–1800, Sun 1400–1800 (Mar–Oct); Mon–Sat 1000–1630, Sun 1400–1630 (Nov–Mar). Admission £1.50 (£2.50 including Roman Baths and Amphitheatre). Take bus 7 to *Caerleon*, 3 miles north. **Caerleon Roman Baths and Amphitheatre** (Cadw), *High St, Caerleon; tel: (01633) 422518.* Open daily 0930–1830 (late Mar to late Oct), Mon–Sat 1400–1600, Sun 1100–1600 (late Oct to late Mar). Admission £1.50 (£2.50 including Caerleon Museum). Take bus 7 to *Caerleon*, 3 miles north. **Penhow Castle** (8 miles east), *Chepstow Rd; tel: (01633) 400800.* Open Wed–Sun and Bank Holiday Mons 1000–1800 (Good Fri to Sept), daily (Aug); Wed 1000–1700 (Oct–Good Fri). Last admission 45 mins before closing. Admission £2.95. Take bus 73.

 Side Track from Newport

CHEPSTOW

TIC: *Bridge St, Chepstow, Gwent NP6 5LH; tel: (01291) 623772.* Open daily 1000–1800 (Easter to end Oct). DP Services offered: local bed-booking service and BABA (latest 1730), advance reservations handled. *Vale of Usk and Wye Valley* brochure is available free and includes an accommodation listing.

Station: Chepstow Station, *Station Rd; tel: (01222) 228000* is walkable from the town centre. Trains run every 2 hrs (very infrequent on Suns) from Chepstow to Newport and Cardiff, and to Gloucester, Cheltenham and Birmingham. There is no taxi rank, for taxis see below.

Getting Around

Attractions are walkable from the centre; the TIC has free town maps and transport timetables. Most local bus services are operated from *Thomas St* by **Red and White** *tel: (01633) 266336* and **Badgerline** *tel: (01272) 553231.* Services are reasonable Mon–Sat, but infrequent after 2000 or on Sun. For taxis call **Field's** *tel: (01291) 624294* or **AB** *tel: (01291) 625696.*

Staying in Chepstow

There is a small choice of hotels, including one in the *FH* chain, and a reasonable range of guesthouse, b. & b. and farmhouse accommodation. It is usually easy to book on arrival. The closest campsite is **St Pierre Caravan Park**,

Portskewett; tel: (01291) 425114, bus 64 or 74 to Caldicot, 2½ miles west.

Sightseeing

A town of narrow, steep streets, Chepstow stands on cliffs at the southern entrance to the Wye Valley. **Chepstow Museum** covers the history of Chepstow and the lower Wye valley area. **Chepstow Castle** guards this strategic position from a dramatic cliff above the Wye; probably the earliest stone castle in the country, it was strengthened over the centuries and stands remarkably complete. The **town walls**, 7 ft thick in places, were designed as an extension to this stronghold.

Tintern Abbey, the subject of one of Wordsworth's most famous poems, is unmissable. This most complete of ruined British monasteries lies in a meadow by the Wye. The restored Norman border castle at **Caldicot** is surrounded by peaceful gardens and a country park; the **Nelson Museum** at Monmouth has memorabilia of Britain's most famous admiral.

Chepstow Castle (Cadw); tel: (01291) 624065. Open daily 0930–1830 (Easter to end Oct); Mon–Sat 0930–1600, Sun 1100–1600 (Nov to end Mar). Admission £2.90. **Chepstow Museum**, Bridge St; tel: (01291) 625981. Open Mon–Sat 1100–1300 and 1400–1700, Sun 1400–1700. Admission £1.

Out of Town

Caldicot Castle, Caldicot; tel: (01291) 420241. Open Mon–Sat 1030–1700, Sun 1330–1700 (Mar–Oct). Admission £1.20. Train to Caldicot, 6 miles south-east. **Nelson Museum**, Market Hall, Priory St, Monmouth; tel: (01600) 713519. Open Mon–Sat 1000–1300 and 1400–1700, Sun 1400–1700. Admission £1. Red and White bus 69 to Monmouth, 12 miles north. **Tintern Abbey** (Cadw), Tintern; tel: (01291) 689251. Open daily 0930–1830 (Easter to end Oct); Mon–Sat 0930–1600, Sun 1100–1600 (Nov–Easter). Admission £2. Red and White bus 69 to Tintern, 6 miles north.

CAMBRIDGE

Settlers have been attracted to this fenland site since prehistoric times, and it was always an important trading centre. But Cambridge's fame rests with its university, reputedly founded in 1209 by a handful of rebel scholars from Oxford; and the colleges, many of which back on to the River Cam, are the town's chief architectural glory. Together with Cambridge's many other fine buildings, they are best explored at a leisurely pace, so that you can savour the atmosphere of a town which has nurtured countless great scientists, philosophers and poets.

Tourist Information

TIC: *Wheeler St, Cambridge CB2 3QB; tel: (01223) 322640.* Open Mon–Fri 0900–1730, Sat 0900–1700 (Nov–Mar), Mon–Fri 0900–1800, Sat 0900–1700 (Apr–Oct); Sun and Bank Holidays 1030–1530 (Easter–Sept). DP SHS Services offered: local bed-booking service (latest 30 mins before closing), BABA (latest 1 hour before closing) for accommodation bookings (be prepared to queue). Guided tours booked, English Heritage passes sold. *Cambridge Official Guide* (including accommodation list) is £2.95, *Where to Stay In and Around Cambridge* is £0.50.

Arriving and Departing

Two fast trains each hour run London Kings Cross–Cambridge taking 52 mins. A slower service runs from London Liverpool Street.

Station

Cambridge Station, *Station Rd; tel: (01223) 311999* (1 mile east of centre). **Guide Friday**, *Station Forecourt; tel: (01223) 62444*, operate an accommodation-finding service (commission charged) 0930–1700. There is a taxi rank and bus 1 runs very regularly into town, Mon–Sat.

Buses

National Express coaches operate from the central bus station on *Drummer St; tel: (01223) 460711.*

Getting Around

Most attractions are within a walkable area. Town and transport maps are available at a small charge from the TIC. Local public transport is quite good in the centre, but very patchy to outlying areas and services are much reduced or do not run in the evenings and at weekends.

Buses

Cambus is the main operator for local buses *tel: (01223) 423554*, most of which start from the bus station on *Drummer St.*

Taxis

The main taxi rank is on *St Andrew's St.*

Staying in Cambridge

Accommodation

It is always advisable to book accommodation in advance, and essential during June–Sept. Availability is affected by the **Cambridge Folk Festival** (last weekend in July), and also by various events out of town, for example the races at Newmarket (dates throughout the summer), and **Mildenhall Air Show** (Aug Bank Holiday). There is a small range of hotels, and a large choice of guesthouse and b. & b. accommodation, with cheaper establishments located 2–3 miles north, south and east of town. The TIC is very busy with accommodation bookings during the summer, especially in the afternoon.

Hotel chains in Cambridge include *DV, FP, HI, MH.* **Cambridge Youth Hostel**, *97 Tenison Rd; tel: (01223) 354601*, open from 1300, is located very close to **Cambridge Station**, 1 mile east of town (bus no. 1). There is also a **YMCA**, at *Gonville Place; tel: (01223) 356998*. The nearest campsite is **Highfield Farm Camping Park**, *Highfield Farm, Long Rd, Comberton; tel: (01223) 262308* (4 miles west), bus no. 118 or 119.

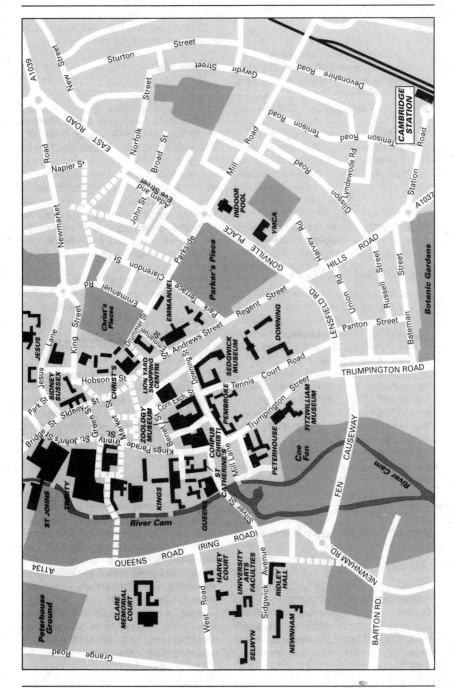

Eating and Drinking

There is a good selection of restaurants of many nationalities, to suit all tastes and pockets. There is a limited selection of vegetarian restaurants, including **King's Pantry**, *9a King's Parade*. The TIC has a list of eating places, cost £0.50.

Communications

The main post office is on *St Andrew's St*, open Mon–Fri 0900–1730 (Wed from 0930), Sat 0900–1230. Post restante facilities are available here.

Money

Thomas Cook bureaux de change are located at *18 Market St* and at *The Grafton Centre*, as well as at Midland Bank, *Market Hill*.

Entertainment and Events

Events and entertainment lists are available from the TIC. There is a detailed listing, *Summer in the City*, that covers what's on July–Sept, and a programme for the **Corn Exchange**. The main entertainment venue is the **Cambridge Corn Exchange**, *Wheeler St; tel: (01223) 357851*, a combination of concert hall, theatre, cinema and pop venue. Other theatres: **Arts Theatre**, *Peas Hill; tel: (01223) 352000*. **ADC Theatre**, *Park St; tel: (01223) 352000*. **Mumford Theatre**, *East Rd; tel: (01223) 352932*. See under Newmarket for horseracing.

Cambridge Folk Festival takes place annually over the last weekend in July, at *Cherry Hinton Hall; tel: (01223) 463346*, 3 miles southeast (bus 4). In June and July there are the **'Bumps' Races**, rowing races on the river *Cam* which take their name from the fact that each boat has to bump the one(s) in front to improve its position in the league tables.

Shopping

The main areas for shopping are **Lion Yard** and **Grafton** shopping centres, and *Sidney St, Rose Crescent, Trinity St, King's Parade, St John's St* and *Green St*. There is also the **Cambridge Market**, *Market Square*, daily from Mon–Sat for general goods, and for local crafts there is the **Craft Market**, *All Saints Gardens*, daily 1000–1700 (June–Sept and from mid-Dec to Christmas), Fri, Sat 1000–1700 (rest of the year).

Sightseeing

Tours

Various sightseeing tours give an excellent introduction to Cambridge, details of which are available from the TIC. **Guide Friday**, *tel: (01223) 62444*, operate a **Cambridge Tour** on their open-topped double-decker buses. Tours run every 15–20 mins (daily except 24–26 Dec), starting at 0945 from Cambridge Station. A ticket (£6) is valid all day, and you can leave and rejoin the tour at any of the stops along the route. Daily public guided walks of the town and colleges are organised by the TIC, and private tours can also be arranged (*tel: (01223) 463290* – from £5).

Punting is another very good way to see Cambridge, and punts, rowing boats and canoes can be hired from the boatyard at *Mill Lane*, either to go along the *Backs* or up river to Grantchester (see below). Boats for the Backs only are on hire from *Quayside*. But beware! Punting is more difficult than the nonchalant experts make it look and you may prefer to take advantage of a chauffeurpunt from *Silver St* or *Magdalene St* (details of the various companies offering chauffeurpunts are available from the TIC). The boatyards are open from Easter to early Oct.

Colleges

There are about 30 colleges scattered around the town, which make up the university. These are private places where people live and study throughout the year. However, visitors are usually welcome to wander freely through the courts, to visit the chapels and in some cases halls and libraries. 'Private' notices should, of course, be respected. Most colleges open from about 0930 until 1630, and in some cases an admission fee is charged; access is generally restricted during examination time, from mid-Apr to late June. Groups must be accompanied by a Cambridge Blue Badge Guide. Public walking tours for individuals start from the TIC.

The majority of the colleges lie to the east of

the river, and a good place to start is along the **Backs**, the west bank of the River Cam which meanders through the town and gives it a semi-rural feel. From here there are classic views of some of the most beautiful colleges. Unmissable is **King's College**, founded by Henry VI: royal patronage is reflected in the splendour of its **Chapel**, arguably the finest Perpendicular (15th-century Gothic) building in England. Its fan vaulting is incomparable; and among its other glories are Rubens' *Adoration of the Magi* (1639), hanging behind the altar, and the brilliantly coloured 16th-century narrative stained-glass windows, depicting scenes from the life of Jesus. Admission to chapel: £2.

Picturesque **Queens' College**, founded by not one queen but two, is unusual for its half-timbered, 16th-century **President's Lodge** and the curious **Mathematical Bridge** over the Cam. This wooden bridge was built without the aid of a single nail in 1749, on mathematical principles; when curious Victorians dismantled it, they had to resort to bolts to hold it together again. Admission £1.

Beautifully proportioned **Clare College** has notable gardens across its elegant bridge, the oldest surviving in Cambridge. Admission £1. **Trinity College**'s 2-acre Great Court is claimed to be the largest university court in the world; apparently this is where Sir Isaac Newton first measured the speed of sound. Trinity's magnificent **Library** by Christopher Wren is open to the public. Admission £1.50. Beyond Trinity lies **St John's**, which has a beautiful Tudor gatehouse: its enclosed river bridge is known as the Bridge of Sighs, after the more famous Venetian bridge on which it was modelled. Within St John's garden and across the river lies the 12th-century **School of Pythagoras**, the oldest house in Cambridge. Admission £1.50.

Further north and around the river bend, **Jesus College**, built on the site of a 12th-century nunnery, has many medieval buildings and spacious, secluded grounds which are a pleasant place to stroll or rest.

Away from the river, highlights among the colleges include **Corpus Christi**, founded in 1352, which has the best surviving early medieval court; the chapel at **Pembroke**, which was Wren's first building; **Emmanuel** chapel, also by Wren, which contains a plaque to former student John Harvard who, after sailing on the *Mayflower*, founded another great university; and **Pepys' Library** at **Magdalene**, where the diarist's collection as well as his shorthand manuscripts are displayed. Interesting modern college buildings include **New Hall** (1954) and **Fitzwilliam College** (1963).

Other Attractions

Apart from colleges, other buildings which should not be missed include the **Round Church**, *Round Church St*, one of only a few circular churches surviving in England: built in 1130, it was based on the shape of the Holy Sepulchre in Jerusalem. Zealous 19th-century restoration has not destroyed its charm.

It is also worth seeking out tiny **St Bene't**, *Bene't St*, which is one of Britain's earliest surviving Saxon churches and the oldest building in Cambridge; while from the tower of **Great St Mary's**, the University Church, there are panoramic views of the whole town.

The **Fitzwilliam Museum**, housed in a grandiose 19th-century edifice, is one of the oldest museums in Britain. It has outstanding collections – including Canaletto, Rembrandt, Turner, Titian and French impressionists; Egyptian, Greek and Roman antiquities; and particularly fine medieval illuminated manuscripts, as well as ivories, miniatures, carvings and armour. **Kettle's Yard** is an eclectic collection of early 20th-century art; its strong appeal (even to those lukewarm about modern art) rests upon the intimate setting of what was the collector's own house, which lends charm and immediacy to the collection. The **Botanical Gardens** provide a peaceful retreat for the foot-weary.

Churches

Great St Mary's Church, *King's Parade*. Open 1000–1630. Admission £1 for the tower, otherwise free. **King's College Chapel**, *King's College; tel: (01223) 331100*. Open 0930–1430 (check times, as they vary according to season and college terms). Admission £2.

Museums and Galleries

Fitzwilliam Museum, *Trumpington St; tel: (01223) 332900.* Open Tues–Fri 1000–1700 (Antiquities and Applied Arts Galleries 1000–1400, Paintings, Fine Arts and Furniture Galleries 1400–1700); Sat 1000–1700, Sun 1415–1700 (all galleries). Admission free.

Folk Museum, *Castle St; tel: (01223) 355159.* Open Tues–Sat 1030–1700, Sun 1400–1700; also open Mon, Apr–Sept. **Kettle's Yard Gallery**, *Castle St; tel: (01223) 352124.* Open Tues–Sat 1230–1730, Sun 1400–1730. Admission free.

Museum of Zoology, *Free School Lane; tel: (01223) 336650.* Open Mon–Fri 1415–1645. Admission free. **Sedgwick Museum**, *Downing St; tel: (01223) 333456.* Open Mon–Fri 0900–1300 and 1400–1700, Sat 1000–1300. Admission free. **Whipple Museum of Science**, *Free School Lane; tel: (01223) 334540.* Open Mon–Fri 1400–1600. Admission free. **University Museum of Archaeology and Anthropology**, *Downing St; tel: (01223) 333516.* Open Mon–Fri 1400–1600, Sat 1000–1230. Admission free. **University Museum of Classical Archaeology**, *Sidgwick Ave; tel: (01223) 335151.* Open Mon–Fri 0900–1700. Admission free.

Parks and Gardens

The Backs, between *Queens Rd* and the River Cam, (open at all times, with the exception of the college grounds). **University Botanical Gardens**, entrances from *Trumpington Rd* or *Hills Rd; tel: (01223) 336265.* Open Mon–Sat 0800–1800, Sun 1000–1800 (closes at dusk in winter). Admission £1.

Out of Town

There are several grand country houses in the vicinity. **Wimpole Hall** is an imposing Georgian mansion, with a large landscaped park and a Home Farm which boasts a wide selection of rare breeds. The palatial Jacobean (early 17th-century) **Audley End House** has many fine interiors, including some by Robert Adam and a magnificent Jacobean great hall, and is set in Capability Brown parkland. **Anglesey Abbey** was built c.1600 on the site of a medieval priory and is outstanding for its beautiful Georgian-style gardens, laid out this century.

Duxford Airfield is home to most of the Imperial War Museum's collection of historic military aircraft, and civil aircraft on display include the prototype *Concorde 01*. Nearer at hand, you can walk (or punt, see above) the 2 miles along the river Granta from *Silver St* to the little village of **Grantchester**, immortalised in Rupert Brooke's poem *The Old Vicarage, Grantchester*; the church clock, thanks to this poet, stands perpetually at ten minutes to three.

Anglesey Abbey and Gardens (NT – 6 miles north-east of Cambridge), *Lode; tel: (01223) 811200.* Open Wed–Sun and Bank Holiday Mons 1100–1730 (end Mar to mid-Oct). Abbey opens 1300. Gardens also open daily mid-July to early Sept. Admission £4.75 (gardens only £3). Take Cambus bus 111.

Audley End House and Park (EH), *Saffron Walden, Essex; tel: (01799) 522842.* Open Wed–Sun and Bank Holiday Mons, grounds 1200–1700, house 1300–1700 (Apr–Sept). Last entry 1 hr before closing. Admission £5.20 (grounds only £2.85). Take Cambus bus 22 or 112 from bay 8 to Saffron Walden (1 hr), then 1-mile walk. Approximately 15 miles south-east of Cambridge.

Duxford Airfield and Imperial War Museum, *Duxford; tel: (01223) 835000.* Open daily 1000–1800 (summer), 1000–1600 (winter). Admission £5.95. Take Cambus bus 103. Twelve miles south.

Linton Zoo, *Hadstock Rd, Linton; tel: (01223) 891308.* Open daily 1000–1800 (or dusk if earlier). Last entry 45 mins before closing. Admission £3.75. Take Cambus bus no. 113 from bay 9 to Linton (30 mins), then 5-min walk. Ten miles south-east of Cambridge.

Wimpole Hall, Farm and Park (NT), *Arrington, near Royston; tel: (01223) 207257.* Hall: open Tues–Thur, Sat, Sun and Bank Holiday Mons 1300–1700 (Apr–Oct). Farm: Tues–Sun and Bank Holiday Mons 1030–1700 (mid-Mar to Oct and weekends in winter). Admission hall only £4.50; farm only £3.50; combined ticket £6. Take Whippet Coaches (*tel: (01480) 463792*) bus 175 to Wimpole, then 2-mile walk. Eight miles south-west of Cambridge.

Side Tracks from Cambridge

ELY

TIC: *Oliver Cromwell's House, 29 St Mary's St, Ely, Cambridgeshire CR7 4HF; tel: (01353) 662062/663653.* Open daily 1000–1800 (Apr–Sept), Mon–Sat 1000–1715 (Oct–Mar). DP Services offered: local bed-booking service (latest 30 mins before closing), advance reservations handled, BABA (latest 1½ hours before closing), guided tours booked. *Discovering East Cambridgeshire* and an accommodation guide are available free.

Station: *Ely Station, Ely Rd; tel: (01353) 662536* is ½ mile south-east of the town centre. There are frequent rail services from Cambridge, taking 15–17 mins.

Getting Around

Most attractions are within easy walking distance of the centre. The TIC can provide free town and transport maps. For general transport enquiries *tel: (01223) 317740*. There is reasonable bus service in town, but services to outlying villages are very patchy. Most services are operated by **Cambus** *tel: (01223) 423554*.

The main taxi rank is at the station, or contact: **AK Taxis** *tel: (01353) 661010*, **S&H Taxis** *tel: (01353) 662117* or **John's Taxis** *tel: (01353) 662772*.

Staying in Ely

It is generally very easy to book on arrival, except during the last weekend of Aug when the **Mildenhall Air Show** takes place. There is a very small choice of hotels, but a large number of b.&b. establishments in Ely and the surrounding area, and three pubs with rooms.

Hotel chains in Ely include *MH*. There is a youth hostel which is open from end May to end Aug: **Ely Youth Hostel**, *Sixth Form Centre, Downham Rd; tel: (01353) 667423*.

The nearest campsite is **Two Acres Caravan and Camp Site**, *Ely Rd, Little Thetford; tel: (01353) 648870*. Two miles south.

Sightseeing

Surrounded by flat East Anglian landscape, Ely was effectively an island until the fens were drained in the 17th and 18th centuries. The small town is dominated by its wonderful **Cathedral**, visible like a mirage from far around: the octagonal 14th-century lantern tower is a miracle of medieval engineering, while the Lady Chapel (1321) is breathtakingly beautiful. The adjacent **Stained Glass Museum** gives an insight into how stained-glass windows are designed and made. **Oliver Cromwell's House**, where England's Lord Protector lived for about 10 years, has been evocatively refurbished, and Ely has many other attractive domestic buildings: various walking tours can be booked through the TIC, which also has leaflets on local walking tours and car trails. The River Ouse here also makes for a pleasant stroll and there is a pretty marina area with a major antiques warehouse and boat hire facilities.

Nearby **Wicken Fen**, the first nature reserve in Britain, is an area of undrained fenland which provides a habitat rich in plant and animal life; **Prickwillow Engine Trust** has working examples of the engines which were once used to drain the fens.

Ely Cathedral; *tel: (01353) 667735*. Open daily 0700–1900 (summer), Mon–Sat 0730–1830, Sun 0730–1700 (winter); no admission during services. Admission £2.80 (including guided tour). **Ely Museum**, *28c High St; tel: (01353) 666655*. Open Tues–Sun 1030–1300 and 1415–1700 (Easter–Sept); Tues–Fri 1130–1530, Sat, Sun 1130–1600. Closed Mon except Bank Holidays. Admission £1. **Oliver Cromwell's House**, *29 St Mary's St; tel: (01353) 662062*. Open daily 1000–1800 (Apr–Sept), Mon–Sat 1000–1715 (Oct–Mar). Admission £1.80. **Stained Glass Museum**, *Ely Cathedral; tel: (01353) 667735*. Open Mon–Fri 1030–1600 (Mar–Oct), Sat 1030–1630, Sun 1200–1500 (all year). Admission £1.50

Out of Town

Downfield Windmill, *Fordham Rd, Soham; tel: (01353) 720333*. Open Sun and Bank Holidays 1100–1700. Admission £0.70. Mon–Sat take bus 116 or 122, Sun bus 19. Four miles southeast. **Prickwillow Engine Trust Museum**, *c/o 25 Main St, Prickwillow, Ely; tel: (01353) 88230*. Static display open 0900 to dusk (Apr–Sept); engine run on specific days. Admission free (donations welcomed). Thur and Sat take bus 127, Sun bus 156. Approximately 4 miles northeast. **Stretham Old Engine**, *Green End Rd, Stretham; tel: (01353) 649210*. Open daily 1130–1700 (Apr–Sept). Admission £1.50. Mon–Sat take bus 109 or 171, Sun bus 19. Four miles south-west. **Wicken Fen National Nature Reserve** (NT), *Lode Lane, Wicken, Ely; tel: (01353) 720274*. Nature Reserve open daily from dawn to dusk. William Thorpe Building open daily from 0900 to dusk. Fen Cottage open Sun and Bank Holiday Mons 1400–1700 (Apr–Oct). Admission £2.50 (cottage only, £0.50). On Sun bus 19 goes to Wicken village, then 1-mile walk. (Approximately 8 miles south of Ely).

KING'S LYNN

TIC: The Old Gaol House, *Saturday Market Pl, King's Lynn, Norfolk PE30 5DQ; tel: (01553) 763044/767711*. Open daily 0915–1700. DP Services offered: local bed-booking service (latest 1650), advance reservations handled, BABA (latest 1630). Guided tours booked and tickets sold for local festivals and events. *King's Lynn Miniguide* and the *West Norfolk What to Do and Where to Stay* guides are free.

Station: King's Lynn Station, *Railway Rd; tel: (01553) 772021* is half a mile east of the town centre, and has a taxi rank. Services are approximately hourly (every two hours on Suns) from Ely to King's Lynn and take about 30 mins.

Bus Station: *Broad St; tel: (01553) 772343*. There are direct coaches from London and Peterborough, and connecting services from all major towns. For details of **National Express** services *tel: (0121) 456 1122*.

Getting Around

Most of the attractions are within easy walking distance, and free town and transport maps are available from the TIC. There is a reasonable bus

service in the centre, but it is rather patchy to outlying areas.

Most buses are operated by **Eastern Counties Omnibus** *tel: (01553) 772343* from the bus station at *Broad St*. Most buses operate a reduced service after 2000 and on Sun. **Explorer** tickets (£4 for daily tickets) cover all Eastern Counties buses in Norfolk.

For taxis, contact: **Gaywood Taxis** *tel: (01553) 764500*; **Glebe Taxis** *tel: (01553) 772616*; **Lynn Cabs** *tel: (01553) 760600*; **Star Cars** *tel: (01553) 761152*; **Taffy's Taxis** *(01553) 760900*.

Staying in King's Lynn

There is a fair range of hotel and guesthouse accommodation, with cheaper rooms located on the edge of town and there are a few pubs with rooms in outlying villages. Accommodation is generally easy to book on arrival, except during the **King's Lynn Festival** in July.

Hotel chains include *BW, Bu, FH*. **King's Lynn Youth Hostel**, *Thoresby College, College Lane; tel: (01553) 772461* is in the town centre, open Thur–Mon from 1700 (Apr–June, Sept and Oct), daily from 1700 (July and Aug), Nov–Mar for group bookings only. The nearest campsite is **Gatton Waters Touring Caravan and Campsite**, *Hillington; tel: (01485) 600643* (8 miles east). Take bus 48.

Sightseeing

From medieval times, King's Lynn was a major port, with strong trading links with Germany. There is still a Germanic feel to some of the many elegant buildings which remain in the old town, bordering the river Great Ouse and along *King St*. The **Custom House** of 1683 (*Purfleet Quay*) is a fine monument to King's Lynn's maritime prosperity. Guided walks are operated by **Blue Badge Guides** year round, *tel: (01553) 765714*, starting from the TIC (price: £2).

The chequered-fronted Trinity Guildhall (1421) is now home to **Tales of the Old Gaol House**, which tells the stories of some of the town's more infamous characters in the original cells of the town gaol; the **Town House Museum** recreates Lynn life from Tudor to recent times; and at the **Caithness Crystal**

Factory you can watch glass being blown – an industry long associated with the area.

Outside town, **Castle Rising Castle**'s great 12th-century keep stands at the centre of even more impressive earthworks; classical **Holkham Hall** houses paintings by Rubens, Van Dyck and Gainsborough, and has a good Bygones Collection as well as a fine deer park by the sea; while **Oxburgh Hall** is a 15th-century moated building with an impressive gatehouse, parterre garden and woodland walks. But the most famous house in the area is the royal country retreat at **Sandringham**, where the personal nature of the rooms offers a glimpse into the home life of the Royal Family. At **Norfolk Lavender** – the largest lavender-grower and distiller in the country – there are guided tours of the distillery and gardens. In July and Aug there is a 'Coastliner' bus from King's Lynn to *Great Yarmouth* along the coast, offering great views.

Caithness Crystal Factory, *Old Medow Rd, Hardwick Industrial Estate; tel: (01553) 76511.* Open Mon–Fri 0900–1700, Sat 0900–1600 (all year); Sun (June–Sept only) 1100–1630. Glass-blowing ends 45 mins before closing. Admission free. Buses 434, 438, 794 and 47 go to within quarter of a mile. (1½ miles south-east of centre.)

King's Lynn Arts Centre and St Georges Guildhall (NT), *2729 King St; tel: (01553) 773578.* Opening hours variable. Admission £0.60 to Guildhall. **Lynn Museum**, *Old Market St; tel: (01553) 775001.* Open Mon–Sat 1000–1700; closed Bank Holidays. Admission £0.60. **St Margaret's Church**, *Saturday Market Pl.* Open daily 1000–1800. Admission free. **St Nicholas Chapel**, *Pilot St.* Key available from True's Yard Museum. Admission free. **Tales of the Old Gaol House**, *Saturday Market Pl; tel: (01553) 763044.* Open daily 1000–1700 (Easter to end Oct), Fri–Tues 1000–1700 (Nov–Easter); last admissions 1615. Admission £2. **Town Museum of Lynn Life**, *46 Queen St; tel: (01553) 773450.* Open Tues–Sat 1000–1700 (1600 in winter); Sun (May–Sept only) 1400–1700. Admission £1. **True's Yard Fishing Museum**, *North St; tel: (01553) 770479.* Open daily 0930–1630. Admission £1.80.

Out of Town

Castle Rising Castle (EH), *Castle Rising; tel: (01553) 631330.* Open daily 1000–1800 (Apr–Oct), Wed–Sun 1000–1600 (Nov–Mar). Admission £1.25. Take bus 410 or 411. Four miles north. **Holkham Hall**, *Wells-next-the-Sea; tel: (01328) 710227.* Open Sun–Thur 1330–1700 (June–Sept), Bank Holiday Mons 1130–1700 (Easter–August). Last admission: 1640. Admission to Hall £3, to Bygones and Park £3 or £5 for inclusive ticket. Take Coastliner bus (Tues–Thur, July and Aug). Thirty miles north.

Houghton Hall, *King's Lynn; tel: (01485) 528569* (13 miles east). Currently closed for major repair work. Telephone for opening times and admission prices. (**Sanders Coaches** service to Hartley, then 1-mile walk.) **Norfolk Lavender**, *Caley Mill, Heacham; tel: (01485) 570384* (13 miles north). Open daily 1000–1700; closed 24 Dec to mid-Jan. Tours daily from May to end Sept. Admission free. Take bus 410 or 411.

Oxburgh Hall (NT), *Oxborough; tel: (01366) 328258.* Open Sat–Wed 1300–1700 (garden 1200–1730) (Apr–Oct), Bank Holiday Mons 1100–1700. Admission £3.80. Buses only go as close as Downham Market (47) or Swaffham (434, 438 or 794), 7–8 miles from the Hall, then taxi. (Fifteen miles south-east from King's Lynn.)

Park Farm, *Snettisham; tel: (01485) 542425.* Open daily 1015–1700 (mid-March to end Oct). Admission £3.50 (£6 including safari). Take bus 410 or 411. Eleven miles north.

Sandringham House, *Sandringham; tel: (01553) 772675* (8 miles north). Grounds open Mon–Sat 1030–1700, Sun and Good Friday 1130–1700; house and museum open Mon–Sat 1100–1645, Sun and Good Friday 1200–1645 (Apr–Sept). During Royal visits the house is closed – check with TIC. Admission £3.50. Take bus 411.

NEWMARKET

TIC: *63 The Rookery, Newmarket, Suffolk CB8 8HT; tel: (01638) 667200.* Open Mon–Thur 0900–1700, Fri 0900–1730, Sat 1000–1700. DP Services offered: local bed-booking service, advance reservations handled, BABA, guided tours booked. Memberships sold for National Trust and English Heritage. Town guide and accommodation list available free of charge.

Station: Newmarket Station, *Green Rd; tel: (01223) 311999*, is half a mile south of the town centre. The station is poorly sited, without amenities and the train service from Cambridge is infrequent; the bus service is better.

Bus Station: National Express coaches operate from the bus station at *The Rookery; tel: (01223) 460711*. There is an hourly Cambus service from Cambridge to Newmarket, taking about 27 mins.

Getting Around

With the exception of the National Stud, racecourses and some trainers' yards (for which there are organised tours), attractions are accessible on foot from the centre. Town and transport maps are available free from the TIC.

Cambus is the main operator for local bus services, which operate from the bus station at *The Rookery; tel: (01223) 460711*. Services are good within the town centre, but rather patchy to outlying areas (there are no buses to the National Stud and racecourses).

The main taxi rank is on the *High St*; taxis can also be hailed on the street, or tel: **Sound City Cars** *tel: (01638) 669966*; **New Tax** *tel: (01639) 561561*; **Streamline** *tel: (01638) 560460*; **Anglia Star Cars** *tel: (01638) 663933*; **New Cab** *tel: (01831) 602681*.

Staying in Newmarket

It is generally possible to book on arrival, except for the Spring Bank Holiday, Mildenhall Air Show weekend and during all race meetings. There is a small range of accommodation available, approximately half in hotels, half in guesthouse and b.&b., plus a number of establishments in the surrounding area.

The closest youth hostels are **Brandon Youth Hostel**, *Bury Rd, Brandon; tel: (01842) 812075*, take Eastern Counties bus 200, 12 miles north; and **Cambridge Youth Hostel** (see under Cambridge). The nearest campsite is at **Rowley Mile Racecourse** *tel: (01638) 663235*, 2 miles south-west of town.

Sightseeing

Newmarket is world-famous for its horse-racing, and this dominates the attractions of the town (race meetings take place at irregular intervals from mid-April to mid-August and from mid-September to mid-October). As many of them can only be visited by prior appointment and are not accessible by public transport, it may be easier to take a guided tour. **Hoofbeats** (Newmarket guide service), *66 Old Station Rd, tel: (01638) 668455* can organise tours to all or some of the following: the Equine Swimming Pool; the Gallops; a Training Yard; the National Horseracing Museum; The National Stud; the British Racing School; Tattersalls Sales and a tour of the town (price £10–£25).

Buildings worth noting in the town centre are the **Rutland Arms Hotel** on *Palace St* and, further along, **Nell Gwynne's House**, home of the mistress of Charles II.

The **National Horseracing Museum** tells the story of the development of horse-racing and has a video of classic races: it also offers **Newmarket Equine Tours**, including visits to the **Gallops, National Stud, Museum, Private Training Yard and town tour** (price £20). You can see horses training daily on *Newmarket Heath*, west of the town, from 0600 to 1230; visitors should remain in their cars, parking quietly off *Moulton Rd* where possible. The seven-mile-long **Devil's Dyke**, an ancient earthwork, probably constructed to defend the Saxon kingdom of East Anglia against its expansionist neighbour, Mercia, can be seen here.

National Horseracing Museum, *99 High St; tel: (01638) 667333*. Open Tues–Sat, Bank Holiday Mons and all Mons in July and August (1000–1700), Sun 1200–1600 (Apr–Nov). Admission £3.30. Tours by arrangement. **The National Stud**, *Newmarket; tel: (01638) 663464*. Tours by appointment only, starting Mon–Fri 1115 and 1430, Sat 1115, Sun 1430 (Apr–Sept). Tour price: £3.50. Two miles south-west of town (no public transport). **Rowley Mile and July Racecourses**. For race enquiries, contact the TIC or the Clerk of the Course, *tel: (01638) 663482*. Two miles south-west of town (no public transport).

CANTERBURY

Three major events have shaped Canterbury's character: the arrival of St Augustine from Rome in 597 to begin the conversion of the English peoples; the brutal despatch of Henry II's 'turbulent priest', Thomas à Becket, in 1170; and German bombing in 1942. Despite the latter, much of the medieval streetscape of this small city survives, clustered around the awe-inspiring cathedral to which Chaucer's pilgrims, among others, journeyed in the Middle Ages. Today, tourists in their thousands follow in their footsteps, visiting the cathedral where the head of the Anglican church presides. Although the city is tiny, allow a whole day to explore it.

Tourist Information

TIC: Canterbury Visitor Centre, 34 St Margarets St, Canterbury, Kent CT1 2TG; tel: (01227) 766567. Open Mon–Sun 0930–1730 (Easter to mid-Oct); Mon–Sat 0930–1700 (mid-Nov to Easter). SHS Services offered: local bed-booking service and BABA (latest 30 mins before closing), advance reservations handled; bureau de change. Tickets booked for local events and festivals, London theatres and major concerts. Canterbury Accommodation Guide is available free from the TIC. **TIC**: Longport Coach Park, Lower Chantry Lane. Open 0930–1700 Mon–Sun (mid-Mar to mid-Oct). Services offered: local bed-booking service (latest 30 mins before closing); bureau de change. Tickets sold for Canterbury's museums and Canterbury Tales (see p. 102).

Arriving and Departing

Station

Canterbury East Station, Station Rd East; tel: (01732) 770111 is five minutes walk south-east to the city centre. It has a taxi rank and a car hire office provided by **S & B Hire**.

Getting Around

Most of Canterbury's attractions are within walking distance of the city centre. Free town and transport maps are available from the TIC.

Buses

Most bus services are operated by **Stagecoach East Kent**, tel: (01227) 766151, from the central bus station in St Georges Lane. Services are good to most areas of the city and surrounding area but are reduced on Sun.

Taxis

The main city taxi rank is on St Georges Lane and taxi companies in Canterbury include **Andycabs Taxis** tel: (01227) 876111; **Cabwise** tel: (01227) 784448; **Laser Cars** tel: (01227) 464422; **Longport Taxi Service** tel: (01227) 458885; **Lynx Taxis** tel: (01227) 464232; **Manhattan Cabs** tel: (01227) 786785; and **Blean Taxis** tel: (01227) 471553.

Staying in Canterbury

Accommodation

There is a reasonable range of hotels on offer in Canterbury and over 80 guesthouse and b. & b. establishments. The majority of the cheaper accommodation is located on the edge of the city centre. It is generally easy to find accommodation on arrival but it is recommended that advance bookings are made during the University Graduation in July and during Cricket Week in Aug.

Hotel chains in Canterbury include BW, FH, MH. There are only three pubs and inns offering accommodation near the city, one of which is in the centre. The other two are located in Chilham, seven miles south-west and Boughton, seven miles west of the city. For budget accommodation **Canterbury Youth Hostel** is located at 54 New Dover Rd; tel: (01227) 462911, close to the city centre. The nearest campsites are **The Camping and Caravanning Club Site**, Bekesbourne Lane; tel: (01227) 463216, 1½ miles east of the city centre on bus routes 613, 1n3, 614 and **The Royal Oak** Broad Oak; tel (01227) 710448, 3 miles north (not accessible by public transport). The TIC has details of campsites around the area.

Eating and Drinking

A list of local restaurants is available free from the TIC. There is a good range of cheaper eating places in Canterbury and most major ethnic specialities are catered for. However there are only two gourmet restaurants in the city and no places specialising in vegetarian meals. *St Peters St* is a particularly good area for restaurants.

Communications

The main post office is located at *28 High St* and has a post restante facility.

Money

Thomas Cook bureaux de change are to be found at *9 High St, Longport Coach Park* and *14 Mercery Ln.*

Entertainment and Events

Entertainment listings can be found in the publication *Fifteen Days*, which is available free and widely distributed throughout the city. Canterbury's main theatre, **The Marlowe**, is located at *The Friars, tel: (01227) 767246,* in the city centre. There are only two nightclubs in Canterbury and one pub with a theatre.

An events listing is available free from the TIC and covers both major and more unusual events taking place around the city, including the **Chaucer Festival**, which is held twice a year, in April and during the summer, at *22 St Peters St* in the city centre. Another major event is the annual **Canterbury Festival** with over 200 events including cathedral concerts, opera, dance, jazz, drama, cabaret, walks, street entertainment, exhibitions and fireworks which are held at various locations in the city over two weeks in Oct (for a full programme contact the *Canterbury Festival Office, Christchurch Gate, The Precincts; tel: (01227) 452853).*

Shopping

Long Market, High St, St Peters St, St Georges St and *The Marlowe Arcade* are all good for gifts, clothes and accessories, whilst antique shops and a further selection of gift ideas can be found on *Palace St* and at *Burgate*. The **Kingsmead Market**, *Kingsmead Rd*, is ¼ mile from the city centre and is held every Wed.

English wines can be sampled and the 'vine trail' walked at **Ash Coombe Vineyard**, *Coombe Lane, Ash; tel: (01304) 813396*, open Thur–Sat 1100–1700, Sun 1200–1600 (Apr–Oct), on bus routes 613 and 614; **Staple Vineyards** *Church Farm, Staple; tel: (01304) 812571*, open Mon–Sat 1000–1700, Sun 1200–1600 (Easter to Christmas), on route 614; and **St Nicholas Vineyard** *Ash; tel: (01304) 812670*, open Sat–Sun 1000–1800 (all year), Mon–Fri 1000–1800 (Apr–Dec), on routes 613 and 614.

Sightseeing

Head first for the **Cathedral**. You approach it along historic *Mercery Lane*, entering the precinct via the ornate, heraldic **Christ Church Gate**. This magnificent cathedral, the heart of the Anglican church, dates from Norman times: highlights include the amazingly beautiful 12th- and 13th-century stained glass; the largest Norman crypt in the country; the central tower ('Bell Harry'), and the tomb of the Black Prince. You can also see the site of the shrine of St Thomas à Becket in Trinity Chapel; and an altar in the north transept marks the spot where he was martyred by Henry II's over-zealous knights. Just beyond the cathedral, have a look at the unusual Norman exterior staircase of the ancient **King's School**.

The city itself is compact, lying mostly within the bounds of the city wall, which was built in the 13th and 14th centuries on Roman foundations. Long stretches of wall survive, but only one gate, the **West Gate**, survived World War II bombing: this now contains an interesting arms museum. The city's Roman history is explained at the **Roman Museum**, which includes the remains of a town house with fine mosaics. Little remains from the time when St Augustine arrived on his mission to the Saxons from Rome in 597, but there is Saxon work in the ruins of **St Augustine's Abbey**, as well as the remains of a later Norman church. Further up *Longport* is **St Martin's Church**, parts of which date back to the 6th century and

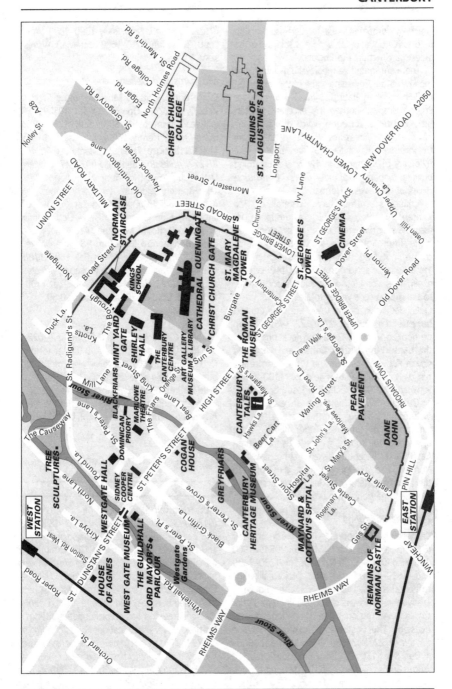

which was probably in use for Christian worship before St Augustine arrived: it is said to be the oldest parish church in England.

There are some fine medieval buildings along the River Stour, including some of the 'hospitals' built to accommodate pilgrims. The lovely Poor Priests' Hospital houses the excellent **Canterbury Heritage Museum**, which displays many of the city's treasures; while 13th-century **Greyfriars**, the first English friary built by the followers of St Francis in 1267, is a charming building spanning the river. **Eastbridge Hospital** preserves a Norman hall.

Chaucer's 14th-century masterpiece, *The Canterbury Tales*, in which a group of ill-assorted pilgrims tell each other stories *en route* from Southwark to Canterbury is, of course, not forgotten here. **The Canterbury Tales** purports to provide a 14th-century experience, complete with sounds and smells, to bring Chaucer's verses to life.

Guided walks of the town from the **Canterbury Guild of Guides**, *tel: (01227) 459779*, can be booked at the TIC. Joining locations are at the **Canterbury Visitor Centre** and **Longport Coach Park**. Walks from the **Visitor Centre** are run daily at 1400 (Easter to Nov), 1100 (June–Sept) and 2000 (Fri in July and Aug only).

Outside town, **Chilham** is an exceptionally picturesque village, with a central square surrounded by timbered Tudor houses. From one side of the square, a gate leads to **Chilham Castle**, a 17th-century hexagonal house with a Norman keep: though the house is not open to the public, there are lovely terraced and woodland gardens, with lakeside walks.

Historical Buildings

Canterbury Cathedral, *The Precincts; tel: (01227) 762862*. Open Mon–Sat 0845–1900 (summer), 0845–1700 (winter); Sun 1230–1430 and 1630–1730 (all year). Occasionally the cathedral is closed to visitors at short notice, it is advisable to always check opening times prior to visit. Admission: free (but donation requested). **The Eastbridge Hospital**, *The High St; tel: (01227) 471688*. Open Mon–Sat 1000–1700, Sun 1300–1700. Admission: free. **St Augustine's Abbey**, (EH) *Longport; tel:*

(01227) 767345. Open daily 1000–1800 (Apr–Sept); Tues–Sun 1000–1600 (Oct–Mar). Admission: £1.50.

Museums and Galleries

Canterbury Heritage Museum, *Stour St; tel: (01227) 452747*. Open Mon–Sat 1030–1700 (all year, last entry 1600); Sun 1330–1700 (June–Oct, last entry 1600). Admission: £1.50. **The Canterbury Tales**, *St Margarets St; tel: (01227) 454888*. Open daily 0930–1730 (Mar–Oct); 1000–1630 (Nov–Feb). Admission: £4.75. **The Roman Museum**, *Butchery Lane; tel: (01227) 452747*. Open Mon–Sat 1030–1700 (all year); Sun 1330–1700 (June–Oct). Admission: £1.40. **Royal Museum, Art Gallery and Buffs Regimental Museum**, *18 High St; tel: (01227) 452747*. Open Mon–Sat 1000–1700. Admission: free. **West Gate Museum**, *St Peters St; tel: (01227) 452747*. Open Mon–Sat 1100–1230 and 1330–1530. Admission: £0.60.

Out of Town

Chilham Castle Gardens, *Chilham; tel: (0227) 765155*. Open daily from 1100 (Easter to mid-Oct). Admission: £3. Six miles west of Canterbury, take bus 410 to Chilham village. **Howletts Wild Animal Park**, *Bekesbourne; tel: (01303) 264647*. Open daily 1000–1700 (1600 winter). Admission: £6.50, 2 miles east on bus 613/614.

- - - - - - - - - - - - - - -
 Side Track from Canterbury

DOVER

TIC: *Townwall St, Dover, Kent CT16 1JR; tel: (01304) 205108*. Open daily 0900–1800. DP SHS Services offered: local bed-booking service and BABA (£3 booking fee or 10% commission on first night taken), advance reservations handled. Tickets sold for ferries, National Express and Euroline and theatres; AA and YHA memberships sold. *White Cliffs Country Guide* is free and has accommodation listings. **Station**: Dover Priory Station, *Folkestone Rd; tel (01732) 770111* is 10-mins walk north-west of the town centre and has a taxi rank.

Trains run every ½ hour from Canterbury East

to Dover Priory and vice versa (every hour on Suns). Fastest journey time is 18 mins.

Ferries and Hovercraft: ferries to Calais are operated by P & O European Ferries *tel: (01304) 203388* and Stena Sealink *tel: (01233) 647047*, from the Eastern Docks in Dover; ferries operate at least hourly throughout the year. Buses run every 45 mins between the station and the Eastern Dock's terminal from 0545 to 0115 and are timed to coincide with ferry arrivals. Ferry tickets can be purchased at the terminal or at the TIC. Two **Thomas Cook** bureaux de change can be found at the Eastern Docks. Hoverspeed, *tel: (01304) 240241*, operate hovercraft and SeaCat services from the Hoverport on the *Western Docks*. A regular bus service runs between the station and hoverport. (See pp. 12–13 for further details of Channel crossings.)

Getting Around

Most of Dover's attractions are within walking distance of the town centre. Pick up free town and transport maps from the TIC. Most bus services are operated by **Stagecoach East Kent**, *tel: (01304) 240024*, from the central bus depot on *Pencester Rd*. Services are good in the town centre and there are regular buses to other main towns in the area but services are patchy to rural villages nearby. Reduced services operate after 2000. For local taxis contact **A2B** *tel: (01304) 225588*; **Central Cars** *tel: (01304) 240441*; **Coastal Cars** *tel: (01304) 206155*; **Dover Taxis** *tel: (01304) 201915*; **Invicta** *tel: (01304) 240604*; **New Street Cars** *tel: (01304) 242526*; and **Star Taxis** *tel: (01304) 242526*.

Staying in Dover

There is not a wide choice of hotels in Dover, but there is a good range of guest-house and b. & b. establishments, mostly located in the town centre. The only inn with accommodation is at *St Margarets-at-Cliffe*, 4 miles east on bus route 90. It is generally easy to find accommodation on arrival, except during July and August (and particularly after 1800).

Hotel chains in Dover include *FH, MH* and *TI*. For budget accommodation try the **Dover Youth Hostel**, *306 London Rd; tel: (01304) 201314*, open 1300–2100, or the **YMCA**, *Leyburne Rd; tel: (01304) 206138*, open from 1700. The closest campsites are at **Hawthorne Farm**, *Martin Mill; tel: (01304) 852658*, 3 miles north-east on bus route 593; **St Margarets Country Club**, *Reach Rd, St Margarets-at-Cliffe; tel: (01304) 853262*, 3 miles east on bus route 90; **Little Satmar Holiday Park**, *Wine House Lane, Capel-le-Ferne, Folkestone; tel: (01303) 251188*, 5 miles west on bus route 90; and **Varne Ridge Caravan Park**, *145 Old Dover Rd, Capel-le-Ferne, Folkestone; tel: (01303) 251765*, 5 miles west on bus route 90.

There is a good choice of cheaper eating establishments in Dover, mostly located in the town centre, but only one gourmet restaurant and no places specialising in vegetarian food.

The main post office is on *Biggin St*, open Mon–Fri 0900–1730, Sat 0900–1230. A post restante facility is available.

Entertainment listings can be found in the TIC's events list and in the two local newspapers *Dover Express* (price £0.40) and *East Kent Mercury* (price £0.30), which are available at local newagents. An events listing is available free from the TIC.

Sightseeing

Millions of people pass through Dover, the gateway to England, *en route* for foreign pastures; but for centuries its role, as guardian of the shortest sea passage to the Continent, was to keep invaders out. **Dover Castle** is one of the most impressive medieval fortresses in Western Europe. You can spend hours exploring here, taking in the labyrinth of underground passages known as **Hellfire Corner**, a secret operations HQ during World War II.

The best view of the famous White Cliffs is from a boat, but a walk up the East Cliff footpath above Eastern Docks will bring you to the parkland of **Langdown Cliffs**: on a clear day you can spy France, 22 miles away, or just watch the ships come and go. Back in town, the **White Cliffs Experience** is an exciting, multimedia show which tells the story of Britain through the eyes of Dover; entry includes admission to **Dover Museum**. The exceptionally well-preserved **Roman Painted House** has wonderful frescoes.

Free guided walks from **White Cliffs Countryside Project**, *tel: (01304) 241806*, start at various locations around the town and can be booked at the TIC. If time permits an excursion, take in **Deal** and **Walmer Castles**, both forts built by Henry VIII in the 1530s: whereas Deal preserves its martial character, Walmer has the gentler atmosphere of a stately home, with attractive formal gardens.

Dover Castle and **Hellfire Corner** (EH) *Castle Hill; tel: (01304) 201066*. Open daily 1000–1800 (Apr–Oct); 1000–1600 (Nov–Mar). Admission: £5.25.

Dover Museum *Market Sq; tel: (01304) 201066*. Open daily 1000–1730. Admission: £1.20.

Langdown Cliffs (NT) *Upper Rd; tel: (01892) 890651*. Open Sat–Sun and Bank Holidays 1400–1700 (Apr–Oct). Admission: £1.

Old Town Gaol *Dover Town Hall, Biggin St; tel: (01304) 242766*. Open Weds–Sat 1000–1630, Sun 1400–1630 (all year); Mon–Tues 1000–1630 (May–Oct). Admission: £3.20.

Roman Painted House *New St; tel: (01304) 203279*. Open Tues–Sun and Bank Holiday Mon 1000–1700; Mon 1000–1700 (July–Aug). Admission: £1.50.

The White Cliffs Experience *Market Sq; tel: (01304) 214566*. Open daily 1000–1700 (Apr–Oct); 1000–1500 (Nov–Mar). Last admission one hr before closing. Admission: £4.99.

Out of Town

Deal, 7 miles north-east on bus route 90. **Deal Castle**, *The Stand, Deal; tel: (01304) 372762*. Open daily 1000–1800 (Apr–Oct); Wed–Sun 1000–1600 (Nov–Mar). Admission: £2. **Maritime and Local History Museum**, *St Georges Rd, Deal; tel: (01304) 369576*. Open daily 1400–1700 (June–Sept). Admission: £0.50. **The Salter Collection**, *18 Gladstone Rd, Deal; tel: (01304) 361471*. Open Mon–Tues 1400–1800, Sun 1500–1800 (May–Sept). Admission: £1.50. **Time Ball Tower**, *Seafront, Deal; tel: (01304) 201200*. Open Tues–Sun 1000–1700 (June–Aug). Admission: £1.10.

Folkestone, 6 miles south-west, either 20 mins on train or on bus route 90. **Kent Battle of Britain Museum**, *Hawkinge Airfield, Nr Folkestone; tel: (01303) 893140*. Open daily 1000–1700 (Easter to Oct). Admission: £2.50. Four miles north on bus route 16 from Folkestone. **Eurotunnel Exhibition Centre**, *High St, Cheriton, Nr Folkestone; tel: (01303) 270111*. Open daily 1000–1800 (Apr to mid-Oct); 1000–1700 (mid-Oct–Mar). Admission: £3. Two miles north from Folkestone on bus route F2. **Hythe**, 10 miles south-west, take bus 90 to Folkestone then bus 11. **Port Lympne Wild Animal Park**, *Lympne, Hythe; tel: (01303) 264647*. Open daily 1000–1700. Admission: £6.50. Take bus 10 from Folkestone. **St Margaret's Bay**, 3 miles east on bus route 90. **The Bay Museum**, *St Margaret's Bay; tel: (01304) 852764*. Open Tues–Thur and Sat–Sun variable opening hours (June–Sept and occasional days in Apr and May). Admission: £0.60. **The Pines Gardens**, *St Margaret's Bay; tel: (01304) 852764*. Open daily 1000 to dusk. Admission: £1.

Sandwich, 10 miles north-east on bus route 94. **Precinct Toy Museum**, *38 Harnet St, Sandwich; tel: (01304) 369576*. Open Mon–Sat 1030–1630 (Easter to Sept); Sat 1400–1630 (Oct). Admission: £1. **Richborough Castle**, *Richborough Rd, Sandwich; tel: (01304) 612013*. Open daily 1000–1800 (Apr–Oct). Admission: £1.80. **Sandwich Guildhall**, *New St, Sandwich; tel: (01304) 617197 (Town Clerk's office)*. Open for guided tours Tues–Thur at 1100 and 1430. Admission: £1. **Stour River Bus**, *Sandwich Quay, Sandwich; tel: (01304) 820171*. Open Thur–Sun (Easter to mid-Sept, normally four sailings a day). Round trip to Richborough: £3. **White Mill Folk Museum**, *Ash Rd, Sandwich; tel: (01304) 612076*. Sun 1030–1200 and 1430–1730, Bank Holiday Mon 1430–1730 (Easter to mid-Sept). Admission: £1. **Walmer**, 6 miles north-east on bus route 90. **Walmer Castle**, (EH) *Kingsdown Rd, Walmer; tel: (01304) 364288*. Open daily 1000–1800 (Apr–Oct); 1000–1600 (Nov–Dec). Admission: £3.

Connection: London

The quickest service from Dover to London is half-hourly – to Charing Cross via Ashford – and takes 1 hr 40 mins.

CARDIFF

The Welsh capital, Cardiff is a city whose relatively recent growth owes much to the influence of the Earls of Bute in the 19th century. It was their interest in the iron and coal industries which transformed the town into what was, during the heyday of the South Wales coalfield, the greatest coal port in the world. Although the Welsh coal industry has now shrunk beyond recognition – the Rhondda Heritage Park providing a glimpse into the ways of life formerly associated with it – Cardiff itself retains a cosmopolitan air, with good cultural and shopping facilities. Its public spaces and buildings, many of the most impressive of which date from around the turn of the century, have a well-cared-for look, and it is worth allowing a day or two to explore.

Tourist Information

TIC: Cardiff Central Station, *Central Square, Cardiff, South Glamorgan CF1 1QY; tel: (01222) 227281/668750.* Open Mon–Sat 0900–1830, Sun 1000–1600, Bank Holidays 1000–1700 (Apr–Sept); Mon–Sat 0900–1730, Sun 1000–1600 (Oct–Mar). DP Services offered: local bed-booking service, BABA (latest 30 mins before closing, £1 fee taken for Wales, £5 for London, £3 for rest of UK), bureau de change. British Heritage Pass and Cadw 7-day Explorer Pass sold. *Cardiff, Capital of Wales* and *Cardiff Accommodation* are available free.

Arriving and Departing

Cardiff Central Station, *Central Square; tel: (01222) 228000* is in the centre of town, and has a taxi rank and a TIC (see above).

Getting Around

Free town and transport maps are available from the TIC. Most of the attractions in town are within walking distance or an easy bus journey from the city centre. Local train services also go from the centre to the suburbs.

Buses

Most services operate from **Central Bus Station**, *Central Square*. The two main local operators are **Cardiff Bus** *tel: (01222) 396521* and **Cardiff Bluebird** *tel: (01222) 398700.* Services are good in the city centre and to the suburbs, running until 2300 on the most popular routes with reduced services on Suns. Cardiff Bus have a 'Capital Day-Out' ticket for £3 a day, covering all their bus services.

Taxis

The main taxi ranks can be found at *Central Station, The Hayes, Park Place* and *St Mary St.* Taxis can also be hailed in the street.

Staying in Cardiff

Accommodation

There is a good range of accommodation in all categories, with cheaper establishments located on the edge of the city in the suburbs of *Whitchurch* and *Heath* and in *Llandaff,* 2.4 miles north. It is generally possible to book on arrival, except during Rugby International weekends between late Jan and early Mar.

Hotel chains in Cardiff include *Ca, Cp, FH, Fr, Ja, Ma, MC, MH.*

For accommodation bookings you can also contact **Cardiff Marketing Ltd**, *PO Box 48, Cardiff CF1 1XQ; tel: (01222) 395173*; fax: *(01222) 377653* (10% deposit taken).

For budget accommodation: **Cardiff Youth Hostel**, *2 Wedal Rd, Roath Park; tel: (01222) 462303*, opens daily from 1500 (Mar–Oct), Mon–Sat from 1500 (Jan, Feb and Nov). Take bus 78, 80 or 82 from Central Station. Also **Cardiff YWCA**, *126 Newport Rd; tel: (01222) 497379*, open 0900–1300 and 1800–2200.

The closest campsites are: **Lavernock Point Holiday Estate** (5 miles south), *Fort Rd, Penarth, South Glamorgan; tel: (01222) 707310.* Take bus P4, P5 or P8 from the centre. **Tredegar House** (10 miles east), *Newport; tel: (01633) 815880.* Take bus 30.

Eating and Drinking

There is a very good range of restaurants in all price categories, with the most expensive in the city centre, and cheaper places in the areas of *Roath, Cathays* and *Canton*. Vegetarian restaurants include: **Crumbs Salad Restaurant**, *33 Morgan Arcade* (not open evenings) and **Celtic Cauldron**, *4749 Castle Arcade* (for Welsh and vegetarian food). Also renowned for good Welsh food is **Blas-Ar-Gymru** (A Taste of Wales), *48 Crwys Rd, Cathays; tel: (01222) 382132* (booking recommended). Try some **'Brains'** beer, the distinctive local brew!

Communications

The main post office is at *24 Hill St, The Hayes; tel: (01222) 232410*, open Mon–Fri 0900–1730, Sat 0900–1630, and has post restante facilities.

Money

Thomas Cook bureaux de change are located at *16 Queen St* and *St Davids Centre*, and at Midland Bank, *56 Queen St*, and British Airways, *99 St Mary Street*.

Entertainment

Various entertainment listings are available free from the TIC, including *Buzz, Capital Choice* and *What's On Wales*. There is a wide variety of clubs and pubs, catering for all tastes.

Music and Theatre

The main concert halls are **St David's Hall**, *The Hayes; tel: (01222) 371236* and **Cardiff International Arena**, *Bute Terrace; tel: (01222) 224488*. For theatre, there is **New Theatre**, *Park Pl; tel: (01222) 394844* (home of Welsh National Opera) and **Sherman Theatre**, *Senghennydd Rd; tel: (01222) 230451*.

Sport

Cardiff Arms Park, *Westgate St; tel: (01222) 390111* is the venue for Wales' home international rugby matches and **Wales National Ice Rink**, *Hayes Bridge Rd; tel: (01222) 397198* is home to the **Cardiff Devils** ice hockey team.

Events

The following popular events take place at *St David's Hall*: **Welsh Proms** in July; **Welsh Singer of the Year Competition** in June; **Welsh Harp Festival** every two years in June. **Cardiff Summer Festival** takes place around the city in Aug. The **Home International Rugby Season** takes place at *Cardiff Arms Park* over two weekends between Jan and Mar, during which time accommodation is very difficult to find.

Shopping

Cardiff has many Edwardian arcades, department stores, malls, indoor and outdoor markets. The main shopping centres are **St David's Centre, Capitol Centre, Queen's West, St David's Market** and **Central Market**. **Cardiff Market**, *St Mary's St*, is a daily indoor market; **Splott Market**, *East Tyndall St, Splott*, takes place on Suns; and **Jacob's Antique Market**, *West Canal Wharf*, is best visited on Thur and Sat, 0900–1730.

Sightseeing

Cardiff Castle has Roman stonework in its outer walls and an 11th-century keep, but its character is overwhelmingly Victorian, thanks to the 3rd Marquess of Bute, who transformed it in the mid-19th century in the most lavish of styles; the result is an opulent, mock-medieval interior. The **National Museum of Wales** has excellent collections, including particularly fine French Impressionist paintings, and an Evolution of Wales exhibition; and in the Cardiff Bay area, attractions include **Techniquest**, one of the largest hands-on science centres in the country, ideal for children. From the city centre, you can take a lovely riverside walk to **Llandaff Cathedral**: originally Norman, the cathedral was reconstructed after it was heavily bombed in 1941, and has a striking sculpture by Epstein of Christ in Majesty.

Highly recommended outside town is the **Welsh Folk Museum**, where buildings ranging from a toll gate to a chapel have been assembled from all over Wales in 100-acre St Fagan's Park to give an insight into Wales' rural

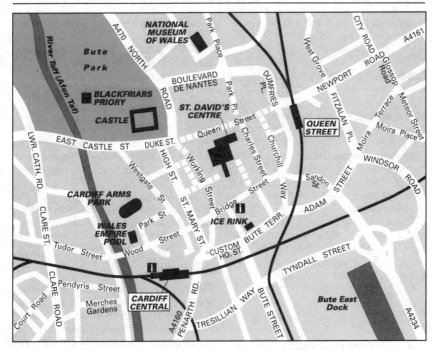

past. Like Cardiff Castle, **Castell Coch** was extensively altered by the 3rd Marquess of Bute and his architect William Burges: the result is a fairytale castle, its conical sandstone towers rising romantically from the Welsh hillside.

The **Rhondda Heritage Park** is one of many ex-collieries in South Wales where tourism has taken over from heavy industry; here, the original colliery buildings have been converted to provide a record of a coal-mining community, and ex-miners act as tour guides.

There are bus tours of the city operated by **Leisurelink** *tel: (01222) 522202*, which start from Central Station, price £4. Boat trips of the *Bristol Channel* area are run by **Waverley Excursions** *tel: (01446) 720656*. They start from *Penarth Pier*, cost from £7.95, and can be booked at the TIC. For details of guided walks contact **International Tourism Services** *tel: (01374) 116560* or **Cardiff Official Guides** *tel: (01222) 811970*.

Castles and Churches

Cardiff Castle, *Castle St; tel: (01222) 822083.*

Open daily 1000–1800 (May–Sept), 1000–1630 (Nov–Feb), 1000–1700 (Mar, Apr and Oct). Admission: £3.30.

Llandaff Cathedral (2 miles north-west), *The Green, Llandaff; tel: (01222) 564554.* Open daily 0700–1900. Admission: free, donations welcomed. Take bus 21a, 33, 62c, 65c or 133 from Central Bus Station, or 25 from *Castle St.*

St John's Church, *The Hayes; tel: (01222) 395231.* Open Sun–Thur 0800–1800, Fri and Sat 0800–1630. Admission: free, donations welcomed.

Museums

Industrial and Maritime Museum (1 mile south), *Bute St; tel: (01222) 481919.* Open Tues–Sat 1000–1700, Sun 1430–1700. Admission: £1.50. Take bus 8 or 8b from *Wood St*, or 7, 7a or 7e from *Queen St.*

National Museum of Wales, *Civic Centre, Cathays Park; tel: (01222) 397951.* Open Tues–Sat 1000–1700, Sun 1430–1700.

Techniquest (science museum; 1 mile south), *72 Bute St, Pier Head, Cardiff Bay; tel:*

City Map–Sightseeing–Out of Town

(01222) 460211. Take bus 8 or 8b from *Wood St*, or 7, 7a or 7e from *Queen St.*

Out of Town

Castell Coch (Cadw), *Tongwynlais; tel: (01222) 810101.* Open daily 0930–1830 (Mar–Oct); Mon–Sat 0930–1600, Sun 1100–1600 (Nov–Mar). Admission: £2. Take bus 26 or 136 from Central Bus Station to *Tongwynlais*, 4 miles north-west.

Rhondda Heritage Park, *Lewis Merthyr, Coed Cae Rd, Trehafod, Rhondda; tel: (01443) 682036.* Open 1000–1800 (closed Mon, Oct–Easter). Admission: £4.95. Take train to *Trehafod* (30 mins), 17 miles north-west.

Welsh Folk Museum, *St Fagan's; tel: (01222) 569441.* Open daily 1000–1700 (closed Sun Nov–Mar). Admission: £4. Take bus 32 from Central Bus Station or 56 from *Castle St* to *St Fagan's*, 6 miles west.

 Side Track from Cardiff

CAERPHILLY

TIC: *Park Lane, Caerphilly, Mid Glamorgan CF8 1AA; tel: (01222) 851378.* (Due to move April 1995 to: *The Twyn, Castle St*, same tel). Open daily 1000–1800 (Apr–Oct). DP Services offered: local bed-booking service and BABA (latest 30 mins before closing), advance reservations handled. *Rhymney Valley* including an accommodation guide is available free.
Station: Caerphilly Station, *Cardiff Rd; tel: (01222) 228000* is ½ mile north of the centre, and has a taxi rank. There are frequent rail services from Cardiff to Caerphilly, the journey taking about 15 mins.

Getting Around

A free town map is available from the TIC. **Caerphilly Castle**, the town's main attraction, is an easy walk from the centre.

Most bus services are operated from *Station Terrace*, by **Cardiff Bus** *tel: (01222) 396521* and **Caerphilly Bus** *tel: (01222) 396521.* The service is good in the centre and to Cardiff, but patchy

to outlying areas, with very few buses on Sun.

There is a taxi rank at the station, or you can contact: **Brad Cars** *tel: (01222) 885000;* **Castell Cars** *tel: (01222) 869333;* **Civic** *tel: (01222) 851011;* **Caerphilly Cars** *tel: (01222) 868686* or **BTM Taxis** *tel: (01222) 885808.*

Staying in Caerphilly

There is a very limited range of accommodation: one hotel and about seven guesthouse and b. & b. establishments. It is generally possible to book on arrival, except during the peak holiday period.

For the nearest youth hostel, see Cardiff. The closest campsite is **Cwmcarn Forest Drive Campsite**, *Nant Carn Rd, Cwmcarn, Crosskeys; tel: (01495) 272001.* Eight miles north-east (no public transport from Caerphilly).

Sightseeing

Caerphilly is a small town famous for its castle and its crumbly cheese (much of the latter is now made elsewhere, but traditional cheese-making skills are still demonstrated – ask at the TIC for details). The massive 13th-century **Castle** is an extraordinary sight: with its seemingly impregnable series of concentric stone and water defences, it is one of Western Europe's most powerful fortresses. Its leaning tower famously outleans Pisa's. At **Llancaiach Fawr Living History Museum**, stewards in 17th-century guise provide an insight into the life of a Civil War stronghold.

Caerphilly Castle (Cadw), *Castle St; tel: (01222) 883143.* Open daily 0930–1830 (end Mar to end Oct), Mon–Sat 0930–1600, Sun 1100–1600 (end Oct to end Mar). Admission: £2.

Out of Town

Castell Coch (see Cardiff). **Llancaiach Fawr Manor** (living history museum), *Nelson, Treharris; tel: (01433) 412248.* Open Mon–Fri 1000–1700, Sat, Sun 1000–1800 (last admission 1½ hours before closing). Admission: £3.50. Take bus C16 to *Nelson*, 9 miles north.

CARDIFF to PEMBROKE

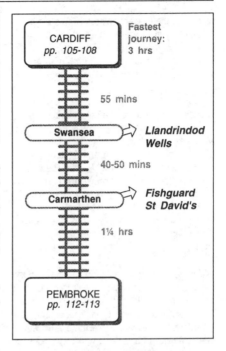

Winding along the often spectacular south coast of Wales, this itinerary features some of the most impressive medieval castles in the province, as well as the boathouse on Carmarthen Bay where Wales' most famous modern poet, Dylan Thomas, spent his final years. A long scenic side-track takes you into mid-Wales to the Victorian spa town of Llandrindod Wells.

TRAINS

ETT table: 531

 Fast Track

A through train runs daily from Cardiff Central to Pembroke, leaving Cardiff in the morning and taking 3 hrs. Other trains are available throughout the day by changing at Swansea – services are much reuced on Suns and vary considerably between summer and winter.

 On Track

Cardiff–Swansea

At least one Inter-City train per hour links the two principal cities of Wales. The journey takes 55 mins and departs from Cardiff Central. Suns services commence in late morning.

Swansea–Carmarthen

An aproximately hourly service operates from Swansea to Carmarthen (less frequently on Sun). The journey takes 40–50 mins.

Carmarthen–Pembroke

Eight trains a day (4 on Summer Suns, 2 in winter) makes the hour and a quarter long journey between Carmarthen and Pembroke.

SWANSEA

TIC: *Singleton St, Swansea, West Glamorgan SA1 3QG; tel: (01792) 468321.* Open Mon–Sat 0930–1730. DP SHS Services offered: local bed-booking service, BABA (latest 1700), advance reservations handled, guided tours booked. *Swansea Bay, Mumbles and Gower* holiday guide is free and has an accommodation listing. **Station:** Swansea Station, *High St; tel: (01792) 467777* is just outside the town centre and has a taxi rank.

Ferries: There are ferry connections from Swansea to Cork in Ireland. For details contact **Swansea-Cork Ferries** *tel: (01792) 456116.*

Getting Around

Most attractions in the town are within a walkable distance of the centre. Free town and transport maps are available from the TIC.

Most local bus services are run by **SWT** *tel: (01792) 580580* from **Quadrant Bus Station,** off *Westway.* Coverage is good in the centre and to outlying areas, but there are no Sun services to the Gower Peninsula. There is a daily 'Multiride' ticket for unlimited travel on SWT buses in Swansea, costing £2.50.

The main taxi ranks are at *St Mary's Church*, *Whitewalls* and off *King's Way*.

Staying in Swansea

There is a good choice of hotel and guest-house accommodation both in Swansea and in Mumbles and the Gower Peninsula. It is generally easy to book on arrival. Hotel chains in Swansea include *FC, Hn, Ja, Ma*. The closest youth hostel is **Port Eynon Youth Hostel** (12 miles west), *Port Eynon, Gower; tel: (01792) 390706*. Take bus 18a (Mon–Sat). There are various campsites situated on the Gower Peninsula: contact the TIC for details.

Sightseeing

Wales' second largest city, Swansea is a busy industrial port, where oil terminals have ensured continuing prosperity after the decline of coal. The docklands have been made into an attractive marina with a **Maritime and Industrial Museum** complex, which includes a complete working woollen mill, floating exhibits and displays on Swansea's maritime history. **Glynn Vivian Art Gallery** has a fine collection of the rare and richly decorated Swansea china and **Swansea Museum** covers archaeological, natural and local history; the impressive glass pyramid at **Plantasia** houses over 5000 typical plants. A statue in **Dylan Thomas Square** and eponymous theatre commemorate Wales' most famous modern poet, born in Swansea in 1914.

Swansea, the pretty village of **Mumbles**, and the unspoilt **Gower Peninsula** offer a wide variety of magnificent bays, beaches and cliffs. **Oystermouth Castle**, which overlooks Mumbles, is an impressive 13th-century ruin, while further into the peninsula the **Gower Heritage Centre** offers an insight into the area's history. At Port Talbot, **Margam Park's** many acres of parkland and forest are a notable beauty spot, while nearer at hand **Clyne Gardens** are famed for their azalea and rhododendron display in May.

Glynn Vivian Art Gallery, *Alexandra Rd; tel: (01792) 655006*. Open Tues–Sun and Bank Holidays 1030–1730 (last admission 1710). Admission free. **Maritime and Industrial Museum**, *Museum Sq; tel: (01792) 650351*. Open Tues–Sun and Bank Holidays 1030–1730 (last admission 1710). Admission free. **Plantasia**, *Parc Tawe; tel: (01792) 474555*. Open Tues–Sun and Bank Holidays 1030–1730 (last admission 1710). Admission £1. **Swansea Museum**, *Victoria Rd; tel: (01792) 653763*. Open Tues–Sun and Bank Holidays 1030–1730 (last admission 1710). Admission free.

Out of Town

Clyne Gardens (3 miles south-west), *Blackpill; tel: (01792) 302420*. Open daily dawn–dusk. Admission free. Bus 1, 2 or 3. **Dylan Thomas' Boat House** (see Carmarthen p. 112). **Gower Heritage Centre** (7 miles south-west), *Parkmill, Gower; tel: (01792) 371206*. Open Sat, Sun 1000–1800. Admission £1.50. Bus 18a. **Margam Park** (10 miles east), *Port Talbot; tel: (01639) 881635*. Open daily 1000–1730 (Apr–Sept). Last entry 1600. Admission £3.10. Brewer's bus 66 and X1. **Oystermouth Castle** (4 miles south-west), off *Newtown Rd, Mumbles; tel: (01792) 368732*. Open daily 1100–1700 (Apr–Sept). Admission £0.80. Bus 1, 2, 3.

 Side Track from Swansea

LLANDRINDOD WELLS

TIC: Old Town Hall, *Temple St, Llandrindod Wells, Powys LD1 5DL; tel: (01597) 822600*. Open Mon–Fri 0900–1800, Sat, Sun 1000–1800 (summer); Mon–Fri 0900–1700 (winter). DP Services offered: local bed-booking service, advance reservations handled, BABA (latest 30 mins before closing). Cadw membership and local theatre tickets sold. *Heart of Wales*, including accommodation listing, available free. **Station**: Llandrindod Wells station, *Station Crescent; tel: (01597) 822053* is in the town centre. There is no taxi rank: for taxis, contact one of the companies listed below. Four trains on weekdays, 3 on summer Suns (Jun to Sep only) run between Swansea and Llandrindod; the journey takes around 2½ hrs.

Getting Around

Most of the attractions are out of town, and a free transport map and town map (£0.10) are available from the TIC. Local bus and rail services are infrequent, with no evening bus services and limited Sunday trains and buses. For general transport enquiries *tel: (01597) 822600*. The main bus companies are **Roy Brown's** *tel: (01982) 552597*, **Crossgates Motors** *tel: (01597) 851226*, **Trans Cambria** *tel: (01352) 700250* and **Post Bus** *tel: (01597) 822925*, and most buses operate from the *High St*. For taxis contact: **Adeys** *tel: (01597) 822118* or **Grimwood** *tel: (01597) 822864*.

Staying in Llandrindod Wells

Llandrindod Wells has a small selection of hotels, including one in the hotel chain *Mp*, and a good range of b. & b. and guesthouses. It is usually possible to book on arrival, except during the **Royal Welsh Agricultural Show** – the biggest agricultural show in Wales – at *Builth Wells* in July and the **Victorian Festival** in Aug.

The nearest campsites are: **Disserth Farm Caravan Park**, *Disserth, Howey; tel: (01597) 89277* (Roy Brown's bus to *Howey*, 2 miles south, then ½-mile walk); and **Park Motel Caravan and Camping** (3 miles north) *Crossgates; tel: (01597) 851201* (Crossgates bus).

Sightseeing

The detour to Llandrindod Wells on the Heart of Wales Railway Line provides an opportunity to see some of the wild and remote Cambrian mountains. Llandrindod Wells was one of three popular inland spas in the area in Victorian times (you pass through another, Llanwrtyd – see below – en route), and has retained its period elegance. The town's heyday is celebrated during the **Victorian Festival** in Aug, when the streets come alive with street entertainers and horse-drawn vehicles. Further along the line to the north east, Knighton is a picturesque base for hillwalking as it stands on **Offa's Dyke**, the earth bank and ditch built c.784 by Offa, King of Mercia, to mark the boundary between Mercia and Wales (it now follows the Welsh border).

The adventurous can take the postbus to Rhyader, and walk the mountain road to the **Elan Valley Visitor Centre**: this explains the construction of the spectacular chain of Edwardian reservoirs in the valley, which supply water to Birmingham. You can watch lead crystal glassware being produced by master craftsmen at **Welsh Royal Crystal**.

Llandrindod Wells Museum, *Temple St; tel: (01597) 824513*. Open Thur–Tues 1000–1230 and 1400–1630 (Apr–Sept), Mon–Fri 1000–1230 and 1400–1630, Sat 1000–1230 (Oct–Mar). Admission free.

Out of Town

Knighton (20 miles north-east by train to *Knighton*). **Offa's Dyke Visitor Centre and TIC**, *Knighton; tel: (01547) 528753*. Open daily 0900–1730 (Apr–Oct), Mon–Fri 0900–1300 and 1400–1700 (Nov–Mar). Admission free.

Cambrian Woollen Mill, *Llanwrtyd Wells; tel: (01591) 610211*. Open daily 0930–1630. Admission £3.

Rhayader (10 miles north-west, by Post Bus). **Elan Valley Visitor Centre**, *Elan Valley*, near Rhayader; *tel: (01597) 810898*. Open 1000–1800 (mid-Mar to end Oct). Admission free. Three miles from Rhayader (walk or taxi).

Welsh Royal Crystal, *5 Brynberth Industrial Estate, Rhayader; tel: (01597) 811005*. Open daily 0900–1700. Admission £2.

CARMARTHEN

TIC: *113 Lammas St, Carmarthen, Dyfed SA31 3AQ; tel: (01267) 231557/221901*. Open daily 0930–1730 (Easter–Nov), Tues–Sat 1000–1630 (Nov–Easter). DP Services offered: local bed-booking service, advance reservations handled, BABA. Guided tours booked, tickets for local events sold. *Coast and Countryside in Carmarthenshire* including an accommodation listing available free.

Station: Carmarthen Station, *Station Rd; tel: (01267) 235803* is on the edge of town, on the south side. There is no taxi rank (for details see 'Taxis' below). There are frequent bus connections to the centre.

Getting Around

With the exception of **Carmarthen Museum**, attractions are within easy walking distance of the centre. Free transport maps are available from the TIC. The local bus service is reasonable within the town, but very infrequent to outlying areas, and there are no buses after 1800 or on Suns. Most services operate from the bus station on *Blue St.* For bus enquiries *tel: (01267) 231817.*

There is a taxi rank on *Lammas St,* or contact: **Carmarthen Taxi Company** *tel: (01267) 237704*; **Chris Cars** *tel: (01267) 234438.*

Staying in Carmarthen

There is a small range of hotel and b.&b. accommodation, including one hotel chain, *FP.* It is generally possible to book on arrival, except during the **Agricultural Show** – one of the largest in Wales – in the second week of Aug. The closest campsites are **Pant Farm Caravan Park** (2 miles east), *Llangunnor; tel: (01267) 235665* (take bus B4300) and **Church House Farm** (4 miles south), *Llangain, near Llansteffan; tel: (01267) 83274* (bus 227 then ½ mile walk).

Sightseeing

This ancient county town on the banks of the river Towy retains some steep and narrow streets, a **Roman Amphitheatre** which once seated 5000, and a Norman **Castle**, of which an impressive gatehouse survives. **Carmarthen Museum** offers an insight into the history of the region, which is prime agricultural country, and **Oriel Myrddin Art Gallery** contains changing displays of local arts and crafts.

For information about guided walks, starting from **St Peter's Civic Hall**, *tel: (01267) 232075.* **Carmarthen Castle** (ruin). Open Mon–Fri 1000–1630. Admission free. **Carmarthen Museum**, *Abergwili; tel: (01267) 231691.* Open Mon–Sat 1000–1630. Admission £0.50. Take bus 280, 1½ miles east. **Oriel Myrddin Art Gallery**, *Church La; tel: (01267) 222775.* Open Mon–Sat 1030–1645. Admission free. **Roman Amphitheatre** (remains), *Priory St.* Open at all times. Admission free.

Out of Town

Thirteen miles south-west of Carmarthen, on the coast at the attractive town of Laugharne, is the **Boat House**, where Dylan Thomas, Wales' most famous 20th-century poet, spent his last years. The Boat House, *Dylan's Wall, Laugharne; tel: (01994) 427420* opens 1000–1800 (Easter to end Oct) – reduced opening hours in winter, please ring to confirm. Admission £1.60. Take bus 222 to *Laugharne.*

Museum of the Welsh Woollen Industry, *Drefach Felindre, Llandysul; tel: (01559) 370929.* Open Mon–Fri 1000–1700 (also Sat Easter–Sept). Admission £1. Take bus 460, 461 or 462 to *Drefach Felindre,* 15 miles north.

Cenarth, famous for its Falls, is also well known for coracle (Celtic fishing boat) fishing; the **National Coracle Centre and Flour Mill**, *Cenarth Falls; tel: (01239) 710980,* explains this ancient art. Open Sun–Fri 1030–1730 (Easter to end Oct). Admission £1.50. Take bus 460 or 461 to *Cenarth,* 19 miles north.

_____

Side Tracks from Carmarthen

The small port of **Fishguard**, linked by ferry to the Republic of Ireland, has a pretty upper town huddled on a hillside.

Station: Fishguard Harbour Station, *Fishguard Harbour; tel: (01437) 764361* is 1 mile south of the centre. The **Town Service** bus goes into the centre every 30 mins; there is no taxi rank. There are only two trains between Carmarthen and Fishguard Harbour running solely in connection with the Irish ferry services.

Ferries: Fishguard Harbour is 1 mile south of the centre. **Stena Sealink Line** *tel: (01348) 872881* operates ferries from Fishguard to Rosslare twice daily (see p. 12). There are good rail links from Fishguard Station, which is located at the harbour.

The tiny city of **St David's** is easily accessible and a lovely place to explore. Attractions in St David's, 15 miles south-west, can be reached by bus no. 411 from Fishguard (journey time 50–60 mins), Mon–Sat only: there are impressive remains of the 14th-century **Bishop's Palace** and the (restored) Norman **Cathedral** has a rich interior. From here there are frequent boats to and around **Ramsey Island**, which provides sanctuary for seabirds and grey seals; and you can also explore the **Pembrokeshire Coastal Path** (the Pembrokeshire Coast is one of Wales' national parks).

PEMBROKE

TIC: *Commons Rd, Pembroke, Dyfed SA71 4EA; tel: (01646) 622388.* Open daily 1000–1730 (Easter to end Oct), Tues, Thur and Sat 1000–1600 (end Oct to Easter). DP Services offered: local bed-booking service, BABA. *Tenby and South Pembrokeshire Holiday Guide* is free and includes an accommodation listing. **National Park Information Centre**, *Westgate Hill; tel: (01646) 682148.*
Station: Pembroke Station, *Upper Lamphey Rd; tel: (01792) 467777* is half a mile west of the town centre. Taxis sometimes wait outside the station, but it is advisable to book in advance.

Getting Around

Most attractions are walkable from the centre, and free town and transport maps are available from the TIC. Local bus operators are **Silcox Motors** *tel: (01646) 683143*, **South Wales Transport** *(01792) 580580* and **Bus Dyfed** *tel: (01267) 251817*. Bus services are good to major towns, but less frequent to rural areas. Services are reduced after 1700, and there are none after 1900 or on Suns. There is no town taxi rank. For taxis contact **Castle Cars** *tel: (01646) 622440*; or **East End Cars** *tel: (01646) 681457*.

Staying in Pembroke

There is a limited choice of hotel and b. & b. accommodation, including one hotel in the *BW* chain, and some farm accommodation in the outlying area. It is advisable to book in advance from June–Sept. The closest budget accommodation is **Manorbier Youth Hostel** (5 miles south-east), *Manorbier; tel: (01834) 871803,* open daily (early July to early Sept). Take bus 358 or 359. The closest campsite is **Windmill Campsite**, *St Daniel's Hill; tel: (01646) 682392,* 1 mile south of town (no public transport).

Sightseeing

This small town has one of the largest castles in south Wales. Built by the Normans, it has an 80 ft-high circular keep, and is surrounded by water on three sides.

Pembroke is within the stunningly unspoilt **Pembrokeshire Coast National Park**, and is a good place from which to explore the coastal path. Other impressive fortresses include the magnificent Norman **Manorbier Castle** on its lovely moated site, and imposing **Carew Castle**, which has a restored tidal mill dating from 1558 and a Celtic cross nearby. Ruined, 13th-century **Lamphey Palace** was once a residence of the bishops of St Davids. Tenby is an attractive seaside resort, very busy in summer: the **Tudor Merchant's House**, a fine 15th-century building, recalls a period of maritime prosperity.

Boat trips to *Skomer Island* are run by **National Parks Authority** *tel: (01646) 682148*, departing from *Martin's Haven*, price £5 plus landing fees. **Dragon Marine Cruises** *tel: (01834) 844151* also organise boat trips, departing from *Hobb's Point, Pembroke Dock*, price £5.

Pembroke Castle, *Main St; tel: (01646) 684585.* Open daily 0930–1800 (Apr–Sept), 1000–1700 (Mar and Oct), 1000–1600 (Nov–Feb). Admission £2.

Out of Town

Carew Castle, Cross and Mill, *Carew; tel: (01646) 651657.* Open daily 1000–1700 (Easter–Oct). Admission £2 (castle), £1.50 (mill). Bus 361 to *Carew*, 4 miles north-east. **Lamphey Bishops Palace** (CADW), *Lamphey; tel: (01646) 672224.* Open at all times. Admission £1.50 when manned (free in winter). Bus 358 or 359 to *Lamphey*, 2 miles east.

Manorbier Castle, *Manorbier; tel: (01834) 871394.* Open daily 1030–1730 (Easter–Sept). Bus 358 or 359 to *Manorbier*, 5 miles south-east.

Tudor Merchant's House (NT), *Quay Hill, Tenby; tel: (01834) 842279.* Open Mon–Fri 1100–1745, Sun 1400–1800 (Apr–Oct). Admission £1.60. Bus 358 or 359 to *Tenby*, 10 miles east.

St David's–Pembroke   **113**

CARLISLE

Guarding the western end of England's border with Scotland, Carlisle is well worth a day's stopover to appreciate its castle, museum and cathedral; it also has some excellent shops.

TIC: *Old Town Hall, Carlisle, Cumbria CA3 8JH; tel: (01228) 512444.* DP SHS Open Mon–Sat 0930–1700 (Sept–May); Mon–Sat 0930–1800, Sun 1100–1600 (June, July); Mon–Sat 0930–1830, Sun 1100–1600 (Aug). Services offered: local bed-booking service and BABA (latest 30 mins before closing), advance reservations handled, guided tours booked, bureau de change. *Stay a While in Carlisle* is free and includes an accommodation list.
Station: Citadel Station, *Court Sq; tel: (01228) 44711* is 5 mins walk south of the town centre and has a taxi rank.

Getting Around

The town's attractions are within easy walking distance of the centre, and a free town map is available from the TIC. It is advisable to avoid the *Botchergate* area on Saturday evenings. Most of the local bus services are operated from the bus station on *Lonsdale St* by **Cumberland Motor Services** *tel: (01946) 63222*, and are good within the town and to many outlying areas, but reduced after 1800 and on Suns.

Staying in Carlisle

There is a good range of hotel, guest-house and b. & b. accommodation, including hotels in the *Co, FP, MC, Sw* chains. It is generally easy to book on arrival, but best to book in advance during July and Aug. The closest youth hostel is **Etterby House**, *Etterby; tel: (01228) 23934*, open mid-Feb to Oct. Take bus no. 62, 2 miles north. The nearest campsite is **Orton Grange**, *Wigton Rd; tel: (01228) 710252*, bus no. 300, 4 miles south-west.

Sightseeing

Carlisle's turbulent history is well told at **Tullie House**, the city's excellent museum and art gallery, and a good starting point. Across the street lies **Carlisle Castle**, bleak but imposing, with its long history of military occupation, warfare and sieges – don't miss the graffiti (supposedly carved by prisoners) on the top floor of the keep. There are some interesting streets and alleys around the red sandstone **Cathedral**, which has a curiously truncated, but lovely, Norman nave; the choir has an outstanding east window and a striking, restored 19th-century ceiling. Carlisle is a good base from which to explore the western end of **Hadrian's Wall** – **Birdoswald Roman Fort** is well preserved and has splendid views over the Irthing valley. There are impressive remains of a 13th-century keep and later buildings at picturesque **Brougham Castle**. Guided walks (from £1) and coach tours (from £7) of Carlisle and the surrounding area (including bus tours of *Hadrian's Wall* and the *Lake District*) can be booked through the TIC.

Carlisle Castle (EH), *Castle Way; tel: (01228) 591922.* Open daily 1000–1800 (Apr–Oct), 1000–1600 (Nov–Mar). Admission £2. **Carlisle Cathedral**, *Castle St; tel: (01228) 48151.* Open Mon–Sat 0745–1815, Sun 0745–1700. Admission free. **Guildhall Museum**, *Greenmarket; tel: (01228) 34781.* Open Tues–Sun 1100–1600 (Good Friday to end Sept). Admission £0.50. **Tullie House Museum and Art Gallery**, *Castle St; tel: (01228) 34781.* Open Mon–Sat 1000–1700, Sun 1200–1700. Admission £3.30.

Out of Town

Birdoswald Roman Fort, *Gilsland, Brampton; tel: (01697) 747602.* Open daily 1000–1730 (Easter to end Oct). Admission £1.75. Take Hadrian's Wall coach tours in summer, or school bus during term-time, 16 miles east. **Brougham Castle** (EH), *nr Penrith; tel: (01768) 62488.* Open daily 1000–1800 (Apr–Oct). Admission £1.25. Bus no. 104, 20 miles south. **Lanercost Priory** (EH), *Lanercost; tel: (01697) 73030.* Open daily 1000–1800 (Apr–Sept). Admission £0.80. Bus no. 685 or train to *Brampton*, then 2-mile walk. Twelve miles east.

CARLISLE to GLASGOW

The On Track route from the border stronghold of Carlisle to Scotland's second city enables you to explore one of Scotland's most distinctive lowland areas, and one indelibly associated with her celebrated national poet Robert Burns.

TRAINS

ETT tables: 550, 589

 Fast Track

InterCity trains to Glasgow Central follow a different route to that given below, taking just under 1½ hrs.

 On Track

Carlisle–Dumfries–Kilmarnock–Glasgow

Trains run approx. every 2 hrs (less on Sun). Carlisle–Dumfries: 36 mins; Dumfries–Kilmarnock: 1 hr 10 mins (change at Kilmarnock for Ayr); Kilmarnock–Glasgow: about 40 mins.

DUMFRIES

TIC: *Whitesands, Dumfries DG1 2SB; tel: (01387) 253862.* Open daily 1000–1700 (Apr–May), 0930–1800 (June–Aug), 1000–1700 (Sept–Oct), 1000–1230, 1330–1630 Mon–Sat (Nov–Mar). DP SHS services offered: local bed booking service (10% of cost of first night commission taken), BABA (£2.75 fee and 10% commission) – the TIC can be busy from 1600 onwards with accommodation bookings. Historic Scotland Explorer tickets, National Express Coach tickets and bus tour tickets to other areas may also be purchased. The *Dumfries and Galloway Holiday Guide* is free from the TIC.

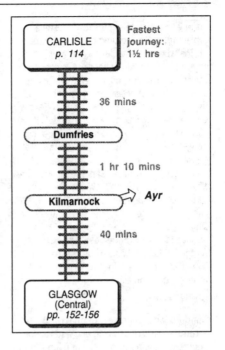

Station: Dumfries, *Lovers Walk*, is 1 mile north of the *High St* and has public transport connections to the centre as well as a taxi rank.

Getting Around

The majority of attractions in the town are within a walkable area of the centre and the TIC will provide a free town map. Travelling by bus in Dumfries and the surrounding area is generally easy, even at night and on Sat. Buses are less frequent on Sun however. General transport enquiry no: *tel: (0345) 090510.* Most buses operate from the central bus depot at *Whitesands* and the main bus companies are **Western Buses** *tel: (01387) 253496,* **McEvans** *tel: (01387) 710357* and **Gibsons** *tel: (01576) 470225.*

The main town centre taxi rank is in *Munches St.* Registered taxi companies include **Beehive Taxis** *tel: (01387) 269069* and **Radio Taxis** *tel: (01387) 255050.*

Staying in Dumfries

There are few large independent hotels and no

major branded hotels in the town. Instead, there is plentiful b. & b. accommodation, the majority of the cheaper establishments being on the edge of the centre. Generally it is easy to find accommodation on arrival, with the exception of Bank Holidays. There are no youth hostels in the local area but the **Dumfries and Galloway College of Technology,** Heath Hall, tel: (01387) 261261 can provide b. & b. accommodation at budget prices. The TIC can provide information on local campsites. The closest campsites to the town centre include **Barnsoul Farm Park,** Shawhead; tel: (01387) 730249. Take the bus to the village (infrequent service) and walk the last mile to the campsite. Seven miles from Dumfries.

Also **Park of Brandedleys,** Crocketford; tel: (01556) 690250. Sparse bus service nos. 501 and 503 from Dumfries to Kirkcudbright, 9 miles from Dumfries.

Sightseeing

Dumfries and Galloway is one of the most accessible parts of Scotland and also one of the warmest, allowing palm trees to flourish on the mild western coast. It is known as the 'Southern Highlands' because of its rich countryside and spectacular views. Bus tours and guided walks are possible in Dumfries – visit the TIC for more information.

The town itself has a wealth of museums covering a range of interests, for example **Dumfries Museum**, with its Camera Obscura in the windmill tower overlooking the town, and **The Robert Burns Centre** where the story of the poet is told with the aid of audio-visual presentations. Further associations with Burns can be found at **Burns House**, where he lived. Dumfries' oldest house – **The Old Bridge House** – can be found right next to the 15th-century **Devorgilla Bridge**, which is now a museum of everyday life. Surrounding attractions to visit include the **Old Blacksmith's Shop** at Gretna Green, the famous site of runaway marriages and **Threave Gardens** is particularly pleasant in spring.

Robert Burns Centre, Mill Rd; tel: (01387) 264088. Open Mon–Sat 1000–2000, Sun 1400–1700 (Apr–Sept), Tue–Sat 1000–1300, 1400–1700 (Oct–Mar). Admission £0.80. **Dumfries Museum and Camera Obscura,** The Observatory; tel: (01387) 253374. Open Mon–Sat 1000–1300, 1400–1700, Sun 1400–1700 (Apr–Sept). Admission £0.80. **Burns House**, Burns St; tel: (01387) 255297. Open Mon–Sat 1000–1300, 1400–1700, Sun 1400–1700. Closed Sun and Mon (Oct–Mar). Admission £0.80. **Devorgilla Bridge**, Whitesands. Open all year. Free admission.

Out of Town

Gretna Blacksmith's Shop, Gretna Green; tel: (01461) 338441. Open daily all year, 0900–2000 (summer), 0900–1800 (winter). Admission £1.00. Take the Western Bus no. 79 to Gretna Green, 20 miles south east of Dumfries. **Drumlanrig Castle and Country Park,** Thornhill; tel: (01848) 330248. Open Mon–Sat 1100–1700, Sun 1300–1700 (end Apr–end Aug). Admission £4.00. Take the Western Bus nos 236 and 246, 18 miles north of Dumfries. **Threave Gardens,** Castle Douglas; tel: (01556) 502575. Open daily 0930–1700 (Apr–Oct). Admission £3.00. Take the Western Bus no. 81 or contact McEwans Coaches on tel: (01387) 266528. Twenty miles south-west of Dumfries.

– –

 Side Track from Kilmarnock

AYR

TIC: Burns House, Burns Statue Sq, Ayr KA7 1UP; tel: (01292) 288688. Open Mon–Sat 0915–1700 (Oct–Apr), Mon–Sat 0915–1800, Sun 1000–1800 (May, June, Sept), Mon–Sat 0915–1900, Sun 1000–1900 (July–Aug). DP services offered: local bed-booking service, BABA, Bureau de change, guided tours booked. Ayrshire Scotland's Holiday Country is available free and includes an accommodation listing.

Station: Ayr Station, Burns Statue Sq; tel: (0345) 212282 is in the town centre and has a taxi rank.

Getting Around

The attractions in town are all within walking

distance of the centre. Free town maps are available from the TIC. The main bus operator is **Western Stagecoach**, *tel: (01292) 264643.* Services are good in the town centre but patchy in outlying areas. Reduced services run after 1800 and on Sun. The main taxi rank is at at the station. For details of registered taxi companies contact the TIC.

Staying in Ayr

There is a good range of accommodation, particularly b. & b. establishments and guesthouses. It is generally easy to book accommodation on arrival, except during July and Aug. The TIC has details of youth hostels and campsites in the area – the nearest youth hostel is **Ayr Youth Hostel**, *Craigweil Road, Ayr; tel: (01292) 262322.* Open Feb–Oct. The nearest campsite is **Heads of Ayr**, *Dunure Rd, Ayr; tel: (01292) 442269,* 5 miles south of Ayr.

Sightseeing

Long stretches of beach, superb sports and recreational facilities and family entertainment have helped make Ayr one of Britain's premier coastal resorts, as well as a good base for touring. Ayr's sandy beaches will keep the family occupied all day, as will **Wonderwest World**, Scotland's largest theme park. Under cover on the same site, the **Wondersplash Waterworld** with its blue lagoons and rushing flumes offers adventure for everyone.

Away from the excitement of a theme park, **Culzean Castle, Loudoun Hall** and **Dean Castle and Country Park**, provide the ideal opportunity to soak up some of Ayr's history, architecture and countryside. Ayr is well known for its connections with Scotland's national poet, Robert Burns. **Burns' Cottage and Museum** and **Burns' Monument and Gardens** are in nearby Alloway. For the sports lover, Ayr is the home of the Scottish Grand National horse race and one of the finest golf courses, at **Belliesle Estate**.

The TIC can book bus tours and boat trips. Guides and guided walks are available.

Auld Kirk, *off High St; tel: (01292) 262938.* Open Tue, Thur 1930–2030 (July–Aug). Admission free. **Loudoun Hall**, *Boat Vennel, off Cross,*

Scotland's National Poet

The enduring popularity of **Robert Burns** (1759–96) is reflected in the 'Burns Night' celebrations still enjoyed worldwide on his birthday, 25 Jan. A farmer's son, Burns worked on farms for most of this life, but the publication of his *Poems, Chiefly in the Scottish Dialect* in 1786 brought immediate success. Later he avidly collected and wrote Scottish traditional songs, and is best remembered for some of his lyrical pieces such as *Auld Lang Syne.*

Literary pilgrims can follow a Burns Trail in Alloway, now a suburb of Ayr, where the whitewashed thatched cottage where he was born is now a museum. Further south, the house where he died in Dumfires contains memorabilia; and he, his wife and their five sons are buried in St Michael's Churchyard.

Ayr; tel: (01292) 282109. Open Mon–Sat 1000–1700 (July–Aug). Admission free.

Out of Town

Culzean Castle (NT) and Country Park, *by Maybole; tel: (01655) 760274.* Castle open daily 1030–1730 (Apr–Oct), country park open all year. Admission £6.50. 12 miles south of Ayr. Nearest town is Maybole (1 mile from castle). Excursions available – ask at the TIC. **Dean Castle and Country Park**, *Kilmarnock; tel: (01563) 22702.* Open all year. Admission £2; 1 mile from the centre, take bus no. 4 from central bus station. **Burns Cottage and Museum, Monument and Garden**, *Alloway; tel: (01292) 441215.* Cottage open all year, gardens open Apr–Oct. Admission £2.20. Three miles from town centre, take bus no. 61 from central bus station. **Scottish Maritime Museum**, *Irvine; tel: (01294) 278283.* Open daily (Apr–Oct). Admission £2; ½ mile from the centre.

Wonderwest World, *Dunure Rd, Ayr; tel: (01292) 265141.* Open daily May–Oct. Admission £5. Five miles south from the town centre, take bus no. 61 from central bus station.

CHESTER

Lying just outside the Welsh border, Chester was originally a Roman stronghold, and a flourishing medieval port before the tidal estuary of the Dee silted up from the 15th century. This legacy has left the best-preserved city wall in England, and an exceptional architectural heritage within it, which Chester has an enviable record for preserving. Allow a couple of days to do it justice.

Tourist Information

TIC: *Town Hall, Northgate St, Chester, Cheshire CH1 2HJ; tel: (01244) 317962, 324324, 313126.* Open Mon–Sat 0900–1700 (Nov–Apr), Mon–Sat 0900–1930 (May–Oct), Sun 1000–1600 (all year). DP Services offered: local bed-booking service and BABA (latest 30 mins before closing), advance reservations handled, guided tours booked. Bookings made for bus tours and chauffeur-driven tours, YHA and Cadw membership; tickets sold for theatre and events. Free *Chester Visitor Guide* includes accommodation listing. Accommodation bookings busiest from 1500–1700; for bookings also *tel: (01244) 318356.*

TIC: *Chester Visitor Centre, Vicar's Lane; tel: (01244) 351609.* Open 0900–1900 (Nov–Mar), 0900–2100 (Apr–Oct). DP Services offered: local bed-booking service (latest 1700 winter, 1900 summer), advance reservations handled, BABA (latest 1700), guided tours booked, bureau de change. Bookings made as at TIC above, plus National Express tickets.

TIC: *Chester Railway Station, Station Rd; tel: (01244) 322220.* DP Services offered: local bed-booking service, BABA, guided tours booked.

Arriving and Departing

Station
Chester Railway Station, *Station Rd; tel:* *(01244) 346737* is 1 mile east of the town centre, with a connecting bus running every 10 mins (30 mins evenings and Suns). Facilities: TIC (see above), taxi rank and car hire (**Europcar** at *Brook St*, 5 mins walk, *tel: (01244) 312893*).

Buses
Regional buses and National Express operate from the bus station on *Delamere St; tel: (01244) 602666,* in the centre.

Getting Around

Local and regional bus transport is regular and frequent, with good evening coverage in town, but limited evening and Sun services to outlying areas. For enquiries *tel: (01244) 602666.*

Chester also offers a **Women's Safe Transport Service**, pre-booked door-to-door service from 1830–2400, Mon–Sat, *tel: (01244) 300996,* and the **Chester Dial-a-Ride** service for disabled people unable to use ordinary buses, *tel: (01244) 301301.* Free town and transport maps are available from the TICs.

Buses
Most local services operate from the **Bus Exchange Point** on *Princess St,* and are run by a number of different companies.

Taxis
The main rank is at the Bus Exchange Point, *Princess St;* taxis can be hailed on the street.

Staying in Chester

Accommodation
Chester and the surrounding area can provide an extremely wide choice of accommodation in all categories, particularly b. & b. It is usually easy to book on arrival, except during the Chester Races (held on specific dates from May–Sept, check with TIC).

Hotel chains in Chester include *BW, FC, Ja, MC, MH, Mn.* The majority of cheaper rooms can be found in the suburbs *Hoole* and *Hough Green* (1½ miles east and west of centre). For self-catering accommodation, contact **Chester Holiday Homes**, *PO Box 799, Chester CH1 3GB; tel: (01270) 610633.*

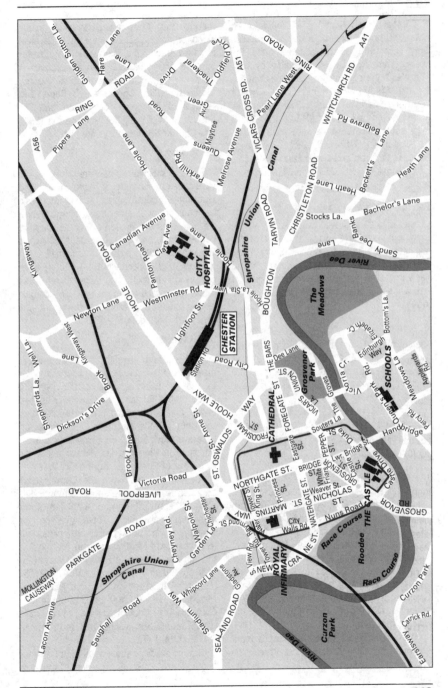

Chester Youth Hostel is at *Hough Green House, 40 Hough Green; tel: (01244) 680056.* Open from 1500 (closed Dec to early Jan). The nearest campsites are all accessible by bus: **Thornleigh Park Farm**, *Ferry Lane, Sealand Rd; tel: (01244) 371718.* 1½ miles west. **Chester Southerly Caravan Park**, *Balderton Lane, Marlston-cum-Lache; tel: (01244) 270791.* 3 miles south. **Birchbank Farm**, *Stamford Lane, Christleton; tel: (01244) 335233.* 3 miles east. **Fairoaks Caravan and Camp Park**, *Rake Lane, Little Stanney; tel: (0151) 355 1600.* 3 miles north.

Eating and Drinking

Chester is well endowed with eating places, from gourmet to take-away. The main areas for restaurants are around *Eastgate St, Watergate St, Lower Bridge St* and *Northgate St.* The TIC has a free restaurant guide. Cheshire cheese (in red, white and blue) and fresh Dee salmon are local specialities.

Communications

The main post office is on *St John St,* open Mon–Fri 0900–1730 (Wed from 0930), Sat 0900–1230 and post restante facilities are available.

Money

Thomas Cook bureaux de change: *10 Bridge St,* and at Midland Bank, *47 Eastgate St.*

Entertainment and Events

The TIC has a free monthly *What's On* guide, and there are listings in the local papers. The main arts venue is **Chester Gateway Theatre**, *The Forum, Hamilton Place; tel: (01244) 340392,* and the main spectator sports venue is **Chester Racecourse**, *The Roodee; tel: (01244) 323170* for the famous Chester horse races, the oldest in the country.

Chester also has a large number of discos, winebars, two multi-screen cinemas and **Alexander's Jazz Theatre**, *Rufus Court off Northgate St,* for live music.

The following are some of Chester's more important annual events: **Chester Races**, *The Racecourse, The Roodee* – May–Sept (held on

specific dates). **Chester Regatta** (oldest in the world) on the *River Dee* in June. **River Carnival and Raft Race** on the *River Dee* in July. **Chester Summer Music Festival**, *various locations in town,* in July. **Literature Festival**, *various locations,* in Oct. **Lord Mayor's Show and Festival of Transport**, *City Centre and The Roodee,* in May. Every five years (next in 1997), **The Chester Mystery Plays** are held.

Shopping

The main shopping areas are *Foregate St, Watergate St, Eastgate St, Northgate St* and *Grosvenor Precinct* (covered mall). Chester has a large number of antique shops, many of which are on Watergate St. Don't miss the **Cheshire Candle Shop**, *Bridge St Row,* or the **Cheshire Workshops**, *Burwardsley, Tattenhall; tel: (01829) 70401,* open daily 1000–1700 (8 miles east by car or taxi) – the largest hand-carved candle manufacturer in Europe. For bargain hunters there is a Mon–Sat market at *The Forum,* off *Northgate St.*

Sightseeing

Chester is a fairly compact city which rewards the stroller. The ideal way to get your bearings is to walk the two-mile circuit of the city walls. Much of the Roman wall survives, with two towers and gates added in the Middle Ages. Look out for the elaborate, if anachronistic, **Eastgate Clock** (1897) on *Eastgate St* and the exhibition in **King Charles' Tower** about the long siege of Chester during the Civil War.

Alternatively, start with the **Chester Heritage Centre**, which gives an excellent introduction to the city's history, or with one of the many tours available – boat trips on the attractive river and canal are particularly recommended. Most tours can be booked through the TIC: **Guide Friday** bus tours (£5), trips on **Bithell's Boats** *tel: (01244) 325394* (£3), canal trips and cruises from **Mill Hotel**, *Milton St; tel: (01244) 350035* (from £1). **Chester City Council** guided town walks (£1.95) and 'Ghost Hunter Trail Tours' Thurs–Sat 1930 (May–Oct).

Historic buildings abound, but don't miss the famous **Rows** – two tiered galleries of walkways and shops, built in medieval and Tudor times in elaborate half-timbered style. The principal Rows are *Eastgate, Northgate, Watergate* and *Bridge St*, and they now form a thriving shopping area, somewhat incongrously housing many high street names. A life-size recreation of the Rows in Victorian times can be seen at the **Chester Visitor Centre**. **Chester Castle** dates from Norman times, but what remains is principally 19th-century restoration: the castle now houses the **Military Museum**, which has memorabilia of the Cheshire Regiment. Chester's squat, sandstone **Cathedral** is mainly 14th-century, though it was well restored in the 1870s; it has some fine medieval woodcarving. The three bridges spanning the Dee – the **Old Dee Bridge** (*Lower Bridge St*), the elegant **Suspension Bridge** (*The Groves*) and **Grosvenor Bridge** (*Grosvenor St*) are also worth a look.

Roman finds are well displayed at the **Grosvenor Museum** (which also has good paintings and silver collections and Georgian and Victorian period rooms), and you can see part of the largest Roman **amphitheatre** in Britain outside Newgate on *Vicar's Lane*. At **Roman Deva Experience**, a Roman galley transports visitors to a recreation of Roman Chester. Chester also has a good **Toy Museum**, which boasts among its antique playthings a vast collection of Dinkey and Lesney cars.

Out of town, **Chester Zoo** is one of the best in Britain, with its animals in semi-natural enclosures. Further north at Ellesmere Port the **Boat Museum**, occupying a historic canal dock, has the world's largest floating collection of canal craft, large and small, some of which can be boarded. Ruined 13th-century **Beeston Castle** has unusual crusader-like defences and stupendous, panoramic views; on the next hill lies **Peckforton Castle**, a fine 19th-century mock-medieval fortress complete with a vaulted Great Hall and a minstrels' gallery. Both castles are landmarks visible from miles around, rising above the Cheshire Plain.

Churches and Cathedrals

Chester Cathedral, *St Werburgh St; tel: (01244) 324756*. Open daily 0700–1830.

Admission free. **St John's Church and St John's Ruins**, *Vicar's Lane; tel: (01244) 350607*. Open Mon–Sat 0930–1730, Sun 0800–2000. Admission free.

Museums

Cheshire Military Museum, *The Castle; tel: (01244) 327617*. Open daily 0900–1700; closed 18 Dec to 2 Jan. Admission £0.50. **Chester Heritage Centre**, *Bridge St Row; tel: (01244) 321616*. Open Mon–Sat 1100–1700, Sun 1200–1700. Admission £1. **Chester Toy Museum**, *13a Lower Bridge St; tel: (01244) 346297*. Open daily 1100–1700. Admission £1.50. **Chester Visitor Centre**, *Vicar's Lane; tel: (01244) 351609*. Open daily 0900–1800. Admission free. **Deva Roman Experience**, *Pierpoint Lane, off Bridge St; tel:(01244) 343407*. Open daily 0900–1700. Admission £3.80. **Grosvenor Museum**, *Grosvenor St; tel: (01244) 321616*. Open Mon–Sat 1030–1700, Sun 1400–1700. Admission free. **King Charles' Tower and Water Tower**, *City Walls; tel: (01244)321616*. Open daily 1100–1600 (mid-June to mid-Sept). Admission £0.40 for King Charles' and £0.90 for Water Tower. **On the Air, Broadcasting Museum & Vintage Sound Shop**, *42 Bridge St Row; tel: (01244) 348468*. Open daily 1000–1700. Admission £1.95.

Out of Town

Beeston Castle (EH), *Beeston*. Open 1000–1800 (Apr–Oct), 1000–1600 (Nov–Mar). Admission £2. Bus 64, C83, L2 to *Beeston*, 6 miles east. **Boat Museum**, *Ellesmere Port; tel: (0151) 355 5017*. Open daily 1000–1700 (Oct–Apr); Sat–Weds 1000–1600 (Nov–Mar). Admission £4.50. Bus 2, 2c, 3, 4, 11c, 12c, 36, 100, 853, C76,X3, X8, 702 to *Ellesmere Port*, 6 miles north. **Chester Zoo**, *Upton-by-Chester; tel: (01244) 380280*. Open 1000–1900 (last admission 1730). Admission £6.50. Bus 11c, 12c, 36,40, 40a, 853, C41, C43, X20, 2 miles northeast. **Peckforton Castle**, *Peckforton, near Tarporley; tel: (01829) 260930*. Open daily 1000–1800 (Easter to mid-Sept). Admission £2.50. Bus (infrequent) C83 to *Peckforton*, 10 miles east.

CHESTER to BANGOR

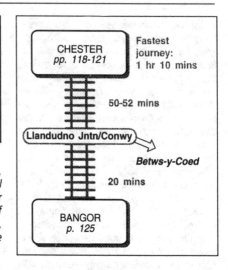

Snaking along the rugged north coast of Wales, this itinerary takes in the massive medieval castles of Conwy and Caernarvon – the latter the scene of the investiture of the Prince of Wales in 1969. It also covers Betws-y-Coed, gateway to the mountainous drama of the Snowdonia National Park.

TRAINS

ETT table: 555

 Fast Track

One train per hour (extras at times, but less frequent on Suns) runs between Chester and Bangor, taking between 1 hr 10 mins and 1 hour 20 mins depending on stops.

 On Track

Chester–Conwy–Bangor

The regular service from Chester to Bangor calls at Llandudno Junction (and a few call at Conwy on request 2 mins later). Alternatively, Conwy is a 15 min-walk across the road bridge (great views) from Llandudno Junction. There is also a regular, more convenient bus service stopping nearby. The Chester–Bangor service takes 50 mins to Llandudno Junction and a further 20 mins to Bangor.

CONWY

TIC: Castle Buildings, *Castle St, Conwy, Gwynedd LL32 8LD; tel: (01492) 592248.* Open daily 0930–1800 (end Mar to end Oct), Mon–Sat 1000–1600, Sun 1100–1600 (end Oct to end Mar). DP Services offered: local bed-

booking service and BABA (latest 30 mins before closing), advance reservations handled. *Conwy Towers Above* is available free of charge. **Station**: Conwy Station, *Rosemary Lane; tel: (01492) 585151* is in the centre of town. There is no taxi rank (see below for taxi information).

Getting Around

Attractions are walkable from the centre. The TIC has free town maps and timetables. Most local bus services are operated by **Crosville Cymru** *tel: (01492) 596969.* Services are good, but reduced after 1800 and on Suns in winter. There is a taxi rank at *Lancaster Sq*, or contact **Elwyn's Taxis** *tel: (01492) 592344.*

Staying in Conwy

There is a small range of hotels, including one in the *FC* chain, and a reasonable choice of guesthouse and b. & b. accommodation. It is generally easy to book on arrival. The closest youth hostel is **Rowen Youth Hostel** (5 miles south), *Rhiw Farm, Rowen; tel: (01492) 530627* (closed winter); bus 19. The nearest campsite is **Conwy Touring Park**, 1½ miles south on the B5106 road; *tel: (01492) 592856;* take bus no. 19.

Sightseeing

Conwy has probably the most complete surviving medieval walls of any town in Britain, although surprisingly few old buildings remain within it (the oldest is the carefully refurbished 14th-century **Aberconwy House**). Conwy's glory is Edward I's **Castle**, dominating the town with its massive towers and barbicans; seemingly hewn from its narrow rocky promontory, this is one of Wales' finest and most complete fortresses. You can walk around the **town walls** from here.

Ask at the TIC for the *Conwy Town Trail* leaflet, which guides you to the most important sights, including Telford's delicate, drawbridge-like suspension bridge (1827) and the Stephenson rail bridge (1848). On the pretty harbour-front you can see what is reputedly Britain's smallest house. River trips are also available; for details see notices on The Quay or *tel: (01492) 592284*. Out of town in the lush Conwy Valley; **Bodnant Garden** is one of the finest in Britain, with the bonus of views across to Snowdonia.

Aberconwy House (NT), *Castle Street; tel: (01492) 592246*. Open Wed–Mon 1100–1730 (last entry 1700). Admission £1.80.

Conwy Butterfly Jungle, *Bodlondeb Park; tel: (01492) 593149*. Open daily 1000–1730 (Apr–Sept), 1000–1600 (Oct). Admission £2.50.

Conwy Castle and Town Walls (Cadw), *Castle St; tel: (01492) 592358*. Open daily 0930–1830 (end Mar to end Oct), Mon–Sat 0930–1600, Sun 1100–1600 (end Oct to end Mar). Admission £2.90.

Out of Town

Bodnant Garden (NT), *Tal-y-Cafn; tel: (01492) 650460*. Open daily 1000–1700 (last Admission 1630) (mid-Mar to end Oct). Admission £3.60. 10-min walk to *Llandudno Junction*, then bus 25, 5 miles south.

- - - - - - - - - - - - - - - - - - - -

 Side Track from Conwy

BETWS-Y-COED

TIC: Snowdonia National Park Visitor Centre, *Y Stablau, Betws-y-Coed, Gwynedd LL24 0AH; tel: (01690) 710426*. Open daily 1000–1800 (Apr–Oct), 1000–1700 (Nov–Mar). DP Services

offered: local bed-booking service and BABA (latest 15 mins before closing), advance reservations handled. Guided tours booked, Cadw membership sold. *Betws-y-Coed Guide*, which includes an accommodation listing, costs £0.80. **Station**: Betws-y-Coed Station, *Station Rd; tel: (01492) 585151* is in the town centre. There is no taxi rank (see below for taxi information). There are about 6 services daily from Llandudno Junction, taking around 25 mins.

Getting Around

Attractions are mainly outside Betws-y-Coed. Free transport maps are available from the TIC. Most local buses are operated by **Crosville** *tel: (01492) 596969*, **Selwyns** *tel: (01492) 640814* and **D & G** *tel: (01248) 600787*. Services are reasonable, but there are none in the evenings. **Road Runner Travel** *tel: (01690) 710521*.

Staying in Betws-y-Coed

There is a small range of hotel accommodation in the town and a very good choice of guesthouse and b. & b. accommodation. It is generally easy to book on arrival, except over Easter. The closest youth hostels are **Capel Curig** (5 miles west), *Plas Curig; tel: (01690) 4225*; take bus no. 19 or 65, and **Lledr Youth Hostel** (4 miles south-west), *Pont y Pant; tel: (01690) 6202*; take bus 69 or 84. There are two campsites in the town, at **Hendre Farm** (no telephone) and **Riverside** *tel: (01690) 710310*.

Sightseeing

Lying at the meeting place of three valleys, Betws-y-Coed makes a perfect – though busy – place from which to explore the Snowdonia National Park, with its dramatic mountains, lakes and forest trails. Guided walks are available starting from the TIC, and the public transport 'Sherpa' bus 19 is a good sightseeing route. This is an ideal base for country walking – eg. to the famous **Swallow Falls** nearby.

Apart from walking, narrow gauge railways offer the best means of seeing the scenery. The **Snowdon Mountain Railway** travels to the summit of Snowdon, Wales' highest peak, while the **Ffestiniog Railway** takes a spectacular route from Blaenau Ffestiniog, once the heart of Snowdonia's slate industry to Porthmadog. Victorian mining conditions have been recreated at the **Llechwedd Slate Caverns**. At **Power of Wales**, Merlin is your guide on a journey through Welsh history, and you can also visit Dinorwig, the largest underground pumped storage power station in Europe.

Betws-y-Coed Motor Museum, tel: (01690) 710760. Open daily 1000–1800 (Easter–Oct). Admission £0.90. **Conwy Valley Railway Museum**, tel: (01690) 710568. Open daily 1015–1730 (Easter–Oct), Sat, Sun 1030–1630 (winter). Admission £1. **Swallow Falls**. Open at all times. Admission £0.40 (through turnstile). Two miles west on A5; take bus no. 19.

Out of Town

Ffestiniog Railway (13 miles south) – see Private Railways, pp. 339–340. **Llanberis Lake Railway** (13 miles west), *Llanberis; tel: (01286) 870549.* Open Mon–Thur (early Mar to late Oct), Fri and Sun (May–Sept), Sat (July and Aug), telephone for exact times. Admission £3.60. Bus 19 to *Llanberis*. **Llechwedd Slate Caverns** (13 miles south) *Blaenau Ffestiniog; tel: (01766) 830523.* Open daily 1000–1715 (Mar–Sept), 1000–1615 (Oct–Feb). Admission £4.70 for single tour. Train to *Blaenau Ffestiniog*. **Portmeirion** – see Portmeirion, at the end of this chapter. **Power of Wales** (13 miles north-west), *Llanberis; tel: (01286) 870636.* Open 0930–1800 (June to mid-Sept). Includes trips to an underground hydroelectric power station. Admission £5. Bus 19 to *Llanberis*. **Snowdon Mountain Railway**, *Llanberis; tel: (01286) 870223.* See Private Railways, pp. 339–340. Open mid-Mar to end Oct, telephone for exact times. Fare £13.20. Bus no. 19 to *Llanberis*, 13 miles west.

BANGOR

TIC: *Theatr Gwynedd, Deiniol Rd, Bangor, Gwynedd LL57 2TL; tel: (01248) 352786.* Open Mon–Sat 0930–1700, also Sun (July and Aug only) (Easter to end Sept). Services offered: local bed-booking service and BABA (latest 1630), advance reservations handled. *Bangor*

Guide costs £0.50, and a free accommodation list is also available.

Station: Bangor Station, *Holyhead Rd*; tel: (01407) 769222 is half a mile south-west of the centre and has a taxi rank.

Getting Around

With the exception of **Penrhyn Castle**, the town's attractions are walkable from the centre. Free town and transport maps are available from the TIC. Anglesey and the North Wales coast are accessible by train, and there is a bus service for Bangor and surrounding areas. Bus services (reduced on Suns and after 2000) are run by **Crosville**, tel: (01248) 370295. The main taxi rank is on *Ffordd Gwynedd*.

Staying in Bangor

It is usually easy to book on arrival. There is a small choice of hotels, and a larger range of b. & b. and guesthouse accommodation. For budget accommodation there is a youth hostel at *Tan-y-Bryn*; tel: (01248) 353516. The closest campsites are **Woodside**, *Holyhead Rd*; tel: (01248) 362618, 1 mile west, and **Treborth Hall** (2 miles west), *Treborth Hall Farm*; tel: (01248) 364104. Take bus no. 4, 57 or 62.

Sightseeing

This university city, lying between the mountains of Snowdonia and the island of Anglesey, has a small but charming **cathedral**, restored by Sir George Gilbert Scott in the 1870s; the tranquil **Bible Garden** beside it is planted with trees, shrubs and flowers referred to in the Bible. A ½ mile walk from the *High St* takes you to the plateau at the top of **Bangor Mountain**.

Bangor is a good base from which to explore some of Wales' finest castles. Two miles outside Bangor lies mock-Norman **Penrhyn Castle**; built in 1820–45, it has a richly decorated Victorian interior and lovely gardens. Hugely impressive **Caernarfon** was the mightiest of the fortresses built by Edward I after his conquest of Wales, while across on Anglesey, moated **Beaumaris Castle** is the most perfect example of a concentrically planned castle in Britain.

The large island of Anglesey itself, lying across the Menai Strait and spanned by two great bridges built by Telford and Stephenson, has many good beaches. Overlooking the Strait, **Plas Newydd** is an 18th-century house in unspoilt surroundings, with lovely lawns and parkland. Boat trips leave from *The Pier* daily in the summer.

Bangor Cathedral, *High St; tel: (01248) 370693.* Open daily 0645–1800. Admission free. **Bangor Museum and Art Gallery**, *Ffordd Gwynedd; tel: (01248) 353368.* Open Tues–Sat 1200–1630. Admission free. **Bangor Pier**, *Garth Point; tel: (01248) 352421.* Open 0830–2130 (summer), 1000–1600 (winter). Admission £0.20. **Bible Garden**, *Ffordd Gwynedd.* Open at all times. Admission free. **Penrhyn Castle** (NT), *Llandygai; tel: (01248) 353084.* Open Wed–Mon 1200–1700 (Apr–Oct), 1100–1700 (July and Aug). Last admission 1630. Grounds open 1100–1800. Admission £4.40. Take bus 54 from Bangor Town Clock. One mile east.

Out of Town

Beaumaris Castle (Cadw), *Beaumaris, Anglesey; tel: (01248) 810361.* Open daily 0930–1830 (late Mar to late Oct), Mon–Fri 0930–1600, Sun 1100–1600 (late Oct to late Mar). Admission £1.50. Take bus 57 (10 miles north). **Caernarfon Castle** (Cadw), *The Square, Caernarfon; tel: (01286) 677617.* Open daily 0900–1800. Admission £3.50. Take bus 5a. Nine miles south-west. **Plas Newydd** (NT), *Llanfairpwll, Anglesey; tel: (01248) 714795.* Open Sun–Fri 1200–1700 (Apr–Sept), Fri and Sun 1200–1700 (Oct). Last admission 1630. Admission £3.80. Take bus 42. Eight miles south-west. **Llanberis Lake Railway, Power of Wales** and **Snowdon Mountain Railway** – see Betws-y-Coed, p. 123

 Side Track from Bangor

PORTMEIRION

Tourist Information: Hotel Portmeirion, *Portmeirion, Gwynedd LL48 6ET; tel: (01766) 770228.*

Stations: the nearest mainline station to Portmeirion is approximately 20 miles north at **Bangor**. Access from here can be made by train to Blaenau Ffestiniog and then by the private Festiniog Railway (when running) to Minffordd or, much quicker, by bus (5/5A Bangor–Caernarfon, 1/2 Caernarfon–Porthmadog). The closest local railway stations to Portmeirion are Porthmadog, and Minffordd (within 2 miles) both on the **Cambrian Coast Line** from Shrewsbury. The Hotel can arrange for taxis to meet you on arrival.

Staying in Portmeirion

The main hotel has 14 rooms, and there are a further 24 rooms and suites in various locations throughout the village. In addition, there are 16 cottages suitable for families wishing to stay for a week or more on a self-catering basis. The village is open as an attraction daily from 0930–1730. Admission £3 (£1.50 Nov–Mar). There are various shops and a self-service restaurant – non-residents can also eat in the Hotel Portmeirion dining room. Due to the many steps and steep slopes, the village is not well suited to visitors in wheelchairs.

Sightseeing

This bizarre village – given popular fame by the cult British TV series *The Prisoner* – is well worth a day's detour. It was the product of the imagination of one man – Sir Clough Williams-Ellis, a Welsh architect who dreamed of creating a perfect village which would not mar the beauty of its natural setting.

His fantastic creation, built between 1925 and 1972, has a distinctly Italianate flavour, with its colourful domes and towers, castle and lighthouse, cobbled squares and pastel-coloured villas, and the plush hotel serving as a focus. The site, a little rocky peninsula overlooking Cardigan Bay, has miles of paths through its deep, subtropical woodlands, leading to rocky coves and sandy beaches along the headland.

EDINBURGH

Edinburgh, Scotland's gracious capital, is steeped in history. Much of its past is associated with the tragic Mary, Queen of Scots, and many of the ancient buildings date from her time. The city offers a feast of things to see and do and is so compact that all its contrasting sights can easily be explored on foot, from the courtyards and cobbles of the Old Town to the leafy avenues and Georgian houses of the New Town. The city's many distinguished buildings helped it gain its title of 'The Athens of the North'.

All the traditional images of Scotland can be found in Edinburgh: tartan, bagpipes, fine malt whisky and dramatic scenery. Its rich cultural heritage includes many exiting events and festivals held throughout the year; highlights are the spectacular Edinburgh International Festival and Edinburgh Festival Fringe.

Tourist Information

Edinburgh and Scotland Information Centre, 3 Princes Street EH2 2QP; tel: (0131) 557 1700, fax: (0131) 557 5118. Open Mon–Sat 0900–1800 (Nov–Mar), Mon–Sat 0900–1800, Sun 1100–1800 (Apr and Oct), Mon–Sat 0900–1900, Sun 1100–1900 (May, Jun and Sept), Mon–Sat 0900–2000, Sun 1100–2000 (Jul and Aug). DP services offered; local bed-booking service available, £3 booking fee plus 10% deposit, BABA £2.75 booking fee plus 10% deposit. Self catering booking service. There is a ticket system so be prepared to queue for accommodation bookings. Guided tours can also be booked. Bureau de change available. Lothian Region Transport Coach Tours and Passes, Guide Friday, Rabbies Trail Burners, Blue Banana tours, Scotline, Citylink, SMT, National Express tickets and passes, Scotrail Rovers and pass, can all be booked here. Also walking tours of the city and Scottish evenings at various hotels. Theatre and concert hall tickets for Royal Lyceum, The Traverse, Theatre Workshop and The Queens Hall. The Great British Heritage Pass, Historic Scotland Pass and NT Scotland Touring Pass are sold here. Ticket Hotline tel: (0131) 558 1072.

Edinburgh Holidays (including accommodation listing) and The Essential Guide to Edinburgh are available free and separate area accommodation listings are sold at £0.25. The TIC also has a wide range of guides, maps, souvenirs and videos of Edinburgh and Scotland for sale.

Tourist Information Desk, Edinburgh Airport; tel: (0131) 333 2167, fax: (0131) 335 3576. Open Mon–Sat 0900–1800, Sun 0930–1700 (Nov–Mar), Mon–Sat 0900–2130, Sun 0930–2130 (Apr–Oct). DP service offered; local bed-booking and BABA (see main TIC above for charges). Full range of tickets and guides as for main TIC.

The Lothian Coalition of Disabled People, 13 Johnston Ter; tel: (0131) 220 6855, publish a collection of useful leaflets on access for people with disabilities. The leaflets cover cinemas, theatres and concert halls, hotels, museums and art galleries and restaurants. **Artsline** is an arts and disability organisation; for further information tel: (0131) 229 3555.

Arriving and Departing

Waverley Station, tel: (0131) 556 2451, is in the city centre. **Hertz Rent-a-Car** has a car hire office there and there is a taxi rank at the station.

Getting Around

Many of the attractions in the town are within a walkable area of the centre. Free transport maps are available at the TIC and from **Traveline,** St Giles St; tel: (0131) 225 3858. Public transport is very good both in the city and to outlying areas, running frequent, comprehensive and cheap services from early morning until late in the evening. After midnight special hourly night service buses take over.

Buses

Lothian Region Transport (LRT), whose buses

are maroon coloured *tel: (0131) 225 3858* and **SMT,** whose buses are green and white, *tel: (0131) 558 1616* are the main companies offering bus services in and around the city. Most services start from the central bus station in *St Andrew Sq.* Daily, weekly and monthly passes are available from both companies but are not interchangeable

Taxis

The main taxi rank is **Waverley Cabs** at *Waverley Station; tel: (0131) 557 5559* and it is possible to hail taxis in the street. Other taxi companies are **Capital Castle Taxis,** *tel: (0131) 228 2555;* **Radiocabs,** *tel: (0131) 225 9000;* **Central Radio Taxis,** *tel: (0131) 229 2468;* **City Cabs,** *tel: (0131) 228 1211.* Many taxis in Edinburgh can take wheelchairs, indicated by the wheelchair sign attached to the front.

Staying in Edinburgh

Accommodation

It is always a good idea to book accommodation in advance, especially in August and Septtember, but it is usually possible to book on the day. There is an enormous range of accommodation in and around the city, from large chain and independent hotels to small hotels, guesthouses and b. & b. establishments. The majority of cheaper accommodation is on the edge of the city centre and in suburbs like *Portobello, and Joppa* (3 miles east), and *Costorphine* (4 miles west). Availability is affected by the **Edinburgh Festival, Edinburgh Fringe Festival, Edinburgh Tattoo and Edinburgh Film Festival,** all of which take place in August and Septtember. Hotel chains in Edinburgh include: *Forte Grand, MH, Ic, Ho, SC, Sh, Nv, North British Trust Hotels*

There are nine youth hostels in Edinburgh, including **SYHA Youth Hostel,** *18 Eglinton Cres; tel: (0131) 337 1120,* open all year, all day until 0200. Vacate rooms by 1000. Bus 26, 31, 69, 85 and 86 from TIC to Palmerston Place; **Princes Street Hostel,** *3 West Register St; tel: (0131) 556 6894,* open all year, daily May–Oct, 2 minutes walk from bus and train stations. **Belford Youth Hostel,** *6/8 Douglas Gdns; tel:*

(0131) 225 6209 is in the city centre and open all year round. The TIC has a free list of youth accommodation. The SYHA Head Office is at *161 Warrender Park Rd; tel: (0131) 229 8660,* open for enquiries Mon–Fri 0900–1700, Sat 0900–1230.

The nearest campsites are **Mortonhall Caravan Site,** *Frogston Rd East; tel: (0131) 664 1533.* Take bus 11 from Princes St, garden side beyond the Scott Monument. **Silverknowes Caravan Park,** *Marine Dr; tel: (0131) 312 6874.* Take Bus 8A up to 1800 hours, bus 14 after 1800 from North Bridge. **France Caravan Park,** *219 Old Dalkeith Rd; tel: (0131) 666 2326,* On A7 road from Edinburgh to Newcastle upon Tyne, 3 miles south of the city centre. **Fordel Camp Site,** *Lauder Rd, Dalkeith, Midlothian; tel: (0131) 660 3921,* 9 miles south of Edinburgh.

Eating and Drinking

Edinburgh has a huge and varied selection of restaurants in and around the city. It is possible to eat good food quite cheaply, as well as choosing one of the many gourmet eating places. The TIC has a free list of restaurants, pubs and wine bars in the centre and in outlying areas. There are a number of restaurants offering Scottish fare, including haggis and Scotch beef. There are at least two vegetarian restaurants, **Helios Fountain,** *7 Grassmarket; tel: (0131) 229 7884* and **Henderson's Salad Table and Wine Bar,** *94 Hanover St; tel: (0131) 225 2131.* Recently a branch of **Harry Ramsden's,** the famous fish and chip restaurants, opened at *Newhaven Harbour; tel: (0131) 551 5566.* As well as haggis, sample shortbread, Scotch whisky and Edinburgh Rock while visiting the city.

Communications

The main post office is on *2–4 Waterloo Pl* and has post restante facilities.

Money

Centrally located **Thomas Cook** bureaux de change include *79A Princes St* and *Waverley Steps, Princes St,* as well as in the British Airways office at *30/32 Frederick St.*

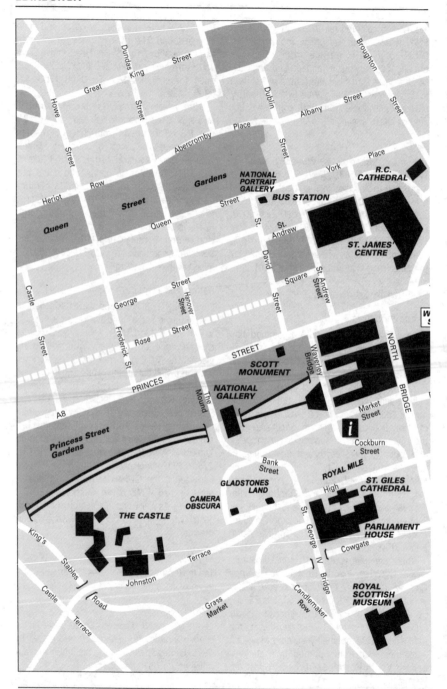

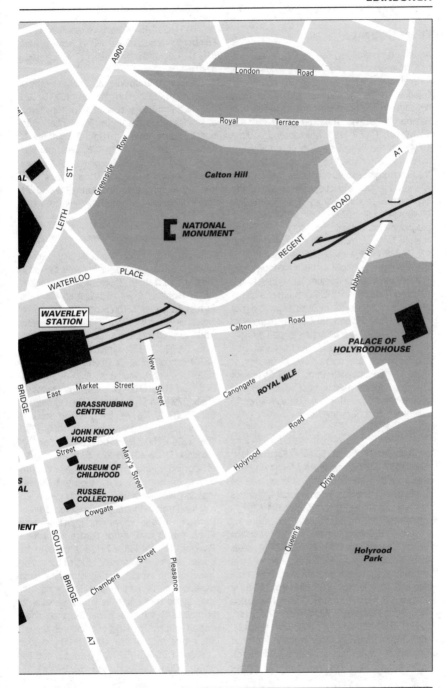

Entertainment

An entertainments list, *Day by Day*, is available free from the TIC and *The List Magazine*, a fortnightly guide to events in Edinburgh and Glasgow, is also available at the TIC or from newsagents. The latest performance venue, **The Edinburgh Festival Theatre**, *13–29 Nicolson St; tel: (0131) 662 1199*, which opened in June 1994, has the largest stage in Britain and is a major venue for concerts and opera. Many of the **Edinburgh Festival** events are held here, as well as other top productions. Any bus from the city centre stops nearby. **The Edinburgh Playhouse**, *tel: (0131) 557 2590*, offers a programme of musicals, pop, rock and comedy acts all the year round. **The Usher Hall**, *tel: (0131) 228 1155*, with its 2700-seat auditorium, is Edinburgh's principal orchestral concert hall. The **Meadowbank Stadium**, *London Rd; tel: (0131) 661 5351*, is Scotland's premier athletics arena. It is about 15 minutes from the city centre by bus. **Hillend Ski Centre**, *Biggar Rd; tel: (0131) 669 0404*, is Britain's longest artificial ski slope. Edinburgh has six municipal golf courses which are open daily. A full list of these can be obtained from the TIC, free of charge. Other entertainment and nightlife venues can be found in the *Essential Guide to Edinburgh*, free from the TIC.

Events

Scottish International Science Festival, *tel: (0131) 557 4296* is held in April for about three weeks, with workshops and talks as well as family events. **Scottish International Children's Festival**, *22 Laurie St; tel: (0131) 554 6297* (1 week in May) is the best theatre for children.

Royal Highland Show, *Royal Highland Centre, Ingliston; tel: (0131) 333 2444*, takes place annually in June. It is Scotland's main agricultural show, but also a flower show, craft fair and food exhibition. **Edinburgh Military Tattoo**, *22 Market St, Box Office: The Tattoo Tickets Sales Office, 31/33 Waverley Bridge; tel: (0131) 225 1188, Credit Card Hotline tel: (0131) 225 3661*. Annual outdoor military display at Edinburgh Castle held in August. **Edinburgh International Jazz Festival**, *116 Canongate; tel: (0131) 557 1642*. Held annually in August. **Edinburgh International Film Festival**, *tel: (0131) 228 2688*. International film festival held in August

Edinburgh International Fringe Festival, *Box Office: 180 High St; tel: (0131) 226 5257/5259*. Three weeks of non-stop events at various venues in August/Septtember. **Edinburgh International Festival**, *Box Office: 21 Market St; tel: (0131) 226 4001 and from mid-Apr (0131) 225 5756*. Celebration of the arts, theatre, opera, music and dance. Takes place annually in Aug/Sept. **Hogmanay**, *tel: (0131) 557 1700*, a celebration of the New Year, held on 30/31 Dec and 1 Jan.

Shopping

The main area for shopping in the city is Princes Street, which has all the major stores as well as some specialist shops. There are shops specialising in Highland Dress and Scottish woollens, such as **Burberrys & The Scotch House**, *39–41 Princes St*. Open Mon–Sat 0930–1730; **Kinloch Anderson**, *Commercial St/Dock St, Leith*. Open Mon–Sat 0900–1730; **James Pringle Weavers**, *70/74 Bangor Rd, Leith*. Open Mon–Sat 0900–1700 (Nov–Mar), Mon–Sat 0900–1730 (Apr–Oct), Sun 1000-1700 (all year); **The Cashmere Shop**, *379 High St (opposite St Giles Cathedral); tel: (0131) 225 5178*, has a varied stock of quality cashmere. Open Mon–Sat 1000–1730, Sun 1200–1600. **John Dickson & Son**, *21 Frederick St; tel (0131) 225 4218* are retailers of sporting clothing, fishing tackle and guns, trading for over 170 years. **Ingliston Market**, *Ingliston*, is 10 miles west of the city centre. It is a general market that takes place every Sunday. Edinburgh is also known for crystal and the **Edinburgh Crystal Visitor Centre** at *Eastfield, Penicuik; tel: (01968) 675128* is open to the public. They have 30-minute tours of the factory showing the secrets of glassmaking from glassblowing to cutting and engraving. The shop in the centre has the largest selection of Edinburgh Crystal, plus a woollen shop and a display entitled 'The Story of Edinburgh Crystal'. The centre is open daily 1000–1700 and tours are Mon–Fri 0900–1530 (all year), Sat and Sun 1100–1500 (May–Sept). Also in the city is the

Scotch Whisky Heritage Centre, *354 Castlehill, Royal Mile; tel: (0131) 220 0441*. Open daily 1000–1700. It brings the history of Scotland's national drink vividly to life with a distillery tour and an audio-visual display. **The Scottish Experience and Living Craft Centre** *High St; tel: (0131) 557 9350*, offers the opportunity to see craftsmen at work making kilts, bagpipes and Aran sweaters, weaving tartan or 'throwing' pots. Also Scottish jewellery and sgian shubhs (dirks). Open daily 1000–1800.

Sightseeing

Historic Edinburgh is dominated by its imposing castle and has attractions to suit all tastes and ages. At the heart of the **Old Town** is **The Royal Mile** with its wonderful medieval architecture. This ancient street leads from the Castle to the **Palace of Holyroodhouse**, once the home of Mary, Queen of Scots and the scene of many dramatic events in her life; it is still the Sovereign's official residence in Scotland and the state rooms and historic apartments are open to the public except when the Royal Family are in residence. Perched high on Castle Rock is 12th-century **Edinburgh Castle** – probably Scotland's most famous sight. It was here, in 1566, that Mary, Queen of Scots gave birth to James VI of Scotland (later to become James I of England). Within the Castle's ancient battlements are the Crown Jewels of Scotland and the giant cannon *Mons Meg*. Listen out for the daily 1 o'clock gun fire from the castle ramparts.

The Old Town has many buildings of interest: medieval **John Knox House** (associated with Knox – Scotland's religious reformer); **Gladstone's Land** – a typical 17th-century tenement building; and 12th-century **St Giles Cathedral**, the High Kirk of Edinburgh. The **People's Story** reconstructs the life of Edinburgh people from the 18th century onwards and the **Museum of Childhood** was the first in the world to be devoted to the history of childhood. A couple of streets away from the Royal Mile is the **Royal Museum of Scotland** which has varied collections ranging from natural history and science to decorative arts. Also off the Royal Mile is the **Russell Collection of Early Keyboard Instruments**, an important collection of harpsi-

chords, clavichords, organs, etc, and the **Brass Rubbing Centre**, located in an old Edinburgh church. Edinburgh's **Camera Obscura** offers a unique city tour from inside the giant 1850s camera, though the city's best vantage points are **Calton Hill**, with its collection of monuments, and **Arthur's Seat**, an extinct volcano.

Edinburgh has a well-planned Georgian (18th century) **New Town** which has attractive squares, elegant shopping thoroughfares and several art galleries; the nation's major collections are held at the **National Gallery of Scotland** and the **National Gallery of Modern Art**, whose 20th century paintings include works by Picasso and Matisse. The **Scottish National Portrait Gallery** houses portraits of famous people – like Bonnie Prince Charlie and Robert Burns – who helped shape Scotland's history. Most of the city's main shops are located in **Princes Street** and nearby **Princes Street Gardens** offer a peaceful retreat away from the bustle of city life. Located at the east end of Princes Street is the towering **Scott Monument**, a 200ft-high Gothic spire commemorating the Scottish writer, Sir Walter Scott, which was built in 1840–6 and offers excellent views over the city. More gardens, complete with glasshouses and ponds, can be found at the famous **Royal Botanic Garden**.

In Charlotte Square is the **Georgian House**, a Robert Adam masterpiece and a typical example of New Town architecture. Westwards, beyond Princes Street and Charlotte Square, the pace of life quietens; here is St Stephen Street with its antique shops, the peaceful **Water of Leith** in its tree-shaded valley, and picturesque **Dean Village**, a former milling community. The **Clan Tartan Centre** at Leith Mills enables visitors to discover their Scottish heritage, from clan links to full Highland dress. Also not far from the city centre is **Edinburgh Zoo,** which includes a large penguin enclosure and many endangered species, and the fascinating **Royal Observatory**

To the west of Edinburgh are two of Scotland's finest stately homes: **Dalmeny House** with its superb collections and beautiful grounds, and **Hopetoun House**, with its splendid architecture, state apartments and woodland walks. Just across the famous Forth

Shopping–Sightseeing **131**

Road Bridge is **Deep Sea World**, the largest aquarium of its kind in the world. The **Scottish Agricultural Museum** at Ingliston depicts the life and work of Scotland's countryside over the last 200 years, and at the **Almond Valley Heritage Centre** there are farm animals, museum attractions and nature trails. South of Edinburgh are delightful **Craigmillar Castle**, once a retreat of Mary, Queen of Scots, and **Edinburgh Butterfly and Insect World** with free-flying butterflies in a tropical environment. Yet farther south is the **Scottish Mining Museum**, where former miners guide visitors round the displays at the old Lady Victoria Colliery.

Tours and Walks

Guide Friday, tel: (0131) 556 2244, and **Lothian Region Transport**, tel: (0131) 220 4111, operate regular open-top bus tours of the city starting from Waverley Bridge. Tickets are available for the whole day, with passengers being able to alight at any stop on the route and then reboard later to continue the tour. Tickets are available on the buses or from the TIC, cost £6. A cruise under the spectacular Forth Bridge starts from Hawes Pier, South Queensferry and can be booked through **Maid of the Forth**, tel: (0131) 331 4857, cost £6.25. To arrive at the pier take Eastern Scottish bus from St Andrew Square or Lothian Region bus 40. There are a number of city walking tours available including **Mercat Ghost and History Walks** tel: (0131) 661 4541. These are historical day walks and evening ghost walks, starting from Mercat Cross, by St Giles, Royal Mile, cost £4. **Audio Walking Tours**, tel: (0131) 220 3030, will give you over 500 years of history in 50 minutes with headphones and a printed guide in eight languages. **Robin's Edinburgh Tours**, tel: (0131) 661 0125, offer daily tours of the historical Old Town during the day and ghost walks at night, starting from the TIC. Other tours can be found in *The Essential Guide to Edinburgh*, available from the TIC. **The Scottish Tourist Guides Association** will undertake coach and walking tours in up to 17 foreign languages, tel: (0131) 661 7977.

Historic Buildings

St Giles Cathedral, *High St, Royal Mile; tel: (0131) 225 9442.* Open daily 0900–1900 (summer), 0900–1700 (winter). Admission free. **Edinburgh Castle**, *Castlehill; tel: (0131) 244 3101.* Open daily 0930–1800 (Apr–Sept), 0930–1700 (Oct–Mar). Admission £5. **Palace of Holyroodhouse**, *Canongate; tel: (0131) 556 1096.* Open Mon–Sat 0930–1715 (summer), Mon–Sat 0930–1615 (winter). The Palace is closed on a regular basis for Royal Family visits; check before visiting. Admission £3.50.

The Georgian House, *Charlotte Sq; tel: (0131) 225 2160.* Open Mon–Sat 1000–1700, Sun 1400–1700 (Apr–23 Oct), **Gladstone's Land**, *477B Lawnmarket; tel: (0131) 226 5856.* Open Mon–Sat 1000–1700, Sun 1400–1700 (Apr–23 Oct). Admission £2.50. **John Knox House**, *45 High St; tel: (0131) 556 9759.* Open Mon–Sat 1000–1630. Admission £1.25.

Zoo

Edinburgh Zoo, *Costorphine Rd; tel: (0131) 334 9171.* Open daily 0900–1800 (Apr–Sept), 0900-1630 (Oct–Mar). Admission £4.80.

Themed Attractions

Camera Obscura, *Castlehill; tel: (0131) 334 9171.* Open daily 0930–1800 (Apr–Oct), 1000–1700 (Nov–Mar). Admission £2.90. **Royal Observatory Visitor Centre**, *Blackford Hill; tel: (0131) 668 8405.* Open daily 1200–1730 (Apr–Sept), Sat–Thu 1300–1700, Fri 1300–2100 (Oct–Mar). Admission £2. **Scott Monument**, *East Princes St; tel: (0131) 529 4068.* Open Mon–Sat 0900–1800 (Apr–Sept), Mon–Sat 0900–1500 (Oct–Mar). Admission £1.

Garden

Royal Botanic Garden, *Inverleithen Row; tel: (0131) 552 7171.* Open daily 1000–1600 (Nov–Feb), 1000–1800 (Mar, Apr, Septt and Oct), 1000–2000 (May–Aug). Admission free.

Art Galleries and Museums

National Gallery of Scotland, *The Mound; tel: (0131) 556 8921.* Open Mon–Sat 1000–1700,

Sun 1400–1700. Admission free. **National Gallery of Modern Art**, *Belford Rd; tel: (0131) 556 8921*. Open Mon–Sat 1000–1700, Sun 1400–1700. Admission free. **Scottish National Portrait Gallery**, *1 Queen St; tel: (0131) 556 8921*. Open Mon–Sat 1000–1700, Sun 1400–1700. Admission free. **The People's Story Museum**, *Canongate, Royal Mile; tel: (0131) 529 4057*. Open Mon–Sat 1000–1700 (Oct–May), 1000–1800 (Jun–Sept) and Sun 1000–1700 during Edinburgh Festival only. Admission free. **Museum of Childhood**, *42 High St, Royal Mile; tel: (0131) 529 4142*. Open Mon–Sat 1000–1700 (Oct–May), 1000–1800 (Jun–Sept) and Sun 1400–1700 during Edinburgh Festival dates only. Admission free. **Royal Museum of Scotland**, *Chambers St; tel: (0131) 225 7534*. Open Mon–Sat 1000–1700, Sun 1200–1700. Admission free. **Brass Rubbing Centre**, *Trinity Apsye, Chalmers Close* (off *Royal Mile); tel: (0131) 556 4364*. Open Mon–Sat 1000–1700 (Oct–May, Mon–Sat 1000–1800 (June–Sept), Sun 1200–1700 only during Edinburgh Festival. **The Russell Collection of Early Keyboard Instruments**, *St Cecilia's Hall, Niddry St, Cowgate; tel: (0131) 650 2805*. Open Wed and Sat 1400–1700. Admission £1.

Out of Town

Wildlife

Deep Sea World, *North Queensferry, Fife; tel: (01383) 411411*. Open daily 0930–1800 (end Mar–Jun, Sept/Oct), daily 0930–2000 (Jul/Aug), Mon–Fri 1000–1600, Sat/Sun 1000–1800 (Nov–Mar). Admission £4.50. Situated 10 miles north of Edinburgh. Take train from Waverley to North Queensferry. **Edinburgh Butterfly and Insect World**, *Melville Nursery, Lasswade, Midlothian; tel (0131) 663 4932*. Open daily 1000–1730 (Mar–Oct), 1000–1700 (Nov–Feb). Admission £3.25. Take bus no. 3 from the city centre, takes 20 minutes.

Historic Buildings

Dalmeny House, *South Queensferry, West Lothian; tel: (0131) 331 1888*. Open Sun 1300–1730, Mon/Tue 1200–1730 (May–Sept).

Admission £3.40. Situated 7 miles west of Edinburgh off A90. Take bus to South Queensferry from St Andrew Sq. **Hopetoun House**, *South Queensferry, West Lothian; tel: (0131) 331 2451*. Open daily 1000–1730 (Apr–early Oct). Admission £3.80. The house is 7 miles west of Edinburgh, take the A90 and turn off onto A904 just before Forth Bridge and follow the signs. No public transport. **Craigmillar Castle**, *Craigmillar Castle Rd; tel: (0131) 661 4445*. Open Mon–Sat 0930–1830, Sun 1400–1830 (Apr–Sept), Mon–Wed, Sat 0930–1630, Sun 1400–1630 (Oct–Mar). Situated 2 miles south of central Edinburgh, off Edinburgh-Dalkeith Road, take bus no. 33 from North Bridge.

Heritage Centre

Almond Valley Heritage Centre, *Livingston Mill, Millfield, Livingston, West Lothian; tel: (01506) 414957*. Open daily 1000–1700. Admission £1.50. Off A705 Livingston to Whitburn road, reached from junction 3 of M8 motorway, or SMT bus no 27 from Edinburgh city centre.

Clan Tartan Centre, *Leith Mills, 70/74 Bangor Rd, Leith; tel: (0131) 553 5161*. Open Mon–Sat 0900–1700 (1730 Apr–Nov), Sun 1000–1700. Admission free. Buses 10, 22 or 25 from *Princes St* take 10–15 mins.

Museums

Scottish Agricultural Museum, *Ingliston; tel: (0131) 333 2674*. Open daily 1000–1700 (Apr–Sept), Mon–Fri 1000-1700 (Oct–Mar). Admission free except during Royal Highland Show. Near Edinburgh Airport, take airport bus and follow signposts. **Scottish Mining Museum**, *Lady Victoria Colliery, Newtongrange, Midlothian; tel: (0131) 663 7519*. Open daily 1000–1600 (Apr–Sept). Situated 10 miles south of Edinburgh on A7.

Connection: Glasgow

Trains run between Edinburgh Waverley and Glasgow Queen St every half-hour (hourly on Sun mornings) – journey time 50 mins (1 hr 10 mins on Sun).

EDINBURGH to ABERDEEN

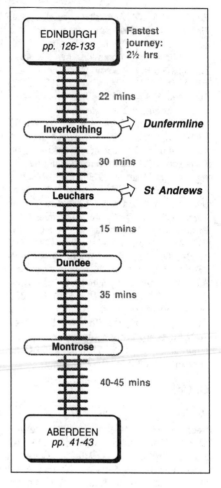

EDINBURGH pp. 126-133	Fastest journey: 2½ hrs

22 mins

Inverkeithing → *Dunfermline*

30 mins

Leuchars → *St Andrews*

15 mins

Dundee

35 mins

Montrose

40-45 mins

ABERDEEN pp. 41-43

Connecting the Scottish capital with the 'granite city' of Aberdeen, this route follows the east coast of Scotland for much of its length, affording some striking views. It provides a jumping-off point for the venerable seaside town of St Andrews, famous for being the home both of golf and of Scotland's most ancient university.

TRAINS

ETT table: 600

 Fast Track

An hourly service (two hourly on Sun) operates between Edinburgh and Aberdeen taking about 2½ hrs for the journey.

 On Track

Edinburgh–Leuchars–Dundee

The roughly hourly service from Edinburgh to Dundee stops at Leuchars. Change at Leuchars for St Andrews. Edinburgh to Leuchars takes about 1 hr; Leuchars to Dundee 13–14 mins.

Dundee–Montrose–Aberdeen

Two trains every hour (one per hour on Suns) link Dundee to Aberdeen, calling at Montrose en route. Dundee to Montrose takes 35 mins, Montrose to Aberdeen 40–45 mins.

- - - - - - - - - - - - - - - - - - -

 Side Track from Leuchars

ST ANDREWS

TIC, *70 Market St, St Andrews KY16 9NU; tel: (01334) 472021/474609. Open Mon–Fri 0930–* 1700, Sat 1100–1700 (Nov–Mar), Mon–Sat 0930–1700, Sun 1400–1700 (Apr, May, Oct), Mon–Sat 0930–1800, Sun 1100–1700 (Jun–Sept), Mon–Sat 0930–1900, Sun 1100–1700 (July, Aug). DP services offered: local bed booking service, BABA, bureau de change, theatre bookings, guided tours booked. *St Andrews and NE Fife Holiday Guide* is free.
Station: Leuchars, *Fife; tel: (01382) 228046* (6 miles west) is the closest and has a taxi rank.

Getting Around

Most attractions in town are walkable from the

town centre. Free town maps are available from the TIC. The main bus operator is **Fife Scottish Buses**, *City Rd; tel: (01334) 474238*. Services are relatively frequent around the town but less so outside the town, with a reduced service after 2000 and at weekends. The main taxi rank is at the bus station, *City Rd*. Registered taxi companies are: **Jay Taxis**, *tel: (01334) 476622* and **Williamsons**, *tel: (01334) 476787*.

Staying in St Andrews

The majority of accommodation is in b. & b. and guest-houses, although there are a couple of large independent hotels. It is generally easy to book except during July and Aug. The TIC has information on campsites in the area – the nearest are **Cairnsmill Caravan Park**, *Largo Rd; tel: (01334) 473604*, 1 mile south of the centre; **Craigtoun Meadows**, *Mount Melville; tel: (01334) 475959* 2 miles south west and **Kinkell Braes**, *tel: (01334) 474250*, a mile south on A9.

Sightseeing

Historic St Andrews is the 'home of golf' and also has the oldest university in Scotland. The famous **Royal and Ancient Golf Club**, founded in 1754, overlooks the **Old Course** (the world's oldest golf course). The fascinating **British Golf Museum** chronicles 500 years of golfing history. The **Open Golf Championships** take place in July. St Andrews also offers beaches and historic attractions, like ruined **St Andrews Castle** with its 'bottle dungeon' and 'secret passage'. More underground mysteries are uncovered in **Scotland's Secret Bunker**, the former Government nuclear war HQ for Scotland.

Bus tours available from: **Fife Scottish**, *tel: (01334) 474238* who operate city tours on open top buses, and **North Fife Travel**, *tel: (01334) 850255*. Boat trips available from **Anstruther Pleasure Trips**, *tel: (01333) 310103* and guided walks/guides can be booked through **Scottish Tourist Guides**, *tel: (01334) 850638*.

St Andrews Castle, *The Scores; tel: (01334) 477196*. Open Mon–Sat 0930–1800, Sun 1300–1800 (Apr–Sept). Admission £2. **St Andrews Cathedral**, *North St; tel: (01334) 472563*. Open Mon–Sat 0930–1800, Sun 1300–1800 (Apr–Sept). Admission £1.50. **St**

Andrews **Sealife Centre**, *The Scores; tel: (01334) 474786*. Open daily 1000–1800 (Sept–Jun), 0900–2100 (July–Aug). Admission £4.25. **British Golf Museum**, *Golf Pl; tel: (01334) 478880*. Open daily 1000–1700 (Mar–Apr), 1000–1900 (May–Oct), 1000–1600 (Nov–Feb). Admission £3.50. **St Andrews Museum**, *Kinburn Pk; tel: (01334) 477706*. Open 1100–1800 (Apr–Sept). Admission free. **Botanic Gardens**, *tel: (01334) 477178*. Open 1000–1900 (May–Sept), 1000–1600 (Oct–Mar). Admission £1.

Out of Town

Scottish Fisheries Museum, *Anstruther; tel: (01333) 310628*. Open daily 1000–1730 Mon–Sat, 1100–1700 Sun. Admission £2; bus 95 to *Leven*. **Scottish Deer Centre**; *tel: (01333) 810391*. Open daily 1000–1700 (Mar–Oct), 1000–1800 (Jul–Aug). Admission £4.00; bus 23, 3 miles from *Cupar*. **Scotland's Secret Bunker**, *Anstruther; tel: (01333) 310301*. Open daily 1000–1800 (Apr–Oct), Sat–Sun (Nov–Mar). Admission £3.75; bus no. 61. **Falkland Palace**, *Falkland; tel: (01337) 857397*. Open 1100–1730 Mon–Sat, 1330–1730 Sun (Apr–Oct). Admission £4; bus no. 23 or X59 to *Crouper* and then bus no. 66 to *Falkland*. **Praytis Farm Park**, *Leven; tel: (01333) 350209*. Open all year. Admission varies; bus no. 95 to *Leven*.

- - - - - - - - - - - - - - - - - - - -

DUNDEE

TIC: *4 City Sq, Dundee DD1 3BA; tel: (01382) 434664/434284*. Open Mon–Sat 0830–2000, Sun 1100–2000 (May, Jun, Sept), Mon–Sat 0830–2100, Sun 1100–2100 (Jul–Aug), Mon–Fri 0900–1800, Sat 1000–1200 1300–1600 (Oct–Apr). DP services offered: local bed-booking, BABA, guided tours booked, bureau de change. *Dundee – City of Discovery* (including accommodation listings) is available free.

Station: Dundee Station, *Riverside Dr; tel: (01382) 228046* is located in the city centre, and has car hire and a taxi rank.

Getting Around

Most attractions are within a walkable area

from the centre. Town maps are available free from the TIC, whilst transport maps are available free from the transport providers. Local public transport is good in the city centre and to outlying areas. A reduced service runs on Sun whilst buses stop running at 2330.

Strathtay Scottish is the main operator for local buses *tel: (01382) 228054* and operates from the central bus depot, *Seagate Station*. The main taxi ranks are located at *Nethergate* or *Commercial Street*, and the TIC can provide details of registered taxi companies.

Staying in Dundee

It is generally easy to book accommodation on arrival, except during July and Aug (due to university graduation). There is a large range of guest-houses and b. & b. on offer, with several large hotels also available. Cheaper accommodation is available on the outskirts. The nearset campsite is **Tayview East Holiday Park**, *Monifieth; tel: (01382) 532837*, and is located 7 miles east of the city centre. Accessible by bus/train. Dundee has a variety of ethnic eating places, as well as several gourmet restaurants.

Entertainment and Events

Events and entertainment lists are available free from the TIC. There are also two local publications, the *Courier* and the *Advertiser* (both £0.28). Dundee has three theatres: **Dundee Repertory Theatre**, *Tay Sq; tel: (01382) 223530*; **Little Theatre**, *Victoria Rd; tel: (01382) 225885* and **Whitehall Theatre**, *Bellfield St; tel: (01382) 822684*. There are also several cinemas in Dundee, one of which is the **Odeon Multiplex Cinema**, *Stack Leisure Park, Harefield Rd; tel: (01382) 400855*. The TIC can provide information on the other cinemas. Dundee also possesses several night clubs – current details from the TIC.

Dundee Summer Festival takes place annually during 24 June–22 July at various venues throughout the city. **Dundee Water Festival** follows, 5–13 Aug, various locations. In the summer, the **Dundee Jazz and Blues Festival** fills the theatres and pubs with music. There's also the **Guitar Festival**, the **Folk Festival**, the **Children's Festival** and the **Grand**

Parade – not to mention the **Broughty Ferry Gala** and **East of Scotland Sheepdog Trials**.

Sightseeing

Dundee has a long association with the sea, a source of prosperity through trade. Dundee made its fortune from 'jam, jute and journalism'. The Victorian merchants and industrialists left a fine legacy of homes and civic buildings. Typical of the exuberant Neo-Gothic styles are the **Cathedral Church of St Paul** and the **McManus Galleries**, which house a magnificent collection of Scottish Victorian art, as well as an excellent museum explaining the growth of Dundee through the centuries. The award-winning **Discovery Point Visitor Centre** introduces the **Discovery** herself, the Dundee-built research ship. There's more maritime history at **Victoria Dock**, where you can board the **Frigate Unicorn**, the oldest British-built warship afloat.

Dundee has 4000 acres of open space. Enjoy the peace and quiet of **Templeton Woods**, go horse riding or view native Scottish wildlife at **Camperdown Country Park**, or picnic on **Belgay Hill**. Garden enthusiasts will enjoy browsing around the exotic plant collections at the **University Botanic Garden**.

The TIC can book bus tours, boat trips and guided walks, which give an excellent insight into Dundee. **Scottish Tourist Guides Association** *tel: (01382) 434664* offer guided tours around Dundee.

Discovery Point, *Discovery Quay; tel: (01382) 201245*. Open daily 1000–1800. Admission £4. **Frigate Unicorn**, *Victoria Dock; tel: (01382) 200900*. Open Mon–Sat 1000–1700. Admission £3. **McManus Galleries**, *Albert Sq; tel: (01382) 434000*. Open Mon–Sat 1000–1700. Admission free. **Cathedral Church of St Paul**, *High St; tel: (01382) 224486*. Open Mon–Fri 1000–1600. Admission free. **Dundee Parish Church**, *Nethergate; tel: (01382) 226271*. Open Mon, Tue, Thu, Fri 1000–1200. Admission free.

Mills Observatory, *Balgay Pk; tel: (01382) 667138*. Open Tue–Fri 1500–2200, Sat 1400–1700 (Oct–Mar), Tue–Fri 1000–1700, Sat 1400–1700 (Apr–Sept). Admission free, 1½ miles from the centre. **Boughty Castle Museum**, *Boughty*

Ferry; tel: (01382) 776121. Open Mon 1100–1300, 1400–1700, Tue–Thu, Sat 1000–1300, 1400–1700, Sun 1400–1700. Admission free, 3 miles east.

Dundee University Botanic Garden, *Riverside Dr; tel: (01382) 566939.* Open (Mar–Oct) Mon–Sat 1000–1630, Sun 1100–1600; (Nov–Feb) Mon–Sat 1300–1500, Sun 1100–1500. Admission £1, 2½ miles west.

Camperdown Country Park, *Coupar Angus Rd; tel: (01382) 434624.* Open daily 24 hours. Admission free (charge for Wildlife Centre), 3 miles north-west.

Granny Shaws Sweetie Factory and Visitor Centre, *Fulton Rd, Wester Gourdie Industrial Estate; tel: (01382) 610369.* Open 1 June–30 Sept daily 1130–1600, winter Wed only 1330–1600. Admission £0.75. Three miles north-west.

Out of Town

Barry Mill (NT), *Barry, Carnoustie; tel: (01241) 856761.* Open Good Friday–30 Sept daily 1100–1700, 1–22 Oct Sat/Sun 1100–1700. Admission £1.50; 9 miles east.

Glamis Castle, *Estates Of-fice, Glamis; tel: (01307) 840242.* Open 1 Apr–30 Oct daily 1030–1730. Admission £4.50, 12 miles north. Limited access by public transport.

MONTROSE

TIC, *The Library, High St; tel (01674) 72000.* Open Mon–Sat 1000–1700 (Apr, May and Sept), Mon–Sat 0930–1730 (Jun–Aug). Local bed-booking and BABA service offered, deposit required. *The Angus Adventure* (including accommodation listings) is available free.

Station: Montrose Station, enquiries *tel: (01382) 228046*, is in the town centre and taxis can be found outside the station.

Getting Around

Attractions in the town are within walkable distance except for **House of Dun**, which is a short bus ride away. The TIC has free transport maps available. **Strathtay Buses** *tel: (01674) 672805* is the main bus company for the area. They run daily services to Brechin and Dundee, hourly during the week, less often at weekends.

Staying in Montrose

There are a few mid-range and small hotels and numerous guest-houses in the area. It is not difficult to book accommodation on arrival but as the TIC is not open in the winter it would be better to call **Arbroath TIC** in the Oct–Mar period, *tel: (01241) 872609.* There are a number of campsites in and around Montrose – further details from the TIC. The nearest are **South Links Caravan Park**, *Trail Dr; tel: (01674) 672026* near the beach, 5 minutes from the town, and **Lauriston Caravan Site**, *St Cyrus; tel: (01674) 85316.* St Cyrus is 6 miles north of Montrose on A92 Dundee to Aberdeen road; Bluebird bus no. 10 stops nearby.

Sightseeing

The merchants of Montrose, an old-established prosperous seaport, built some outstanding private and public buildings. The oldest part of the town occupies a unique position, on a broad peninsula between the sea and the tidal basin of the River North Esk. The **Museum** has good displays of local history, including the Pictish Stones. Visitors with an interest in sculpture will enjoy the **William Lamb Memorial Studio**, with a selection of the works of this Montrose sculptor and etcher.

Montrose Museum, *Panmure Pl; tel (01674) 673232.* Open Mon–Sat 1000–1700. Admission free. **William Lamb Memorial Studio**, *24 Market St; tel: (01674) 673232.* Open Sat 1400–1700 (Jul–Aug). Admission free.

Out of Town

House of Dun, nr *Montrose; tel: (01674) 810264.* Open daily 1330–1730 (Easter–22 Oct) except Jul–Aug 1100–1730. Admission £3. **Brechin Museum**, *St Ninians Sq, Brechin; tel: (01307) 68813.* Open Mon, Wed 0930–2000, Tue, Thu 0930–1800, Fri, Sat 0930–1700. Admission free; daily bus from Montrose.

St Cyrus National Nature Reserve, *Old Lifeboat Station, Nether Warburton; tel: (01674) 813736.* Open Tue–Sun 0930–1730 (May–Sept). Admission free. Daily bus from Dundee, via Montrose, stops in St Cyrus, reserve is signposted.

Dundee–Montrose

EDINBURGH to INVERNESS

This route incorporates some of the most scenic railway journeys in the whole of Britain, taking you through the heart of the Scottish Highlands and giving access to the skiing facilities of the Cairngorms, the much-publicised mysteries of Loch Ness, and the still more remote charms of the Isle of Skye and the Outer Hebrides.

TRAINS

ETT table: 605

 Fast Track

Four or five through trains a day (two or three on Suns) operate between Edinburgh and Inverness; other services are available by changing trains at Perth. Journey time is about 3½ hrs by through train, 4 hrs if a change at Perth is necessary.

 On Track

Edinburgh–Stirling

Edinburgh to Stirling has two trains each hour on weekdays with a journey time of 48 mins. On Suns, the service is hourly and a change of train is necessary at Falkirk Grahamston; journey time is extended to 55 mins.

Stirling–Perth

An hourly service (2 hourly on Suns) links Stirling to Perth. Journey time is 32 mins.

Perth–Aviemore–Inverness

Eight trains a day run between Perth and Inverness (roughly two-hourly but with some longer gaps of up to three hours). All trains call at Aviemore. Perth to Aviemore takes about 1 hr

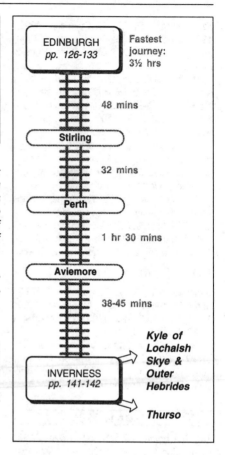

30 mins, and Aviemore to Inverness takes 38–45 mins.

STIRLING

TIC: *41 Dumbarton Rd, Stirling FK8 2QQ; tel: (01786) 475019 fax: (01786) 471301.* Open 1 Apr–29 May, Mon–Sat 0900–1700, Sun 1000–1700, 30 May–3 Jul, Mon–Sat 0900–1800, Sun 1000–1700, 4 Jul–4 Sep, Mon–Sat 0900–1930, Sun 0930–1830 and 5 Sep–18 Sep, Mon–Sat 0900–1900, Sun 1000–1700. DP SHS services offered: local bed-booking service; 10% deposit to be paid in advance, BABA 10% of first night as a deposit or £2.75. Accommodation bookings are particularly busy from 1600–1700.

TIC, Royal Burgh Visitor Centre: *Castle Esplanade, Stirling FK8 1EH; tel: (01786) 479901.* Open Jan–Feb, daily 0930–1700, 1 Apr–3 Jul, daily 0930–1800, 4 Jul–4 Sept, Mon, Wed, Thu, Fri, Sat and Sun 0900–1830, Tue 0900–2100, 31 Oct–31 Mar Mon–Sun 0930–1700.

TIC, Stirling Pirnhall: *Granada Service Area, M9/M80, Junction 9; tel: (01786) 814111.* Open 1 Apr–29 May daily 1000-1700, 30 May–3 Jul daily 0930–1800, 4 Jul–4 Sept daily 0930–1900, 5 Sept–25 Sept daily 1000–1800 and 26 Sept–30 Oct daily 1000–1700.

The *Loch Lomond Stirling and the Trossachs* guide is available for 50p (free to postal enquirers) and includes accommodation listings. **Dial-a-Journey** offers a transport service for visitors who have a mobility problem, from 0645–2315; *tel: (01786) 465355.*

Station: Stirling Station, *Goosecroft Rd; tel: (01786) 464754* is in the town centre. There is a taxi rank.

Getting Around

Most of the attractions in the town are within a walkable area of the centre except National Wallace Monument and Bannockburn Heritage Centre. **Midland Bluebird** buses operate from *Stirling Bus Station, Goosecroft Rd; tel: (01786) 473763.* For timetable enquiries, *tel: (01324) 613777.* Public transport is good in the town centre but infrequent to outlying areas on Sundays. Taxi ranks can be found at *Stirling BR Station* and *Murray Pl*, in the town centre.

Staying in Stirling

There is a reasonable range of accommodation in Stirling, mostly concentrating on b.&b. establishments. The nearest youth hostel is **Stirling Youth Hostel**, *St John St; tel: (01786) 473442.* The TIC is able to provide information on campsites. The nearest are: **Auchenbowie Caravan Site**, *Auchenbowie; tel: (01324) 822141* (4 miles south-west) and **Witches Craig**, *Blairlogie; tel: (01786) 474947* (4 miles east). Neither is accessible by public transport.

Sightseeing

Stirling, the 'Gateway to the Highlands', is dominated by its hilltop castle, below which is an historic old town with many fine buildings. The imposing fortress of **Stirling Castle** was a royal palace and focal point of Scotland's Wars of Independence; the views from the ramparts take in the hills of the Trossachs and the Ochils, the Forth estuary and the sites of seven battlefields, including Bannockburn. Visitors can learn the story of Stirling at the **Royal Borough of Stirling Visitor Centre**. Other attractions include the **Smith Art Gallery and Museum**, which houses an extensive collection of local art and artefacts, and the magnificent **Church of the Holy Rood**.

Heading out of Stirling, visit **Scotland's Mill Trail Visitor Centre** to learn all about the area's woollen industry, and hear tales of the infamous Highland outlaw and folk-hero, Rob Roy Macgregor, at the **Rob Roy and Trossachs Visitor Centre**.

Bus tours, operated by Midland Bluebird, guided walks and guides can be booked through the TIC. The Callander–Aberfoyle bus route is particularly good for sightseeing. The **Heritage Tour Bus** takes in many of the attractions listed.

National Wallace Monument, *Abbey Craig, Causeway Head; tel: (01786) 472140.* Open Mar–Oct, daily 1000–1700; Jul–Aug 0930–1800. Admission £2.35; 1½ miles away, take bus nos 51, 52 and 58 (Heritage Tour Bus). **Stirling Castle**, *tel: (0131) 244 3101.* Open Apr–Sept, daily 0930–1800; Oct–Mar, daily 0930–1730. Admission £3.50. (Heritage Tour Bus). **Bannockburn Heritage Centre**, *Glasgow Rd; tel: (01786) 812664.* Open Mar–Oct, daily 1000–1730; 31 Jan–31 Mar daily 1100–1800. Admission £1.80. 2 miles west. Bus 81, 14 and 39. **Royal Burgh of Stirling Visitor Centre**, *Castle Esplanade; tel: (01786) 479901.* Open Apr–Sept, daily 0930–1800; Oct–Mar, daily 0930–1730. Admission free. (Heritage Tour Bus)

Cambuskenneth Abbey, *Cambuskenneth; tel: (0131) 244 3101.* Open Apr–Sept, Mon–Sat 0930–1830, Sun 1430–1830. Admission free. **Church of Holy Rood**, *Spittal St.* Open May–Sept, daily 1000–1700. Admission free. (Heritage Tour Bus).

Smith Art Gallery and Museum, *Dumbar-*

Stirling   **139** ton Rd; tel: (01786) 471917. Open Apr–Sept, Tue–Sat 1030–1700, Sun 1400–1700; Nov–Mar, Tue–Fri 1200–1700, Sat 1030–1800, Sun 1400–1700. **MacRoberts Arts Centre**, Stirling University; tel: (01786) 461081. Open all year. Admission variable.

Out of Town

Scotland's Mill Trail Visitor Centre, Glentana Mill, West Stirling St, Alva; tel: (01259) 769696. Open Jun–Sept, daily 0900–1800; Oct–Dec, daily 1000–1700. Admission free. Eight miles east. Not accessible by public transport. **Rob Roy and Trossachs Visitor Centre**, Ancaster Sq, Callander; tel: (01877) 330342. Open Jan–Feb, Sat & Sun 1000–1800; Mar–May, daily 1000–1700; Jun, daily 0930–1900; Jul/Aug, daily 0900–2230; Sept, daily 0930–1900; Oct, daily 1000–1700; Nov/Dec, Mon–Fri 1000–1600, Sat & Sun 1000–1700. Admission £2. 16 miles north. Bus 59 or 'Trossachs Trundler Bus'.

  Castle Campbell, Dollar; tel: (0131) 244 3101. Open Apr–Sept, Mon–Sat 0930–1830, Sun 1430–1830; Mar–Oct, Mon–Sat 0930–1630, Sun 1400–1630, closed Thur afternoons and Fri in winter. 12 miles east. Bus no. 23. **Doune Castle**, Doune; tel: (01786) 841742. Open Apr–Sept, Mon–Sat 0930–1830, Sun 1400–1830; Oct–Mar, Mon–Sat 0930–1600, Sun 1400–1630. Closed Thur afternoons and Fri in winter. Admission £2. 7 miles northwest. Bus no. 59 or 'Trossachs Trundler Bus'.

PERTH

TIC: 45 High St, Perth; tel: (01738) 638353. Open 0900–1700 Mon–Sat (Oct–Mar), 0900–1800 Mon–Sat, 1200–1800 Sun (Apr–Jun), open daily 0900–2000 (Jul–Sept). DP services offered: local bed-booking services, BABA, bureau de change. Tickets booked for the theatre and Military Tattoo. In and Around Perth and Perthshire Guide are available free. **Station:** Perth Station, Leonard St, Perth; tel: (01738) 637117 is in the town centre and has a taxi rank and car hire facilities.

Getting Around

Most attractions in the town are walkable from the centre. Free town maps are available from the TIC. The main bus operator is **Scottish Citylink** tel: (01738) 633481. Services are good to the town centre and provincial towns, except on Sundays, with a limited service after 1800. The main taxi rank is located in Mill St. For details of registered taxi companies contact the TIC.

Staying in Perth

The accommodation available is mostly guesthouses with several mid-range hotels. Cheaper accommodation is available 1 mile from the town centre. It is generally easy to book on arrival except during mid-Feb and July and Aug (due to the bull sales and the peak season). The TIC has details of youth hostels in the area – the nearest is **Perth Youth Hostel**, Glasgow Rd, Perth; tel: (01738) 623658. Open from Feb–Aug. The TIC also has details on campsites – the nearest is **Cleeve Caravan Park**, Glasgow Rd; tel: (01738) 639521, 2 miles west of the centre.

Sightseeing

The small, ancient city of Perth, once called St. Johnstoun, is beautifully situated on the broad River Tay, the longest river in Scotland. Once the capital of Scotland, its regal importance meant that kings were crowned at nearby **Scone Palace**, which was rebuilt in 1808 by William Atkinson for the 3rd Earl of Mansfield. Today, the palace contains a wealth of fine painting, French furniture, clocks, porcelain and ivory objects. Wool and glass are important industries in Perth so **Caithness Glass** and **Lower City Mills** are a must. Perth is well known for its winter sports such as curling, ice skating and skiing and is also an ideal base for exploring the Highlands. The TIC can book bus tours and guided walks.

  Scone Palace, Scone; tel: (01738) 552300. Open Mon–Sat 0930–1700, Sun 1330–1700 (Mar–Oct). Admission £4.50. **Caithness Glass**, Inveralmond; tel: (01738) 637373. Open daily Mon–Sat 0900–1700, Sun 1300–1700. Admission free. **Lower City Mills**, West Mill St; tel: (01738) 627958. Open Mon–Sat 100–1700 (Apr–Oct). Admission £1. **Branklyn Garden**, Dundee Rd; tel: (01738) 625535. Open daily

0930–sunset (Mar–Oct). Admission £2.50. **Fergusson Art Gallery**, *Marshall Pl; tel: (01738) 441944.* Open Mon–Sat 1000–1700 (Jan–Dec). Admission free.

Out of Town

Blair Castle, *Blair Atholl, nr Pitlochry; tel: (01796) 481207.* Open daily 1000–1800 (Apr–Oct). Admission £4.50. Take the train from Perth to Blair Atholl. 32 miles north-west of Perth. **Glamis Castle**, *Glamis, By Forfar; tel: (01307) 840242* (see Dundee p. 137). **Huntingtower Castle**, *Huntingtower by Perth; tel: (0131) 244 3101.* Open Mon–Sat 0930–1800, Sun 1400–1800 (Apr–Sept), Mon–Sat 0930–1600, Sun 1400–1600 (Oct–Mar). Admission £1.50. Bus from Scott Street, Perth to *Huntingtower.* 4 miles west. **Glenturret Distillery**, *The Hosh, Crieff; tel: (01764) 652424.* Open Mon–Sat 0930–1600, Sun 1200–1600 (Mar–Dec), Mon–Fri 1130–1600 (Jan–Feb). Admission £2.75. Bus from Perth to Crieff. 18 miles west of Perth.

AVIEMORE

TIC: *Grampian Rd, Aviemore, Inverness-shire PH22 1PP; tel: (01479) 810363. Accommodation booking tel no (01479) 810454.* Open daily 0900–1800 (0900–2000 July and August). DP and SPS services offered. Local bed-booking service (£1 plus 10% commission charged). BABA (£2.75 plus 10% deposit). Advance reservations handled. Self-catering accommodation and guided tours also booked. Bureau de change. Tickets sold for Scottish City Link and National Express coaches. *Aviemore and Spey Valley* (including accommodation list) is available free. Visitor's guide also available free.
Station: Aviemore Station, *tel: (01345) 212282* is in the town centre, and has a taxi rank.

Getting Around

The attractions in town are all within walking distance of the centre, except Rothiemurchus Estate, which is 1 mile out of the town. A free town map is available from the TIC. There are limited bus services within the surrounding area. **Scottish Citylink Coach Service Enquiries**, *tel: (01463) 711000.* **National Express Coaches**,

tel: *(01738) 33481.* The main taxi rank is at the railway station.

Staying in Aviemore

There are a lot of large and mid-range hotels, and also a large number of guest-houses and b.& b. establishments. It is generally easy to find accommodation on arrival, except in mid-Feb and late July/early Aug. National hotel chains in Aviemore include *St.*

The closest youth hostel is **Aviemore SYHA**, *Grampian Rd; tel: (01479) 810345,* which is open all day (booking office closes at 2330). It is a 5-min walk from the railway station. The nearest campsites are: **Campgrounds of Scotland**, *Coylumbridge; tel: (01479) 810120* is 2 miles out of the town on the Cairngorm Chairlift Bus route. **Dalraddy Holiday Park**, *by Aviemore; tel: (01479) 810330* is 3 miles out of the town; access is difficult by public transport.

Sightseeing

Aviemore is a purpose-built resort, with a large range of entertainment and facilities on hand. In addition, there is easy access into the Cairngorms, including **Glen More Forest Park**, **Craigellachie National Nature Reserve**, and the **Cairngorm ski slopes**. The area is very important for its distinctive landscape, animals, plants and rocks. There are many opportunities to learn about and enjoy the outdoors, for example at the **Cairngorm Reindeer Centre**, and the **Highland Wildlife Park**. There are several large estates, such as **Alvie & Dalraddy Estate** and **Rothiemurchus Estate**, which offer activities such as guided walks and tours, fishing and shooting. Visitors can also follow whisky trails to visit the numerous distilleries within the area. Throughout the summer there are various Agricultural and Highland shows where you can experience the local culture and traditions. The area is also well known for its winter sports facilities, including skiing, snowboarding and skating.

Highland Discovery Tours, *tel: (01479) 811478* offer bus tours (starting from Inverness). Prices from £12. **Jacobite Cruises** *tel: (01463) 233999* offer boat trips (starting from Inverness). Prices from £8. The **Cairngorm**

Chairlift Company, *tel: (01479) 861261* offer guided walks, starting from the Cairngorm car park (May–Oct). Free of charge.

Santa Claus Land theme park, *Aviemore Mountain Resort; tel: (01479) 810624*. Open daily 1000–1800. Admission £3 (3-4 year olds), £3.50 (5-13 year olds), £4 (14+ years). Family tickets £15 (2 adults plus 2 children), £17.50 (2 adults plus 3 children). **Rothiemurchus Estate**, *Coylumbridge; tel: (01479) 831609*. Open daily 0900–1700 (except Christmas Day). One mile east of the town centre on the road to the ski slopes (regular bus route).

Out of Town

Alvie and Dalraddy Estate, *Kincraig, Kingussie; tel: (01540) 651255*. 7 miles from the town on regular bus route. **Ruthven Barracks**, *Kingussie*. Ruined castle, 20 miles south of the town on regular bus route. **Highland Folk Park**, *Newtonmore; tel: (01540) 673551*. Twenty miles south of the town on regular bus route.

INVERNESS

TIC: *Castle Wynd, Inverness IV2 3BJ; tel: (01463) 234353, fax: (01463) 710609*. Open Mon–Sat 0900–1700, Sun 1000–1600 (Jan–May, Oct–Dec); Mon–Sat 0900–1800, Sun 100–1700 (Jul), Mon–Sat 0900–2030, Sun 0930–1800 (Jul–Sept). DP SHS Services offered: Local bed-booking service (£2 booking fee), BABA (£2.75 booking fee). Guided tours booked, Bureau de change, National Express, Scottish Citylink, P&O and car hire booked. *Welcomeness* tourist guide available free.

Station: Inverness Station, *Station Sq, Academy St; tel: (01463) 238924* is in the town centre, and has a taxi rank and car hire.

Getting Around

The attractions in town are within walking distance of the town centre. Free town maps are available from the TIC. The main bus operator is **Inverness Traction** *tel: (01463) 239292*. Services are good in town and some rural areas but patchy in some outlying areas. Reduced services run after 2000 and on Sun. The main taxi rank is at the station.

Staying in Inverness

There is a good range of accommodation available, particularly b.&b. It is generally easy to book on arrival, except during late July and the first two weeks in Aug. The TIC has details of youth hostels in the area; the nearest is **Inverness Youth Hostel**, *Old Edinburgh Rd; tel: (01463) 231771*. There is also a campsite in the area – **Bught Caravan and Camping Site**, *tel: (01463) 236920*, 1 mile west of the centre.

Sightseeing

Built around the River Ness, overlooked by **Inverness Castle**, Inverness is an elegant town; in summer the streets are blooming with over a thousand barrels, tubs and hanging baskets. The town is famous for Loch Ness and its legendary inhabitant, and well known for the Highland Games, Inverness Tattoo and the Northern Meeting Piping Competition.

Loch Ness is a freshwater lake, 24 miles long, 1 mile wide and 750 ft deep. You can hire a cabin cruiser or just get out your binoculars and scan the loch for the elusive monster. Bus tours and boat trips can both be booked at the TIC. The **Loch Ness Centre** at Drumnadrochit has the most exhaustive body of scientifically gathered evidence about the creature that has captured the imagination of the world.

The unique 1885 **Amazon Museum Ship** was the summer home of actor Arthur Lowe while the **Floral Hall** offers a magnificent floral experience when you stroll along winding paths through sub-tropical landscape. The **Culloden Visitor Centre** marks the spot where 'Bonnie Prince Charlie' was defeated in 1746, in the last battle fought on British soil. The rich tradition of Highland music can be experienced at **Balnain House** with interactive exhibitions and videos and live music some evenings.

Amazon Museum Ship, *Clachnaharry; tel: (01463) 242154*. Open 0900–1700. Admission £1.50. **Floral Hall**, *Bught Nurseries, Bught Pk; tel: (01463) 724224*. Open Mon–Fri 100–2000, Sat–Sun 1000–1700. Admission free. **Scottish Kiltmaker Centre**, *Huntly St; tel: (01463) 222781*. Open Mon–Sat 0900–2130, Sun 1000–1730. Admission £2. **St Andrews**

Cathedral, *Ardross St.* Open dawn till dusk. Admission free. **Balnain House**, *Huntly St; tel: (01463) 715757.* Open Tue–Sun 1000–1700. Admission £3. **Inverness Castle and Flora MacDonald Monument**, *Castle St.* Admission free.

Out of Town

Loch Ness Centre, *Drumnadrochit; tel: (01456) 450573.* Open daily 0900–1930. Admission £4.00. Sixteen miles south-east of town centre; take bus no. 16 from Inverness bus station or daily tour (runs all year round) from TIC (price starts from around £6). **Culloden Battlefield and Visitor Centre (NTS)**, *Culloden; tel: (01463) 780607.* Open daily 0900–1800. Admission £1.80. Five miles east of Inverness; take bus no. 12 or open-top bus tour run by Guide Friday May–Sept (*tel: (01456) 224000*).

 Side Tracks from Inverness

KYLE OF LOCHALSH

TIC: *Car Park, Kyle of Lochalsh, Ross-shire; tel: (01599) 534276 or 534371.* Open Mon–Sat 0915–1730 (Apr–May), Mon–Sat 0915–1900 (Jun–Jul, Sept), Mon–Sat 0900–2130 (Aug), Mon–Sat 0930–1730 (Oct). Also open Sun 1230–1630 (Jul–Aug). DP SHS services offered: local bed booking and BABA (10% commission taken).

Station: Kyle of Lochalsh Station, *Station Rd*, is situated in the centre of the town, near to the TIC. For rail enquiries, *tel: (01599) 534205.* Three or four trains operate each day between Inverness and Kyle of Lochalsh, the journey taking 2 hrs 30 mins–2 hrs 40 mins (see ETT table 597). The Kyle of Lochalsh to Inverness railway line is one of the most scenic journeys in Britain; 82 miles long, it was built between 1862 and 1897 and was the most expensive railway ever built at the time.

Getting Around

The TIC will provide a free town map although most attractions in the area are far enough out of Kyle of Lochalsh to require the use of a car or

Skye and the Western Isles

Lying off the north-west shore of Scotland, these islands with their deeply indented coastlines, dramatic moors and mountains offer some of Scotland's most remarkable scenery. **Skye** is currently linked to the mainland by ferry (Mallaig–Armadale or Kyle of Localsh–Kyleakin), though a bridge is under construction. It is the largest of the Inner Hebridean group, and apart from the towns and main attractions is little touched by tourism, remaining the domain of serious climbers and walkers. The central part is dominated by the dramatic, bare peaks of the **Cuillin Hills**, beyond which is the capital Portree; near the ferry terminal in Armadale is the **Clan Donald Centre**, housing an exhibition on the Lords of the Isles and Scottish culture.

Sprawling beyond Skye's finger-like peninsulas are the **Western Isles** or Outer Hebrides, a long chain of islands which, with the exception of Harris–North Uist and South Uist–Barra, are linked by causeways. As on Skye, buses are rare beasts, so anyone wishing to explore will need to hire a car (from Lewis' capital, Stornaway). The main islands, **Lewis** and **Harris**, stretch 130 miles from north to south. Distinctly different in landscape, they both have an unforgettable light and atmosphere: the treeless, desolate peat moorlands of Lewis in the north gradually give way to the wild and rugged mountains of Harris to the south, whle the western, Atlantic seaboard has miles of magnificent, almost white sandy beaches. Everywhere there are reminders of ancient habitation, none more mysterious than the **Callanish Stones** – contemporary with Stonehenge and just as spectacular, but without the crowds. Untouched by organised tourism, the Western Isles are an escapist paradise.

public transport. The main bus companies are **Scottish Citylink** *tel: 0141-332 9644* and

Highland Scottish Omnibuses tel: (01463) 233371. Generally the bus services become patchy in outlying areas and most buses stop after 1700. The ferry to the Isle of Skye (Kyleakin) runs regularly from Kyle of Lochalsh all year, but on the island buses run infrequently even in high season and never on Sun.

Staying in Kyle of Lochalsh

There is a very limited range of hotels in the town but b.&b. is more plentiful. There is no youth hostel in the vicinity. The TIC can provide information on local campsites which include **Balmacara Woodlands Campsite**, Forest Enterprise, The Sq, Balmacara; tel: (01599) 566321. The site is 3 miles east of the town and can be reached by Highland Scottish Bus no. 970 to Inverness, which passes Balmacara on the main road.

Sightseeing

Kyle of Lochalsh is a busy shipping village with views across to the beautiful **Isle of Skye**. To the south-east is **Eilean Donan Castle** in a picturesque promontory setting surrounded by lochs; it dates from 1220 and is now a museum.

Eilean Donan Castle, Dornie. Open daily 1000–1800 (Easter–Sept). Admission £1.50. Take the bus no. 970, which passes Dornie en route. Nine miles south-east. **Lochalsh Woodland Gardens**, Balmacara Estate, nr Kyle of Lochalsh; tel: (01599) 86325. Open daily 0900– sunset. Admission £1.00. Take the bus no. 970 which passes Balmacara on the way. Three miles east.

THURSO

TIC: Riverside, Thurso; tel: (01847) 892371. Open Mon–Sat (Apr–Oct) hours vary according to demand. Services offered: local bed-booking, BABA and P & O ferry reservations. Caithness & Sutherland Where to Stay, What to Do has accommodation listings and is available free.
Station: Thurso Station is ½ mile from the town centre and has a taxi rank. Three trains run each day between Inverness and Thurso, taking about 3 hr 40 mins for the journey (ETT table 597).

Getting Around

The attractions in town are all within walking distance of the centre, except for Thurso Castle ruins, which are about 2 miles from the town centre. Town and transport maps are available from the TIC for a small charge. The main bus operator is **Highland Bus and Coach** tel: (01847) 896123. Services are good in the town centre, but patchy in outlying areas. There is no service available at night time. The main taxi rank is at Princess Street.

Staying in Thurso

A good range of accommodation is available, particularly b.&b. establishments. Cheaper accommodation can be located in the town centre. It is generally easy to book on arrival, except during peak season, July and Aug. The TIC has details of campsites in the area – the nearest is **Thurso Municipal Caravan Site**, Gillock Park, Thurso; tel: (01955) 603761, ½ mile north-west of the centre.

Sightseeing

Modest though Thurso is today, this was in medieval times the principal port for the trade between Scotland and Scandinavia and in the 14th century of such importance that its weights and measures were adopted throughout Scotland. Later the town became busy with the flatstone industry. An ideal location for the watersports enthusiast and avid walker, Thurso offers a wide range of watersports, from waterskiing to fishing. With **John O'Groats**, the most northerly point on the British mainland, only a stone's throw away, there are many different rambling trails for the walker to pursue. In addition to these activities there is a vast array of bird life and other wildlife.

Caithness Glass, Airport Industrial Estate, Wick. Open Mon–Sat 0900–1700, Sun 1100– 1700 (Jun–Sept). Admission free. **St Peters Church**, nr the harbour. Open daily. Admission free. **Thurso Heritage Museum**, Town Hall, High St. Open Mon–Sat 1000–1300, 1400– 1700 (Jun–Sept). Small admission charge.

- -

EXETER

Exeter is an ancient city, and though its centre was heavily bombed during World War II and has been largely rebuilt, it still has its share of old buildings, including the unscathed cathedral and some elegant Georgian terraces. A university city, Exeter is also a lively cultural centre with an excellent arts festival.

Tourist Information

TIC: *Civic Centre, Paris St, Exeter, Devon EX1 1RP; tel: (01392) 265700.* Open Mon–Fri 0900–1700, Sat 0900–1300 and 1400–1700. DP Services offered: local bed-booking service and BABA £1.75 and £2.75 booking fee taken respectively (latest 30 mins before closing). YHA membership, tickets for National Express buses and day trips from local coach operators sold. *Exeter Visitor Guide* is available free and includes an accommodation listing.

Arriving and Departing

Exeter St David's Station, *Bonhay Rd; tel: (01392) 433551* is a mile north-west of the city centre and has a taxi rank. A minibus shuttle service to the centre, on bus route N, runs every 10 mins during the day and every 20 mins in the evening (0700–2325).

Getting Around

The majority of attractions are within walking distance. A free town map and transport map is available from the TIC and from local transport providers.

Most bus services within Exeter and to the surrounding area are on minibuses which are run by **Devon General Ltd**, *tel: (01392) 56231*, from the central bus station on *Belgrave Rd*. The minibuses provide an excellent service during the day with between five and ten minutes frequency on all routes. A reduced service operates after 1800 and there are no services after 2330 or on Suns. An 'Exeter 1-day Freedom ticket' is available directly from bus drivers after 0900 (price £2.05).

The main taxi rank is located outside Debenhams store on *Sidewell St.*

Staying in Exeter

Accommodation

There is a good range of accommodation of all types in Exeter, and the majority of guesthouses and b. & b. establishments are located in the city centre. It is generally easy to find accommodation on arrival in the city, except during mid-July due to the Exeter Festival and University Graduation. Hotel chains in Exeter include *BW, FP, MC.* For budget accommodation the **Exeter City Hostel** (YHA) is at *4749 Countess Wear Rd; tel (01392) 873329,* open daily from 1700–1000. Take minibus route K south from the *High St.* The closest campsites to Exeter are **Castle Brake Holiday Park,** *Woodbury; tel: (01395) 232431,* 8 miles south-east on **Devon Buses** route 385; **Kennford International Caravan Park,** *Exeter; tel: (01392) 833046,* 5 miles south on bus route X39; **Haldon Lodge Farm Camping and Caravan Park,** *Clapham, Kennford; tel: (01392) 832312,* 4½ miles south, not on any public transport route; and **Springfield Holiday Park,** *Tedburn Rd, Tedburn St Mary; tel: (01647) 24242,* 7 miles west, no access by public transport.

Eating and Drinking

Exeter has a good choice of gourmet and cheaper restaurants (including ethnic specialities), inns and wine bars serving food, mostly located in the city centre. Vegetarian restaurants include **Herbies,** *North St; tel: (01392) 58473,* **The Crystal Cafe,** *117 Fore St; tel: (01392) 410759* and **Toppers Fish & Vegetarian Restaurant,** *41 Fore St; tel: (01392) 874707.* Don't miss trying Devon cider or a cream tea with local clotted cream.

Communications

The main post office is on *Bedford St*, open Mon–Fri 0900–1730, Sat 0900–1300, and has a post restante facility.

Entertainment and Events

Entertainment and event listings can be found in *What's On* and *Exeter Events*, both available free from the TIC.

The **Northcott Theatre**, *Stoker Rd; tel: (01392) 54853/211080*, is a professional regional theatre which presents a wide range of plays, musicals, films and concerts with regular visits from touring opera and dance companies (10 mins from city centre on minibus route H).

Two of the main annual events taking place in Exeter are the **Devon County Show** at *Westpoint* during mid-May, 5 miles east of the centre, and the **Exeter Festival** which takes place around the city in early July.

Sightseeing

Miraculously, Exeter's inspiring **Cathedral** escaped the German bombing of the city: it is one of the best preserved in England and Devon's finest building. You can't miss its twin Norman towers, the west front with its remarkable 14th-century sculptures, or the striking, vaulted nave; but hunt out the 14th-century Bishop's Throne (made without nails) and the exotically carved choir stalls. The *Cathedral Close* is a quiet haven, bounded on one side by a surviving part of the old city wall. Exeter's **Guildhall** is reputedly the oldest municipal building in Britain, built in 1330. A guided tour of the **Underground Passages** offers the unusual experience of walking through medieval, subterranean waterducts, which supplied spring water to the city. Of Exeter's museums, the **Maritime Museum** is highly recommended: it has a collection of over 170 historic vessels from around the world, from Chinese junks to Venetian gondolas, and many can be boarded.

In the surrounding area, take your pick from 18th-century **Killerton House**, which has a good collection of period costumes, a lived-in feel, and a well-planted and extensive estate; and 14th-century **Powderham Castle**, much restored in the 19th century, which has richly furnished state rooms and a beautiful rose garden, with views over the ancient deer park to the Exe estuary.

Free guided walks around the city are operated by **Exeter City Council's Guided Tours** service (*tel: (01392) 265700* to book); the main joining location is the *Royal Clarence Hotel, Cathedral Close*. A leaflet detailing the walks available and starting times is available from the TIC. A variety of bus tours can be booked at the TIC from May–Sept, including **Red Bus Services**, who operate an open-top bus tour of the city (price £3), and all-day coach excursions around the surrounding area from **Dartline, Hookways Greenslade** and **Turners Tours**. Boat trips from **Southern Company** depart from *Exeter Quay* from May–Sept and can also be booked at the TIC (price £2.50). A list of **West Country Tourist Board Blue Badge Guides** can be obtained from the TIC.

Historic Buildings

Exeter Cathedral, *Cathedral Close; tel: (01392) 55573.* Open daily from 0715 (except during services); guided tours available (May–Oct). Admission free (but £2 donation suggested). The Guildhall, *High St; tel: (01392) 77888* (contact the Mayor's Secretary). Open Mon–Fri 1000–1700 (subject to civic functions). Admission free. **St Nicholas Priory,** *The Mint, off Fore St; tel: (01392) 265858.* Open Tues–Sat 1000–1300 and 1400–1700 (Easter to Oct). Admission £1. **Underground Passages,** off *High St; tel: (01392) 265887.* Open Mon–Sat 1000–1700 (Easter to Oct); Tues–Fri 1400–1700, Sat 1000–1700 (Nov to Easter). Admission £2.25. (NB the passages are very narrow and are not suitable for anyone prone to claustophobia.)

Museums

Maritime Museum, *The Haven; tel: (01392) 58075.* Open daily 1000–1700 (Apr–Sept); 1000–1600 (Oct–Mar). Admission £3.75. Take minibus G south from the *High St* to *The Quay*. **Quay House Interpretation Centre,** *46 The Quay; tel: (01392) 265213.* Open daily 1000–1700 (Easter to Oct). Admission Free. Take minibus G south from the *High St* to *The Quay*. **Royal Albert Memorial Museum,** *Queen St; tel: (01392) 265858.* Open Mon–Sat 1000–1730 (Easter to Oct); Tues–Sat 1000–1730 (Nov to Easter). Admission free to main museum; variable charges for exhibitions.

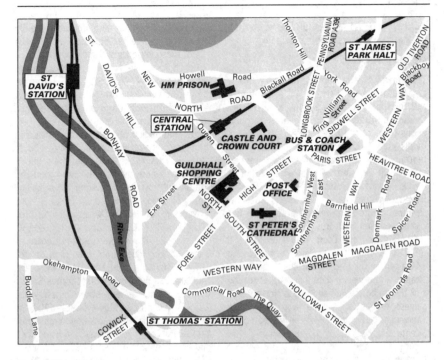

Out of Town

Becky Falls, *Manaton, nr Bovey Tracey; tel: (0164722) 259.* Open daily 1000–1800 (Easter to Nov), closes at dusk if earlier. Admission £3.50 per car. Fifteen miles west, limited access by public transport. **Creally Country,** *Creally Park, Sidmouth Rd, Clyst St Mary; tel: (01395) 233200.* Open daily 1000–1800 (mid-Mar to Oct); 1100 to dusk (Nov–Dec). Admission £3.85. Take *Exeter* to *Sidmouth* bus 52, 5 miles south-east. **Killerton House and Gardens** (NT), *Broadclyst; tel: (01392) 881345.* House open Mon and Wed–Sun 1100–1730, Tues closed (Apr–Oct); Garden and Park open daily during daylight hours (all year). Admission: house and grounds £4.60; grounds only £2.80. Seven miles north-east on bus route 375 or take bus 54 to *Killerton Turn*, then 1 mile walk. **Powderham Castle,** *Kenton; tel: (01626) 890243.* Open Mon–Fri and Sun 1000–1700, Sat closed (Apr–Sept). Admission £3.95. Eight miles south on bus routes 85 and 85A.

 Side Track from Exeter

BARNSTAPLE

TIC: *North Devon Library, Tuly St, Barnstaple, Devon EX31 1EL; tel: (01271) 388583 or 388584.* Open Mon–Fri 0900–1900, Sat 0930–1700, closed Bank Hols. DP SHS services offered: local bed booking (10% deposit taken), BABA (10% deposit), ferry tickets sold. The TIC may be particularly busy with accommodation bookings between 1600–1800. The *Barnstaple Town Guide* costs £0.80 and the *North Devon Guide* and accommodation listings are free.
Station: Barnstaple Station, *Junction Rd,* ½ mile south-west of the centre, is the terminus of the Tarka Line – a particularly scenic 40-mile branch line which starts at Exeter St David's Station. In summer there are about a dozen trains a day, fewer on Suns and in winter. Journey time varies from 1 to 1½ hrs. All rail enquiries *tel: (01752)*

221300. Four bus services run into town from the station and there is also a taxi rank.

Getting Around

The majority of attractions are within a walkable distance of the town centre. A free town map and transport map can be obtained at the TIC. **Devon County Council** run a general transport enquiry no., *tel: (01271) 382800* (Mon–Fri). Barnstaple's bus services are plentiful and regular. However, there are limited services after 1900 and no services after 2300. A limited service operates on Suns. The central Bus Station is situated in *The Strand* and most services operate from here. The two main bus companies are **Red Bus North Devon** *tel: (01271) 45444* and **Filers Travel** *tel: (01271) 863819*. A daily 'Day Explorer' ticket costing £4.50 can be used on all Red Bus North Devon services and a weekly 'Red Rider' ticket costing £13.50 can be used on all Red Bus North Devon services except to Plymouth and Exeter. The main town centre taxi rank is in *Boutport St.*

Staying in Barnstaple

It is always advisable to book accommodation in advance and essential in Sept–Oct. There are few hotels in Barnstaple. Cheaper b. & b. accommodation can be found on the edge of town and in the suburbs of Newport (1½ miles east) and Sticklepath (1 mile south-west). The nearest youth/budget accommodation is **Instow Youth Hostel**, *Worlington House, New Rd, Instow; tel: (01271) 860394*, 6 miles west of Barnstaple by Red Bus North Devon nos. 1, 2 or B, or Filers Travel bus 301. The TIC can provide details on local campsites.

Sightseeing

The attractive town of Barnstaple is an ideal centre for touring North Devon; the 'Tarka Trail' takes in the surrounding countryside, featured in Henry Williamson's novel, *Tarka the Otter*. The **Museum of North Devon** displays the natural and human history of the region and incorporates the **Royal Devon Yeomanry Museum**. Nearby attractions include the unique **Lynton and Lynmouth Cliff Railway**, and **Dartington Crystal**, makers of exquisite hand-

made glassware. A little more unusual is the **Big Sheep**, an all-weather attraction with sheep racing, sheepdog trials and sheep-milking.

Coach tours are available with **Loverings Coaches**, *tel: (01271) 863673*, which start from the Bus Station and cost £4.00–6.00. **Guided Walks of Historic Barnstaple**, *tel: (01271) 388584*, conduct walks from the TIC. For further information on walks and on boat trips from Ilfracombe or Bideford to Lundy or South Wales, visit the TIC in Barnstaple. The summertime bus service no. 300 is also good for sightseeing, since it travels along the coast and through Exmoor.

Museum of North Devon, *The Sq; tel: (01271) 46747* Open Tue–Sat 1000–1630. Admission £1. **Barnstaple Heritage Centre**, *St Annes Chapel, Paternoster Row, High St; tel: (01271) 46747*. Open Tue–Sat 1000–1300, 1400–1630. Admission £0.50. **Sanders Sheepskin Works and Tannery**, *Pilton Causeway; tel: (01271) 42335*. Open Mon–Fri 0900–1700, Sat 0915–1200. Free entry and free tours. **Brannam's Pottery**, *Roundswell; tel: (01271) 43035*. Open Mon–Fri 0900–1600. Admission £2.75 inc tour. Take the Red Bus North Devon no. 71, 1½ miles southwest.

Out of Town

Watermouth Castle, *Watermouth, nr Ilfracombe; tel: (01271) 867474*. Opening times vary – ask at the TIC. Admission £4.50. Take the Red Bus North Devon no. 30 (destination Berrynarbor); 12 miles north. **Dartington Crystal**, *Great Torrington; tel: (01805) 624233*. Open Mon–Fri 0930–1530. Admission £2.20. Take the red bus North Devon no. 71; 12 miles south. **The Big Sheep**, *Abbotsham, nr Bideford; tel: (01237) 472366*. Open daily 1000–1800. Admission £3.50. Take the Red Bus North Devon no.1, 2 or B or the Filers Travel bus no. 301 to Bideford and change to the Filers Travel bus no. 319 to the Big Sheep; 11 miles south-west. **Lynton and Lynmouth Cliff Railway**, *Lynton; tel: (01598) 52318*. Open Mon–Sat 0800–1900 (Mar–Nov), Sun 1000–1900 (May–end Sep). Admission £0.35. Travel on the Red Bus North Devon no. 310 to Lynton; 18 miles north-east.

EXETER to PLYMOUTH

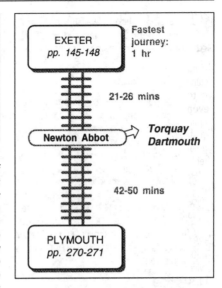

This scenic route skirts the southern fringes of Dartmoor – perhaps the wildest of England's National Parks – and provides a springboard for discovering the rugged and desolate beauty of a wilderness which has supported human habitation since prehistoric times. By contrast, a side track to the Victorian seaside resort of Torquay gives access to the more sedate charms of the so-called 'English Riviera', while another to Dartmouth brings you to the spectacular banks and hidden creeks of the Dart estuary.

TRAINS

ETT table: 510

 Fast Track

At least one train per hour runs between Exeter St Davids and Plymouth. Journey times are between 1 hr and 1 hr 10 mins. On Sun the service does not start until midday.

 On Track

Exeter–Newton Abbot–Plymouth

Most trains from Exeter to Plymouth call at Newton Abbot en route. If not, then a following slower train will. Journey times; Exeter to Newton Abbot 21–26 mins; Newton Abbot to Plymouth 42–50 mins (10–15 mins longer on Sun).

- - - - - - - - - - - - - - - - - - - -

Side Tracks from Newton Abbot

TORQUAY

TIC: *Vaughan Pde, Torquay, Devon TQ2 5JG;*

tel: *(01803) 297428.* Open Nov–Mar Mon–Sat 0900–1700, April–Oct Mon–Sat 0900–1800 DP SHS Services offered: local bed-booking service (latest 1700, booking fee), BABA (latest 1600, booking fee), tickets booked for theatre, bus, AA and British Rail. *The English Riviera Guide* (including accommodation list) is free.

Station: Torquay Station, *Rathmore Rd; tel (01752) 221300* is ½ mile away from the main shopping centre. There is a taxi rank. Bus nos 12 and 100 run into town. Services from Newton Abbot to Torquay and to Paignton (see under Dartmouth overleaf) are at least hourly – journey times are 11 mins to Torquay and 16 mins to Paignton. Be careful on return journeys from Torquay – some trains on Sats in summer will be going straight through Newton Abbot to the Midlands! Ask station staff if in doubt.

Getting Around

The majority of attractions in the town are within a walkable area of the centre. Town maps are available at a small charge from the TIC, whilst transport maps are available free of charge.

The main bus operator is **Bayline** tel: *(01803) 613226.* Services are good in the town centre and between towns every day up to 2300. A one-day 'Explorer' ticket, available daily after 0900, costs £5.95 for adults and £3.95 for children and OAPs. The main taxi rank is on *Cary Pde.*

Staying in Torquay

There is a good range of accommodation available, particularly mid-range hotels and guesthouses. Cheaper accommodation is located in the outlying villages, in particular in the *Avenue Rd* area. It is relatively easy to book on arrival, except during Jul and Aug (due to school holidays). Accommodation can also be booked through the **Torquay Hotels and Catering Association**, *12 Walnut Rd; tel: (01803) 605808.* The TIC has details of campsites in the area – the nearest is **Manor Farm**, *Daccombe; tel: (01803) 328294*, 3 miles north of the centre.

Sightseeing

The palm-fringed English Riviera town of Torquay has elegant Victorian terraces, sandy beaches, well-kept gardens and a continental feel. The town is associated with crime writer Agatha Christie, born here in 1890, and both **Torquay Museum** and **Torre Abbey** have special exhibitions on her life. **Bygones** takes a nostalgic look at life in Victorian times and **Kent's Cavern** has showcaves dating from 2,000,000 BC! The neighbouring resort of Paignton is home to popular **Paignton Zoo**, one of the largest in the country.

Wallace Arnold, *tel: (01803) 211729* offer various bus tours and boat trips can be arranged by **Western Lady**, *tel: (01803) 852041* from *Princess Pier.*

Babbacombe Model Village, *Hampton Ave; tel: (01803) 328669.* Open daily from 1000. Admission £3.40. **Kent Cavern**, *Ulsham Rd; tel: (01803) 294059.* Open all year. Admission £3.25. **Torquay Museum**, *529 Babbacombe Rd; tel: (01803) 293975.* Open Mon–Fri, Sun afternoons. Admission £1.75. **Torre Abbey**, *The Kings Dve; tel: (01803) 293593.* Open Apr–Oct. Admission £2.50.

Out of Town

Paignton Zoo, *Totnes Rd, Paignton; tel:* *(01803) 527936.* Open all year, 1000–1600 (last admission 1500). Admission £4.30 (winter rate) £5.95 (summer), family ticket available. Three miles, bus no. 80. See also p. 151. **Paignton and Dartmouth Steam Railway**, *Queens Park Station, Paignton (adjacent to British Rail); tel: (01803) 553760.* Open Apr–Oct. Admission £5. Three miles west. Bus 12, 100. **South Devon Railway**, *Buckfastleigh; tel: (01364) 642338.* Open Apr–Oct. Admission £5.90. Ten miles west. Train (via Newton Abbot) to Totnes and walk over footbridge to Totnes Riverside Station. Bus no. 80 runs direct from Paignton to Totnes town centre. **Compton Castle**, *Marldon, Paignton; tel: (01803) 752466.* Open Apr–Oct. Admission £2.60. Five miles west. **Bradley Manor**, *Newton Abbot; tel: (01392) 881691.* Open Apr–Sept (Wed only). Admission £2.60. Eight miles north. Bus no. 12. **Bygones**, *Fore St; tel: (01803) 326108.* Open daily from 1000. Admission £2.50. Two miles north. Bus no. 32.

DARTMOUTH

TIC: *The Engine House, Mayor's Avenue, Dartmouth, Devon TQ6 9YY; tel: (01803) 834224. Accommodation booking tel: (01803) 834959.* Open Mon–Sat 1000–1600 (1 Jan–31 Mar and 1 Oct–31 Dec), Mon–Sat 0930–1730, Sun 1000–1600 (1 Apr–30 Sept). DP SHS services offered: local bed booking, BABA (10% commission taken); some concessions to attractions sold. A copy of the guide *Welcome to Dartmouth 1995* is available free at the TIC and contains accommodation listings.

Station: General railway enquiries *tel: (01752) 221300.* There is no railway station in Dartmouth – the nearest is **Paignton Station**, *Station Sq, Paignton*, which is approximately 6 miles north of Dartmouth. For services from Newton Abbot, see previous page. There is a taxi rank outside the station.

Alternatively, travel to **Kingswear** and then take the ferry across the River Dart to Dartmouth. In summer (June–Sept) the **Paignton & Dartmouth Steam Railway** runs from Paignton to Kingswear; or you can catch the Bayline Bus no. 200, which runs frequently in the summer from Paignton to Kingswear and about four times a day during the winter.

Getting Around

Most attractions are within a walkable distance from the centre. A free transport map is freely available from the TIC. Bus services tend to be good in the centre but patchy to outlying areas. There are few buses operating after 1800 and a reduced service runs at the weekends.

There is no central bus depot in Dartmouth but most services start from the South Embankment in the town centre. The two main bus companies are **Western National** tel: (01752) 222666 which actually operates from Dartmouth and **Bayline** tel: (01803) 613326 which runs from the Kingswear side of the River Dart only. It is possible to buy a one-day 'Explorer' ticket for Bayline bus services, available daily after 0900 – an adult ticket costs £5.95.

A taxi rank is situated on the South Embankment in Dartmouth. Registered taxi companies include **ABP Taxis** tel: (01803) 862424 and **Carr's Private Hire Taxis** tel: (01803) 835035.

Staying in Dartmouth

There are few hotels of any type in Dartmouth – one national chain is represented. Cheaper accommodation in guesthouses and b. & b.s is plentiful and can be found in the town centre. There are also several inns offering accommodation, in the villages of Blackawton (5 miles west) and Dittisham (2 miles north). Though it is generally easy to find accommodation, it is advisable to book in advance during the **Regatta**, which takes place in late Aug.

The TIC can provide campsite information. **Little Cotton Campsite**, Little Cotton; tel: (01803) 832558 is 1 mile north and accessible by the 'Park and Ride' bus which leaves from the South Embankment. **Leonards Cove Campsite**, Stoke Fleming; tel: (01803) 770206 is accessible by the no. 93 Plymouth Bus and lies 3 miles south of Dartmouth.

Sightseeing

Dartmouth lies near the mouth of the river Dart,

in an area of outstanding natural beauty – countryside and moorlands on one side, a scenic coastline on the other. The remains of **Dartmouth Castle** date from the 15th century and **Dartmouth Museum** is full of local information. Fun for all ages can be had at **Woodlands Leisure Park**, and to the north-west is the rugged and desolate beauty of **Dartmoor National Park**, famous for its wild ponies and prehistoric remains.

Boat trips from Dartmouth to Totnes are popular. **River Link** tel: (01803) 834488 or (01803) 862735 operate all year but by appointment only Nov–Easter. **Red Cruises** tel: (01803) 832109 operate services Mar–end Oct which last 1–1½ hours and start at the North and South Embankments. Town guided tours are available – contact **Peter King**, tel: (01803) 832611.

Dartmouth Castle, Castle Rd; tel: (01803) 833588. Open daily 1000–1300, 1400–1800 (1 Apr–30 Sept), closing at 1600 (1–31 Oct), Wed–Sun only (1 Nov–31 Mar). Admission £2.00. Just under 1-mile walk or take the castle ferry (running Whitsun–end Sept).

Thomas Newcomen Engine, Mayors Ave; tel: (01803) 834224. Open Mon–Sat 0930–1730, Sun 1000–1600 (Apr–end Sept), Mon–Sat 0930–1600 (Oct–end Mar). Admission £0.50. **Dartmouth Museum**, The Butterwalk; tel: (01803) 832923. Open Mon–Sat 1100–1700 (Apr–end Oct), Mon–Sat 1200–1500 (Nov–end Mar). Admission £0.80.

Out of Town

Paignton and Dartmouth Steam Railway, Queens Park Station, Paignton; tel: (01803) 553760. Open Sun, Tue, Thu (1 Apr–31 May, 1–31 Oct), daily according to timetable (1 Jun–30 Sept). Join the train at Kingswear by taking the passenger ferry across the river.

Paignton Zoo (see Torquay, p. 150), bus no. 3 from Paignton bus station. **Woodlands Leisure Park**, Blackawton; tel: (01803) 7112598. Open daily 0930–dusk. Admission £3.75. Take the Totnes bus no. 89 from Dartmouth, which passes the entrance. Six miles north.

GLASGOW

Glasgow is a great Scottish city, enjoying a reputation as one of Europe's most vibrant cultural capitals, as well as being a bustling, sprawling commercial and industrial complex. Renowned for the range and quality of its fine art museums and galleries, it is alive all year round with a programme of arts and entertainment.

Tourist Information

TIC: *35 St Vincent Pl, Glasgow G1 2ER; tel: (0141) 204 4400.* Open Mon–Sat 0900–1800 (Oct–May), Sun 1000-1800 (Apr–Sep), Mon–Sat 0900–1900 (Jun and Sep), Mon–Sat 0900–2000 (July and Aug). SHS service offered, local bed-booking service at cost of 10% of total booking, BABA fee £2.75 plus 10% of total booking. Very busy for bookings during July and Aug. Theatre tickets, Scottish Tourist guides city walks, boat trips, city tours booked. The TIC sells many kinds of public transport tickets and passes, as well as Scottish Youth Hostel membership, Young Scots Cards and car hire. The *Greater Glasgow Official Quick Guide* costs £1 and *Where to Stay* £0.90.

TIC: *Glasgow Airport, Tourist Information Desk (International Arrivals) Paisley PA3 2ST; tel (0141) 848 4440.* Open daily 0730–1800. Local bed-booking service and BABA offered. Rail tickets to all stations in Scotland sold, also Great British Heritage Pass.

TIC: *Town Hall, Abbey Close, Paisley PA1 1JS; tel: (0141) 889 0711.* Open Mon–Fri 0900–1300 and 1400–1700 (Apr and May), Mon–Sat 0900–1800 (Jun–Sep).

Arriving and Departing

Airport

Glasgow Airport is situated in Renfrew, just 8 miles from the city centre. There is a coach every 20 minutes from the airport (£2 single) and an airport bus links the airport to Paisley Gilmour Street Station from where there is a train every 10 minutes to Glasgow Central (£2 single).

Stations

The main stations are **Glasgow Central**, *Gordon St*, and **Glasgow Queen Street**; for rail enquiries *tel: (0141) 204 2844.* There is a shuttle bus service between the two stations, cost £0.35. Glasgow Central Station has a **Hertz Rent-a-Car** desk and a courtesy telephone when the desk is not manned. There are taxi ranks outside both stations.

Getting Around

There are many attractions within walking distance of the centre but a few are not so close, and public transport such as buses and the excellent underground system are good ways of getting around. The TIC has free town and transport maps and transport maps can also be obtained from the **Travel Centre**, *St Enoch Sq; tel: (0141) 226 4826.*

Buses

The main bus company, **Strathclyde Buses Ltd**, operates from *Buchanan Bus Station, Killermont St; tel: (0141) 332 7133.* Services are good in the city centre; outlying area services are good during the day but less frequent in the evening and at weekends. There are some night services to most areas.

Underground

Glasgow has a small underground railway system – there are 15 stations serving the central area of the city and a flat fare of £0.50 is charged for any length of trip.

There are a number of special tickets for the transport system. **Day Tripper**, at £11 for 2 adults and £6 for one adult, covers most rail bus services in Strathclyde (except Argyll). The **Glasgow Roundabout** and **Roundabout Plus** tickets offer unlimited travel for one day on the underground and Scotrail services in Glasgow for £3. The Roundabout Plus ticket costs £5 and includes the Discovering Glasgow Guided Bus Tour. The **Underground Heritage Trails** is £1.60 and offers unlimited trips on the under-

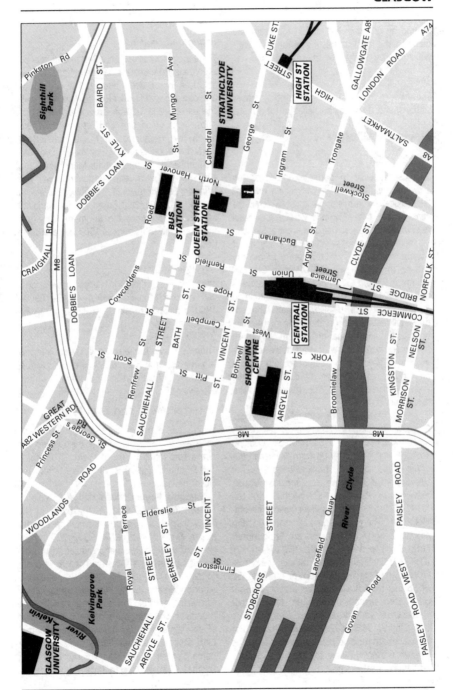

ground on one day. Included in the ticket is a guide to the most interesting historic buildings which can be reached by the underground.

Taxis

The two main taxi ranks are at the railway stations, and taxis may be hailed in the street.

Staying in Glasgow

Accommodation

It is usually easy to book accomodation on arrival in the city except in May when **Mayfest** takes place and in July and August, which is the peak holiday time. **Thomas Cook** has a hotel reservation bureau at Glasgow Central Station.

There is a large selection of all types of accommodation both in the centre of the city and on the outskirts. Hotel chains in Glasgow include BW, Cp, FC, Hn, Ma, MC, ST and Sw. It is possible to find budget accommodation in most areas. There is also a small range of budget inns situated on the edge of the city, towards the airport and in Cumbernauld, which is 12 miles from the city. It is advisable to arrive quite early if you wish to find accommodation on the day, as it can be difficult later in the evening, particularly in the guesthouse and b. & b. range.

The **Scottish Youth Hostel Association**, Glasgow Hostel, 7/8 Park Terrace; tel: (0141) 332 3004 is open daily 0700–0200 (last booking 2330). Buses 44 and 59 go from Buchanan Bus Station and bus 11 from Queen St. The **University of Glasgow** at Cairncross House, Kelvinhaugh Park and Kelvinhaugh St; tel: (0141) 330 5385 have summer holiday accommodation. There are four campsites in and around Glasgow, the nearest are **Craigenmuir Park**, Campsie View, Stepps; tel: (0141) 779 4159/2973. Open all year, take a train from Queen Street station to Stepps or a no. 40, 50 or 56 bus from Buchanan Bus Station and get off at Stepps, then a 10-minute walk. **Balgair Castle Caravan Park**, Overglins, Fintry, Stirlingshire; tel: (01360) 860283, is 18 miles north of the city but there is no public transport to it. The Greater Glasgow Where to Stay guide has the addresses of other sites.

Eating and Drinking

There are plenty of cafés and restaurants serving everything from Scottish to international cuisine at prices to suit every budget. The city's pubs and bars are well-known for their character and friendliness. The TIC can provide a free list of pubs, cafés, wine bars and restaurants. There are a few restaurants in the centre serving vegetarian food as part of their menu. If you are an admirer of Charles Rennie Mackintosh, the Glasgow architect and designer, visit **The Willow Tea Room**, 217 Sauchiehall St; tel (0141) 332 0532. Housed in an original Mackintosh building, the Room de Luxe has been restored to its original 1903 lilac and silver decor.

Communications

The main post office is in George Sq, Glasgow and is open Mon–Fri 0830–1745, Sat 0900–1900. It has poste restante facilities.

Money

Thomas Cook bureaux de change: Glasgow Airport; Glasgow Central Station; 50 Sauchiehall St; 15–17 Gordon St; 66 Gordon St. (British Airways office).

Entertainment and Events

What's On, a free monthly list of events and entertainment is available from the TIC and The List, a fortnightly listing of events in Glasgow and Edinburgh (see p. 126), costs £1 from the TIC or newsagents.

Glasgow Royal Concert Hall, 2 Sauchiehall St; tel: (0141) 227 5511 is the home of the Royal Scottish National Orchestra. **The Theatre Royal**, Hope St; tel: (0141) 332 9000 is the home of Scottish Opera and regular host to the Scottish Ballet. **The Citizens Theatre**, Gorbals St; tel (0141) 429 0022 is Glasgow's innovative repertory theatre. Scottish dance nights, known as ceilidhs, are held in lively venues all over the city. **Ibrox Stadium**, Edminston Dr, is the home of the famous soccer team Rangers Football Club, while **Celtic Park**, 95 Kerrydale St, is the home of their equally well-known rivals Celtic Football Club. **Hampden Park** is the national football stadium where international matches are played.

Mayfest is an international festival of theatre, dance, music, the visual arts and film and takes place in various venues for three weeks in May each year. The **World Pipe Band Championships** takes place annually in August at *Bellahouston Park*. The **Gourock Highland Games** is held in *Gourock Park* every May. The **Glasgow International Folk Festival** and **Jazz Festival** are held annually in June and July.

Shopping

Glasgow is a city with fine shopping facilities, from elegant malls to small boutiques. *Princes Sq* and the *Italian Centre, John St* and *Ingram St* are the areas for designer-name shops, whilst *St Enoch Centre*, the largest glass-covered shopping centre in Europe, has 80 stores as well as a food-court. The **Barras Market** in *54 Calton Entry*, near *Princes Sq*, is a craft market and is open Sat and Sun 1900–1700.

Sightseeing

Glasgow is a city of great architectural contrast. Charles Rennie Mackintosh is the city's most celebrated architect: the **Glasgow School of Art, Hill House, The Mackintosh House (Hunterian Museum), Queen's Cross Church** and the **Museum of Education** are different examples of his Art Nouveau work. **Glasgow Cathedral** is a superb example of 12th-century architecture while the grandeur of the **City Chambers** in *George Sq*, built in 1883 in the Italian Renaissance style, is testament to the opulence of Victorian Glasgow. The **Art Gallery and Museum** are world-famous, whilst the **Burrell Collection**, a priceless collection of paintings and objets d'art, is housed in a superb building in Pollok Country Park. The oldest house in the city, **Provand's Lordship**, built in 1471, now houses a collection of period furniture.

Discovering Glasgow day tours from open-topped buses can be booked at the TIC. They start from *George Sq* and cost £4.50. **Strathclyde Buses** do day tours in the summer *tel: (0141) 636 3190*. Paddle steamer **Waverley** offers boat trips on the Clyde from *Anderston*

Quay from £9.95, also **Caledonian Macbrayne** do daysavers on the Clyde to Bute and Tarbert *(0475) 650100*. **Glasgow City Walks** do guided walks of the city daily May-Sep, contact *(0141) 942 7929*. Also, **Clyde Helicopters** *tel: (0141) 226 4261* offer spectacular aerial tours of Glasgow and beyond. The **Citilink Smart Card** is a discount ticket for students, under 25s and over 60s on Citilink services, cost £7.

Art Galleries and Museums

Glasgow Art Gallery and Museum, *Kelvingrove, Argyll St; tel: (0141) 221 9600*. Open Mon–Fri 1000–1700, Sun 1100–1700. Admission free. **Museum of Transport**, *Kelvin Hall, 1 Bunhouse Rd; tel: (0141) 221 9600*. Open Mon–Sat 1000–1700, Sun 1100–1700. Admission free. **Burrell Collection**, *Pollok Country Park, 2060 Pollokshaws Rd; tel: (0141) 649 7151*. Open Mon–Sat 1000–1700, Sun 1100–1700. Admission free. **Hunterian Art Gallery and Museum**, *University Ave; tel: (0141) 330 4221/5431*. Open Mon–Sat 09300–1700. Admission free. **People's Palace**, *Glasgow Green; tel: (0141) 554 0223*. Open Mon–Sat 1000–1700, Sun 1100–1700. Admission free. **Pollok House**, *Pollok Country Park, 2060 Pollokshaws Country Park; tel: (0141) 0274*. Open Mon–Sat 1000–1700, Sun 1100–1700. Admission free. **Hagg's Castle**, *100 St Andrew's Dr; tel: (0141) 427 2725*. Open Mon–Sat 1000–1700, Sun 1100–1700. Admission free. **St Mungo Museum of Religious Life and Art**, *2 Castle St; tel: (0141) 553 2557*. Open Mon–Sat 1000–1700, Sun 1100–1700. Admission free. **Headquarters of the Charles Rennie Mackintosh Society**, *Queen's Cross Church, 870 Garscube Rd; tel: (0141) 946 6600*. Open Tue, Thu and Fri 1200–1700, Sun 1430–1700. Admission free. **Museum of Education**, *Scotland St; tel: (0141) 429 1202*. Open Mon–Sat 1000–1700, Sun 1400–1700. Admission free. **McLellan Galleries**, *270 Sauchiehall St; tel: (0141) 331 1854*. Open Mon–Sat 1000–1700, Sun 1100–1700. Admission charge varies with exhibition.

Historic Buildings

Glasgow Cathedral, *Castle St: (0141) 552 6891*. Open Mon–Sat 0930–1300, 1400–

1600, Sun 1400–1600 (daily to 1800 Apr–Sept). Admission free. **Provands Lordship**, *3 Castle St; tel: (0141) 552 8819*. Open Mon–Sat 1000–1700, Sun 1100–1700. Admission free. **The Tenement House**, *145 Buccleuch St; tel: (0141) 333 0183*. Open daily 1400–1700 (Mar–end Oct). Admission £2. **Hutchesons' Hall**, *158 Ingram St; tel: (0141) 552 8391*. Open Mon–Fri 0930–1700, Sat 1000–1600. Admission free. **City Chambers**, *George Sq.* Tours Mon–Fri 1030 and 1430. Admission free. **University of Glasgow and its Visitor Centre**, *University Ave; tel: (0141) 330 5511*. Open Mon–Sat 0930–1700. Admission free. **Glasgow School of Art**, *167 Renfrew St; tel: (0141) 353 4526*. Guided tours Mon–Fri 1100 and 1400, Sat 1030 (tours restricted in winter). Admission free.

Out of Town

Paisley Museum and Art Galleries, *High St, Paisley; tel: (0141) 889 3151*. Open Mon–Sat 1000–1700. Admission free. Eight miles south west of Glasgow. Take the train from Glasgow Central to Paisley Gilmour Street Station. **Summerlee Heritage Park**, *West Canal St, Coatbridge; tel: (01236) 431261*. Open daily 1000–1700. Admission free. Eight miles east of Glasgow, take the train from Glasgow Queen Street to Sunnyside. **Custom House Museum**, *Custom House Quay, Greenock; tel: (01475) 726331* Open Mon–Fri 1000–1230, Sun 1330–1630. Admission free. This is 25 miles west of Glasgow, by train from Glasgow Central to Greenock. **Glengoyne Distillery**, *Dumgoyne, near Killearn; tel: (01360) 50254*. Tours by arrangements. Admission £3. Take Midland bus no. 10 from Buchanan Bus Station. **New Lanark World Heritage Village**, *New Lanark Mills, Lanark; tel: (01555) 661345*. Open daily 1100–1700. Admission £2.75. The distillery is 20 miles south east – take the train from Glasgow Central to Lanark. **Hill House,** *Upper Colquhoun St, Helensburgh; tel: (0436) 73900*. Open daily 1330–1730 (Apr–Dec). Admission £3. Take the train from Glasgow Queen Street to Helensburgh Lower.

GLASGOW to OBAN

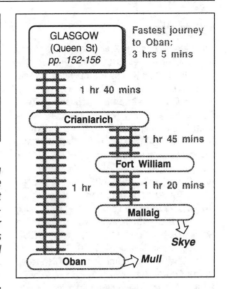

GLASGOW (Queen St) pp. 152-156

Fastest journey to Oban: 3 hrs 5 mins

1 hr 40 mins

Crianlarich

1 hr 45 mins

Fort William

1 hr

1 hr 20 mins

Mallaig

Skye

Oban

Mull

Striking north-west from Glasgow and skirting the 'bonny banks' of Loch Lomond, this route passes through some of Scotland's most majestic scenery, and provides excellent opportunities for exploring this south-western corner of the Highlands. Oban and Mallaig also serve as points of departure for the Isles of Mull and Skye, two of the jewels of the Inner Hebrides.

TRAINS

ETT table: 593

 On Track

The service between Glasgow and Oban consists of three trains daily (only one on winter Suns). The journey from Glasgow Queen Street to Oban takes around 3 hrs 5 mins. All trains call at Crianlarich, where some divide for Oban (usually the front) and Fort William and/or Mallaig (usually the rear) portions – make sure you are in the correct half of the train. The various journey times are: Glasgow Queen Street to Crianlarich 1 hr 40 mins; Crianlarich to Oban 1 hr; Crianlarich to Fort William 1 hr 45 mins; Fort William to Mallaig 1 hr 20 mins.

FORT WILLIAM

TIC: *Cameron Sq; tel: (01397) 703781.* Open Mon–Thur 1000–1600, Fri 1000–1700, and Sat, Sun if there's skiing. DP SHS Services offered: local bed-booking service (latest 5 mins before closing), BABA (latest 15 mins before closing). *Essential Guide* (including accommodation list) is free. *Best of Fort William & Lochaber* brochure (with accommodation list) is also free.

Station: Fort William Station, *Transport Centre;*

tel: (01397) 703791 is north side of the town centre, and has a taxi rank.

Getting Around

Most attractions are not walkable from the centre. A town map is available free from the TIC. Transport information is available in person or by phone from the TIC. Local public transport is excellent in the centre, although trips to some rural areas would require planning in advance. **Highland Bus and Coach Station** is one of the main operators for local buses *tel: (01397) 702373.* The main taxi rank is in the *High St.*

Staying in Fort William

There is a good range of accommodation, particularly guesthouses and b. & b.s. Cheaper accommodation is located mainly in the town centre and outlying areas. It is easy to book on arrival in most months, but advance booking is essential during Aug and Christmas/New Year. The nearest youth hostel is **Glen Nevis Youth Hostel**, *Glen Nevis; tel: (01397) 702336,* open daily 0700–2300, 3 miles south from Fort William. The TIC has details of campsites in the area; the nearest is **Glen Nevis Caravan & Camping Park,** *Glen Nevis; tel: (01397) 702191,* 2½ miles north-east of the town centre.

Sightseeing

There are various sightseeing tours and guided walks on offer, details of which are available from the TIC. Boat trips are operated by **Seal Island Cruises,** tel: (01397) 705589.

Clan Cameron Museum, Achnacarry, Spean Bridge; tel: (01397) 772473. Open daily 1400–1700 (Easter–mid Oct). Thirteen miles north of Fort William. Admission £1.50. **West Highland Museum,** Cameron Sq; tel: (01397) 702169. Open Mon–Sat 1000–1300, 1400–1700, Jul–Aug 0930–1730, 1400–1700 Sun. Admission £1.50. **Treasures of the Earth,** Mallaig Rd; tel: (01397) 772283. Open daily 1000–1700, during summer 0930–1900. Admission £2.50. **Ben Nevis Distillery,** North Rd; tel: (01397) 700200. Open daily 0900–1700, 2 miles north of the town centre. Admission free. **Glen Nevis Visitor Centre,** Glen Nevis; tel (01397) 705922. Open 0900–1800 (summer). Two miles from the town centre. Admission free.

Out of Town

Kinlochlaich House and Gardens, Appin, Argyll; tel: (01631) 73342. Open Mon–Sat 0930–1730, Sun 1030–1730 (Apr–Oct), Mon–Sat 0930–1700 (mid Oct–Mar), 25 miles south of Fort William. Admission free. **Mallaig Marine World,** The Harbour, Mallaig; tel: (01687) 462292. Open daily 0900–1900, except Christmas, Boxing Day, New Year, late Jan and early Feb). Admission £2.50.

 Connection: Mallaig to Isle of Skye

A Caledonian MacBrayne ferry runs from Mallaig to **Armadale,** on the Isle of Skye, twice daily (with an extra sailing on July–Aug weekdays). A bus connects Armadale with **Kyleakin,** from where it is possible to get another ferry to **Kyle of Lochalsh** on the mainland (see Edinburgh–Inverness route, p. 144).

OBAN

TIC: Boswell House, Oban; tel: (0631) 63122,

fax: (01631) 64273. Open Mon–Sat 0900–1730, Sun 0900–1600 (May–mid Jun), Mon–Sat 0900–1900, Sun 0900–1600 (mid Jun–mid Sept, except Jul/Aug, when open to 2100 Mon–Sat), Mon–Thur 0900–1730, Fri 0900–1700 (Winter – closed at 1300 for lunch) TIC opening hours may change in 1995. DP, SHS services offered, local bed-booking service £1 booking fee, BABA £2.75 booking fee. Guided tours booked. West Highlands and Islands of Argyll brochure and an accommodation list are available free.

Station: Oban Station, tel: (01631) 63083 is in the town centre. There is a taxi rank outside the station.

Getting Around

The majority of attractions are within walking distance of the town centre. Free town and transport maps are available from the TIC. There are several bus companies serving the area, **Oban and District;** tel: (01631) 628561/63244, **Gaelic Bus;** tel: (018552) 229, **Highland Bus Co,** tel: (01397) 702373 are the main ones. Services are good in the whole area, with reduced services after 1700.

Staying in Oban

There is a wide range of accommodation of all types in and around the town centre. It is generally easy to find accommodation on arrival, except at bank holidays and during the peak holiday season, mid-July to end of Aug, when it is imperative to book. There is one youth hostel in the area, **Oban Youth Hostel,** The Esplanade, in the centre of the town. The closest campsite is **Oban Camping and Caravan Park,** Gallanoch Farm, Gallanoch Rd tel: (01631) 66624. It is very close to Oban station.

Sightseeing

Oban is an attractive Victorian port and holiday resort, with a busy harbour. The waters around Oban are perfect for sailing and the town is also a well-known centre for sub-aqua diving. Bus tours and boat trips can be booked through the TIC. One of the most popular visitor attractions on the west coast is the **Oban Sea Life Centre,** which offers the chance to come face to face with some amazing sea creatures. The unique location of **Oban Distillery Visitor Centre** in the town centre makes it one of Scotland's most unusual and interesting distilleries. Forty miles south of Oban is **Inveraray Castle**, home of the Duke and Duchess of Argyll. Also in Inverary is the **Arctic Penguin Maritime Experience**, in a 1911 three-masted schooner, featuring an on-board cinema with breathtaking archive film. A contrast of experiences is offered by 19th-century **Inveraray Jail**, with its Torture, Death and Damnation exhibition, and **Argyll Wildlife Park**, where you can enjoy a walk around 60 acres of hill, forest and wildfowl marsh.

Oban Distillery, *Oban; tel: (01631) 64262.* Open Mon–Fri 0930–1700. Admission charge. **Oban Sea Life Centre**, *Barcaldine; tel: 90631) 172386.* Open daily 0900–1800 (Easter–Nov, but open to 1900 Jul–Aug), Sat and Sun 0900–1700 (Dec–Feb, daily over Christmas/New Year). Admission £4.35. The centre is 10 miles from Oban; Gaelic Bus and Oban and District buses to Fort William stop at the Sea Life Centre.

Argyll Wildlife Park, *Inveraray; tel: (01499) 302213.* open daily 0930–1800 (Apr–end Oct). Admission £3.25. Inveraray is 40 miles south of Oban. The Oban–Glasgow bus service of West Coast Motors runs 2–3 times a day from Oban railway station and stops in Inveraray. The park is 1 mile from Inveraray town. **Arctic Penguin Maritime Heritage Centre**, *The Pier, Inveraray; tel: (01499) 302213.* Open daily 1000–1800 (Easter–Nov), 1000–1600 (Nov–Easter). Admission £6.25. In centre of Inveraray. **Inveraray Castle**, *Argyll Estates Office, Cherry Pk; tel: (01499) 302203.* Open Mon–Thur, sat 1000-1200 and 1400–1700, Sun 1300–1700 (Apr–Jun, Sept–mid Oct), Mon–Sat 1000–1700, Sun 1300–1700 (Jul–Aug). Admission £5.50. **Inveraray Jail**, *Church Sq; tel: (01499) 302381.* Open daily 0930–1800. Admission £3.95.

- - - - - - - - - - - - - - - - - - -

 Side Track from Oban

ISLE OF MULL

TIC: *Main St, Tobermory, Isle of Mull, Argyll PA75 6NU; tel: (01688) 302182.* Open Mon–

Sun 0900–1730 (Summer), Mon–Fri 1000–1600 (Winter).

Ferries: from Oban, take the ferry to either **Craignure** or **Tobermory** (foot passengers only). Caledonian MacBrayne, *Ferry Terminal, Railway Pier, Oban; tel: (01631) 62285* operate at least two ferries a day – one every 2 hrs in the summer.

Buses: Services on the Island are sparse and infrequent, and there are none after 1800. In particular, there are no services to Ulva, which is the starting point for several boat trips out to neighbouring islands.

Sightseeing

Tobermory has become famous through the centuries as the site where the Spanish galleon *Florida* was sunk, starting a hunt for lost treasure that continues even today. This small, attractive town is a perfect base from which to explore the Isle of Mull – an island rich in both culture and landscape, and surprisingly large in size. The TIC has details of a wide range of accommodation.

Hill walking is extremely popular here, but for those with less time to spend, **Bowman Coaches**, *tel: (01680) 812313*, operate various bus tours of the Isle from Oban on the mainland from Apr–Oct – a circular tour costs £12.00. A day tour including a visit to windswept **Iona** costs £14.00 (which includes the 5-min ferry crossing from Fionnphort), where visitors will discover the Abbey.

Turus Mara Boat Company *tel: (01688) 400242* run half-day and full-day boat trips from Ulva Port, on the west of the island to **Staffa Island** (site of the stunning basalt formations of **Fingal's Cave**) and **Lunga**, a bird spotter's paradise, costing £10.00–£23.00.

Back on Mull, no visit would be complete without visiting Craignure, best known for its two castles, **Duart** and **Torosay**, the latter being linked to Craignure by the miniature **Mull and West Highland Railway**. Finally for a little culture, spend the evening at the **Mull Little Theatre**, *Dervaig; tel: (01688) 400267*, Britain's smallest professional theatre which performs to an audience of just 37 people.

- - - - - - - - - - - - - - - - - - -

LONDON

Buckingham Palace, the Tower of London, the Houses of Parliament – few capital cities have buildings so closely linked with their country's image in the eyes of the world. You will need at least four days to see the most important tourist attractions, but London is far more than just the sum of these. A vast, exciting city where the pace of life can seem frenetic, it has many quieter parts, almost villages, worth seeking out within it; for Londoners, these neighbourhoods, together with London's great parks, are the parts which stir the affections and give the city its enormous charm.

Tourist Information

The **British Travel Centre** (BTC), *12 Lower Regent Street, London SW1Y 4PQ* (tube: *Piccadilly Circus*). Open Mon–Fri 0900–1830, Sat, Sun 1000–1600 (extended opening on Sat from mid-May to Sept). DP Services offered: local b. & b. service and BABA (£5 booking fee charged, and redeemable deposit of first night's accommodation usually taken). Latest bookings 30 mins before closing. Advance reservations handled. *Tel: 930 0572,* for **Expotel Reservations** at the BTC. Guided tours, theatre tickets and transport tickets booked. Comprehensive information in many languages on travel, accommodation, events and entertainment is available.

TIC: *Victoria Station Forecourt, London SW1V 1JU* (tube: *Victoria*). Open Mon–Sat 0800–1900, Sun 0800–1700. DP Services offered: as above. Victoria TIC is extremely busy from June–Sept, so expect to queue.

Further TICs are also to be found at: **Heathrow Airport**, *Terminal 3 Arrivals Concourse*. DP Services offered: as for Victoria TIC (see above). Heathrow Airport, *Terminals 1, 2 and 3 Underground Station Concourse*. Open daily 0830–1800. DP Services offered: as for

Victoria TIC (see above). **Liverpool Street Station**, *Liverpool St, EC2* (tube: *Liverpool St*). Open Mon 0815–1900, Tues–Sat 0815–1800, Sun 0830–1645. DP Services offered: as for Victoria TIC (see above). **Selfridges**, *Oxford St, W1* (tube: *Bond St*). Open store hours. DP Services offered: as for Victoria TIC (see above). **Waterloo International**, *Arrivals Hall, SE1*. DP Services offered: as for Victoria TIC (see above).

Arriving and Departing

Airports

Heathrow Airport is 15 miles west of central London, about 45 mins from central London by tube on the Piccadilly tube (Underground) line, single fare £3.10. (There are two tube stops at Heathrow, one for Terminals 1, 2 and 3, and one for Terminal 4, so it is important to check which terminal your flight leaves from before you travel home.) Alternatively, Airbus routes A1 and A2 run to central and west London, (journey time from 50–85 mins), single fare £5; *tel: 222 1234.* There are also regular Speedlink coach services connecting Heathrow with Gatwick (1 hr) and Stansted (1 hr 20 mins) airports, single fare approximately £14. There is a TIC located by the underground station for Terminals 1, 2 and 3 (see above). Taxis into central London cost approximately £30–35. General enquiries: Terminal 1 *tel: 745 7702/ 3/4*; Terminal 2 *tel: 745 7115/6/7*; Terminal 3 *tel: 745 7412/3/4*; Terminal 4 *tel: 745 4540*.

Gatwick Airport is 27 miles south of central London. Gatwick Express trains depart for Victoria Station every 15 mins from 0530–2000, then every 30 mins until 2300, and hourly throughout the night, (journey time 30 mins, 45 mins at night), single fare £8.60; *tel: 928 5100.* The Flightline 777 bus service runs hourly to Victoria Coach station from 0520–2200 (journey time 60–70 mins), single fare £7.50; *tel: 668 7261.* There are regular coach services operated by Speedlink and Jetlink between Heathrow and Gatwick, journey time 60 mins, fare from £9.50–£14. Taxis into central London cost approximately £40–£45. There is a TIC on the arrivals concourse of the South Terminal; however, if you are coming into London by train, use the TIC at Victoria Station for London accommodation bookings (see above). For enquiries *tel: (01293) 535353/560108.*

London Stansted Airport is 37 miles north-east of central London. Stansted Express trains go direct to Liverpool Street station, where there is a TIC. Trains run every 30 mins from 0600–2300 (first train Sat 0700, Sun 0730), journey time 41 mins, single fare £10; *tel: 928 5100.* There are currently no bus services running from Stansted to London, but Cambridge Coach Service and Speedlink bus services connect Stansted with Heathrow (1 hr 20 mins) and Gatwick (2 hrs 20 mins), single fare from £11–£13.50; *tel: (01279) 663018.* Taxis into central London cost approximately £40–£45. For enquiries *tel: (01279) 662379 or 662520.*

Stations

There are 16 British Rail stations in central London (most are linked to tube stations of the same name). The most important are: **Victoria** (*tel: 928 5100).* Victoria is the terminal of the Gatwick Express and also covers the south coast towns. Victoria is also home to a number of useful information desks, such as the British Rail International Rail Centre, the main London Tourist Board TIC and a hotel-booking desk. There is a Travellers' Aid office on platform 10, which can help with all sorts of problems, including lost passports.

Charing Cross (*tel: 928 5100)* covers the Kent coast and Dover ferry port trains. Traditionally covering the south-western region, **Waterloo** (*tel: 928 5100)* handles trains to Portsmouth for boat services to France and Spain. It is also the London terminal for Eurostar international trains (see p. 14). **King's Cross** (*tel: 278 2477)* currently handles services to the north-east and Scotland. Other main stations include: **Euston** (*tel: 387 7070)* for trains to the west Midlands, north Wales, north-west England and Scotland; **Liverpool St** (*tel: 928 5100)* for trains to eastern England, including boat trains to Harwich for ferries to the Netherlands; **Paddington** (*tel: 262 6767)* for trains to Wales and western England; **St Pancras** (*tel: 387 7070)* for trains to Sheffield and the east Midlands.

The following is a list of the appropriate telephone enquiry numbers for rail travel from London to different areas of the country: eastern England, Essex, south, south-east *tel: 928 5100*; Yorkshire, north-east, east coast *tel: 278 2477*; Midlands, north Wales, north-west England, west coast *tel: 387 7070*; west of England, south Wales: *tel: 262 6767.*

Buses

Victoria Coach Station *Buckingham Palace Rd, SW1; tel: 730 0202,* is the main London terminal for long-distance coaches, approximately 10 mins walk from the rail station and tube. Tickets for most services need to be bought before boarding the coach. Tickets for National Express services covering England and Wales can be bought at the coach station daily, 0600–2400. Credit card bookings can be made by telephone on *tel: 730 3499.* National Express cover bus travel around England and Wales, daily except 25 December.

Green Line buses (*tel: 668 7261)* connect central London with towns and villages in the surrounding counties. Buses depart from *New Coach Road, Bulleid Way,* just off *Eccleston Bridge, SW1,* approximately 10 mins walk from Victoria station, and tickets can be bought from the driver when boarding.

Getting Around

The first thing you should do on arrival is arm yourself with a good street guide: try the *A–Z Map of London* (available for £1.95 from most newsagents). This covers the central area on a scale of 6 in. to the mile, highlights places of interest and has maps showing the West End cinemas and theatres. For more detail and a much wider area, buy the full A–Z and *Nicholson Street Guides,* also available from most newsagents.

Free bus and tube maps and other information about London Transport (LT), including the various types of tickets, are available in most tube stations. (The official map of the underground system is included in the colour map section at the end of this book.) If you draw a blank, try the main LT office in **St James's Park** tube station (*tel: 222 1234* 24 hours a day).

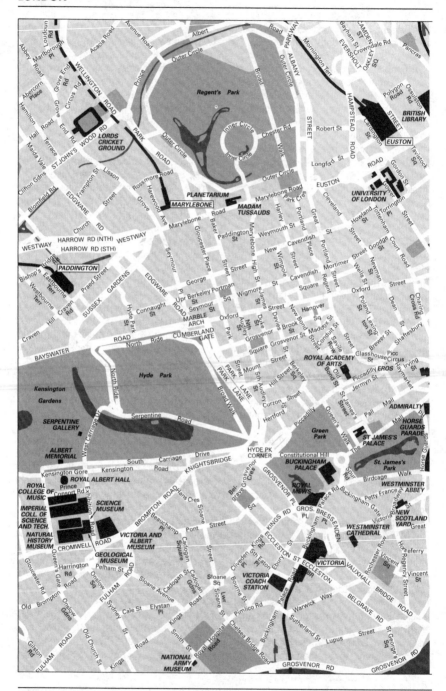

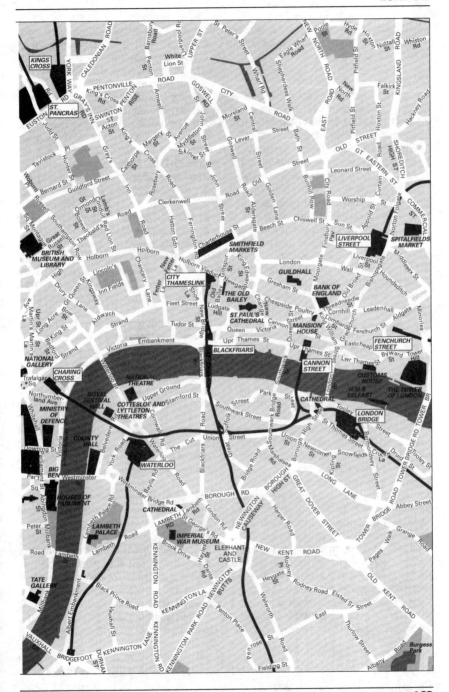

Travel during rush hour (primarily Mon–Fri 0715–0915 and 1630–1830) is no fun at all, so avoid it if you can.

Tickets

Transport in London is arranged in a series of concentric circles (zones) spreading out through the suburbs. A ticket for Zones 1 and 2 should cover most tourist destinations.

Single tickets are expensive in comparison to Travelcards (one-day Travelcards are £2.70 for zones 1 and 2, £3.20 for all zones; available from most stations and many newsagents). These cover all public transport services within London, giving you the freedom to hop on and off buses, tubes and some local trains. One-day Travelcards can be bought and used only after 0930 (for travel before 0930 ask for an LT card) and are not valid for travel on night buses (designated 'N'); for travel before 0930 use an LT card. Travelcards valid for a week, a month, three months or a year can be used at any time.

The Underground

Commonly known as 'the tube', London's underground railway (subway) system is extensive, efficient and usually the quickest and most foolproof way to get around. On the down-side, it can be dirty, impossibly crowded and claustrophobic during rush hours. The hours of operating vary slightly from line to line, but most services run Mon–Sat from 0530 to around midnight and Sun 0700–2330. Smoking is forbidden anywhere on the Underground.

Each line is designated by a name and a colour, and maps of the network are found at frequent intervals throughout stations. Platforms are clearly labelled to show if the trains are north-, south-, east- or west-bound. As an additional help, destination boards on the platforms and the front of the train give the final stop. Keep your ticket handy: there are occasional inspections and you need to put the ticket through a turnstile machine to get out of the station. Anyone found travelling without a valid ticket is fined £10 on the spot.

Buses

London's bright-red double-decker buses have become a tourist attraction in their own right. (Not all buses are red, however, so look out for the number irrespective of the colour!) The roads are often congested and travel can be slow, but you will get a much clearer idea of how London fits together from a bus than if you travel underground. Some of the routes (e.g. nos. 12 and 11) are excellent for sightseeing and the view from the top deck is always great. Most services run: Mon–Sat 0600–2400 and Sun 0730–2300. Restricted services operate on several routes through the night. Night bus stops have blue and yellow signs.

Older buses have an open platform at the back and a conductor to issue tickets. More modern buses have doors at the front, and you must pay the driver (or show your Travelcard) before you take your seat. Keep your ticket until you reach your destination as there are random checks. Buses do not always go the full length of their route, so check the destination board on the front or back.

There are bus stops every few hundred yards throughout central London, with the relevant bus numbers clearly shown on each. There are two types of stop: the compulsory stop (white background) and the request stop (red background). The bus will stop without being hailed at the compulsory stop, unless it is full. At the request stop the bus will not halt unless you put your arm out to flag it down or ring the bell if you are on board. There are also single-deck Red Arrow buses with ticket machines on entry (you must have the exact change for your fare).

Taxis

London's famous 'black' cabs are often covered in advertisements and may not always be black, but their shape is nevertheless distinctive. Fares are not cheap, but taxis are metered and the drivers have to pass a rigorous test on their knowledge of London. There are extra (metered) charges for: a lot of baggage; more than one passenger; travelling in the evening (after 2000) or at weekends. It is usual practice to give the driver a tip of about 10 to 15 per cent on top of the fare.

There are taxi ranks at key positions, but you can also hail them in the street. When a taxi is free, the yellow light at the front saying 'TAXI' is on. Avoid the unlicensed minicabs which tout for business on the street and at mainline stations (licensed minicabs can only be booked by telephone).

Staying in London

Accommodation

London has an enormous range of accommodation, from world-renowned hotels with extremely high prices, such as the Ritz and Savoy, to budget hotels and youth hostels (see below). All the major international hotel chains are represented. Further down the scale, there are plenty of small hotels, ranging from the completely unacceptable to clean establishments with modest facilities. Prices start at around £25 per person for something half-way decent. The *Paddington, Victoria* and *Earl's Court* areas, in particular, have a good range. The best bet for cheap accommodation is the **Hostelling International (HI)** organisation, which has seven hostels in London. If you are not already a member, full details can be obtained from their central information office, *tel: 248 6547.*

The British Travel Centre and and all other central London TICs (see beginning of chapter for details) operate a booking service for all types of accommodation in London and throughout Britain.

Thomas Cook have hotel booking desks at the following rail stations: Gatwick Airport, Kings Cross, Victoria (two locations) and Waterloo.

Other hotel booking services include: **British Hotel Reservation Centre**, *10 Buckingham Palace Road, SW1; tel: 828 2425/6.* **Hotel Booking Service Ltd**, *4 New Burlington Place, W1; tel: 437 5052.* **Hotel Finders**, *20 Bell Lane, NW4; tel: 202 7000/0988.* **Hotelguide**, *The Coach House, 235 Upper Richmond Road, SW15; tel: 780 1066.* **Hotelpacc Group Services**, *Hotelpacc House, 40/46 Headfort Place, Hyde Park Corner, SW1; tel: 235 9696.*

The **London Tourist Board**'s credit card booking service (*tel: 824 8844*) will reserve and book accommodation by telephone (Access and Visa credit cards only) in over 500 hotels and guest houses at a wide range of prices within a 20-mile radius of central London. For telephone bookings through the **British Travel Centre** call Expotel Reservations on *tel: 930 0572.*

Camping in central London is not possible. The parks are locked in the evening and patrolled until they re-open. The city spreads for miles in every direction and the nearest campsites are some way out of town. For more information, contact the **Camping and Caravanning Club**, *Greenfields House, Westwood Heath, Coventry CV4 8JH; tel: (01203) 694995.*

Communications

Post offices are usually open Mon–Fri 0900–1730 and Sat 0900–1230, although some small branches close for lunch. A limited range of stamps is available from many shops and hotels. The post office near Trafalgar Square (*24/28 William IV St, WC2 4DL; tel: 930 9580*) is a major branch that has a poste restante facility. It is open Mon–Fri 0830–1830.

London **telephone** numbers have two area codes: (0171) for the centre, and (0181) for outlying areas, both followed by seven digits. The area code is always needed if phoning from outside the London telephone area, but within London is *not* needed if phoning another number in the same area.

NOTE: In this chapter, all phone numbers quoted without an area code are (0171) area – just dial the seven-digit number given, unless phoning from an (0181) or out-of-London number, in which case add the (0171).

Eating and Drinking

London is a superb hunting ground for food, with restaurants of every conceivable type, from traditional British to those of countries you probably couldn't pin-point on a map. The cost is equally varied: from fast-food chains, where you can get something filling for around £2, to places with no prices on the menu that may cost more than you would spend on food in a month.

In the **West End**, *Soho* and *Covent Garden* offer a good choice of restaurants. Soho is also the centre of London's **Chinatown**, one of the largest in Europe, based in the area around

Wardour St (tube: *Leicester Sq*). Slightly away from the centre, *Queensway, Victoria* and *Earl's Court* areas are very lively in the evenings, with a wide range of cheap and cheerful eating places.

Places with a menu in several languages or displaying a Union Jack are designed for tourists and tend to be over-priced and poor quality.

There are pubs (public houses) on almost every street, including historic inns reputed to have been frequented by everyone from Ben Jonson to Charles Dickens. There are several books devoted to the subject and even organised 'pub crawls', which combine a historic walk with an evening's drinking. If this appeals to you, just turn up at *Temple* tube station at 1930 any Friday evening and join **London Pub Walks** *(tel: 883 2656)* for one of their organised tours.

Money

There are banks and bureaux de change on virtually every main street. **Thomas Cook** bureaux de change can be found in every area of London, and at all the London airports.

Embassies and Consulates

Australia: *Australia House, Strand, WC2B 4LA; tel: 379 4334.*
Canada: *Consular Section, 1 Grosvenor Square, W1X 0AB; tel: 258 6316.*
Republic of Ireland: *Irish Embassy General Office, 17 Grosvenor Place, SW1; tel: 235 2171.*
New Zealand: *New Zealand House, 80 Haymarket, SW1Y 4TQ; tel: 930 8422.*
USA: *24 Grosvenor Square, W1A 1AE; tel: 499 9000.*

Security

Unfortunately, London is just as prone to street crime as most major cities and you should exercise customary caution. There are the usual number of pickpockets, bag-snatchers, con-men and so on. It is reasonably safe to walk around the city centre in the late evening, as streets are well-lit and generally busy, but women on their own should avoid the King's Cross area.

Entertainment

There are several publications listing London's entertainments, of which the best are the weekly magazines *Time Out* (£1.50) and *What's On in London* (£1), available from all newsagents. The daily *Evening Standard* also has excellent theatre and cinema listings.

Nightlife

Almost everything is on offer, including jazz clubs, discotheques, gay clubs and pub entertainment. Most clubs offer one-night membership at the door. There is often a dress code, which might be a jacket and tie or could just depend on whether you fit the club's image. Jeans and trainers are out, no matter what. The larger rock venues are all a little way out of the city centre, as are many of the pubs with the best entertainment. The chief problem is that almost the entire city shuts by midnight. Those places which do stay open late (mostly nightclubs) usually increase their entrance charges at around 2200 and many places charge more at weekends.

Theatres

London is one of the world's greatest centres of theatre and music. In addition to the Royal National Theatre complex (*South Bank Centre* – see below) and the **Royal Shakespeare Company**, *Barbican Centre, EC2; tel: 638 8891* (tube: *Barbican*), there are about 50 theatres in central London. A great number of these are closely grouped in the *West End*.

West End theatre tickets are expensive, but there is a kiosk in *Leicester Square* (the south side) which sells half-price tickets for performances the same day, to personal callers only. There is a limit of four tickets per person, payment is by cash only, and opening times are Mon–Sat from 1200 for matinees, 1430–1830 for evening performances. If you want to book ahead, go to the theatre itself or book at a TIC, as most agents charge a hefty handling fee. Seats for the big musicals are often hard to get, but it's always worth queuing for returns.

Away from the centre, a number of fringe theatres offer small-scale or alternative productions at reasonable prices, and many areas have their own theatres which stage important productions. From May–Sept is the **Open Air**

Theatre Season, *Inner Circle, Regent's Park, London NW1; tel: 486 2431* (tube: *Regent's Park/Baker St*), a season of Shakespearean plays, set against the magnificent natural backdrop of Regent's Park – weather permitting!

Music

London is renowned as a musical centre. This has long been true of classical music, but applies also to pop and jazz. Five symphony orchestras make London their home and many more visit the capital. There are classical music concerts in a wide variety of venues, from cheap lunch-time performances in churches to major programmes in famous venues. The major classical venues are the **Royal Festival Hall**, **Queen Elizabeth Hall** and the **Purcell Room** on the *South Bank* (see below); the **Barbican Hall** at the *Barbican Centre, EC2; tel: 638 8891* (tube: *Barbican*); the **Wigmore Hall**, *36 Wigmore Street, W1; tel: 935 2141* (tube: *Bond St*); **St John's Smith Square**, *Westminster, SW1; tel: 222 1061* (tube: *Westminster*); the **Royal Albert Hall**, *Kensington Gore, SW7; tel: 589 8212* (tube: *South Kensington;* bus nos 9, 9A, 10, 52 or C1). If you are in London in July–Sept, try to get to the Proms (Henry Wood Promenade Concerts), a superb series of concerts at the Royal Albert Hall. There are standing-room tickets at low prices for those prepared to queue.

The South Bank Centre (tube: *Embankment*, plus a walk over Hungerford Bridge; or *Waterloo* slightly closer, but with a less pleasant walk) is an outstanding entertainment complex. Attractions include: the **National Theatre** (three different auditoriums) *tel: 928 2252*; the **National Film Theatre (NFT)** *tel: 928 3232*; **Museum of the Moving Image (MOMI)** – a must for cinema buffs, *tel: 401 2636* (see p.172); **Hayward Gallery**, *tel: 928 3144*, for frequent exhibitions of contemporary art, (see p.172); **Royal Festival Hall** (musical performances from symphonies to jazz), **Queen Elizabeth Hall** and **Purcell Room** (both set aside for solo and small group performances) *tel: 928 8800*. Prices are slightly lower than in the *West End* and there are free performances in the lobby of the NT and in the foyer of the Royal Festival Hall.

Ronnie Scott's Club, *47 Frith Street, W1; tel: 439 0747,* (tube: *Leicester Square/Piccadilly Circus*) is a well-known jazz venue, as are the **100 Club**, *100 Oxford Street, W1; tel: 636 0933* (tube: *Tottenham Court Road*); the **Bass Clef**, *35 Coronet Street, N1; tel: 729 2476/2440* (tube: *Old Street*) and **Pizza Express Dean Street**, *10 Dean Street, W1; tel: 437 9595* (tube: *Tottenham Court Rd*).

Pop and rock fans are also very well catered for, with many of London's larger venues such as **Wembley Arena** and **Wembley Stadium**, *Empire Way, Wembley; tel: 900 1234* (tube: *Wembley Park*); **Hammersmith Apollo**, *Queen Caroline Street, W6; tel: 741 4868* (tube: *Hammersmith*) and the **Forum** (formerly the Town and Country Club), *9/17 Highgate Rd, NW5; tel: 284 2200* (tube: *Kentish Town*) staging concerts by international stars.

Ballet and Opera

Lovers of ballet will not be disappointed if they visit the **Royal Opera House**, *Covent Garden, WC2; tel: 240 1066*, home to the Royal Ballet; **Sadler's Wells Theatre**, *Rosebery Ave, EC1; tel: 278 8916*, which plays host to visiting dance troupes of international fame performing both traditional ballet and contemporary dance; or the **London Coliseum**, *St Martin's Lane, WC2; tel: 836 3161*. Several companies (the Royal Ballet, English National Ballet, the Birmingham Royal Ballet and the Rambert Dance Company (contemporary dance) perform at various venues in the capital throughout the year.

For opera, visit the **Royal Opera House** (see above for details), base for the Royal Opera, or the **London Coliseum** (see above for details), which is the home of the English National Opera, whose performances are sung in English.

Cinema

There are dozens of cinemas in the *West End* and there is often a discount for the first showing on weekdays. Most are expensive and you will find the same films at a lower price a little way out of the centre.

Events

There are countless events taking place in the

capital throughout the year, from royal pageantry to major exhibitions to sporting events. The publications *Time Out* and *What's On in London* (see Entertainment section) will tell you what is currently happening.

Shopping

The **West End** is full of famous shopping areas. Perhaps the best-known shopping street in London is **Oxford Street** (tube: *Oxford Circus*), with its numerous fashion shops and many large department stores. Directly off Oxford Street is **Regent Street** (tube: *Oxford Circus/Piccadilly Circus*), lined with elegant buildings and noted for its high-quality British clothing shops, such as Aquascutum, Austin Reed and Burberry. Two particularly famous shops on *Regent St* are Hamley's, one of the best known toy shops in the world, and Liberty, which specialises in fine fabrics and silk scarves. For exclusive designer clothes, jewellery, antiques, art galleries, the auction house Sotheby's and up-market window shopping, try **Bond Street** (tube: *Bond St*). The 60s mecca **Carnaby St** (tube: *Oxford St*) is now full of souvenir shops and downmarket fashion emporia.

Piccadilly (tube: *Piccadilly Circus*) has Simpson's high-quality clothes shop, Lillywhite's with its extensive range of sports wear and equipment, and Fortnum & Mason, one of the world's great department stores, particularly famous for its food hall. **Jermyn Street** (running parallel to *Piccadilly*) is famous for its shirtmakers, fashion and jewellery shops and for Floris, which has been blending perfume on site since 1730.

Knightsbridge (tube: *Knightsbridge*) is another very famous and up-market shopping area, with Harrod's, London's most illustrious department store, The Scotch House, famous for its Scottish knitwear, and Harvey Nichols, an exclusive department store specialising mainly in high-class fashion.

Kensington High Street (tube: *Kensington High St*) has a good selection of trendy clothes shops as well as **Kensington Market** and **Hyper Hyper**, which has many individual units selling casual and off-beat clothing. The **King's Road** (tube: *Sloane Square*) is excellent for young fashion.

Covent Garden (tube: *Covent Garden*) is an elegant covered shopping area in the former fruit and vegetable market, with restaurants, bars and shops, trendy boutiques, market stalls and street entertainers well worth a visit.

Streets specialising in certain goods include **Hatton Garden** for jewellery; **Charing Cross Road** for books; **Tottenham Court Road** for hi-fi, radio equipment and furnishings, **Kensington Church Street** for (expensive) antiques, and **Chancery Lane** for the London Silver Vaults, an underground arcade of over 30 shops selling silver, jewellery, china, glass and objets d'art.

Some of London's street markets are tourist attractions in themselves, and are the perfect hunting ground for those in search of a bargain. Amongst the best are **Portobello Road,** *W11* (tube: *Ladbroke Grove/Notting Hill Gate*), Mon–Sat for foodstuffs, household goods and fashions, Sat for antiques, Fri, Sat for the flea market, bric-a-brac and secondhand clothes; **Petticoat Lane,** *Middlesex St, E1,* (tube: *Aldgate/Aldgate East* or *Liverpool St*) Sun morning (best early) for clothes and household goods; **Camden Lock,** *NW1,* (tube: *Camden Town/Chalk Farm*) all week, best Sun, for crafts, antiques, bric-a-brac, fashion and jewellery; **Greenwich Antique Market,** between *Greenwich High Rd* and *Burney St, SE10,* (BR: *Greenwich*), Sat, Sun for antiques, bric-a-brac, second-hand clothes and books.

Sightseeing

The listing below is of necessity very selective, and is by type of attraction. It is a brief overview dealing with the main sites by area, as this is probably the most convenient way of seeing London. Details of sights mentioned are given by category from p. 172 onwards.

The West End

Just about at the centre of London lies pigeon-filled **Trafalgar Square**, scene of New Year's Eve revelries and home to the famous **Nelson's Column**, guarded by Landseer's four redoubtable bronze lions. The north side of the square is filled by the **National Gallery**, which has one of the most comprehensive collections of paintings in the world, some displayed in the brilliant new

Sainsbury Wing. Just around the corner, thousands of faces from British history stare down from the walls of the **National Portrait Gallery**. On the east side of the square is **St Martin-in-the-Fields** church, built on simple classical lines in the 1720s.

The area south and west of Trafalgar Square is the hub of tourist (and political) London; if you can, visit this part either first thing in the morning or late afternoon. Down *Whitehall* are most of the Government offices; after **Horse Guards**, where members of the Household Cavalry stand guard, *Downing Street* heads off to the right (protected by its forbidding new gates). The austere **Cenotaph** in the middle of *Whitehall* honours Britain's war dead.

Whitehall leads down to *Parliament Square*, the heart of Westminster. Dominated by **Big Ben's** clock tower are the **Houses of Parliament**, built by Sir Charles Barry in the 1860s in flamboyant Gothic revival style to replace the old Palace of Westminster, which had been destroyed by fire. You can watch the (often unseemly) spectacle of democracy in action at certain times from the Strangers' Gallery of the House of Commons (be prepared to queue); the more somnolent House of Lords is easier to get into. Walk across *Westminster Bridge* for classic views of the Houses of Parliament and river.

Across Parliament Square lies **Westminster Abbey**: built mainly by Henry III, this is the burial place of the great and the good. Don't miss the Chapel of Henry VII (1503), the Stone of Scone and the Coronation Chair, Poet's Corner, and the Grave of the Unknown Warrior. The restful abbey cloister includes the beautiful **Chapter House** (the monks' meeting place), famous for its superb tiled floor and wall paintings.

Heading west of here along *Birdcage Walk*, or alongside the lake in lovely **St James's Park**, brings you to the surprisingly unprepossessing, but unmissable, **Buckingham Palace**. In Aug and Sept, a series of rooms are open to the public; the **Queen's Gallery** has a changing display from the Royal Collection; and the **Changing of the Guard** is another bit of London pageantry which has to be seen.

North of the Palace lies the pleasantly unstructured *Green Park*, and heading back towards *Trafalgar Square* again, the aristocratic *St James's* quarter lies between the *Mall* and *Piccadilly*: this is the home of many 'gentlemen's clubs' and of high-class emporia. **Rock Circus** near *Piccadilly Circus* celebrates pop rock music from the 1950s to the 90s with a lively combination of animatronics, wax effigies and music; while halfway along *Piccadilly* lies the **Royal Academy of Arts**, venue for major art exhibitions including its massive annual summer show of contemporary art. Millbank runs south of Parliament Square, and it is worth a small detour to visit the **Tate Gallery**, which has Britain's greatest collection of British and modern art in well-arranged galleries, including the superb Turner collection in the new Clore Gallery.

The City

The Square Mile, as it is known, now London's financial and business centre, was where the Romans founded the original *Londinium*. Some roads are frenetic on weekdays but it is quieter on Sats and deserted on Suns, although some museums and churches remain open then; time your visit according to whether or not you want to see the City in action. Located alongside a piece of Roman wall, the **Museum of London** gives an excellent introduction to the capital, telling its story in a 'time-walk' display from Roman times to the present.

The medieval City was almost totally destroyed by the Great Fire in 1666; the 311-step **Monument** stands 61 yards from the spot where it started in *Pudding Lane*. When the City was rebuilt, its medieval streets and alleys and their names were retained, so that now towering office buildings line the likes of *Bread St*, *Poultry* and *Threadneedle St*. Famously, Sir Christopher Wren was commissioned to design 51 new churches, some of which – characterised by their elegance and space – are among the earliest surviving buildings in the City (e.g. **St Bride's**, *Fleet St*, **St Stephen Walbrook**, *Walbrook*). Wren's masterpiece, completed in 1710, was **St Paul's Cathedral**, probably Britain's most powerful monument. Though

---

Sightseeing   **169**

now hemmed in by modern office buildings, it still manages to dominate London's skyline with its great dome. You need a good head for heights to climb the 259 steps to the Whispering Gallery (where whispered words will carry around the inside face of the dome), and even more nerve for the climb to the Stone Gallery and above it the Golden Gallery, more than 400 ft up; but there is no better panorama of London than that to be beheld from here.

West of the City are the peaceful Inns of Court of legal London; the **Temple Church**, the finest surviving circular church in England, is another undervisited delight (off *Fleet St*; usually open Wed–Sat 1000–1600, Sun 1300–1600).

The **Tower of London**, founded by William the Conqueror, still has the power to evoke its bloody history, with its gruesome associations with former prisoners (such as the Little Princes, Sir Walter Raleigh, Guy Fawkes). The greatest Norman fortress in the kingdom, it has 20 towers, the oldest of which, the White Tower, houses St John's Chapel and the Armouries. The dazzling **Crown Jewels** have recently been redisplayed, and a block on Tower Green marks the spot where many a famous head has been abruptly parted from its owner. Jovial 'Beefeaters' in traditional dress still stand guard (their free tours are recommended). Be prepared for queues. Adjacent **Tower Bridge** is another unmistakable London landmark; you can walk across the upper level. South of the river in gloomy vaults near London Bridge station, the **London Dungeon** recreates scenes of horror, punishment, torture and witchcraft – not recommended for sensitive souls.

Bloomsbury and Covent Garden

The quarter which gave its name to the literary and artistic set of the early 20th century still has a distinctly intellectual flavour. This is the home of the **British Museum**, repository of the infamously pilfered Elgin Marbles, Egyptian mummies, Magna Carta and the Sutton Hoo burial hoard. The Museum is vast: to avoid cultural indigestion, buy a plan or guide and home in on a few galleries at a time.

Much of Bloomsbury consists of Georgian and Regency squares and terraces, gracious and elegant. To the south, Covent Garden (see 'Shopping' above), once London's vegetable market, is a busier but equally pleasant place to stroll; the **London Transport Museum** has exhibits to climb aboard.

Regent's Park

This is a good area to head for with children. The **Park** itself is one of London's finest open spaces, while John Nash's elegant Regency terraces surround it (one of London's few attempts at grandiose architectural schemes). Within the Park, through which runs the Regent's Canal, are a boating lake and **London Zoo**, which has managed to survive recent threats of closure. Westwards along *Marylebone Road* lies **Madame Tussaud's**, the ultimate waxwork experience (be prepared to queue).

Kensington and Chelsea

South Kensington is the home of three of London's great museums, all housed in resplendent Victorian buildings. The **Natural History Museum** is famous for its superbly displayed dinosaurs; its galleries use computer displays, life-size models and a Discovery Centre to enhance the exhibits. The Earth Galleries include a simulated earthquake. The **Science Museum** has always been famous for its hands-on exhibits – 'Launch Pad' is designed especially for children to try their own experiments. The **Victoria and Albert Museum** has a staggering collection of applied art from many civilisations, ranging from Raphael's Cartoons to Persian carpets.

Heading north up *Exhibition Rd* past the ornate circular **Royal Albert Hall** will bring you to **Hyde Park** and contiguous **Kensington Gardens**, together cutting a great green swathe through the heart of London. Here you can simply lounge, or row on the famous Serpentine. At the park's north-east corner are **Marble Arch** and **Speaker's Corner**, where free speech can be heard in action on Suns and summer evenings.

Chelsea, which lies to the south, is one of London's most fashionable quarters, and the streets near the river (*Cheyne Walk, Cheyne Row* and *Tite St*) are a lovely place to wander and spot the blue plaques which are affixed to the former homes of famous London residents at every turn.

South of the Thames

The South Bank arts complex (see p.167) contains the exciting **Museum of the Moving Image**, which employs the hi-tech displays you would expect from a museum of film and television. South of here lies the impressive **Imperial War Museum**, which as well as displaying war paintings, armour and weapons post-1914, includes reconstructions of the Blitz and of a World War I trench (minus the mud), which vividly evoke the horror of their subject.

Guided Tours and Walks

Special tourist buses, some open-topped, offer an excellent introduction to all London's major sights and many provide a running commentary during the journey. Major departure points for the **Original London Sightseeing Tour** run by London Coaches (duration 90 mins) are *Marble Arch, Victoria, Haymarket* and *Baker Street*. Buses run all year except 25 December, approximately every 30 mins in winter and every 10 mins in summer; the tour price is £9 for adults. A *London Plus* ticket offers tours where you can hop on and off at more than 20 stops all day. Tickets can be bought on board the bus, from London TICs, or *tel: 828 7395*. For further information *tel: 828 6449*. (Some of the ordinary bus routes, e.g. no.12, are also excellent for sightseeing.)

Exploring on foot is one of the best ways of getting to know a place well, and there are several companies offering conducted walking tours on various themes. Generally tours start from tube stations, are at a leisurely pace and cost from £4. Some of the companies offering walking tours are **Footsteps UK Multilingual Walks**, *tel: (01860) 688693;* **The Original London Walks**, *tel: 624 3978;* **London Pub Walks**, *tel: 883 2656*.

River Journeys

A cruise on the river is a wonderful opportunity to see London from a different perspective, across the wide expanse of the Thames. In central London there are piers at *Westminster, Charing Cross* (tube: *Embankment*) and at the *Tower of London*. Boats sail eastwards from these (downstream) to Greenwich, Docklands and the Thames Barrier at Woolwich, and westwards (from *Westminster Pier* only) to Hampton Court, Richmond and Kew. Take a single or return trip, buying your tickets at the pier from which you travel. Ask at the pier for prices and times of sailings, or pick up a leaflet at any TIC in London.

In addition to these regular services there are special cruises by night to see the illuminated buildings on the banks, lunch cruises or evening cruises with dinner and disco cruises. **Bateaux London** *tel: 925 2215*, **Catamaran Cruisers** *tel: 839 3572/2349*, **Tidal Cruises** *tel: 839 2164*, **Westminster Passenger Service Association** *tel: 930 2062/4097*, **Campion Launches** *tel: 305 0300*, and **Tower Pier Launches** *tel: 488 0344* are a few of the companies offering riverboat cruises.

Churches and Cathedrals

St Paul's Cathedral, *Ludgate Hill, EC4; tel: 248 2705* (tube: *St Paul's*). Open Mon–Sat 0900–1600, galleries 1000–1615; On Suns open for worship only. Admission £3 to Cathedral, £2.50 for galleries.

Westminster Abbey, *Parliament Square, SW1; tel: 222 5152* for details of services (tube: *Westminster/St James's*). Abbey open Mon–Fri 0900–1600, Sat 0900–1400 and 1545–1700, subject to services; visitors admitted to Nave and Cloisters between services on Sun (admission: free). Various opening times Mon–Sat for Choir, Transepts, Royal Chapels, Chapter House and College Garden (admission: £4). Comprehensive 'Super Tours' (£7) available Mon–Sat; bookings can be made at Enquiry Desk in the Abbey, or *tel: 222 7110*.

Art Galleries

Hayward Gallery, *South Bank Centre, SE1; tel: 928 3144* (tube: *Waterloo/Embankment*). Open daily 1000–1800, Tues and Wed until 2000; closed between exhibitions. Admission varies according to exhibition. **National Gallery**, *Trafalgar Square, WC2; tel: 839 3321* (tube:

Charing Cross/Leicester Square). Open Mon–Sat 1000–1800, Sun 1400–1800. Admission free except for special exhibitions in Sainsbury Wing.

National Portrait Gallery, *St Martin's Place, WC2; tel: 306 0055* (tube: *Charing Cross/ Leicester Square*). Open Mon–Sat 1000–1800, Sun 1200–1800. Admission free except for special exhibitions. **Royal Academy of Arts**, *Burlington House, Piccadilly, W1; tel: 439 7438* (recorded information service *tel: 439 4996/7*) (tube: *Piccadilly Circus/Green Park*). Open daily 1000–1800 (last admission 1730). Admission charge varies depending on the exhibition.

Tate Gallery, *Millbank, SW1; tel: 887 8000* (recorded information service *tel: 887 8008*) (tube: *Pimlico*). Open Mon–Sat 1000–1750, Sun 1400–1750. Admission free except for special exhibitions. **Wallace Collection**, *Hertford House, Manchester Square, W1; tel: 935 0687* (tube: *Bond Street*). Eighteenth-century paintings and furniture. Open Mon–Sat 1000–1700, Sun 1400–1700. Admission free, voluntary donations welcomed.

Museums

British Museum, *Great Russell St, WC1; tel: 636 1555* (recorded information service *tel: 580 1788*) (tube: *Russell Square/Holborn/Tottenham Court Rd*). Open Mon–Sat 1000–1700, Sun 1430–1800. Admission free. **Imperial War Museum**, *Lambeth Road, SE1; tel: 416 5000* (tube: *Lambeth North*). Open daily 1000–1800. Admission £3.90.

London Dungeon, *28/34 Tooley St, SE1; tel: 403 7221* (tube: *London Bridge*). Open daily Apr–Sept 1000–1730, Oct–Mar 1000–1630. Admission £6.95. **London Transport Museum**, *Covent Garden, WC2; tel: 379 6344* (tube: *Covent Garden*). Open daily 1000–1800 (last admission 1715). Admission £3.95.

Madame Tussaud's, *Marylebone Rd, London NW1; tel: 935 6861* (tube: *Baker St*). Open daily 1000–1730. Admission £7.95. **Museum of London**, *London Wall, EC2; tel: 600 3699* (tube: *Barbican/St Paul's/Moorgate*). Open Tues–Sat 1000–1800, Sun 1200–1800; closed Mondays (except Bank Holidays). Admission £3.50.

Museum of the Moving Image, *South Bank, Waterloo, SE1; tel: 401 2636* (tube: *Waterloo/ Embankment*). Open daily 1000–1800. Admission £5.50.

Natural History Museum, *Cromwell Rd, South Kensington, SW7; tel: 938 9123* (tube: *South Kensington*). Open Mon–Sat 1000–1800, Sun 1100–1800. Admission £5. **Rock Circus**, *London Pavilion, Piccadilly Circus, W1; tel: 734 7203* (tube: *Piccadilly Circus*). Open daily 1000–2200, except Tues 1200–2200. Admission £6.95. **Science Museum**, *Exhibition Rd, SW7; tel: 938 8000* (tube: *South Kensington*). Open Mon–Sat 1000–1800, Sun 1100–1800. Admission £4.50 (free after 1630). **Victoria and Albert Museum**, *Cromwell Rd, SW7; tel: 938 8500* (tube: *South Kensington*). Open Tues–Sun 1000–1800, Mon 1200–1800 (last admission 17.50). Admission: suggested voluntary donation of £4.50.

Sights

Buckingham Palace, *The Mall, SW1; tel: 930 4832* (tube: *Victoria/St James's Park*). Open daily Aug and Sept only, 0930–1730. Admission £8. **The Queen's Gallery**, *tel: 799 2331*, open Tues–Sat 1000–1700, Sun 1400–1700 (last admission 1630); closed Mondays (except Bank Holidays). Admission £3. The **Royal Mews**, *tel: 799 2331*, has the Royal carriages, horses and equipage. Open Wed 1200–1600 Oct–Mar, Tues–Thur 1200–1600 Apr–Sept (last admission 1530). Admission £3.

Changing of the Guard, *Buckingham Palace, SW1*, takes place at 1130 daily during the summer, and on alternate days in winter; and at *Horse Guards, Whitehall, SW1* (tube: *Westminster/Embankment/Charing Cross*), the mounted guard changing ceremony by the Household Cavalry takes place daily Mon–Sat 1100, Sun 1000. (The musicians do not play in very wet weather, and times are subject to alteration. It is advisable to get there early.)

Houses of Parliament are at *Parliament Square, SW1; tel: 219 4272* (tube: *Westminster*). If you want to hear a debate in the House of Commons Strangers' Gallery (156 seats), queue at St Stephen's Entrance for admission Mon–Thur from approximately

1615, Fri from approximately 1000. (Open only when Parliament is in session, usually mid-Oct to July, except the weeks after Christmas and Easter.) **The Monument**, *Monument St, EC3; tel: 626 2717* (tube: *Monument*). Open Mon–Fri 0900–1740, Sat, Sun 1400–1740. Admission £1.

Tower of London, *Tower Hill, EC3; tel: 709 0765* (tube: *Tower Hill*). Open Mon–Sat 0900–1800, Sun 1000–1800. Admission £7.95. The 700-year-old ceremonial locking of the main gates of the Tower, the **Ceremony of the Keys** takes place at 2140. Free passes can be obtained by writing at least 2 months in advance to: *Ceremony of the Keys, Waterloo Block, HM Tower of London EC3N 4AB*. Applications must be accompanied by a stamped addressed envelope or international reply coupon. Present your pass at the main gate at 2130.

Statues and Monuments

Eros in *Piccadilly Circus, W1*. **Nelson's Column** in *Trafalgar Sq, W2*. **Sir Winston Churchill** in *Parliament Sq, SW1*. **Victoria Memorial** opposite *Buckingham Palace, SW1*. **Duke of Wellington** on *Hyde Park Corner, SW1*. **Cenotaph**, *Whitehall, SW1*.

Parks and Zoos

The Royal Parks are the property of the Crown. Originally the grounds of Royal homes or palaces, they cover over 6000 acres of London, they are open from sunrise to sunset and admission is free. In central London these include **Hyde Park** and **Kensington Gardens**, home to **Kensington Palace** (*tel: 937 9561*, open Mon–Sat 0900–1615, Sun 1100–1615. Admission £4.50); **Regent's Park** containing **London Zoo** (*tel: 722 3333*, open daily 1000–1730, last admission 16.30. Admission £6.95); **Green Park** and **St James's Park**.

Hampstead Heath, *NW3*, (tube: *Hampstead*) is a high open space covering 800 acres with natural park and woodland, which has long been very popular with Londoners. It provides a great vantage point from which to view the whole city, and in summer there are open-air concerts at **Kenwood** (EH), *Hampstead*

Lane, NW3; tel: 413 1443 (tube: *Golders Green* and bus 210 or *East Finchley* and Kenwood courtesy shuttle bus, approx every 20 mins).

Out of Town

Just outside central London and accessible by train, bus or boat (see River Journeys) are, to the west, the magnificent **Royal Botanic Gardens** (Kew Gardens), *Richmond, Surrey; tel: 940 1171*. This collection of rare specimens from the world over, spread over a tranquil 300 acres, is second to none: the famous glasshouses include the extraordinary Palm House, completed in 1848, where you can look down from the dome on a tropical plantation. This part of London is also rich in gracious mansions which, once country retreats, are now pleasant oases in the midst of suburbia. Visible across the river from Kew is **Syon House**, which was remodelled in the 18th century by Robert Adam; the grounds, landscaped by Capability Brown, contain some rare and unusual trees as well as a famous observatory, built in 1820. Even more elaborate Adam interiors can be seen at **Osterley Park House** close by: the house is set in a 140-acre landscaped park, with ornamental lakes.

The superb Tudor palace, **Hampton Court**, is at *East Molesey, Surrey; tel: (0181) 781 9500* (train from Waterloo to Hampton Court station); **Osterley Park** (National Trust), *Isleworth, Middlesex; tel: (0181) 560 3918* (tube: *Osterley*) and **Syon House**, *Brentford; tel: (0181) 560 0881* (tube: *Gunnersbury*, then take bus 237 or 267 to Syon Park). Heading the other way, spend a day at riverside **Greenwich**, home to the **National Maritime Museum, Royal Naval College, Old Royal Observatory, Queen's House**, *tel: 858 4422* and the **Cutty Sark and Gipsy Moth IV**, *tel: 858 3445*.

It is also easy to visit **Windsor** as a day-trip from London. Trains run from Waterloo roughly every half hour, the journey time being about 45 mins. Details of Windsor can be found on p. 208, on the London–Oxford route. Many other places near London are covered in our routes from London elsewhere in the book, and can be alternatively treated as day trips by train from London.

LONDON to BATH

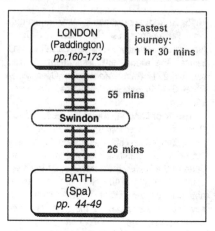

LONDON (Paddington) pp.160-173

Fastest journey: 1 hr 30 mins

55 mins

Swindon

26 mins

BATH (Spa) pp. 44-49

This route offers a fast track journey from the capital to the elegant Georgian spa town of Bath, as well as an 'on track' alternative calling at Swindon, formerly one of the world's major railway towns and now an excellent base for visiting some of Britain's most remarkable prehistoric sites.

TRAINS

ETT table: 530

 Fast Track

An hourly service (with additional trains at certain times of the day) connects London Paddington with Bath Spa. Journey time 1 hr 30 mins.

On Track

London–Swindon

Two trains every hour operate between London Paddington and Swindon and take about 55 mins.

Swindon–Bath

One train an hour makes the 26 mins run from Swindon to Bath Spa.

SWINDON

TIC: *37 Regent St, Swindon, SN1 1JL; tel: (01793) 530328.* Open Mon–Sat 0930–1730. DP services offered: local bed-booking service. *Swindon Visitors Guide* available free.
Station: Swindon Station, *Station Rd; tel: (01793) 536804* is in the town centre and has a taxi rank.

Getting Around

The attractions in town are all within walking distance of the centre. Free town maps are available from the town centre.

The main bus operator is **Swindon and District,** *tel: (01793) 522243.* Services are good in the town centre, with a reduced service after 2000 and on Sundays. One-day 'Explorer' and 'Rover' tickets are available.

The main taxi ranks are at the station and *Newbridge Sq.* For details of registered taxi companies contact the TIC.

Staying in Swindon

The best range of accommodation on offer is in the mid-range hotels and b. & b. establishments. Cheaper accommodation can be found around the town centre and the bus and rail stations. It is generally easy to book on arrival except for the last weekend in July (because of the International Air Tattoo). There are no youth hostels in Swindon but the TIC can provide details of local campsites.

Hotel chains in Swindon include: *DV, FC, Hn, Ib, Ma* and *MC.*

Sightseeing

Swindon is where the West Country meets the Cotswolds, a lively modern town surrounded by some of England's finest countryside and most famous attractions. For 150 years Swindon was one of the world's great railway towns, a heritage celebrated at the Railway Museum and Railway Village.

The **Great Western Railway Museum** and **Railway Village** are dedicated to the era of steam. Manuscripts, personal items and first editions can be viewed at the **Richard Jefferies Museum**, Swindon, the birthplace of this famous writer on the English countryside. Collections on archaeology, geology, natural history and social history can be seen at the **Swindon Museum**. There are many attractions within a short distance of Swindon, one of them being the famous **White Horses**, cut into the chalk hillsides. The 'Hackpen Horse' is closest to Swindon (5 miles south). Others can be seen at Marlborough, Alton Barnes, Cherhill, Westbury and Pewsey. The **Avebury Stone Circle**, built around 4000 years ago, and second only to Stonehenge among Britain's prehistoric sites, is 10 miles south of the town. The TIC can book bus tours.

Art Gallery and Swindon Museum, *Bath Rd, Old Town; tel: (01793) 493188.* Open Mon–Sat 1000–1700, Sun 1400–1700. Admission free. **Great Western Railway Museum**, *Farringdon Rd; tel: (01793) 493188.* Open Mon–Sat 1000–1700, Sun 1400–1700. Admission £2.10. **Richard Jeffries Museum**, *Coate Water, Marlborough Rd; tel: (01793) 493188.* Open first and third Sun of each month 1400–1700. Admission free.

Coate Water Country Park, *Coate Water, Marlborough Rd; tel: (01793) 490150.* Open all year. Admission free. Bus nos 13, 14 from Fleming Way. **Lydiard House and Country Park**, *Lydiard Park, Lydiard Tregoze; tel: (01793) 770401 (house), (01793) 771419 (park).* Open Mon–Sat 1000-1300, 1400–1730, Sun 1400–1700. Winter early closing 1600. Country park open all year. Admission £0.50. Bus no. 1 from Fleming Way.

Out of Town

Barbury Castle Country Park, *Marlborough Downs, Marlborough.* Open daily all year. Admission free. Take Thamesdown bus no. 49. Four miles south. **Avebury Manor**, *Avebury, Marlborough; tel: (01672) 539388.* Open 26 Mar–30 Oct daily 1100–1730. Closed Mon and Thurs. Admission £2.10. Thamesdown bus no. 49. 10 miles south. **Corsham Court**, *Corsham; tel: (01249) 712214.* Open Jan–Nov daily except Mon and Fri 1400–1630, from Good Friday to Sept 1400–1800. Admission £3.50 (house and gardens), £1.50 (gardens only). Take bus from Chippenham to Bath, then bus no. 231 or 232. **Highclere Castle**, *Highclere, Newbury; tel: (01635) 253210.* Open July–Sept Wed–Sun 1100–1800. Closed 9/10 July. Admission £5.00 (house and gardens), £3.00 (gardens only). 29 miles east. Take the train to Newbury.

Avebury Stone Circle, *Avebury, Marlborough; tel: (01672) 539250.* Open all year. Admission free. Take Thamesdown bus no. 49 or Wiltshire & District bus no 5.

Ancient Landscapes

The rural landscape of south-western England has survived little changed for centuries, relatively untouched by urbanisation, industrialisation or modern cultivation. This has left a countryside littered with ancient monuments and some of the finest prehistoric landscapes in Western Europe, which powerfully evoke the presence of the peoples who farmed this land thousands of years ago.

The Wiltshire Downs are a particularly rich landscape. The world famous monuments at **Stonehenge** and **Avebury** are astonishing feats of prehistoric engineering, and should be on any itinerary. But there are many other equally fascinating sites clustered around Avebury: they include the enigmatic **Silbury Hill** – the largest man-made mound in Europe – the **West Kennet Long Barrow**, a vast chambered tomb, and nearby ceremonial **West Kennet Avenue**. Both Wiltshire and Dorset boast some famous hill carvings, most famously the lewd **Cerne Abbas Giant**, north of Dorchester; while on the outskirts of that town are the massive earthworks of **Maiden Castle**, the finest Iron Age hill-fort in Britain and extraordinarily evocative of another age.

LONDON to BIRMINGHAM

This route connects London with the nation's second largest city and hub of the Midlands, once Britain's industrial heartland. It also includes two of the country's most visited towns: Stratford-upon-Avon, the birthplace of William Shakespeare; and Warwick, the site of one of England's most magnificent castles.

TRAINS

ETT tables: 540

 Fast Track

Two fast trains each hour (one per hour on Suns) depart London Euston for Birmingham New Street, taking 1 hr 40 mins (2 hours 10 mins on Suns). There are also 2 direct trains daily (not on Suns) from London (Paddington) to Stratford-upon-Avon, taking 2¼ hrs.

∿∿ On Track

London–Coventry

Two fast trains per hour (hourly on Suns) run between London Euston and Coventry, taking 1 hr 12 mins (30 minutes longer on Suns).

Coventry–Leamington Spa

An almost hourly weekday service (much reduced on Suns) links Coventry to Leamington Spa, taking 17 mins. Change at Leamington for trains to Warwick.

Leamington Spa–Warwick–Stratford

Ten trains a day (5 on Suns, summer only) make the 4-min journey from Leamington to Warwick and the 20-min journey from Warwick to Stratford-upon-Avon.

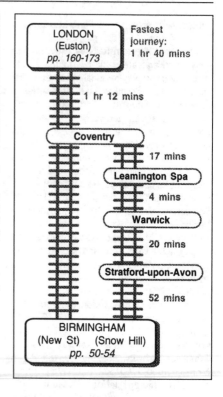

Stratford–Birmingham

An hourly service runs to and from Birmingham (Snow Hill), taking 52 mins. There are five trains on Sundays from June to September.

COVENTRY

TIC: *Bayley Lane, Coventry, West Midlands CV1 5RN; tel: (01203) 832303/4.* Open Mon–Fri 0930–1700 (–1630 Nov–Mar), Sat, Sun 1000–1630; all Bank Holidays 1000–1630. DP Services offered: local bed-booking service (latest 30 mins before closing), AR, BABA (latest 30 mins before closing), GT. Tickets for Arts Centre and events sold. Main guide *Coventry Can Do It* is free and includes list of accommodation.

Station: Coventry Station, *Station Square; tel: (01203) 555211* is ¼ mile south of the town centre, connected by a regular bus link. There is also a taxi rank.

Bus Station: Pool Meadow Bus Station, *Fairfax St* (within the city centre) is the main coach and bus depot, both for local and national routes. For general enquiries about all bus and train services in the West Midlands, *tel: (01203) 559559* (Centro Hotline) or *tel: (01203) 223116* (West Midlands Travel).

Getting Around

Most attractions are within walkable distance of the town centre; town and transport maps are available free from the TIC. There is a good local bus service throughout the city and well into Warwickshire, run mainly by West Midlands Travel (see above); services are reduced in the evenings and on Sundays. The main taxi ranks are at the rail and bus stations and on *Ironmonger Row*. Taxis can also be hailed in the street.

Staying in Coventry

There is a good range of hotel and guesthouse accommodation, but very little in the way of b. & b.s. Cheaper establishments can be found on the edge of the town, and there is generally no problem with booking on arrival, except during the Royal Agricultural Show in early July.

Hotel chains include *Ca, DV, FC, Hn, Nv, PL.* For closest HIs see Birmingham (p. 50) and Stratford. There is a campsite just 1½ miles south of the town: **Canley Ford Milk Bar**, *Canley Ford*, off *Kenilworth Rd; tel: (01203) 675286.* Take the Kenilworth bus. For other nearby campsites ask at the TIC.

Sightseeing

A bright, modern industrial city, Coventry is probably best known for the fact that it was blitzed in 1940. Its two **cathedrals** stand as a powerful symbol of Coventry's regeneration: Spence's **St Michael's Cathedral**, a memorable work of modern architecture, was built next to the haunting ruins of the medieval cathedral.

Though much of Coventry's post-war development is depressing, the city makes the most of the remnants of its past, and it's worth seeking them out: in the cathedral quarter is **St Mary's Guildhall** with Tudor almshouses nearby; and the medieval buildings of **Spon St**

have been brought together and expertly restored. In **Broadgate** stands the statue of Lady Godiva, who famously rode naked through the city streets in protest at the high taxes imposed by her husband. Guided walks are organised by the **Coventry Guild of Guides**, *tel: (01203) 832303* and can be booked at the TIC, price £1.50. Modern art is well represented at the **Herbert Art Gallery and Museum**, with paintings by Lowry and sculptures by Moore. Coventry was once the hub of Britain's motor industry, and the **Museum of British Road Transport** has the largest collection of its kind. The **Toy Museum** has toys and games from the 18th century onwards, while civil and military aircraft spanning 70 years are displayed at the **Midland Air Museum**. Out of town, **Coombe Abbey Country Park** is pleasantly laid out around the abbey remains, while **Ryton Organic Gardens** are nationally renowned.

Buildings and Statues of Historic Interest

Coventry Cathedral and Visitor's Centre, *Priory Row; tel: (01203) 227597.* Cathedral open Mon–Sat 0930–1800 (winter –1700), Sun 1200–1630; Visitor Centre Mon–Sat 1000–1630 (winter –1600), Sun 1200–1630. Admission £2.50. **Lady Godiva's Statue**, *Broadgate.* **St Mary's Guildhall**, *Bayley Lane; tel: (01203) 833041.* Open daily 1000–1700 (Apr–Sept); closed occasionally for civic functions. Admission £1. **Spon Street** (expertly restored buildings of medieval character); *tel: (01203) 832773/5.*

Museums and Galleries

Coventry Toy Museum, *Much Park St; tel: (01203) 227560.* Open daily 1200–1800. Admission £1.50. **Herbert Art Gallery and Museum**, *Jordan Well; tel: (01203) 832381.* Open Mon–Sat 1000–1730, Sun 1400–1700. Admission free. **Museum of British Road Transport**, *St Agnes Lane, Hales St; tel: (01203) 832425.* Open daily 1000–1700. Admission £2.95.

Out of Town

Coombe Abbey Country Park (4 miles east), *Brinklow Rd, Binley; tel: (01203) 453720.* Park open daily 0730 to dusk; visitor centre open daily 0900–1900 (Apr–Sept), 0900–1700 (Oct–Mar), closed 25 Dec. Take bus 913 (15–20 mins). **National Motorcycle Museum** (10 miles west), *Coventry Rd, Bickenhill, Solihull; tel: (01675) 443311*. Open daily 1000–1800; closed 24–26 Dec. Admission £3.75. Take bus 900 towards Birmingham (approximately 40 mins).

Royal Agricultural Society of England, *National Agricultural Centre, Stoneleigh Park; tel: (01203) 696969* for the Royal Agricultural Show in early July. **Ryton Organic Gardens**, *Ryton-on-Dunsmore; tel: (01203) 303517*. Open daily 1000–1730 (last admission 1700 or dusk if earlier); closed Christmas week. Admission £2.50. Take bus towards Rugby from Coventry (bus stop P4 at bus station), get out at *Wolston Village*, 5 miles south east (15–20 mins) and then ½-mile walk west.

WARWICK

TIC: The Court House, *Jury St, Warwick CV34 4EW; tel: (01926) 492212*. Open daily 0930–1630. DP SHS Services offered: local bed-booking service (latest 1615), AR, BABA (latest 1600). Free accommodation list available; accommodation booking *tel: (0926) 498647*. *Warwick Official Town Guide* (£0.40).
Station: Warwick Station, *Station Rd; tel: (01203) 555211* (¼ mile from town centre).
Bus Station: *Market Place; tel: (0121) 6224373*. National Express run direct bus services between Warwick and London, Glasgow, Bristol and many other places.

Getting Around

Most attractions are within walking distance of the town centre. There is good local bus transport to Coventry, Leamington Spa, Kenilworth, Stratford and surrounding villages, operated by **Midland Red** and **Stratford Blue** *tel: (01788) 535555*, and **Warwickshire Buses** *tel: (01926) 414140*. There are no services after 2030, and only reduced services on Sundays. The main bus stop is in the *Market Place*. It is possible to buy a Day Explorer ticket (£3.50), which covers all services. There is a taxi rank in the *Market Place* and taxis can also be hailed in the street.

Staying in Warwick

There is a small range available, with cheaper accommodation to be found on the edge of the town centre. Only one hotel chain (*Hn*) is represented. It is usually easy to book a room on arrival, with the exception of July, during the Royal Show and Warwick Arts Festival, and Aug during the Folk Festival, when it is advisable to book in advance. The nearest youth hostel is in Stratford. There are various nearby campsites in Warwick, including **Caravan Club Site**, *Hampton Rd; tel: (01926) 495448*.

There is a good selection of eateries particularly of cheaper restaurants and pubs serving hot food, and many cafés and tearooms. There are also regular medieval banquets throughout the year in the Undercroft of the Castle, *tel: (01926) 495421*.

The main post office is situated on the *Old Square*, open Mon–Fri 0900–1730, Sat 0900–1230 (no post restante facilities available here).

Entertainment and Events

A free entertainments listing, *What's On in Warwick*, is available from the TIC and local newspapers give details. There is little nightlife in Warwick – just one nightclub, **Astoria's**, at the *Globe Hotel, Theatre St*, and the **Warwick Folk Club** at the *Punchbowl, The Butts*. The main venue for theatre and music is **Warwick University Arts Centre**, *Gibbet Hill, Coventry; tel: (01203) 524524*, 7 miles away by bus X16 or 539 (45 mins). At Kenilworth there is the **Talisman Theatre**, *Barrow Rd, Kenilworth; tel: (01926) 56548* and **Priory Theatre**, *Rosemary Hill, Kenilworth; tel: (01926) 55301*, 5 miles north east by bus X16 or 539 (30 mins). Recently Priory Theatre have begun to stage some open-air performances at Warwick Castle during the summer.

Warwick Festival is an annual arts festival covering two weeks in July, at various venues around the town *tel: (01926) 410747* (Warwick Arts Society). **Warwick Folk Festival** in Aug is another big event, taking place at many different venues *tel: (01203) 678738*. Both events affect visitor numbers considerably, so it is advisable to book accommodation in advance. The TIC has a free events listing.

Shopping

Thurs is early closing day in Warwick. The main shopping streets are *Market Place, Swan St, Brook St, Smith St, Jury St* and *West St*. There is also an abundance of antique shops and centres. There is a weekly Saturday market in the *Market Place*, and in July and Aug a Sunday market for crafts and antiques. At **Hatton Country World**, *George's Farm, Hatton; tel: (01926) 842436*, converted farm buildings house craft workshops. Open daily 1000–1730, 4½ miles north of town; take a taxi from Warwick.

Sightseeing

Try to pick a quiet time to visit **Warwick Castle**, one of the most popular visitor attractions in England. Its curtain wall and tower defences are intact, while the state rooms (inhabited until the 1970s) are rich in treasures and – be warned – peopled with lifelike wax models. There are also dungeons and a torture chamber for the ghoulish, and a fine armour display. The extensive grounds have a Victorian rose garden and woodland walks; the best view of the castle, towering above the Avon, is from Castle Bridge.

Warwick's compact centre is remarkably harmonious: much of it was rebuilt in the 18th century after a fire in 1694. *Northgate St* has some lovely façades. The fine **Court House** (1714), as well as housing the TIC, has the **Warwickshire Yeomanry Museum and Warwick Town Museum** in its cellars. It is easy to tell how far the fire spread from where the half-timbered houses begin: none is more charmingly irregular than **Lord Leycester Hospital**, by the medieval **West Gate** at the end of the *High St*, which is still used as a soldiers' rest home. **Oken's House** is a fine Elizabethan timber-framed house, home to a superb collection of dolls, including automata and dolls' houses, while **St John's Museum** specialises in folk life and costume. **St Mary's Church** is renowned for its outstanding 15th-century

chapel housing the lavish tomb of Richard Beauchamp. To the north-west of town, some interesting early industrial buildings have been conserved by the Saltisford Canal Trust.

Guided walks are available, and can be booked through the TIC. There are no organised bus tours, but the Stratford Blue bus 18 takes a scenic route through local villages to Stratford. Out of town, the dramatic ruin of once mighty **Kenilworth Castle** forms a peaceful contrast to Warwick's fortress: Sir Walter Scott used it as a romantic backcloth for his novel **Kenilworth** (1821), a fictionalised account of Elizabeth I's visit here. **Charlecote Park** dates from the 1550s – Shakespeare allegedly poached deer here, and there are still herds in the park.

Historic Buildings

Lord Leycester Hospital and the Master's Garden, *High St; tel: (01926) 491422*. Hospital open daily 1000–1700 (summer), 1000–1600 (winter). Admission £2.25. Garden open Sat 1400–1700 (Easter to Oct). Admission £1. **Warwick Castle**; *tel: (01926) 495421/408000*. Open daily 1000–1800 (Apr–Oct), 1000–1700 (Oct–Mar), weekends during Aug 1000–1900; closed 25 December. Admission £7.50 (busy when special events on at castle.)

Churches

Collegiate Church of St Mary, *Old Square; tel: (01926) 400771*. Open daily 1000–1800 (summer), 1000–1600 (winter). Admission free.

Museums and Galleries

Oken's House and Doll Museum, *Castle St; tel: (01926) 495546*. Open Sat 1000–1600 (Jan–Mar), Mon–Sat 1000–1600, Sun 1400–1700 (Apr–Oct). Admission £1. **Warwickshire Museum**, *Market Hall, Market St; tel: (01926) 412501*. Open Mon–Sat 1000–1730 (all year), Sun 1400–1700 (May–Sept). Admission free. **Warwickshire Yeomanry Museum and Warwick Town Museum**, *The Cellars, Court House, Jury St; tel: (01926) 492212*. Open nearly every Fri, Sat, Sun and Bank Holiday Mon, 1000–1300, 1400–1600 (Easter to end Sept). Admission free.

Out of Town

Charlecote Park (NT), *Charlecote; tel: (01789)* 470277. Open Fri–Tues 1100–1800 (Apr to end Oct); closed Good Friday. Admission £4. Take bus 18 to *Charlecote*, 5 miles south. **Kenilworth Castle** (EH), *Kenilworth; tel: (01926) 52078.* Open Mon–Sun 1000–1800 (Apr–Oct); Tues–Sun 1000–1600 (Oct–Mar). Very busy on special event days. Admission £1.80. Bus X16 or 539 to *Kenilworth*, 5 miles north. **Wellesbourne Watermill**, *Kineton Rd, Wellesbourne; tel: (01789) 470237.* Thurs–Sun and Bank Holidays 1030–1700 (Mar–Sept, Sun only Oct–Nov). Admission £2. Bus 18 to *Wellesbourne*, 5 miles south, then 1½ miles from village. **Wellesbourne Wartime Museum**, *Wellesbourne Airfield, Wellesbourne; tel: (01789) 470237.* Open Sun 1000–1600 and some Bank Holidays. Directions as for Welles-bourne Watermill.

STRATFORD-UPON-AVON

TIC: *Bridgefoot, Stratford-upon-Avon, Warwickshire CV37 6GW; tel: (01789) 293127/297319.* Open Mon–Sat 0900–1800, Sun 1100–1700 (Mar–Oct), Mon–Sat 0900–1700 (Nov–Mar). DP SHS Services offered: local bed-booking service (latest 15 mins before closing), advance reservations handled, BABA (latest 1630), guided tours booked, bureau de change. Tickets booked for Guide Friday Tours, Shakespeare Properties. Great British Heritage Pass and Town Heritage Pass sold. Ask for free town guide *Stratford-upon-Avon, Shakespeare's Country* and accommodation guide. For accommodation booking *tel: (01789) 415078* (busiest Fri and Sat mornings). **Guide Friday Tourism Centre**, *Civic Hall, 14 Rother St; tel: (01789) 294466.* Open 0845–1900 (summer), 0845–1730 (winter). DP Services offered: local bed-booking service and BABA (£3 booking fee), guided tours booked (with discounts on Shakespeare Properties). Local events booked.
Station: Stratford-upon-Avon Station, *Alcester Rd; tel: (0121) 643 2711* or *(01203) 555211* is ½ mile from the town centre. There is a car hire desk (**Hertz**) and a taxi rank at the station.
Bus Station: there is no bus depot, but most buses and coaches operate from *Bridge St* and *Wood St* in the town centre. For National Express enquiries *tel: (0121) 622 4373.*

Getting Around

Free town and transport maps are available from the Bridgefoot TIC. Local bus services are good in the town centre but less frequent to outlying areas.

Tickets

Weekly **Blue Rider** tickets, for use only on **Stratford Blue** buses within Stratford, are available for £4.25 from the bus driver.

Buses

Local services (Stratford Blue buses) run from *Bridge St* and *Wood St; tel: (01788) 535555.* Buses X16 (to Coventry), 18 (to Leamington) and X20 (to Birmingham) operate a reduced service on Sun, other buses Mon–Sat only.

Taxis

Taxi ranks can be found at *Bridgefoot, Bridge St, Union St* and *Rother Market* (near White Swan Hotel). The TIC has a list of registered taxi companies. (**Stratford Taxis** *tel: (01789) 415888* offer wheelchair transport.)

Staying in Stratford

Accommodation

There is a very large range of accommodation in and around the town, including farmhouse and self-catering. Stratford itself offers predominantly guest-house accommodation. During July and Aug and over Bank Holiday weekends it is necessary to book in advance. Hotel chains in Stratford include *BW, FC, MC, MH*. Cheaper accommodation can be found on the outskirts of town (*Alcester Rd, Shipston Rd, Evesham Rd* and *Evesham Pl*).
    Stratford-upon-Avon HI is at *Hemmingford House, Alveston; tel: (01789) 297093.* Take bus 18 from *Bridge St*, just 1½ miles along the *Tiddington Rd*. There are various campsites within easy reach of town: **Avon Caravan Park**, *Warwick Rd; tel: (01789) 293438.* Take Bus X16, 1 mile east. **Dodwell Park**, *Evesham*

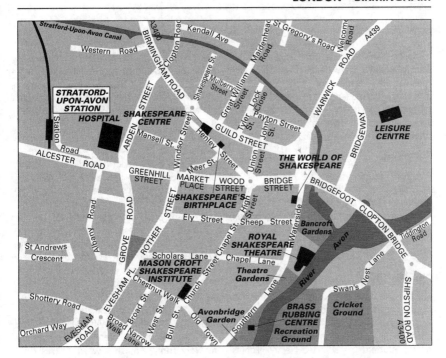

Rd; tel: (01789) 204957. Take bus 218, 2 miles south-west. **Stratford Racecourse**, Luddington Rd; tel: (01789) 267949. Take bus 218, 1½ miles south-west. **The Elms Camp**, Tiddington; tel: (01789) 292312. Take bus 18, 1½ miles north-east.

Eating and Drinking

The TIC has a free list of places to eat and drink in Stratford. The range is good, with approximately six gourmet restaurants, and plenty of cheaper options, including a wide choice of pubs. Places nearer to the town centre are predictablymore expensive; the largest concentration of restaurants is in High St and Sheep St. There is a vegetarian restaurant, **Café Natural**, in Greenhill St.

Communications and Money

The main post office is on Henley St, open Mon–Fri 0900–1730, Sat 0900–1230. Post restante facilities are available. **Thomas Cook** bureau de change at Midland Bank, 13 Chapel St.

Entertainment and Events

The TIC has its own free entertainments listing, as well as the Visitor Magazine (free) and Herald Press (£0.25), for details of what's on. In addition to the excellent theatres for which Stratford is famous, there are four nightclubs, and a great number of pubs.

The Royal Shakespeare Company at **The Royal Shakespeare Theatre** (ticket availability depends on performance and performance times; it is best to book 2–3 months in advance, but check with the box office to see if there are any returns for on-the-day performances) and **Swan Theatre**, Waterside and **The Other Place**, Southern Lane; tel: (01789) 414999, have performances nightly from Mar–Jan, matinées on Thurs and Sat. For horse-racing enthusiasts, there is **Stratford Racecourse**, Luddington Rd; tel: (01789) 267949, bus 218, 1 mile south-west.

Every year on 23 April, or the Sat closest to it, the **Shakespeare's Birthday Celebrations** take place, with various events in the town centre (some free). Details from *Shakespeare Birthplace Trust, Henley St; tel: (01789) 204016.* Visitors come from all over the world to participate. **Stratford Festival**, a wide-ranging, non-Shakespeare-related festival of performance art attracting internationally renowned artists, takes place for two weeks in July at various venues around the town; *tel: (01789) 267969.* Admission prices vary according to events.

Shopping

The main shopping streets are *High St, Bridge St, Bell Court* and *Bard's Walk*. There is a general Friday market on *Rother St*, and for those who are interested a cattle market on *Alcester Rd* every Thurs. You may notice the unusual resin figures crafted by local artists in some of Stratford's shops.

Sightseeing

The claim to fame of this small market town in central England rests on one accident of birth: England's greatest playwright was born here in 1564, in the upstairs room of a timber-framed house. Stratford has attracted literary pilgrims ever since the Bard's death, and the Shakespeare connection is inescapable from pub and café names to the main tourist attractions which have a link, however tenuous, with the man himself. Stratford is now a mecca for coach parties, so if your enjoyment is likely to be marred by having to share the experience with hordes of others, time your visits before 1100 or after 1600. By far the best way of understanding Shakespeare is to see one of the plays in performance, and at the **Royal Shakespeare Theatre** they are performed regularly by one of the great theatre companies; so if you can, arrange an overnight stop, or catch a matinée.

There are five main 'Shakespeare' properties in and around Stratford (for admission arrangements, see below). In Stratford itself, **Shakespeare's Birthplace** contains Bard memorabilia and Elizabethan exhibits, and admission includes the adjacent BBC Television Costume Exhibition. **Hall's Croft**, an impressive gabled house with a beautiful walled garden, was the home of Dr John Hall, who married Shakespeare's daughter Susanna; it has an exhibition on medicine in Dr

Hall's time and a display of furniture. Only the foundations remain of **New Place**, where Shakespeare spent his final years and died in 1616; an Elizabethan garden marks the site, and entry is through **Nash's House**, a museum of local history and furniture. Out of town are the two big draws: **Anne Hathaway's Cottage** is in fact a substantial thatched farmhouse, where Anne Hathaway lived with her wealthy family before her marriage to Shakespeare – arranged to reveal Tudor domestic life, it has a pretty garden. The childhood home of William's mother, **Mary Arden's House**, was 'restored' in the 19th century, and its extensive outbuildings house displays of farming and rural life.

Still on the Shakespeare theme, well worth visiting is the **Royal Shakespeare Company Collection**, where props and costumes reveal the changing fashions in Shakespeare productions. For **Royal Shakespeare Company Theatre Tours**, *tel: (01789) 296655.* Mon–Fri 1330 and 1730 (–1730 only on matinée days), Sun 1230, 1345, 1445, 1545. Also Mon–Sat after evening performance. Price: £3.80. The beautiful **Holy Trinity Church** is where Shakespeare was baptised and is buried.

Stratford is not quite exclusively geared to Shakespeare. The mother of John Harvard, founder of Harvard University, lived at modest **Harvard House** (1596); the **Teddy Bear Museum** has every conceivable kind of stuffed ursine creature, including the original Sooty; and the **Butterfly Farm** has some 1000 exotic (live!) species. The banks of the River Avon and canal are a pleasant place to stroll.

Out of town, **Ragley Hall**, a fine Palladian mansion in a 400-acre park, is a refreshing contrast to half-timbered Stratford; **Coughton Court** is a splendid, winged Tudor gatehouse, with two churches and a lake in its grounds. The **Heritage Motor Centre** tells the story of the UK motor industry from the 1890s to the present, with a huge collection of historic cars and many themed displays.

Several battles were fought in this area during the English Civil War, and **Edgehill Battle Museum** at Farnborough Hall re-creates the period.

Various **tours** are available to give a good

introduction to Stratford and the surrounding area. Bus tours are operated by **Guide Friday**, *Civic Hall, 14 Rother St; tel: (01789) 294466*, daily except 24–26 Dec, every 15 mins (summer), every 30–60 mins (winter). Tour tickets are valid all day, allowing you to jump on and off at places of interest on the route, including all five Shakespeare Properties (for which tour-ticket holders get discounted admission). Buses depart from various stops in town. Price: £7. (Cotswold Tour also available, daily 1330, price: £14.) The TIC can also book river cruises, guided walks and individual guides.

The Shakespeare Properties

There are three in-town houses (admission to all three: £5 for visitors undertaking the Town Walking Tour), and two out-of-town houses (admission to all five: £7.50).

Anne Hathaway's Cottage, *Shottery; tel: (01789) 292100*. Open Mon–Sat 0900–1730, Sun 1000–1730 (summer); Mon–Sat 0930–1600, Sun 1030–1600 (winter). Admission £2.20. Take frequent Stratford Blue **Avon Shuttle** bus from Bridge St, or signed 1-mile walk from Evesham Place. **Hall's Croft**, *Old Town; tel: (01789) 292107*. Open Mon–Sat 0930–1700, Sun 1030–1700 (summer); Mon–Sat 1000–1600, Sun 1330–1600 (winter). Open from 1330 on 1 Jan. **Mary Arden's House and Shakespeare's Countryside Museum**, *Wilmcote; tel: (01789) 293455*. Open Mon–Sat 0930–1700, Sun 1030–1700 (summer); Mon–Sat 1000–1600, Sun 1330–1600 (winter). Admission £2. Train to Wilmcote Station, 3½ miles, then a 5 minute walk. **New Place/Nash's House**, *Chapel St; tel: (01789) 292325*. Open Mon–Sat 0930–1700, Sun 1030–1700 (summer); Mon–Sat 1000–1600, Sun 1330–1600 (winter). Open from 1330 on 1 Jan. **Shakespeare's Birthplace**, *Henley St; tel: (01789) 204016*. Open Mon–Sat 0900–1730, Sun 1000–1730 (summer); Mon–Sat 0930–1600, Sun 1030–1600 (winter). Open from 1330 on 1 Jan. Admission £2.60.

Other Sights

Holy Trinity Church, *Old Town; tel: (01789) 266316*. Open Mon–Sat 0830–1800 (Nov–Feb 1600), Sun 1400–1700. Last admission 20 mins before closing. Admission to see Shakespeare's grave: £0.50. **Harvard House**, *High St; tel: (01789) 292325*. Open daily 1000–1600 (May–Oct). Admission £1.

Royal Shakespeare Company Collection, *Swan Theatre, Waterside; tel: (01789) 296655*. Open Mon–Sat 0915–2000, Sun 1200–1630; 1100–1600 Nov–Mar. Admission £1.70 (free for those attending Swan Theatre same evening). **Stratford Brass Rubbing Centre**, *Avonbank Garden, near Holy Trinity Church; tel: (01789) 29767*. Open daily 1000–1800 (Easter to end Oct). Admission free (brass rubbing fee from £1.50–£10). **Teddy Bear Museum**, *Greenhill St, near Market Pl; tel: (01789) 293160*. Open daily 0930–1800. Admission £1.95. **World of Shakespeare**, *Waterside; tel: (01789) 269190*. Open daily 0930–2130 (summer), 0930–1700 (winter). Admission £3.50. **Stratford-upon-Avon Butterfly Farm**, *Tramway Walk, Swan's Nest Lane; tel: (01789) 299288*. Open daily 1000–1800 (–dusk in winter). Admission £3.25.

Out of Town

Coughton Court (NT), *Alcester; tel: (01789) 400777*. Open 1330–1730 (weekends in Apr, and Sat–Wed May–Sept), 1330–1700 (weekends in Oct), 1230–1730 Bank Holidays. Admission £4.50. Bus 208 or 228. Nine miles north-west.

Edgehill Battle Museum, in the grounds of **Farnborough Hall** (NT), *Farnborough; tel: (01926) 332213*. Open Wed and Sat 1400–1800. Admission £1. No public transport connection, 16 miles from town. **Heritage Motor Centre**, *Gaydon; tel: (01926) 641188*. Open daily 1000–1800 (Apr–Oct), 1000–1630 (Nov–Mar). Admission £5.50. Thirteen miles from town. Public transport is infrequent – yellow Grazby Coaches bus from *Wood St* goes once a day, check times with Centre before travelling.

Ragley Hall (8 miles north-west), *Alcester; tel: (01789) 762090*. Open 1200–1700 (house), 1000–1800 (garden and park); closed Mon and Fri except Bank Holiday Mons, garden and park open daily in July and Aug. Admission £5. Bus 208 or 228.

LONDON to BRIGHTON

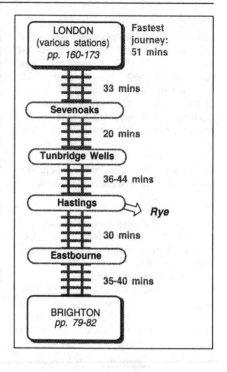

This route offers two alternative ways of travelling between London and the celebrated Regency resort of Brighton. The on track alternative takes you through the heart of Kent, a country whose rolling green countryside has earned it the title of 'the garden of England' and which is particularly rich in historic associations and stately homes. Among other attractions, the route also visits Hastings, the town which gave English history its best known date.

TRAINS

ETT table: 505 (Brighton), 501 (Hastings)

→ Fast Track

On weekdays hourly 'Capital Coast Express' trains run from London Victoria to Brighton. These trains take 51 mins for the journey. Another, hourly, slower train also runs every day from London Victoria, and two trains (increasing to four on weekdays in May 1995) between Kings Cross (Thameslink), Blackfriars and London Bridge stations to Brighton.

On Track

London–Sevenoaks

Four fast trains (three on Suns) run between London Charing Cross, Waterloo (East) and London Bridge stations and Sevenoaks. The trains take 32–33 mins.

Sevenoaks–Tunbridge Wells

Two trains every hour (weekdays – only one on Suns) link Sevenoaks with Tumbridge Wells. The journey takes 20 mins.

Tunbridge Wells–Hastings

Two trains every hour (weekdays – only one on Suns) run between Tunbridge Wells and Hastings taking 36–44 mins.

Hastings–Eastbourne

Two hourly trains (weekdays), one on Suns operate between Hastings and Eastbourne, taking 30 minutes.

Eastbourne–Brighton

Two through trains each hour (weekdays) operate between Eastbourne and Brighton. A third service is available with a change of trains at Lewes. Journey time is 35–40 mins. On Suns there is one service per hour but a change of train at Lewes is necessary almost every time. Journey time is 45 minutes.

SEVENOAKS

TIC: Buckhurst Lane, Sevenoaks, Kent TN13

1LQ; tel: (01732) 450305. Open Mon–Sat 1000–1300, 1400–1630 (Nov–Mar), Mon–Sat 1000–1700 (Apr–Oct), Sun 1000–1300 (Jul–Aug). DP SHS Services offered: local bed-booking service (10% commission fee), BABA (10% commission fee and latest booking 30 mins before closing), Great British Heritage Pass sold. *Heart of Kent Holiday Guide* which includes accommodation listings is free.

Station: Sevenoaks Station, *London Rd; tel: (01732) 770111* is ½ mile north of the town centre and Sevenoaks can be reached by the Kentish Bus nos 402, 406, 420, 425, 426.

Getting Around

Free town maps and transport details are available from the TIC. A free transport map can also be obtained from the Kentish Bus Station, *Buckhurst Lane; tel: (01732) 743040.* General bus transport enquiry no: *(0800) 696996.* **Kentish Bus Company** *tel: (0474) 321300,* is the main operator for local bus services, most of which start at the Bus Station in Buckhurst Lane. The main town taxi rank is outside the bus station.

Staying in Sevenoaks

Hotel accommodation is very limited in Sevenoaks but b. & b. is more plentiful, particularly on the edge of town. During the summer season, it is generally difficult to find any accommodation without pre-booking and the TIC tends to be very busy from 1300 onwards. The closest budget accommodation is **Kemsing Youth Hostel**, *Church Lane, Kemsing, Kent TN15 6LU; tel: (01732) 761341,* which is open all year excluding Jan and open Fri–Sat only in Feb, Nov, Dec, and can be reached by Kentish Bus nos. 425, 426, 435, and 436. The TIC has details of campsites in the area.

Sightseeing

A commuter town, Sevenoaks nevertheless has a rural atmosphere – you are in the Heart of Kent, farming country famous for its fruit orchards and hop production.

The **Vine** at Sevenoaks is one of the oldest cricket grounds in the country and has been the site of the famous seven oak trees for many generations. Sevenoaks is dominated by the National Trust property **Knole House**, which is the largest private house in England, complete with a 100- acre deer park. The surrounding countryside is packed with historic properties, such as **Chartwell**, home of Sir Winston Churchill and **Hever Castle**, where Anne Boleyn spent her childhood and **Penshurst Place**, birthplace of Sir Philip Sydney.

Knole House (NT), *tel: (01732) 450608.* Open Wed, Fri–Sun and Bank Hol Mon, 1100–1700, Thu 1400–1700 (1 Apr–29 Oct). Last admission 1600. Admission £4.00.

Out of Town

Chartwell, (NT), *Westerham; tel: (01732) 866368.* House opening times: Sat–Sun, Wed 1100–1700 (Mar & Nov), Tue–Thu, Sat–Sun & Bank Hol Mon 1100–1730 (Apr–Oct). Garden and Studio opening times: Tue–Thu, Sat–Sun and Bank Hol Mon 1100–1730, last admission 1630 (Apr–Oct). Closed 14 Apr and Tue following Bank Hol Mon. Admission £4.50 (House and gardens), £2.50 (House only), £2.00 (Gardens only). Take the Kentish Bus no. 425 from Sevenoaks to Westerham followed by a 2 mile walk. 8 miles west of Sevenoaks.

Hever Castle, *Hever, Edenbridge; tel: (01732) 866796.* Open daily (14 Mar–5 Nov), 1200–1800 (Castle), 1100–1800 (Gardens). Last admission 1700. Admission £5.70 (castle and gardens), £4.30 (gardens only). Take the train from Sevenoaks to Hever station and walk the last mile. 10 miles south-west of Sevenoaks.

Penshurst Place and Gardens, *Penshurst, Tonbridge; tel: (01892) 870307.* Open Sat–Sun (1–26 Mar, Oct), daily (27 Mar–1 Oct), 1100–1800 (Grounds), 1200–1730 (House). Last admission 1700. Admission £4.95 (house and gardens), £3.50 (gardens only). Take the train to Tunbridge Wells and then the Maidstone and District Bus no. 231/233 out to Penshurst, which passes Penshurst Place. 8 miles south of Sevenoaks.

TUNBRIDGE WELLS

TIC: *The Old Fish Market, The Pantiles, Tunbridge Wells, Kent TN2 5TN; tel: (01892)*

515675. Open Mon–Fri 0900–1700, Sat 0930–1730, Sun and bank holidays 1000–1600. DP Services offered, local bed-booking service, BABA (latest one hour before closing) - charge made of 10% of cost of first night. Tickets sold for Local Assembly Hall, British Heritage Pass and A Day at the Wells. *Heart of Kent* holiday guide (including accommodation list) is free.
Station: Tunbridge Wells, *Mount Pleasant; tel: (01732) 770111* is central, and has a taxi rank.

Getting Around

Town and transport maps are available free of charge at the TIC. There are bus and train services covering the town and the surrounding region, but Sun services are very restricted. For further information *tel: (0800) 696996.* The main taxi rank is at the railway station.

Staying in Tunbridge Wells

There is a small number of hotels and guest-houses, and a larger choice of b.&b. establishments. It is usually easy to find accommodation on arrival, but is more difficult during Jul and Aug, on bank holiday weekends, and especially during the Georgian festivities in Aug. Hotel chains in the area include *Ja.* The nearest campsite to the town centre is **Mabledon Farm**, 6 miles north of town centre, *tel: (01732) 352407.* Take bus no 214, 215, 216 or 217 towards Tonbridge.

Sightseeing

The spa town of Royal Tunbridge Wells was at its most fashionable as a resort from the 17th to 19th centuries and was a favourite with royal visitors. **A Day at the Wells** depicts the lively high society goings-on of Georgian (18th-century) Tunbridge Wells and spa water is still served by the traditional Dipper at the **Chalybe-ate Spring**. There are speciality shops in the historic colonnaded shopping mall known as **The Pantiles**, setting for a variety of entertainment during the summer, including the Georgian Festivities in July/Aug.
    A Day at the Wells, *Corn Exchange, The Pantiles; tel: (01892) 546545.* Open daily 1000–1700 (Apr–Sep); daily 1000–1600 (Oct–Mar). Admission £3.75. **Tunbridge Wells Museum**

and Art Gallery, *Civic Centre, Mount Pleasant; tel: (01892) 547221.* Open Mon–Sat 0930–1700 all year, except bank holidays and Easter Saturday. Admission free. **Chalybeate Spring,** *The Pantiles; tel: (01892) 548861.* Open daily 1000–1700 (14 Apr–31 Oct). Admission free (£0.25 for glass of spa water).

Out of Town

Chiddingstone Castle, *Chiddingstone, Eden-bridge; tel: (01892) 870347.* Open Tue–Sat 1400–1730, Sun & bank holidays 1130–1730 (Jun–Sep); Sun & bank holidays 1130–1730, Wed & Easter Sat 1430–1730 (Apr–May & Oct); closed for special events. Admission £3.50. 5 miles north west of the town. Take bus nos 232 or 234 to Chiddingstone.

HASTINGS

TIC: *4 Robertson Ter, Hastings TN34 1JE; tel: (01424) 781111.* Open May Mon–Fri 0930–1700, Sat 1000–1700; Oct–Easter Mon–Sat 0930–1700; Sep Mon–Fri 0930–1700, Sat 1000–1700; Jul–Aug daily 0930–1800; Jun Mon–Fri 0930–1700, Sat 1000–1730. DP SHS Services offered: local bed-booking service (latest 15 mins before closing), BABA (latest 15 mins before closing). *Hastings Holiday Guide* (including accommodation list) is £0.50. *1066 Country Discover Hastings* brochure (with accommodation list) is free. Coaches booked and theatre tickets for Hastings and Eastbourne. **Fishmarket TIC,** The Stade, Old Town, Hastings TN34 1E2; tel: (01424) 781111. Open Nov/Feb Sat/Sun 1100–1600; Dec–Jan Sun 1100–1600; Oct Fri–Sun 1000–1700; Sep daily 0930–1700, closed Mon; Jul–Aug daily 0930–1800, Sat 0930–1900; Jun/May daily 0930–1700, closed Mon.
Station: Hastings Station, *Station Approach; tel: (01732) 77011* is central and has a taxi rank.

Getting Around

Free town and transport maps are available from the TIC. Local public transport is quite good in the centre, but very patchy in outer areas. National Express buses operate from the central bus station on *Queens Rd; tel: (01345)*

581457. The main bus operator is **South Coast Buses**, *tel: (01345) 581457.* The main taxi rank is at *Havelock Rd.*

Staying in Hastings

There is a good range of accommodation available, particularly guesthouses and b. & b. Cheaper accommodation is located mainly in the town centre. It is generally easy to book on arrival, but it is essential to book accommodation in advance in Jul–Aug. Availability is affected by the **Morris Dance Festival** in May and the half-marathon on March 12.

Hastings Youth Hostel, *Guestling Hall, Rye Rd, Guestling; tel: (01424) 812373,* is open from 1700. Closed Jan–mid-Feb. Hourly bus service from town centre or station. The TIC has details of **campsites**. The nearest are: **Shearbarn Holiday Park,** *Barley Ln; tel: (01424) 423583,* approx. 4 miles from the centre (take bus no. 20 from the centre to Harold Road); and **Stalkhurst Cottage,** *Ivyhouse Ln; tel: (01424) 439015,* 3 miles from the town centre.

Sightseeing

The attractive seaside town of Hastings is an ideal base for exploring the Sussex coast and countryside. The Old Town nestles between two hills (which can be climbed by **cliff railways**), and has picturesque old houses and narrow, winding streets. On West Hill is ruined **Hastings Castle** which brings to life the events of the most famous date in Hastings' – and perhaps Britain's – history. The Battle of Hastings, at which William the Conqueror defeated King Harold to establish the Norman dynasty in England, took place inland at **Battle**, where you can visit the battlefield itself and the ruins of the **Abbey** William built in thanksgiving for his victory.

There are various sightseeing tours which give an excellent introduction to Hastings, details of which are available from the TIC.

Hastings Castle, The 1066 Story, *West Hill; tel: (01424) 781112/422964.* Open daily (Easter-Sep), 1000–1700 (Oct to Easter), closed Jan 3, Feb 3, Dec 24-26. Admission £2.50.

Fisherman's Museum, *Rock-a-Nore Rd, Old Town; tel: (01424) 461446.* Open Mon–Fri

1030–1700, Sat & Sun 1430–1700 (May–Sep). Admission free. **Flower Makers Museum,** *Shirley Leaf and Petal Company, 58A High St, Old Town; tel: (01424) 427793.* Open Mon–Fri 0930–1630, Sat 1000–1630, Sundays by arrangement only. Admission £1. **The Hastings Embroidery,** *Town Hall, Queens Rd; tel: (01424) 781111.* Open Mon–Fri (Oct–end Apr) 1130–1500, 1000–1630 (May–Sep). Admission £1.25. **Shipwreck Heritage Centre,** *Rock-a-Nore Rd, Old Town; tel (01424) 437452.* Open 1030–1700 (Easter–end Sep). Admission £2.50. **Smugglers Adventure, St Clements Caves,** *West Hill; tel: (01274) 631756.* Open daily 1000–1730 (Easter–Sep), 1100–1630 (Oct–Easter). Follow the signs on all major roads to the car park on the beach at Pelham Place and then take the West Hill Cliff Railway to the top of the West Hill. Admission £3.80.

Hastings Sealife Centre, *Rock-a-Nore Rd, Old Town; tel: (01424) 718776.* Open daily (except Christmas Day) 1000–1800 (2100 in Summer Holidays). Admission £4.25.

Out of Town

Battle Abbey, *Battle; tel: (01424) 773792.* Open daily 1000–1800 during 1 Apr–31 Oct and 1000–1600 during 1 Nov–31 Mar. Take bus 4/5 (Maidstone-Hastings). Admission £1.80. **Camber Castle,** *Camber; tel: (01424) 775705.* Open Wed, Fri, Sun 1000–1700 (Apr–30 Sep). 1½ miles from Rye station. Take bus no. 11 to Camber. Admission £2. **Pevensey Castle,** *Pevensey; tel: (01323) 762604.* Open daily 1000–1800 (1 Apr–31 Oct), 1000–1600 (1 Nov–31 Mar). Take bus no. 28 or 29 from Eastbourne. Admission £1.80.

– – – – – – – – – – – – – – – – – – – –

 Side Track from Hastings

RYE

TIC: *Heritage Centre, Strand Quay, Rye, East Sussex TN31 7AY; tel: (01797) 226696.* Open daily 0900–1730 Apr–end Oct, Mon–Fri 1100–1300, Sat, Sun 1000–1600 Nov–Mar. DP, SHS services offered: local bed-booking service (latest 15 mins before closing), BABA (latest 30

mins before closing), guided tours available on tape. Hoverspeed, Country Holidays, Derwyns Coaches can be booked. *Rye Colour Guide* (including accommodation listing) is £1.50, *Rye 1066* town guide and *Simply Rye* are available free.

Station: Rye Station, *Station Approach;* tel: *(01732) 770111,* is central and has a taxi rank.

Getting Around

Free town and transport maps are available from either the TIC or East Sussex County Council. Several bus companies cover the town and outlying areas, with reduced services after 1700 and a limited service at weekends – **Local Rider,** tel: *(01273) 474747;* **Maidstone and District Bus Company,** tel: *(01634) 832666;* and **South Coast Buses,** tel: *(01345) 581457.* All companies offer a one-day Explorer ticket costing £5.50, which can be used on all services in the town. There are also some weekly and monthly tickets available. The main taxi rank is at the station.

Staying in Rye

There is a good range of accommodation, including a number of mid-range hotels and pubs in the centre. Cheaper accommodation can generally be found on the edge of town. It is generally easy to book accommodation on arrival except for Sat or Bank Holiday weekends and during Aug. Hotel chains in Rye include *BW* and *FC.* The closest hostel accommodation is **Guestling Youth Hostel,** *Guestling Hall, Rye Rd, Guestling, Hastings;* tel: *(01424) 812373),* open Feb–Nov. Take South Coast bus no. 11 from Rye to Guestling. There is one campsite near the town – **Rolveden Farm,** *Love Ln;* tel: *(01797) 222311,* 5 mins walk, ½ mile north-west of the town. The TIC are able to supply addresses of other campsites in the area.

Sightseeing

Rye now lies 2 miles inland but was once a coastal town, rife with smugglers. Narrow, cobbled streets, like *Mermaid St* and *Watchbell St,* are lined with interesting old houses; visit the **Mermaid Inn** – dating from 1420 it is one of England's oldest pubs. Find out more at the **Rye**

Town Model – Sound and Light Show, where the history of Rye is dramatically brought to life. East of Rye is the **Romney, Hythe and Dymchurch Railway,** a popular miniature railway whose steam trains are replicas of full-size locomotives. One of England's most fascinating gardens, and a Lutyens-designed house, are at **Great Dixter,** and **Bodiam** offers an excellently preserved medieval castle.

Jane Fraser Hay, *tel: (01424) 882343* offers guided walks of the town at £3, starting from the Heritage Centre. Events in the town include the **Rye Festival** in Sept and the **Medieval Festival** in Aug.

Rye Town Model – Sound and Light Show; *Heritage Centre, Strand Quay;* tel: *(01797) 226695.* Open Sat, Sun 1030–1530 (Nov–Easter), daily 0930–1700 (Easter–end Oct). Admission £2, shows every half-hour. **Rye Castle and Rye Museum,** *Gungarden;* tel: *(01797) 226728.* Open Sat, Sun 1100–1600 (Nov–Mar), daily 1030–1730 (Apr–Oct). Admission £1.50. **Lamb House,** *West St,* tel: *(01892) 890651 Regional National Trust Office.* One-time home of novelist Henry James. Open Wed, Sat 1400-1800 (1 Apr–29 Oct). Admission £2

Out of Town

Bodiam Castle, *Bodiam, Robertsbridge;* tel: *(01580) 830436.* Open Tue–Sun 1000–dusk (Nov–Dec), daily 1000-1800 or dusk (18 Feb–31 Oct). Admission £2.50. Take Eastbourne Bus 28 to Eastbourne via Bodiam, 6 miles north east of Rye. **Great Dixter,** *Northiam;* tel: *(01797) 252878.* House open Tue–Sat and BH 1400-1700, gardens open Sun 1100–1700 Jun-Aug. Admission £3.50 house and Gardens, £2.50 gardens only. **South of England Rare Breeds Centre,** *Highlands Farm, Woodchurch, near Ashford;* tel: *(01233) 861493.* Open Tue–Sun 1030–1630 (Oct–Easter), daily 1030–1730 (Easter to 30 Sep). Admission £3. Take train to Ashford (Kent), then bus 295 to the farm (2 buses per day Mon-Sat), 6 miles north east of Rye. **Romney, Hythe and Dymchurch Railway,** *New Romney Station, New Romney;* tel: *(01797) 362353.* Open Sat, Sun (Mar and Oct), daily (Apr–Sep), check with railway for exact times. Admission £7.30 return fare Hythe to Dungeness. Take Eastbourne bus 28 or South Coast Bus 711 to New Romney.

EASTBOURNE

TIC: *Cornfield Rd, Eastbourne BS21 4QL; tel: (01323) 411400*. Open Mon–Sat 0930–1730, Sun 0930–1300 (summer only). DP and SHS services offered. Services offered: local bed-booking service and BABA, £2.50 booking fee. Suggestions given for accommodation.
Station: Eastbourne Station, *Terminus Rd; tel: (01273) 206755* is central and has a taxi rank.

Getting Around

The majority of attractions are within walking distance of the town centre, with the exception of **Sovereign Centre** and **Fort Fun**. Free town and transport maps are available from the TIC. Bus services are operated by **Eastbourne Bus Company** and **South Coast Buses**. For general enquiries, *tel: (01323) 416416*. The services is generally good both in town and to outlying areas. Reduced service after 1800 and restricted service on Sundays. Saver tickets include the 'Explorer', but cannot be used on Eastbourne Buses. The main taxi ranks are at the railway station and *Bolton Rd*.

Staying in Eastbourne

Eastbourne has a good range of accommodation of all types located throughout the town, with a choice of cheaper establishments. It is advisable to book in advance during 19–24 June because of the **Direct Line Insurance Ladies Tennis Tournament**. For budget accommodation: **Eastbourne Youth Hostel**, *East Dean Rd; tel: (01323) 721081* is on bus route 712. The TIC can supply a list of campsites. Hotel chains include: *DV, BW, Pr, Fr, Co*.

Entertainment and Events

Eastbourne is a major entertainment centre, with an impressive choice of theatres, cinema screens and dozens of music and dance venues.

Major annual events in Eastbourne include **Eastbourne International Folk Festival**, at various venues 5–8 May; **Fiesta '95 Weekend**, including **Grand Prix Power Boat Racing** and **Eastbourne Carnival**, on the seafront and various venues 8–9 July; **Airbourne '95 RAF Show** including the Red Arrows aerobatic team, various venues 17–20 August. **1812 Firework Nights**, *Redoubt Fortress* July–mid Sept. A full list is obtainable from the TIC.

Sightseeing

Eastbourne is an unspoilt seaside town of charm and elegance and an ideal touring base. There are dozens of stately homes, manor houses, vineyards, castles and gardens within reach. Children enter the world of Long John Silver at **Treasure Island**, an award-winning adventure theme park. The **Eastbourne Miniature Steam Railway** circles Southbourne Lake, with its swans, ducks, geese and wild flowers. The **Redoubt** is a circular fortress built in 1810 to guard against Napoleonic invasion and houses three important military exhibitions – the Queen's Royal Irish Hussars, the Royal Sussex Regiment and the Combined Services. The **Lifeboat Museum** features life-saving vessels from the early days of the fishing industry to the high-tech modern boats. The **Museum of Shops** displays over 50,000 items in authentic settings, giving a fascinating insight into the everyday life of yesteryear.

Bus tours and guided walks are bookable at the TIC. The local bus no. 3 to the cliffs of **Beachy Head** during the summer is a good sightseeing tour.

Towner Art Gallery, *High St; tel : (01323) 411688*. Open Wed–Sat 1000–1700, Sun 1400–1700. Admission £2. **Redoubt Fortress**, *Royal Pde; tel: (01323) 410300*. Open Easter–end Oct. Admission £1.70. **Museum of Shops**, *Cornfield Ter; tel: (01323) 737143*. Open 12 Feb–Christmas. Admission £2. **Lifeboat Museum**, *Grand Pde; tel: (01323) 730717*. Open mid Mar–Dec. Admission free. **Butterfly Centre**, *Royal Pde; tel: (01323) 645522*. Open Mar–Oct. Admission £2.25. **Treasure Island**, *Royal Pde; tel: (01323) 411077*. Open Mar–Oct daily. Admission £1.30. **Eastbourne Miniature Steam Railway**, *Lottbridge Drove; tel: (01323) 520229*. Open daily in summer, weekends during spring and autumn. Admission £1.

Rye–Eastbourne

LONDON to CANTERBURY

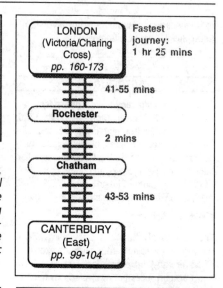

LONDON
(Victoria/Charing Cross)
pp. 160-173

Fastest journey: 1 hr 25 mins

41-55 mins

Rochester

2 mins

Chatham

43-53 mins

CANTERBURY (East)
pp. 99-104

On its way to the cathedral city of Canterbury, one of the two greatest centres of ecclesiastical life in the British Isles, this route takes in the twin towns of Rochester, with its imposing Norman Castle and associations with the novelist Charles Dickens, and Chatham, whose glorious naval past is recaptured at the Historic Dockyard.

TRAINS

ETT table: 500

 Fast Track

A half-hourly service operates from London Victoria to Canterbury East taking from 1 hr 25–1 hr 50 mins. On the faster services, care needs to be taken to ensure that you join the Dover portion of the train (usually the rear 4 coaches) as the train divides into two at Faversham. On Sun one through train taking 54 minutes provides the service.

 On Track

London–Rochester–Chatham

Rochester is served by one fast and two slower trains on weekdays (one slow train only on Sun) each hour from London Victoria, and two slow trains per hour from London Charing Cross. Journey times are 41–55 mins from Victoria and 63 mins from Charing Cross. There are at least five trains (four on Sun) per hour between Rochester and Chatham, taking only 2 mins.

Chatham–Canterbury

Two trains an hour link Chatham with Canterbury East, taking 43–53 mins.

ROCHESTER AND CHATHAM

TIC: *Eastgate Cottage, Eastgate, High St, Rochester, Kent ME1 1EW; tel: (01634) 843666.* Open Mon–Sat 1000–1700 (Jan–Jun), daily 1000–1700 (Jul–Aug), Mon–Sat 1000–1700 (Aug–Dec). DP SHS services offered: local bed booking (10% commission taken and latest booking at 1630), BABA (10% commission taken and latest booking at 1600). The *Rochester upon Medway Visitors Guide* is available at the TIC for £0.20 and the *Rochester upon Medway Accommodation Guide* is available free.

Station: Rochester Station, *High St*; Chatham Station, *Railway St.* There is a taxi rank outside Rochester Station.

Getting Around

The attractions in Chatham and Rochester (except Chatham Historic Dockyard) are within a walkable distance from either town, since the towns are only separated by ½ mile, 10–15 mins walk. Local public transport is good between Rochester and Chatham. There are, however, reduced services on Sun. Buses nos. 140 and 141 from Star Hill in Rochester run to Chatham's Pentagon Shopping Centre. The whole area becomes very congested during the Summer

Festivals – dates are shown below. A free town and transport map is available from Rochester TIC. The general enquiry tel no. for buses in Kent is *(0800) 696996*. The bus depot for Rochester and Chatham is situated in the **Pentagon Shopping Centre**, Chatham, and the main bus company which operates from here is the **Maidstone & District Bus Company**, tel: *(01634) 832666*. 'Freedom Tickets' purchased daily can be used all day on Maidstone & District buses.

Staying in Rochester and Chatham

There is a variety of accommodation in the area, the majority being b. & b. However, there are several large independent hotels and national chains include *BW, FP* and *St.* Generally it is easy to find accommodation on arrival except during festival times – **Chimney Sweeps Festival** (6–8 May), **Dickens Festival** (1–4 Jun), **Medway Arts Festival** (22–30 Jul), **Norman Rochester Festival** (26–28 Aug) and the **Steam Festival** (9–10 Sept). There are no youth hostels in the area but Rochester TIC will provide information on campsites. The nearest is **Woolman's Wood Campsite**, *Rochester Rd, Bridgewood; tel: (01634) 867685*. Take the no. 101 bus to Maidstone from Chatham Pentagon Centre and get off at the Bridgewood roundabout – 3 miles south.

Sightseeing

The city of Rochester sits on the banks of the river Medway; its landmark, **Rochester Castle**, stands in a strategic position overlooking the river and has one of the finest Norman keeps in the country. **Rochester Cathedral**, founded in 604, is the second oldest in England; the present building is predominantly Norman. Rochester features in several of the novels of Charles Dickens, who spent many years in the area – the **Charles Dickens Centre**, in Elizabethan **Eastgate House**, brings to life the characters and scenes he created. **Chatham Historic Dockyard**, once an important naval base, is now a working museum where ropes and flags are still being made. Its 'Wooden Walls' gallery recreates life in the Dockyard of 1758 using sights, sounds and smells. South of

Chatham are many more attractions: fairytale **Leeds Castle**, set on a lake surrounded by magnificent parkland, and 15th-century **Stoneacre**, a half-timbered manor house.

The **City of Rochester Society** *tel: (01634) 721886 (evenings)* runs free guided walks in Rochester from Good Fri–end Sept every Sat, Sun and public holiday. The walks last approximately 1½ hours and start at the Dickens Centre. Group guides are also available from the **City of Rochester Society** and **Travellers in Time;** *(01634) 849355*.

Rochester Castle, *The Keep, Castle Hill; tel: (01634) 402276*. Open all year daily 1000–1600 (2 Jan–31 Mar and 1 Nov–31 Dec), 1000–1800 (1 Apr–31 Oct). Admission £2.50. **Rochester Cathedral**, *The Precinct, Rochester; tel: (01634) 843366*. Open all year, Sun–Fri 0730–1800, Sat 0730–1700. Visiting restricted during services. Admission free but a £2.00 donation suggested. **Charles Dickens Centre and Eastgate House**, *High St, Rochester; tel: (01634) 844176*. Open daily 1000–1730. Admission £2.60. **Chatham Historic Dockyard**, *Dock Rd, Chatham; tel: (01634) 812551*. Open daily 1000–1700 (1 Apr–29 Oct), Wed, Sat–Sun 1000–1600 (Nov). Last admission 1 hour before closing. Admission £5.60. From Chatham Pentagon, take the Maidstone & District bus no. 100 which runs every 20–30 mins, 3 miles north east of Rochester.

Out of Town

Leeds Castle, *Leeds, Maidstone; tel: (01622) 735616*. Open all year daily – Park: 1000–1700, Castle: 1100–1730 (Mar–Oct); Park: 1000–1500, Castle: 1015–1530 (Jan–Feb and Nov–Dec). Take the no. 101 bus from Chatham to *Pudding Lane*, Maidstone. Walk to the *High St* and catch the East Kent Bus no.10 from there to Ashford – this passes Leeds Castle. Fourteen miles south east.

Stoneacre (NT), *Otham, Maidstone; tel: (01622) 861861*. Open Wed and Sat 1400–1800 (1 Apr–30 Oct). Admission £2.00. Last admission 1700. Travel from Chatham to Maidstone on bus no. 101 and then take the Maidstone & District bus no. 12B to the village of Otham. Twelve miles south-east.

LONDON to EXETER

This chapter offers a choice of two routes between London and Exeter. The first takes you via Taunton, the county town of Somerset and the starting point for an interesting side track by private railway to picturesque Dunster. The alternative goes via the cathedral city of Salisbury – jumping-off point for Britain's premier prehistoric monument, Stonehenge – and offers side tracks to the ancient Dorset towns of Shaftesbury and Sherborne, and to the unspoilt seaside resort of Lyme Regis.

TRAINS

ETT table: 510, 511

→ Fast Track

Ten to 15 trains a day run from London Paddington to Exeter St Davids; there are some long gaps in the service, especially around midday. Additional journeys are possible via Bristol Temple Meads (change trains). Journey times are around 2 hr 25 mins with the fastest train, the 'Cornish Riviera', taking a little over 2 hrs. There is one 'Pullman' service available each way Mon–Fri leaving Exeter in the early morning and departing Paddington in the early evening. Trains on this route can get very crowded at peak holiday periods and advance seat reservation is strongly recommended.

∿ On Track

London–Taunton–Exeter

All the expresses from London to Exeter call at Taunton, with the sole exception of the 'Cornish Riviera'. London to Taunton takes about 2 hrs, Taunton to Exeter St David's takes 25–30 mins.

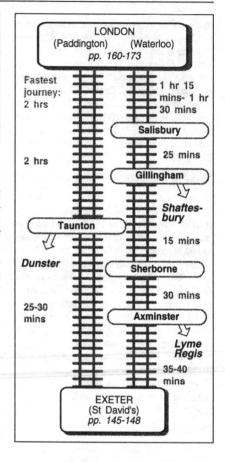

London–Salisbury

An hourly service (some longer gaps on Sun) operates from London Waterloo to Salisbury, taking between 1 hour 15 and 1 hour 30 mins.

Salisbury–Gillingham–Sherborne–Axminster–Exeter

Fifteen trains a day (roughly two-hourly, with additional early and late services) run between Salisbury and Exeter St Davids calling at Gillingham (Dorset), Sherborne and Axminster en route. Salisbury to Gillingham takes about 25 mins, Gillingham to Sherborne 15 mins, Sherborne to Axminster 30 mins and Axminster to Exeter 30–45 mins.

TAUNTON

TIC: *The Library, Corporation St, Taunton, Somerset TA1 4AN; tel: (01823) 274785.* Open 0930–1730 Mon, Tues and Thur, 0930–1900 Wed and Fri, 0930–1600 Sat, 1000–1600 Bank Holiday Mon. DP SHS Services offered: local bed-booking service and BABA (latest 30 mins before closing). Guided tours booked, tickets sold for the theatre, concerts, Bath and West show and Waverley Steamship. *The Welcome to Taunton Deane brochure is free and includes an accommodation listing.*
Station: Taunton Station, *Station Approach; tel: (01823) 251331* is a mile north of the town centre and has a taxi rank. **Southern National Ltd** runs a shuttle service between the station and the town centre on bus routes L and M.

Getting Around

Taunton's attractions are within walking distance of the town centre, and a free town map is available from the TIC.

Most services within Taunton are operated by **Southern National Ltd** *tel: (01823) 272033* from the Bus Station on *Tower St.* Southern National and a number of other companies also operate services to outlying areas and throughout the county. **Somerset County Council** operates a central bus enquiry number on *(01823) 255696.* Bus services are good in the town centre but infrequent to outlying country areas. Most bus services cease after 1800 and Sun services only operate on selected routes. A variety of daily and weekly bus passes are available including the daily 'Explorer' pass covering all **Southern National** and **Red Bus** services across Somerset, west Dorset and north and mid-Devon (price £4.50 adult). The main taxi rank in Taunton is located on *Corporation St*

Staying in Taunton

There is a reasonable range of accommodation in Taunton including hotels in the *FH* and *Prestige* chains. The majority of guesthouse and b. & b. accommodation is located to the edge of the city centre and in outlying areas. There are a number of pubs and inns offering accommodation mostly located in the villages around

Taunton, including **Hatch Beauchamp,** 6 miles south-east on Southern National bus nos 26, 31 and 32; **Stoke St Gregory,** 9 miles east on Southern National bus no. 51 and **Trull,** 3 miles south on Southern National bus route 24. Accommodation may be difficult to find between May–Oct, and after 1800 throughout the year. The closest campsites to Taunton are **Holly Bush Farm,** *Culmhead; tel: (01823) 421515,* 5 miles south-east; **Ashe Farm Caravan and Camping Site,** *Thornfalcon; tel: (01823) 442567,* 4 miles south-east on Southern National bus route 31; **Gamlin's Farm,** *Greenham, Wellington; tel: (01823) 672596,* 8 miles south; and **Quantock Orchard Caravan Park** *Crowcombe; tel: (01984) 618618,* 11 miles north-west on bus route 28.

Sightseeing

This small county town has some fine buildings and pleasant streets. Part of the restored Norman **Castle** houses the **Somerset County Museum,** while the 15th-century parish church of **St Mary's** with its sandstone tower is a Taunton landmark. Other old buildings include **Gray's Almshouses** in East St, dating from 1635. **Welcome West** *tel: (01823) 331010* operates guided walks of Taunton at £1.50 and also offers individual guides on request; both walks and guides can be booked at the TIC.

The Vale of Taunton Deane is prime cider-making country: **Sheppy's** is a traditional farm where the cider-making process is well explained (and can be sampled). To the east of Taunton are the Somerset levels, an important habitat for wetland flora and fauna: the **Willow and Wetlands Visitor Centre** gives a good insight into this area and its industries, including basket weaving. Finally a trip on the **West Somerset Railway** (see p. 338) offers a fine opportunity to see the Quantock Hills, a little-known area of quiet pastoral beauty and small villages, which inspired the poet Coleridge.

Although there are no organised bus tours of the area, Southern National's bus nos 28 from Taunton to Minehead and 29 from Taunton to Wells (see p. 48) are particularly scenic.

Horse racing meetings are held at **Taunton Racecourse** *Orchard Portman; tel: (01823)*

337172, on various dates between Sept–Apr and the town is also home to **Somerset County Cricket Club** *The County Ground; tel: (01823) 272946* which hosts matches Apr–Sept.

St Mary's Church *Church Sq.* Open daily. Admission free. **Somerset County Museum** *Taunton Castle, Castle Green; tel: (01823) 255504.* Open Mon–Sat 1000–1700. Admission £1.50. **Somerset Cricket Museum** *7 Priory Ave; tel: (01823) 275893.* Open Mon–Fri 1000–1600. Admission £0.60 (on first-class match days access to the museum is only available on purchase of a ground ticket). **Vivary Park** Open daily. Admission free. May be busy in Aug during **Taunton Flower Show**, which is held here.

Out of Town

Cricket St Thomas Wildlife and Leisure Park *Cricket St Thomas, Chard; tel: (01460) 30755.* Open daily 1000–1800 (Apr–Oct), 1000–1700 (Nov–Mar, closes at dusk if earlier). Admission £6.80, 18 miles south. **Gaulden Manor,** *Manor House, Tolland; tel: (019847) 213.* Open Thur, Sun and Bank Holiday Mon 1400–1730 (May–Sept). Admission £2.80 (house and garden), £1.25 (garden only). Ten miles north-west, no public transport. **Hatch Court,** *Hatch Beauchamp; tel: (01823) 480120.* House open Thur, Sun and Bank Holiday Mon 1400–1730 (mid-June to mid-Sept); Garden open Thur 1430–1730 (June–Sept). Admission £3 (house and garden), £1.50 (garden only). Six miles south-east on Southern National bus routes 26, 31 and 32. **Hestercombe Gardens** *Cheddon Fitzpaine; tel: (01823) 337222.* Open Mon–Fri 0900–1700 (all year), Sat–Sun 1400–1700 (May–Sept). Admission £2. Take Southern National bus nos 23 or 24, 2½ miles north of Taunton.

Sheppy's Farmhouse Cider *Three Bridges, Bradford-on-Tone; tel: (01823) 461233.* Open Mon–Sat 0830–1830 (May–Sept), Mon–Sat 0830–1800 (Oct–Apr), Sun 1200–1400 (Apr–Dec). Admission £1.50. Take Southern National's bus 22B or Harding Coaches' bus 802, 3 miles south. **Willow and Wetlands Visitor Centre** *Meane Green Court, Stoke St Gregory; tel: (01823) 490249.* Open Mon–Fri 0900–1700 (tours only); Mon–Fri 0900–1700,

Sun 1000–1700 (shop). Admission £2. Nine miles east on Southern National's bus no. 51.

 Side Tracks from Taunton

DUNSTER

Dunster can be reached as a stop on the privately owned **West Somerset Railway,** *The Railway Station, Minehead; tel: (01643) 704996.* Open Sat–Sun (mid-Mar to mid-Apr and Nov), Tues–Thur and Sat–Sun (Mid-Apr to May and Oct), daily (June–Sept). Timetable varies, *tel: (01643) 707650* for details. Return ticket from Bishop's Lydeard (5 miles north-west of Taunton) £7.70; through tickets are available from Taunton BR station, via a special (but very limited) bus link.

Dunster is a small and picturesque market town, dominated by **Dunster Castle (NT),** *tel: (01643) 821314,* open daily, except Thur and Fri, 1100–1600. Admission adults £4.60, children £2.30. The town owed its past property to the wool trade, an unusual relic of which is the octagonal 17th-century **Yarn Market** in the *High St.* Nearby is the partially ruined but atmospheric **Cleeve Abbey (EH),** *tel: (01984) 40377.* Open daily 1000–1800 (Apr–Oct), Wed–Sun 1000–1600 (Nov–Mar). Admission adults £1.80, children 90p.

SALISBURY

TIC: *Fish Row, Salisbury, Wiltshire SP1 1EJ; tel: (01722) 334956.* Open Oct–April Mon–Sat 0930–1700; May Mon–Sat 0930–1700, Sun 1100–1600; June and Sept Mon–Sat 0930–1800, Sun 1100–1600; July and Aug Mon–Sat 0930–1900, Sun 1100–1700; July and Aug Mon–Sat 0930–1900, Sun 1100–1700. DP and SHS services offered. Services offered: local bed-booking service and BABA (latest booking 1700), 10% of first night booking. Guided tours booked. **National Express** and **Explorer** tickets sold and local theatre tickets. Free town and accommodation guides available. There is an additional TIC at **Salisbury Station**.

Station: Salisbury Station, *South Western Rd; tel: (01703) 229393* is situated ¼ mile west of town centre. The TIC operates during the summer season offering local bed-booking service. There is a taxi rank outside the station.

Getting Around

The majority of attractions in Salisbury are within walking distance of the town centre. Free town and bus maps are available from the TIC. Bus services are operated by **Wilts & Dorset** from *Endless St; tel: (01722) 336855*. The service is generally good in the town centre and patchy to outlying areas. Saver tickets include 'Explorer'. The main taxi rank is in *New Canal*.

Staying in Salisbury

Salisbury has a good range of centrally located accommodation of all types. There are several cheaper hotels and a wide choice of guesthouses and b.&b. establishments. There are also several pubs offering accommodation in the town centre. Pre-booking is recommended during June–Sept. Hotel chains in Salisbury include: *FC, BW, MH, Re*.

For budget accommodation: **Salisbury YHA**, *Milford Hill House, Milford Hill; tel: (01722) 327572*. The TIC can provide information on campsites. The closest accessible by public transport is **Hudsons Field Campsite**, *Castle Rd* (A345), 1½ miles north and accessible by public transport. Open Apr–Sept.

There are three luxury restaurants in Salisbury and the majority of restaurants are situated in the *Market Sq* vicinity. Several pubs offer very good food. Vegetarians are catered for at **Sunflowers**, *2/4 Ivy St*.

Entertainment and Events

The TIC produces a free monthly entertainment listing, *Periscope*. **The City Hall**, *Malthouse Ln; tel: (01722) 327676* is an entertainment centre attracting a variety of quality events and national tours. **Salisbury Playhouse**, *Malthouse Ln; tel: (01722) 320333* has a good theatre programme and **The Medieval Hall**, *The Cathedral Close; tel: (01722) 324731* is an important venue for chamber music and theatre. There is also a cinema. Major annual events in Salisbury include the **Salisbury Festival** (13–29 May in 1995) and **St George's Festival** (16–23 Apr). A free events listing is available from the TIC.

Sightseeing

Two miles north of the present city are the massive ramparts of **Old Sarum**, an Iron Age hillfort successively used by Romans, Saxons and Normans. In the early 13th century, the inconvenience of its windswept site led to the foundation of New Sarum beside the River Avon, and thus was born modern Salisbury, arguably the most beautiful cathedral city in Britain.

Salisbury's **cathedral** is the purest example of Early English style: it was built entirely between 1220 and 1258, apart from the spire, the highest in the country, which was added 1334–80. The intrepid can climb the 360 steps up the tower to the base of the (leaning) spire, for views of the Close and Old Sarum. Take time also to explore the cloister, the octagonal chapter house with its medieval frieze carved with scenes from Genesis and Exodus and the peaceful, walled **Cathedral Close**. The latter preserves a happy mix of 13th–18th-century houses. These include **Mompesson House**, built in 1710, which has fine plasterwork, Queen Anne furniture and a collection of rare 18th-century drinking glasses; and **Malmesbury House**, where the composer Handel once lived. The **Salisbury and South Wiltshire Museum** also lies within the Close in 13th-century King's House: it has many archaeological treasures from Old Sarum and Stonehenge, as well as a reconstructed pre-NHS doctor's surgery. There are historic areas to explore beyond the Close as well: north of the Cathedral towards **Market Square** is a network of medieval streets and alleys, with many overhanging half-timbered houses. Guided walks can be arranged by the TIC (price £2 adult, £1 child) and Registered Guides.

A trip from here to **Stonehenge** is a must: this is Britain's most famous prehistoric monument, and though from afar the stones may appear disappointingly small, you quickly come to appreciate that this mysterious edifice represents an extraordinary feat of prehistoric engineering. Nearer in time and space, 17th-century **Wilton House** boasts Inigo Jones' famous Double Cube Room, and a renowned art collection including paintings by Breughel, Rubens and Van Dyck; **Breamore House** is a fine manor house built in 1583, with a good museum of coaches and steam engines.

Salisbury Cathedral, *The Close; tel: (01722) 328726.* Open 2 Jan–30 April, 1 Sept–23 Dec daily 0800–1830; 1 May–31 Aug daily 0800–2030. Admission free, but donations requested. **Malmesbury House**, *15 The Close; tel: (01722) 327027.* Open 5 April–30 Sept Tues–Sat 1000–1700. Admission £3. **Mompesson House**, *Choristers Green, The Close; tel: (01722) 335659.* Open 26 Mar–30 Oct Sat–Wed 1200–1730. Admission £3. **Salisbury & South Wiltshire Museum**, *The King's House, 65 The Close; tel: (01722) 332151.* Open all year Mon–Sat 1000–1700; 3 July–mid-Sept Sun 1400–1700. Admission £2.50.

Out of Town

Breamore House, *Breamore, Fordingbridge; tel: (01725) 512233.* Open 1–30 April Tues, Wed, Sun; 1 May–30 June, 1 July–30 Sept Tues–Thurs, Sat and Sun; 1–31 Aug daily 1400–1730. Admission £4. Nine miles south. Bus no. 38 then 1½ mile walk. **Stonehenge and Old Sarum**, *Amesbury; tel: (01980) 623108.* Open 1 April–31 Sept daily 1000–1800; 1 Oct–31 Mar daily 1000–1600. Admission £2.85. Nine miles north of Salisbury. Wilts & Dorset bus no. 3. **AS Tours** *tel: (01980) 862931* operate tours to Stonehenge. Bookings can be made at the TIC. **Wilton House**, *Wilton; tel: (01722) 743115.* Open 29 Mar–30 Oct daily 1100–1800 (last admission 1700). Admission £5.50 or £2.50 for grounds only. Three miles west. Bus nos 60, 61.

- - - - - - - - - - - - - - - - - - - -

 Side Track from Gillingham

SHAFTESBURY

TIC: *8 Bell St, Shaftesbury, Dorset SP7 8AE; tel: (01747) 853514.* Open: Apr–Oct, Mon–Sun 1000–1700; Nov–Mar, Mon–Fri, 1000–1300,

Sat 1000–1700. DP service offered: local bed-booking service, BABA (latest time for local booking 1630) commission 10% of first night's charge. *Shaftesbury Official Guide* is £0.15, *North Dorset Where To Stay in Shaftesbury & District* is free.

Station: Gillingham (Dorset), *Station Rd, Gillingham; tel: (01703) 229393 or (0171) 928 5100* is 4½ miles north-west of the centre on B3081 road. There is a taxi rank, and Southern National bus no. 59, Mon–Sat, to Shaftesbury.

Getting Around

Most attractions are within a walkable area from the centre. Town and transport maps are available from the TIC. Local public transport is available in the centre and to nearby towns but is sporadic, with no service after 1900 Mon–Sat and no service on Suns. **Wiltshire & Dorset Bus Co**, *tel: (01722) 336855;* **Southern National Bus Co**, *tel: (01935) 76233;* **National Express Coaches**, *tel: (01202) 551481.* Explorer tickets available daily in advance, family ticket £8.00, adult £4.00, child under 14 years £2.00, senior citizen over 60 years £2.95. The main taxi rank is in the *High St*, near the Town Hall.

Staying in Shaftesbury

It is advisable to book accommodation in advance, particularly late Aug and early Sept because of the **Great Dorset Steam Fair**. Hotel chains include *BW* and *FP*, and there are four smaller hotels and 50 guest-houses and b. & b. premises within a 10-mile radius of Shaftesbury, as well as seven pubs offering accommodation. The nearest campsites are: **Shaftesbury Football Club**, *Coppice St; tel: (01747) 824767 (daytime), (01747) 853990 (after 1830),* a ¼ mile from *High St*; **Blackmore Vale Caravan Park**, *Sherborne Causeway; tel: (01747) 852573,* 2 miles along A30; **Thorngrove Centre**, *Common Mead Ln, Gillingham; tel: (01747) 822242 (daytime), (01747) 825384 (evenings/weekends),.* 5 miles. Southern National bus no. 59.

Sightseeing

Shaftesbury, one of England's oldest towns, offers wonderful views over the Blackmore Vale.

It appears in Thomas Hardy's novels under the name of 'Shaston'. The town's attractions are close to each other: much photographed **Gold Hill** is a picturesque, steeply cobbled street, and the ruined medieval **Abbey** was founded by King Alfred the Great. Nearby **Stourhead** dates from the 18th century; the house contains fine works of art and the famous landscaped gardens are a series of lakes, temples and vistas.

Shaftesbury Museum, *Gold Hill; tel: (01747) 852157.* Open 14 Apr–30 Sep 1100–1700; 1 Oct–Easter Sun 1100–1700. Admission £0.90. **Shaftesbury Abbey & Museum**, *Abbey Walk; tel: (01747) 852910.* Open: 14 Apr–1 Oct 1000–1730; 2–29 Oct, Sat–Sun 1000–1730. Admission £0.90.

Out of Town

Old Wardour Castle, *nr Tisbury, Salisbury: tel: (01747) 870487.* Open daily Apr–Oct 1000–1800, Nov–Mar, Wed–Sun 1000–1600. Admission £1.35. Eight miles east. Bus no. 26. **Stourhead House & Garden**, *Stourton, Warminster; tel: (01747) 840348.* Open: (house) Apr–Oct, Sat–Wed 1200–1730 (last admission 1700 or dusk if earlier); (garden) all year, daily 0900–1900 or dusk if earlier. On 19–22 Jul the garden closes at 1700 for a Fête Champêtre. Admission £7.50 house and garden.

SHERBORNE

TIC: *3 Tilton Court, Digby Road, Sherborne, Dorset DT9 3NL; tel: (01935) 815341.* Open: Mar–Oct, Mon–Sat 0930–1730; Nov–Feb, Mon–Sat 1000–1500. DP SHS services offered: local bed-booking service, BABA, guided tours booked. *West Dorset Accommodation Guide* is available free, *Sherborne Visitor Guide* is £0.40. **Station:** Sherborne Station, *Station Approach; tel: (0117) 929 4255* is a 5-minute walk from the town centre and has a taxi rank.

Getting Around

The majority of attractions in town are within walking distance of the centre. Free transport maps are available from the TIC. The main bus operator is **Southern National**, *tel: (01935)*

76233. There are regular services during the day around the town, but the service is virtually non-existent after 2200 and on Sun. The main taxi rank is located outside the station.

Staying in Sherborne

The majority of accommodation in Sherborne consists of b. & b. establishments and a couple of mid-range hotels. The cheaper accommodation can be found on the edge of the town centre. It is generally easy to book on arrival, except during Bank Holiday periods. The TIC has details of **campsites** in the area – the nearest is **Giants Head Caravan and Camping Park**, *Old Sherborne Rd, Cerne Abbas; tel: (01300) 341242,* 12 miles south of the centre.

Sightseeing

The lovely medieval buildings of Sherborne are dominated by **Sherborne Abbey**, founded in 705 AD and once a Benedictine Abbey Church. This small country town has two castles: **Sherborne Castle**, a furnished house built by Sir Walter Raleigh in 1594, and 12th-century **Sherborne Old Castle**, now a romantic ruin. Out of town visit **Montacute House**, a late 16th-century house with notable Long Gallery and Great Hall, and **Sparkford Motor Museum**, with over 200 old cars and motorcyles. The TIC can book bus tours, boat trips and guided walks.

Sherborne Castle, *tel: (01935) 813182.* Open Thu, Sat, Sun 1200–1730 (Apr–Sep). Admission £3.60. **Sherborne Abbey**, *tel: (01935) 812452.* Open daily 0900–1800 (May–Sep), 0900–1600 (Oct–Apr). Admission free. **Sherborne Museum**, *Abbey Gate House; tel: (01935) 812252.* Open Tue–Sat 1030–1630, Sun 1430–1630 (Mar–Oct). Admission 50p. **The Almshouse of St John the Baptist and John the Evangelist**, *Half Moon St; tel: (01935) 813245.* Open May–Sept, Tue, Thu–Sat 1400–1600. Admission nominal.

Out of Town

Conservation Worldwide, *Compton House; tel: (01935) 74608.* Open Apr–Oct, daily 1000–1700. Admission £3.50. Three miles west of town centre. **Montacute House**,

Montacute, Somerset; tel: (01935) 823289. Open May–Oct, Wed–Mon 1200–1730. Admission £4.70. Eight miles west. **Fleet Air Arm Museum**, *RNAS Yeovilton, Ilchester, Somerset; tel:(01935) 840565.* Open daily 1000–1430 (Jan–Mar, Nov–Dec), 1000–1700 (Apr–Oct). Admission £5.50. Ten miles north-west of the centre. **Sparkford Motor Museum**, *Sparkford, Yeovil, Somerset; tel: (01963) 440804.* Open daily 0930–1730. Admission £3.85. Nine miles north of town centre.

 Side Track from Axminster

LYME REGIS

TIC: *Guildhall Cottage, Church St, Lyme Regis, Dorset DT7 5BS; tel: (01297) 442138.* Open daily 1000–1700 (Apr, Oct), Mon–Fri 1000–1800, Sat–Sun 1000–1700 (May–Sep), Mon–Fri 1000–1600, Sat 1000–1400 (Nov–Mar). SHS services offered: local bed-booking service, BABA. Tickets booked for excursions, theatres and local attractions. *Lyme Regis the Pearl of Dorset* and accommodation listings are available free.
Station: The nearest main line station is Axminster, 5 miles north-west of the town centre, which has a taxi rank.

Getting Around

The majority of attractions in the town are within a walkable area of the centre. A free transport map is available from the TIC. The main bus operator is **Southern National**, *tel: (01823) 272033.* A good town shuttle service operates, with an hourly service to outlying areas. Services operate 0600–2000. Tickets available are 'Welfarer' (for senior citizens), 'Explorer' and 'Silver'. The main taxi rank is located at *The Square, Broad St.*

Staying in Lyme Regis

There is a good range of guesthouses and b.&b. establishments to choose from, with cheaper accommodation available in the town centre. It is generally easy to book accommodation on arrival, except during July and Aug.

The TIC has details of **campsites** in the area. The nearest are: **Hook Farm**, *Gore Ln, Uplyme; tel: (01292) 442801,* 1 mile west of the centre; **Wood Farm**, *Axminster Rd, Charmouth; tel: (01297) 560697,* two miles north; and **Newlands**, *Charmouth; tel: (01297) 560259,* 2 miles east.

Sightseeing

The seaside town of Lyme Regis was a fashionable resort in the 18th and 19th centuries; a regular visitor was Jane Austen, who set part of her novel *Persuasion* here. The harbour is sheltered by the stone breakwater known as **The Cobb**, site of the fascinating **Lyme Marine Aquarium**. The area is a paradise for fossil collectors and there is an excellent display at the **Philpot Museum**. Out of town is **Forde Abbey and Gardens**, whose house is an interesting blend of several styles.

The TIC can book bus tours, boat trips and guided walks.

Dinosaurland, *Coombe St; tel: (01297) 443541.* Open all year. Admission £2.50. **Lyme Marine Aquarium**, *The Cobb; tel: (01297) 443678.* Open daily 1000–dusk (Apr–Oct). Admission £1.10. **Lyme Regis Philpot Museum**, *Bridge St; tel: (01297) 443370.* Admission £0.50. **New World Tapestry**, *Guildhall, Bridge St.* Open various times throughout the year, but check with the TIC. Admission free.

Out of Town

Pecorama, *Underleys, Beer, Seaton; tel: (01297) 21542.* Open all year. Admission £2.85, 8 miles west, bus no. 899. **Seaton Electric Tramway**, *Riverside Depot, Harbour Rd, Seaton; tel: (01297) 20375.* Open daily (Mar–Oct). Admission £3.70, 7 miles west, bus no. 899. **Moores Biscuit Factory**, *Morcombelake; tel: (01297) 489253.* Open Mon–Fri 0900–1700, 5 miles east, bus no. 31. **Forde Abbey and Gardens**, *nr Chard; tel: (01460) 220231.* Gardens/nursery open all year 1000–1630; abbey open 1 Apr–end Oct Wed, Sun and public holidays 1300–1630. Admission £4.50 (Gardens only £3.25). Bus no. 31 to Chard 10 miles away, then 3 miles by taxi.

LONDON to NORWICH

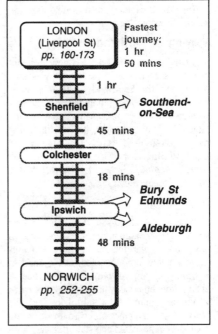

This route passes through the heart of East Anglia to link the nation's capital with the unofficial one of the region. Taking in another one-time capital – the Roman city of Colchester – it gives access to 'Constable Country' as well as to the Suffolk coast at Aldeburgh, famous for its annual arts festival.

TRAINS

ETT table: 580

 Fast Track

Express trains link London Liverpool Street and Norwich (every hour on weekdays, two-hourly on Suns taking 1 hr 50 mins–2 hours.

 On Track

London–Shenfield–Colchester

Direct trains from London to Colchester are frequent and take about 1 hr 10 mins. Two trains each hour run between Shenfield and Colchester, with journey times of 45 mins.

Colchester–Ipswich–Norwich

Two trains per hour link Colchester–Ipswich (18 mins) and one per hour Ipswich–Norwich (48 mins).

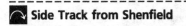 **Side Track from Shenfield**

SOUTHEND-ON-SEA

TIC: *19 High St, Southend-on-Sea, Essex SS1 1DZ; tel: (01702) 215120.* Open Mon–Sat 0930–1700. DP SHS Services offered: local bed-booking service (latest 1630), advance reservations handled, BABA (latest 1600). *Southend-on-Sea* and accommodation guide are available free.

Station: there are two stations in Southend, Southend Victoria Station, *Victoria Ave; tel: (01702) 611811* on the edge of the town centre, and Southend Central Station, *Clifftown Rd; tel: (01702) 611811* in the centre. Both have a taxi rank. There are regular services daily from London Liverpool Street and Shenfield to Southend Victoria Station, Southend Central has services to London Fenchurch Street. The journey from London takes an hour and from Shenfield about 30 mins.

Getting Around

The majority of attractions are within easy walking distance of the centre. Free town and transport maps are available from the TIC. There is good bus coverage of the town, and good bus and train coverage of outlying areas.

Most buses operate from the bus station at *York Rd.* For enquiries *tel: (01702) 434444.*

The main taxi rank is on *London Rd.* Taxis can also be hailed in the street.

Staying in Southend-on-Sea

It is generally easy to book on arrival, except over the second May Bank Holiday weekend, and during the **Southend Airshow** in June. There is a fair range of hotels and guest-houses, with the cheaper establishments located on the edge of town and along the seafront. The nearest campsite is **Eastbeach Caravan and Camping Site**, *East Beach, Shoeburyness; tel: (01702) 292466*, which is 4 miles east (take a train to *Shoeburyness*).

Sightseeing

A popular seaside resort, Southend is best known for its autumn illuminations and its 1.3-mile long **pier**, the longest in the world. Its attractions are family-oriented: at the **Sea Life Centre**, you can view marine life (including sharks) from an underwater tunnel; **Peter Pan's Playground** offers all the fun of the fair; and **Never Never Land** recreates children's favourite characters in animated and static displays. *Royal Terrace* preserves a glimpse of the town's faded Regency elegance.

The TIC has information on bus tours and boat trips on the Thames Estuary. The **South-end-on-Sea Shuttle Train** is a good way to see the sights, running between the Sea Life Centre and Cliffs Pavillion every 30 mins from 1000–1730, single fare: £1.50.

Never Never Land, *Western Esplanade; tel: (01702) 460618*. Open weekends Easter–Nov, daily during school holidays 1100–2200. Admission £1.80. **Peter Pan's Playground**, *Western Esplanade; tel: (01702) 468023*. Open daily 1100–2200 (summer), open weekends and school holidays all year, 1100–1800 (winter). Admission £0.40 per ride or £5.99 for unlimited rides. **Southend Pier**, *Southend Seafront; tel: (01702) 215622*. Open Mon–Fri 0800–2100, Sat, Sun 0800–2200 (summer); daily 0815–1600 (winter). Admission £1.20 (£1.75 including pier train). **Southend Sea Life Centre**, *Eastern Esplanade; tel: (01702) 462400*. Open daily from 1000 (variable closing times). Admission £4.25.

Out of Town

Hadleigh Castle, *Hadleigh; tel: (01702) 551072*. Open from dawn to dusk. Admission free. Take bus nos 1, 2 or 3 to *Hadleigh*, 9 miles west.

COLCHESTER

TIC: *1 Queen St, Colchester, Essex CO1 2PJ; tel: (01206) 712920*. Open Mon–Fri 0900–1700, Wed from 1000; Sat, Sun 1000–1700 (June-Sept), Sat only 1000–1300 (Oct–May). DP Services offered: local bed-booking service (latest 30 mins before closing), advance reservations handled, BABA, guided tours booked, YHA membership sold. *People Are Talking About Colchester*, the main guide, and *Where to Stay and Eat* are available free.

Station: Colchester North Station, *North Station Rd; tel: (01206) 564777* is 1½ miles north of the town, with bus connections on routes 67, 77, 78 and 178 to the centre. There is also a taxi rank.

Bus Station: local buses and national coaches operate from *Queen St*. For National Express enquiries *tel: (01206) 571321*.

Getting Around

With the exception of **Colchester Zoo**, the town's attractions are within walking distance of the centre. Town and transport maps are available free from the TIC.

The main local bus operator is **Eastern National** *tel: (01206) 571321*, and most buses start from the bus station on *Queen St*. There is a good transport service in town and locally, but not so good for outlying villages. Frequency is much reduced after 2030.

The main taxi ranks are at the bus station on *Queen St*, and on the *High St*.

Staying in Colchester

There are about 12 hotels and 60 b.&b. establishments to choose from, with the cheaper places located in the suburbs of *Stanway*, 3 miles east, and *Lexden*, 1½ miles west. There are also a few pubs with rooms in the surrounding area. It is generally easy to book on arrival, with the exception of university graduation in July, and **Cricket Week** in Aug. Hotel chains in Colchester include *FP, MH, RH.*

Colchester Youth Hostel, *East St; tel: (01206) 867982,* is open daily in July and Aug, Mon–Sat Apr–June, Tues–Sat Mar, Sept and Oct; closed Nov–Feb. The closest campsite is **Colchester Camping and Caravan Park,** *Cymbeline Way, Lexden; (01206) 45551.* Approximately 1½ miles west (30-min walk or bus nos 53, 82 or 133).

Sightseeing

Colchester claims to be Britain's oldest recorded town, with settlement here by the 5th century BC. Settled by the Romans, captured and burnt by the powerful Iceni tribe and their queen Boudicca (Boadicea), and then recaptured, it became the capital of Roman Britain. Now a busy university town, within commuting distance of London, it has retained some of its old buildings and character. Its history is imaginatively displayed at the excellent **Castle Museum,** which is actually inside the Norman castle, with its massive keep. There are four smaller museums as well including **Hollytrees Museum** – a collection of toys, costume and decorative arts – and **Tymperley's Clock Museum,** a display of Colchester-made clocks within a restored 15th-century house. Other buildings worth a look are ruined **St Botolph's Priory** (*St Botolph's St*) and the **Roman wall**. There are guided walks from June–Sept, departing from the TIC at 1400 (1100 on Sun), organised by **Colchester Borough Council,** *tel: (01206) 712920,* price: £1.50. **Colchester Borough Transport** *tel: (01206) 764029* run bus tours in July and Aug at 1100, 1330 and 1500, starting from *Castle Park* main gates, price: £4. Both can be booked through the TIC.

West of town, **Hedingham Castle** has a great Norman keep and peaceful woodland and lakeside walks; trips on a steam train can be enjoyed nearby at the **Colne Valley Railway**. To the south, **Layer Marney Tower** boasts the tallest Tudor gatehouse in England, as well as a rare breeds farm; and for nature lovers **Fingringhoe Wick Nature Reserve** on the

Colne estuary is a haven for sea birds. Just north of Colchester lies the **Stour Valley,** which inspired John Constable, perhaps England's best loved landscape artist, to paint many of his most famous works; the village of **Dedham** and **Flatford Mill** (1¼-mile walk from Dedham) have managed to survive the attentions of visitors.

Colchester Castle Museum, *Castle Park, High St; tel: (01206) 712931.* Open Mon–Sat 1000–1700 (all year); also Sun 1400–1700 (Mar–Nov). Admission £2.50. **Colchester Zoo** (2 miles south of centre), *Maldon Rd; tel: (01206) 330253.* Open daily 0930–1800 (closes one hour before dusk Oct–Apr). Admission £6. Take bus nos 118 or 119. **Hollytrees Museum,** *High St; tel: (01206) 712931.* Open Tues–Sat 1000–1200 and 1300–1700. Admission free.

Natural History Museum, *High St; tel: (01206) 712931.* Open Tues–Sat 1000–1300 and 1400–1700. Admission free. **Social History Museum,** *Trinity St; tel: (01206) 712931.* Open Tues–Sat 1000–1200 and 1300–1700 (Apr–Oct). Admission free. **Tymperleys Clock Museum,** *Trinity St; tel: (01206) 712931.* Open 1000–1300 and 1400–1700 (Apr–Oct). Admission free.

Out of Town

Colne Valley Railway Museum (15 miles west), *Castle Hedingham; tel: (01787) 461174.* Open 1000–1700 (Mar–Dec). Admission £2 (£4 on steam days). Take bus no. 88 to *Halstead,* then bus no. 89 to *Castle Hedingham* (good connections). **Dedham Rare Breeds Centre** (10 miles north-west), *Mill Rd; tel: (01206) 323111.* Open daily 1000–1730 or one hour before dusk (Mar–Dec). Admission £2.50. Take bus no. 87 to *Dedham.*

East Anglian Railway Museum (10 miles west), *Chappel and Wakes Colne Station; tel: (01206) 242524.* Open 0930–1700. Admission £2 (£4 on steam days). Hourly train service from Colchester. **Fingringhoe Wick Nature Reserve** (5 miles south), *Fingringhoe; tel: (01206) 729687.* Open Tues–Sun 0900–1700 (–1800 in summer). Admission free, donations welcomed. Take bus no. 76.

Hedingham Castle (15 miles west), *Castle Hedingham; tel: (01787) 60261.* Open daily

1000–1700 (Easter–Oct). Admission £2.50. Take bus no. 88 to *Halstead*, then bus no. 89 to *Castle Hedingham* (good connections). **Layer Marney Tower**, *Layer Marney; tel: (01206) 330784*. Open Sun–Fri 1400–1800 (Apr–Sept), Bank Holidays 1100–1800. Admission £3. Take bus nos 118 or 119 to *Roundbush Corner*, then 1-mile walk. (Six miles south of Colchester).

IPSWICH

TIC: *St Stephen's Church, St Stephen's Lane, Ipswich, Suffolk IP1 1DP; tel: (01473) 258070.* Open Mon–Sat 0900–1700. DP SHS Services offered: local bed-booking service, advance reservations handled, BABA, guided tours booked. Tickets for local events and excursions and HI membership sold. *Ipswich and District* is free by post or £0.50 at the TIC, and includes an accommodation list.
Station: Ipswich Station, *Burrell Rd; tel: (01473) 693396* is ½ mile south of the town centre and has a taxi rank.

Getting Around

The majority of attractions in the town are within easy walking distance of the centre. Free town and transport maps are available from the TIC. For general transport enquiries *tel: (01473) 265676*.

Ipswich Buses *tel: (01473) 232600* operate most local services from *Tower Ramparts*. Services are good within the town and to some outlying districts.

The main taxi ranks are at *Ipswich Railway Station, Lloyds Ave* and the *Old Cattle Market*. Taxis can also be hailed in the street.

Staying in Ipswich

There is a reasonable selection of hotel accommodation including one in the *Nv* chain, and a good range of b. & b. and guest-house establishments. It is generally easy to book on arrival.

For budget accommodation there is a **YMCA** at *169 Norwich Rd; tel: (01473) 254816* and *2 Wellington St; tel: (01473) 252456*; and a **YWCA** at *43 Fonnereau Rd; tel: (01473) 214554*. The closest campsites are **Orwell**

Meadows, *Priory Lane, Nacton; tel: (01473) 726666* and **Priory Park**, *Priory Lane, Nacton; tel: (01473) 727393*, both 4 miles south-east. Bus no.2 to roundabout beyond airport, then 10-min walk.

Sightseeing

Ipswich is a busy port which has an interesting Victorian dockland: the **Ipswich Wet Dock Maritime Trail** gives a good insight into this historic area of the town. Although much of Ipswich was built or rebuilt in the 19th century, 12 medieval churches survive – ask at the TIC for the *Historic Churches Trail* leaflet. Other interesting buildings include the elaborately plastered **Ancient House** (1670), now housing a bookshop, and **Christchurch Mansion** (1548),

---

Landscape Painters

Britain has excelled in landscape painting, and no landscape in Britain has impressed artists so profoundly as the East Anglian countryside. Thomas Gainsborough (1727–88) was inspired by his native Suffolk landscape, and his birthplace at Sudbury is now a musuem. Fifty years later, John Constable (1776–1837) was to immortalise the villages, churches and winding valleys of the Suffolk–Essex border in paintings so familiar they are part of the national consciousness. Constable was born in **East Bergholt**, and nearby **Flatford Mill** and **Dedham** are surprisingly unchanged since they featured in his paintings: Willy Lott's cottage by the millpond is still recognisably the setting for *The Haywain*. Visit **Christchurch Mansion Museum**, Ipswich for a good collection of both artists.

Further north, the flatter landscape, immense skies and dramatic light of Suffolk and Norfolk inspired the Norwich school of painters. Their work, especially the powerful paintings of John Crome (1768–1821) and John Sell Cotman (1782–1842), is especially well represented at the **Norwich Castle Museum**.

---

which has period rooms and a good art collection, including some Constables and Gainsboroughs. Guided walks (Tues 1415 May–Sept) can be booked at the TIC.

There is an unusual, restored 18th-century **Tide Mill** at the attractive and unspoilt small market town of **Woodbridge**. Boat trips on the **Waverley Steamer** can be booked at the TIC, and in summer Ipswich Buses operate a circular tour of the area.

Ancient House, *Buttermarket*, open Mon–Sat 0900–1730. Admission free. **Christchurch Mansion and Wolsey Art Gallery**, *Christchurch Park; tel: (01473) 253246*. Open Tues–Sun 1000–1700. Admission free.

Ipswich Museum, *High St; tel: (01473) 213761*. Open Tues–Sat 1000–1700. Admission free. **Ipswich Transport Museum**, *Old Trolley Bus Depot, Cobham Rd; tel: (01473) 832260*. Open 1100–1630 on specific days (one Sun each month, Easter–Oct), ask TIC for details. Courtesy bus from *Tower Ramparts* on open days. Two miles east.

Out of Town

Woodbridge Tide Mill, *Woodbridge; tel: (01473) 626618*. Open daily 1100–1700 (Easter and May–Sept), Sat, Sun 1100–1700 (Oct). Admission £0.80. Bus nos 80, 81, 82 or 83 to Woodbridge, 8 miles north-east.

- - - - - - - - - - - - - - - - - -
 Side Tracks from Ipswich

BURY ST EDMUNDS

TIC: *6 Angel Hill, Bury St Edmunds, Suffolk IP33 1UL; tel: (01284) 764667/757083*. Open Mon–Fri 0930–1730, Sat, Sun 1000–1500 (summer); Mon–Fri 1000–1600, Sat 1000–1300 (winter and Bank Holidays). DP Services offered: local bed-booking service and BABA (latest 30 mins before closing), advance reservations handled, guided tours booked. Membership sold for YHA, National Trust, Great British Heritage Pass. Concert tickets and local travel booked. *Visitor's Guide* including accommodation listing, £0.99.

Station: Bury St Edmunds Station, *Station Hill;*

tel: (01473) 693396 is just ¼ mile north of the town centre, and there is a bus connection but no taxi rank. There are at least 5 services daily from Ipswich to Bury St Edmunds, taking around 30–40 mins.

Getting Around

The majority of Bury's attractions are within walking distance of the centre. The TIC can provide free town and transport maps. For general local transport enquiries *tel: (01473) 253734*.

A number of bus companies operate local services, which are good in the town centre, but variable to the outlying areas. There are no evening services except for the Nightrider buses in the town centre.

The main taxi rank is on *Cornhill*. Taxis can be hailed in the street, or for a list of registered taxi companies, contact the TIC.

Staying in Bury St Edmunds

Bury has very few hotels – they include a *BW* – but a good number of b. & b. establishments. It is generally easy to book on arrival. The nearest campsites are **The Dell Touring Park**, *Beyton Rd, Thurston; tel: (01359) 270121*, 3 miles east of Bury – take Eastern Counties bus no. 85 to Beyton, then a 10-min walk – and **Snuff Box Farm**, *Bradfield Combust; tel: (01284) 828164*, 5 miles south of the town – take Chambers bus no. 27 towards Lavenham and get off at Cockfield turning.

Sightseeing

This unassuming cathedral town, which retains its 12th-century street plan, is easy to see on foot and the TIC organises guided walks of the town (cost: £2). There are some attractive streets, and many particularly splendid Georgian buildings, including the **Athanaeum** (*Angel Hill*) and **Theatre Royal**, which reflect the town's 18th-century prosperity. **Moyse's House Museum** contains a wonderfully eccentric collection within a rare 12th-century house. The 18th-century **Theatre Royal** is one of the oldest and smallest working theatres in the country.

The town's name comes from a 9th-century

martyred Saxon king; on the strength of his shrine the medieval **abbey** became one of the most powerful in England. Its fragmentary but graceful ruins form the centrepiece of the award-winning floral **Abbey Gardens**; bizarrely, later houses have been built into the church's west front. Two fine gatehouses remain: the magnificent 14th-century Great Gate and the Norman one, which forms the belfry of the adjacent 16th-century **St Edmundsbury Cathedral** (worth visiting for its hammerbeam roof).

Just outside town (see below), extraordinary **Ickworth House**, with its 100-ft high oval rotunda, boasts a fine art collection; while within **West Stow Country Park** is a reconstructed Anglo-Saxon settlement, built on the excavated site of an actual one.

Art Gallery, *Market Cross, Cornhill; tel: (01284) 762081.* Open Tues–Sat 1030–1630. Admission £0.50. **Abbey Visitor Centre** (EH), *Samson's Tower, West Front, Abbey Precinct; tel: (01284) 763110.* Open daily 1000–2000 (June–Aug), 1000–1800 (May and Sept), 1000–1700 (April and Oct); Wed and Sat 1000–1600, Sun 1200–1600 (Nov–Mar). Admission free. **Manor House Museum**, *Honey Hill; tel: (01284) 757072.* Open Mon–Sat 1000–1700, Sun 1400–1700. Admission £2.50. **Moyse's Hall Museum**, *Buttermarket; tel: (01284) 757072.* Open Mon–Sat 1000–1700, Sun 1400–1700. Admission free. **Nowton Park**, *Nowton Road; tel: (01284) 757068.* Open dawn until dusk. Admission free. **St Edmundsbury Cathedral**, *Angel Hill; tel: (01284) 754933.* Open 0830–2000 (June–Aug); 0830–1800, Fri until 1900 (Sept–May). Admission free. **Theatre Royal** (NT), *Westgate St; tel: (01284) 769505.* Open Mon–Fri 1000–2000, Sat 1200–2000 (except during rehearsals and performances). Admission to look at theatre is free.

Out of Town

Ickworth House (NT), *Horringer; tel: (01284) 735270.* Open weekends and Bank Holidays 1330–1730 (Easter–Oct), Tues, Wed and Fri 1330–1730 (May–Sept). Admission £4.30. Eastern Counties bus no. 143 to Horringer then 1-mile walk (3 miles south-west of Bury).

West Stow Country Park and Anglo Saxon Village, *West Stow; tel: (01284) 728718.* Park open 0800–1700 (summer), 0800–2000 (winter); village open daily 1000–1700, last entry 1615. Admission village £2.50, park free. Eastern Counties bus no. 155 to Lackford, then 2-mile walk (6 miles west of Bury).

ALDEBURGH

TIC: *The Cinema, High St, Aldeburgh, Suffolk IP15 5AU; tel: (01728) 453637.* Open Mon–Fri 0900–1715, Sat, Sun and Bank Holidays 1000–1715 (Mar–Oct). DP SHS Services offered: local bed-booking service and BABA (latest 1645); advance reservations handled. Very busy for accommodation bookings on Fri and Sat. YHA, Ramblers Association and National Trust memberships sold; National Express coach tickets sold. *Suffolk Coast Holiday Guide*, including an accommodation listing, is free.

Station: the nearest station is at Saxmundham (*Station Approach, Saxmundham; tel: (01473) 693396*), which is 7 miles west of Aldeburgh and accessible from Ipswich by a two-hourly train service taking about 37 minutes. At Saxmundham there is a taxi rank and an Eastern Counties bus connection, bus nos 80 or 81, to Aldeburgh.

Getting Around

The majority of attractions which can be visited from Aldeburgh are not within walking distance and public transport is fairly patchy and irregular. The TIC can provide free town and transport maps and advise you on the best routes to take. For general transport enquiries *tel: (01473) 265676.*

The main local bus company is **Eastern Counties** *tel: (01473) 253734*, and buses generally operate from the *High St*. Services are quite regular to main towns and centres, but very infrequent to rural villages, with much-reduced timetables in the evenings and on Sundays. **National Express** *tel: (01223) 460711* service 081 runs to *Aldeburgh Moot Hall*.

There are two taxi companies: **Alde Taxis** *tel: (01728) 453637* and **Pickering Pick-Ups** *tel: (01728) 452092.*

Staying in Aldeburgh

Aldeburgh is very popular for weekend breaks, and it is generally advisable to book in advance for Saturday nights from June–Sept, particularly during the **Aldeburgh Festival** in June. There are three hotels, eight b. & b.s and three pubs offering rooms. Cheaper accommodation is located both in the town centre and on the outskirts of town. Hotel chains in Aldeburgh include BW, FH.

Blaxhall Youth Hostel, Heath Walk, Blaxhall; tel: (01728) 688206. This is 5 miles south of Saxmundham, but very difficult to reach by public transport: bus nos 80 or 81 via Saxmundham, or bus no. 99 from Saxmundham to Stratford St Andrew, then 2-mile walk to Blaxhall.

Nearest campsites: **Church Farm Caravan and Camping Site** (1 mile north of Aldeburgh), Thorpeness Rd; tel: (01728) 453433. Take bus nos 80 or 81. **Cakes and Ale Park**, Abbey Lane, Leiston; tel: (01728) 831655. Take bus nos 80 or 81 from Aldeburgh to Leiston, then ½-mile walk (5 miles north-west of Aldeburgh).

Sightseeing

This quietly fashionable seaside resort is famous for its annual music festival in June, founded by the composer Benjamin Britten, who made the town his home. The festival is now divided between the town and **Snape Maltings** (6 miles away), which is a collection of attractive converted granaries and malthouses surrounded by Suffolk marshes, housing one of Europe's finest concert halls.

The seafront at Aldeburgh itself makes for a pleasant walk, both for the scenery, and for its vernacular buildings. Close to the beach is the quaint **Moot Hall**, a 16th-century building housing a museum of Aldeburgh's history. There are good views from the **Town Steps** and up the hill (Victoria Rd) is the fine **parish church**, where Britten is buried.

Five miles south of Snape, in the pretty village of Orford, now cut off from the sea by Orford Ness, is the magnificent keep of **Orford Castle**, built by Henry II; while inland is picturesque **Framlingham Castle**, 12th-century

like Orford but complete with its curtain wall and 13 towers topped by bizarre Tudor chimneys. Along the coast north of Aldeburgh, **Sizewell Visitor Centre** explains how power is generated at this well-known nuclear power station.

Bus tours of the area are organised by **Belle Coaches** tel: (01728) 830414 and **Happy Wanderers** tel: (01728) 830358, starting from Aldeburgh, Saxmundham and Leiston. There are also several companies offering river trips on the Alde Estuary and River Deben: **Lady Florence** tel: (01831) 698298, **Jahan** tel: (01473) 736260, **Snape** tel: (01728) 688303 and **Regardless** tel: (01394) 450637. Prices start from £3 an hour.

Moot Hall Museum, Market Cross Place. Open 1430–1700 (weekends in Apr and May, daily June and Sept); daily 1030–1230 and 1430–1700 (July and Aug). Admission £0.35.

Out of Town

Framlingham Castle (EH), Framlingham; tel: (01728) 724189. Open daily 1000–1800 (Apr–Oct), daily 1000–1600 (Nov–Mar). Admission £1.80. Bus nos 80 or 81 to Saxmundham, and then 82 to Framlingham. (About 14 miles northwest). **Orford Castle** (EH), Orford; tel: (01394) 450472. Open daily 1000–1800 (Apr–Oct), daily 1000–1600 (Nov–Mar). Admission £1.80. No public transport from Aldeburgh (about 30 mins drive).

Sizewell Visitor Centre, Sizewell, Leiston; tel: (01728) 642139. Open daily 1000–1600. Admission free. Take bus nos 80 or 81 from Aldeburgh to Leiston, then 2-mile walk. (About 5 miles north of Aldeburgh). **Snape Maltings Riverside Centre**, Snape; tel: (01728) 688303 and **Concert Hall**, tel: ((01728) 452935. Open all year 1000–1800. Admission free (except for concerts). Snape is about 6 miles west of Aldeburgh (Eastern Counties bus no. 123 or National Express 081: however, buses are very few and far between, so it is better to drive or take a taxi). The administrative headquarters for the Aldeburgh Festival and other concert series held at Snape Maltings is **The Aldeburgh Foundation**, High St, Aldeburgh.

LONDON to NOTTINGHAM

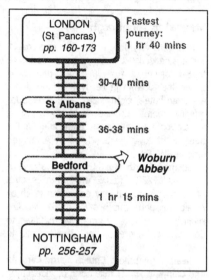

On its way to the East Midlands city of Nottingham, this route enables you to visit the cathedral town of St Albans and to sample the wildlife and artistic splendours of Woburn Abbey, for centuries the home of the Dukes of Bedford.

TRAINS

ETT tables: 560

 Fast Track

London St Pancras to Nottingham takes around 1 hr 40 mins–1 hr 50 mins, the fastest train being 'The Robin Hood'. One to two trains each hour operate the service.

 On Track

London–St Albans

This 30–40 mins journey is operated by at least 4 trains per hour. Train leave from London Bridge and Kings Cross Thameslink stations.

St Albans–Bedford

Four trains per hour run between St Albans and Bedford. The journey time is 36–38 mins.

Bedford–Nottingham

Bedford to Nottingham takes 1 hr 15 mins. There is a train every 2 hrs on Mon–Fri. Through trains are rare at weekends and most journeys require a change of train at Leicester.

ST ALBANS

TIC: *Town Hall, Market Place, St Albans, Hertfordshire AL3 5DJ; tel: (01727) 864511/*

842632. Open Mon–Sat 0930–1730 (Apr–Oct), Sun 1030–1630 (end July to mid-Sept); Mon–Sat 1000–1600 (Nov–Mar). DP Services offered: local bed-booking service and BABA (10% deposit plus booking fee charged, latest booking 30 mins before closing). *St Albans Official Guide* costs £0.75.

Station: City Station, *Station Way*; tel: *(01582) 27612* is just under a mile east of the centre. Buses into town run from the station, and there is a taxi rank. The main rank is on *St Peters St*.

Sightseeing

Bustling St Albans has some very well preserved buildings and streets (especially medieval *French Row* and Georgian *Fishpool St*). It was an important Roman city: **Verulamium Park** covers its site and contains part of the Roman wall, a good hypocaust (underfloor heating) and the excellent **Verulamium Museum**, where the collection includes some well preserved mosaics. The distinctive Norman **Cathedral** has a glorious (and immensely long) nave and a tower of pillaged Roman brick. Guided walks can be organised through the **Association of Honorary Guides** tel: *(01727) 833001* (£20 for up to 25 people). There are also free public walks on Sun from Easter–Sept, meeting at the medieval **Clock Tower** at 1500.

The internationally renowned **Garden of the Rose** is a paradise for rose lovers; further afield, 17th-century **Hatfield House** has some important portraits of Elizabeth I in its fine collection, as well as recreated formal, scented and knot gardens.

Some of the attractions in town are not within walking distance of the centre. The TIC can provide free transport maps. For transport enquiries *tel: (01992) 556765* or *(01462) 438138* or *(01923) 684784*.

Cathedral and Abbey Church of St Albans, *Sumpter Yard, Sumpter Yard; tel: (01727) 860780*. Open daily 0900–1745 (1845 in summer), services permitting. Admission free. **Clock Tower**, *Market Place; tel: (01727) 853301*. Open Sat, Sun and Bank Holidays 1030–1700 (Easter to mid-Sept). **Museum of St Albans**, *Hatfield Rd; tel: (01727) 819340*. Open Mon–Sat 1000–1700, Sun 1400–1700. Admission free. **Roman Theatre**, *Bluehouse Hill; tel: (01727) 835035/855000*. Open daily 1000–1700 (1600 in winter). Admission £1. Bus no. 300, 1½ miles west. **St Albans Organ Museum**, *320 Camp Rd; tel: (01727) 851557*. Open Sun 1400–1600. Admission £2. Bus no. S2, 2 miles east. **Verulamium Museum**, *St Michael's St; tel: (01727) 819339*. Open Mon–Sat 1000–1730, Sun 1400–1730. Admission £2.50. Bus no. 300, 1½ miles west.

Out of Town

Gardens of the Rose, *Chiswell Green Lane, Chiswell Green; tel: (01727) 850461*. Open Mon–Sat 0900–1700, Sun 1000–1800. Admission £4. Bus nos 733, 724 or 339 to *Chiswell Green*, 3 miles south-east. **Hatfield House**, *Old Hatfield; tel: (01707) 262823/265159*. Open Tues–Sat 1200–1600, Sun 1330–1700. (Very busy during the Living Crafts Exhibition in May). Admission £4.70. There are about 12 buses to Hatfield, including no. 300, 7½ miles east. **De Havilland Mosquito Aircraft Museum**, *Salisbury Hall, London Colney; tel: (01727) 822051*. Open from first Sun in Apr to last Sun in Oct. Thur 1400–1730, Sat, Sun 1030–1730. Admission £3. Bus nos 84, 356, 357, 358, 600 or 602 to *London Colney*, 3½ miles south. **Luton Hoo**, *Luton; tel: (01582) 22955*. Open Fri–Sun (Apr–

mid-Oct) and Bank Holidays. Gardens open 1200, Wernher Collection opens 1330 (Bank Holiday Mons 1030); last admissions 1700. Admission £5. Bus no. 321 to *Luton*, 9 miles north.

 Side Track from Bedford

WOBURN ABBEY

There are various ways of getting to **Woburn Abbey** by public transport from Bedford (15 miles south-west). The best options, in June–Sept at least, are a train to *Bletchley* and then Leisure-Link bus no. 604 from *Bletchley Bus Station* to Woburn Abbey, approximately 25 mins (bus operator is **Challenger Transport** *tel: (01582) 561307*), or a Leisure-Link bus no. 600 from *Bedford Bus Station* to Woburn Abbey, approximately 35 mins (bus operator is **Buffalo Travel**, *tel: (01525) 712132*). Other possibilities are trains to Ridgmont or Milton Keynes, and then bus journeys from those points.

Woburn Abbey, *Woburn; tel: (01525) 290666*. House: open Sat, Sun 1100–1600 (Jan–Mar); Mon–Sat 1100–1645, Sun 1100–1745 (Apr–Oct). Park: open Sat, Sun 1030–1545 (Jan–Mar); Mon–Sat 1000–1645, Sun 1000–1730 (Apr–Oct). Last admission to house 45 mins before closing. Admission £6.50.

Woburn has been home to the Dukes of Bedford since Henry VIII gave them the Abbey after the Dissolution. The mansion, remodelled in the 18th century, contains a magnificent collection of Old Masters – including works by Rembrandt, Gainsborough, Reynolds and a superb sequence of Canalettos – and of French and English 18th-century furniture. In the 3000-acre Deer Park nine species of deer roam freely; one area within the grounds forms Woburn's famous **Safari Park** (drive-through).

There is also a 50-shop antiques centre at the Abbey *tel: (01525) 290350*. Open daily 1000–1730 (summer), 1100–1630 (winter). Admission £0.20. The attractive village of Woburn, outside the Abbey park, offers accommodation, eating and more shopping opportunities.

LONDON to OXFORD

This route connects the capital with one of Britain's (and the world's) greatest university cities. On the way you can visit Windsor, the town from which the Royal Family takes its name and whose magnificent castle has been a royal residence for more that half a millenium. Another side track brings you to Henley-on-Thames, a picturesque riverside town which hosts the world-famous rowing event, the Henley Royal Regatta.

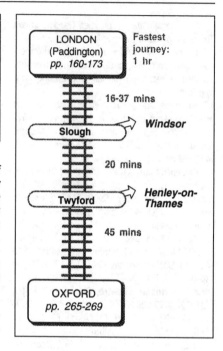

LONDON (Paddington) pp. 160-173

Fastest journey: 1 hr

16-37 mins

Slough ⟹ **Windsor**

20 mins

Twyford ⟹ **Henley-on-Thames**

45 mins

OXFORD pp. 265-269

TRAINS

ETT table: 525

→ **Fast Track**

Hourly 'Turbo Express' trains run from London Paddington to Oxford, taking about 1 hr.

 On Track

London–Slough

Five trains per hour (weekdays), three on Suns link London Paddington with Slough. Timings vary from just 16 mins (fast 'Turbo Expresses') to 37 minutes by the slowest train.

Slough–Twyford

Two trains per hour (weekdays), one on Suns run between Slough and Twyford, taking about 20 mins. At Twyford change trains to reach Henley-on-Thames.

Twyford–Oxford

One train an hour (weekdays) runs between Twyford and Oxford, taking 45 mins for the journey. On Suns a change of train at Reading is necessary.

~ **Side Track from Slough**

WINDSOR

TIC: *High Street, Windsor, Berkshire SL4 1LH; tel: (01753) 852010, fax: (01753) 833450.* Open Mon–Sat 0930–1700 and Bank Holidays; Sun 1000–1600 (Nov–March); Mon–Sat 0930–1830, Sun 1000–1730 (Apr–Oct). DP SHS Services offered: local bed-booking service (latest 15 mins before closing); local bed-booking service available, £2.50 booking fee plus a 10% deposit, BABA £4 booking fee. National Express coach tickets and National Heritage passes sold. A *Royal Windsor Visitor Guide* is available at £1.50, but does not have accommodation listings. In addition to this there is a *Royal Windsor Country Guide* for £0.50.
Station: Windsor and Eton Central Station is in the centre and is a museum in its own right. A frequent shuttle service runs between Slough and Windsor (connections from London).

Getting Around

Most of the attractions in the town are within a walkable area of the centre.

General bus enquiries can be made at the *Brunel Bus Station, tel: (01753) 524144*. The major bus operator is **Beeline** and their number is the same as above. There are services to Heathrow Airport every 30 mins; London, Victoria and Reading every hour. Bus services are reduced after 2000 and after 2200 there are very few. **Buzz cards** are available which cover most of the town's transport system and can be bought weekly or monthly. Local buses are excluded.

The main taxi rank is on *Thames St* (outside the castle). Registered taxi companies include **Five Star,** *tel: (01753) 858888*; **Eton Taxis,** *tel: (01753) 866576* and **Windsor Radio Cars,** *tel: (01753) 841414*.

Staying in Windsor

Although Windsor is an easy day's return trip from London (see p. 172 for best route), it does offer a choice of accommodation for those who want to make it a base. It is always advisable to book accommodation in advance in the second week of May and from mid June–Sept. Availability is affected by the **Ascot Races,** *(20–23 June 1995)* and the **Royal Windsor Horse Show,** *(provisional dates 10–14 May 1995)*.

There is a small range of hotels, a large choice of b.&b. establishments and a few pubs and inns offering accommodation in the town centre. The majority of cheaper accommodation is located in the town centre and in the suburbs which are 1–2 miles west of the centre. There are two major chain hotels: *FP* and *Ma.*

Enquiries for youth hostel accommodation should be made direct to **Windsor Youth Hostel,** *Edgware House, Mill Ln, tel: (01753) 861710*. The TIC is able to provide information on the three campsites surrounding Windsor; however, the closest is approximately 5 miles away. You can reach **Amerden Camping and Caravan Site** on *Old Marsh Ln, Dorney Reach; tel: (01628) 27461* by train to Taplow Station and then there is a 1-mile walk.

Sightseeing

Picturesque Windsor grew in Victorian times and many of its buildings date from that period. **Windsor Castle,** England's largest, has been a royal residence for over 500 years and the Queen often stays there. The Castle stands in a commanding position with stunning views over **Windsor Great Park,** the river **Thames** and **Eton,** home of the famous public school, **Eton College,** founded in 1440 by Henry VI.

Outside Windsor is beautiful **Savill Garden,** where over 35 acres of woodland and borders offer something to see whatever the season. **Dorney Court,** a fine Tudor manor house dating from about 1440, includes 400 years of family portraits. Horse-lovers should head for the **Courage Shire Horse Centre,** a working stable with prize-winning shire horses, and to famous **Ascot Racecourse,** home of the important Royal Ascot race meeting which dates back to 1711.

Bus tours by **Guide Friday,** *tel: (01753) 855755*; boat trips by **French Bros Ltd,** *tel: (01753) 851900* and **Salters Steamers,** *tel: (01753) 865832*. Guided walks and guides for groups only with **Windsor Guide Services,** *tel: (01753) 852010*. The **White Bus Service** operates good routes for sightseeing.

Windsor Castle, *tel: (01753) 868286*. Open daily 1 Mar–31 Oct 1000–1700 (last entry 1600) and 1 Nov–28 Feb 1000–1600 (last entry 1500). Admission Mon–Sat £8 and Sun £5. **Dorney Court,** *Dorney; tel: (01628) 604638*. Open Easter weekend, Sun, Mon Tues, June–Sept, May Day Bank Holiday, 1400–1730. Admission £3.50. **Crown Jewels of the World Museum,** *Peascod St; tel: (01753) 833773*. Open 28 Mar–31 Oct 1100–1600. Admission is £3.50.

Out of Town

Savill Garden, *Wick Ln, Egham, tel: (01753) 860222*. Open all year except Christmas Day and Boxing Day, 1000–1800 (1900 on weekends or at sunset). Admission is £3.20. **Ascot Racecourse,** *Ascot; tel: (01344) 22211*. Admission £5–£25. **Courage Shire Horse Centre,** *Cherry Garden Ln, Maidenhead; tel: (01628) 824848*. Open 1030–1700 (last entry 1600), (18 Mar–31 Oct), Admission £2.80. Access is by

Beeline buses, tel: (01753) 524144. **Eton College,** Eton High St, Eton, tel: (01753) 671177. Opening times vary according to term times. Admission £3.50. **Thorpe Park,** Staines Rd, Chertsey, tel: (01932) 569393. Open 1000–1800 (Easter–31 Oct). Admission £11.25.

 Side Track from Twyford

HENLEY-ON-THAMES

TIC: Town Hall, Market Place, Henley-on-Thames, Oxfordshire RG9 2AQ; tel: (01491) 578034. Open daily 1000–1900 (Apr–Sept); daily 1000–1600 (Oct–Mar); closed Christmas and New Year. DP SHS services offered, local bed-booking service (10% commission or £2.50 booking fee charged), BABA (latest 30 mins before closing – 10% commission charged). Late afternoon is particularly busy for accommodation bookings. The Henley-on-Thames Official Guide is £0.75. An accommodation guide, Henley Visitor, is available free of charge.
Station: Henley-on-Thames Station, Station Rd; tel: (01734) 595911 is in the town centre and has a taxi rank. There are hourly train services (half hourly at times on Mon to Fri) from Twyford.

Getting Around

The attractions in the town are all within walking distance of the centre. Town maps (price £0.25) and free transport maps are available from the TIC. Public transport is good in the town centre, but patchy to other outlying areas, and is reduced in the evenings and on Suns. The main taxi rank is in Falaise Sq, near the entrance to the Greys Rd car park.

Staying in Henley-on-Thames

There are only a few hotels in the town, but there is a large number of b. & b. establishments in the town and the surrounding area. There are also several pubs and inns in the town centre which offer accommodation. Accommodation is generally easy to find on arrival, except during the **Henley Royal Regatta** (see Sightseeing).
The following campsites are nearest to the town. **Swiss Farm International Camping,** Marlow Rd; tel: (01491) 573419. ½ mile out of the town. Take Reading Buses nos 328, 329 or 330. **Four Oaks Caravan Site,** Marlow Rd; tel: (01491) 572312. ½ mile out of town. Take Reading Buses nos 328, 329 or 330.

Sightseeing

Henley-on-Thames is full of picturesque streets – like New Street and Hart Street – with delightful 18th- and 19th-century buildings. The **Town Hall**, **St Mary's Church** and 18th-century **Henley Bridge**, with its five arches, are of architectural and historical interest. Boat trips are available in the summer, and can be booked via **Hobbs & Sons Ltd**, Station Rd; tel: (01491) 572035. The international rowing event **Henley Royal Regatta**, tel: (01491) 572153, takes place during the last week in June/first week in July; and the **Henley Festival of Music and The Arts**, tel: (01491) 411353, during the first/second week in July, when there are orchestral concerts, cabaret acts, jazz, dancing, marching bands and fireworks.

Nearby houses of note include 17th-century **Fawley Court**, designed by Sir Christopher Wren and with grounds by 'Capability' Brown, **Greys Court**, set in beautiful parkland and dating in part from the 14th century, and **Stonor House**, which dates back to 1190 and contains many rare items.

Fawley Court, Marlow Road; tel: (01491) 574917. Open Wed, Thur and Sun 1400–1700 (Mar–Oct). Admission £2.00. One mile north of the town centre. Take Reading Buses nos 328, 329 or 330. **Greys Court** (NT), Greys Green; tel: (01491) 628529. House open Mon, Wed & Fri 1400–1800 (last admission 1730) (Apr–Sept). Grounds open Mon, Tues, Wed, Fri 1400–1730 (last admission 1730) (Apr–Sept). Admission £3.80. 2 miles north west of the town centre. No access by public transport. **Stonor House**, Stonor; tel: (01491) 638587. Open Sun 1400–1730 (Apr–Sept); Wed 1400–1730 (May–Sept); Thurs 1400–1730 (Jul–Aug). Admission £3.20. 5 miles north-west of the town centre, on Yellow Bus route no. M24 (runs Tues, Thurs, Fri and Sat only).

LONDON to SOUTHAMPTON

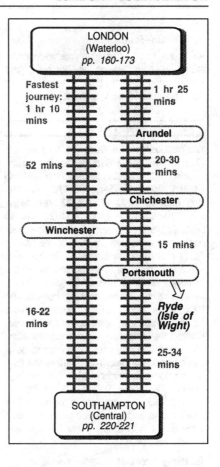

This route offers a choice of travelling directly, with the option of stopping at Winchester, ancient capital of the Saxon kingdom of Wessex, or taking a more meandering path through Sussex, visiting Arundel and its grand castle, the cathedral city of Chichester, and Britain's premier naval town of Portsmouth, with the opportunity of a short ferry trip to the picturesque Isle of Wight.

TRAINS

ETT table: 502 (direct), 508/9 (via Chichester)

Fast Track

On weekdays hourly fast trains link London Waterloo and Southampton Central, taking around 1 hr 10 mins, supplemented by hourly slower trains taking 1 hr 30 mins. On Suns the service is hourly and the journey time up to 2hrs.

On Track

London–Winchester

On weekdays one fast train and two slower trains run hourly between London Waterloo and Winchester, taking 52 mins. On Suns there is only one hourly train, taking up to 1 hr 30 mins.

Winchester–Southampton

Three trains each hour (one on Suns) link Winchester to Southampton Central. Journey time varies between 16 and 22 mins (weekdays) and 28 mins on Sundays.

London–Arundel

The hourly trains from London Victoria to Arundel take about 1 hr 25 mins.

Arundel–Chichester

One train every hour (weekdays) links Arundel to Chichester. It divides at Barnham, with the Portsmouth portion (at the front of the train) serving Chichester. On Suns (and sometimes during the week) an actual change of train at Barnham is necessary. Journey time from Arundel to Chichester is 20 mins (direct), 30 mins if you need to change.

Chichester–Portsmouth

Two trains every hour run from Chichester to Portsmouth and Southsea station, taking 25–34 mins. Many trains carry on to Portsmouth Harbour station.

Portsmouth–Southampton

An hourly fast train operates between Portsmouth Harbour (calling at Southsea) and Southampton Central. Journey time is about 45 mins (up to 55 mins on Sundays).

WINCHESTER

TIC: *The Guildhall, The Broadway SO23 9LT; tel: (01962) 840500/848180; accommodation booking tel: (01962) 867871; fax (01962) 841365.* Open Mon–Sat 1000–1700 (Apr and Oct), Mon–Sat 1000–1730 (2–22 May), Mon–Sat 1000-1800, Sun 1100–1400 (23 May–30 Sep). DP, SHS services offered: local bed-booking service (latest 15 mins before closing) £2 fee plus 10% of first nights' accommodation – queue at designated booking desk, which can be busy in late afternoon; BABA (latest 30 mins before closing). Guided tours are booked, and there is a bureau de change. Publications include a free list of self-catering accommodation and the *Winchester Visitor Guide* (including accommodation list), price £1. A large range of other guides is on sale. Youth Hostels and local theatre tickets can be booked.

Station: Winchester Station, *Station Rd; tel: (01703) 229393,* is very close to the centre. The station has its own information centre, including some tourist information. There is a taxi rank outside the station.

Getting Around

The majority of attractions in town are within a walkable area of the centre. Town and transport maps are available free of charge from the TIC and from the rail station. Local public transport services are good in the town centre at all times and to outlying areas the Mon–Sat services are good but Sun services are limited. Services run up to 2300 Mon–Sat.

Stagecoach (Hampshire Bus) is the main operator, *tel: (01256) 464501);* most services starting from the bus station on *The Broadway.* Some services are run by Hampshire County Council under contract. These services will display the 'County Bus' sign. Hampshire CC information *tel: (01962) 870500.*

Staying in Winchester

It is advisable but not essential to pre-book accommodation, but it may be difficult to find rooms if you arrive late in the evening. There is a range of high-to-medium-priced hotels in the city but cheaper accommodation is mostly found outside the immediate city centre. Hotel chains in Winchester include *FC* and *MH.*

Winchester Youth Hostel, *City Mill; tel: (01962) 853723)* is located very close to the TIC. There are a number of campsites in the area, and the TIC has a free list available. The closest is **River Park Leisure Centre,** *Gordon Rd; tel: (01962) 869525,* which is 5 mins walk from the TIC. **Morn Hill,** *tel: (01962) 869877* is 2 miles west of the city; the Stagecoach 67 bus passes close by.

There is a good selection of restaurants of all nationalities, listed in the *Winchester Visitor Guide.* There are no specialist vegetarian restaurants but many places include vegetarian dishes on their menus. Most eating places can be found in the *Jewry St, City Rd* and *High St* areas. The **Richoux Restaurant,** *God Begot House, 101 High St; tel: (01962) 841790* is in a 14th-century building and features the Richoux Patisserie.

The main post office is on *Middlebrook St,* open Mon–Fri 0900-1730, Sat 0900–1900. Poste restante facilities are available.

Entertainment and Events

A bi-monthly list of events, *What's on in Winchester,* is available from the TIC free of charge. **Theatre Royal,** *Jewry St; tel: (01962) 843434,* is a major entertainment venue showing films, plays, comedy and pop concerts. **Winchester Folk Festival** takes place every Apr at the Guildhall, *The Broadway.* **The New Forest Agricultural Show** is another annual event, taking place in Jul/Aug in Brockenhurst, which is about 1 hr drive west of Winchester. However, public transport to the venue is not good from Winchester.

Shopping

The main areas for shopping are in the *High St* and *Brooks Centre,* where all the main shops and department stores can be found. *The Minstrels* has a range of independent and special interest shops. There is a general market in *Market Car Park*, every Wed, Fri and Sat. **Kingswalk Antiques Market**, *Kingswalk; tel (01962) 862277*, is held on Mon–Sat from 0900. The TIC has a free list of antique shops and markets in the Winchester area.

Sightseeing

Winchester was London's predecessor as capital of England and many early English kings are buried in **Winchester Cathedral**. The first cathedral on this site was begun in AD 642 by King Cenwealh of Wessex; the present structure, started in 1079, contains many ancient treasures and is thought to be the second longest medieval building in the world. Nearby are the ruins of **Wolvesey Castle** (the old Bishops' Palace), once the home of the Bishops of Winchester. The city is also famous for **Winchester College**, one of the oldest public schools in Britain, founded in 1382. Further along College Street is the house where the novelist, Jane Austen, died in 1817; she is buried in the cathedral.

What is said to be the famous **Round Table** of King Arthur is proudly displayed in the 13th-century **Great Hall**, the only visible part that remains of the medieval castle. Winchester has five magnificent military museums, four of which – including the **Royal Hussars Museum** and the **Gurkha Museum** – are at the Peninsula Barracks. All the military museums contain displays and collections depicting the past and present activities of the regiments.

South-east of Winchester is **Marwell Zoological Park**, a large zoo set in over 100 acres of parkland and specialising in the breeding of endangered species. To the east, at Chawton, is **Jane Austen's House**, which has a large collection of memorabilia. She lived here in 1809–1817, writing many of her famous novels.

Walking tours of the city start from the TIC daily from Apr–Oct, last 1½ hours and cost £2 *tel: (01962) 840500* for information. Guided tours can also be booked at the TIC, suiting most requirements. Foreign language speakers are available. The *Walk Round* guide from the TIC is a good way to see the city.

Winchester Gallery, *Park Ave; tel: (01962) 852500*. Open Tue–Fri 1000-1630. Admission free. **Royal Hussars Museum**, *Peninsula Barracks, Romsey Rd; tel: (01962 863751*. open Tue–Fri 1000–1300 and 1400–1700, Sat and Sun 1200–1600. Admission £1.50. **Gurkha Museum**, *Peninsula Barracks, Romsey Rd; tel: (01962) 842832*. Open Tue–Sat and BH Mon 1000-1700. Admission £1.50. **Intech**, *Hampshire Technology Centre, Romsey Rd; tel: (01962) 863791*. Open daily 1000-1600. Admission free **Westgate Museum**, *High St; tel: (01962) 848269*. Open Mon–Fri 1000-1700, Sat 1000-1300 and 1400–1700, Sun 1400–1700 (Closed Mon Feb–Mar and Oct). Admission free. NOTE: Steep stairwell access. **City Museum**, *The Square; tel: (01962) 863064/868269*. Open Mon–Fri 1000–1700, Sat 1000–1300 and 1400–1700, Sun 1400–1700 (Closed Mon Oct–Mar). Admission free. **Royal Hampshire Regiment Museum**, *Serles's House, Southgate St; tel:(01962) 863658*. Open Mon–Fri 1000–1230 and 1400–1600, Sat, Sun and BH Mons (Summer) 1200–1600. Admission free.

Winchester Cathedral, *tel: (01962) 852500*. Open Tue–Fri 1000–1630. Admission free. **Winchester College**, *College St; tel: (01962) 868778*. There are tours to the public areas 2–3 times a day. Admission £2. **Great Hall**, *off High St; tel: (01962) 846476*. Open daily 1000–1700 (Apr–Oct), 1000–1600 (Nov–Mar). Admission free. **Hospital of St Cross**, *St Cross Rd; tel: (01962) 851375*. Open 0930–1230 and 1400–1700 (Summer), 1030–1200 and 1400–1530 (Winter). Admission £1.50. **City Mill**, *Bridge St; tel: (01962) 870057*. Open 1100–1645 (Apr–Sep), shop open all day. Admission £0.90. **Wolvesey Castle**, *College St; tel: (01962) 854766*. open daily 1000–1300 and 1400–1800 (Apr–Sep), daily 1000–1600 (Oct). Admission £1.50

Out of Town

Romsey Abbey, *Romsey; tel: (01794) 513125*. Open daily 0830–1830. Admission by donation. 10 miles south-west from Winchester, take Stagecoach bus 66 (Mon–Sat), X65 Sun. **Avington Park**, *Itchens Abbas; tel: (01962)*

779260. Open Sun and BH 1430–1730 (May–Sep). Admission £2.50. 5 miles south east, Stagecoach buses 64 or 453. **Mottisfont Abbey and Gardens** (NT), *Mottisfont, near Romsey; tel: (01794) 341220.* Gardens open Sat–Wed 1200–1800 (Apr,May,Jul–Oct), 1200–2030 (Jun); House (Whistler Room only) Tue,Wed and Sun 1300-1700. Admission £2. Stagecoach bus nos 66, X66 and 900 stop nearby. **Jane Austen's House**, *Chawton, Alton; tel: (01420) 83262.* Open Sat & Sun 1100–1630 (Jan–Feb), Wed–Sun 1100–1630 (Nov, Dec and Mar), daily 1100–1630 (Apr–Oct). Admission £2. Bus 214 or 215 from Winchester, alight in village. **Sir Harold Hillier Garden and Arboretum**, *Jermyns Ln, Ampfield, near Romsey; tel: (01794) 368787.* Open daily 1030–1800 (Apr–Oct), 1030–1700 (Nov–Mar). Admission £3. Situated 9 miles south west of the city; take Stagecoach bus 900. **Marwell Zoological Park**, *Marwell, Coldon Common; tel: (01962) 777406.* Open daily 1000–1800 (1700 in winter). Admission £6. Six miles from Winchester; no public transport available.

ARUNDEL

TIC, *61 High St, Arundel, West Sussex BN18 9AJ; tel: (01903) 882268.* Open Mon–Fri (except Wed) 0930–1530, Wed 0930–1230, Sat–Sun 1000–1500 in winter, Mon–Fri 0900-1700, Sat–Sun 1000–1700 in summer. Opening hours extended to 1800 in Jul–Aug. SHS services offered: local bed booking (10% deposit and latest booking 30 mins before closing), BABA (10% deposit or £2.15 fee and latest booking 30 mins before closing). A free *Sussex by the Sea* brochure, which includes accommodation listings is available at the TIC.

Station: Arundel Station, *Station Rd* is ½ mile east of the centre and there is a taxi rank outside. General rail enquiries *tel: (01273) 206755.*

Getting Around

Most attractions in town can be reached by foot from the centre. A free town map is available from the TIC and a free transport map can be obtained from **Public Transport Section, West Sussex County Council**, *County Hall, Chichester PO19 1RH.* Arundel is too small to require public transport within the town but there are hourly bus services (and train services) to nearby Littlehampton, Worthing and Bognor Regis.

The primary bus company operating in Arundel is **Stagecoach**, *tel: (01903) 237661.* There is no bus depot. Generally the buses travelling in the Bognor direction leave from the river bank and buses for Littlehampton and Worthing leave from the High St. There are no evening bus services and only a limited Sunday service.

There are taxi ranks in *Mill Rd* and at *Arundel Station* but it is advisable to call **Castle Cars**, *tel: (01903) 884444.*

Staying in Arundel

Accommodation establishments are limited in number and range. The majority are b. & b. and there are no large independent or chain hotels in Arundel. With the exception of the Arundel Festival period (25 Aug–3 Sep in 1995), it is generally easy to find accommodation on arrival. **Arundel Youth Hostel**, *Warningcamp, nr Arundel; tel: (01903) 882204,* 1¼ miles from the town centre, offers the nearest budget accommodation. There are around five campsites within 5 miles, about which the TIC has information. These include **Ship and Anchor Marina**, *Station Rd, Ford; tel: (01243) 551262.* The nearest rail station is situated at Ford, approx ½ mile away. 2 miles south-west of Arundel. **White Rose Touring Park**, *Mill Lane, Wick, Littlehampton; tel: (01903) 716176* is accessible by Stagecoach Bus no.11 (hourly) and lies 2½ miles south of Arundel.

Sightseeing

Arundel is a historic and picturesque town on the banks of the river Arun. **Arundel Castle** had a turbulent past but now the fairy-tale castle offers stunning views of the surrounding countryside from its battlements, turrets and a massive keep. At Littlehampton visitors can take **The Body Shop Tour** to find out more about this company's popular, environmentally-friendly products.

River Arun Cruises *tel: (01243) 265792 or*

(01903) 884663 offer boat trips starting from Arundel and Littlehampton which cost £3–£5 return depending on the trip.

Arundel Castle, *tel: (01903) 883136.* Open Mon–Fri, Sun 1100–1600 (Apr–Oct). Admission £4.50. **Wildfowl and Wetlands Centre,** *Mill Rd; tel: (01903) 883355.* Open daily 0930–1730 (closes 1630 in winter). Admission £3.95.

West Sussex Brass Rubbing Centre, *61 High St; tel: (01903) 850154.* Open Tue–Sun 1000–1700. Admission free but fee for brass rubbing. **Arundel Museum and Heritage Centre,** *61 High St; tel: (01903) 882344.* Open Mon–Sat 1100–1700, Sun 1400–1700 (Easter–Oct). Admission £1. **Arundel Toy and Military Museum,** *23 High St; tel: (01903) 507446.* Open daily Jun–Sep (telephone for confirmation). Admission £1.25.

Out of Town

Amberley Museum, *Amberley; tel: (01798) 831370.* Open Wed–Sun and Bank Hols 1000–1700 (Mar–Nov), daily during school holidays. Admission £4.50. Take the train to Amberley. 4 miles north. **The Body Shop Tour,** *Watersmead, Littlehampton; tel: (01903) 731500.* Open Mon–Fri – book in advance. Admission £3.50. Take the Stagecoach Bus no. 11 to Littlehampton then bus no. 700 or 701 to Watersmead. 3 miles south-east.

CHICHESTER

TIC: *29A South St, Chichester, West Sussex PO19 1AH; tel: (01234) 775888.* Open Mon–Sat 0915–1715; Suns April–Sept 1000–1600. DP and SHS services offered. Services offered: local bed-booking and BABA (latest 15 mins before closing), HI membership, tickets for special concerts and coach excursions. Free *Chichester Visitors Guide* and accommodation listing available.

Station: Chichester Station, *Southgate; tel: (01703) 229393* or *(01273) 206755* is in the town centre and has a taxi rank.

Getting Around

The majority of attractions are within walking distance of the town centre, with the exception of the **Mechanical Music & Doll Collection**. You should avoid **Goodwood** during the last week in July because of the race-going crowds, unless you are actually going races. Free town and transport maps are available at the TIC and station. There are many bus services operating in Chichester. Enquiries are handled by **West Sussex County Council Transport Co-ordinator,** *tel: (01243) 777556.* The services to outlying towns are quite good but services to smaller villages are patchy. Most routes are well covered during the day but operate less frequently during the evenings and on Sun. Saver tickets include the 'Explorer', which can be used daily or weekly. The main taxi rank is at the railway station.

Staying in Chichester

Chichester has quite a good range of accommodation located throughout the city and its outlying areas. Hotel chains in Chichester include: *Ja, FG, Country Club, St.*

There is a wide range of b.&b. establishments and cheaper hotels can be found on the edge of town and in the nearby countryside. Pre-booking is recommended during July because of the Goodwood races. Self-catering bookings are handled by **Baileys,** *17 Shore Rd, East Wittering; tel: (01243) 672217/673748.*

For budget accommodation, the nearest youth hotels are in Portsmouth (15 miles) and Arundel (12 miles). The closest campsites are: **Southern Leisure Centre,** *Vinnetrow Rd; tel: (01243) 787715* (2 miles away, accessible by bus – families and couples only); **Ellscott Nursery,** *Sidlesham Ln, Birdham; tel: (01243) 512003* (4 miles away, accessible by bus). Further lists obtainable at the TIC.

Entertainment and Events

The **Chichester Festival Theatre** has a Summer Festival Season of plays and musicals with all-star casts; and in the winter a variety of ballet, concerts and bands. **Glorious Goodwood** horse racing takes place at the end of July, and during the summer **Polo** is played at *Midhurst*.

Major events in Chichester include **Chichester Festival of Music Dance & Speech**, 11 Feb–11 Mar and the Summer Festival Season at

---

Arundel–Chichester   **215**

the **Chichester Festival Theatre**, *Oaklands Pk*, end Apr–end Sept, which features plays and musicals with all-star casts; the **British Open Polo Championships** take place at Cowdray park, *Midhurst*, 25 June–16 July; **Glorious Goodwood** is a premier horse-racing event at Goodwood racecourse, 25–29 July.

Sightseeing

Chichester Cathedral is an eye-catching sight, its spire, visible for miles around, rising high above South Downs farmland. Close up, it does not disappoint. Much of the encircling Roman wall remains, partly rebuilt in medieval times, and the **Wall Walk** is a good way of orienting oneself; the four main streets within it meeting at the ornate 16th-century **Market Cross** are also Roman in origin. **Chichester District Museum** provides a good introduction to the area's Roman and later history.

The **Cathedral**, mainly Norman and early English, has a graceful nave, some superb Norman sculpture, and an unusual detached bell tower. Both within the tranquil precinct and elsewhere there are some fine 18th-century houses, particularly in the area around **Pallant House**, which has good collections of porcelain and modern British art.

Fishbourne Roman Palace is the largest Roman residence ever discovered in Britain: it boasts many remarkable mosaic floors and a reconstructed dining room. At the well-sited **Weald and Downland Open Air Museum**, over 35 rescued rural buildings including a 19th-century schoolhouse, medieval watermill and Tudor market hall have been reconstructed; nearby **West Dean Gardens** have a peaceful downland setting. The collection at **Tangmere**, a famous Battle of Britain airfield, spans 70 years of military aviation.

Bus tours are available and are bookable at the TIC. **Chichester Harbour Water Tours**, *tel: (01243) 786418*, operate boat trips around the picturesque harbour, but they are not bookable. Guided walks are bookable at the TIC; the pleasant four-mile path along the Canal to Chichester Harbour is rich in wildlife.

Chichester Cathedral, *West St; tel: (01243) 782595*. Open all year (except during services).

There are many concerts during the first three weeks in July. Admission free but donation expected. **Chichester District Museum**, *Little London; tel: (01243) 784683*. Open all year Tues–Sat 1000–1730. Admission free. **Pallant House**, *North Pallant; tel: (01243) 774557*. Open all year Tues–Sat 1000–1730. Admission £2.50.

Out of Town

Fishbourne Roman Palace, *Salthill Rd, Fishbourne; tel: (01243) 785859*. Open mid-Feb–mid-Dec daily from 1000; rest of year – Sun only. Admission £3.40. Two miles away, take bus or train. **Goodwood House**, *Goodwood; tel: (01243) 774107*. Open April–Sept Sun and Mon (Tues–Thurs in Aug) 1400–1700. Closed to public last week in July. Admission £3.40. Four miles away; not accessible by public transport.

Mechanical Music and Doll Collection, *Church Rd, Portfield; tel: (01243) 785421/372646*. Open April–Sept Sun–Fri 1300–1700; winter, Suns 1300–1700 (closed Dec). Admission £2. Two miles, accessible by bus. **Stansted Park**, *Rowlands Castle, Hants; tel: (01705) 412265*. Open May–Sept Sun, Mon, Tues 1400–1730. Admission £3.50. Eight miles away (Emsworth). Not accessible by public transport.

Tangmere Military Aviation Museum, *Tangmere; tel: (01243) 775223*. Open Feb–Nov daily from 1000. Admission £2.50. Three miles away. Accessible by bus. **Weald & Downlands Open Air Museum**, *Singleton; tel: (01243) 811348*. Open Mar–Oct daily; winter, Wed, Sat and Sun from 1100. Admission £4. Five miles. Accessible by bus. **West Dean Gardens**, *West Dean; tel: (01243) 811301*. Open Mar–Oct daily 1100–1800. Admission £2.50. Five miles. Accessible by bus.

PORTSMOUTH

TIC, *The Hard, Portsmouth PO1 3QJ; tel: (01705) 826722 and (01705) 838382*. Open 0930–1745 daily (Apr–end Oct), 0930–1715 daily (end Oct–end Mar). DP SHS services offered: local bed booking (10% or £2.00 booking fee and latest booking ½ hour before closing), BABA (10% commission taken and latest booking ½ hour before closing). May-flower Theatre, Southampton and Kings Thea-tre, Portsmouth tickets sold. The brochure *Portsmouth – Flagship of Maritime England* is available free of charge from the TIC and contains accommodation listings. Three other TICs are located in Portsmouth – *102 Commer-cial Rd, Portsmouth PO1 1EJ; tel: (01705) 838382*. Open Mon–Sat 0930–1745 (Apr–end Oct), Mon–Sat 0930–1715 (end Oct–end Mar). *Clarence Esplanade, Southsea, PO5 3ST; tel: (01705) 832464*. Open 0930–1745 (Apr–Sep). *Continental Ferryport, Rudmore Roundabout, PO2 8QN; tel: (01705) 838635*. Open 0600–0730, 1830–2230 (Apr–Sep), winter times vary according to ferry services.

Station: There are two main-line stations in Portsmouth. Portsmouth and Southsea Station, *Station St*, is situated in the town centre, with a taxi rank outside. Portsmouth Harbour Station, *The Hard*, is 20 mins walk from centre of town. A frequent service connects the two stations. *General rail enquiry tel no. (01703) 229393.*

Getting Around

The city centre and surrounding towns are covered by frequent and reliable bus services, which run at reduced times between 1800–2300 and all day Sundays. Most attractions, however, are within walking distance of the town centre and the TIC will provide free town and transport maps. Bus route maps are also freely available from local bus operators.

The central bus depot is situated at *The Hard* and the main bus companies which operate from here are **People Provincial** *tel: (01329) 232208*, **Red and Blue Admiral** *tel: (01705) 650967*, **Stagecoach Coastline Buses** *tel: (01705) 498894*, **Hampshire Buses** *tel: (01962) 852352* and **Southampton City Buses** *tel: (01703) 553011*. A Portsmouth Transit ticket can be bought either daily or weekly for £1.95 or £7.00 respectively and can be used around the city.

Staying in Portsmouth

It is generally easy to find accommodation on arrival in Portsmouth, with the exception of the annual VE Weekend (early May), when places can get fully booked. The majority of accom-modation establishments are b. & b. and guest-houses, but there are also many large independent hotels. National chains represented in Portsmouth include *Co, FC, Ma, Hn* and *Mn*. The majority of cheaper accommodation lies 1½ miles south of the city centre in Southsea. **Portsmouth Youth Hostel,** *Wymering Manor, Cosham, Portsmouth; tel: (01705) 375661* is open all year and can be reached by taking the train to Cosham Station or by Blue Admiral Bus nos. 1A/1B/1C/3/4 or a Peoples Provincial Bus nos. 48/49 from Portsmouth centre. A short walk from either of the railway stations in Portsmouth is the **YMCA,** *Penny St; tel: (01705) 864341* which is open all year round. The TIC will provide information on local campsites and the nearest include **Southsea Caravan Park,** *Melville Rd, Southsea; tel: (01705) 735070*, 1½ miles south east of the centre and accessible by Blue Admiral bus no.16 or Peoples Provincial bus no.116.

Sightseeing

The seaside city of Portsmouth offers beaches, historic ships and maritime museums. **Ports-mouth's Historic Dockyard** – traditional home of the Royal Navy – is now a centre of maritime heritage, with the **Royal Navy Museum** and three historic ships: Henry VIII's *Mary Rose* (sunk in 1545 and raised from the seabed in 1982); Nelson's flagship *HMS Victory*, which fought at the Battle of Trafalgar in 1805; and Queen Victoria's *HMS Warrior*, 1860.

Southsea is Portsmouth's seaside resort and is the setting for **Southsea Castle** and the **D-Day Museum** which, together with the magnificent **Overlord Embroidery**, tells the D-Day story. Portsmouth is an ideal touring base; not far away are **Staunton Country Park**, with gardens, lake and animal farm, and **Porchester Castle**, with its intact Roman walls.

Guide Friday operate a bus tour around Portsmouth for about £5.00. There are various joining locations and the TIC will provide further details. Boat trips are also possible with **Butchers Blue Boats,** *tel: (01705) 822584*, which leave daily from The Hard between Easter

---

Portsmouth   **217**

and Oct. A 45-min trip costs £2.20. **Portsmouth Tourism Guiding Services** offer guided walks and can be booked at The Hard TIC. There are also free **Guildhall Guided Tours** *tel: Civic Information desk on (01705) 834092*, which run on Mon, Wed and Fri 1000 and 1130 (May–Sep). The Blue Admiral Bus no.25 is good for sightseeing since it runs along the seafront.

Portsmouth Historic Ships (HMS Victory, HMS Warrior and Mary Rose), *HM Naval Base, The Hard; tel: (01705) 839766*. Open daily 1000–1730 (Mar–end Oct), 100–1700 (Nov–Feb). Admission £4.75 (1 ship), £9.00 (2 ships), £13.00 (3 ships). **D-Day Museum and Overload Embroidery**, *Clarence Esplanade; tel: (01705) 827261*. Open daily 1000–1730 (last admission 1630). Admission £3.60. Bus no. 40, 41, 1, 1A, 4 from the city centre to Southsea Shopping Centre. 2 miles south east of Portsmouth centre. **Charles Dickens Birthplace Museum**, *393 Commercial Rd; tel: (01705) 827261*. Open Mon–Fri 1300–1700, Sat–Sun 1100–1700 (Apr–Sep). Admission £1.00. **Portsmouth Sea Life**, *Clarence Esplanade; tel: (01705) 734461*. Open daily 1000–1800 (extended to 2100 in the summer) but closed for refurbishment 2 Jan–31 Mar. Admission £4.25. Blue Admiral Bus no.25 along the seafront in the summer. 2 miles south east.

Out of Town

Portchester Castle, *Castle St, Portchester; tel: (01705) 378291*. Open daily 1000–1800 (Apr–Sep), 1000–1600 (Oct–Mar). Admission £2.00. Take the no.57 bus from Commercial Rd outside Portsmouth and Southsea Station. 10 miles north-west. **Staunton Country Park**, *Middle Park Way, Havant; tel: (01705) 453405*. Open daily 1000–1700 (summer), 1000–1600 (winter). Admission £2.90. Bus no. 21 from The Hard depot passes the park entrance. 14 miles north east.

- - - - - - - - - - - - - - - - - - -

 Side Track from Portsmouth

RYDE (ISLE OF WIGHT)

TIC: *14 The Esplanade, Ryde PO33 2DY; tel: (01983) 562905*. Open daily during summer (from Easter) 0900–1730, July–Aug until 1930; Winter 1000–1500, closed Tues and Suns. Services offered: local bed-booking service with 10% of first night as deposit; advance reservations handled; BABA, self-catering reservations. Bookings made for theatre, Bus Rover tickets, boat trips. AA and RAC membership arranged. *Isle of Wight Holiday Guide* available free of charge. This TIC is particularly busy 1200–1400.

Station: Ryde Pier Head Station, *Ryde Pier; tel: (01703) 229393* is situated 1 mile north of town centre. There is a taxi rank at the station. Ryde Esplanade Station, *Ryde Esplanade: tel: (01703) 229393* is situated ½ mile north of town centre and has a taxi rank. Ryde St Johns Station, *Ryde St Johns*, is situated 1 mile east of town centre. AVIS car hire are represented at this station.

Ferries: There are regular sailings daily from Portsmouth Harbour to Ryde Pier Head, the journey takes about 20 mins. Wight Link Ferries, *tel: (01705) 827744* and Hovertravel, *tel: (01983) 811000 (Ryde); (01795) 8111000 (Southsea)* will help with your travel enquiries and arrangements.

Getting Around

The majority of attractions in Ryde are within walking distance of the town centre. Free transport and town maps (summer only) are available from the TIC and *Things to See and Do* is obtainable from **Southern Vectis Bus Company**, *tel: (01703) 562264*. The majority of services in and around the town are operated by Southern Vectis (see 'Getting Around'). Buses operate all over the island. The only remaining public train service is that between Ryde, Sandown and Shanklin. Generally the bus service is very good. All main routes operate until 2230 and the 'Night Clubber' bus runs from 2300 visiting all the main towns on the island. 'Rover Tickets' for both bus and train are available. The main taxi rank is located near the TIC on *The Esplanade*.

Staying in Ryde

Accommodation in Ryde and the surrounding areas mainly consists of guesthouses and b. & b.

establishments and is generally easy to book on arrival except during the August Bank Holiday. There are no youth hostels in Ryde but there are two campsites within 2½ miles. These are: **Beaper Farm**, *Sandown Rd; tel: (01983) 615210* (bus 16 every 30 mins, 2½ miles northeast); and **Pondwell Campsite**, *Seaview Rd; tel: (01983) 612330* (bus 7 every 30 mins, 2½ miles east).

Entertainment and Events

LA Bowling Alley, *The Esplanade; tel: (01983) 617070*. Open all year, evenings 2200–0200. **Ice Skating Rink**, *The Esplanade; tel: (01983) 615155*. Open all year daily 1100–1300; 1400–1700 (public sessions). Admission £2 adults, skate hire 50p. **Waltzing Waters**, *Old Leisure Centre, Brading Rd; tel: (01983) 811333*. Open Mon–Fri, shows every hour on the hour until 1600. Admission £3. Bus 16 or 6 miles south.

The premier event of the Isle of Wight calendar is **Cowes Week** in Aug, Britain's most important yachting regatta.

Sightseeing

Ryde offers all the pleasures of a traditional seaside town, and has miles of sandy beaches with safe bathing as well as attractive parks and gardens. The town owes much of its atmosphere to spectacular growth during Victorian times, when the ½-mile-long pier and many elegant houses were built. The main thoroughfare of *Union Street* sweeping down to the seafront is lined with cafés, gift shops, fashion boutiques and antique shops.

The island itself, 21 miles west–east and 13 miles north to south, is a popular holiday destination, offering pleasant scenery as well as the usual seaside attractions, and the excellent bus services make it one of the easiest parts of Britain to explore without a car. There are plenty of safe, sandy beaches and many marked footpaths across the chalk downlands.

It was Queen Victoria who made the island fashionable by building **Osborne House** here, overlooking the Solent, as a seaside retreat: this elaborate Italianate villa, her favourite home, is richly decorated and gives a remarkably intimate glimpse of the family life of Victoria, Albert and their many children. In the gardens is the charming Swiss Cottage, a chalet where the royal children learnt the arts of cookery and gardening. Inland are the impressive ruins of **Carisbrooke Castle**, best known as Charles I's prison before his execution: the castle dates from Norman times and offers much to see, including fine views from the ramparts and a 16th-century waterwheel worked by donkeys.

The east coast of the island is the most developed. Heading south down the Ryde–Shanklin railway towards the great sweep of Sandown Bay, Brading has a good **Wax Museum**, which occupies a timber-framed house of c.1500. **Shanklin Cline**, a picturesque cleft in the high chalk downs, is a popular walking spot.

To the west of the island is the pretty port of **Yarmouth**, with its castle built by Henry VIII guarding the harbour. The **Freshwater Peninsula** beyond tapers to the dramatic chalk pinnacles known as the **Needles**, with the inevitable pleasure park nearby. Part of the peninsula is known as **Tennyson Down** after the Victorian poet, who walked here daily from his home, Farringford, in Freshwater (now a hotel).

For steam railway buffs there is a direct interchange with the Ryde–Shanklin line at Smallbrook junction for the **Isle of Wight Steam Railway**, which runs 5 miles west to Wootton using restored engines and rolling stock from the original railway.

Bus tours are available, bookable at the TIC, from **Southern Vectis** *tel: (01983) 562264*. Tours start from the bus station and cost from £10 for a full day. Bus 7 is an island explorer with commentary. **Solent & White Line Cruises**, *tel: (01983) 564602* operate boat trips from the end of the pier. Price £8.95 (£4.95 child) for half day. Bookable at the TIC.

Out of Town

Carisbrooke Castle (EH), *Newport; tel: (01983) 522107*. Open 1 Oct–1 April 1000–1600; 1 April–30 Sept 1000–1800. Admission £3.20. Bus to Newport then short walk. Seven miles west. **Osborne House (EH)**, *East Cowes; tel: (01983) 200022*. Open 1 Apr–31 Oct daily

1000–1700. Admission £5.50 adults. Bus 4 to East Cowes. Four miles north-east. **Wax Museum**, High St, Brading, Sandown; tel: (01983) 407286. Open 1 May–30 Sept, Mon–Sun 1000–2200; 1 Oct–31 April, Mon–Sun 1000–1700. Bus 16 or train to Brading, 2–3 miles south. **Isle of Wight Steam Railway**, The Station, Haven Street; tel: (01983) 882204. Phone for train running times. Take train to Smallbrook Junction. **Yarmouth Castle**, Yarmouth; tel: (01983) 760678. Open 1 Apr–30 Sept, daily 1000–1800. Admission £1.70. Bus no. 7 or 7A to Yarmouth, 15 miles west.

SOUTHAMPTON

TIC: Above Bar, Southampton, Hampshire SO9 4XF; tel: (01703) 221106. Open Mon–Wed, Fri–Sat 0900–1700, Thu 1000–1700 and Bank Hols (May–Aug). DP services offered: local bed booking service (10% commission taken and latest booking 15 mins before closing), BABA (10% commission taken and latest booking at 1600). Mayflower Theatre and Muffield Theatre tickets sold. The Southampton Visitors Guide is available free and includes accommodation listings.
Station: Southampton Central Station, Blechynden Ter; tel: (01703) 229393 is ½ mile to the west of the town centre and there is a taxi rank outside.

Getting Around

Most attractions are within walking distance from Southampton town centre. A town map with local transport details is provided inside the back cover of the Visitors Guide available from the TIC. Local public transport by bus is excellent and very frequent in the city centre and good to surrounding towns and villages. Most city services operate until 2200, including Sundays (but on a reduced frequency).

There is no central bus station in Southampton but buses tend to terminate around the city centre (Pound Tree Rd, Castle Way, Bargate Rd, Vincents Walk). **City Buses**, tel: (01703) 553011 provide services mostly in the city centre and the **Solent Blue Line**, tel: (01703) 226235

covers a wider region.

There are taxi ranks outside Marlands Shopping Centre, in the High St and along Bedford Pl. Registered taxi companies include **Radio Taxis,** tel: (01703) 333992, **Streamline Taxis,** tel: (01703) 223355 and **Shirley Cabs**, tel: (01703) 510410.

Staying in Southampton

It is generally easy to find accommodation on arrival in the city, with the exception of the second and third weeks in September during the Southampton Boat Show. There is a wide range of accommodation types, particularly mid-range hotels and guesthouses. National hotel chains represented in Southampton include Nv, Hn, Ib and MH, and there is also a number of large independent hotels.

The majority of cheaper accommodation lies on the outskirts of the centre (Hill Lane/Howard Rd). Local accommodation-finding agencies (excluding the TIC) include **Break South Holidays**, Business Park, Rushington, Totton; tel: (01703) 663966, who can book all types of accommodation in advance and offer weekend breaks and discounted midweek bookings. **Town or Country**, The Old Rectory, School Rd, Bursledon; tel: (01703) 405668 is a self-catering agency and does not charge a booking fee.

Budget/youth accommodation is offered at the **YMCA**, Cranberry Place; tel: (01703) 221202, just ½ mile north of the centre and the **YWCA**, Bellevue Rd; tel: (01703) 227155, also ½ mile north of the city centre.

The TIC can provide information on campsites but there is also a **Forestry Commission** (New Forest) camping enquiry tel no., (01703) 283771. The nearest campsite is a Forestry Commission Site, Lyndhurst Rd, Ashurst; tel: (01703) 283771, which is 6 miles west of Southampton. Take the train to Lyndhurst Road Station or the Solent Blue Line Bus nos. 56 or 56A which passes the site entrance. There is also **Riverside Park**, Satchel Ln, Hamble; tel: (01703) 453220. Take the City Bus nos. 16,17A or Solent Blue Line Bus 29A to Hamble Square and then walk the last ½ mile to the site. 6 miles east of Southampton.

Sightseeing

The historic port of Southampton has a rich heritage and is the cultural centre for the region. Learn about the city's history and monuments by taking the **Walls Walk** – a walkway round the remains of the well-preserved medieval town walls. Southampton has several excellent museums: the **Tudor House Museum** is a beautiful timber-framed building displaying the domestic and social life of Victorian and Edwardian England; and the **Maritime Museum** portrays the heyday of the port of Southampton, when it was home to famous transatlantic liners such as the *Queen Mary* and *Queen Elizabeth*; it also features a *Titanic* exhibition. Explore Southampton's lively waterfront at **Ocean Village** and **Town Quay**, with shops, entertainment and dozens of sailing boats.

North-west of Southampton is **Paulton's Park** – a leisure park with gardens, lake, exotic birds and over 40 attractions. To the east are the picturesque remains of **Netley Abbey**, a Cistercian Abbey founded in 1239. west of Southampton is the historic house of **Beaulieu Abbey**, home of the **National Motor Museum**.

There are various sightseeing tours which give an excellent introduction to Southampton. **Guide Friday** offer bus tours which can be booked at the TIC. Boat trips can be taken from *Ocean Village* with the company **Blue Funnel**, *tel: (01703) 223278*. Prices depend on the length and destination of the cruise. Visitors can join the free guided walks which start at *The Bargate*. Alternatively, guides can be hired from the **Southampton Tourist Guides Association**; *tel: (01703) 868401* and cost around £15.00 per guide with a maximum of 30 people per guide.

The ferry which operates from the city to Hythe every half-hour is another good way to see the Southampton area. Southampton is also famous for its free balloon festival which takes place every first weekend in June.

Tudor House Museum, *St Michael's Sq, Bugle St; tel: (01703) 332513*. Open Tue–Fri 1000–1200, 1400–1700, Sat 1000–1200, 1400–1600, Sun 1400–1700. Admission:

£1.50. **Maritime Museum**, *The Wool House, Bugle St; tel: (01703) 223941*. Open Tue–Fri 1000–1700, Sat 1000–1600, Sun 1400–1700 (Apr–Sep). Admission: £1.50. **Medieval Merchants House** (EH), *58 French St; tel: (01703) 221503*. Open 1000–1800 (Apr–end Sep). Admission: £1.80.

Out of Town

Paulton's Park, *Ower, nr Romsey; tel: (01703) 814442*. Open daily 1000–1830 (15 Mar–31 Oct) with earlier closing in spring and autumn. Admission: £6.50. Take the Wiltshire and Dorset Bus no. 7 which runs every hour. 6 miles north west of Southampton. **New Forest Butterfly Farm**, *Longdown, Ashurst; tel: (01703) 292166*. Open daily 1000–1700 (Mar–end Oct). Admission: £3.50. Take the Solent Blue Line Bus 56/56A to Deerleap Lane and walk the last mile. 5 miles west of Southampton. **Longdown Dairy Farm**, *Deerleap Ln, Longdown, Ashurst; tel: (01703) 293326*. Open daily 1100–1700 (8 Apr–29 Oct). Admission: £3.50. Take the Solent Blue Line Bus 56/56A to Deerleap Lane and walk the last mile. 5 miles west of Southampton.

National Motor Museum, *Beaulieu, Brockenhurst; tel: (01590) 612345*. Open daily 1000–1800 (14 Apr–30 Sep), 1000–1700 (1 Oct–13 Apr). Admission: £7.50. Either take the ferry or bus (nos.8, 9, 38, or 39) to Hythe then change to bus no.112 to Beaulieu. 7 miles south west of Southampton. **Netley Abbey** (EH), *1 Abbey Hill, Netley; tel: (01703) 453076*. Open daily 1000–1800 (1 Apr–31 Oct), Sat–Sun 1000–1600 (1 Nov–31 Mar). Admission free. Take the City Bus no.16 which runs every half-hour. 3 miles east of Southampton.)

– – – – – – – – – – – – – – – – – – – –

 Side Track from Southampton

THE NEW FOREST

TIC: *High St, Lyndhurst, Hampshire, SO43 7NY; tel: (01703) 282269*. Open daily 1000–1800 (Apr–Sep), 1000–1700 (Oct–Mar). DP services offered: local bed-booking service, BABA. *Where to Stay 1995* is available free.

Station: Lyndhurst Road Station is situated 4 miles north-east of Lyndhurst. Although no taxi rank exists, it is possible to travel into Lyndhurst town on the Southampton–Lyndhurst bus, no. 56, which stops on the main road just a short walk away. Beaulieu Road Station is 4 miles north-west of Beaulieu but has no taxi rank and no bus services at all; to reach Beaulieu, take bus no. 123 from Lyndhurst.

For rail enquiries contact **Southampton Station**, tel: (01703) 229393.

Getting Around

Free town maps of Lyndhurst, the forest's 'capital', and details on transport around the New Forest are available from the TIC. It is possible to catch the **Wightlink Ferry** tel: (01705) 827744 from Lymington for the day to the **Isle of Wight** (see under Ryde for more details of the Isle Wight).

The main bus company is **Wiltshire and Dorset**, tel: (01590) 672382, which operates from **Lymington Bus Station**, High St, Lymington. Services are run hourly or half hourly (depending on the destination).

The main taxi rank is located at the main car park in Lyndhurst. Registered taxi companies include: **AA Taxis** tel: (01703) 864310, **Ask Taxis** tel: (01703) 283686, **Lymington Taxis** tel: (01590) 672842 and **Fritham Taxis** tel: (01703) 814441.

Staying in the New Forest

A good range of accommodation is available, particularly b. & b. establishments. It is generally easy to book on arrival, except at Bank Holidays.

The TIC has information on **youth hostels** and **campsites**. The nearest youth hostel is **Burley Youth Hostel**, Cottimore House, Cott Ln, Burley, Ringwood; tel: (01425) 403233. Open from 1700. The nearest campsite is **Ashurst Campsite** (Forestry Commission), The Queens House, High St, Lyndhurst; tel: (01703) 283771.

Sightseeing

English monarchs from William the Conqueror onwards have protected and enlarged this area, originally for the pleasures of hunting. Customs and institutions peculiar to the New Forest dating from the Middle Ages survive to this day. 'Forest' originally did not imply continuous woodland, and in fact the area contains woods linked by moorland and villages. It is well known for its unique woodland scenery, coastal views, ponies and wildlife. A circular bus tour around Lyndhurst can be booked with **Home James** tel: (01703) 282269, costing £4.50. **Hurst Castle Ferry and Cruises** tel: (01425) 610784 operate boat trips from Keyhaven to Hurst Castle, which cost £2.20, and **Encounter Walks** guided walks costing £6.50 can be booked at the TIC. Lyndhurst TIC also has details on public transport routes which are particularly good for sightseeing. Bus routes 56 and 112 take in many of the sights listed below.

New Forest Museum and Visitor Centre, Main Car Park, High St, Lyndhurst; tel: (01703) 283914. Open daily 1000–1800 (Apr–Sep), 1000–1700 (Oct–Mar). Admission: £2.50. **St Michaels All Angels Church**, High St, Lyndhurst; tel: (01703) 282154. Opening times depend on service times. **Kristen Pottery and Craft Shop**, High St, Beaulieu; tel: (01590) 612064. Open daily 1030–1730 (high season), Tue–Sun 1030–1730 (mid season), Sat–Sun only in winter – phone for confirmation. Free admission.

Out of Town

The National Motor Museum and **Beaulieu Abbey** are accessible from Lyndhurst by bus 56 or 112 or 123. 7 miles south-east. For full details of the museum, see under Southampton. **Paulton's Park**, can be reached by bus no. X34 or 180 (summer only). 6 miles north (more details under Southampton) **Exbury Gardens**, Exbury Village; tel: (01703) 899422. Open daily (Feb–Oct). Admission: £4.50 (in season), £2.00 (out of season). 7 miles south. **Longdown Dairy Farm**, Deerleap Lane, Longdown, Ashurst; tel: (01703) 293313. Open daily 1100–1700 (Mar–Oct). Admission: £3.50. Take bus 56 or 56a. 4 miles east. **Eling Tide Mill**, Eling Toll Bridge, Totton; tel: (01703) 869575. Open Wed–Sun 1000–1600. Admission: £1.15. Take bus no. 31 to Totton. 6 miles east.

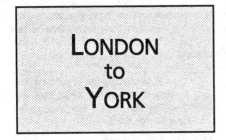

LONDON to YORK

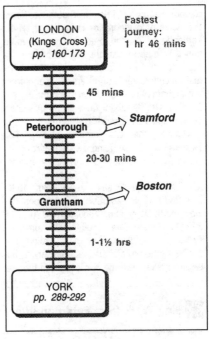

One of the country's principal rail arteries, this route links the capital to what was for centuries Britain's second city. A side track from the cathedral city of Peterborough brings you to Stamford and one of England's most magnificent historic houses, Burghley House.

TRAINS

ETT table: 570

 Fast Track

This route currently offers the fastest and most modern rail services in Britain. Two 'IC225' trains run each hour taking between 1 hr 46 mins and 2 hrs (2 hrs 20–2hrs 46 mins on Sun). 'Pullman' service (see p. 29) is offered to passengers travelling first class on three morning Mon–Fri trains to London and three evening return services.

On Track

London–Peterborough

Two or three express trains on weekdays, (2 on Suns) run each hour between London King's Cross and Peterborough taking around 45 mins (50 mins–1 hr 10 mins on Sun) for the journey.

Peterborough–Grantham

Services are shared between Regional Railways and InterCity: the former are more frequent and take 30 mins; the latter are roughly two-hourly but are faster at 20 mins. On Sun a reduced service is provided by both operators.

Grantham–York

Only three through trains run on weekdays (one

on Sun) from Grantham to York, taking just over 1 hour. The number of journeys can be increased however, by changing trains at Doncaster. Journey time approximately 1 hr 30 mins.

PETERBOROUGH

TIC: Peterborough Town Hall, *Bridge St, Peterborough PE1 1HA; (01733) 317336.* Open Mon–Fri 0900–1700; Bank Holiday Mons and Sat 1000–1600. Services offered: BABA, local bed-booking service, advance reservations handled, guided tours booked. *Where to Stay in Peterborough*, including an accommodation list, and *In and around Peterborough* are available free.

Station: Peterborough Station, *Station Rd; tel: (01733) 68181* is central and has a taxi rank.

Sightseeing

If you have time to spare while waiting for a train to Stamford, pay a visit to **Peterborough Cathedral** (about 10 mins walk from the station). Begun in 1118, the church was given the status of cathedral by Henry VIII in 1541. Katherine of Aragon, Henry's first Queen, is buried here and it was the original burial place of Mary Queen of Scots. Amongst the cathedral's architectural features are the magnificent West Front with its huge arches, and the Eastern Building with its superb fan vaulting. A Visitors Centre explains the building's history.

Outside the city centre is **Flag Fen Excavations**, an on-going archaeological excavation with a recreation of a Bronze Age farm. **Peterborough Cathedral** *Cathedral Sq; tel: (01733) 345064.* Open Mon–Sat 0800–1930, Sun 0800–1800. Admission: free (donations welcomed). **Flag Fen**, *Fengate, tel: (01733) 313414.* Open daily 1100–1700, admission £1.95 (winter) £2.80 (summer). Although it can be reached by an infrequent bus service, it is easier to take a taxi the 3 miles east to the site.

_ _ _ _ _ _ _ _ _ _ _ _ _ _ _ _ _ _

 Side Track from Peterborough

STAMFORD

TIC: Stamford Arts Centre, *37 St Mary's St, Stamford, Lincolnshire PE9 2DL; tel: (01780) 55611.* Open Mon–Sat 0930–1700; Bank Holiday Mons and Sun 1000–1500 (Apr–Sept). DP Services offered: local bed-booking service and BABA (latest 15 mins before closing), advance reservations handled, guided tours booked. *Going Places* including an accommodation list is available free.

Station: Stamford Station, *Station Rd; tel: (01733) 68181* is central. Taxis are usually available. A more or less hourly train service runs between Peterborough and Stamford, taking 12 mins. On Suns there are no trains before midday.

Getting Around

With the exception of **Burghley House**, the town's attractions are within easy walking distance of the centre. Free town and transport maps are available from the TIC. For general transport enquiries *tel: (01780) 66131*.

Services are good to Peterborough, but poor elsewhere, with no evening services and few on Suns. The main bus companies are **Delaine** *tel: (01778) 423866*, **Kimes** *tel: (01529) 7251* and **Viscount** *tel: (01733) 54571*, and most services operate from *Sheepmarket.*

Taxis often wait at the station and on *Red Lion Sq,* or you can contact **Direct Line** *tel: (01780) 481481*, **Merritt** *tel: (01781) 66155* or **Star Taxis** *tel: (01780) 62345.*

Staying in Stamford

There is a very small range of hotels, including one in the *GH* chain, and a good number of guesthouses, pubs with rooms and b. & b. establishments. Cheaper accommodation can be found both in the centre and the suburbs. It is generally easy to book on arrival except during the **Burghley Horse Trials** (end Aug–mid-Sept).

For budget accommodation the closest is **Thurlby Youth Hostel**, *16 High St, Thurlby, Bourne; tel: (01778) 425588*, open Fri–Wed (Apr–Oct). Take Delaine bus service to *Thurlby,* 11 miles north-east. The closest campsite is **Road End Farm**, *Great Casterton; tel: (01780) 63417*, 1 mile north (easiest to walk).

Sightseeing

Stamford is generally regarded as the finest stone-built town in England, its wealth of medieval and Georgian buildings forming an extraordinarily unspoilt whole. Highlights include five medieval churches, such as Perpendicular **St Martin's** (*High St, St Martin's*), and **Brownes Hospital**, one of the finest surviving medieval almshouses in England; but there are delights around every corner.

You do not have to leave Stamford to visit a magnificent country house: **Burghley House** (approx. 30 mins walk) is the vast palace built by Elizabeth I's chief minister, William Cecil, Lord Burghley. Famous international horse trials are held here each year (early Sept).

Blue Badge Guides offer guided walks of the town, starting from the TIC on Sat and Sun in summer (price: £1.50).

Brewery Museum, *All Saints St; tel: (01780) 52186*. Open Wed–Fri 1000–1600, Sat, Sun 1000–1800 (Mar to mid-Oct). Last admission 30 mins before closing. Admission: £1.20.

Brownes Hospital (historic building), *Broad St; tel: (01780) 51226.* Open Sat, Sun 1100–1700 (May–Sept). **Burghley House,** *Stamford; tel: (01780) 52451.* Open daily 1100–1700 (Apr–Sept). Admission: £5.10. One mile south-east. (Easiest to walk or take a taxi.) **Stamford Museum,** *Broad St; tel: (01780) 66317.* Open Mon–Sat 1000–1700, Sun (summer only) 1400–1700. Admission: £0.40.

Out of Town

Belton House (see Lincoln p. 261). **Belvoir Castle** (see Nottingham p. 257). **Grantham House** (see Lincoln p. 261).

- - - - - - - - - - - - - - - - - - - -

Side Tracks from Grantham

BOSTON

TIC: Blackfriars Arts Centre, *Spain La, Boston, Lincolnshire PE21 6HP; tel: (01205) 356656.* Open Mon–Sat 0900–1700. Services offered: local bed-booking service and BABA (latest 1630). The main guide, *Boston: The Original* and an accommodation listing are available free. **Station**: Boston Station, *Station Approach, Boston; tel: (01305) 363281* is in easy walking distance, just west of the town centre, and has a taxi rank. Around a dozen trains on weekdays, (four on Suns) each day link Grantham and Boston with journey times of just under 1 hr.

Getting Around

The majority of attractions are within walking distance of the centre, and a free town map is available from the TIC. For general transport enquiries, contact the **Transport Hotline** *tel: (01205) 310010.*

Bus services are good within the town but patchy to outlying areas, and services are reduced after 1800.

The main taxi rank is on *Market Pl.* Taxis can be hailed in the street, and details of registered companies can be obtained from the TIC.

Staying in Boston

There is a very small range of accommodation (hotel, b. & b. and guesthouse) in town, and there are a number of b & b establishments and four pubs with rooms in the surrounding area. However, it is generally easy to book on arrival, except during school summer holidays.

Orchard Park Caravan Park, *Hubbert's Bridge; tel: (01205) 290328*, is 3½ miles north-west of Boston (take a train to Hubbert's Bridge, then a half-mile walk). The TIC has details of additional camping and caravan sites further from Boston.

Sightseeing

This still busy inland port is less well known than the town in Massachusetts named after it by the Puritans, who departed here in 1630. An earlier attempt to escape led to the Pilgrim Fathers' imprisonment in the 15th-century **Guildhall**, now a museum of Boston's history and maritime heritage.

Boston has some pleasant buildings, the most famous of which is **St Botolph's Church**: its 272 ft tower, the 'Boston Stump', is the region's best known landmark, and the church itself is magnificent in both size and detail. On the edge of town, five-sailed **Maud Foster Windmill** is the tallest working mill in England.

For details of river cruises down *The Haven* and out into *The Wash*, contact the TIC. There is a lively market in the town centre on Wed and Sat (on Wed there is also an open-air auction).

Blackfriars Arts Centre, *Spain La; tel: (01205) 363108.* Open Mon–Sat 1000–1800. Admission: free. **Guildhall Museum**, *South St; tel: (01205) 365954.* Open Mon–Sat 1000–1700; Sun (Apr–Sept only) 1330–1700. Admission: £0.90. **Maud Foster Windmill**, *Willoughby Rd; tel: (01205) 352188.* Open Wed 1000–1700, Sun and Bank Holidays 1400–1700. Admission: £1.20. **Pilgrim Fathers Memorial** (monument), *Fishtoft* (4½ miles south-east of Boston). Admission: free. Not accessible by public transport. **St Botolph's Church**, *Market Pl; tel: (01205) 362864.* Open daily 0900–1630 and for services on Sun. Admission: free (£2 to climb the Tower).

Out of Town

Belton House, Grantham House and **Tattershall castle** (see Lincoln p. 261).

MANCHESTER

Manchester is a new city by British standards, having developed as one of the centres of the Industrial Revolution. Much spruced up in recent years to counteract its once dour image, it boasts first-class museums and lively nightlife; and some superb countryside, historic houses and parks lie surprisingly close by. It is also the centre of a network of rail connections and a convenient touring base for the north-west.

Tourist Information

TIC: *Manchester Visitor Centre, Town Hall Extension, Lloyd St, Manchester M60 2LA; tel: (0161) 234 3157/8.* Open Mon–Sat 1000–1730, Sun and Bank Holiday Mons 1100–1600. DP SHS Services offered: local bed-booking service (latest 30 mins before closing), BABA (10% commission plus £1.50 booking fee, latest bookings 1 hr before closing), bureau de change. *Manchester Visitor Guide* (£0.80); free accommodation guide. The TIC is busy for bookings Thur–Sat, 1600–1730. **TIC**: *International Arrivals Hall, Terminal 1, Manchester Airport; tel: (0161) 436 3344.* Open 0800–2100. DP Services offered: local bed-booking service, advance reservations handled. National Express and Flightlink tickets sold. **TIC**: *International Arrivals Hall, Terminal 2, Manchester Airport; tel: (0161) 489 6412.* Open 0930–1230. DP Services offered: as for Terminal 1.

Arriving and Departing

Airport

Manchester Airport, 10 miles south of centre; *tel: (01839) 888747 (international arrivals), (01839) 888757 (domestic).* **Rail connections** into *Piccadilly Station* in the centre run every 10–15 mins (every 20 mins on Sun), journey time 20 mins, fare: £2.10. There are direct rail links from the airport to Liverpool, the north-east and to north-west resorts. **Bus connections** into the centre run every 30 mins (daytime), every hour (evenings and Suns); journey time 50 mins. **Finglands** bus 747 goes to *Stevenson Sq*, fare: £1.50. **GM Buses** 44 and 105 go to *Piccadilly Bus Station*, fare: £1.80. **Taxi rank** *tel: (0161) 499 9000.*

Stations

There are two stations, linked by shuttlebus and the Metrolink: **Piccadilly Station**, off *London Rd; tel: (0161) 832 8353*, is the mainline station and is central; it has a taxi rank and **Hertz** car hire office *tel: (0161) 236 2747*. **Victoria Station**, *Victoria Station Approach*, off *Corporation St; tel: (0161) 832 8353* is for suburban trains. It is on the north side of the centre and has a taxi rank. Use the new Metrolink tram system to travel between the main stations.

Buses

From **Chorlton Street Coach Station** in the centre, National Express coaches serve a large number of destinations, *tel: (0161) 228 3881.*

Getting Around

For general transport enquiries *tel: (0161) 228 7811*. The city centre and surrounding suburbs are well served by Metrolink, and there are also reasonable bus and train services both within the city and to outlying towns. The TIC can provide free town and transport maps. Most in-town attractions are within walking distance of the centre.

Tickets

There is a weekly **County Card**, covering buses and trains only, fare £19. **Rail Ranger** tickets offer a day's unlimited train travel in the Greater Manchester area after 0930, cost £2.

Trams

Metrolink is an excellent tram system running every 10 mins from Altrincham in the south to Bury in the north, with eight stations in the city centre. *Tel: (0161) 205 2000.*

Buses

The main bus depot is **Piccadilly Bus Station**,

Piccadilly; tel: (0161) 228 7811. There are a great number of bus companies operating, two of the main ones are **GM Buses South** tel: (0161) 273 3300 and **GM Buses North** tel: (0161) 627 2828.

Taxis

Main taxi ranks are at *Albert Sq* and *Whitworth St West*. Black taxis can be hailed in the street. There are 54 private minicab companies, and three black cab companies: **Airtax** tel: (0161) 489 2313; **Mantax** tel: (0161) 236 5133; **Taxifone** tel: (0161) 236 9182.

Staying in Manchester

Accommodation

The Manchester district has over 18,000 bed spaces across all accommodation categories so it is never a problem finding somewhere to stay on arrival. There is a good choice of larger hotels in the city centre and cheaper b. & b., guesthouse, pub and self-catering accommodation can be found in the suburbs, particularly to the south (Chorlton, Didsbury and Fallowfield).

Hotel chains include *FC, FP, HO, Hn, MC, MH, Ra*. Opening early in 1995 is **Manchester Youth Hostel**, *Potato Wharf, Castlefield; tel: (01727) 855215*. The closest campsites are **Hollybank Caravan Park**, *Rixton, Warrington, Cheshire; tel: (0161) 775 2842*, take bus 10 to *Warburton Bridge* (12 miles west); **Elm Beds Caravan Park**, *Elm Beds Rd, Poynton, Stockport, Cheshire; tel: (01625) 872370*, take bus 191 to *Poynton* (13 miles south) from Cross St; **Capesthorne Hall**, *Siddington, near Macclesfield, Cheshire; tel: (01625) 861779*, bus 130 to *Macclesfield* (15 miles south).

Eating and Drinking

The choice of restaurants is overwhelming. There are over 20 nationalities represented in the centre, and 14 restaurants have a listing in the *Good Food Guide*. There are cheap places to eat all over town. Manchester has the largest Chinese population in Britain outside London, and subsequently its own **Chinatown** in the centre, with an excellent selection of oriental cuisine. **Rusholme** (*Wilmslow Rd*) is the Indian

equivalent, with an enormous choice of Asian restaurants. For vegetarian, try **On the Eighth Day**, *109 Oxford Rd* or **Govindas**, *244 Deansgate*. There is now also a **Harry Ramsden's** in Manchester (*1 Water St, tel: (0161) 832 9144*), famous for fish and chips. The TIC has a free *Food and Drink Guide*. Manchester's local specialities are Boddington's Beer, Vimto (fizzy blackcurrant drink) and Eccles Cakes (round pastry cake filled with currants).

Communications

The main post office is at *26 Spring Gardens*. Open Mon–Fri 0830–1800, Sat 0830–1300. Post restante facilities are available for travellers.

Entertainment

The main entertainment magazine for Manchester is *City Life*, £1.20 from newsagents or TICs. The city has an enormous choice of things to do, from music and theatre to nightclubs and sporting clubs. The following list is just a sample.

Theatre, Opera and Ballet

Contact Theatre, *Oxford Rd; tel: (0161) 274 4400* (theatre). **Green Room**, *Whitworth St West; tel: (0161) 236 1677* (fringe theatre, cabaret). **Palace Theatre**, *Oxford Rd; tel: (0161) 242 2503* (theatre, ballet, opera). **Royal Exchange**, *St Ann's Sq; tel: (0161) 833 9833* (theatre). **Royal Northern College of Music**, *124 Oxford Rd; tel: (0161) 273 4504* (opera, ballet, jazz). **Opera House**, *Quay St; tel: (0161) 242 2509* (theatre, musicals, opera, dance).

Music

Apollo Theatre, *Ardwick St; tel: (0161) 236 9922* (concerts). **BBC Philharmonic**, *New Broadcasting House, Oxford Rd; tel: (0161) 200 2001* (classical). **G-Mex**, *Windmill St, Mosley St; tel: (0161) 834 2700* (international exhibitions and events centre, also major pop concerts). **The Hallé**, *Free Trade Hall, Peter St; tel: (0161) 834 1712* (classical). For clubs (music, sport and social) consult the TIC *Visitor Guide* (see p. 226).

Sport

Manchester City Football Club, *Main Rd; tel: (0161) 226 1191*. **Manchester United Football**

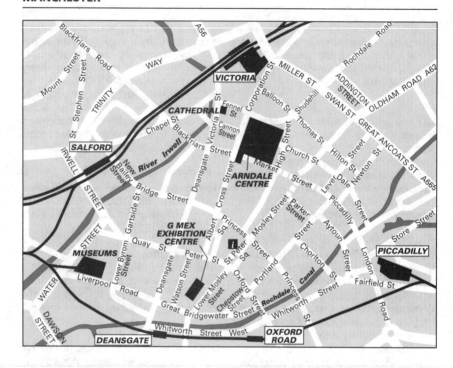

Club, *Old Trafford;* tel: *(0161) 872 0199.* Metrolink to *Old Trafford.* **Lancashire County Cricket Club**, *Old Trafford;* tel: *(0161) 848 7021.* Metrolink to *Old Trafford.*

Events

Look out for the following: **Lord Mayor's Parade**, *City Centre*, in June (free); **Manchester to Blackpool Cycle Ride**, starts *Albert Square,* July (spectators free); **Boddington's Manchester Festival of Television and the Arts**, *various venues*, for three weeks in Sept (admission varies); **Castlefield Carnival**, a three-week outdoor carnival in *Castlefield* in Sept (free). The TIC issues a free events list.

Shopping

The **Arndale Centre** is the city's largest covered shopping centre. Main shopping streets are *Cross St* and *Market St*, into *Piccadilly* and the pedestrianised area of *St Ann's Sq* and *King St.* There is also the Mon–Sat **Arndale Market** at the *Arndale Centre*, and **Castlefield Street Market**, *Castlefield* on Sun and Mon, every Bank Holiday weekend. For crafts, there is **Manchester Craft Centre**, *17 Oak St*, Mon–Sat 1000–1730.

Sightseeing

To get a flavour of Manchester's 19th-century grandeur, take a bus tour: buildings worth noting are the Victorian Gothic **Town Hall** (*Albert Sq*) and **Royal Exchange Theatre**. One-hour guided bus tours of Manchester run daily at 1000, 1100, 1200, 1400, 1500 from May–Sept, departing from *Central Library, Peter St;* tel: *(01565) 650102.* Price: £4.50. Alternatively, boat trips on the canal system provide a good insight into how Manchester's wealth was created: contact **Bridgewater Packetboat Service** tel: *(0161) 748 2680;* **Egerton Narrowboats** tel: *(0161) 833 9878;* **Irwell and Mersey Packet Boat Company** tel: *(0161) 736 2108.* A variety of guided walks are also available with **Blue Badge Guides**, from £2; contact the TIC for details. An attraction unique to Manchester is the **Granada Studios Tour**, where you can enter the world of film and television through the sets of popular programmes. The excellent **Museum of Science and Industry** offers everything from steam engines to a 'hands-on' visitor centre, on the site of the world's oldest passenger station. Both these attractions are within the **Castlefield** area, recently developed as an Urban Heritage Park around Manchester's canal basin; this is a good area to walk round, with its own **Visitor Centre** (*Liverpool Rd*). There is a celebrated collection of Pre-Raphaelite paintings at the **City Art Galleries**, while for soccer enthusiasts the **Manchester United Museum and Tour Centre** is a must.

Further afield, **Tatton Park** and **Lyme Park** are huge country estates, while **Quarry Bank Mill** offers working industrial history in a sylvan setting; all days out in themselves. At **Jodrell Bank**, as well as the famous radio telescope, are a planetarium, science exhibition and arboretum. **Last Drop Village** is a 'living' village recreated from 18th-century farm buildings, with a craft centre and village-style shops.

Cathedrals

Manchester Cathedral, *Deansgate; tel: (0161) 833 2220*. Open daily 0745–1730 (sometimes – 1600 on Sun). Admission: free.

Historic Houses

Wythenshawe Hall, *Wythenshawe Park, Northenden; tel: (0161) 236 5244*. Open in summer, telephone for details. Admission: free.

Museums and Galleries

Charter Street Ragged School, *142 Dantzic St; tel: (0161) 832 5016*. Open Mon–Fri 1000–1600. Admission: £1. **City Art Galleries**, *Mosley St; tel: (0161) 236 5244*. Open Mon–Sat 1000–1745, Sun 1400–1745. Admission: free. **Granada Studios Tour**, *Water St; tel: (0161) 832 9090* or *833 0880*. Opening times vary, telephone for details. Admission: £9.99. Admission: £1.75, take bus 135. **Manchester Museum**, *University of Manchester, Oxford Rd; tel: (0161) 275 2634*. Open Mon–Sat 1000–1700. Admission: free.

Manchester United Museum and Tour Centre, *Old Trafford; tel: (0161) 877 4002*. Open Tues–Sun 0930–1600 and most Bank Holiday Mons. Admission: £2.95, (£4.95 with tour). Metrolink to *Old Trafford*. **Metropolitan Gallery**, *Grosvenor Building, Cavendish St; tel: (0161) 247 1708*. Open Mon–Fri 1000–1800 during term time. Admission: free. **Museum of Science and Industry**, *Liverpool Rd; tel: (0161) 832 1830/2244*. Open daily 1000–1700. Admission: £3.50. **Museum of Transport** (2 miles north), *Boyle St, Cheetham; tel: (0161) 205 2122*. Open Wed, Sat, Sun and Bank Holidays 1000–1700. Admission: £1.75; bus 135. **Royal Northern College of Music**, *124 Oxford Rd; tel: (0161) 273 6283*. Open Mon–Sat 1000–2200, Sun 1000–1700. Admission: free. **Whitworth Art Gallery**, *University of Manchester, Oxford Rd; tel: (0161) 273 4865*. Open Mon–Sat 1000–1700 (–2100 Thur). Admission: free.

Out of Town

Dunham Massey Hall (National Trust), *near Altrincham, Cheshire; tel: (0161) 941 1025*. Open Sat–Wed 1200–1700, garden 1100–1730. Admission: £4.50. Metrolink to *Altrincham*, then bus 38 or taxi. Three miles from Altrincham. **Jodrell Bank Science Centre and Arboretum**, *Lower Withington, near Macclesfield, Cheshire; tel: (01477) 571339*. Open daily 1030–1730 (summer), Sat, Sun 1100–1630 (winter). Admission: £3.50. Take the hourly Crewe train from Piccadilly to Goostrey (about 25 mins), then 2-mile walk.

Last Drop Village (15 miles north), *Bromley Cross, Bolton, Lancashire; tel: (0204) 591131*. Opening times vary according to attraction. Admission: free. Train (half-hourly service departs from both Piccadilly and Victoria) to Bolton, and then taxi 4 miles. **Lyme Park** (National Trust), *Disley, Stockport, Cheshire; tel: (01663) 762023*. Park open daily 0800–2030; gardens open 1100–1700; house open Sat–Wed 1330–1700, last admission 1630 (Apr–Oct). Admission: £2.50 (house and garden). Take train to *Disley* (hourly service departing from Piccadilly), then 2-mile walk or bus 361. **Quarry Bank Mill** (National Trust), *Styal, Cheshire; tel: (01625) 527468*. Open

1100–1800. Admission: £4.50. Train to *Styal* (one service daily from Piccadilly in the early morning) station, then 20-min walk (12 miles). **Tatton Park**, *Knutsford, Cheshire; tel: (01565) 750260.* Mansion open 1200–1600 (Apr–Oct), park 1030–1800 (1700 in winter). Admission: £2.50 for mansion. Train to *Knutsford* (half-hourly from Piccadilly), then 2½-mile walk.

- -

 Side Track from Manchester

SOUTHPORT

TIC: *112 Lord Street, Southport, Merseyside PR8 1NY; tel: (01704) 533333.* Open Mon–Fri 0930–1730, Sat, Sun and Bank Holidays 1000–1600. DP SHS Services offered: local bed-booking service and BABA (latest 30 mins before closing), advance reservations handled, guided tours booked. Tickets sold for theatre, attractions and travel. The main guide costs £0.50 and includes an accommodation listing. **Station**: Southport Station, *Chapel St; tel: (0151) 709 9696* is in the town centre and has a taxi rank. There are hourly train services from Manchester Piccadilly to Southport.

Getting Around

Most attractions are walkable from the centre. The TIC has free town and transport maps. Local bus services are run by **Merseybus** (*tel: (01704) 536137*) and are generally good, although reduced after 2000 and on Suns.

Taxis can be hailed in the street, or call: **Yellow Tops** *tel: (01704) 531000*; **All White** *tel: (01704) 537777*

Staying in Southport

Accommodation

There is a wide choice of accommodation, particularly smaller hotels, b.&b. and guest-houses, and the cheaper places are in the town centre. It is generally easy to book on arrival, except during the **Southport Flower Show** – the UK's premier flower show, held in Victoria Park – in Aug. Hotel chains in Southport include *BW, FP.* The closest campsite is **Brooklyn**

Country Club (3 miles north), *Gravel Lane, Banks; tel: (01704) 28534* take bus X8 or X27.

Sightseeing

This gracious Victorian resort has extensive sands and dunes, an artificial boating lake, well-laid-out parks, and the second longest pier in Britain. *Lord St*, a conservation area, is a fine thoroughfare with canopied shops. Within the town, **Southport Railway Centre** has a large collection of working locomotives, buses and trams. Much of the surrounding area was once marshland, and **Martin Mere** is a large wetland bird sanctuary, offering good hides and an attractive visitor centre. **Rufford Old Hall** is one of the finest 16th-century buildings in Lancashire.

Open-top bus tours operate regularly May–Aug, and can be booked through the TIC. **Beach Aviation** *tel: (01704) 547811* offer pleasure flights from *Southport Sands* (from £9.50). **Southport Pleasureland**, *Southport Sands; tel: (01704) 532717.* Open daily 1100–2000 (June to early Sept). Funhouse indoor play area open weekends in winter, 1200–1700. Admission: separate charges for each ride.

Southport Railway Centre, *Derby Rd; tel: (01704) 530693.* Open Sat, Sun 1100–1700 (June–Sept), Mon–Fri 1300–1700 (June and first week Sept), Mon–Fri 1030–1630 (July and Aug); Sat, Sun 1300–1700 (Oct–May). Admission: £1.50 (£2 on steam days). **Southport Zoo**, *Prince's Park; tel: (01704) 538102.* Open daily 1000–1800 (closing times vary according to season – check). Admission: £2.50.

Out of Town

Rufford Old Hall (National Trust), *Rufford, nr Ormskirk; tel: (01704) 821254.* House open daily Sat–Wed 1300–1700, garden Sat–Wed 1200–1730 and Sun 1300–1730 (Apr–Oct). Admission: £3 (£1.60 garden only). Bus 347/357. Ten miles east. **Wildfowl and Wetlands Centre**, *Martin Mere, Burscough, Ormskirk, Lancashire; tel: (01704) 895181.* Open daily 0930–1730 (1600 in winter). Admission: £3.95. Take bus run by ABC Travel *tel: (01704) 576033* (summer only). Ten miles south-east.

- -

MANCHESTER to CARLISLE

This route between the heart of North-West England and the Scottish borders provides a jumping-off point for the romantic beauty of the Lake District, as well as for the earthier pleasures of Blackpool, the North-West's most enduringly popular seaside resort. Continuing northwards, you enter the border country, once so hotly disputed between England and Scotland, now so tranquil – though the fortress at Carlisle (p. 114) bears witness to its turbulent past.

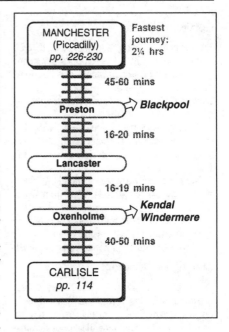

MANCHESTER (Piccadilly) pp. 226-230	Fastest journey: 2¼ hrs

45-60 mins

Preston → *Blackpool*

16-20 mins

Lancaster

16-19 mins

Oxenholme → *Kendal Windermere*

40-50 mins

CARLISLE pp. 114

TRAINS

ETT tables: 550

 Fast Track

Five trains run between Manchester Piccadilly and Carlisle (three on Sun), taking 2¼ hrs. Additional services are available by changing at Preston.

On Track

Manchester–Preston

Two to three trains per hour run from Manchester Piccadilly to Preston, the journey taking 45–60 mins.

Preston–Lancaster

Frequent but irregularly timed trains link Preston to Lancaster taking 16–20 mins.

Lancaster–Oxenholme

One or more trains per hour (less on Sun) run between Lancaster and Oxenholme Lake District, taking 16–19 mins.

Oxenholme–Carlisle

One or two trains run hourly (very few on Suns), taking 40–50 mins.

- - - - - - - - - - - - - - - - - - - -

 Side Track from Preston

BLACKPOOL

TIC: *1 Clifton St, Blackpool, Lancashire FY1 1LY; tel: (01253) 21623/25212.* Open Mon–Sat 0900–1700, Sun 1000–1545 (Mar–Nov); Mon–Thur 0845–1645, Fri 0845–1615, Sat 0900–1700 (Nov–Mar). DP SHS Services offered: local bed-booking service (no fee taken), busiest times for booking are from 1200–1400. *Blackpool Festival* brochure including accommodation listing is free.

Station: Blackpool North Station, *Talbot Rd; tel: (01772) 259439* is in the town centre and has a taxi rank.

Bus Station: National Express operate from *Lonsdale Rd* (summer), *Talbot Rd* (winter).

Getting Around

For general transport enquiries *tel: (01253) 23931*. The majority of Blackpool's attractions are within easy walking distance or a couple of miles from the centre, and the town is well served by local trams and buses. A free transport map is available from the TIC.

Blackpool has had **trams** since 1885. The current network is 12 miles long, stretching from *Starr Gate* to *Fleetwood*, along the seafront.

Most local services are operated by **Blackpool Transport** *tel: (01253) 23931* from *Talbot Rd.*

The main taxi rank is on *Talbot Square*, and taxis can also be hailed on the street. The TIC has details of further registered taxi companies.

Staying in Blackpool

There are approximately 2800 hotels and guesthouses in the town, and generally it is not a problem finding somewhere to stay on arrival. However, during the **Blackpool Illuminations** (Sept–Nov), especially at weekends, it is advisable to book ahead. Hotel chains in Blackpool include *Mp*. Accommodation can also be booked through the **Blackpool Hotel and Guest House Association**, *87a Coronation St; tel: (01253) 21891* (commission charged).

There are various campsites within easy reach of town; the following are all approximately 3–4 miles inland, accessible by the Blackpool to Preston bus (further campsite details from the TIC): **Gillett Farm**, *Peel Rd, Peel; tel: (01253) 761676*; **Mariclough-Hampsfield**, *Preston New Rd; tel: (01253) 761034*; **Pipers Height**, *Peel Rd, Peel; tel: (01253) 763767*; **Underhill Farm**, *Preston New Rd; tel: (01253) 763107*.

Sightseeing

A mecca for holidaymakers and day-trippers, Blackpool is *the* major seaside resort in north-west England. It developed from the mid-18th century to cater for the huge numbers of workers from crowded industrial Lancashire, and millions still arrive during the summer season for traditional seaside fun. Along the famous **Golden Mile** of beach with its three

piers (the north pier is open all year), are any number of amusements, dominated by the 518-ft **Blackpool Tower**, a smaller copy of the Eiffel Tower, which boasts an 'indoor theme park' as well as a renowned ballroom at its foot. If state-of-the-art stomach-churning rides are your passion, then **Blackpool Pleasure Beach** is for you.

For a contrast to the relentless fun, try the **Grundy Art Gallery**, which has a good 19th- and 20th-century British collection. Inland from the beach, **Stanley Park** is a fine green oasis with traditional floral displays, lake and model village; nearby **Blackpool Zoo Park** is a modern zoo with over 400 animals.

Seagull Coaches operate bus tours of the area, which can be booked through the TIC. The tram is also a pleasant way to see the 7-mile promenade, and view the famous **Illuminations** (Sept–Nov).

Blackpool Pleasure Beach (2 miles south), *South Promenade; tel: (01253) 341033.* Open 1100 until late (Easter–Nov). No entrance fee. Take tram or bus no. 40.

Blackpool Tower, *Promenade; tel: (01253) 22242.* Open daily (summer), weekends (winter). Admission £6.95. **Blackpool Zoo Park** (2 miles east), *East Park Drive; tel: (01253) 725610.* Open 1000–dusk. Admission £3.80. Take bus no. 21. Open 1000 until late. Admission £3.99. Take tram or bus no. 40.

Grundy Art Gallery, *Queen St; tel: (01253) 751701.* Open Mon–Sat 1000–1700. Admission free. **Stanley Park** (23 miles east), *Westpark Drive; tel: (01253) 762341.* Open daily. Admission free. Take bus no. 21.

LANCASTER

TIC: *29 Castle Hill, Lancaster, Lancashire LA1 1YN; tel: (01524) 32878.* Open Mon–Sat 1000–1700, Sun (Bank Holiday weekends only) 1000–1600 (Apr–June and most of Sept); Mon–Sat 0930–1800, Sun 1000–1600 (July to early Sept); Mon–Sat 1000–1600 (Oct–Mar). DP SHS Services offered: local bed-booking service and BABA (latest 30 mins before closing), advance reservations handled, guided tours booked, bureau de change. Tickets booked for local events, YHA membership sold. *Lancaster The Legacy* and an accommodation guide are available free.

Station: Lancaster Station, *Meeting House Lane; tel: (01524) 32333* is just west of the town centre, and has a taxi rank.

Getting Around

Most of the attractions are within easy walking distance of the centre, and free town and transport maps are available from the TIC. The area has a good rail network. For general transport enquiries *tel: (01524) 841656.*

Most local buses are operated by **Ribble** *tel: (01524) 424555*, from the bus station on *Damside St*. Services are good in the centre, to Morecambe, and to some outlying villages.

The main taxi rank is by the bus station on *Damside St*, or contact **Lancaster Radio Taxis** *tel: (01524) 844844*; **City Cabs** *tel: (01524) 35666*; **John's Taxis** *tel: (01524) 845210* or **Tiger Taxis** *tel: (01524) 844122.*

Staying in Lancaster

There are a few hotels in Lancaster including the chains *FC* and *Pr*, and a small choice of b. & b., guest-house and pub accommodation, with cheaper places located on the edge of town. It is generally easy to book on arrival.

The closest youth hostel is **Arnside Youth Hostel** (10 miles north), *Oakfields Lodge, Redhills Rd, Arnside, Carnforth; tel: (01524) 761781* (train to *Arnside*).

One of the nearest campsites is **Detrongate Farm** (3 miles north), *Bolton-Lee-Sands, Carnforth; tel: (01524) 732842*, bus nos 55 or 555.

Sightseeing

A grey city with a historic heart, Lancaster is dominated by its massive **Castle**: the keep dates from c.1170 and the **Shire Hall** contains a fine heraldic display. Also on the hill is the **Priory Church of St Mary**, mainly late 14th- and 15th-century – don't miss the magnificent carved choir stalls.

The **Maritime Museum**, housed in the fine 18th-century Customs House on the Quay, is a reminder that this was once a great port; while

the grand, domed **Ashton Memorial** (1909) stands in a fine city park which has an exotic butterfly collection. Other museums include the **Cottage Museum**, furnished as an artisan's house of c.1820, and **Judges' Lodgings**, which contains both a collection of furniture by Gillow, the famous Lancaster cabinetmaker, and a museum of childhood. Gillow furniture is also among the treasures at neo-Gothic **Leighton Hall**, which is set in fine parkland.

The TIC can provide information on bus tours, guided walks (including walks across the vast – and treacherous – sands of **Morecambe Bay**), canal cruises and boat trips.

Grange-over-Sands is a charming seaside town with an Edwardian promenade, an ornamental lake and a view across Morecambe Bay to Lancaster (25 miles north-west; 30 mins by train).

At Morecambe, **Frontierland** is a theme park which will have particular appeal to Wild West fans.

Ashton Memorial and Butterfly House, *Williamson Park; tel: (01524) 33318*. Open daily 1000–1700 (Easter–Sept), Mon–Fri 1000–1600, Sat, Sun 1300–1600 (Oct–Easter). Admission £3.50 (memorial only, £0.50).

City Museum, *Market Sq; tel: (01524) 64637*. Open Mon–Sat 1000–1700. Admission free. **Cottage Museum**, *15 Castle Hill; tel: (01524) 64637*. Open daily 1400–1700 (Easter to end Sept). Admission £0.50.

Judges' Lodgings, *Church St; tel: (01524) 32808*. Open Mon–Sat and Bank Holiday Suns 1400–1700 (Easter–June and Oct), Mon–Fri 1000–1300 and 1400–1700, Sat and Sun 1400–1700 (July–Aug). Admission £1.

Lancaster Castle, *Shire Hall, Castle Hill; tel: (01524) 64998*. Open Sat, Sun 1030–1700, last tour 1600 (Easter to end Oct). Also open for tours on weekdays when Crown Courts are not in operation. Admission £2.50.

Lancaster Maritime Museum, *St George's Quay; tel: (01524) 64637*. Open daily 1100–1700 (Easter–Oct), 1400–1700 (Nov–Easter). Admission £1.50.

Lancaster Priory, *Castle Hill; tel: (01524) 65338*. Open daily 0930–1700. Admission free.

St Peter's Cathedral, *St Peter's Rd; tel:*

(01524) 61860. Open daily 0800–1900. Admission free.

Out of Town

Frontierland Western Theme Park, *Morecambe; tel: (01524) 410024.* Open mid-March to end Oct (times vary according to season). Admission £6.99. Train to *Morecambe*, 4 miles north-west.

Leighton Moss Wildlife Park, *Myers Farm, Silverdale, Carnforth; tel: (01524) 701601.* Open daily 1000–1700. Admission £3. Train to *Silverdale*, 8 miles north. **Leighton Hall** (8 miles north), *Carnforth; tel: (01524) 734474.* Open Tues–Fri and Sun 1400–1700 (May–July and Sept), 1130–1700 (Aug). Last tour 1630. Admission £3.30. Bus nos 55 or 55a to *Peter's Hill, Yealand Conyers*, then ½-mile walk.

Steamtown Railway Centre, *Warton Rd, Carnforth; tel: (01524) 732100.* Open daily 0900–1700 (Easter–Oct), 1000–1600 (Oct–Easter). Admission £2.10 (static days), £3.50 (full steam days). Bus nos 55, 55a or 555, or train to *Carnforth*, 8 miles north.

Ulverston, 40 mins by train, 35 miles north-west. Pretty market town with cobbled streets, birthplace of Stan Laurel and home to the **Laurel and Hardy Museum**, *Upper Brook St; tel: (01229) 582292.* Open daily 1000–1600. Admission £2.

 Side Tracks from Oxenholme

KENDAL

TIC: *Highgate, Kendal, Cumbria LA9 4DL; tel: (01539) 725758.* Open Mon–Sat 0900–1700 (all year), Sun 1000–1600 (Easter–Oct). DP Services offered: local bed-booking service, advance reservations handled (except for Bank Holidays), BABA (latest 30 mins before closing). Guided tours booked, coach tickets sold. *Kendal Mini Guide* costs £0.45, *Where to Stay in South Lakeland* costs £0.85.

Station: Oxenholme Station, *Oxenholme; tel: (01539) 720397* is the closest mainline station (2 miles south-east of Kendal) and has a taxi rank. There are local trains between Oxenholme,

Kendal and Windermere and a regular mini-link bus service connecting Kendal and Oxenholme.

Getting Around

Most of Kendal's attractions are within easy walking distance of the centre. Free town and transport maps are available from the TIC. Local bus services are good within the town and on the main route through the Lake District, but patchy to outlying areas, and poor on Sun.

Most local bus services are operated by **Cumberland Motor Services** *tel: (01946) 63222* from *Blackhall Rd*. There is a daily or 4-day 'Explorer Ticket' available (£4.99 or £12.99 respectively) for use on all their services.

The main taxi rank is on *Market Place*, or contact **AA Taxis** *tel: (01539) 740205*; **Ace Taxis** *tel: (01539) 733430*; **Airport Taxis** *tel: (01539) 724658*; **Blue Star Taxis** *tel: (01539) 723670*; **Castle Taxis** *tel: (01539) 726233* (further taxi details available from the TIC).

Staying in Kendal

There are very few hotels in Kendal, but a good choice of b. & b., guest-house and pub accommodation, with cheaper establishments located in the town centre. It is generally possible to book on arrival, except over Bank Holidays, high summer, Christmas and New Year, when the area is extremely busy.

Kendal Youth Hostel is at *118 Highgate; tel: (01539) 724066*, open daily (mid-Mar to mid-Sept), Sun and Mon (mid-Sept to mid-Mar) plus specific dates over Christmas and New Year. The closest campsites are **Millcrest** (1½ miles north), *Skelsmergh, Shap Rd; tel: (01539) 741363*, bus no. 43 and ½-mile walk, and **Ashes Lane Caravan and Camping Park** (3 miles north), *Stavely; tel: (01539) 821119*, bus no. 555 and ½-mile walk.

Sightseeing

Well-known for its major products – mint cake and shoes – Kendal lies just south of the **Lake District National Park**, and is a good base from which to visit the rolling fells of the southern Lakes. There are numerous full-day and half-day bus tours of the Lake District on offer, which can be booked at the TIC. **Supertours** collect from Kendal as well as from *Windermere* and *Ambleside*. The no. 555 bus service from Lancaster to Keswick is a good sightseeing route.

Quieter than some other Lakeland towns, Kendal has some fine 17th- and 18th-century buildings and some excellent museums for the (frequent) rainy days: at **Abbot Hall**, the **Art Gallery** includes paintings by Turner, Romney and Ruskin, while the **Museum of Lakeland Life and Industry** captures the area's working and social life.

Kendal Museum has a gallery devoted to Alfred Wainwright, famed for his Lakeland guidebooks; modern tapestries from 15 countries celebrating the Quaker movement, which began in this area, are exhibited in an old meeting house at the **Quaker Tapestry**. There are pleasant strolls to be had along the River Kent, and many good fell walks within an easy radius – enquire at the TIC.

Five miles from Kendal, Elizabethan **Levens Hall** has a famous topiary garden where the trees were first shaped in 1694; nearby **Sizergh Castle** has a 60-ft high 14th-century tower and a limestone rock garden.

Abbot Hall Art Gallery, *Kirkland; tel: (01539) 722464*. Open Mon–Sat 1030–1700, Sun 1400–1700 (end Mar to Oct); reduced hours in Nov and Dec. Admission £2.50. **Abbot Hall Museum of Lakeland Life and Industry** (all details as for Art Gallery above).

Kendal Castle (ruin, south of *Castle St*). Open at all times. Admission free. **Kendal Museum of Natural History and Archaeology**, *Station Rd; tel: (01539) 721374*. Open Mon–Fri 1030–1700, Sun 1400–1700 (late Mar to end Oct); Mon–Fri 1100–1600, Sat, Sun 1200–1500 (early Jan to late Mar); reduced hours in Nov and Dec. Admission £2.50.

Kendal Parish Church, *Kirkland; tel: (01539) 721248*. Open daily until 1630 (Apr–Oct) and most mornings during winter months. Admission free.

Kendal Reptiles, *117 Sticklandgate; tel: (01539) 721240*. Open Mon–Sat 1000–1700, Sun 1100–1600. Admission £2.25. **Quaker Tapestry**, *New Rd; tel: (01539) 722975*. Open

Mon–Sat 1000–1700, Sun 1400–1700 (May–Oct). Admission £2.

Out of Town

Lakeland Wildlife Oasis, *Hale, Milnthorpe; tel: (01539) 563027*. Open daily from 1000. Admission £2.85. Four miles south (no public transport).

Levens Hall and World Famous Topiary Garden (5 miles south), *Levens; tel: (01539) 560321*. Open Sun–Thur 1100–1700 (Apr–Sept); steam collection 1400–1700. Admission £3.90. Bus nos 553, 554 or 555.

Sizergh Castle (NT), *Sizergh; tel: (01539) 560070*. Open Sun–Thur 1330–1730 (Apr–Oct). Admission £3.30. Bus no. 555 to *Brettargh Halt*, then ½-mile walk. Three miles south.

WINDERMERE

TIC: *Victoria St, Windermere, Cumbria LA23 1AD; tel: (01539) 446499*. Open daily 0900–1800 (Easter–Oct), 0900–1700 (Nov–Easter). DP Services offered: local bed-booking service and BABA (latest 15 mins before closing), guided tours booked, bureau de change. *Windermere and Bowness Mini Guide* costs £0.75, *Where to Stay in South Lakeland* costs £0.85. **Lake District National Park Office**, *Glebe Rd, Bowness-on-Windermere; tel (01539) 442895*. Open 0930–1730 (Easter–Oct), Sat, Sun 1000–1600 (Nov and Dec). DP Services offered: as above.

Station: Windermere Station, *Station Precinct; tel: (01539) 720397* is on the northern edge of the town and has a taxi rank. The W1 bus service connects with Bowness, the southern area of the town.

Getting Around

Most of the attractions are within an area of just over a mile across. Free town and transport maps are available from the TIC. Local bus services are good within the town and on the main route through the Lake District, but patchy to outlying areas, and poor on Suns.

Most local bus services are operated by **Cumberland Motor Services** *tel: (01946) 63222*. There is a daily or 4-day 'Explorer

Ticket' available (£4.99 or £12.99 respectively) available for use on all their services.

The main taxi rank is outside the station, or you can contact **Coopers Cabs** *tel: (01539) 445282;* **Cumbria Taxis** *tel: (01539) 445246;* **Lakes Taxis** *tel: (01539) 446777.*

Staying in Windermere

There is a good choice of accommodation of all sorts, including hotels in the *FH* and *MC* chains. It is generally possible to book on arrival, except over Bank Holiday weekends and in high summer.

Windermere Youth Hostel, *High Cross, Bridge Lane, Troutbeck; tel: (01539) 443543* is open daily (closed Tues in low seaon, and early Nov to late Dec). Bus nos W1 or 555 to *Troutbeck Bridge*, then ½-mile walk (2½ miles north). The nearest campsite is **Limefitt Park**, *Patterdale Rd, Troutbeck; tel: (01539) 432300.* Take bus no. 517 (limited summer service), 3½ miles north.

Sightseeing

On the eastern side of Lake Windermere, Britain's largest lake, Windermere town's Victorian villas and hotels bear witness to its established appeal. There are many viewpoints within walking distance, including **Orrest Head** – reached via the path beside the Windermere Hotel. A 1½-mile walk or bus ride will take you down to Bowness, the tourist trap on the lake shore; but even commercialisation cannot spoil the character of this vast expanse of water, with its wooded islands and shores.

Boat trips will take you up and down the lake (at a price), connecting at Lakeside with the **Lakeside and Haverthwaite Railway**. The ferry from *Ferry Nab Rd* to the quiet western shore takes you within reach of **Hill Top**, the tiny cottage (avoid peak times) where the children's writer and book illustrator Beatrix Potter wrote many of her Peter Rabbit stories; in Bowness itself, the **World of Beatrix Potter** brings the stories to life with delightful 3D tableaux. Her local fame rested more upon her devotion to rearing the unique and ancient Lakeland breed,

the Herdwick sheep; these ultra-hardy animals are encountered on every Lakeland walk and their wool is used in a multitude of items of clothing sold in local stores.

There are countless places to walk within easy reach – the **Brockhole National Park Visitor Centre** provides the best introduction to the area. Devotees of the Lakes' romantic poet, William Wordsworth, can visit **Dove Cottage** at Grasmere, where he wrote much of his best-known poetry; the poignant evidence of poverty displayed in his early home (including walls papered with newspapers of the day) contrasts with the grander **Rydal Mount**, where he spent his last years, standing near busy but charming Ambleside.

Numerous full-day and half-day bus tours, guided walks and boat trips can all be booked at the TIC. **Windermere Steamboat Museum**, *Rayrigg Rd; tel: (01539) 445565.* Open daily 1000–1700 (Easter–Oct). Admission £2.80. **World of Beatrix Potter**, *Rayrigg Rd, Bowness; tel: (01539) 488444.* Open daily 1000–1830 (Easter–Sept), 1000–1600 (Oct–Easter). Admission £2.85.

Out of Town

Brockhole National Park Visitor Centre (3 miles north-west), *Windermere; tel: (01539) 446601.* Open daily 1000–1700 (late Mar to ealy Nov). Admission free. Bus no. 555.

Dove Cottage (Wordsworth's home), *Grasmere; tel: (01539) 435544.* Open daily 0930–1730 (closed mid-Jan to mid-Feb). Bus no. 555 to *Grasmere*, 8 miles north-west.

Hill Top (NT), *near Sawrey, Ambleside; tel: (01539) 36269.* Open Sat–Wed 1100–1700 (Apr–Oct), last admission: 1630. Admission £3.30. Bus nos 505 or 506 to Bowness Pier, then ferry and 2-mile walk. Four miles south-west. **Rydal Mount** (Wordsworth's home), near *Ambleside; tel: (01539) 433002.* Open daily 0930–1700 (Mar–Oct), 1000–1600 Nov–Feb. Admission £2. Bus no. 555. Seven miles north-west.

MANCHESTER to CHESTER

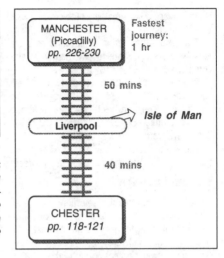

MANCHESTER (Piccadilly)
pp. 226-230

Fastest journey: 1 hr

50 mins

Liverpool

Isle of Man

40 mins

CHESTER
pp. 118-121

From one of the greatest manufacturing towns of the Industrial Revolution this route takes you via the once-thriving port of Liverpool – birthplace of the Beatles and point of departure and arrival for millions travelling to and from Ireland and the United States – to the distinctive half-timbered charm of Chester.

TRAINS

ETT tables: 551, 554, 555, 585

 Fast Track

An hourly service (much reduced on Suns) links Manchester Piccadilly to Chester. The direct route takes just under 1 hour and does not go via Liverpool.

 On Track

Manchester–Liverpool

Two services per hour (hourly on Suns) run from Manchester Piccadilly to Liverpool Lime Street, taking 50 mins. An hourly service also runs from Manchester Victoria taking about an hour.

Liverpool–Chester

Two trains an hour every day of the week take 40 mins from Liverpool Lime Street to Chester.

LIVERPOOL

TIC: *Merseyside Welcome Centre, Clayton Sq, Liverpool, Merseyside L1 1QR; tel: (0151) 709 3631.* Open Mon–Sat 0930–1730, Bank Holidays 1000–1700. DP SHS Services offered: local bed-booking service, advance reservations handled, BABA, guided tours booked, bureau de change. Tickets booked for theatre, local events, National Express and YHA membership sold. *Pocket Guide* £0.25; free accommodation listing. *Atlantic Pavilion, Albert Dock; tel: (0151) 708 8854.* Open 1000–1730. DP SHS Services offered: local bed-booking service, advance reservations handled, BABA, guided tours and tickets for theatre and local events booked.

Station: Lime Street Station, *Lime St; tel: (0151) 709 9696* is central and has a taxi rank. **Bus Station**: there are good express connections to Liverpool, particularly from Manchester, Birmingham and London. For **National Express** *tel: (0161) 228 3881*, services arrive at *Brownlow Hill* (at the side of the Adelphi).

Ferries: services to the Isle of Man are operated by **Isle of Man Steam Packet Co**, *tel: (01624) 661661*, and to Ireland by **Norse Irish Ferries**, *tel: (01232) 779090*; also ferries across the Mersey. All from *Liverpool Pier Head*.

Getting Around

The majority of attractions are within walkable distance of the city centre. There is good train and bus coverage of the city and surrounding area, with reduced frequency in the evenings and on Sun. For local travel enquiries *tel: (0151) 236 7676* (Merseytravel). **Shopmobility**, *Clayton Sq; tel: (0151) 708 9993*. DP SHS Service offering battery-powered scooters and wheelchairs to people with mobility problems, for use in the city centre.

The central bus station for local buses is on *Paradise St*; services are run by many different companies.

Regular **ferries** cross the Mersey to the Wirral Peninsula *tel: (0151) 236 7676* (**Merseytravel**), and there are ferry cruises to see the waterfront daily in summer (£2.75), *tel: (0151) 630 1030*. Both leave from *Liverpool Pier Head*.

There are approximately eight taxi ranks in the centre; taxis can also be hailed in the street.

Staying in Liverpool

There is a reasonable selection of hotel accommodation in and around the city, but not very much in the way of guest-house and b. & b. It is generally easy to find accommodation on arrival, except during the **Grand National** in April. Hotel chains in Liverpool include *Ca, MC, MH*. There is one private hostel, **Embassie Youth Hostel**, *1 Faulkner Sq; tel: (0151) 707 1089*, open 24 hrs. (For nearest HI hostel, see Chester, p. 118). The nearest campsite is at **Abbey Farm**, *Dark Lane, Ormskirk; tel: (01695) 572686*. Train to *Ormskirk*.

Liverpool has the oldest **Chinatown** in Europe, just outside the city centre, as well as restaurants of many nationalities, and to suit all pockets. **Lark Lane** is also a popular and lively area (likened to New York's Greenwich Village), with a good choice of eating places (take the train to *St Michael's*), as is the **Cavern Quarter**.

The main post office is at *2333 Whitechapel*, open Mon–Fri 0900–1730, Sat 0900–1230. Post restante facilities are available.

Entertainment and Events

Liverpool has an enormous choice of evening entertainment. The TIC has a free entertainment list, *In Touch*. The main Liverpool entertainment guide *L Scene* costs £1 from newsagents or the TIC. Local papers also carry listings.

MGM 8 Screen Cinema, *Edge Lane Retail Park; tel: (0151) 252 0550*. For music: **Bluecoat Arts Centre**, *School Lane; tel: (0151) 708 9050*. **The Cavern Club**, *Matthew St; tel: (0151) 236 9091* (where The Beatles first played). **Royal Liverpool Philharmonic Orchestra**, *Hope St;*

tel: (0151) 709 3789. Nightclubs: **The Grafton**, *West Derby Rd; tel: (0151) 263 2303*. Spectator Sports: **Aintree Racecourse**, *Ormskirk Rd; tel: (0151) 5232600* (where the Grand National is held in April). **Everton Football Club**, *Goodison Park; tel: (0151) 521 2020*. **Liverpool Football Club**, *Anfield Rd; tel: (0151) 263 2361*. Theatres include: **Liverpool Empire**, *Lime St; tel: (0151) 709 1555* (the city's main theatre). **Liverpool Playhouse/Studio**, *Williamson Sq; tel: (0151) 709 8363* (Britain's oldest continuing repertory theatre). **Flora Pavilion**, *Promenade, New Brighton, The Wirral; tel: (0151) 639 4360* (the Wirral's largest theatre).

A few of the city's more important annual events are: the **Grand National**, *Aintree Racecourse* (see above) in April; **Liverpool Festival of Comedy** (various venues) in June; the **Mersey River Festival** in June (Europe's largest water-based festival, taking place around the *River Mersey* and *Albert Dock*); the **Beatles Convention**, *Adelphi Hotel*, in August; and the **Mathew Street Festival** in Aug.

Shopping

There are three modern precincts: *Clayton Sq, St John's Centre* and *Cavern Walks*, as well as the shopping areas of *Bold St, North John St* and *Whitechapel*. The beautifully restored *Albert Dock* is also popular for shopping. There are a number of excellent markets including: **Quiggins Centre**, *School Lane*, Mon–Sat 1000–1800; **St John's Market**, *Eliot St*, Mon–Sat; **Stanley Dock Sunday Market**, 1½ miles north of *Pier Head*, 0900–1600.

Sightseeing

Best known as the birthplace of the Beatles, and home of the Grand National and two famous football clubs, Liverpool is a surprisingly attractive city (despite a reputation for deprivation) with a vibrant atmosphere. The 1-hr **City Sightseeing Tour** is a good introduction to the city, and for Beatles fans there is a 2-hr **Magical History Tour**. Both are by bus; further details from the TIC. For a cruise on the Mersey, contact *Mersey Ferries, tel: (0151) 630 1030*.

In the 18th century Liverpool developed from what was a fishing village into Europe's most important Atlantic seaport; the huge **Royal Liver Building** (1911) still dominates the Mersey waterfront. Other fine municipal buildings reflecting Liverpool's former wealth can be seen around *William Brown St*, such as the **Walker Art Gallery**, which houses an internationally renowned collection of European art. **St George's Hall** (1854, *Lime St*) is one of the finest neo-classical buildings in the country. The vast Victorian Gothic **Anglican cathedral** is the largest Anglican cathedral in Britain, but is exhilaratingly well-proportioned. Climb the tower for views to Wales.

The **Albert Dock**, once bustling with shipping, now teems with a different sort of life: the visitors to its thriving complex of museums, exhibitions and shops. Outstanding are the **Merseyside Maritime Museum**, which traces the history of Liverpool's shipping, and the **Tate Gallery**, housing the national collection of modern art and sculpture in the north. Cartoon fans will enjoy **Animation World**, which includes hands-on displays.

Just outside town, **Speke Hall**, incongruously set next to a housing estate and backing on to the airport runway, is a lovely timbered Elizabethan house with fine Victorian interiors, attractive gardens and woodland. Across the Mersey on the Wirral peninsula is the garden village of **Port Sunlight** – precursor of garden cities – which was built by William Hesketh Lever in 1888 for his soap factory workers. The **Heritage Centre** tells the story of the community and the **Lady Lever Art Gallery** houses a collection of 18th- and 19th century decorative arts.

Cathedrals

Liverpool Cathedral, *St James Rd; tel: (0151) 709 6271*. Open 0800–1830. Admission free, donations welcomed; access to top of tower £2.50. **Metropolitan Cathedral of Christ the King** (Roman Catholic), *Mount Pleasant; tel: (0151) 709 9222*. Open daily 0800–1800 (Suns in Winter 1700). Admission free, donations welcomed.

Museums and Galleries

Animation World, *Britannia Pavilion, Albert Dock; tel: (0151) 707 1828*. Open daily 1000–1800. Admission £3. **Beatles Story**, *Britannia Vaults, Albert Dock; tel: (0151) 709 1963*. Open 1000–1800 (extended in summer, reduced in winter). Admission £4.45. **Liverpool Museum and Planetarium**, *William Brown St; tel: (0151) 207 0001*. Open Mon–Sat 1000–1700, Sun 1200–1700. Admission free. **Merseyside Maritime Museum; Museum of Liverpool Life; Anything to Declare? H M Customs and Excise Museum**, *Albert Dock; tel: (0151) 207 0001*. Three museums under one roof. All open daily 1030–1730 (last admission 1630). Admission £2.50 (includes admission to all three). **Tate Gallery**, *The Colonnades, Albert Dock; tel: (0151) 709 0507*. Open Tue–Sun 1000–1800 and Bank Holiday Mons. Admission free (special exhibitions £1). **Walker Art Gallery**, *William Brown St; tel: (0151) 207 0001*. Open Mon–Sat 1000–1700, Sun 1200–1700. Admission free. **Western Approaches** (secret wartime headquarters), *1 Rumford St; tel: (0151) 227 2008*. Open daily 1000–1600. Admission £3.99.

Out of Town

Knowsley Safari Park, *Prescot Rd, Prescot; tel: (0151) 430 9009*. Open 1000 to dusk (Mar–Oct). Admission £8. Accessible by public transport (train to *Prescot*), but car needed for touring park 6 miles east. **Lady Lever Art Gallery**, *Port Sunlight, Wirral; tel: (0151) 645 3623*. Open Mon–Sat 1000–1700, Sun 1200–1700. Admission free. Train to *Port Sunlight*, 5 miles west. **Port Sunlight Heritage Centre**, *95 Greendale Rd, Port Sunlight, Wirral; tel: (0151) 644 6466*. Open daily 1000–1600 (summer), 1200–1600 (winter). Admission £0.20. Train to *Port Sunlight*, 5 miles west. **Speke Hall** (NT), *The Walk; tel: (0151) 427 7231*. Open Tues–Sun and Bank Holiday Mons 1300–1730 (Apr–Oct), Sat, Sun 1300–1630 (Nov to mid-Dec). Admission to house and garden: £3.40. Take bus 32, 82, 80, H26 to *Speke Hall Ave*, 9 miles south of centre. **Sudley Art Gallery** (2 miles south), *Mossley Hill Road; tel: (0151) 207 0001*. Open Mon–Sat 1000–1700, Sun 1200–1700. Admission free. Bus 20, 21, 32, 82 or train.

MANCHESTER to YORK

Crossing the Pennines, this route takes in the industrial towns of Bradford and Leeds, and the spa of Harrogate, a byword for northern gentility. It also provides access to Haworth, an area forever associated with the Brontës, and to the World Heritage Site at Fountains Abbey.

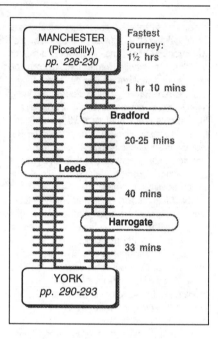

MANCHESTER (Piccadilly) *pp. 226-230* — Fastest journey: 1½ hrs

1 hr 10 mins

Bradford

20-25 mins

Leeds

40 mins

Harrogate

33 mins

YORK *pp. 290-293*

TRAINS

ETT table: 551, 552, 567

 Fast Track

The route between Manchester and York is served by two through trains each hour. Journey time for the trip from Manchester Piccadilly to York is about 1½ hrs (longer on Sun) and bypasses Bradford and Harrogate.

On Track

Manchester–Bradford

Trains run every half-hour (hourly on Suns) between Manchester Victoria and Bradford Interchange, taking 1 hr 10 mins.

Bradford–Leeds

Trains run every 15 mins (half-hourly on Suns) from Bradford Interchange to Leeds; the journey time is 20–25 mins.

Leeds–Harrogate

There is a train every 30 mins (reduced to hourly or even two-hourly on Suns) between Leeds and Harrogate and the journey takes 40 mins.

Harrogate–York

One train every hour (eight trains only on Suns, starting around midday) operates between Harrogate and York. Journey time is 33 mins.

BRADFORD

TIC: *National Museum of Photography, Film and Television, Pictureville, Bradford BD1 1NQ; tel: (01274) 753678.* Open daily 0930–1730 (closed 24-27 Dec). DP Services offered: local bed-booking services, BABA, 'Haworth and Ilkley' guide books and an accommodation guide are available free.

Station: Bradford Interchange, *Bridge St; tel: (01274) 732237* is in the town centre, and has a taxi rank.

Getting Around

Most attractions are within a walkable area from the centre. Town and transport maps are available free from the TIC and the station. The main bus operator is **Yorkshire Rider Ltd,** *tel: (01274) 732237*. Services are quite good within the town. The main taxi rank is at the station.

Staying in Bradford

There is a good range of accommodation

---

available, particularly guesthouses and b. & b.s. Cheaper accommodation is located mainly in outlying villages. It is generally easy to book on arrival. A good option for budget accommodation is **Haworth Youth Hostel,** Longlands Hall, Longlands Dr, Lees Ln, Haworth; tel: (01535) 642234, open from 1700. Take bus nos 663, 664 or 665 from Bradford town centre. The TIC has details of **campsites** in the area, including **Dobrudden Caravan Park,** Baildon Moor, Baildon; tel: (01274) 581016, 7½ miles north of the centre.

Bradford is notable for the number of restaurants serving food from the Indian subcontinent, said to be the highest per head of population of any British town.

Sightseeing

Wool and Bradford are almost synonymous, such was its importance in the 19th century as a central market after the Industrial Revolution brought steam power to the wool trade. Like many small market towns that exploded into industrial cities almost overnight, Bradford's architecture is a mixture of grand civic buildings and factories. Few traces remain of the town's past, but one obvious exception is the Cathedral. Set on a rise, its detailed carvings – particularly the 20 angels that support the nave roof – catch the eye.

Bradford has a long and proud transport heritage and a number of attractions which make an interesting tour. You can step into the world of colour at the award-winning **Colour Museum**, or see the world's biggest lens and smallest camera, the world's best snapshot and the first-ever photographic likenesses at the **National Museum of Photography, Film and Television**.

For a different kind of experience, visit Bradford's gothic Victorian cemetery at **Undercliffe** and its ornate tombstones with weeping angels, marble obelisks and even an Egyptian tomb with sphinxes. Some of the mausoleums are listed as protected buildings because of their architectural significance.

The nave and arches of **Bradford Cathedral** date from the 1500s; major extensions were built in the 1950s and 1960s. Visitors are welcome at services and may walk around the Cathedral when services are not being held.

Once the home of the remarkable Brontë family, the **Brontë Parsonage** in Haworth is now an intimate museum. This is where the writers of Jane Eyre and Wuthering Heights lived. The small Georgian parsonage has rooms furnished as in the Brontës' day, with displays of their personal treasures, their pictures, books and manuscripts.

In nearby Shipley is Europe's largest collection of the works of Bradford-born artist **David Hockney**. Also in Shipley, a brick-roofed former spinning room in Titus Salt's Victorian woollen mill has been transformed into the **1853 Gallery**. In nearby Keighley is the **Cliffe Castle Museum**. Wealthy wool baron Henry Butterfield made Cliffe Castle his home and part of the building is still furnished and decorated in the lavish style of the 1880s. The museum specialises in natural history, geology and local history.

Bradford Cathedral, Church Bank; tel: (01274) 728955. Open daily 0800–1800. Admission free. **Colour Museum,** Grattan Rd; tel: (01274) 390955. Open Tues–Fri 1400–1700, Sat 1000–1600, closed public holidays. Admission: adults £1.10, children under the age of 15 years and senior citizens 65p. **National Museum of Photography Film and Television,** Pictureville; tel (01274) 727488. Open Tues–Sun 1030–1800 and Bank Holiday Mondays. Admission free. **Undercliffe Cemetery,** Undercliffe Ln; tel: (01274) 642276. Open daily.

Out of Town

Bolling Hall, Bolling Hall Rd; tel: (01274) 723057. Open Tues–Sun 1000–1700 (Oct–Mar), 1000–1800 (Apr–Sep). Closed Monday except Bank Holidays. 2 miles from town centre. Take bus 621 from the Bradford Interchange Depot to East Bowling. Admission free. **Bradford Industrial and Horses At Work Museum,** Moorside Mills, Moorside Rd; tel: (01274) 631756. Open Tues–Sun 1000–1700, closed Monday except Bank Holidays. 3½ miles from town centre. Take bus no. 614/634 from Market Street, or 608/609 from Bank Street, to Eccleshill. **Cliffe Castle Museum,** Spring

Gardens Ln, Keighley; tel: (01274) 758230. Open Tues–Sun 1000–1700 (Oct–Mar), 1000–1800 (Apr–Sep), closed Monday except Bank Holiday. 10 miles from town centre. Take bus nos 663, 664 or 665 from Bradford Interchange Depot to Keighley.
East Riddlesden Hall (NT), *Bradford Rd, Keighley; tel: (01535) 607075.* Open 26 Mar–30 Oct, Sat–Wed 1200–1700. Approximately 8 miles from town centre. Take bus nos 663, 664 or 665 from Bradford Interchange Depot to Keighley. **Brontë Parsonage,** *Church St off Main St, Haworth; tel: (01274) 531163.* Open all year except 3 weeks in January and February. Take bus nos 663, 664 or 665 from Bradford Interchange Depot to Haworth. Admission: adults £3.60, senior citizens and students £2.60, children under 16 years of age £1.10.
1853 Gallery, *Salts Mill, Victoria Rd, Saltaire, Shipley; tel: (01274) 531163.* Open daily 1000–1700 except Christmas and Boxing Day. Take bus no 622 or 669 from Bradford Interchange Depot to Shipley. 4 miles from Bradford. Admission free.

LEEDS

TIC: *19 Wellington St, West Yorkshire LS1 4DG; tel: (0113) 247 8301/2.* Open Mon–Fri 0930–1700, Sat 0930–1230; 1330–1600. DP Services offered: local bed-booking service and BABA (booking fee or 10% commission on first night taken), advance reservations handled one day ahead only. The TIC can book self-catering in the Leeds area in advance. The TIC books guided tours and sells National Express tickets. The guides *Leeds Always* and *Where to Stay in Leeds* are available free. A Women's Travel Group is in operation to assist disabled and elderly female visitors.
Station: Leeds City Station *City Sq; tel (0113) 2448133* is located in the town centre. The TIC is moving to the station premises in March 1995. There is a taxi rank and **Hertz** car hire is represented at the station.

Getting Around

The majority of Leeds attractions are within walking distance of the town centre, with the exception of **Lotherton Hall** and **Temple Newsam**. Free town and transport maps are available from the TIC.

It is recommended that Temple Town Rd is avoided at night.

A good bus service runs throughout the city to all areas, operated by **Yorkshire Rider Co,** *tel: (0113) 242 9614,* from the central bus depot on *Wellington St.* Lotherton Hall at the extreme east of the city is not served by public transport. A reduced service operates after 2000 and Sundays. Bus service stops 2330–2400. A night bus operates hourly from 0100–0300. Saver tickets for bus and train include the 'Metro Rover'.

The main taxi ranks are at *Leeds Station.* The city has 150 registered taxi companies.

Staying in Leeds

There are approximately 30 mid-range hotels in Leeds and 25 guest-houses and b. & b. establishments. The cheaper accommodation is to be found close to the university at Headingley, 4 miles north of Leeds. There are a number of inns offering accommodation 3–5 miles around city centre. It is generally easy to find accommodation on arrival except during July and August particularly after 1800. Hotel chains in Leeds include *FC, Hn, Ho* and *Ma.* The nearest youth hostel is in York.

There are several campsites within 10 miles of the city: **Roundhay Park,** *Princes Ave; tel: (0113) 2266 1850,* 4 miles north-east. **Moor Lodge Caravan Park,** *Blackmore Ln, Bardsey; tel: (01937) 572 424,* 5 miles north-east on Wetherby Rd. **Rudding Holiday Park,** *Follisfort, Harrogate; tel: (01423) 870439,* 10–12 miles north-east.

Sightseeing

The city of Leeds has some impressive Victorian buildings, including the **Corn Exchange**, which now houses speciality shops and exhibitions, and the magnificent **Town Hall**. East of the Town Hall are the **Leeds City Art Gallery** and **Leeds City Museum**; the former houses paintings, sculptures and one of the best 20th-century collections in the country, while the latter includes an excellent natural history gallery and displays of Roman artefacts.

The city's revitalised waterfront at **Granary Wharf** offers canalside shops, restaurants, craft stalls and street entertainers. On a river island site is 19th-century **Thwaite Mills**, a fully restored water-powered grinding mill complete with waterwheels. Leeds' **Roundhay Park** – a large, natural park – is a popular venue for outdoor events during the summer. The Park is also home to **Tropical World**, a paradise of indoor tropical forests, tumbling waterfalls and clear pools, complete with butterflies, fish and exotic birds.

The area around Leeds boasts a rich variety of historic houses. **Temple Newsam House** is a Tudor–Jacobean mansion with a splendid collection of decorative arts, set in parkland with many outdoor attractions. Edwardian **Lotherton Hall** is also a treasure trove of decorative arts and costumes and has a fine bird garden. Spot yet more birds at **Harewood House and Bird Garden**, an 18th-century stately home with impressive art collection, set in grounds landscaped by 'Capability' Brown and housing aviaries with 150 bird species.

Boat trips are operated by **Yorkshire Hire Cruises**, tel: (0113) 2456195. Trips start from Leeds Waterfront and cost £1.50 adult, £1 child. Guided walks of the city are organised by Leeds County Council, price £2 adult, £1 child and guides are available. All these facilities can be booked at the TIC.

Leeds City Art Gallery, The Headrow; tel: (0113) 2247 8248. Open all year Mon–Fri 1000–1730; Wed 1000–2100; Sat 1000–1600. Admission free. **Leeds City Museum**, The Headrow; tel: (0113) 2247 8275. Open Tues–Fri 1000–1730; Sat 1000–1600. Closed June and Mons. Admission free. **Thwaite Mills Industrial Museum**, Thwaite Ln, Stourton; tel: (0113) 2249 6453. Open all year Tues–Sun 1000-1700. Admission £2.

Temple Newsam House, city centre; tel: (0113) 2264 7321. Open all year Tues–Sun 1030–1730. Admission £2. Bus 27 to city centre. **Roundhay Park**, Princes Ave; tel: (0113) 2266 1850. Open all year. Admission free. **Tropical World**, Coral Gdns, Roundhay Park; tel: (0113) 2266 1850. Open all year

1030–dusk. Admission free.

Out of Town

Kirkstall Abbey, Kirkstall Rd; tel: (0113) 2275 5821. Open all year. Admission free. 3 miles west (A65). **Lotherton Hall**, Aberford; tel: (0113) 2281 3259. Open all year, Tues–Sun 1030–1730. Admission £1.20. Metro bus no 63 or 64 from Leeds to Swan Inn at Aberford. **Harewood House**, Harewood; tel: (0113) 2288 6225. Open 13 Mar–31 Oct daily. Admission £5.75. 7 miles from Leeds, served by West Yorkshire Buses.

HARROGATE

TIC: Royal Baths, Assembly Rooms, Crescent Rd; tel: (01423) 525666; fax: (01423) 525669. Open Mon–Fri 0900-1715, Sat 0900-1230 (Oct–May), Mon–Sat 0900–1800, Sun 1400–1700 (Jun–Sep). DP services offered. Local bed-booking service available for 10% of first night's booking, BABA, self catering booked. Tickets for local events sold. Harrogate District guide sold at £0.50, accommodation listing available free of charge.

Station: Harrogate Station, Station Pde; tel: (01132) 448133 is in the city centre. There is a taxi rank outside.

Getting Around

Most attractions are within a walkable area of the centre, but the town is very busy durng conference times and the **Spring Flower Show** in April. A free town map is available from the TIC and a transport map can be obtained from **Harrogate and District Transport**, 3-4 Station Rd; tel: (01423) 527984

There are several bus companies operating in the area, including **Abbotts**, tel: (01677) 422858, **Harrogate and District**, tel: (01423) 52798, and **Stephenson Nationwide Travel**, tel: (01347) 838990. For general bus enquiries tel: (01423) 527984. Services are good both within the town and to outlying districts, with fewer services after 2200 hours and on Sundays. The TIC has a free booklet on transport in and around Harrogate. The main taxi rank is in James St.

Staying in Harrogate

There are a number of large chain and independent hotels and some cheaper hotels in the centre; the majority of guesthouses and b. & b. establishments are on the edge of the town. Hotel chains in Harrogate include *FC, MC, MH, Pr* and *Sw.*

It is generally easy to find accommodation on the day of arrival except when there is a conference at the Harrogate International Centre, so it is a good idea to check before planning a stay.

There are four **campsites** in the area: **Bilton Park**, *Village Farm, Bilton Ln; tel: (01423) 863121,* 1½ miles out of Harrogate; **High Moor Farm Park**, *Skipton Rd: tel: (01423) 563637,* 3 miles out of town; **Rudding Holiday Park**, *Follifoot; tel: (01423) 870439,* 2 miles out of town; and **Ripley Caravan Park**, *Ripley; tel: (01423) 770050.* There is no public transport except to Ripley – bus nos 23, 36 and 36a have a regular service on weekdays, occasional on Suns.

Sightseeing

Harrogate has a rich spa heritage and a modern role as a cosmopolitan visitor venue, epitomised by the successful international conference and exhibition centre set amidst parks and gardens. The town has the reputation as one of the most florally attractive towns in Britain.

Following the discovery of the first mineral spring in 1571 the town evolved as a fashionable spa. The **Royal Pump Room**, built in 1842 to enclose the Old Sulphur Well and once the main watering hole for spa visitors, has now been painstakingly restored as a museum. **Harlow Carr Botanical Gardens**, set in 68 acres, are the most prestigious in the North of England and headquarters to the Northern Horticultural Society. Coach tours can be booked through **Wrays**, *tel: (01423) 522466,* and tours start from St Mary's Walk. Free guided walks can be arranged through the TIC or **Harrogate Council**, *tel: (01423) 500600 ext 3212.* Out of town, the romantic ruins of 12th-century **Fountains Abbey**, set amid magnificent gardens, are a World Heritage Site.

Royal Pump Room Museum, *Royal Pde; tel: (01423) 503340.* Open Mon–Sat 1000–1700, Sun 1400–1700 (Apr–Oct), Mon–Sat 1000–1600, Sun 1400–1600 (Nov–Feb). Admission £1. **Harlow Carr Botanical Gardens**, *Crag Ln; tel: (01423) 565418.* Open daily 0930–1700 or dusk (Nov–Feb), 0930–1800 (Mar–Oct). Admission £3.20.

Out of Town

Lightwater Valley (theme park), *North Stainley, Ripon; tel: (01765) 635321.* Open Easter to Oct daily Jun–Aug, days and times vary rest of time. Admission £8.95. Five minutes from A1 on A6108 Masham to Leyburn road. There are many buses from Harrogate to Ripon and from Ripon there is a special bus service X36 that runs to the theme park in July and Aug.

Fountains Abbey and Studley Royal, *Ripon; tel: (01765) 608888.* Open daily 1000–1900 (Apr–Sep), 1000–1700 (Oct–Mar) Closed Fri Nov–Jan. Admission £4. Nine miles north west of Harrogate on B6252, off A61 near Ripon. West Yorkshire bus no. 806 runs on Sun and bank holidays in summer only. **Knaresborough Castle**, *Castle Grounds; tel: (01423) 5033410.* Open daily 1030–1730 (Easter and May–Sep). Admission £1. Regular train services from Harrogate, also bus nos 1, 2, 55, 55a, 56, 57 and H174 run a regular service.

Allerton Park, *Knaresborough; tel (01423) 330927.* Open Sun and BH Monday 1300-1700 (Easter–Sep). Admission £3. Located on A59, just off A1. Numerous bus services from Harrogate stop ¼ mile from house. **Mother Shipton's Cave and Petrifying Well**, *High Bridge, Knaresborough: tel: (01423) 864600.* Open daily 0930–1745 (Easter–Halloween), 1000-1645 (Halloween–Easter). Admission £3.95. Bus service from Harrogate every 10 minutes; alight at the caves.

Ripley Castle, *Ripley; tel: (01423) 770152.* Open, Castle and Garden Sat,Sun 1130–1630 (Apr,May,Oct), Thu–Sun 1130–1630 ((Jun,Sep), daily 1130–1630 (Jul, Aug). Gardens open all year. Admission house and gardens £3.75, gardens only £2.25. Situated 3½ miles from Harrogate. Bus nos 36, 36a and 36c run half-hourly to Ripley.

NEWCASTLE

A busy industrial city, Newcastle lies at the heart of a sprawling conurbation along the Tyne. It has more to offer than appears at first sight: its Norman castle, medieval quayside, fine 19th-century streets and squares and many museums plus the north-east's best shops repay at least a day's visit.

Tourist Information

Newcastle City and Tourist Information Service is based at *Central Library, Princess Square, Newcastle, Tyne & Wear NE99 1DX; tel: (0191) 2610691/2611405.* Open Mon, Thur 0930–2000, Tues, Wed, Fri 0930–1700, Sat 0900–1700; closed Bank Holiday Sats, Suns and Mons. Services offered: DP, SHS (latest 15 mins before closing), BABA (latest 30 mins before closing), GT. Theatre, tours, travel and events booked, YHA membership and Great British Heritage Pass sold. Busiest times of day for room bookings 1200–1400 (also *tel: (0191) 2611405*). Main guide and mini guide free. **Central Station TIC**, *Main Concourse, Central Station, Neville Street; tel: (0191) 2300050/ 2300030.* Open Mon–Sat 1000–2000, Sun 1000–1700 (June–Sept), Mon–Sat 1000–1700 (Oct–May). Services offered as above.

Arriving and Departing

Station

Central Station, *Neville St; tel: (0191) 2326262* is just ½ mile from the city centre, an easy walk, or take the Metro to *Monument.* The station has a TIC (see above), car hire (Hertz *tel: (0191) 2611052*) and taxi rank.

Buses

Arriving by bus you come in to the main coach station in the town centre: *Gallowgate; tel: (0191) 2616077.*

Ferries

North Sea ferry services arrive at the *International Ferry Terminal, Royal Quays,* 8 miles east of the town centre, with bus connections to and from Central Station for each sailing. For services to Bergen and Stavanger in Norway, **Colour Line** *tel: (0191) 296 1313.* For Esbjerg in Denmark, Hamburg in Germany and Gothenburg in Sweden, **Scandinavian Seaways** *tel: (0191) 2936262.*

Getting Around

Most attractions are within walking distance of the town centre, and town and transport maps are available from the TIC.

Newcastle and the surrounding area are very well served by public transport. Network Travel Tickets which cover the whole town's transport system are £3 for a Day Rover, £10.30 for an all-day weekly ticket.

Metro and Buses

There is an efficient Metro light rail system (underground in the centre) and four bus stations serving different companies that cover all areas. Most buses and the Metro run a reduced service in the evenings and on Suns, with last services between 1100 and 1130. General bus and Metro enquiries *tel: (0191) 2325325.*

Taxis

The main taxi rank is at Central Station, and it is also possible to hail black taxis in the street.

Staying in Newcastle

Accommodation

There are a reasonable number of hotels in the middle range, but not much in the way of b. & b. or pub accommodation. Cheaper accommodation is situated a couple of miles out of the town centre, in the suburbs of *Jesmond, Heaton, Fenham* and *Spital Tongues.* Accommodation is generally easy to find on arrival (during TIC opening hours) except during university graduation (July) and the Great North Run (Sept).

Hotel chains include *FC, Cp MC, Nv* and *Sw.* For budget accommodation there is **Newcastle Youth Hostel**, *Jesmond Rd; tel: (0191) 2812570.* Open 1700–1000 (Feb–Dec). Metro to *Jesmond* or bus 33.

The closest campsites are as follows: **Newcastle Racecourse Campsite**, *High Gosforth Park; tel: (0191) 2363258,* take bus 42, 43, 44 or 45 (5 miles north). **Lizard Lane Campsite**, *Marsden, South Shields; tel: (0191) 4544982.* Metro to *South Shields*, then bus 22 (10 miles south-east). **Sandhaven Campsite**, *Bents Park Road, South Shields; tel: (0191) 4545594.* Metro to *South Shields* (10 miles south-east).

Eating and Drinking

The TIC has an excellent *Eating Out* guide for £0.50, detailing Newcastle's wide range of eating places, with a good selection of vegetarian restaurants and more unusual international cuisine. Good areas are *Stowell St* (for Chinatown), *Bigg Market* and *Quayside*. Newcastle Brown Ale is a local speciality.

Communications

The main post office is at *Sidgate, Eldon Square*, open Mon–Fri 0900–1730, Sat 0900–1230; post restante facilities are available.

Entertainment and Events

Entertainment leaflets, *Paint it Red* (free) and *Two Fortnites* (£0.40) are available from the TIC and some other outlets. Newcastle has five theatres, the most important being the **Theatre Royal**, *Grey St; tel: (0191) 2322061,* which hosts the Royal Shakespeare Company in Feb and Mar.

City Hall, *Northumberland Rd; tel: (0191) 2612606* is the main venue for classical music, and there is an abundance of other live music of all sorts in the many, lively pubs and clubs (see the TIC's free *Nightlife* listing).

If you are visiting in June, don't miss **The Hoppings**, *Town Moor*, which is Europe's largest travelling fair – over a mile long (1 mile from the centre by bus or Metro).

The annual **Great North Run** in Sept is a half marathon from Newcastle to South Shields, claimed to be the biggest fun-run in Europe.

Shopping

Newcastle is a regional shopping centre for the north-east with **Eldon Square, Eldon Garden** and **Monument Mall** forming a large shopping area in the town centre, featuring many department stores and chain stores, specialist shops and boutiques. Easily accessible by bus or Metro to *Monument*. The most popular street market (of which there are a few) is **Quayside Market**, open every Sun 0930–1400. **Blackfriars Craft Centre**, *Monk St*, is a 13th-century Dominican friary with a working potter and a variety of locally produced goods.

Serious shoppers shouldn't miss the **Metro Centre** at Gateshead (frequent trains from Newcastle rail station, 7-min journey) said to be Europe's largest shopping mall.

Sightseeing

Many of Newcastle's oldest buildings are found near the river Quayside; **Sandhill** is the historic heart of the city, and **Bessie Surtees House** consists of two rare 16th- and 17th-century merchants' houses. From the top of the Norman **Castle Keep** (with 19th-century battlements) there are good views of the six bridges across the Tyne: the two most famous are Robert Stephenson's double-decker **High Level Bridge** (1849), for both rail and road, and the 1920s single-span **Tyne Bridge**, almost ½ mile long.

St Nicholas Cathedral has a delicate lantern tower of 1470; and *Grey St* and *Grainger St* show Victorian town planning at its best. For an introduction to the town, there are bus tours and guided walks (**City Guides**, *tel: (0191) 261 0691*, starting from Central Library and other points), and boat trips (**River Tyne Cruises**, *tel: (0191) 251 5920*, starting from *Quayside*).

Of the museums and galleries, the **Laing Art Gallery** has the north-east's main art collection, the **Museum of Antiquities** houses many finds from Hadrian's Wall, and **Newcastle Discovery** has a plethora of galleries aimed at families.

Away from Tyneside, the landscape is very rural. **Alnwick Castle** is a magnificent border fortress dating back to Norman times, with lavish Renaissance interiors; the stone soldiers on the battlements probably never fooled

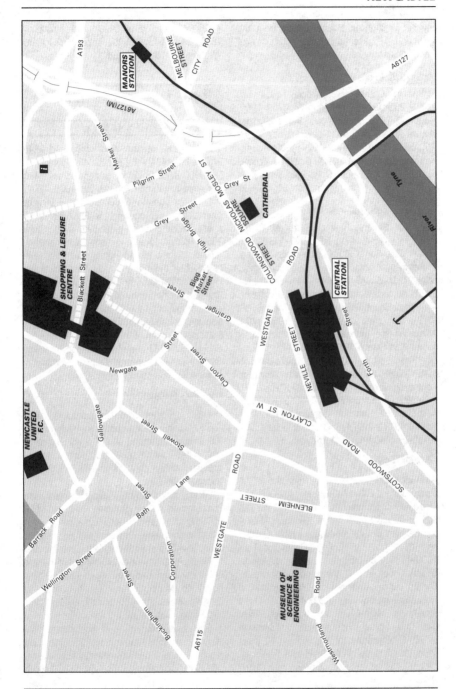

anyone. **Wallington House**, dating from the 17th and 18th centuries, has 100 acres of woodlands and lakes.

Historic Buildings

St Nicholas Cathedral, *St Nicholas Square; tel: (0191) 232 1939*. Open Mon–Fri 0700–1900, Sat 0800–1600, Sun various. **Bessie Surtees House**, *41–44 Sandhill, Quayside; tel: (0191) 2611585*. Open Mon–Fri 1000–1600. Admission free. **Castle Keep**, *Castle Garth, St Nicholas St; tel: (0191) 2327938*. Open Tues–Sun 0930–1730 (–1630 Oct–Mar). Admission £1.

Museums and Galleries

Laing Art Gallery, *Higham Place; tel: (0191) 2327734*. Open Mon–Fri 1000–1730, Sat 1000–1630, Sun 1430–1730. Admission free. **Museum of Antiquities**, *Newcastle University; tel: (0191) 2227844*. Open Mon–Sat 1000–1700. Admission free. **Newcastle Discovery**, *Blandford House, West Blandford Square; tel: (0191) 232 6789*. Open Mon–Sat 1000–1700. Admission free. **Newcastle United Museum**, *St James' Park; tel: (0191) 2328361*. Open Mon–Fri 1000–1600, Sat 1000–1400 (very busy on match days). Admission £1. **Trinity Maritime Centre**, *29 Broad Chare, Quayside; tel: (0191) 2614691*. Open Mon–Fri 1100–1515 (Apr–Oct). Admission £1. **Hancock Museum**, *Great North Rd; tel: (0191) 2227418*. Open Mon–Sat 1000–1700, Sun 1400–1700. Admission £1.

Out of Town

Alnwick Castle, *Alnwick; tel: (0665) 510777*. Open daily 1100–1700 Easter to Oct and weekends in summer. Admission £4. Take bus 501 or 505, 30 miles north. **Hadrian's Wall** – see Hexham p. 249. **Wallington Hall**, *Cambo; tel: (01670) 74283*. Open daily except Tues 1300–1730 (Apr–Oct) plus summer weekends. Grounds open all year. Weekend bus service to Cambo, 23 miles north-west. **Washington Old Hall**, *Washington; tel: (0191) 4166879*. Open Sun–Thurs 1100–1700, last admission 1630 (Apr–Oct); open Good Friday. Admission £2.20. Take bus X4 to Washington, 10 miles south. **Washington Wild Fowl and Wetlands Centre**, *District 15, Washington; tel: (0191)*

4165454. Open daily 0930–1730 (winter – 1630). Admission £3.40. Take bus X4 to Washington, 10 miles south.

 Side Track from Newcastle

HEXHAM

TIC: *Hallgate, Hexham, Northumberland NE46 1XD; tel: (01434) 605225/652348*. Open Mon–Sat 0900–1800 (mid-May to Sept, closes 1830 from mid-July to end August), Sun 1000–1700; rest of year Mon–Sat 0900–1700. SHS Services offered: local bed-booking and BABA (latest 15 mins before closing, particularly busy from 1500–1800), advance reservations handled, guided tours booked. Tickets sold for Newcastle Theatre Royal and local bus excursions. *Hadrian's Wall Country Holiday Guide* is £0.50 (free to postal enquiries) and includes an accommodation listing. For accommodation bookings *tel: (01434) 652348*.

Station: Hexham Station, *Station Rd; tel: (0191) 232 6262* is a short distance from the centre and has a taxi rank. Trains run frequently from Newcastle, taking about 30 mins.

Getting Around

The TIC has free town and transport maps. There is a bus service between Hexham and Haltwhistle connecting all the major Hadrian's Wall sites, which operates during school summer holidays only. Call the TIC for general transport enquiries.

Most bus services depart from the **Priestpopple Bus Station**, *tel: (01434) 602061*, and are operated by a number of different companies. National Express coaches connect with the Northumbria bus service 685 to Hexham via Newcastle (45 mins) and Carlisle (95 mins). Services run hourly to Carlisle, half-hourly to Newcastle and less frequently to outlying areas. There are no services after 1700 or on Suns.

The main taxi rank is at Priestpopple Bus Station, or you can contact the following registered taxi companies: **Bateys** *tel: (01434) 602500*; **Dodds** *tel: (01434) 603362*; **Acomb** *tel: (01434) 605068;* or **Henshaw Garage** at *Bardon Mill* for Hadrian's Wall Sites, *tel: (01434) 344272.*

Staying in Hexham

There is a small selection of hotels including one chain (*Sw*), a good number of b. & b. establishments on the edge of town, and pubs with rooms in the outlying villages (*Corbridge, Haydon Bridge, Slaley, Acomb* and *Allendale*). It is generally easy to find accommodation on arrival. The nearest youth hostel is **Acomb**, *Main St, Acomb; tel: (01434) 602864.* Take bus 880, 881 or 882, 2 miles from town centre. The nearest campsites are: **Riverside Leisure**, *Tyne Green Road; tel: (01434) 604705*, (½ mile north); **Hexham Race Course**, *High Yarridge; tel: (01434) 606847*, (2 miles south of town, bus to within 1 mile); **Heathergate Country Park**, *West Farm Cottage, Lowgate; tel: (01434) 602827*, take 688 bus (2 miles south-west).

Sightseeing

Hexham is a good base from which to explore the best bits of **Hadrian's Wall**: the 74-mile barrier which served as ancient Rome's northern frontier. **Housesteads Fort** is deservedly the most popular spot, for its dramatic ridge site, outstanding views across open moorland and the walk along the Wall to Steel Rigg. **Chesters** also has a beautiful site and a famous Roman bathhouse. Hexham itself is a small, attractive market town preserving many fine medieval buildings, including the 12th-century **Abbey**: very well preserved, it has some superb medieval wood carving.

Bus tours of the area are run by **Rochester and Marshall**, *tel: (01434) 600263*, and start from the bus station, price from £5.50. **Hexham Guild of Guides**, *tel: (01434) 605225*, conduct guided walks starting from the TIC, in return for a donation to the Guild. Bus tours and walks can be booked at the TIC. (The **Wright Brothers** bus service 888 (Newcastle–Hexham–Keswick) is also good for sightseeing.)

Border History Museum, *The Old Gaol*, near *The Marketplace; tel: (01434) 652349.* Open daily 1000–1630 (Easter–Oct), Sat–Tues 1000–1600 (Feb–Easter and Nov). Admission £1.30.

Hexham Abbey, *Beaumont St; tel: (01434) 602031.* Open daily 0900–1900 (May–Sept), 0900–1700 (Oct–Apr). Admission free.

Out of Town

Aydon Castle, *Corbridge; tel: (01434) 632450.* Open daily 1000–1800 (Apr–Sept). Admission £1.80. Train or bus 685 or 602 to Corbridge then 2-mile walk or taxi (6 miles east). **Cherryburn** (NT), *Mickley, Stocksfield; tel: (01661) 843276.* Open daily except Tues, 1300–1700 (Apr–Oct). Admission £2.50. Take bus 602 to *Mickley* (10 miles east). **Chesters Roman Fort** (EH), *Chollerford; tel: (01434) 681379.* Open daily 1000–1800 (Apr–Sept), 1000–1600 (Oct–Mar). Admission £2. Take bus 880 to *Chollerford* (5 miles north). (Mid-July to early Sept take 890 Hadrian's Wall Bus).

Corbridge Roman Site (EH), *Corbridge; tel: (01434) 632349.* Open daily 1000–1800 (Apr–Sept), Wed–Sun 1000–1600 (Oct–Mar). Admission £2. Take train or bus 602, 685 or 687 to *Corbridge* (3½ miles east). **Housesteads Roman Fort** (EH, NT), *Bardon Mill; tel: (01434) 344363.* Open daily 1000–1800 (Apr–Sept), 1000–1600 (Oct–Mar). Admission £2.20. Take train or 685 bus to *Bardon Mill*, then 3½-mile walk or taxi (12 miles north-west). (Mid-July to early Sept take 890 Hadrian's Wall Bus.)

Prudhoe Castle (EH), *Prudhoe; tel: (01661) 833459.* Open daily 1000–1800 (Apr–Sept), Tues–Sun 1000–1600 (Oct–Mar). Take train or bus 602 to *Prudhoe* (12 miles east). **Roman Army Museum**, *Carvoran, Greenhead; tel: (01697) 747485.* Open daily from 1000 – check seasonal variations in closing times (Mar–Oct), Sat, Sun 1000–1600 (Feb, Nov). Admission £2.50. Take 685 bus to *Greenhead*, then ½-mile walk (20 miles west). (In high season bus 602 from Haltwhistle and 890 Hadrian's Wall Bus.) **Vindolanda** (Roman fort and museum), *Chesterholm, Bardon Mill; tel: (01434) 344277.* Open daily from 1000 until 1600–1830 depending on season (Feb–Nov). Admission £3. Train or bus 685 to *Bardon Mill*, then 1½-mile walk or taxi (16 miles north-west). (In high season bus 602 from Haltwhistle and 890 Hadrian's Wall Bus.)

_ _

NEWCASTLE to EDINBURGH

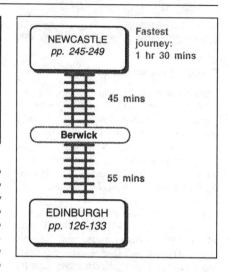

For much of its length this route between the unofficial capital of the north-east and the actual capital of Scotland follows the bleakly beautiful Northumberland coast, taking in the windswept isolation of Holy Island and the much fought-over border town of Berwick-on-Tweed, its ramparts a striking reminder that you are crossing what was once the front line between warring nations.

TRAINS

ETT tables: 570

→ Fast Track

One train each hour runs from Newcastle to Edinburgh, taking 1 hr 30 mins–1 hr 40 mins.

On Track

Newcastle–Berwick–Edinburgh

About half of the Newcastle–Edinburgh trains call at Berwick-upon-Tweed en route, giving an average service of one train every 2 hrs. Journey times from Newcastle to Berwick are 45 mins and from Berwick to Edinburgh 55 mins.

BERWICK-UPON-TWEED

TIC: *Castlegate Car Park, Berwick-upon-Tweed, Northumberland TD15 1JS; tel: (01289) 330733;* accommodation booking number (01289) 330733. Open Mon–Sat 0930–1900, Sun 1000–1800 (Easter–Oct); Mon–Sat 1000–1600 (Nov–Easter). DP Services offered: local bed-booking service (latest 30 mins before closing), BABA (latest 1 hr before closing), tickets booked for opera, boats, one-off

events. *Berwick Holiday Guide* £0.50. Free accommodation listing available.

Station: Berwick Station; *tel: (01289) 306771* is ½ mile north-west of the centre; it stands on the site of Berwick's castle.

Getting Around

A free town map is available from the TIC. All the in-town attractions are within easy walking distance of the centre.

Buses give good coverage in the town centre, but are rather patchy to outlying areas. **Northumbria Buses** *tel: (01289) 307283* and **Lowland Scottish** *tel: (01289) 307461* run local services from the central bus depot at *Marygate*, from which regional and national coach and bus services also operate. Taxis and car hire are both available; ask at the TIC for details.

Accommodation

Accommodation is easily available in and around Berwick, in all price categories. The nearest youth hostel is **Wooler YHA** (16 miles), *30 Cheviot St, Wooler; tel: (01668) 281365.* Take Northumbria bus 464 or 470 to Wooler (approximately 45 mins). The nearest campsite is **Marshall Meadow House Campsite**, *Marshall Meadows; tel: (01289) 307375.* Open Mar–Oct. Just a couple of miles outside Berwick; take the bus towards Edinburgh.

Sightseeing

Lying on the unspoilt Northumbrian coastline, this border town changed hands between England and Scotland 13 times before 1482. The **Elizabethan ramparts** encircling the old town – the first in Europe designed to incorporate cannon – are exceptionally well preserved, and the 2-mile walk round them is highly recommended; guided tours are available in summer. From **Meg's Mount** there is a splendid view of Berwick and the River Tweed, spanned here by the **Three Bridges** that include the 17th-century 15-arched bridge, and Stephenson's railway bridge (which you will already have crossed). **Berwick Barracks** is distinctive because it recreates what life was like in Britain's first purpose-built army barracks, designed by Vanbrugh in 1717.

Public transport access to outlying places is not straightforward in most instances; it might be worth hiring a car, so as not to miss out. Give priority to **Holy Island** (which can only be reached at low tide across a causeway; check tide times first!), where you can see **Lindisfarne Priory**, cradle of Christianity in northern England, and romantic and picturesque **Lindisfarne Castle**. Further south lies spectacularly sited **Bamburgh Castle**, while from nearby Seahouses you can take a boat trip to the windswept seabird and seal sanctuary on the **Farne Islands**. Still further south, the isolated shell of **Dunstanburgh Castle**, rising gently from its rocky promontory, resounds to the cries of seabirds.

Further attractions lie inland, the number of castles reflecting the constant threat to peace in the Border area in medieval times. **Chillingham Castle**, dating back to the 12th century, has been restored and includes an arms and armour collection, while the ruins of 14th-century **Etal Castle** lie near the site of the Battle of Flodden (1513); adjacent **Lady Waterford Hall** has beautiful 19th-century Biblical murals. **Paxton House**, a Palladian country mansion, is used as an outstation by the National Galleries of Scotland.

The **Barracks Museums and Art Gallery** (EH), *The Parade; tel: (01289) 304493/330044/* 307426. Open Tues–Sun 1000–1600 (Oct–Mar), daily 1000–1800 (Apr-Sept). Admission £2.20. **Cell Block Museum and Town Hall**, *Marygate; tel: (0289) 330900.* Open for tours twice daily, Mon–Fri. Admission £1. **Wine and Spirit Museum,** *Palace Green; tel: (01289) 305153.* Open daily 0900–1700. Admission free.

Out of Town

Paxton House, *just outside Paxton Village; tel: (01289) 386291.* Open daily Good Friday to end Oct, house 1200–1700, grounds 1000–sunset. Admission £3.50 to house, £1.50 to grounds. Take bus from Berwick to *Paxton*, and ask to be dropped off at turning for Paxton House, then 1 mile's walk. **Etal Castle** (EH), *Etal; tel: (01890) 820332.* Open daily 1000–1800 (Apr–Oct). Admission £2. Take the 267 bus from Berwick to *Wooler* via *Millfield*, 12 miles south west of Berwick. See also nearby **Ford** estate, for **Lady Waterford Hall,** *tel: (01890) 820524.*

Lindisfarne Priory (EH), *Holy Island; tel: (01289) 89200.* Open daily 1000–1800 (Apr–Oct), daily 1000–1600 (Nov–Mar) (subject to tide times; check tables at TIC or property). Admission £2.20. Take bus 477 from Berwick. Fourteen miles south east. **Lindisfarne Castle** (NT), *Holy Island; tel: (01289) 89244.* Open daily except Fri, 1300–1730. Admission £3.40. Travel details as for Priory, above. **Bamburgh Castle,** *Bamburgh; tel: (01668) 214208.* Open daily 1100–1700 (Easter–Oct) – times do vary, so check before going. Admission £2.50. Take a bus from Berwick. Approximately 20 miles south east. **Farne Islands** (NT); *tel: (01665) 721099.* Open Easter–Oct. Accessible by boat tour from Seahouses harbour. Tours can be booked at the harbour, price £5. Takes 1 hour by 501 bus from Berwick, change at *Belford*. **Chillingham Castle,** *Chillingham; tel: (01668) 5359.* Open daily except Tues 1330–1700 (May–Sept). Admission £3.30. Bus 510 to *Chillingham* is a Sun service only. **Dunstanburgh Castle** (EH), *tel: (01665) 576231.* Open daily 1000–1800 (Apr–Oct), 1000–1600 (Nov–Mar). Admission £1.25. Take bus 401 from Berwick to *Craster*, then 1½-mile walk. Approximately 35 miles south-east of Berwick.

Berwick-Upon-Tweed

NORWICH

Norwich is a beautiful and ancient city with a proud tradition of independence. From St James Hill, above the city on Mousehold Heath, the buildings of old Norwich can be seen clustered around the cathedral within the circle of the city walls and the river. The streets, alleys and many medieval churches illustrate the long-standing prosperity of Norwich. The city is also an ideal touring centre for the Norfolk countryside.

Tourist Information

TIC: The Guildhall, Gaol Hill, Norwich, Norfolk NR2 1NF; tel: (01603) 666071; after-hours tel: (01603) 761082. Open Jun–Sep Mon–Sat 0930–1800, Oct–May Mon–Sat 0930–1730. Services offered: local bed-booking service and BABA. The guide Norwich and the Norfolk Countryside is available free and includes accommodation listings.

Arriving and Departing

Thorpe Station Thorpe Road; tel: (01603) 632055 is 1 mile south-east of the city centre and has a taxi rank. There is a bus into the centre departing from the stops on the hill to the right of the entrance every few minutes (less frequently at night and on Sundays).

Getting Around

The majority of the city's attractions are within walking distance of the town centre, except for the **Sainsbury Centre**. A free route map for local bus services is available at the TIC, Bus Station, Norfolk Bus Information Centre and libraries. At the TIC you can also buy a more detailed Routefinder Map of the main attractions and the surrounding area (price £1.80).

Buses

The majority of services in and around the city are operated by **Eastern Counties** from the

Central Bus Station, Surrey St; tel: (01603) 761212. Additional services, particularly outside the city centre, are operated by a number of other companies. Information on all of the city's bus services can be obtained from the **Norfolk Bus Information Centre**, Advice Arcade, 4 Guildhall Hill; tel: (01603) 613613, open Mon–Fri 0900–1700. Most routes are well covered during the day but operate less frequently during the evenings and on Sun. Saver tickets include the Evening and Sunday Rover ticket, which can be used on all buses, and the Centrerider, Citywide and Sixer tickets, which can be used on evening and weekend Eastern Counties services.

Taxis

The main taxi ranks are at Guildhall Hill and Thorpe Station.

Staying in Norwich

Accommodation

Norwich has a good range of accommodation of all types located throughout the city and its outlying areas. There are several cheaper hotels in the city centre and a wide choice of b. & b. establishments, most of which are on the outskirts. A number of farmhouses offer accommodation in the surrounding countryside. For budget accommodation: **Norwich Youth Hostel**, Turner Rd; tel: (01603) 627647, on bus route 19 (daytime); **YMCA**, 48 St Giles St; tel: (01603) 620269 and **YWCA**, 61 Bethel St; tel: (01603) 622059, both in the city centre. The closest camping site is on Martineau Lane, Lakenham; tel: (01603) 620060 on bus routes 9, 28 and 31 (daytime); 32 and 59 (Evenings and Sun).

Eating and Drinking

There is a wide selection of eating establishments in all price ranges in the city centre and the majority of establishments offer a choice of vegetarian dishes.

Communications

The main post office is on Davey Place, and has a post restante facility. Open 0900–1730.

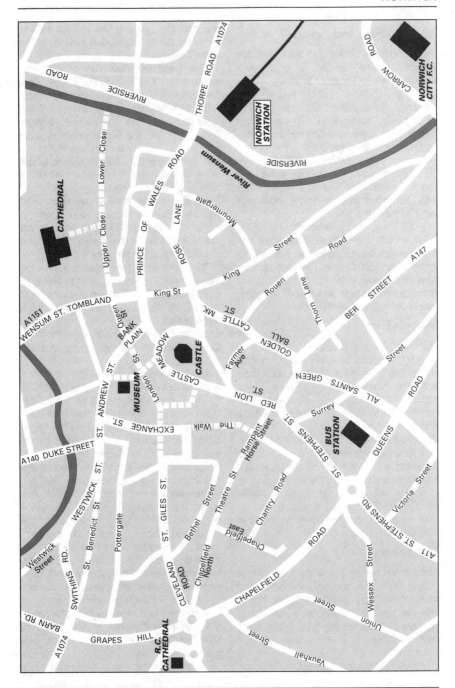

Entertainment and Events

Theatres in Norwich include: **Maddermarket Theatre,** *St Johns Alley; tel: (01603) 629921;* **Norwich Puppet Theatre,** *St James, White-friars; tel: (01603) 629921;* **Sewell Barn Theatre,** *Constitution Hill; tel: (01603) 617991* and **Theatre Royal.** *Theatre St; tel: (01603) 630000.* **Norwich City Football Club** is on *Carrow Rd; tel: (01603) 612131.*

Norwich has a number of nightclubs and discos, mostly located in the city centre, with two in *Tombland* and two on *Prince of Wales Rd;* it also offers four arts centres and a wide range of leisure facilities.

Major annual events in Norwich include the **Royal Norfolk Agricultural Show,** *Royal Norfolk Showground, Costessey, Norwich* on bus routes 19 and 20 in June; **The Lord Mayor's Street Procession,** in the city centre in July and **Norwich Arts Festival,** *St Andrew's and Blackfriar's Hall, George Street* in October.

Shopping

The main shopping streets in Norwich are *St Benedict* for specialist clothes and furniture stores; *Elm Hill* and *Tombland* for craft shops, bookshops and jewellers; *St Giles St* for antiques and bookshops; *Bridewell Alley,* home to the **Mustard Shop** (the condiment is a traditional Norwich product); *London St* for clothes and jewellers shops; *Castle Mall,* a 7-acre site adjacent to **Norwich Castle,** with over 75 shops, and *Magdalene St,* the oldest and longest shopping street in the city.

A large open-air market is held in *Market Place* (adjacent to the TIC) on Mon–Sat, with a wide variety of stalls selling everything from books to cheese, tea and coffee.

Sightseeing

Norwich was already at important town at the time of the Norman conquest, and during most of the Middle Ages rivalled London and York in size and wealth. This has left a heritage of medieval buildings, including the cathedral, the castle and over 30 fine churches, which is unequalled by any British city.

Norwich Cathedral, founded in 1069, has fine decorated work in the cloisters (1297–1430) and carved 15th–century choir stalls; the Visitor Centre has audio-visual displays.

The Riverside Walk, along the River Wensum to Carrow Bridge, passes **Cow Tower,** formerly a river tollhouse and prison, **Pulls Ferry,** the 15th-century watergate to the Cathedral Close, and the medieval **Bishops Bridge.** Elm Hill is a winding cobbled street with antique and craft shops, leading to the area next to the cathedral, **Tombland,** whose name has nothing to do with graves but comes from an old word for market.

Norwich Castle provides an example of Norman military architecture second only to the Tower of London. The **Castle Museum** has one of the country's finest regional collections of natural history, archaeology and art.

The church of **St Peter Mancroft,** near the market place, was founded in 1430 and is an exceptionally beautiful and imposing example of Perpendicular Gothic style. Facing the church is the **Guildhall,** dating from the same period, which was the seat of the city's council until the **City Hall,** now dominating the market place, was built in 1938.

Guided walking tours around historic Norwich can be booked at TIC, and last about 1½ hrs. Tours depart from the TIC on Sat at 1430 (Apr–Oct); Mon–Sat 1430, Sun and Bank Holidays 1030 (June–Sept) plus Mon–Sat at 1030 (Aug). Cost: £1.80. An after dark tour by foot or by coach of Floodlit Norwich is also available from the TIC. Individual **Blue Badge Guides** can be arranged through the TIC.

The **Sainsbury Centre for Visual Arts** houses the remarkable Sainsbury Collection in the superb building designed by Sir Norman Foster and Partners. Over 1000 paintings, sculptures and ceramics are on display.

Some 15 miles north of the city is **Blickling Hall,** a magnificent 17th-century red brick house with superb State Rooms, beautiful garden and its own inn, The Buckinghamshire Arms.

A different kind of nostalgia is provided by the daily musical recitals at **The Thursford Collection,** near Fakenham, featuring nine giant fairground organs.

To the north and east of the city lies a long

and varied coastline of saltmarshes, cliffs and wide sandy beaches. One of the main attractions near Norwich is the **Norfolk Broads**, 200 miles of lakes and waterways created by medieval peat and turf digging, now providing a haven for wildlife as well as a popular venue for cruises.

Historic Buildings

Norwich Cathedral, *Cathedral Close; tel: (01603) 764385/767617.* Open Mon–Sun 0730–1800 (Mid-Sept to Mid-May), Mon–Sun 0730–1900 (Mid-May to Mid-Sept). Admission free. **St Peter Mancroft Church,** *St Peters St; tel: (01603) 610443* Open daily 1000–1630. Admission free. **Dragon Hall,** *115–123 King St; tel: (01603) 663922* Open Mon–Sat 1000–1600 (Apr–Oct); Mon–Fri 1000–1600 (Nov-Mar). Admission £1. **Guildhall,** *TIC, Gaol Hill.* See TIC details for opening times.

Art Galleries and Museums

Assembly House, *Theatre St; tel: (01603) 626402* Open Mon–Sat 1000–2200. Admission free. **Norwich Gallery,** *Norwich School of Art and Design, St George's St; tel: (01603) 610561* Open Mon–Fri 1000–1800, Sat 1000–1800 for exhibitions only. Admission free. **Sainsbury Centre for Visual Arts,** *University of East Anglia, Watton Rd; tel: (01603) 56060.* Tue–Sun 1200–1700 (closed during university's Christmas break). Admission £1. 3 miles west of the city centre on Bus Routes 12, 14, 23, 26, and 27 (Mon–Sat); 33 and 34 (Sun). **Bridewell Museum,** *Bridewell Alley; tel: (01603)667231.* Open Mon–Sat 1000–1700. Admission £1.40 (joint ticket gives admission over two days to Bridewell, Strangers Hall, Regimental and St Peter Hungate museums). **Royal Norfolk Regimental Museum,** *Old Shire Hall, Castle Meadow; tel: (01603) 223649.* Open Mon–Sat 1000–1700. Admission: see Bridewell and Castle Museums. **St Peter Hungate Church Museum and Brass Rubbing Centre,** *Princes St; tel: (01603) 667231.* Open Mon–Sat 1000–1700. Admission £0.50 or joint ticket – see Bridewell Museum. **Strangers Hall Museum of Domestic Life** *Charing Cross; tel: (01603) 667229.* Open Mon–Sat 1000–1700. Admis-

sion: see Bridewell Museum. **Castle Museum,** *Castle Meadow; tel: (01603) 223624.* Open Mon–Sat 1000–1700, Sun 1400–1700. Admission £2.20 (includes Regimental Museum). Battlement and Dungeon Tours are £1.50 – *tel: (01603) 223628* to book. **John Jarrold Printing Museum,** *Whitefriars.* Open Mon–Sun 1000–1200 and 1400–1600 (July–Sept). Admission free. **The Mustard Shop Museum,** *Bridewell Alley; tel: (01603) 627889.* Open Mon–Sat 0930–1700. Admission free.

Parks and Gardens

Castle Gardens, *Castle Meadow.* **Chapel Field Gardens,** *Chapel Field Rd* (city centre gardens). **City Hall Gardens,** *St Peters St* (War Memorial Gardens). **Elm Hill Riverside Gardens,** *Elm Hill.* **Ketts Heights** (wildlife haven). Entrances in *Ketts Hill* and *Gas Hill;* take bus route 31 from city centre, 30 to city centre.

Out of Town

Blickling Hall, (NT) *Blickling; tel: (01263) 733084.* Hall open Tues–Wed and Fri–Sun and Bank Holidays 1300–1700 (Apr–Oct). Garden open Tues–Wed and Fri–Sun and Bank Holidays 1200–1700 (Apr–Oct); daily 1200–1700 (Jul–Aug). Hall and garden admission: £4.90, Sun and Bank Holidays £5.50; Garden: £2.50. 15 miles north of Norwich on Eastern Counties Bus Routes 751 and 753 (very limited service). **Pensthorpe Waterfowl Park,** *Fakenham; tel: (01328) 851465* Open Sat–Sun 1100–1700 (Jan to mid-Mar); Mon–Sun 1100–1700 (mid-Mar to Dec). 1 mile from Fakenham by Eastern Counties Bus no. 450 or 454. **The Thursford Collection,** *Thursford, Fakenham; tel: (01328) 878477* Open Mon–Sun, Apr–Oct; times vary, so check for details). 1 mile off A148, Eastern Counties Bus no. 450 or 454.

Norfolk Broads boat trips of 1–3 hrs are run by **Southern River Steamers** (*tel: 01603 624051*) and depart daily from *Elm Hill Quay* at 1100 for the River Yare and 1415 for the Norfolk Broads (Easter to Sept), or 15 mins later from *Thorpe Station Quay.* **Broad Tours Ltd** in Wroxham, *tel: (01603) 782207,* offer Broads cruises and boat hire; take Eastern Counties bus no 51, 55, 717 or 724 to Wroxham.

NOTTINGHAM

Best known as the (real or mythical) home of Robin Hood, Friar Tuck and Maid Marian, Nottingham was also once the centre of a thriving lace industry. It has a lively and cosmopolitan atmosphere, many good museums, and plenty to see in the surrounding area.*

Tourist Information

TIC: *14 Smithy Row, Nottingham NG1 2BY; tel: (0115) 947 0661/935 0730*. Open Mon–Fri 0830–1700, Sat 0900–1700, Sun 1000–1600 (Apr–Sept); closed Sun (Oct–Mar). DP SHS Services offered: local bed-booking service (latest 30 mins before closing), BABA (latest 1 hour before closing). Guided tours booked, tickets sold for local theatre and concerts. The *Robin Hood Country Holiday Guide* and an accommodation guide are available free.

Arriving and Departing

Station: Nottingham Midland Station, *Carrington St; tel: (01332) 32051*, is just ¼ mile south of the centre, and has a taxi rank. Buses to the town centre pass the station every few minutes but take longer than the walking time due to traffic congestion.

Getting Around

Apart from **Wollaton Hall** and **Green's Mill**, attractions are within easy walking distance of the centre. Free town and transport maps are available from the TIC. There is good public transport within the city and to most nearby towns, but a much less frequent service to outlying villages. Services are reduced after 1815 and on Sun. For general transport enquiries contact **Nottingham City Transport**, *tel: (0115) 950 3665*, or the **Busline**, *tel: (0115) 924 0000*.

Most local buses are operated by **Trent**

Buses *tel: (0115) 924 0000* and **Bartons Buses** *tel: (0115) 924 0000* or *(01332) 292200* from the city centre. A Dayrider daily ticket covers all services for £2.

The main taxi ranks are on *Market Sq.*, and at *the Victoria Centre* and *Midland Station*. Black and white **Streamline** taxis can be hailed in the street.

Staying in Nottingham

There is a good range of hotels and guest-houses, with most of the cheaper accommodation located in the suburbs of *West Bridgford* (2–3 miles south-east) and *Beeston* (4–5 miles west). It is generally easy to book on arrival, except during the **Nottingham Goose Fair** in Oct. Hotel chains in Nottingham include *FC, Ho, MC, MH, St*. For budget accommodation, there is the **YMCA**, *4 Shakespeare St; tel: (0115) 947 3068*, open 0800–2200 and **Nottingham Igloo**, *110 Mansfield Rd; tel: (0115) 947 5250*, open 0800–1000 and 1600–2400 (take bus 70, 72 or 73 from *Queen St* or 15, 16, 17, 18, 19, 88 or 89 from *Trinity Sq*). The closest campsite is **Holmepierrepont Caravan and Camping Park**, *Adbolton La, Holmepierrepont; tel: (0115) 982 1212*, take city bus 85 from *Market Sq*, 3 miles south.

Sightseeing

Nottingham Castle (not Prince John's home, but a mainly 17th-century rebuild) was where Charles I raised his standard at the start of the Civil War; the **Castle Museum** within tells the town's story. At the foot of the sandstone rock upon which the castle stands is one of the most plausible of the contenders for the title of oldest pub in England, the **Trip to Jerusalem**. Several museums focus on the lace and textile industries, notably the **Lace Hall**, which has working machinery and audiovisual demonstrations to explain the making of Nottingham lace; and the **Museum of Costume and Textiles**, which displays costumes from the 1730s to the 1960s in period room settings. Other museums include **Brewhouse Yard Museum**, which depicts Nottingham life in post-medieval times, and the **Canal Museum**, which uses dioramas, models and audiovisual programmes to relate the history of the River Trent. **Tales of Robin Hood** takes visitors in adventure cars on a search for the legendary hero, while **Green's Mill** is a working tower mill. You will be hard pressed to spot a goose at the annual **Goose Fair** in Oct, which is now a bumper fun-fair with both traditional and modern rides and sideshows.

For the literary, poetic memorabilia are preserved at **Newstead Abbey**, the suitably romantic ancestral home of Lord Byron, and the **D.H. Lawrence Birthplace Museum**, a humble Victorian terrace in the Nottinghamshire coalfield, gives an insight into the novelist's early childhood. North of the city, **Sherwood Forest Country Park** comprises the small remnant of what was once a great forest, including the ancient and massive **Major Oak**. **Southwell Minster**, east of Nottingham, is one of the most beautiful Norman churches in the country.

Robin Hood bus tours *tel: (0115) 962 2312* leave from Nottingham Castle at 1330 on Wed, Thur and Sat, price £15. There are guided walking tours of the town on Sat at 1400 (June–Sept), or contact the **Blue Badge Guides** *tel: (0115) 987 1961*. For details of tours of Nottingham's network of caves and tunnels, contact the TIC.

Brewhouse Yard Museum, *Castle Boulevard; tel: (0115) 948 3504 ext. 3600*. Open daily 1000–1700. Admission: Mon–Fri free, Sat, Sun and Bank Holidays £1. **Canal Museum**, *Canal St; tel: (0115) 959 8835*. Open Wed–Sat 1000–1200 and 1300–1745, Sun 1300–1745 (Apr–Sept); Wed, Thur, Sat 1000–1200 and 1300–1645, Sun 1300–1645 (Oct–Mar). Admission: free. **Green's Mill and Science Centre**, *Windmill Lane; tel: (0115) 950 3635*. Open Wed–Sun and Bank Holiday Mons 1000–1700. Admission: free. **The Lace Hall**, *High Pavement; tel: (0115) 948 4221*. Open daily 1000–1700. Admission: £2.75. **Museum of Costume and Textiles**, *51 Castle Gate; tel: (0115) 948 3504*. Open 1000–1745 (Apr–Sept), 1000–1645 (Oct–Mar). Admission: free.

Nottingham Castle and Gardens, *Castle Rd; tel: (0115) 948 3504*. Open daily 1000–1700. Admission: Mon–Fri free, Sat, Sun and Bank Holidays £1. **The Tales of Robin Hood** (themed museum), *3038 Maid Marion Way; tel: (0115) 948 3284*. Open daily 1000–1630 (Easter–Oct), 1000–1530 (Nov–Easter). Admission: £4.25.

Wollaton Hall, Park and Natural History Museum (3 miles west), *Wollaton; tel: (0115) 928 1333*. Open Mon–Sat 1000–1700, Sun 1300–1700 (Apr–Sept); Mon–Sat 1000–1630, Sun 1330–1630 (Oct–Mar). Park open 0800–dusk. Admission: Mon–Fri free, Sat, Sun and Bank Holidays £1. Take bus 35, 36, 37 or 38 from *Friar Lane*, or 11, 11a, 11b, 11x or 25 from *Upper Parliament St*.

Out of Town

Belvoir Castle, near *Grantham, Leicestershire; tel: (01476) 870262*. Open Tues–Thur and Sat 1100–1700, Sun and Bank Holidays 1100–1800 (Apr–Sept). Admission: £4. Take Sherwood Forest Bus Service 240 (Sun only, mid-May to mid-Sept). Approximately 20 miles south-east. **D.H. Lawrence Birthplace Museum**, *8a Victoria St, Eastwood; tel: (01773) 763312*. Open daily 1000–1700 (Apr–Oct), 1000–1600 (Nov–Mar). Take Trent bus R11, R12 or R13 from Victoria Bus Station to *Eastwood*, 8 miles north-west. **Holme Pierrepont Hall**, *Holme Pierrepont; tel: (0115) 933 2371*. Open 1400–1730, Sun (June), Thur and Sun (July), Tues, Thur, Fri Sun (August) and Easter, spring and summer Bank Holidays, Sun–Tues, 1400–1800. Admission: £2.75. Take city bus 85 from *Market Sq* to *Holme Pierrepont*, then ½-mile walk. Five miles south-east. **Newstead Abbey**, *Linby; tel: (01632) 793557*. Grounds open daily dawn–dusk. House open daily 1200–1700 (Apr–Sept), last entry 1600. Admission: £3.50 (gardens only, £1.60). Take bus 63 or X2 from Victoria Bus Station to *Ravenshead*, 8 miles north. **Sherwood Forest Country Park and Visitor Centre**, *Edwinstowe, near Mansfield; tel: (01623) 823202*. Park open daily, dawn–dusk. Visitor Centre open daily 1030–1600 (winter), 1030–1700 (summer). Take bus 33 from Victoria Bus Station to *Edwinstowe*, 20 miles north. **Southwell Minster**, *Bishop's Drive, Southwell; tel: (01636) 812649*. Open daily 0800–1900 (summer), 0800–dusk (winter). Admission: free. Take Barton's Pathfinder bus S1S from *South Parade* to Southwell, 14 miles north-east.

NOTTINGHAM to SCARBOROUGH

This route takes you through the rural heart of Lincolnshire, via the historic cathedral city of Lincoln, to Humberside and, beyond, to Scarborough, England's oldest seaside resort.

TRAINS

ETT table: 585, 520, 551, 574, 569, 565, 566

 Fast Track

No through service exists between Nottingham and Scarborough. The fastest route is via Sheffield and York, with a change of train needed in both cities. By this route the journey takes about 4 hrs.

 On Track

Nottingham–Lincoln

An hourly service links Nottingham to Lincoln Central, trains taking around 1 hr. Sunday service is summer only, less frequent and does not start until mid-afternoon.

Lincoln–Hull

The journey from Lincoln to Hull involves a change of train at Doncaster. There are nine trains a day (no service on Sun) between Lincoln and Doncaster (taking 50 mins) and an hourly service (much reduced on Suns) between Doncaster and Hull, taking 1 hr.

Hull–Beverley

Two trains an hour (very few on Suns) operate between Hull and Beverley, taking 12 mins for the journey.

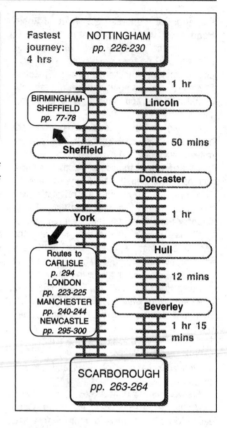

Beverley–Scarborough

The service between Beverley and Scarborough takes 1 hr 15 mins (trains every 1½–2 hours). Only six trains run on summer Suns, none in winter.

LINCOLN

TIC: *9 Castle Hill, Lincoln LN1 3AA; tel: (01522) 529828/564506.* Open Mon–Thur 0900–1730, Fri 0900–1700, Sat, Sun and Bank Holiday Mons 1000–1700. SHS Services offered: local bed-booking service (latest 15 mins before closing), BABA (latest 30 mins before closing). Guided tours booked and tickets sold for local events and concerts. *Lincoln Official Guide* costs £1.80, and the *Lincoln: Where to Stay* guide is free.

Station: Lincoln Central Station, *St Mary's St; tel: (01302) 340222*, is central and has a taxi rank.

Getting Around

Lincoln's attractions are within walking distance of the town centre, and free town and transport maps are available from the TIC. For general transport enquiries *tel: (01522) 553134*, for bus and train times *tel: (01522) 553135*.

The main operator of local services is **Lincoln City Transport/Lincolnshire Roadcar Company** *tel: (01522) 532424*. A **Day Out** ticket covering all their routes costs £3.70. Most services start from **City Bus Station**, *Broadgate*, and coverage is good in the town centre and to nearby villages and larger towns, but rather patchy to smaller villages. Reduced services operate on Suns and Bank Holidays.

The main taxi rank is outside the station; taxis can be hailed in the street.

Staying in Lincoln

There is a good selection of hotels and b. & b. and guest-house accommodation in the town. Cheaper places can be found in the centre, in the *South Park* area (1 mile south) and in the suburb of *North Hykeham* (about 3 miles south). It is usually easy to book on arrival, except during the **Lincolnshire Show** in June, **Lincoln Christmas Market** around the second week in Dec, and over the May and Aug Bank Holidays. Hotel chains in Lincoln include *FP* and *Ma*.

For budget accommodation there is **Lincoln Youth Hostel**, *South Park; tel: (01522) 522076*, open from 1700; **Lincoln YMCA**, *St Rumbold St; tel: (01522) 511811*, open all day and **Bishop Grosseteste College**, *Newport; tel: (01522) 527347*, for accommodation in the Easter and summer holidays. The closest campsites are: **Hartsholme Country Park** (3½ miles south-west), *Skellingthorpe Rd; tel: (01522) 686264*, take bus 29; and **Shortferry Caravan Park** (6 miles east), *Ferry Rd, Fiskerton; tel: (01526) 398021*, take bus 15.

The TIC can provide a free list of local restaurants. The biggest concentration of restaurants, and also the most expensive, are in the *Uphill* area, near the Cathedral and the Castle. There is a good range of cheaper eating places in the centre. Local specialities are Lincolnshire sausage, stuffed chine (ham stuffed with parsley), plum bread and haslet.

The main post office is on *Guildhall St*, open Mon–Fri 0900–1730, Sat 0900–1230 (offers post restante facilities).

Entertainment and Events

The monthly publication *Splash*, which gives details of what's on, costs £1 from newsagents or the TIC. Details are also given in local papers.

For drama, there is the **Theatre Royal**, *Clasketgate; tel: (01522) 525555*. For concerts there is **The Lawn**, *Union Rd; tel: (01522) 560330*, which is the venue used by the **East of England Orchestra**, and **Lincoln Cathedral**, *tel: (01522) 544544*. Some pubs have live music and there is a nightclub, **Ritzy 1 & 2** on *Silver St*.

A free annual events list is available from the TIC. The **Lincolnshire Show** takes place annually in the third week of June at the *Lincolnshire Showground*. Admission is £6, and it is essential to pre-book accommodation during this event. **Lincoln Christmas Market** takes place annually around the second week in Dec, in the *Uphill* area. The **Lincoln Mystery Plays** take place in the Cathedral in Aug.

Shopping

The main shopping centre is the **Waterside Centre** in the lower city. *Bailgate* in the upper city, around the Cathedral, is another shopping area, particularly aimed at tourists. *Steep Hill*, which joins the upper and lower areas, has a range of antiques and collectors' shops, craft centres and second-hand book shops. There is a general market from Mon–Sat: **Lincoln Central Market**, *Market Area, Sincil St*.

Sightseeing

Lincoln was developed by the Romans as *Lindum Colonia*, to command the meeting of their military roads Ermine St and Fosse Way, and later became the centre of the largest and wealthiest bishopric in England. The focal point of Lincoln is still the **Cathedral**: its triple towers stand out for miles around, drawing the eye from the vast Lincolnshire skies. One of the

Lincoln   **259**

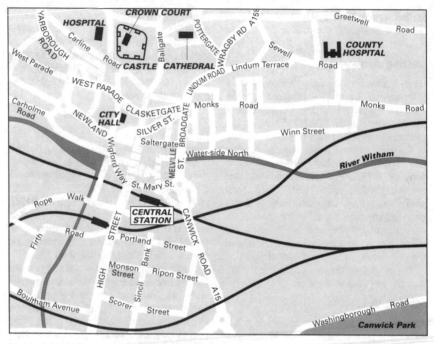

finest Gothic buildings in Europe, it lives up to all expectations, from the carved angels on the breathtaking west front to the elaborate decoration of the Angel Choir – look for the carving of the infamous Lincoln Imp amongst the angels.

The cathedral crowns the old city, which is tightly packed on the end of a high plateau above the River Witham; its steep cobbled streets deserve a day's exploration. Below the cathedral lie the ruins of the medieval **Bishop's Palace**, and around the rest of *Minster Yard* are attractive medieval and Georgian houses. Across from the west façade of the cathedral beyond *Exchequergate* is the much restored but extensive Norman **castle**. Head down the unimaginatively but accurately named *Steep Hill* to see **Jew's House and Court**, among the best surviving examples of medieval domestic architecture (c.1170).

Below the hill the city is unremarkable, but a range of museums are worth seeking out, including the **Museum of Lincoln Life**, the region's largest museum of social history, and

the attractions of the **Lawns** complex, which has pleasant grounds in which to stroll or picnic. There are also substantial remains of the Roman settlement.

The many country houses in the surrounding area testify to its agricultural wealth. **Dodding-ton Hall** is a mellow Elizabethan manor house, with lovely walled rose gardens and fascinating Georgian interiors; further afield, the more formal **Belton House** (1684–88) has acres of parkland and splendid furnishings and decoration throughout.

Lincoln City Tours *tel: (01522) 522255*, with live commentary by a Blue Badge guide, run daily from May–Sept (also Sat, Sun and Bank Holidays during Apr and Oct), departing from the Cathedral West Door every hour on the hour from 1000–1500. Tickets cost £3 and are valid all day, so you can leave and rejoin the tour at any time. **Cathedral City Cruises** *tel: (01522) 546853* offer boat tours from *Brayford Pool* (Apr–Sept); tickets £3. There are also daily guided walks starting from the TIC throughout July and Aug, price £1.

Lincoln Cathedral, *Minster Yard; tel: (01522) 544544.* Open from 0740–1800 (– 1600 Sun). Suggested entry donation £2.50. Lincoln Castle, *Castle Hill; tel: (01522) 511068.* Open Mon–Sat 0930–1730, Sun 1130–1730 (closes 1600 in winter). Admission £2. Bishop's Old Palace (EH), *Minster Yard; tel: (01522) 527468.* Open daily 1000–1800 (Apr–Sept). Admission £0.85. Ellis's Windmill, *Mill Rd.* Open every weekend in summer, every second and fourth weekend of the month in winter, 1400–dusk. Admission £0.70. Hartsholme Country Park and Swanholme Lakes (3½ miles south-west), *Skellingthorpe Rd; tel: (01522) 686264.* Open at all times. Admission free. Take bus 29. Incredibly Fantastic Old Toy Show, *26 Westgate; tel: (01522) 520534.* Open Tues–Sat 1100–1700, Suns and Bank Holiday Mons 1200–1600 (Easter–Oct), weekends and school holidays 1100–1700 (Oct–Christmas). Admission £1.50.

Jew's House and Court, *The Strait; tel: (01522) 521337.* (Viewing from outside only.) The Lawn (Visitor and Conference Centre), including Sir Joseph Banks Conservatory and Aquarium, Charlesworth Centre. Museum of Lincolnshire Life, *Burton Rd; tel: (01522) 528448.* Open Mon–Sat 1000–1730; Sun 1000–1730 (summer), 1400–1730 (winter). Admission £1. National Cycle Museum, *The Lawn, Union Rd; tel: (01522) 545091.* Open daily 1000–1700. Admission £1. Stonebow and Guildhall, *High St; tel: (01522) 564507.* Open first Sat of each month, 1000–1200 and 1400–1630 or by appointment. Admission free. Usher Art Gallery, *Lindum Rd; tel: (01522) 527980.* Open Mon–Sat 1000–1730, Sun 1430–1700. Admission £0.80.

Out of Town

Battle of Britain Memorial Flight Museum, *RAF Coningsby, Coningsby; tel: (01526) 344041.* Open Mon–Fri 1000–1630. Admission £3. Take bus 502 to *Coningsby,* 26 miles south-east. Belton House (NT), *Belton, near Grantham; tel: (01476) 66116.* Open Wed–Sun and Bank Holiday Mons 1300–1730 (Apr–Oct), last admission 1700. Gardens open 1100. Admission £4.30. Take bus 601 to *Belton,* 25 miles

south. Doddington Hall, *Doddington; tel: (01522) 694308.* Open Sun, Wed and Bank Holiday Mons 1400–1800 (May–July and Sept), Sun–Fri 1400–1800 (Aug). Admission £3.50. Take bus BD1 to *Doddington,* 4 miles southwest. Gainsborough Old Hall, *Parnell St, Gainsborough; tel: (01427) 612669.* Open Mon–Sat 1000–1700 (all year); Sun 1400–1730 (Easter–Oct). Admission £1.50. Take bus EG3 or 352 to *Gainsborough,* 25 miles northwest.

Grantham House (NT), *Castlegate, Grantham.* Open by written appointment only, Wed 1400–1700 (Apr–Sept), to: Major General Sir Brian Wyldbore-Smith, Grantham House, Castlegate, Grantham NG1 6SS. Admission £1.50. Take bus 601 to *Grantham,* 28 miles south. Tattershall Castle (NT), *Tattershall; tel: (01526) 342543.* Open Sat–Wed and Bank Holiday Mons 1030–1730 (Apr–Oct), Sat, Sun 1200–1600 (Nov to mid-Dec). Take bus 502 to *Tattershall,* 26 miles south-east.

HULL

TIC: *75–76 Carr Ln, Hull HU1 3RQ; tel: (01482) 223559.* Open Mon 1000–1800, Tues–Sat 0900–1800, Sun 1300–1700. DP SHS Services offered: local bed-booking service (10% commission taken and latest booking 30 mins before closing), BABA (10% commission taken and latest booking 30 mins before closing). Membership sold for YHA and the adjoining box office sells tickets for most venues in Hull. *Where To Stay and What To Do in Hull* (with accommodation listing) is free.

Station: Hull (Paragon) station, *Ferensway; tel: (01482) 326033* is adjacent to the bus station. It has a taxi rank.

Getting Around

The majority of attractions are within a walkable distance of the town centre, with the exception of the Humber Bridge. Free town and transport maps are available from the TIC. The two main bus operators are Kingston-upon-Hull City Transport *tel: (01482) 222222* and East Yorkshire Motor Services *tel: (01482) 327146,* which are both based at the main

Lincoln–Hull

bus depot in *Ferensway*. Services are very good in the city centre and to some small towns such as Bridlington and Beverley, but rather patchy to others, with more limited evening and Sunday services. The main taxi rank is located at **Hull Station**.

Staying in Hull

It is generally easy to find accommodation on arrival except during the first week in July, owing to the graduation ceremonies at Hull University. There is a wide range of accommodation in the town centre, with cheaper accommodation being mainly situated in the suburbs 1½–2 miles north-west of the centre. Hotel chains include *Ca, FC, Fr,* and *Tl.*

Beverley Friary Youth Hostel, *Friar's Ln, Beverley; tel: (01482) 881751* is only 5 mins walk from Beverley Rail Station. Nearest campsites: **Lakeminster Park,** *Hull Rd, Beverley; tel: (01482) 882655.* Take East Yorkshire bus no. 121 or 122, 7 miles north. **Entick House,** *Ings Ln, Dunswell; tel: (01482) 807393.* Take East Yorkshire bus no. 121 or 122, 5 miles north. **Burton Constable Caravan and Camping Park**, *Old Lodge, Sproatley; tel: (01482) 562508.* Take East Yorkshire bus no. 277 (no evening service), 7 miles north.

Sightseeing

Hull (Kingston upon Hull in full) is a blend of both new attractions, such as **The Humber Bridge** and **Hull Marina**, and of older ones such as the **Old Town**, where Hull began about 800 years ago. Here, historic architecture, quiet narrow lanes, old pubs, colourful barges at anchor, preserved warehouses, formal gardens and wide views of the impressive Humber waterway provide many hours of interest. The city's history is preserved in its many museums – **Town Docks Museum, Streetlife–Hull Transport Museum** and **Wilberforce House** – and the churches of **Holy Trinity** and **St Mary The Virgin**.

Guided walks of the area, incorporating all the surrounding countryside, are organised by **Paul Schofield** *tel: (01482) 878535* and **Keith Daddy** *tel: (01482) 781427.* £1.50 for adults, £0.75 for children.

Ferens Art Gallery, *Queen Victoria Sq; tel: (01482) 593933.* Open Mon–Sat 1000–1700, Sun 1330–1630. Admission free. **Town Docks Museum,** *Queen Victoria Sq; tel: (01482) 593902.* Open Mon–Sat 1000–1700, Sun 1330–1630. Admission free. **Streetlife–Hull Transport Museum,** *High St; tel: (01482) 593956.* Open Mon–Sat 1000–1700, Sun 1330–1630. Admission free. **Wilberforce House and 23/24 High Street,** *High St; tel: (01482) 593923.* Open Mon–Sat 1000–1700, Sun 1330–1630. Admission free.

Holy Trinity Church, *Market Pl; tel: (01482) 324835.* Open Mon–Fri 1000–1600, Sat 0930–1200, Sun 1400–1600 (Easter–Christmas). Admission free. **St Mary The Virgin**, *Lowgate.* Open Tues and Fri 1230–1600. Admission free.

Out Of Town

Humber Bridge, *Hessle.* Open daily. Admission: cyclists and pedestrians free, cars £1.60 (each way). There is an hourly bus service (no. 350) Mon–Sat and 2-hourly Sun from Hull Bus Station. Approx 5 miles west of Hull. **Skidby Windmill,** *Skidby; tel: (01482) 882255.* Open Tues–Sat 1000–1600, Sun 1330–1630 (Easter–Oct), Mon–Fri 1000–1600 (Nov–Easter). Admission £1 Adults, £0.50 Child, Family £2 (2 adults, 2 children). Take bus no. 746 to *Beverley*, then no. 225 or 250 to *Hessle*. (Approx 5 miles north-west). **Burton Constable Hall**, *Burton Constable, Sproatley; tel: (01964) 562400.* Open Sun–Thur 1300–1630 (Easter–Sept). Admission £2.50 Adult, £1.20 Child. No public transport from Hull. (Approx 8 miles north-east).

BEVERLEY

TIC: *Beverley Guildhall, Register Square, Beverley, North Humberside HU17 9AU; tel: (01482) 867430, fax: (01482) 883913.* Fully accessible to disabled people and assistance sought on their behalf. Local bed-booking (latest 30 mins before closing). Advance reservations handled. Local booking fee £1.00 plus 10%, BABA (latest booking 1700 Mon–Fri, 1500 Sat) fee £2.50. Self-catering booked in advance. Guided tours booked. Ticketing agency for localised events/performances. Beverley tourist brochure available free of charge, as well as an accommodation list.

Station: Beverley Station, *Station Sq, Railway St; Tel: (01482) 26033* very close to town centre. There is a taxi rank.

Getting Around

Most attractions are within a walkable area from the centre. Town and transport maps are available from the TIC in advance or by calling in. Buses are operated by **East Yorkshire Bus Company,** *tel: (01482) 27146, near Beverley Station.* Taxis can be hailed in the street.

Staying in Beverley

There is a good range of accommodation and the TIC have details of rooms within a 50-mile radius of Beverley. It is generally easy to find accommodation on arrival, except in May because of the **Beverley Music Festival** and June due to the **Folk Festival**. Hotel chains in Beverley include FP.

Budget accommodation: The Friary, *Friars Ln; tel: (01482 881751).* Accessible by public transport or short walk from town centre. The TIC has details of **campsites** in the area – the following are the nearest: **Lake Minster Park,** *Bleach House Farm, Hull Rd; tel: (01482) 882655.* Take bus 121, 122, 246, 746, 1 mile south of Beverley. **Crown & Anchor,** *Weel Rd, Hull Bridge, Tickton; tel: (0964) 542816).* No direct bus service, take a bus to Tickton Village, 3 miles from Beverley on coast road. **Woodby's Caravan Site,** *Brough Rd, South Cove, Brough HU15 2DB, tel: (0430) 422523);* 8 miles from Beverley on the B1230.

Sightseeing

Beverley is a tranquil and historic market town whose landmark, **Beverley Minster,** is a fine example of Gothic architecture; the current building dates back to 1220. Also of interest is **St Mary's Church,** where a now-famous carving is reputed to have inspired the 'White Rabbit' in Lewis Carroll's *Alice in Wonderland.* The surrounding countryside boasts numerous historic houses and gardens, such as **Burnby Hall Gardens and Museum,** with its magnificent grounds and stunning views.

Beverley Art Gallery, *Champney Rd; tel: (01482) 882255.* Open daily 0930–1730. Admission free. **Museum of Army Transport,** *Flemingate; tel: (01482) 860445).* Open daily 1000–1700. Admission £2.99. *(0831) 204701.* **Beverley Minster,** *tel: (01482) 868540.* Open Mon–Sat 0900–2000 (1600 in winter), Sun 1430–1700. Admission free, donation invited. **St Mary's Church,** *North Bar Within.* Open daily 1000–1600 (later in summer). Admission free.

Out of Town

Hornsea Pottery, *Hornsea; tel: (01962) 534211 ext 204.* Open daily 1000–1700. Admission £3.99. Take bus no. 240/246 to Hornsea (1 hr). **Burnby Hall,** *The Palk, Pocklington; tel: (01759) 302068.* Open daily 1000–1800 (8 Apr–1 Oct), Mon–Fri 1000–1600 (2 Oct–Apr). Admission £2. Travel by bus 746 from Beverley. **Burton Agnes Hall,** *Burton Agnes, Driffield; tel: (01262) 490324.* Open daily 1100–1700 (Apr–Oct). Admission £3. 16 miles from Beverley. Take bus no. 121 or 744 from Beverley via Driffield. **Sledmere House,** *Sledmere, nr Driffield; tel: (01377) 236208.* Open Tue–Thu, Sat, Sun and BH 1200–1630 (Easter–1 Oct). Admission £1.50; 8 miles northeast of Driffield, no public transport link. **Sewerby Hall,** *Sewerby, Bridlington; tel: (01262) 673769.* Open Sat–Tue 1000-1600 (Mar–May and Oct–Dec), daily 1000-1800 (May–Sep. Admission £2. On B1255, transport via skipper minibus service 'S' and Appleby's coaches from the *Promenade/Princess Terrace, Bridlington.*

SCARBOROUGH

TIC: *St Nicholas Cliff, Scarborough, North Yorkshire, YO11 2EP; tel: (01723) 373333.* Open daily 0930–1800 (May–Sep), 1000–1630 (Oct–Apr). DP SHS services offered: local bed booking service (10% commission taken), BABA (10% commission). *Scarborough, Whitby and Filey Holiday 95* brochure and free accommodation listing are available. An accommodation guide for disabled travellers is available from **Disablement Action Group,** *5 West Parade Rd; tel: (01723) 379397.*

Station: Scarborough Station, *Westborough,* is situated in the town centre. There is a taxi rank outside. General railway enquiries can be answered on *tel: (01483) 26033.* Recorded timetable information is available on *tel: (01723) 852141* (Scarborough–Hull), *(01723) 367445* (Scarborough–London), *(01723) 368563* (Scarborough–Leeds).

Getting Around

The attractions in town are all within walking distance of the centre. Free town maps and transport details are available from the TIC.

Bus services are good in the town centre and run frequently to surrounding towns – however, most buses operate reduced services after 2000 (Mon–Sat) and all day Sun. There is no central bus depot. The main bus company in Scarborough is **Scarborough and District** *tel: (01723) 375463* who operate Skipper buses from various points in the town. Other bus companies include **Tees and District** *tel: (01642) 210131,* **United Buses** *tel: (01325) 468771,* and **Yorkshire Coastliner** *tel: (01653) 692556.*

Registered taxi companies include: **Nippy Taxis** *tel: (01723) 370888,* **Castle Taxis** *tel: (01723) 378161* and **Borough Taxis** *tel: (01723) 366144.*

Staying in Scarborough

A good range of accommodation is available, particularly cheaper to mid-range hotels. National chains represented in Scarborough include *Pr* and there are many large independent hotels as well. Cheaper accommodation and rooms in pubs and inns can be found in all areas. Generally it is easy to find accommodation on arrival in the town, except during Jul and Aug and at Bank Holiday weekends. The closest youth hostel is **The White House Youth Hostel,** *Burniston Rd; tel: (01723) 361176,* open all year except 3–31 Jan. Phone Scarborough and District Bus Company; *tel: (01723) 375463* for public transport details. The TIC can provide information on local campsites.

Sightseeing

Lively Scarborough was England's first seaside resort and has been a spa since 1662. Twelfth-century **Scarborough Castle** overlooks two sandy beaches and the town has a wide variety of seaside attractions, such as **Water Splash World,** an exciting water theme park. **Scarborough Millennium** is a journey back through time and the history of the town, 966–1966. West of Scarborough take a steam train ride on the **North Yorkshire Moors Railway** (see Whitby – p. 297) and to the south-west is **Eden Camp** – a modern history theme museum reconstructing scenes from wartime Britain. **Scarborough Fayre Festival** takes place from late May to the end of June.

Appleby *tel: (01723) 366659* operate a bus tour around Scarborough and can be booked at the TIC. The TIC also has information on boat trips and guided walks.

Scarborough Castle (EH), *Castle Rd; tel: (01723) 372451.* Open daily. Admission £1.50. **Millennium,** *Harbourside; tel: (01723) 501000.* Open daily 1000–2200 (lLate May–Sep), 1000–1800 (Oct–Late May). Last admission 1 hour before closing. Admission £3.75. **Sea Life Centre,** *Scalby Mills; tel: (01723) 376125.* Open daily all year from 1000. Admission £4.35. A shuttle bus service runs from the town centre and the station all year and open-top buses run along the seafront to the centre throughout the summer; 2 miles north of Scarborough centre. **Water Splash World,** *North Bay; tel: (01723) 372744.* Open daily (end May–mid Sep). Admission £3.60 (£4.20 July–Sep).

Out of Town

Eden Camp, *nr Malton; tel: (01653) 697777.* Open daily 1000–1700 (Feb–Dec). Last admission 1600. Admission £3.00. Contact United Buses and Yorkshire Coastliner Buses for public transport details; 22 miles south west of Scarborough.

Flamingoland Family Fun Park, *Kirby Misperton, Malton; tel: (01653) 668287.* Open daily (Mar–Oct). Admission £8.00. Buses from Scarborough – contact United Buses and Yorkshire Coastliner Buses for details; 22 miles west of Scarborough.

Scarborough

OXFORD

The world-famous university centre of Oxford offers plenty of attractions for the visitor, from punting on the river Cherwell to the 'dreaming spires' of the university colleges, whose hidden courtyards and neat lawns are a timeless haven of tranquillity. Oxford University was established by 1214 and the city now offers a mix of attractive old streets, riverside walks and historic colleges – with bicycles everywhere!

Tourist Information

TIC: *The Old School, Gloucester Green, Oxford, OX1 2DA; tel: (01865) 726871; fax: (01865) 240261.* Open Mon–Sat 0930–1700; Suns and Bank Holidays in summer 1000–1300, 1330–1530. Out of hours *tel: Tourist Hot-Line (01865) 252664* for recording of the events in and around Oxford. DP services available, local bed-booking and BABA. Bus tours, guided walks and guides booked. Free accommodation listing available.

Woodstock Information Centre, Hensington Rd, Woodstock, Oxfordshire OX20 1JQ; tel: (01993) 811038. DP services available, local bed-booking and BABA.

Station

Oxford Station, *Park End St; tel: (01865) 722333* is approximately ¼ mile west of city centre. **Guide Friday Information Centre,** *tel: (01865) 790522.* Regular bus service into city centre. Taxi rank.

Getting Around

Most attractions are within a walkable distance of the city centre. The bus services within the city centre and outlying areas are excellent. Oxford has the 'Park and Ride' facility whereby you park your car (free) in one of the car parks located on the outskirts of the centre and use the quick and frequent bus service into town.

Free town and transport maps available from the TIC and transport maps from the bus companies (see below).

Buses

Oxford is served by two bus companies. **Thames Transit,** *Horspath Rd, Cowley; tel: (01865) 772250,* have minibuses operating every 4–5 mins throughout the central area of the city and to the surrounding countryside. Most services operate until midnight. Zone Cards are available (there are 4 zones in Oxford) from £4–£14 for one week, depending on zones required. An Explorer daily pass costs £4.50 adult, £2.70 child, £9 for family ticket. The **Oxford Bus Company,** *395 Cowley Rd; tel: (01865) 711312,* have a comprehensive network of CityLink buses servicing the city and many places of interest around the city. Services operate until 2300. Zone Cards are available from £4.50.

Taxis

The main taxi rank is situated at the the station. For a list of registered companies, contact the TIC.

Staying in Oxford

Accommodation

There is a large selection of accommodation of most types in the city centre. **The Oxford Accommodation List,** *250 Iffley Rd, Oxford OX4 4AU,* is the free accommodation information service provided by the Oxford Association of Hotels and Guest Houses, designed to help travellers find a place to stay in Oxford. For a free copy of the list write to the above address.

The nearest youth hostel is **Oxford Youth Hostel,** *Jack Straw's Ln; tel: (01865) 62997.* There are several campsites, the nearest being **Oxford Camping International,** *426 Abingdon Rd; tel: (01865) 246551,* 1½ miles from city centre. 'Red Bridge' Park & Ride buses every 10 minutes until 1900, service bus 35 or 36.

Eating and Drinking

Oxford has a large and varied selection of restaurants. Being a city with many students, it is possible to eat good food quite cheaply, as well as choosing one of the many gourmet eating places. The TIC has a free list of restaurants, pubs and winebars in the centre.

Money

Thomas Cook bureaux de change can be found at the rail station, *5 Queen St* and Midland Bank, *65 Cornmarket St.*

Entertainment and Events

Oxford has two principal theatres. **Apollo Theatre**, *George St; tel: (01865) 244544; group bookings: (01865) 723834.*, is traditionally Oxford's premier venue. Originally built to present music-hall entertainment, the variety continues into the 1990s and audiences enjoy the best from many international professional touring companies. **The Playhouse Oxford**, *11–12 Beaumont St; tel: (01865) 247134*, is an intimate, historic theatre, presenting drama, dance, opera, musicals and concerts in comfortable period surroundings. Oxford also has its own **City of Oxford Orchestra**, *contact: John King, The Old Rectory, Paradise Sq; tel: (01865) 252365.* Established in 1965, the orchestra is now the leading regional orchestra between Bournemouth and Birmingham. It presents regular autumn and spring series of concerts together with an annual 'Prom' season and a season of 'Beautiful Music in Beautiful Places' in such settings as the Holywell Music Room, Merton College Chapel, Sheldonian Theatre and Christ Church Meadows.

The main annual event is the **City of Oxford's Lord Mayor's Parade & Show** which is held in May. For a comprehensive listing of events, contact the TIC.

Shopping

Being a university city, Oxford has a wonderful selection of bookshops, notably **Blackwell's**, *48–51 Broad St; tel: (01865) 792792.* Established in 1879, the shop has an international reputation as one of the finest and largest booksellers in the world. Sixteen departments range over four floors. Nearby are specialist bookshops: the **Art & Poster Shop**, *27 Broad St*, the **Map and Travel Shop**, *53 Broad St*, **The**

Children's Bookshop, *8 Broad St*, and the **Music Shop**, *38 Holywell St*, which also sells sheet music. The main shopping area is compact and easy to explore on foot.

To the north of Oxford's central crossroads – known as *Carfax* – runs *Cornmarket St*, where there are large High Street names, plus many smaller shops and the **Clarendon Shopping Centre**.

West from *Carfax* runs *Queen St*, at the west end of which is the **Westgate Shopping Centre**. Tucked behind the modern facades of *Cornmarket St* is the **Covered Market**, built in 1774 to provide a permanent home for the many stallholders who cluttered up the city streets. Traditionally, this is where the colleges do their shopping. It is a gourmet's paradise, where high quality meat, game and fish can be bought. Lovers of a market atmosphere should also pay a visit to the city's **open market**, held every Wednesday at *Gloucester Green*. In beautifully designed buildings set around the market square, the **Gallery** houses a mixture of specialist shops and restaurants.

Sightseeing

Tours

Bus tours and full-day and half-day excursions to Blenheim Palace, Cotswolds, Stratford-upon-Avon, Bath, Warwick Castle, Stonehenge and Salisbury are available. Also walking tours, including 'Inspector Morse's Oxford', based on the popular TV series, and guides can be booked at the TIC or Guide Friday Information Centre at Oxford Station.

Colleges

Most travellers come to visit the lovely **university colleges** in the heart of Oxford, city of 'dreaming spires'. Most of the colleges are within an easy walk of the centre and are generally open in the afternoons and during vacation time (though closures are liable at short notice). You should respect the fact that these are places of study, and heed privacy notices. A few colleges charge for admission.

Most of the historic colleges lie east of *St Giles/Cornmarket/St Aldate's*. The most famous,

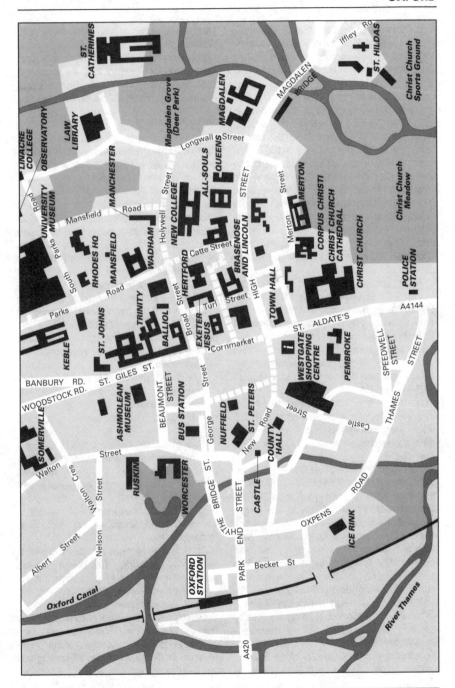

to the south, is **Christ Church** (or 'The House'), founded in 1525 by Cardinal Wolsey. It has the largest quadrangle in Oxford, known as Tom Quad after the bell, Great Tom, in Wren's Tom Tower: Great Tom still rings 101 times at 2105 each night, marking a long-defunct undergraduate curfew. The college chapel doubles as **Christ Church Cathedral**: the smallest cathedral in England, it predates the college, being part of an earlier nunnery dating in part from the 8th century. Its spire was the first in England. Mainly Norman, it has a magnificent Early English chapter house. In Canterbury Quad is **Christ Church Picture Gallery**, which includes Italian, Flemish and Dutch works. College admission £1; Gallery £0.80. To the south and east of Christ Church sprawls the pastoral **Christ Church Meadow**, Oxford's answer to Cambridge's 'Backs'.

East of here along *Merton St* is 13th-century **Merton College**, one of the oldest in Oxford; its peaceful gardens are partly enclosed by the old city wall. Beside *Magdalen Bridge* lies **Magdalen College**, perhaps the most attractive in the city; its buildings have changed little since the 15th century apart from the addition of the harmonious 'New Buildings' in 1733. At sunrise on May Day, the college choir sings from the top of the tower, witnessed by crowds of mostly inebriated students emerging from May Ball revels. Magdalen has its own Deer Park, and there are peaceful walks along the bank of the River Cherwell.

Back along the *High St* are **Queen's College**, with buildings by Wren and Hawksmoor, and **St Edmund Hall**, with a dining hall of 1659; from the 13th-century tower of **St Mary the Virgin**, the university church, is the best view in Oxford. *Queen's Lane* leads you to another gem, **New College**, famed for its gardens, hall and cloisters. The **Bridge of Sighs** spanning *New College Lane*, named after its Venetian counterpart, forms part of **Hertford College**.

Next to the Bodleian Library (see below) is the imposing **Sheldonian Theatre**, designed by Sir Christopher Wren in 1664 to resemble a Roman theatre, and used for university functions and concerts. Westwards along *Broad St* are famous rivals neo-Gothic **Balliol College** and

Trinity College, which has renowned gardens. **Wadham College** along *Parks Rd* has beautiful 17th-century buildings; and worth a slightly longer walk, for a contrast to all the sandstone, is red-brick **Keble College**, once regarded as an eyesore, now seen as a Victorian tour de force.

Other Attractions

A 17th-century gateway leads into Oxford's **Botanic Garden**, which was founded in 1621 and is the oldest in Britain; it includes rockeries, pools and greenhouses full of exotic plant species.

Oxford's **Ashmolean Museum** is the oldest museum in Britain, open to the public since 1683; it houses treasures from the time of early man to 20th-century art, including paintings and ceramics from Europe and the East.

The **Bodleian Library**, the oldest in the world, is one of the five copyright libraries of the UK, receiving a copy of every book published in Britain. Parts of this vast building, including the original Duke Humphrey's Library (1480), are open to the public. The great, domed **Radcliffe Camera** nearby, built in 1737, acts as one of the reading rooms.

The **Oxford University Museum** is the city's natural history museum and has collections dedicated to zoology, entomology and geology, all housed in an imposing Victorian Gothic building.

One of Oxford's newer attractions is the imaginative and informative presentation of **The Oxford Story**; from a moving medieval scholar's desk, you can experience eight centuries of university life – its history, personalities and great events – all brought to life using new technology and audio-visual techniques.

There are many more attractions to visit in the vicinity of Oxford. The **Didcot Railway Centre** relives the golden age of steam and the Great Western Railway. There are over 20 locomotives on display, including steam and diesel engines, and dozens of carriages dating from the 1880s to the 1950s. The ancient village of Cogges is home to **Cogges Manor Farm Museum**, a fascinating display of farming and the countryside complete with stone outbuildings and manor house, furnished as it would have been at the turn of the century. Animals from all over the world can be found at the **Cotswold Wildlife Park** – zebras, rhinos, tigers, etc in spacious paddocks or enclosures, monkeys and penguins in a walled garden area and alligators in a tropical house; other attractions include an early 19th-century manor house, butterfly house and aquarium.

A few miles north of Oxford is the attractive town of **Woodstock**, home of fabulous **Blenheim Palace**. Blenheim was built for warrior hero John Churchill, the 1st Duke of Marlborough, and is the early 18th-century work of Sir John Vanbrugh. It is the only English 'palace' which was not built for royalty and is where Sir Winston Churchill was born; a fascinating Churchill Exhibition includes his birth room. The house offers tours of the wonderful interior, with its fine pictures and furnishings, parkland and gardens by 'Capability' Brown, and many other outdoor attractions. In Park Street, Woodstock, is 16th-century Fletcher's House, home to the **Oxfordshire County Museum**, which tells the story of Oxfordshire through the ages, using a variety of archaeological, craft and industrial exhibits.

Museums, Libraries and Galleries

Ashmolean Museum, *Beaumont St; tel: (01865) 27800*. Open Tue–Sat 1000–1600, Sun 1400–1600, Bank Holiday Mondays 1400–1700. Admission free. **Bodleian Library**, *Broad St; tel: (01865) 277165*. Open Mon–Fri 1030–1130 and 1400–1500, Sat 1030–1130 (14 Mar–Oct), Mon–Fri 1400–1500, Sat 1030–1130 (Nov-13 Mar). Admission with guided tour £3. **Museum of Modern Art**, *30 Pembroke St; tel: (01865) 722733*. Open Tue–Sat 1000–1800, Thu 1000–2200, Fri 1400–1800. Admission £2.50. **Oxford University Museum**, *Parks Rd; tel: (01865) 272950*. Open Mon–Sat 1200–1700. Admission free . **Oxford Story**, *6 Broad St; tel: (01865) 728822*. Open daily 0930–1700 (Apr–Jun, Sep and Oct), 0900–1830 (Jul and Aug). Admission £4.50.

Churches and Cathedrals

Christ Church Cathedral, *St Aldate's; tel:* *(01865) 276154*. Open Mon–Sat 0930–1800, Sun 1130–1730 (Apr–23 Oct), Mon–Sat 0930–1630, Sun 1130–1630 (24 Oct–Mar). Admission free. **St Mary the Virgin**, *High St.*

Garden

Oxford University Botanic Garden, *Rose Ln; tel: (01865) 276920*. Open daily 0900–1700 (Mar–Oct), daily 0900–1600 (Nov–Feb). Admission free (except Jun–Aug, £1).

Out of Town

Museums

Didcot Railway Centre, *Didcot; tel: (01235) 817200*. Open daily 1100–1700 (Apr–Sep), Sat and Sun 1100–1700 (Oct–Mar). Admission £3-£5, depending on whether it is a steam day. Take the train from Oxford to Didcot Parkway station, or Thames Transit buses 302/303/304/305/306/391 from Oxford. **Heritage Motor Centre**, *Banbury Rd, Gaydon, Warwickshire; tel: (01926) 641188*. Open daily 1000–1800 (Apr–Oct), 1000–1630 (Nov–Mar). Admission £5.50. 30 miles from Oxford on B4100, no public transport.

Oxfordshire County Museum, *Fletcher's House, Park St, Woodstock*. Open Tue–Fri 1000–1600, Sat 1000-1700, Sun 1400–1700. Admission free. South Midland bus X50 from Oxford to Woodstock. **Cogges Manor Farm Museum**, *Church Ln, Cogges, Witney; tel: (01993) 772602*. Open Tue–Fri 1030–1730 (Apr–Oct). Admission £3. Take bus from Oxford to Cogges, alight at Wadards Meadow, walk down hill and turn into Church Lane.

Stately Home

Blenheim Palace, *Woodstock; tel: (01993) 811325/811091*. Open daily 1030–1730 (13 Mar–Oct). Admission £7. 8 miles from Oxford, take South Midland X50 from Oxford or train from Oxford Gloucester Green Station to Woodstock.

Wildlife

Cotswold Wildlife Park, *Burford; tel: (01993) 823006*. Open daily 1000-1800 or dusk. Admission £4.20.

PLYMOUTH

Plymouth sits at the mouth of the river Tamar and has been a seaport of note since the 13th century. The city has a rich maritime heritage and in the past many famous explorers have set sail from its natural harbour: Sir Walter Raleigh and Sir Francis Drake sailed from here in Elizabethan times; the Pilgrim Fathers left for the New World in the Mayflower in 1620; and Captain James Cook sailed from here in the 18th century.

Tourist Information

TIC: Island House, 9 The Barbican, Plymouth PL1 2LS; tel: (01752) 264849 or 227865. Open Mon–Sat 0900–1700 all year, also Sun 1000–1600 (Easter–Oct). DP services offered: local bed booking (£2.00 booking fee), BABA (£3.00 booking fee). Heritage passes, local theatre and attractions tickets sold. The Plymouth Guide is available free from the TIC and contains accommodation listings.

Station

Plymouth station, North Road is a 10-min walk north from the city centre. Alternatively the Plymouth City Bus no. 25 runs every 12 mins. Rail enquiries tel: (01752) 221300. Cars can be hired from **Hertz**, tel: (01752) 252000, at the station and there is also a taxi rank outside.

Getting Around

The majority of attractions in Plymouth are within walking distance of the centre. Free town and transport maps are available from the TIC. Generally public transport is good in and around the town during the summer but more patchy to outlying areas in winter. There are reduced services after 2100 and on Sundays.

Western National tel: (01752) 222666 and **Plymouth City Buses** tel: (01752) 662271 operate from Royal Parade and from Breton-side Bus Station, Bretonside.

Taxi ranks are situated in Old Town St, Royal Parade and Raleigh St. Registered taxi companies include **Key Cabs** tel: (01752) 600580 and **Plymouth taxis** tel: (01752) 562033.

Staying in Plymouth

Accommodation

Plymouth has a wide range of accommodation establishments. National chains represented include BW, Ca, Cp, FP, Ja, MH and Nv, whilst the majority of the cheaper accommodation can be found near the sea front and railway station. Though it is generally easy to find accommodation on arrival, it is advisable to book in advance during the 'Navy Days' special event on August Bank Holiday. **Plymouth Youth Hostel**, Belmont House, Devonport Rd, Stoke; tel: (01752) 562189 is open from 1700 and can be reached by City Bus no. 34 or Western National Buses no. 81 or 15A. The TIC can provide information on local campsites which include **Riverside**, Longbridge Rd, Marsh Mills; tel: (01752) 344122, 4 miles away, reached by City Bus no. 20, 21, 22 or 51 and **Smithaleigh Camping Park**, Smithaleigh; tel: (01752) 893194, reached by Western National Bus no. 88, 7 miles east.

Eating and Drinking

The TIC provides a free list of local restaurants, most of which are concentrated in the Barbican area near Sutton Harbour and in Mayflower St/ Cornwall St in the shopping area. There is a wide choice of styles and many tea shops and pubs offer cheap eating. Vegetarian restaurants include **The Arts Centre**, 38 Looe St; **The Cooperage**, Vauxhall St caters for vegetarians and vegans.

Traditional Plymouth Gin is produced in **The Distillery**, Southside St, The Barbican and traditional Devonshire teas with clotted cream are offered in most cafés and restaurants.

Communications

The main post office is at St Andrews Cross and is open Mon–Fri 0900–1700 and Sat mornings. Post restante facilities are available.

Entertainment and Events

The free publication *What's on and Where to Go* is produced monthly. The local *Evening Herald* also has listings. The main theatre venue is the **Theatre Royal**, *Royal Parade; tel: (01752) 267222* and the **Plymouth Pavilions**, *Millbay Rd; tel: (01752) 222200* offers year-round entertainment, skating and swimming. Lively pubs and clubs are concentrated in *Union St*, while quieter nightlife and wine bars can be found in *The Barbican* area.

The **Navy Days** event, when Devonport Dockyard is open to the public, takes place every 2 years on the August Bank Holiday weekend. The dockyard is 2 miles west of the centre and can be reached by City Bus no. 36 or 46 from Royal Parade. Plymouth then becomes very busy and it is advisable to book accommodation in advance.

Shopping

Big stores are located in *Royal Parade, New George St, Old Town St, Cornwall St* and *Armada Way*, while antique and craft shops can be found in the **Barbican.** There is also the large daily undercover **Pannier St Market.**

Sightseeing

Plymouth Hoe, the grassy area overlooking Plymouth Sound, was where Sir Francis Drake casually finished playing his game of bowls before setting out to fight the approaching Spanish Armada in 1588. Situated on the Hoe is **Plymouth Dome**, a high-tech visitor centre where Plymouth's seafaring history is vividly brought to life.

Museum enthusiasts should head for **Plymouth Museum and Art Gallery**, with its displays of local archaeological finds, porcelain and paintings, including some by local artist, Sir Joshua Reynolds. Most of old Plymouth was destroyed during the Second World War, although some of the old town remains around the harbour area of **The Barbican.**

The city is surrounded by glorious countryside and numerous attractions. **Saltram**, an attractive Georgian house built around the remnants of a Tudor mansion, looks out over landscaped grounds to Plymouth Sound. The Cremyll Foot Ferry crosses the river Tamar to Cornwall and **Mount Edgcumbe**, an elegant house set in 800 acres of parkland with wonderful views towards Plymouth.

Bus Tours operated by **Guide Friday**, *tel: (01752) 222221*, cost £4.00 and guided walks of the Royal Citadel, costing £2.50, start at the *Plymouth Dome*. **Plymouth Boat Cruises**, *tel: (01752) 822797*, operate from *Phoenix Wharf, The Barbican*, for £2.80 and **Tamar Cruising**, *tel: (01752) 822105*, start boat trips from *The Mayflower Steps, The Barbican*.

Museums

Plymouth Dome, *The Hoe;,tel: (01752) 600608.* Open daily 0900–1730 (and later in summer). Admission £3.30. **City Museum and Art Gallery**, *Drake Circus; tel: (01752) 264878.* Open Tue–Sat 0900–1700. Admission free.

Wildlife Collection

Plymouth Aquarium, *The Hoe; tel: (01752) 222772.* Open daily 0900–1700, admission £2.00.

Out of Town

Saltram House, *Merafield Rd, Plympton; tel: (01752) 336546.* House open Sun–Thu 1230–1730, Gallery and garden, Sun–Thu 1030–1730 (Apr–end Oct). Admission £5.00 (House and garden), £2.20 (Garden only). Take the Plymouth City Bus no.22 or Plymouth to Torquay Bus no. 128 or 129, 4 miles east.

Mount Edgcumbe, *Torpoint; tel: (01752) 822236.* Gardens and park open all year dawn–dusk. House and Earl's Garden open Wed–Sun, Bank Hols 1100–1730 (Apr–end Oct). Admission £3.50, gardens and park only free. Take the City Bus no. 33 or 34 to the Cremyll passenger ferry over to Torpoint, 6 miles south-west.

Dartmoor Wildlife Park, *Sparkwell; tel: (01752) 837209.* Open all year dawn–dusk. Admission £4.95. Take the Western National Bus nos.58 or 59 from Plymouth to Sparkwell. 8 miles east.

Entertainment–Shopping–Sightseeing–Out of Town   **271**

PLYMOUTH to PENZANCE

For centuries an outpost many days' journey from the capital, Cornwall has a proud and independent history and boasts some of the most spectacular coastal scenery in the British Isles. This route gives access to many of the country's premier attractions, including the fishing village and artists' colony of St Ives and – only a few miles from Land's End – Penzance, mainland Britain's most westerly town.

TRAINS

ETT table: 515

→ Fast Track

A train runs at roughly hourly intervals (with some longer gaps, especially on Sun) throughout the day between Plymouth and Penzance. The through journey takes just under 2 hours.

⤳ On Track

Plymouth–Liskeard–Bodmin Parkway–Par–Truro–St Erth–Penzance

All of the Plymouth to Penzance trains call at these stations en route. Plymouth to Liskeard takes about 25 mins, Liskeard to Bodmin Parkway (some way from Bodmin town) 12 mins, Bodmin Parkway to Par 11 mins, Par to Truro 25 mins, Truro to St Erth 30 mins, and St Erth to Penzance 10–15 mins.

– –

◠ Side Tracks from Liskeard

LOOE

TIC: *The Guildhall, Fore St, East Looe PL13 1AA;* tel: *(01503) 762072. Open Mon–Sat 1000–*

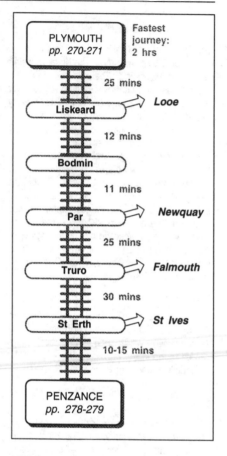

1700 (Apr–Oct). DP services offered: local bed-booking, BABA. *South East Cornwall Guide,* available free.

Station: Looe Station (unmanned), *Station Rd, East Looe* is ½ mile from the centre, and has a taxi rank.

Getting Around

Free town maps are available from the TIC. The main bus operator is **Hambly's** *tel: (01503) 220660.* Services are quite good within the town, but are patchy in the evenings and to outlying areas.

The main taxi rank is in the town centre. For details of registered taxi companies contact the TIC.

Staying in Looe

There is a good range of accommodation, ranging from mid-range hotels to b.&b. establishments. It is generally easy to book on arrival, except during Aug (peak season). The TIC has details of campsites in the area – the nearest is **Camping Caradon**, Trelaume Gds; tel: (01503) 72388. Open daily (Apr–Oct).

Sightseeing

Looe is a fishng port which has long been a tourist centre for Cornwall. Although there are few specific attractions, Looe is overall an attractive town with many old buildings, and wears its tourist commercialisation very well. One unusual attraction is the **The Monkey Sanctuary**, tel: (01503) 262532. Open Apr–Sep Sun–Thu 1030–1700. Admission £3.50.

Out of Town

English China Clay Group, John Keay House, St Austell; tel: (01726) 74482. Open daily all year. Admission free. 15 miles from centre. **Wheal Martyn China Clay Museum**, Carthew, St Austell; tel: (01726) 850362. Open daily 1000–1800 (Apr–Oct). 15 miles from centre. **Kids Kingdom** theme park, Albert Rd, St Austell, Cornwall, PL25 4TZ; tel: (01726) 77377. Open daily 1000–1900 (Apr–Aug). Admission £3.50. 10 miles from centre. **St Austell Brewery Visitor Centre**, St Austell Brewery Company, Trevarthian Rd, St Austell; tel: (01726) 66022. Open by appointment only Mon–Fri 0930–1630 (Apr–Oct). 12 miles from centre.

BODMIN

TIC: Shire House, Mount Folly, Bodmin, Cornwall PL31 2DQ; tel: (01208) 76616. Open daily 1000–1700. DP Services Offered: local bed-booking, BABA. Bodmin Town and Moors Guide available free.

Station: The main railway line runs through **Bodmin Parkway**; tel: (01872) 76244, which is 3 miles from the centre and has a taxi rank.

Getting Around

The majority of attractions in the town are within walking distance of the centre. Free transport maps are available from the TIC. The main bus operator is **Western National**; tel: (01752) 222666. Services are reasonably good within the town but are patchy in some areas. There is a limited service in the evenings and on Sundays. The main taxi rank is in Pool St. Registered taxi companies include: **Bodmin Taxis** tel: (01208) 73000 and **Parnells** tel: (01208) 72880.

Staying in Bodmin

The majority of accommodation is b. & b., with a couple of mid-range hotels. Cheaper accommodation is located mainly in Bodmin Moor. The TIC has details of campsites in the area – the nearest is **Castle Hill**, Bodmin; tel: (01208) 73834, 1 mile north of the centre.

Sightseeing

HIstorically the capital of Cornwall, this small market town lies midway between the county's north and south coasts. The town is linked to Bodmin Parkway station by the steam **Bodmin and Wenford Railway**. Bodmin's military past is reflected in the **Duke of Cornwall Light Infantry Museum** and there are exhibitions on display at the ruined 18th-century **Bodmin Jail**.
Bodmin and Wenford Railway, Harleigh Rd; tel: (01208) 73666. Opening times vary. Admission £4.50. **Duke of Cornwalls Light Infantry Museum**, Castle Canyke Rd; tel: (01208) 72810. Open Mon–Fri 1500–1700. Admission £1. **Bodmin Jail**, tel: (01208) 76292. Open Mon–Fri 1000–1800, Sat 1100–1600 (Apr–Oct). Mon–Fri 1100–1600 (Nov–Mar). Admission £2.80.

Out of Town

Lanhydrock House and Gardens (NT), tel: (01208) 73320. Open: (house) Tue–Sun (Mar–Oct), (gardens) daily during daylight. Admission £5.20. Take bus no. 55. **Pencarrow House**, Washaway; tel: (01208) 841369. Open Sun–Thu 1330–1700 (Apr–May). Admission £3.50. Take bus no. 55. **Tintagel Castle** (EH), Tintagel;

tel: (01840) 770328. Open daily 1000–1800 (Apr–Sep), 1000–1600 (Oct–Mar). Admission £2.10. Take the West National bus to Tintagel.

 Side Tracks from Par

NEWQUAY

TIC: *Municipal Buildings, Marcus Hill, Newquay TR7 1BD; tel: (01637) 871345.* Open Mon–Fri 0900–1700, Sat 1000–1230 (Nov–Mar); Mon–Sat 0900–1800, Sun 1000–1700 (Apr–Sept). DP Services offered: local bed-booking service (10% commission on total stay) and BABA (latest 1 hr before closing), advance reservations handled. Bureau de Change, and Theatre Royal, Cornwall Coliseum and Plymouth Pavilions tickets sold. *Newquay Guide* and *Discover Cornwall* guides are available free of charge and include accommodation listings.

Station: **Newquay Station,** *Cliff Rd; tel: (01637) 877180* is ¼ mile north-east of the town centre and has a taxi rank. Most buses stop at the station en route to the bus station in the town centre.

Getting Around

The majority of attractions are within walking distance of the town centre with the exception of **Lane Theatre** which is two miles out. A free town map is available from the TIC.

The majority of local bus services are operated by **Western National Bus Co** *tel: (01208) 79898* from the central bus depot on *East St.* Services are good in the centre of town, reasonable to nearby towns and very poor to the north coast area. Bus services within Newquay stop at 2230 and most services to outlying areas stop at 1800. From Oct–May there are no services on Sun except a limited service in town. A daily 'Explorer' ticket costs £4.40 and a three day or weekly 'Key West' ticket is available (£13.20 and £22 respectively).

The main taxi rank is located on *Trebarwith Crescent* off *East St* or contact **123 Taxis** *tel: (01637) 851234;* **A1 Taxis** *tel: (01637) 872325;* **Ace Taxis** *tel: (01637) 852121.*

Staying in Newquay

There is a good range of all types of accommodation in Newquay, with over 130 hotels and 100 guest-houses and b.&b. establishments. The majority of cheaper accommodation is located in the town centre. It is generally easy to find accommodation on arrival except in the last week in July and the first week in Aug and over Aug Bank Holiday.

There are no IYHF establishments in Newquay but **hostel** accommodation can be found all year round at **Backpackers,** *69–73 Tower Rd; tel: (01637) 879366;* **Fistral Backpackers,** *Headland Rd; tel: (01637) 873146* and **Towan Backpackers,** *Beachfield Ave; tel: (01637) 874668.* The closest **campsites** are **Port Beach Tourist Park,** *Alexandra Rd, Porth; tel: (01637) 876531,* 1½ miles north-west on bus routes 53 and 53B and **Trencreek Farm Holiday Park,** *Trencreek; tel (01637) 874210,* 1½ miles east; **Mendra Holiday Park,** *Lane; tel: (01637) 875778,* 2 miles east and **Trevelgue Holiday Park,** *Trevelgue Rd; tel: (01637) 851851,* 2 miles north and not accessible by public transport.

Sightseeing

Bus tours of the area are operated by **Western National Bus Co** (see above for details), *tel: (01637) 873222* to book); **Cornishman Coaches** *tel: (01637) 872474,* from £3.30 and **Harris Coaches** *tel: (01637) 873321,* from £2.50; **Grand Tour of Newquay** *tel: (01726) 860345* operates a town bus tour for £2. Bus no. 56 to Padstow (June–Sept only) offers good views along the north coast. Boat trips are available from **Newquay Shooting & Fishing Centre** at £2.50 for an hours pleasure trip, £8 for a half day fishing trip and £22 for shark fishing. Both Western National bus tours and boat trips can be booked at the TIC.

Surfing championships are held over Spring Bank Holiday and during Aug.

Animal World, *Trenance Gardens; tel: (01637) 873342.* Open daily from 1000 (Apr–Oct). Admission £3.90 **Art & Craft Exhibition,** *Trenance Cottages, Trenance Gardens.* Open daily 1000–1730 (Apr–Sept). Admission free.

Blue Lagoon, *Cliff Rd; tel: (01637) 850741.* Open daily 1000–2000. Admission £3. **Fun Factory,** *St Gearges Rd; tel: (01637) 877555.* Open daily 1000–1800. Admission free (chiildren £3). **Sealife Centre,** *Towan Beach Promenade; tel: (01637) 878134.* Open daily from 1000. Admission £4.25 **Tumbletown,** *Gover Lane; tel: (01637) 875610.* Open daily 0900–2200 (May–Sept), 0900–1750 (Oct–Apr). Admission free (children £2). **Tunnels Thro' Time,** *St Michaels Rd; tel: (01637) 873379.* Open: daily 1000–1700 (Apr–Oct). Admission £2.50 **Trenance Gardens** are open all the time. **Waterworld,** *Trenance Gardens; tel: (01637) 875982.* Open daily (times vary, check for details). Admission £4.

Out of Town

Dairyland Farm World, *Tresillian Barton, Summercourt; tel: (01872) 510246.* Open daily 1030–1730 (Apr–Oct). Admission £4.50; 4 miles west no access by public transport. **Lappa Valley Railway** *St Newlyn East; tel: (01872) 510317.* Open daily 1030–1730 (Apr–Oct). Admission £3.95; 6 miles south-east on *Cornishmen Coaches; tel: (01637) 872474,* then 1-mile walk. **The Lost Gardens of Heligan** *Pentewan, St Austell; tel: (01726) 844157/ 843566.* Open daily 1000–1800. Admission £2.60; 25 miles east on bus no. 21. **Trerice Manor** (NT) *St Newlyn East; tel: (01637) 875404.* Open Wed–Mon 1100–1730 (Apr–Sept), 1100–1700 (Oct). Admission £3.60; 4 miles west on Cornishmen Coaches, *tel: (01637) 872474,* then 1-mile walk.

– – – – – – – – – – – – – – – – – –

TRURO

TIC: *Municipal Buildings, Boscawen St, Truro, Cornwall TR1 2NE; tel: (01872) 74555.* Open Mon–Thur 0900–1700, Fri 0900–1645 (Nov–Mar); Mon–Fri 0900–1715, Sat 1000–1300 (Apr–June and Oct); Mon–Fri 0900–1800, Sat 1000–1700 (July–Sept). DP Services offered: local bed-booking service (£1 booking fee, latest 15 mins before closing) and BABA (£2 booking fee, latest 30 mins before closing). Tickets sold for local events. *Truro City Guide* costs £0.50

and the *Truro Accommodation Register* is available free.
Station: Truro Station, *Station Rd; tel: (01872) 76244,* is 1 mile west of the city centre and all buses passing in that direction go into the centre. The station has a taxi rank and **Hertz** and **Scot Hire** car hire offices.

Getting Around

All attractions are within walking distance of the city centre and a free town map is available from the TIC.

Western National Bus Co, *tel: (01209) 719988,* operate services throughout the town and most of the county from the bus station on *Lemon Quay.* Services are good in town but patchy and infrequent to rural areas. Most services are reduced after 1800 and some routes do not operate after 1700 or on Sun. A daily 'Explorer' ticket costs £4.40 and three day or weekly 'Key West' tickets are also available (£13.20 and £22 respectively with reduced rates for senior citizens and children).

The main taxi rank is by the War Memorial on *Boscawen St.*

Staying in Truro

There are no large hotels in Truro and only a few medium sized hotels; however there is a reasonable choice of smaller hotels and guesthouse and b. & b. establishments located both in the city centre and in the outlying villages. Accommodation may be difficult to find at the end of June and beginning of July due to the **Three Spires Music Festival,** and during the peak summer holiday season.

There is no hostel accommodation in Truro. The closest YHA hostels are in *Perranporth; tel: (01872) 337494,* Eight miles west on bus route 87, and in Falmouth, see p. xxx.

The nearest campsites are **Carnon Downs Caravan and Camping Park,** *Carnon Downs; tel: (01872) 560462,* 3 miles south on bus routes 88 or 89; **Leverton Place Caravan and Camping Park,** *Greenbottom; tel: (01872) 560462,* 3 miles west on bus routes 40 or 18; **Summer Valley Touring Park,** *Shortlanesend; tel: (01872) 77878,* 3 miles north on bus route 87 and **Chacewater Park,** *Cox Hill, Chacewater;*

tel: (01209) 820762, 6 miles west on bus route 40 or 18, then a 1-mile walk.

Sightseeing

Once a river port and tin-mining centre, Truro had its heyday in the 18th century, as its elegant and well-preserved Georgian streets (especially *Boscawen St, Lemon St* and *Walsingham Place*) bear witness. The **Royal Cornwall Museum and Art Gallery** offers a good introduction to Cornish history and industry, and boasts a number of Old Masters. Truro's **Cathedral** only had its foundation stone laid in 1880, when Cornwall was finally granted its own bishop; completed in 1910, it is an impressive example of Gothic Revival style.

The gardens in this part of southern Cornwall's so-called 'Riviera' testify to its subtropical climate. **Trelissick Garden** offers unrivalled views of the Fal Estuary, as well as beautiful woodland and sheltered flower gardens. Eighteenth-century **Trewithen House** has a landscaped garden of international fame, containing many rare species, while the nearby **Probus Gardens** specialises in advice on choosing plants to suit their conditions.

Bus tours around the area are available from **F. T. Williams Travel**, *tel: (01209) 717152*; prices range from £3.95 to £5.25. Boat trips ply to and from Falmouth and are operated by **Enterprise Boats**, *tel: (01326) 374241*, at £4.50 for a return ticket.

The annual **Three Spires Music Festival** is held at the end of June and beginning of July. **Boscawen Park**, *Malpas Rd*, is open daily during daylight hours. Admission free.

Royal Cornwall Museum and Art Gallery, *River St; tel: (01872) 72205*. Open Mon–Fri 0900–1700, Sat 1000–1700. Admission £1.20. **Truro Cathedral** *High Cross; tel: (01872) 76782*. Open daily. Admission free (donation requested). **Victoria Gardens**, *St George's Rd*, open daily during daylight. Admission free.

Out of Town

Probus Gardens *Probus; tel: (01726) 882597*. Open daily 1000–1700 (Apr–Sept), Mon and Fri 1000–1600 (Oct–Mar). Admission £1.60. Five miles east on bus no. 24A. **Trelissick Gardens**,

Feock; tel (01872) 862090. Open Mon–Sat 1030–1730 (Mar–Oct). Admission £3 (gardens only). Four miles south. **Trewithen House and Gardens**, *Grampound Rd, Probus; tel: (01726) 882763*. Gardens open Mon–Sat 1000–1630 (Mar–Sept); house open Mon–Tues 1400–1630 (Apr–July). Admission £2.20 (garden) and £2.80 (house). Take bus no. 24A; 5 miles east.

 Side Tracks from Truro

FALMOUTH

TIC: *28 Killigrew St, Falmouth, Cornwall TR11 3PN; tel: (01326) 312300*. Open Mon–Thur 0845–1715, Fri 0900–1645, Sat 0900–1700 (Easter to Sept); Sun 1000–1600 (July–Aug); Mon–Thur 0845–1300 and 1400–1715, Fri 0900–1300 and 1400–1645 (Sept to Easter). DP Services offered: local bed-booking service and BABA (£2.50 booking fee taken, latest booking 1630). Tickets sold for Western National Buses and FT Williams Coaches. The *Falmouth Guide* is available free and includes an accommodation listing.

Station: Falmouth Town Station, *Avenue Rd; tel: (01872) 76244* is in the centre and has a taxi rank. It is known locally as 'The Dell' and is an unmanned station on a branch line from Truro.

Getting Around

Falmouth's attractions are all within walking distance of the town centre. Free town and transport maps are available from the TIC.

The majority of bus services are operated by **Western National**, *tel: (01209) 719988*, and most routes stop on *The Moor* in the town centre. Services are good in town but limited to outlying areas, often requiring a change at either Truro or Penzance. Very limited services operate after 1800 and on Sun. A daily 'Explorer' ticket (£4.40) and three day (£13.20) or weekly (£22) 'Key West' tickets are available from Western National for travel around the surrounding area; however, for travel within town it is better to buy standard tickets.

The main taxi rank is located on *The Moor*.

Staying in Falmouth

There is a very good range of all types of accommodation in Falmouth with the majority of cheaper establishments being located in the town centre and the more expensive hotels being on the seafront and in outlying county-side. It is generally easy to find accommodation on arrival except during **Falmouth Sailing Week** in August. Hotel chains in Falmouth include *BW*.

For budget accommodation: **Pendennis Youth Hostel**, *The Headland; tel: (01326) 311435*. Open Tues–Sat from 1700 (Mar and Sept–Nov); daily (Apr–Aug). Take bus no. 64 from *The Moor* to *Pendennis Castle*. The closest campsites are **Pennance Mill Farm**, *Maenporth, tel: (01326) 312616;* **Tregadna Farm**, *Maenporth, tel: (01326) 250529;* **The Main Valley Caravan and Camping Park**, *Maenporth; tel: (01326) 312190*, all 2 miles south-west on bus route 64 to *Swanpool*, then a ½-mile walk along the coast path; and **Tremorrah Tent Site**, *Swanpool Rd; tel: (01326) 312103*, 1½ miles south-west on bus no. 64.

Sightseeing

The largest town in Cornwall, Falmouth has a vast natural harbour rimmed by grand hotels and mansions and is a popular holiday resort, renowned for its exceptionally mild climate and splendid beaches. Two wonderfully preserved castles built by Henry VIII, **Pendennis** and **St Mawes**, guard the harbour entrance: take the ferry across from one to the other and from Black Rock enjoy the stunning view up the richly wooded Fal estuary. A variety of pleasure cruises and ferries operate from Prince of Wales Pier: **St Mawes Ferry** *tel: (01326) 313813/313201;* **Enterprise Boats** *tel: (01326) 313234* for pleasure boat cruises and the ferry to *Truro;* **Falmouth Passenger Boat Co**, *tel: (01326) 313813;* and **K & S Cruises** *tel: (01326) 376347/211056*, both of which offer pleasure boat cruises and deep sea fishing. **Falmouth Sailing Week**, during the first and second weeks in August, is a major sailing regatta.

A variety of daily and half-daily bus tours around the surrounding area from **F. T. Williams** can be booked at the TIC; prices start at £3.95.

The bus service from Falmouth to Penzance offers particularly good views of the surrounding countryside. A number of gardens in the area boast subtropical species, including **Glen-durgan**, a delightful, informal valley garden, with walled and water gardens and a maze. The **Cornish Seal Sanctuary** is the largest in Europe, rescuing many sick and injured seals and returning them to the wild.

The Art Centre, *Church St; tel: (01326) 314566* (free art exhibitions and musical performances). Opening times and admission charges vary according to the event. **Cornwall Maritime Museum**, *2 Bells Court, Market St; tel: (01326) 316745.* Open Mon–Sat 1000–1600 (Apr–Sept); 1300–1500 (Oct–Mar). Admission £1. **Falmouth Gallery**, *The Municipal Building, The Moor; tel: (01326) 313863.* Open Mon–Fri 1000–1630, Sat 1000–1300. Admission free. **Pendennis Castle**, *Pendennis Headland; tel: (01326) 316594.* Open daily 1000–1800 (Apr–Oct); 1000–1600 (Nov–Mar). Admission £2.10. Take bus no. 64 from *The Moor.* **St Mawes Castle**, *St Mawes; tel: (01326) 270526.* Open daily 1000–1800 (Apr–Oct), 1000–1600 (Nov–Mar). Admission £1.25. **The Princes Pavilion and Gyllyngdune Gardens**, *Melville Rd; tel: (01326) 311277.* Opening times and admission charges vary according to the event.

Out of Town

Cornish Seal Sanctuary, *The Marine Animal Rescue Centre, Gweek, Helston; tel: (01326) 221361.* Open daily 0900–1800 (Apr–Oct); 1000–1700 (Nov–Mar). Admission £4.50; 5 miles south-west on Truronian Bus route 324. **Flambards Village Theme Park**, *Culdrose Manor, Helston; tel: (01326) 574549.* Open daily 1000–1730 (Apr–Oct). Admission £7.95; bus no. 2, 13 miles south-west. **Glendurgan Gardens**, *Mawnan Smith; tel: (01326) 250906.* Open Tues–Sat and Bank Holiday Mon 1030–1730 (Mar–Oct, last admission 1630). Admission £2.50; 4 miles south-west on Truronian Bus route 324. **Trebah Gardens**, *Mawnan Smith; tel: (01326) 250448.* Open daily 1000–1700. Admission £2.50. Four miles south-west on Truronian Bus route 324.

Falmouth

 Side Tracks from St Erth

ST IVES

TIC, *The Guildhall, Street-an-Pol, St Ives, Cornwall TR26 2DS; tel: (01736) 796297.* Open Mon–Thur 0900–1730, Fri 0900–1700 (Jan–mid-May); Mon–Sat 0900–1730 (mid-May–mid-July); Mon–Sat 0900–1800, Sun 1000–1300 (mid-July–Aug); Mon–Sat 0900–1730 (3 Sep–15 Sep); Mon–Thur 0900–1730, Fri 0900–1700 (15 Sep–Dec). SHS Services offered, local bed-booking service (latest 1 hour before closing), BABA – for accommodation bookings be prepared to queue between 1200–1700. *West Cornwall Guide* (including accommodation list) is £1.

Station: St Ives Station, *tel: (01872) 76244* is ½ mile from the town centre, and has a taxi rank.

Getting Around

Attractions are all within walking distance of the centre. A one-day **Explorer** ticket costs from £3.30–£11. A weekly **Keywest** ticket costs from £9.90–£44. For information contact: *tel: (01209) 719988.*

The main bus operator is **Western National** *tel: (01209) 719988.* Services are good within the town, but less frequent to outlying areas, with reduced services after 2000 and on Sun.

Registered taxi companies are as follows: **Goodways** (at the railway station) *tel: (01736) 794437;* **Nicholls** *tel: (01736) 796361;* **St Eia** (01736) 793100. **Dial-a-Car** *tel: (01860) 778818* has facilities for the handicapped.

Staying in St Ives

A good range of accommodation is available, particularly guest-houses and b.&b s. It is usually easy to find accommodation on arrival, except during July, Aug and the beginning of Sept (particularly difficult after 1600 during this period). The nearest campsites are **Ayr Holiday Site,** *Higher Ayr; tel: (01736) 795738,* and **Hellesveor Farm Caravan & Camping Site,** *Hellesveor Farm; tel: (01736) 795738.* Both are within a mile of the town, and accessible by public transport.

Sightseeing

The following companies offer bus tours: **Oates Travel,** *tel: (01736) 795343;* **Western National,** *tel: (01736) 794437;* **Harry Safari,** *tel: (01736) 711427.* Short boat trips are operated by **Paynter,** *tel: (01736) 795505.*

St Ives Tate Gallery, *Porthmeor Beach; tel: (01736) 796226.* Open April–Oct Mon, Wed, Fri, Sat 1100–1900, Tues, Thurs 1100–2100, Sun and Bank Holidays 1100–1700; Nov–Mar Tues 1100–2100, Wed–Sat 1100–1700, Sun 1300–1700. Admission £2.50. **Barbara Hepworth Museum and Sculpture Garden,** *Barnoon Hill; tel: (01736) 796226.* Open April–Oct Mon, Wed, Fri, Sat 1100–1900, Tues, Thurs 1100–2100, Sun and bank holidays 1100-1700; Nov–Mar Tues 1100-2100, Wed–Sat 1100-1700, Sun 1300–1700. Admission £2.50.

St Ives Museum, *Wheal Dream; tel: (01736) 796005.* Open daily from mid-May–30 Sep 1000–1700, and also daily during Easter week 1000–1700. Admission £0.50.

Out of Town

Chysauster Ancient Village, *New Mill, Penzance; tel: (01736) 61889.* Open Apr–Sep daily 1000–1300 and 1400–1800; Oct daily 1000–1300, 1400–1600. Admission £1.40; 7 miles south-west of St Ives. **Wayside Folk Museum,** *Old Mill House, Zennor; tel: (01736) 796945.* Open 2 Apr–30 Sep daily 1000-1800; Oct daily (except Sat) 1100–1700. Admission £1.85; 4½ miles west of St Ives, on the bus to Land's End.

PENZANCE

TIC: *Station Rd, Penzance, Truro, Cornwall TR18 2NF; tel: (01736) 62207.* Open Mon–Fri 0900–1700, 1000–1300 Sat (Oct–May), Mon–Sat 0900–1700 (June–Sept). DP SHS Services offered: local bed-booking service and BABA (£2.25 booking fee, latest one hour before closing), booking services are not available Sats between Oct and May. The *West Cornwall Guide* covering Penzance, St Ives, Hayle and the Land's End Peninsular is available free and includes accommodation listings.

Station: Penzance Station, *Station Rd; tel: (01872) 76244* is in the centre of town and has a taxi rank.

Getting Around

The majority of attractions are within a walkable area from the centre. A free town map is available from the TIC and free transport maps are available from bus and train stations.

The main bus operator is **Western National**, *tel: (01209) 719988*, which offers a good service to St Michael's Mount, Mousehole and St Ives though not so frequent to Land's End. The Promenade is not serviced by bus. For details of taxi companies contact the TIC.

Staying in Penzance

There is a good range of accommodation available, particularly mid-range hotels and guesthouses. It is generally easy to book accommodation on arrival. The closest budget accommodation is **Castle Horwick Youth Hostel**, *tel: (01736) 62666*. The TIC has details of campsites in the area

Entertainment and Events

Events and entertainment lists are available free from the TIC. **Golowan Festival** takes place annually in mid-June, culminating in **Mazey Day** on 25 June. **Marazion 400** celebrates the 400th anniversary of its Charter from 10 to 18 June 1995; and on 24 July–4 Aug the **International 505 Sailing Championships** will be held in *Mount's Bay*.

Minack Theatre and Exhibition Centre, *Porthcurno, tel: (01736) 810181* is open 28 March–30 Oct 1000–1730 (–1630 during Oct). Open-air theatre situated on the south coast, approx. 9 miles from Penzance.

Sightseeing

There is a real sense as you alight here of being right at the end of the line; the railway brings you in along the shore, and seagulls greet you on the harbourside platform. Only 10 miles from Land's End, Penzance is as much a busy market and fishing town as a seaside resort: among its narrow streets *Chapel St*, running from market

to harbour, has some remarkable Georgian houses, most notably the exotic **Egyptian House** of c.1835. The **National Lighthouse Centre** gives a dramatic insight into the history of lighthouses; the **Museum and Art Gallery** includes many works of the important Newlyn School of Artists of the 1880s, while the **Art Gallery** at Newlyn itself houses contemporary art.

Irresistible from here is a trip to **St Michael's Mount**: the great rock is capped by a spectacular castle dating from the 14th century, which contains a maze of narrow passageways. Access is by ferry or on foot across the cobbled causeway at low tide. The atmosphere of **Land's End** itself is marred by a 'visitor attraction', but a short walk south along the cliffs allows you to savour in relative peace some of England's most dramatic coastal scenery. Penzance is also the embarkation point, by ferry or helicopter, for the Isles of Scilly, and day trips by sea and air can be arranged: contact **Isles of Scilly Steamship Co Ltd**, *The Weighbridge, Penzance, tel: (01736) 62009* or **Isles of Scilly Skybus Ltd**, *Land's End Aerodrome, St Just, Penzance, tel: (01736) 787017*.

Penzance and District Museum and Art Gallery, off *Morrah Rd, tel: (01736) 63625*. Open Mon–Fri 1030–1630, Sat 1030–1230. **Trinity House National Lighthouse Centre**, *The Old Buoy Centre, Wharf Rd, Penzance* (adjacent to harbour), *tel: (01736) 60077*. Open daily 1100–1700 Mar–Oct. Admission £2.50.

Out of Town

Newlyn Art Gallery, (approaching *Newlyn*, the gallery is the first building on the sea-side of the coast road from Penzance), *tel: (01736) 63715*. Open Mon–Sat 1000–1700. Admission free.

St Michael's Mount (NT), *Marazion; tel: (01736) 710507*. Open 30 Mar–31 Oct Mon–Fri 1030–1730. From Nov–March as tide and weather permits. Admission £3.50. 10 miles south of St Ives.. **Lands End**, *The Custom House, Land's End, Sennen; tel: (01736) 871812*. Open all year daily from 1000–dusk. Closed Christmas Eve and Christmas Day. Admission £5.50. Approx 12 miles south west of St Ives.

SHEFFIELD

A boom city in the 19th century, when it was a centre for steelmaking and the manufacture of fine cutlery, Sheffield now bears the typical scars of a Victorian town whose heavy industries have drastically declined. Yet it remains prosperous and vibrant, renowned for its entertainment, and access to the Peak National Park by bus is exceptionally easy from here.

Tourist Information

TIC: Peace Gardens, Sheffield, South Yorkshire S1 2HH; tel: (0114) 273 4671/4672. Open Mon–Fri 0930–1715, Sat 0930–1615. DP SHS Services offered: local bed-booking service and BABA (latest one hour before closing), advance reservations handled. Bureau de Change; YHA membership; tickets sold for National Express and local theatres and events. Sheffield Quick Guide is free and includes accommodation listings. **TIC**: Railway Station Concourse, Sheaf St; tel: (0114) 279 5901. Open Mon–Fri 0930–1715, Sat 0930–1615. DP SHS Services offered: local bed-booking service and BABA (latest one hour before closing), advance reservations handled. Bureau de change, tickets sold for local theatres and events.

Arriving and Departing

Sheffield Station, Sheaf St; tel: (0114) 272 6411 is central and has a taxi rank, a courtesy phone for **Hertz** car hire and a TIC (see above).

Getting Around

Most attractions are on the outskirts of the city and accessible by bus from the centre. Free city and transport maps are available from the TIC.

Buses

A good bus service runs throughout the city, operated by **Main Line** from the Transport Interchange, Pond St; tel: (0114) 276 8688.

Reduced services operate between 2000 and 2400 and on Sun. A daily or weekly Travel-master card is available (£1.75 and £3.80).

Taxis

The main taxi rank is located on Barkers Pool and taxis can be hailed in the street. There are over 12 registered taxi companies in Sheffield including **Abbey Taxis** tel: (0114) 275 1111; **Association Taxis** tel: (0114) 272 1462, and **Mercury** tel: (0114) 267 0707.

Staying in Sheffield

There is a good range of all types of accommodation in Sheffield and the outlying area. The majority of cheaper accommodation is located in Millhouses, 3 miles south-west on bus route 97; Broomhill, 1½ miles west on bus route 60; Eccleshall, 1 mile south-west on bus routes 81, 82, 83 and 84; and Grenoside, 4 miles north on bus routes 42 and 53. It can be difficult to find accommodation on arrival if there is a major event being held in the city.

Hotel chains include FH, Ho, Nv, Sw. For budget accommodation try **Sheffield YMCA**, 20 Victoria Rd; tel: (0114) 268 4807 (buses 81, 82, 83 or 84), 1½ miles south-west. The closest **YHA** hostel is **Hathersage Hostel**, Hathersage, Derbyshire; tel: (01433) 650493, 11 miles west on bus 272. The nearest campsite is **Fox Hagg Farm**, Lodge Lane; tel: (0114) 230 5589 (take bus 51, 4 miles west).

Entertainment

Sheffield is home to a number of international sports and entertainment venues, including **Sheffield Arena**, a major venue for indoor pop concerts seating 12,000; **Dunn Valley Stadium**, for international athletics and outdoor pop concerts; **Ponds Forge International Sports Centre**; and the **Crucible Theatre** where the **Embassy World Snooker Championships** are held every April.

Shopping

Meadow Hall Shopping Centre is one of the largest indoor shopping centres in Europe. Use the new tram system from Sheffield city centre, close to the rail station.

Sightseeing

The story of Sheffield's industrial development is well told at the lively **Kelham Island Industrial Museum**: there is working machinery and cutlery craftsmen can be seen at work. Just out of town, the atmospheric **Abbeydale Industrial Hamlet** preserves the 18th-century workshops and machinery of a water-powered scythe and steel works; some of the houses are restored in period style. The **City Museum** has a good display of Sheffield plate and cutlery; it shares a building with the **Mappin Art Gallery**, renowned for its Victorian paintings, which lies in the attractively landscaped **Weston Park**. One of the city's few surviving old buildings, 15th–16th-century **Bishops House**, houses a museum of Sheffield life in Tudor and Stuart times.

Sheffield's fine setting, cradled by seven hills, is a clue to its location on the edge of the Peak National Park: the TIC has details of walks, and rail and bus routes (the Peak is well served by public transport). Bus routes 240 to *Bakewell* and 272 to *Castleton* offer scenic views of the Peak District. Within the city itself there are no organised guided tours or walks, but an individual 'Walkman Tour' can be rented from the TIC for £3; the TIC can also provide details of registered guides in Sheffield.

Abbeydale Industrial Hamlet, *Abbeydale Rd South; tel: (0114) 236 7731.* Open Tues–Sat 1000–1700, Sun 1100–1700. Admission £2.50. Take bus no. 97, 4 miles south-west. **Bishops House Museum,** *Meersbrook Park; tel: (0114) 255 7701.* Open Wed–Sat 1000–1630; Sun 1100–1630. Admission £1. Take bus no. 434 or 439, 3 miles south. **City Museum,** *Weston Park; tel: (0114) 276 8588.* Open Tues–Sat 1000–1700, Sun 1100–1700. Admission free. Take bus no. 52, 1 mile west.

Graves Art Gallery, *Top Floor, Central Library; tel: (0114) 273 5158.* Open Mon–Sat 1000–1700. Admission free. **Kelham Island Industrial Museum,** *Alma St; tel: (0114) 272 2106.* Open Mon–Thur 1000–1600, Sun 1100–1645. Admission £2.50. Take bus no. 47 or 48, ½ mile north-east.

Mappin Art Gallery, *Weston Park; tel:* *(0114) 272 6281.* Open Tues–Sat 1000–1700, Sun 1100–1700. Admission free. Take bus no. 52, 1 mile west. **Ruskin Art and Craft Gallery,** *Norfolk St; tel: (0114) 273 5299.* Open Mon–Sat 1000–1700. Admission free. **Sheffield Cathedral,** *Church St; tel: (0114) 275 3434.* Open daily (times vary according to services, check for details). Admission free.

Out of Town

The Butterfly Farm, *Hungerhill Farm, Woodsetts Rd, North Anston; tel: (01909) 569416.* Open daily 1000–1700 (Apr–Oct); Sat, Sun 1000–1600 (Nov–Mar). Admission £3.75. Take bus 53, 15 miles south-east. Also within reach are **Chatsworth House** and **Haddon Hall** – see Matlock, pp. 77–78.

 Side Track from Sheffield

BUXTON

TIC: *The Crescent, Buxton, Derbyshire SK17 6BQ; tel: (01298) 25106/77889.* Open 0930–1700 (Mar–Oct), 1000–1600 (Nov–Feb); closed 25 Dec only. DP Services offered: local bed-booking service (latest 15 mins before closing), advance reservations handled, BABA (latest 30 mins before closing). Membership sold for YHA, AA, RAC. *Buxton Town Guide* is £0.85. *High Peak Where to Stay* is £0.10. The TIC has details of wheelchairs available for free use through the Buxton Volunteer Bureau.

Station: Buxton Station, *Station Rd; tel: (0161) 832 8353,* is just ¼ mile north of the town centre, within easy walking distance. There is no direct rail link from Sheffield to Buxton. Passengers must take the half-hourly service to Stockport (takes about 40 mins), where they must change for the hourly service to Buxton (also takes about 40 mins).

Getting Around

The majority of attractions are within a walkable distance of the town centre. The TIC can help with travel information, and has maps for sale.

Local bus services are run by a number of different companies; for general enquiries there

Sightseeing–Out of Town–Buxton

is **Busline** tel: (01298) 23098. Services are good within the centre, but rather patchy to outlying areas, with more limited evening and Sunday services, and no coverage of the Goyt Valley.

Main taxi ranks are at Grove Parade and Market Place, and taxis can also be hailed in the street.

Staying in Buxton

There is generally no problem in finding accommodation on arrival, except from mid-July to mid-Aug during the **Opera Festival** and **Gilbert and Sullivan Festival**. There is a good selection of hotels, guesthouses and b. & b.s, with cheaper accommodation about a 10-min walk from the centre.

Hotel chains include BW, Co. Buxton has a youth hostel, at Sherbrook Lodge, Harpur Hill; tel: (01298) 22287, open from 1700. There are many more in the Peak District area – a list is available from the TIC.

There are four campsites in Buxton: **Cold Springs Farm** tel: (01298) 22762; **Grin Low Caravan Club Site** tel: (01298) 77735; **Lime Tree Park** tel: (01298) 22988; **Staden Grange** tel: (01298) 24985.

Sightseeing

Buxton owes its mellow grandeur to its development as a fashionable Georgian spa town (which never quite rivalled Bath). Its many beautiful 18th- and 19th-century buildings easily seen on foot are centred around the lovely hillside **Pavilion Gardens**, which are crowned by the magnificent iron and glass **Pavilion** of 1871 and the Edwardian **Opera House** (tel: (01298) 72190 for box office and information), setting of Buxton's annual festival. The prominent **Devonshire Hospital** (1859) is claimed to have the widest dome in the world. Opposite the (scandalously neglected) Crescent (1780–4) is **St Ann's Well**, where you can sample the Buxton spring water; next to it, the former Pump Room now houses the **Micrarium**, where remote-controlled microscopes allow a close-up look at the natural world. **High Peak Blue Badge Guides** offer a programme of guided walks, starting from the TICs in Buxton and Castleton tel: (01433) 651349.

The town is set high in the **Peak National Park**, which offers over 1600 miles of public footpaths and 80 square miles of open access country. If your time to explore the countryside is limited, on the edge of Buxton the **Country Park** has good views of some typical High Peak scenery plus **Poole's Cavern**, one of the many spectacular caves in the region: this one is rich in amazing rock formations. If you do have time to explore, head for **Castleton**, the heart of High Peak walking country. Of the caves here, **Peak Cavern** is perhaps the most spectacular and is nearest to the village, while the **Speedwell Cavern** has to be visited by boat. For those fit enough for the climb up to Norman **Peveril Castle**, the reward is a truly panoramic view over Castleton and the surrounding hills and moors.

Buxton Micrarium, The Crescent; tel: (01298) 78662. Open 1000–1700 (end Mar to Oct). Admission £2.50. **Buxton Museum and Art Gallery**, Terrace Rd; tel: (01298) 24658. Open Tues–Fri 0930–1730, Sat, Sun 0930–1700. Admission £1.

Poole's Cavern, Buxton Country Park, Green Lane; tel: (01298) 26978. Open daily 1000–1700 (Easter–Oct); closed Wed in Apr, May and Oct. Admission £2.50

Out of Town

Castleton is approximately 8 miles north-east, 35 mins by bus. Bus numbers vary according to day and season so tel: (01298) 23098 for details.

Blue John Cavern and Blue John Mine, Castleton; tel: (01433) 620638/620642. Open daily 0930–1730 or dusk if earlier, (Jan and Feb weather permitting). Admission £4. **Peak Cavern**, Castleton; tel: (01433) 620285. Open daily 1000–1700 (Easter–Oct). Admission £2.80. **Peveril Castle** (EH), Castleton; tel: (01433) 620613. Open daily 1000–1800 (Apr–Oct), 1000–1600 (Nov–Mar). Admission £1.25.

Speedwell Cavern, Castleton; tel: (01433) 620512. Open daily 0930–1730 (1630 in winter). Admission £4.50. **Treak Cliff Cavern**, Castleton; tel: (01433) 620571. Open daily 0930–1730 (1600 in winter). Admission £3.80.

SOUTHAMPTON to WEYMOUTH

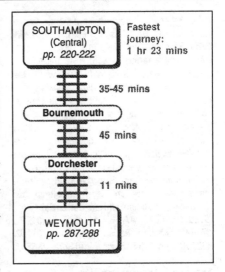

SOUTHAMPTON (Central) pp. 220-222

Fastest journey: 1 hr 23 mins

35-45 mins

Bournemouth

45 mins

Dorchester

11 mins

WEYMOUTH pp. 287-288

This route, beginning in the natural beauty of the New Forest, takes in the chalk hills of Purbeck and the Dorset county town of Dorchester – immortalised as 'Casterbridge' in the novels of Thomas Hardy – as well as some of Britain's most impressive ancient remains, including the Iron Age hill-fort, Maiden Castle. It also visits two of the south coast's most popular seaside resorts, Bournemeouth and Weymouth, the latter a favourite watering-place of King George III.

TRAINS

ETT table: 502

 Fast Track

An hourly service operates between Southampton Central and Weymouth. Trains take 1 hr 23 mins. Sunday services start mid-morning.

On Track

Southampton–Bournemouth

A half-hourly train service each day of the week links Southampton and Bournemouth. Journey times vary from 35 to 45 mins, depending on number of stops.

Bournemouth–Dorchester

Hourly trains (every day) connect Bournemouth with Dorchester South station; journey time 45 mins.

Dorchester–Weymouth

Hourly trains (every day) connect Dorchester South with Weymouth; journey time 11 mins.

BOURNEMOUTH

TIC: *Westover Rd, Bournemouth, Dorset BH1 2BU; tel: (01202) 789789.* Open Sept–mid May, Mon–Sat 0930–1730; mid May–mid July, Mon–Sat 0930–1730, Sun 1030–1700; mid July–early Sept, Mon–Sat 0930–1900, Sun 1030–1700. After hours: 24-hr electronic information unit (touch pad) in TIC window.

DP SHS services offered: local bed-booking service (latest 10 mins before closing), BABA (latest 10 mins before closing). 10% of first night booking. Advance availability information given to clients to book hotels direct. Coach tickets booked, some theatre tickets and AA/ RAC membership. The booklet *Bournemouth – Our Idea of a Holiday* is available for £1, or free by post.

Station: Bournemouth Station, *Holdenhurst Rd; tel: (01202) 292474* is 1 mile north-east of the town centre. There is a taxi rank at the station and **Europcar UK Ltd**, *tel: (01202) 293357*, has an office. There is a bus service into the centre.

Getting Around

The majority of attractions are within walking distance of the town centre. A free transport map is available from the TIC.

Yellow Buses, *tel: (01202) 291288/673555,*

cover Bournemouth, with services to Christchurch and Poole. **Wilts & Dorset**, tel: (01202) 673555, cover Bournemouth, Poole, Christchurch and a radius of approx 40 miles. Both companies operate a 20-min service within the town centre and a 5-mile radius. There is a half-hourly or hourly service to the outlying areas. Both companies are in service until after 2300. Yellow Buses offer the daily or monthly Buzzcard; Wilts & Dorset tickets include the one-day Explorer, 7-day Busabout, Freedom (weekly) and Faresaver (for senior citizens).

The main taxi rank is in the town centre in the square. There are seven registered taxi companies, including **United Radio Cabs**, tel: (01202) 556677; **AA Radio Cars**, tel: (01202) 576621; **Mobile Radio Cars**, tel: (01202) 522500; and **Ariel Taxis**, tel: (01202) 766707.

Staying in Bournemouth

Accommodation

The range and quality of Bournemouth's accommodation is outstanding. There is a choice of country-style retreats set amid wooded valleys, cliff-top hotels with superb sea views, five-star hotels or cosy guest houses to suit all budgets. Bournemouth is at its busiest during Bank Holidays, particularly Aug, and at New Year. Hotel chains in Bournemouth include BW, Co, DV, MC, St and Sw.

Bournemouth Association Hotel, 4 Westover Rd; tel: (01202) 293566/558000, is an agency which can book accommodation. The TIC have lists of campsites. The nearest are: **Mount Pleasant**, Matchans Ln, Christchurch; tel: (01202) 475474. 4 miles east. **Portview Caravan Park**, Matchans Ln, Christchurch; tel: (01202) 474214. 6 miles east. **Heathfield Touring Park**, 'Eulan', Avon Causeway, Christchurch; tel: (01202) 485208. 6 miles north-east. However, none of them is on a public transport route.

Eating and Drinking

There is a wide selection of eating establishments in and around Bournemouth, from exclusive restaurants and luxurious hotels to trendy café bars and traditional village inns.

Entertainment

Bournemouth has a very wide variety of entertainment venues, including four theatres, and guarantees a selection of spectacular shows throughout the season. As part of the national and world tour circuit, Bournemouth's **International Centre** and **Pavilion** attract the big-name stars and West End productions. The **Bournemouth Symphony Orchestra** returns annually to the **Winter Gardens** for a series of summer concerts. Live entertainment is very much part of the scene in pubs, clubs and hotel bars.

Events

Major events in Bournemouth include **Bournemouth Garden and Flower Show**, 12–14 May; **Bournemouth International Festival**, 13–28 May; **Music Makers Festival**, 12–28 May; **Carnival and Regatta**, 29 July–6 Aug; **Kids' Free Fun Festival**, 30 July–28 Aug (all 1995 dates – 1996 dates may vary slightly).

Shopping

Bournemouth is one of the best shopping centres in the south of England. A traffic-free stroll from one end of town to the other takes you through ornate arcades, malls and the recently pedestrianised square. All the main chain and department stores are well represented, as well as shops unique to Bournemouth.

Sightseeing

Bournemouth has a reputation as the 'Garden City by the Sea'. The town is big on entertainment, major events and conferences and offers more quality accommodation than any other seaside resort in England. Its central southerly location means the year-round climate is mild, with above-average sunshine and winds mainly gentle westerlies.

Bournemouth's 7 miles of sandy beaches, set in a sheltered bay, stretch from Hengistbury Head in the east to Alum Chine in the west and are interrupted only by two piers at Boscombe and Bournemouth. The town's 2000 acres of parks and gardens are kept in award-winning form.

The area has plenty to see and do. The **Russell-Cotes Art Gallery and Museum** on Bournemouth's East Cliff is the perfect setting for its lavish collections of Victorian and Edwardian paintings, furniture, decorative and modern art, whilst the **Water Zoo** offers a colourful and informative insight into life in the world's oceans and rivers.

Nearby **Kingston Lacy House** is a fine example of a 17th–century mansion, housing countless valuable art treasures. **Corfe Castle** is the impressive ruin of a Norman castle destroyed by Cromwell's Roundhead troops in 1646. It overlooks a picturesque village of mellowed stone cottages nestling deep in the Purbeck Hills. **Beaulieu** charts a century's motoring achievement with over 250 vehicles and displays. Other attractions include Palace House and Grounds, Abbey ruins, monorail and river cruises to the 18th–century village of **Buckler's Hard**, where ships for Nelson's fleet were built. **Paulton's Park**, near Southampton, is a family leisure park with lots of fun activities in acres of parkland.

Several bus tours are available, all of which are bookable at the TIC. **Waverley & Balmoral Excursions,** tel: *(01202) 720656* do boat trips from *Bournemouth Pier* from £5.95 for a half day. Bookable at the TIC. Free guided walks and **Blue Badge Guides** are also available.

Russell-Cotes Art Gallery and Museum, *Russell Cotes Rd; tel: (01202) 551099.* Open Tues–Sun 1000–1700. Admission: £1. **Shelley Rooms,** *Boscombe Manor, Beechwood Ave, Boscombe; tel: (01202) 551009.* Open Tues–Sun 1400–1700. Admission free. **St Peters Church and Shelley Family Tomb,** *Hinton Rd; tel: (01202) 290986.* **Bournemouth Gardens and Parks, Bourne Stream, Pier, Chines and Promenade** (information from TIC). Centrally located. Other gardens at Boscombe, Southbourne and Westbourne. **Water Zoo,** *Pier Approach: tel: (01202) 295393.* Open daily 1000–2200 (1800 in winter). Admission £1.50.

Expo Centre, (three exhibitions) *Old Christ-church Ln; tel: (01202) 293544.* Open daily 0930–1730. Admission £3.50 per exhibition. **Captain Kids Adventure Playground,** *J J Allen*

Shopping Centre, Old Christchurch Rd; tel: (01202) 290666. Open daily 1000–1800 (2100 during summer hols). Admission £2.50 per child.

Out of Town

Kingston Lacy House and Gardens (NT), nr Wimborne; tel: (01202) 883402. Open Mar–Nov 1200–1830 (closed Thurs & Fri). Admission £5.20. 10 miles north-west. Excursion tours. **Bovington Tank Museum,** *Bovington Camp, Nr Wareham; tel: (01929) 403463.* Open all year, 1000–1700. Admission £4. 20 miles west. Excursion tours.

DORCHESTER

TIC: *1 Acland Rd, Dorchester, Dorset; tel: (01305) 267992/260193.* Open Mon–Fri 1000–1500, Sat 1000–1400 (Nov–Mar); Mon–Sat 0900–1700 (Apr–June and Sept–Oct); Mon–Fri 0900–1800, Sat 0900–1700, Sun 1000–1400 (July–Aug). DP SHS Services offered: local bed-booking service and BABA (latest 30 mins before closing). Tickets are sold for local buses and coaches, theatres and events. *Dorchester Historical Guide and Town Trails* is £0.35 and *West Dorset Where to Stay* and *West Dorset Where to Go* are available free. **Stations**: Dorchester South Station, *Weymouth Ave; tel: (01305) 264423* is ½ mile south of the town centre and has a taxi rank; there is a regular bus service between the station and town centre. Dorchester West Station, *Great Western Rd; tel: (01305) 264423* is ½ mile west of the town centre, but the station has no public transport connections to Dorchester and does not have a taxi rank. Use Dorchester South for Bournemouth, Southampton and Weymouth trains, and Dorchester West for Bristol trains.

Getting Around

The majority of Dorchester's attractions are within walking distance of the town centre with the exception of **Maiden Castle**, which is 2½ miles out of town. A town map is available from the TIC (price £0.10) and free transport maps are available either from the TIC or from **Dorset County Council**.

Bus services are operated by a number of

different companies including **Southern National,** tel: (01823) 272033. Phone the TIC or **Dorset County Council,** tel: (01305) 251000, for information on bus services. There is no bus station in Dorchester but most services stop on Acland Rd. Services are good in the centre of town but patchy to outlying areas. Only a limited service runs after 1800.

The main taxi rank is on Trinity St, and taxi companies in the town include **Abcars** tel: (01305) 269696; **A-Line Taxis/Dorchester Taxi Services,** tel: (01305) 262888, 264747 or 251666, **Fast Cabs,** tel: (01305) 251655, **Petes Cabs,** tel: (01305) 251122, **Starline Taxis,** tel: (01305) 263922, and **Wessex Taxi Hire,** tel: (01305) 251800.

Staying in Dorchester

Accommodation

There are no large hotels in Dorchester and only two smaller ones but, with about 20 b.&b. establishments and 6 pubs and inns offering accommodation located throughout the town and outlying area, it is generally easy to find lodgings on arrival.

The closest campsites to Dorchester are **Sea Barn** and **West Fleet Holiday Farm,** Fleet, Weymouth; tel: (01305) 782218, 7 miles southwest, with only a limited bus service; **Giant's Head Caravan and Camping Park,** Old Sherborne Rd, Cerne Abbas; tel (01300) 341242, 8 miles north with no public transport access; **Sandyholme Holiday Park,** Moreton Rd, Dorchester, 6 miles east; and **The Ranch House,** Osmington Mills, Weymouth; tel: (01305) 832311, 8 miles south on Southern National's bus route 31.

Eating and Drinking

Most restaurants in Dorchester serve English food with a few offering ethnic cuisine; there are no restaurants specialising in vegetarian meals. The best roads for restaurants are High West St and High East St. A list of local restaurants is available free from the TIC.

Dorset Blue Vinney Cheese, Dorchester chocolates and fudge and Moores Dorset Biscuits are all local specialities.

Communications

The main post office is at 43 South St and has a post restante facility.

Entertainment and Events

Entertainment listings can be found in local papers available from newsagents. A listing of major events in West Dorset and the surrounding area is available free from the TIC. The **Dorchester Show,** Came Park, 2 miles east of town, is held every year on the first Sat in Sept.

Shopping

South St, Trinity St, High West St and High East St are particularly good for shopping. The open and covered market in Dorchester is held every Wed between 0800–1500, between Maumbury Rd, Weymouth Ave and Upper Fairfield Rd. The market is one of the largest in the south of England.

Sightseeing

The county town of Dorset, Dorchester seems to have changed little since it featured so prominently as Casterbridge in the novels of Thomas Hardy (1940–1928), whose rather sombre statue broods at the end of High West St. Hardy's last home, max gate, which he designed himself, is in Dorchester but is not open to the public. The **Dorset County Museum** has a reconstruction of his study, plus memorabilia, and is an excellent starting point for exploring Dorset's earlier history, too. For Hardy's birthplace, see under Weymouth.

A 2-mile walk south-west from Dorchester South station brings you to **Maiden Castle,** one of the finest Iron Age forts in Britain: dating from the 1st century BC, this massive defensive earthwork powerfully evokes (as does much of the Dorset landscape) the presence of the pre-Roman British. The castle was captured in around AD 43 by the Romans, who created Durnovaria, the present Dorchester, down the road to supersede it.

Remains of what was an important provincial centre are scattered around the town, including the vast amphitheatre which the Romans created out of **Maumbury Rings,** a Bronze

Age circle (near Dorchester South station).

Incongruously, Dorcester is also home to the **Dinosaur Museum**, Britain's only museum devoted to this subject, complete with touch displays; and the **Tutankhamun Exhibition**, which has a reconstruction of the tomb and facsimile of its contents. But why here?

Some more traditional sights are to be found amidst the rolling Dorset countryside. **Athelhampton House** is a delightfully romantic 15th-century manor house, with lovely gardens surrounded by the River Piddle (*sic*). At **Minterne Gardens** there is a fine collection of rare trees and shrubs: a trip here also allows you a glimpse *en route* of the immodest **Cerne Giant**, the extraordinary Romano-British hill carving of a club-bearing man revealing his all to the inhabitants of the village below.

A variety of guided walks can be booked from the TIC (prices start at £1.50) who also offer individual guide services around Dorchester and the surrounding area.

Dinosaur Museum, *Icen Way; tel: (01305) 269880.* Open daily 0930–1730. Admission £3.50. **Dorset County Museum,** *High West St; tel: (01305) 262735.* Open Mon–Sat 1000–1700 (all year), Sun 1000–1700 (July–Aug). Admission £1.95. **Maiden Castle** (EH), 2 miles south-west off A354 (follow Maiden Castle Road). Open at any reasonable time, admission free. **The Military Museum,** *The Keep, Bridport Rd; tel: (01305) 264066.* Open daily 0930–1700 (Easter to Sept). Admission £1.50. **Tutankhamun Exhibition,** *High West St; tel: (01305) 269571.* Open daily 0930–1730. Admission £3.50.

Out of Town

Athelhampton House, *Athelhampton, Puddletown; tel: (01305) 848363.* Open 1200–1700 Wed, Thurs and Sun (Apr–Oct), Tues (May–Sept) and Mon and Fri (July–Aug). Admission £4.20 (house and garden) and £2.50 (garden only). **Kingston Maurward Park** (1½ miles north-east), *Stinsford; tel: (01305) 264738.* Open daily 1300–1700 (Easter to mid-Oct). Admission £2.50.

Minterne Gardens, *Minterne Magna; tel: (01300) 341370.* Open daily 1000–1900 (Apr–

Oct). Admission £2. Ten miles north. **Millhouse Cider Museum,** *Overmoigne; tel: (01305) 852220.* Open daily 0930–1730. Admission £1. Seven miles south-east, not accessible by public transport.

WEYMOUTH

TIC: *The Pavilion Complex, The Esplanade; tel: (01305) 785747/760804 fax: (01305) 761654.* Open Daily Easter and May Bank Holidays 0930–1830, 17 Apr–Mid June 0930–1700 (1800 Fri), Mid June–Mid Jul 0930–1830, Mid Jul–Sep 0930–2100 (2200 Mon), 28 Aug 0930–2100, Sep–Nov 0930–1700 and Nov–Mar 1000–1600. DP SHS services offered: local bed-booking service (latest 5 mins before closing); 10% deposit to be paid in advance, BABA 10% of first night as a deposit or £3.50 (latest 15 mins before closing). Ferry and coach excursions and National Express bus tickets are available. A Weymouth, Portland and South Dorset guide is available for £1.50 and has accommodation listings. There is also a free guide, *Royal Manor of Portland*.

Station: Weymouth Station, *King St; tel: (01202) 292474.* There is a taxi rank at the station.

Getting Around

Most of the attractions in the town are within a walkable area of the centre. Free transport maps are available from the TIC. The area is well serviced by trains, ferries and buses. For ferry enquiries for travel to the Channel Islands *tel: (01305) 761556.*

Southern National, *King's Statue, The Esplanade; tel: (01305) 783645;* **Wilts & Dorset Bus Company;** *1 Dawson Centre, Poole; tel: (01202) 673555* and trains *tel: (01305) 292474.* Bus services are regular to the town and outlying areas of Portland and Dorchester; however, they are poor to rural villages. There are free market buses in season. Services are limited after 1800. A **Rover** ticket can be purchased which covers the whole town on a weekly or monthly basis.

Taxi ranks can be found at the *Esplanade*. Registered taxi companies: **AB Taxis;** *tel:*

(01305) 760088; **Portline;** *tel: (01305) 821600;* **Bee Cars;** *tel: (01305) 775151;* **Summers;** *(01305) 783571;* **Central;** *(01305) 786600;* **Station;** *(01305) 788888;* **Fleetline;** *(01305) 784252;* **Weytax;** *(01305) 773636.*

Staying in Weymouth

There is an excellent range of accommodation in Weymouth, ranging from large independents to b. & b. establishments. It is always a good idea to book in advance, especially in the **Carnival Week,** in mid-Aug. The majority of cheaper accommodation is located around the town centre. Youth accommodation is provided at the **RSPB Lighthouse,** *Portland; tel: (01305) 778313.* The TIC can provide information on **campsites** surrounding Weymouth, the closest being approximately 2 miles away: **Waterside Holiday Park,** *Bowleaze Cove; tel: (01305) 833103.* Bus no. 503, in summer only. Others include **Pebble Bank,** *90 Camp Road, Wyke Regis; tel: (01305) 774844.* 'F' bus service to White Church plus a ¼-mile walk. **Osmington Mills Holidays,** *Osmington; tel: (01305) 832311.* Bus no. 505, in summer only. **East Fleet Farm,** *Chickerhill; tel: (01305) 785768.* Bus service 'A' plus a 1-mile walk.

Sightseeing

Weymouth is an old harbour town and popular seaside resort, standing on the river Wey. The town is notable for its handsome late Georgian buildings and its beautiful bay. The most striking landmark north of the river and the landlocked harbour is the elaborately painted and gilded statue of **George III** on the Esplanade; the royal seal of approval did much to put Weymouth on the map as a watering-place. Among the good Georgian buildings to the North is the **Gloucester Hotel,** the king's summer home during his visits.

Beyond the fanciful **Jubilee Clock** are, both on the left, **Greenhill Gardens** and **Lodmoor Country Park,** salt marshland kept as a nature reserve.

Chesil Bank is a natural wonder extending from the Isle of Portland, off Weymouth, westwards almost as far as Bridport, some 18 miles. This vast bank of shingle, 40 ft high in places, is unique in Europe. The pebbles which make it up increase in size consistently from the west end to the east. Although the sea deposits the pebbles, there is no agreement among experts as to where they all come from.

It is possible to take bus tours by **Dorset Queen;** *tel: (01305) 852829;* **Bluebird;** *tel: (01305) 786262* and **Barry's;** *tel: (01305) 782149.* For boat trips contact **Condor;** *tel: (01305) 761551.* A book of guided walks is produced by Dorset County Council, price £1.60. Guides are available through the TIC. The area is well known for its watersports.

Special events which visitors should not miss are the **VE Celebrations,** 5–8 May (1995 only), **Summer Spectacular shows,** and the **National Model Ships Regatta,** 15–16 Jul.

Nothe Fort, *Barrack Rd; tel (01305) 787243.* Open 1030–1730. Admission £2. **Portland Castle** (EH), *Castletown; tel (01305) 820539.* Open 1000–1800. Admission £1.80.

Deepsea Adventure and Titanic Story, *Custom House Quay; tel: (01305) 760690.* Open 1000–1700. Admission £3.35. **Portland Museum,** *Wakeham; tel: (01305) 821804.* Open 1030–1700. Admission £1.10. **Bennetts Water Garden,** *Chickerell; tel: (01305) 785150.* Open 1000–1700. Admission £2.75.

Radipole Lake Nature Reserve, *Radipole Lake; tel: (01305) 778313.* Hides, 0800–2000 and nature centre, 0900–1700. **Brewers Quay and Timewalk,** *Hope Sq; tel: (01305) 777622.* Open 0930–1730 (2130 peak season). Admission £3.50, £3 and £1. Model World, *Preston Beach Rd; tel: (01305) 781797.* Open 1000–1800 (2200 in peak season). Admission £2. **Sealife Centre,** *Preston Beach Rd; tel: (01305) 761070.* Open 1000–1800. Admission £4.75.

Out of Town

Thomas Hardy's Cottage (EH), *Lower Bockhampton; tel: (01305) 62366.* The writer's birthplace. Exterior visits from end of garden 1 Apr–31 Oct daily except Thu 1100–1800; interior can be visited by appointment only. Admission £2.50.

YORK

The river Ouse flows through the beautiful and historic city of York. Originally settled by the Romans, followed by the Vikings and the Normans, York became prosperous with the medieval wool trade. Much of York's history can be seen within its city walls, built on Roman foundations and entered by one of four medieval gates. The centre of York is a maze of ancient streets with narrow alleys, known as snickelways. Today, the city is a fascinating mixture of architecture and treasures from Roman, Viking, Norman, medieval and Georgian times up to the present day, and can boast more attractions per square mile than most cities in Britain.

Tourist Information

TIC: York Visitor and Conference Bureau, 6 Rougier St, York YO1 1JA; tel: (01904) 620557. Open Mon–Sat 0900–1800, Sun 1000–1700. DP SHS services offered: local bed-booking service, BABA (latest 30 mins before closing). Advance booking for self-catering holidays. Guided tours booked. *York Official Guide* (including accommodation listing) available free of charge. Bureau de change. Guide Friday Tours. Theatre tickets, National Express and Scottish Citylink tickets booked.

Arriving and Departing

Station: **York Station**, *Station Rd, York; tel: (01904) 642155.* There is a **TIC** on the station, which operates an accommodation finding service. **Hertz** *(tel: (01904) 612586* is represented at the station and there is a taxi rank.

Getting Around

Most attractions are within a walkable distance from the centre. (In deciphering street maps, remember that '-gate' means 'street' in York, as in many other English towns which were Viking

settlements.) A town map is available from the TIC. Local transport is very good in the city. Frequency to outlying areas varies. A Minster Card, covering the whole town's transport system, is available weekly (£7.50) or monthly (£27).

Buses

York Rider, *Rougier St; tel: (01904) 624161*, adjacent to the TIC, is the main operator of local buses, and can supply a free transport map.

Taxis

The main taxi rank is outside York Station; *tel: (01904) 623332.* Registered taxi companies include: **Station Taxis** *tel: (01904) 623332*; **Streamline** *tel: (01904) 638833* and **Fleetways** *tel: (01904) 645333.* Further names are available from the TIC. Taxis can be hailed in the street.

Staying in York

Accommodation

There is a good range of accommodation. The majority of cheaper lodging is to be found on the edge of town and in the suburbs. It is generally easy to book on arrival, except July–Sept, Bank Holidays and 11–25 February (because of the **Jorvik Festival**, see next page). Accommodation ranges from large, mid-range and small hotels to guest-houses and pubs/inns. Hotel chains in York include: *BW, Co, Ja, Pr, MH, St* and *Sw.*

The nearest youth hostel is **Youth Hotel**, *Bishopgate Senior; tel: (01904) 612494.* Open all year, 24 hours a day. The TIC can provide information on campsites. The closest to town are **Rawcliffe Manor Campsite**, *Manor Rd; tel: (01904) 624422.* Take bus 32, 2 miles north; and **Naburn Locks Camping and Caravan Site**, *Naburn; tel: (01904) 728697.* 4 miles south, **Jaronda Travel** runs a bus hourly (no. 42).

Eating and Drinking

There is a good selection of restaurants catering for most tastes. Local traditional dishes include Yorkshire Pudding, Wensleydale Cheese and Yorkshire Curd Tart.

Communications

The main post office is situated in *Lendal*. Open Mon–Fri 0900–1700, Sat 0900–1230. Poste restante facilities are available.

Money

Thomas Cook bureaux de change can be found at the rail station (Inner Concourse) and in the town at *4 Nessgate*, *31 Stonegate* and Midland Bank, *13 Parliament St*.

Entertainment and Events

The publication *York Diary*, detailing entertainments, is available free from the TIC. Main venues are: **York Theatre Royal**, *St Leonard's Pl; tel: (01904) 623568*; **The Barbican Centre**, *Barbican Rd; tel: (01904) 656688*; and **The Grand Opera House**, *Clifford St; tel: (01904) 671818*.

The main event in York is the **Jorvik Festival**, 11–25 Feb, recalling the Viking origins of the city. Many different events take place all over the city throughout the two weeks of the festival; some are free, others have an admission charge. For further information contact Fibbers, *tel: (01904) 651250*. The **Early Music Festival** takes place in July; details from *York Festival Office, PO Box 226, York YO3 6ZU, tel: (01904) 658338*. A full events listing is available free of charge from the TIC.

Shopping

York is a treasure trove for shoppers – the winding medieval streets house famous names in some of the city's most beautiful buildings. Visit **The Shambles**, **Stonegate Walk**, **Petergate** and **Coppergate Centre** for specialist shopping. There is a market in *Market Sq* every day.

Sightseeing

York has many attractions and most of them are within walking distance of each other. In the castle area is the extensive **York Castle Museum**, a fascinating reminder of bygone days complete with reconstructed shop fronts, furnished rooms and hundreds of everyday objects. In the heart of the area is 13th-century

Clifford's Tower, formerly the keep of York Castle, which allows fine views across the city. A few streets away is **York Dungeon**, a museum depicting scenes of execution, torture and other past horrors. Two historic buildings in the area are **Fairfax House**, a fine 18th-century town house with superb furniture collection, and the **Merchant Adventurers' Hall**, a guild hall built in the mid-14th century.

On the site of the excavation of the Viking street of Coppergate is the **Jorvik Viking Centre**. Here, 'time cars' transport visitors through the centuries to the sights, sounds and smells of 10th-century Viking York, complete with houses, market and a quayside. There is also an exhibition of artefacts discovered during the dig.

York's historic city centre is a maze of narrow, twisting streets such as **The Shambles**, with its medieval overhanging houses and shops. **The ARC**, in nearby St Saviourgate, is an Archaeological Resource Centre set in a restored medieval church; it offers 'hands-on' archaeology and the opportunity to try out ancient crafts such as spinning and weaving. Set amidst the city's main shopping streets is **Barley Hall**, a recreated 15th-century home where visitors step back into the time of the Wars of the Roses.

The city is crowned by the superb **York Minster**, England's largest medieval cathedral, which towers above the surrounding streets. It took 250 years to complete, 1220–1470, and is famous for its spectacular windows of medieval stained glass. Nearby is the elegant **Treasurer's House**, originally the home of the Treasurers of York Minster.

The Museum Gardens area is the pleasant location of the **Yorkshire Museum**, which has ancient treasures of Roman, Viking and medieval Yorkshire. In nearby Exhibition Square, the **York City Art Gallery** houses a splendid collection of British and European paintings.

Crossing over the river Ouse, visitors will find the **National Railway Museum**, the largest railway museum in the world. It tells the story of British railways from the 1820s onwards and includes the luxurious carriages used by Queen Victoria and Edward VII, and *Mallard*, the

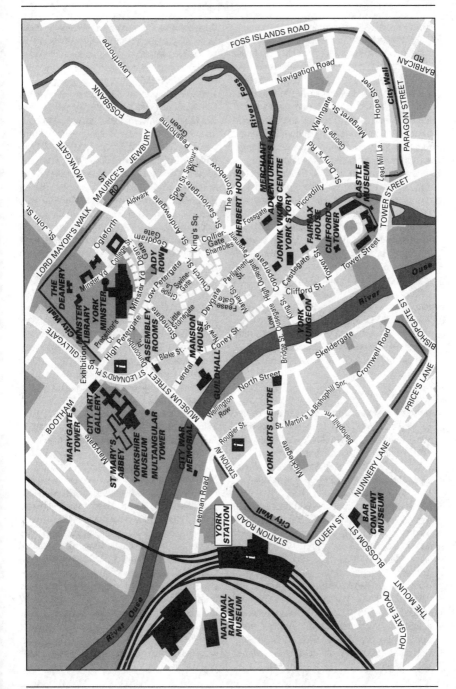

world's fastest steam locomotive.

North-west of York is **Beningbrough Hall**, a beautifully restored Georgian country house with 18th and 19th century exhibits, and to the north-east is 18th-century **Castle Howard**, the home of the Howard family and the largest and most spectacular stately home in Yorkshire. It is filled with family treasures and surrounded by over 1000 acres of parkland with lake and fountains. Castle Howard was the setting for the acclaimed TV drama *Brideshead Revisited*.

Guide Friday *tel: (01904) 640896* operate a York Tour on their open-topped double-decker buses. Tours are daily except 24–26 Dec. Price: £6 adult, £12 family ticket (2 adults and 2 children). **Eddie Brown Tours,** *8 Toer St; tel: (01904) 641737*, run excellent guided tours of Yorkshire by luxury coach. **Yorspeed**, *tel: (01904) 762622/652653*, offer a personalised tour of York. **The Original Ghost Walk of York** conducts nightly walks starting from *Kings Arms Pub, Ouse Bridge, King's Staith; tel: (01904) 764222/(01759) 373090*. Price £2.50 adults, £2 children. **The Victorian Ghost Walk** starts from *James Tea Rooms, 75 Low Petergate; tel: (01904) 640031/640036*. Price: £3.50 adults, £2.50 children.

Museums and Galleries

National Railway Museum, *Leeman Rd; tel: (01904) 621261*. Open Mon–Sat 1000–1800, Sun 1100–1800. Closed 24–26 Dec. Admission £4.20 adults, £2.10 children, £11.59 family ticket (2 + 3). **York Castle Museum,** *The Eye of York; tel: (01904) 653611*. Open Apr–Oct, Mon–Sat 0930–1730, Sun 1000; Nov–Mar, Mon–Sat 0930–1600, Sun 1000. Closed 25,26 Dec and 1 Jan. Admission £3.95 adults, £2.85 children, £11 family ticket. **York City Art Gallery,** *Exhibition Sq; tel: (01904) 623839*. Open Mon–Sat 1000–1700, Sun 1430–1700. Admission free. **Yorkshire Museum**, *Museum Gdns; tel: (01904) 629745*. Open 1 Apr–31 Oct daily 1000–1700, 1 Nov–31 March Mon–Sat 1000–1700, Sun 1300–1700. Admission £3 adults, £1.75 children. **Jorvik Viking Centre,** *Coppergate; tel: (01904) 643211*. Open Apr–Oct, 0900–1900; Nov–Mar 0900–1730. Admission £4.25 adults, £2.10 children. **York**

Dungeon, *12 Clifford St; tel: (01904) 632599*. Open all year daily from 1000. Admission £3 adults, £2 children.

Historic Buildings

York Minster, Information from The Visitors Officer, *Church House, Ogleforth; tel: (01904) 624426*. Voluntary guide service available. Various charges to different parts of the building. **The Arc,** *St Saviourgate; tel: (01904) 654324*. Open Mon–Fri 1000–1700, Sat & Sun 1300–1700. Closed Good Friday, 17 Dec–3 Jan. Admission £3.40 adults, £2.75 children. **Barley Hall,** *Coffee Yd, Swinegate; tel: (01904) 652398*. Open Mon–Sat 1000–1630. Closed Good Friday, 19 Dec–3 Jan. Admission £3.50 adults, £2.50 children. **Clifford's Tower (EH)**, *York Castle; tel: (01904) 646940*. Open Good Friday–31 Oct daily 1000–1800; 1 Nov–31 Mar daily 1000–1600. Admission £1.50 adults, £0.75 children. **Merchant Adventurer's Hall**, *Fossgate; tel: (01904) 654818*. Open 20 Mar–6 Nov daily 0830–1700, 8 Nov–20 Mar daily (except Sun) 0830–1500. Closed 22 Dec–5 Jan. Admission £1.80 adults, £1.50 children. **Treasurer's House** (NT), *Minster Yard; tel: (01904) 624247*. Open 26 Mar–30 Oct daily 1030–1700. Admission £3 adults, £1.50 children. **Fairfax House**, *Castlegate; tel: (01904) 655543*. Open 20 Feb–6 Jan Mon–Sat 1100–1700, Sun 1330–1700. Closed Fridays except in Aug. Admission £3 adults, £1.50 children.

Out of Town

Beningbrough Hall (NT), *Shipton-by-Beningbrough; tel: (01904) 470666*. Open Mar–Oct, Mon–Wed, Sat, Sun & Good Friday; Jul, Aug Friday 1100–1700. Admission £4.50 adults, £2.30 children, £11.30 family ticket. 8 miles north-west of York. **Castle Howard**, *tel: (0653) 648333*. Open Mar–Oct, 1100–1630. Admission £6 adults, £3 children, family ticket available. (£4/£2 for grounds only.) Fifteen miles north-east of York. Both accessible by tour bus, see opposite. **Mouseman Visitor Centre** (furniture store/workshop), *Kilburn; tel: (01347) 868218*. Open 1 Apr–31 Oct Tues–Sun, Bank Hol Mon 1000. Small admission charge. Taxi from Thirsk or York.

YORK to CARLISLE

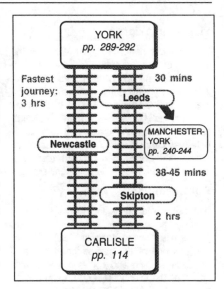

Here are two alternative ways of travelling from York to the border stronghold of Carlisle. The slower is also one of the most scenic railway journeys in England, and provides the perfect opportunity for exploring the Yorkshire Dales.

TRAINS

ETT tables: 551, 552, 562, 563, 570, 575

Fast Track

There is no direct service from York to Carlisle. The quickest route is via Newcastle, with a journey time of around 3 hrs.

On Track

York–Leeds

At least 3 trains an hour (daily) connect York with Leeds. The journey takes about 30 mins.

Leeds–Skipton–Carlisle

One train every half-hour (hourly on Suns) runs from Leeds to Skipton in about 45 mins. However, the Leeds–Carlisle service along the Settle–Carlisle line also stops at Skipton, taking just 38 mins. These trains run every 2 hrs (less frequently on Suns) and take about 2 hrs from Skipton to Carlisle. See next page for a description of this spectacular route.

SKIPTON

TIC: *9 Sheep St, Skipton BD23 1JH; tel: (01756) 792809 and 700679.* Open Mon–Sat 1000–1700, Sun 1400–1700 (Easter–Oct), Mon–Sat 1000–1600, Sun 1300–1600 (Nov–Easter). Services offered: local bed booking (10%

commission taken and latest booking before 1645), BABA (10% commission). There is a staff member with BGL sign language qualifications. Free accommodation listings, but no town tourist brochure, are available.

Station: Skipton Station, *Broughton Rd* is ½ mile east of the town centre and there is a taxi rank outside. General rail enquiries *tel: (01532) 448133.*

Getting Around

The majority of attractions in Skipton are within walking distance of the town centre and the TIC will provide free town maps and transport maps. Bus services serve the town and outlying villages and are generally good. Most bus services operate from **Skipton Bus Station**, located in *Keighley Rd*. The two main bus companies are **Keighley and District** *tel: (01756) 795331* and **Pennine Buses** *tel: (01756) 749215.* Pennine Bus Company offers a 'Pennine Wayfarer' ticket costing £6 a day and Keighley and District Buses have an all-day 'Explorer' ticket costing £4.90. The main town taxi rank is situated at the bus station in *Keighley Rd*. Registered taxi companies include **Central taxis** *tel: (01756) 794757* and **Star Taxis** *tel: (01756) 700505.*

Trains–Skipton

Staying in Skipton

There are few hotels in Skipton – instead the majority of accommodation can be found in guesthouses and b. & b. establishments. While it is generally easy to find accommodation on arrival, the TIC advises visitors to book rooms over Bank Holiday weekends. There is no youth hostel in Skipton and the nearest campsite is **Dalesway Caravan Park**, *Marton Rd, Gargrave; tel: (01756) 749592*, 5 miles north east. Take Pennine Bus no. 580 (Settle) to Gargrave village.

Sightseeing

With its cobbled streets and alleyways, Skipton is an attractive market town and an ideal touring base for the Yorkshire Dales. **Skipton Castle** is one of the best-preserved medieval castles in England and comes complete with dungeon. The town's **Craven Museum** depicts the natural and social history of the Dales area. To the north-east, the majestic ruins of Bolton Priory are the centrepiece of the **Bolton Abbey Estate**, a recreational park ideal for walks. Boat trips along the Leeds and Liverpool Canal are possible from Skipton with **Pennine Boat Trips**, *tel: (01756) 790829*, daily (Apr–end Oct) and cost £2.75.

   Skipton Castle, *High St; tel: (01756) 792442*. Open Mon–Sat 1000–1800, Sun 1400–1800. Admission: £3.20. **Holy Trinity Parish Church**, *High St; tel: (01756) 798804*. Open daily 0900–dusk. Free admission. **Craven Museum**, *Town Hall, High St; tel: (01756) 794079*. Open Mon–Fri 1000–1700, Sat 1000–1200, 1300–1700, Sun 1400–1700 (Apr–Sep), Mon–Fri 1400–1700, Sat 1000–1200, 1330–1630 (Oct–Mar). Admission free.

Out of Town

Bolton Abbey, *Bolton Abbey, Skipton; tel: (01756) 710535*. Open daily dawn–dusk. Admission: £2.50 (car parking). Running on Wed, Fri and Sat only, take the Stagecoach Cumberland bus no. X9 (direction Harrogate) to Bolton Bridge crossroads and walk last ½ mile.

   Cliffe Castle Museum, *Spring Gardens Lane, Keighley; tel: (01756) 618230*. Open Tues–Sun 1000–1800 (Apr–Sep), 1000–1700 (Oct–Mar).

Free admission. Take the Keighley and District bus no. 666/668 from Skipton to Bradford, which passes the gates.

The Settle to Carlisle Railway

Much of this route runs on the Settle to Carlisle line, a stretch of railway that appeals to the tourist for its magnificent scenery as much as it does to the rail enthusiast for its history and engineering excellence. It was built to give the then Midland Railway Co. a faster line to Glasgow. The result, opened in 1876, was a superbly but heavily engineered main line running from Settle Junction, north of Skipton to the outskirts of Carlisle. Today, after surviving a closure threat in the late 1980s, the line is slower than it used to be but the journey can be spectacular (on a clear day).

   After leaving the mill towns of Shipley, Bingley and Keighley, the line begins to climb in earnest, following the River Aire, through sheep-farming country, scored with dry stone walls. From Gargrave to Settle the line skirts the edge of the Yorkshire Dales National Park, crossing into it at Stainforth, where it also joins the valley of the River Ribble on its way down off the high peaks. Now the gradient steepens and the 'Long Drag' (as generations of railwaymen knew it) to Blea Moor begins. The countryside gets progressively wilder; after Helwith Bridge the line rises higher above the river and bursts out on to the magnificent Ribblehead Viaduct across a dry valley. After passing through Blea Moor tunnel the isolated moorland is crossed almost on the level over further dramatic viaducts. At Ais Gill the line reaches its summit at 1167 ft above sea level and begins to fall along Mallerstang Edge to Kirkby Stephen and Appleby. The River Eden joins from the left; from here to Carlisle, it runs through quiet villages like Langwathby, Lazonby and Armathwaite.

YORK to NEWCASTLE

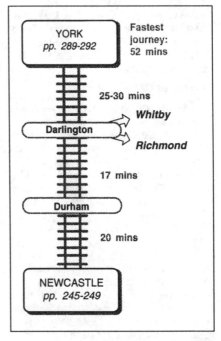

YORK
pp. 289-292

Fastest journey: 52 mins

25-30 mins

Whitby

Darlington

Richmond

17 mins

Durham

20 mins

NEWCASTLE
pp. 245-249

Among its many attractions, this route includes a scenic side track to the fishing port of Whitby – the incongrously picturesque setting for Bram Stoker's novel Dracula – from where you can take the North Yorkshire Moors Railway into the heart of one of the country's most beautiful national parks. It also enables you to visit historic Durham, perhaps Britain's most strikingly situated city and setting for the jewel among her Norman cathedrals.

TRAINS

ETT table: 570

→ Fast Track

The fastest direct services take 52 mins, others take about an 1 hr. There are plenty of trains, even on Suns, but they are irregularly timed.

 On Track

York–Darlington

One or two trains per hour serve this route, taking 25–35 mins.

Darlington–Durham

Two to three trains run hourly (less on Suns), taking 17 mins. Irregular timings can mean some longer gaps.

Durham–Newcastle

This journey takes 20 mins; trains are roughly hourly, with extras at times on weekdays.

DARLINGTON

TIC: *4 West Row, Market Hall, Darlington,*

County Durham DL1 5PL; tel: (01325) 382698/ 368981. Open Mon 1000–1730 (winter 1700), Tue–Fri 0900–1730 (winter 1700), Sat and Bank Holidays 1000–1600. DP Services offered: local bed-booking service and BABA (latest 15 mins before closing), guided tours and some tickets booked. *Darlington Welcome Guide* and *Accommodation Guide* are available free.

Station: Darlington Bank Top Station, *Bank Top; tel: (0191) 232 6262*, is a short distance south-east of the centre. It has an information point for accommodation listings. **Hertz** car hire are represented, and there is a taxi rank.

Getting Around

Transport coverage of the town centre and out of town routes is good. Services to rural areas are reduced after 1800 as are all services on Sun. **Shopmobility**, *Horsemarket; tel: (01325) 461496.* Open 0900–1730. Offers free use of wheelchairs on a daily basis, and a handbook on wheelchair access in the town.

Most local bus services run from Feethams Bus Station and are operated by **United Bus**

Trains–Darlington

Company, tel: (01325) 468771, **Darlington Transport Company**, tel: (01325) 488777, and **Your Bus**, tel: (01325) 351181. The main taxi rank is on Market Sq. For registered taxi companies contact the TIC.

Staying in Darlington

It is generally possible to book accommodation on arrival, except during the **Beer Festival** in March and the **Darlington Dog Show** in September. There is a fair choice of hotel accommodation, and a good number of b. & b. establishments. Hotel chains include Fr, MC, MH, Sw. **Blanche Pease House**, The Arts Centre, Vane Terrace; tel: (01325) 483271 offers hostel-style b. & b. accommodation. Open Mon–Sat 0900–2200.

Sightseeing

The industrial town of Darlington boomed in the 19th century as a pioneering railway and engineering centre: the world's first fare-paying steam train ran from here to Stockton-on-Tees. Even if you don't linger long, at least go and see George Stephenson's pioneering railway engine Locomotion at the **Darlington Railway Centre and Museum**. A programme of guided walks of the town and countryside is available from the TIC, price £1. To the west, the extensive ruined **Barnard Castle**, with its imposing Round Tower, perches high above the Tees in the town which shares its name. West of here, in splendid isolation, is the **Bowes Museum**, purpose-built in French chateau style in 1869 to house a superb collection of decorative art and paintings.

Darlington Art Collections and Museum, Tubwell Row; tel: (01325) 463795. Open Mon–Fri 1000–1300 and 1400–1800 (Thur 1000–1300 only), Sat 1000–1300, 1400–1730. Admission free. **Darlington Railway Centre and Museum**, North Rd Station; tel: (01325) 460532. Open daily 0930–1700, last admission 1630. Admission £1.70. **St Cuthbert's Church**, Church Row, Market Pl; tel: (01325) 482417. Open Mon, Wed, Sat 1100–1500 Apr–Sept. Admission free. **Tees Cottage Pumping Station**, Coniscliffe Rd; tel: (01325) 382698. Steaming and open days on a few weekends

each year, 1100–1700, telephone for details. Admission £1.50.

Out of Town

Barnard Castle (EH), Barnard Castle; tel: (01833) 38212. Open daily 1000–1800 (Apr–Oct), Wed–Sun 1000–1600 (Nov–Mar). Admission £1.80. Take United bus no. 75 to Barnard Castle, 10 miles west. **Bowes Museum**, Barnard Castle; tel: (01833) 690606. Open Mon–Sat 1000–1730, Sun 1400–1700 (winter 1400–1600). Admission £2.50. Take United bus 75 to Barnard Castle, 10 miles west. **Captain Cook Birthplace Museum**, Stewart Park, Marton, Middlesbrough; tel: (01642) 311211. Open 1000–1730 (Apr–Oct), 0900–1600 (Nov–Mar). Admission £1.20. Take United bus no. 268 to Milddlesbrough. Approximately 18 miles away. **Piercebridge Roman Fort**, Piercebridge, near Darlington. Open at all times. Admission free. Take United bus no. 75 to Piercebridge, 4 miles west. **Preston Hall Museum**, Yarm Rd, Stockton-on-Tees; tel: (01642) 781184. Open daily 1000–1700 (summer), 1000–1600 (winter), last admission 30 mins before closing. Admission free. Take United bus no. 268 to Stockton, and then change to the Cleveland bus – 12 miles east. **Raby Castle**, Staindrop; tel: (01833) 660202. Open Sat–Wed Easter Weekend, Wed and Sun (May–June), Sun–Fri (July–Sept), Sat–Tues (May/Spring/Aug Bank Holidays): castle open 1300–1700, gardens 1100–1730. Admission £3.30. Take United bus no. 75 to Staindrop, 12 miles west, then ½-mile walk. **Timothy Hackworth Victorian and Railway Museum**, Soho Cottages, Hackworth Close, Shildon; tel: (01388) 777999. Open Wed–Sun and Bank Holiday Mons 1000–1700 (Easter to end October). Admission £1.30. Take United bus no. X14 to Shildon, 10 miles north-west.

- -

 Side Tracks from Darlington

WHITBY

TIC: Langborne Rd, Whitby, North Yorkshire YO21 1YN; tel: (01947) 602674. Open May–Sept daily 0930–1800; Oct–end-April daily

1000–1230, 1300–1630. DP services offered: local bed-booking service (latest 30 mins before closing), BABA (10% off first night's rate). Free accommodation guide available.

Station: Whitby Station. There is no through service from Darlington; passengers must change at Middlesborough. Services run frequently from Darlington to Middlesborough (taking about 30 mins) but there are only four services daily (no winter Sun service) from Middlesborough to Whitby (taking about 1 hr 30 mins).

Getting Around

Most attractions are within walking distance of the centre. The TIC issues free transport maps. **Tees Buses** is the main operator for local buses. For information contact the Travel Office, *Station Sq; tel: (01947) 602146*. There is a good town service but it is patchy to outlying areas; the night service runs up to 2030 with reduced services at weekends. The centre of the North Yorkshire Moors is not accessible by public transport. The main taxi rank is on *Langborne Rd*, outside the TIC.

Staying in Whitby

Whitby has a good range of accommodation, particularly guest-houses and b. & b.s, which are relatively easy to book on arrival, although less so during July and Aug Bank Holiday. The majority of cheaper hotels are to be found in the West Cliff area. There are approximately 10 pubs/inns in the town centre that offer accommodation. **Whitby Youth Hostel** is located on *East Cliff, Whitby; tel: (01947) 602878*. (This is not accessible by public transport.) The TIC can provide listings of campsites; the nearest is **Sandfield House Farm Caravan Park**, *Sandford Rd; tel: (01947) 602660* – 1 mile away.

Sightseeing

Whitby manages to be both a popular resort and an active fishing port – though crammed with souvenir shops, the steep narrow streets of the old town above the river have much charm. Looming above the harbour on the East Cliff – reached via 199 steps – is the dramatic ruin of

Whitby Abbey, while famous explorer Captain Cook's former home is now a **Memorial Museum**. Whitby is notorious as the setting for Bram Stoker's novel *Dracula*; the ghoulish can follow a Dracula Trail (30p from TIC) or shudder at the waxworks in the **Dracula Experience**. For those interested in Whitby's maritime tradition, the **Whitby Lifeboat Museum** is one of the best of its kind.

The **North Yorkshire Moors Railway** (see private railways, pp. 339–340) allows you to appreciate the fine moorland scenery of the North York Moors National Park. A number of tours operated by **Coastal & Country**, *tel: (01947) 602922*, can be booked through the TIC. Fishing trips can also be arranged. For guided walks, contact Harry Collett, *tel: (01947) 602138*. **Captain Cook Memorial Museum**, *Grape Lne; tel: (01947) 601900*. Open Easter–31 Oct. Admission £1.50. **Dracula Experience**, *9 Marine Pde; tel: (01947) 601923*. Open Mar–Oct. Admission £1.75. **Museum of Victorian Whitby**, *Venus Trading, Sandgate: tel: (01947) 601221*. Open all year. Admission £1.75. **St Mary's Parish Church**, *East Cliff; tel: (01947) 603421*. Open all year. Admission free. **Whitby Abbey** (EH), *East Cliff; tel: (01947) 603568*. Open all year. Admission £1.50. **Whitby Lifeboat Museum**, *Pier Rd*. Open irregular hours. Admission free. **Whitby Museum and Art Gallery**, *Pannett Pk; tel: (01947) 602908*. Open all year. Admission £1.

Out of Town

Flamingo-land, *Kirby Misperton; tel: (01653) 668287*. Open 27 Mar–2 Oct. Admission £8 (25 miles south-west; Yorkshire Coastliner bus to Pickering). **North Yorkshire Moors Railway**, *Pickering Stn and Grosmont Stn; tel: (01751) 472508 (Pickering); (01947) 895359 (Grosmont)*. Open Mar–Oct and 'Santa Special' December weekends. Admission £8.50 return, £6.90 single; 8 miles to Grosmont (train), 21 miles to Goathland (Yorkshire Coastliner 840).

RICHMOND

TIC: *Victoria Rd, Richmond, North Yorkshire DL10 4JE; tel: (01748) 850252 or 825994.*

Open daily 0930–1730 (Apr–Oct), Mon–Sat 0930–1630, Sun 1030–1530 (Nov–Mar). DP services offered: local bed booking and BABA (10% commission and latest booking 30 mins before closing). Swaledale Festival tickets sold. *Wensleydale and Swaledale Holiday Guide* is available free and contains accommodation listings. A separate *Places to Stay* brochure can also be obtained from the TIC.

Station: the nearest station is Darlington Station, *Victoria Rd, Darlington*, 12 miles north east. Take United Bus no 24 or 25 to Richmond.

Getting Around

With the exception of the castle and the Georgian Theatre Royal, most attractions are outside the town centre. Local public transport by **United Automobile Services**, *tel: (01325) 465252*, is good.

Staying in Richmond

It is generally easy to find accommodation on arrival in Richmond and there is a wide range of establishments in the local area, particularly b. & b.s. National chains represented include *Co* and *Fr*. The nearest youth accommodation is at the **Grinton Lodge Youth Hostel** (8 miles away), *Grinton; tel: (01748) 884206*, which is open after 1700 (Mar–Dec). The TIC will provide details of local campsites. **Swale View Caravan Park**, *Reeth Rd, Richmond; tel: (01748) 823106* is 1 mile west of the centre and **Brompton on Swale Caravan and Camping Park**, *Brompton on Swale, Richmond; tel: (01748) 824629* is situated 3 miles east of Richmond and accessible by United buses 24 and 25.

Sightseeing

Richmond is an attractive market town dominated by ruined 11th-century **Richmond Castle**, which offers wonderful views across the Vale of York. The **Green Howards' Museum** is a regimental museum with displays of uniforms and campaign relics from 1688 onwards. Richmond's **Georgian Theatre** is one of England's oldest theatres; originally built in 1788, it has since been restored and re-opened; the **Theatre Museum** contains interesting memorabilia. West of Richmond, the

Swaledale Folk Museum uses lively displays to depict the past lifestyles of the local Dales people. **Guided walks are arranged by the TIC and can be booked on tel: (01748) 850252.**

Richmond Castle, *Richmond; tel: (01748) 826738*. Open all year Tue–Sun 1000–1300, 1400–1600. Admission £1.80. **Richmondshire Museum**, *Ryder's Wynd; tel: (01748) 825611*. Open daily 1100–1700 (Apr–Nov). Admission £0.80. **Green Howards' Museum**, *Trinity Church Sq; tel: (01748) 822133*. Open Mon–Fri 0915–1630 (Feb), Mon–Sat 0915–1630 (Mar–Nov), also Sun 1400–1630 (Apr–Oct). Admission £1. **Georgian Theatre Royal and Museum**, *Victoria Rd; tel: (01748) 823021*. Open Mar–Dec (Theatre), Apr–Oct (Museum). Admission £1.

Out of Town

Yorkshire Museum of Carriages and Horse-drawn Vehicles, *Yore Mill, Aysgarth Falls, Leyburn; tel: (01748) 823275*. Open daily 1100–1700 (Easter–Oct). Admission £2. Take United Bus no.26 from Richmond to Leyburn, 8 miles south-west. **Swaledale Folk Museum**, *Reeth Green, Reeth; tel: (01748) 884373*. Open daily 1030–1730 (Easter–end Oct). Admission £0.95. Take the United bus no. 30. Eight miles west. **Dales Countryside Museum**, *Station Yard, Hawes; tel: (01969) 667494*. Open daily 1000–1700 (Apr–end Oct). Admission £1.50; United Bus 26 to Hawes, 20 miles south-west.

— — — — — — — — — — — — — — — — — — — —

DURHAM

TIC: *Market Pl, Durham DH1 3NJ; tel: (0191) 384 3720/384 7641*. Open Mon–Fri 1000–1730, Sat 0930–1730 (June and Sept); Mon–Sat 0930–1830, Sun 1400–1700 (July and Aug); Mon–Fri 1000–1700, Sat 0930–1300 (Oct–May). DP Services offered: local bed-booking service, advance reservations handled, BABA (latest 30 mins before closing). Local theatre tickets sold. *County Durham Holiday Guide* is free, and includes an accommodation listing.

Station: Durham Station, *North Rd; tel: (0191) 232 6262* is in the centre of town and has a taxi rank.

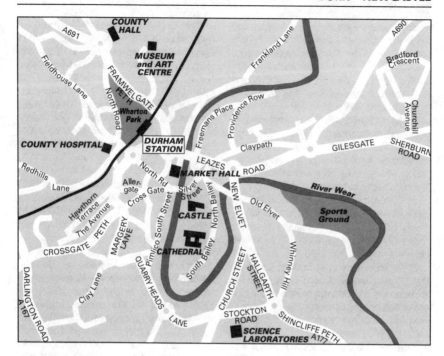

Getting Around

The majority of attractions are within a walkable area of the centre. Free town and transport maps are available from the TIC. For information on bus and train services contact the **Transport Enquiries Helpline** *tel: (0191) 383 3337*.

Most of the local bus services are operated from the bus station at *North Rd*, by a number of different companies. Services are good within the town, and reasonable to outlying areas, but reduced in the evenings and on Suns. There are taxi ranks on *North Rd* and at the station.

Staying in Durham

There is a small choice of hotels, including the hotel chain *Sw*, and a good range of b.&b. and guest-house accommodation. It is usually easy to book on arrival, except during university graduation in June, and beginning of university term in Oct.

Durham Youth Hostel *Sixth Form Centre, The Sands, Providence Row; tel: (01629) 825850* in the centre has budget accommoda-

tion for six weeks in July and Aug, open 1000–2300. Other cheap accommodation is available in the colleges during student holidays (details in the TIC's accommodation guide). The closest campsite is **Grange Camping and Caravan Site**, *Meadow La, Carville; tel: (0191) 384 4778*. Two miles north-east; take Weir Buses 220 or 222 to *Carville High St* then ½-mile walk.

Entertainment and Events

What's On in Durham is a free events list produced by the TIC. Further events details are available free in the *Durham Advertiser*. The **Miner's Gala** (dating back to 1891) takes place annually in July, with marching bands and banners paraded through the city streets. In June there is the **Durham Regatta**.

Sightseeing

Durham's setting, in a wooded loop of the River Wear, and its magnificent cathedral, make it one of England's most visually memorable cities. Being so small, and with restricted traffic access, medieval streets and alleys, riverside paths and the footbridges that are among seven bridges spanning the Wear. There are especially good views from *South St.* **Blue Badge** guided walking tours of the city, Fri–Sun (July and Aug), Sat (June and Sept), leave the TIC at 1415, (tickets £2) *tel: (0191) 384 3720.*

Durham Cathedral is the greatest piece of Norman church architecture in Britain – no other cathedral has preserved so much of its Norman character, and the rich ornamentation on the pillars and arcades is unforgettable. The **Treasury Museum** houses the coffin and cross of St Cuthbert, the most revered of northern saints. Across *Palace Green,* **Durham Castle,** begun c.1070, guards the approach to the historic city: now part of England's third oldest university, it was until 1836 the seat of the powerful Prince Bishops of Durham, and has a fine Norman chapel. Among Durham's other attractions is the **Oriental Museum,** the only one in Britain devoted to its subject.

In the surrounding area there are reminders both of a distant medieval way of life at tranquil **Egglestone Abbey** and **Finchale Priory,** and of the more recent industrial past at the **Beamish North of England Open Air Museum,** a careful recreation of a northern town in the early 1900s, complete with trams.

Durham Castle, *Palace Green; tel: (0191) 374 3800.* Open for guided tours Mon–Sat 1000–1200 and 1400–1630, Sun 1400–1630 (Easter holidays and July–Sept); Mon, Wed, Sat 1400–1630 (other times of year). Admission £1.50. **Durham Cathedral,** *North Bailey; tel: (0191) 386 2367.* Open 0715–2000 (May–Sept), 0715–1800 (Oct–Apr). Admission free. (See also Treasury Museum below.) **Durham Heritage Centre,** *St Mary le Bow Church, North Bailey.* Open 1400–1630 (Easter week daily, then weekends to end May, daily June to late Sept); 1130–1630 (early July to end Aug). Admission £0.70. **Durham University Museum of Archaeology,** *Old Fulling Mill* (between Framwelgate and Prebends Bridges); *tel: (0191) 374 3623.* Open daily 1230–1500 (Nov–Mar), 1100–1600 (Apr–Oct). Admission £0.80. **Durham University Oriental Museum,** *Elvet Hill Rd; tel: (0191) 374 2911.* Open Mon–

Fri 0930–1300 and 1400–1700. Admission £1. Take United bus 6 or 722 to *South Rd,* or Gardiners bus 41 to *Elvet Hill Rd.* Two miles south. **Little Museum of Gilesgate,** *Vane Tempest Hall, Gilesgate; tel: (0191) 386 2200/ 8099.* Open Sat, Sun 1400–1700 (Apr–Oct). Last admission 1630. Admission £0.40. **Treasury Museum,** *Durham Cathedral, North Bailey; tel: (0191) 386 2367.* Open Mon–Sat 1000–1630, Sun 1400–1630. Admission £1.

Out of Town

Auckland Castle, *Bishop Auckland; tel: (01388) 601627.* Open Sun, Wed, Thur and Bank Holiday Mons 1400–1700, Tues 1000–1230 (May to mid-Sept); Sats 1400–1700 (in Aug only). Last admission 30 mins before closing. Admission £2. Take United/OK Travel bus 6 to *Bishop Auckland,* 10 miles south-west. **Beamish North of England Open Air Museum,** *Beamish; tel: (01207) 231811.* Open daily 1000–1700 (mid-Mar to Oct). Extended opening to 1800 (early July to early Sept). Tues–Thur, Sat, Sun 1000–1600 (Nov to mid-Mar). Last admission 1 hour before closing. Admission £6.99 (winter £2.99). Take Diamond bus 720 from *Millburngate.* (There is also a special summer bus service from Durham station.) Six miles north-west. **Finchale Priory,** *Brasside; tel: (0191) 386 3828.* Open daily 1000–1800 (Apr–Oct), otherwise open but unattended. Admission £0.80 when attended, otherwise free. Take Gardiner's bus 737 to *Cocken Lodge* and cross the river by footbridge, or United bus 62, 62a, 63 or 64 to *Brasside,* then 1-mile walk. Four miles north. **Rokeby Park,** near Barnard Castle; *tel: (01833) 37334.* Open Mon, Tues 1400–1700 (June to early Sept), groups by arrangement at any time. Last admission 1630. Admission £3. Take Barnard Castle Coaches 78 or 79 to park entrance. Twenty-two miles south west. **Whitworth Hall,** near *Spennymoor; tel: (01388) 720849/ 817419.* Open Sat, Sun and Bank Holiday Mons (Easter to end Aug), Mon, Tues, Wed (July and Aug), Sun only (Sept): Grounds 1100–1800; Hall 1300–1700. Admission £4. Take United/OK Travel bus 6 to *Four Lane Ends,* then 1½-mile walk. Seven miles south.

BELFAST

In spite of all it has been through in the past quarter-century, Belfast still manages to carry the self-satisfied air of a city prosperous at the height of the British Empire – which it was. This superficial impression is conveyed by its wealth of ornate Victorian buildings, including the splendid Grand Opera House and the marvellously overblown Crown Liquor Saloon. The capital of Northern Ireland, Belfast offers a wide range of recreation, entertainment, cultural activities and excellent shopping.

Tourist Information

Northern Ireland Tourist Board Information Office, *St Anne's Court, 59 North St, Belfast BT1 1NB; tel: (01232) 246609*. Open Mon–Fri 0900–1715, Sat 0900–1400. Helpful staff and lots of maps and information, free and for sale, covering the whole province. There is a well-stocked souvenirs/gifts section. Services offered: local accommodation reservations, BABA, GULLIVER, bureau de change.

Arriving and Departing

Airport

Belfast International Airport, *tel: (0184 94) 22888*, is at Aldergrove, 19 miles west of the city and has an NITB information bureau, money-changing facilities and an airside duty-free shop. An Airbus shuttle operates half-hourly Mon–Sat 0640–2220, hourly Sun 0715–1015, from Aldergrove to Great Victoria St Bus Station, taking about 40 minutes (price £3.50).

Stations

Central Station, *East Bridge St; tel: (01232) 230310* is just east of the city centre and serves all destinations in Northern Ireland as well as Dublin. There are no left luggage facilities because of security precautions.

Ferries

Most Irish Sea ferry services dock at *Larne Ferryport*, 20 miles north of Belfast, with a rail connection into Central Station. For services to Stranraer in Scotland: **Stena Sealink**, *tel: (01232) 327525* and **Hovercraft SeaCat**, *tel: (0141) 204 2266*; to Cairnryan, Scotland, **P&O European Ferries**, *tel: (01581) 2276*. Two other services dock at *Donegall Quay* in Belfast Harbour. For Liverpool, **Norse Irish Ferries**, *tel: (01232) 779090*; for Douglas, **Isle of Man Steam Packet Co**, *tel: (01232) 351009*. For details of ferry crossings, see pp. 12.

Buses

Ulsterbus, *tel: (01232) 320011*, runs express services to 21 towns in the province from **Great Victoria St Bus Station**. From here, **Bus Éireann** also runs services to the Republic.

Getting Around

Belfast has much of interest within walking distance of **Donegall Square** in the city centre, but some major attractions are farther out. However, the city and outlying areas are covered by an excellent bus service; pick up a route map from the NITB information bureau.

Buses

Donegall Square is the starting point for most city bus routes, *tel: (01232) 246485* for information. Fares are charged on a zone system, starting at 40p for city centre travel. A multi-journey ticket costs from £2.90 and can be purchased at newsagents and other shops.

Taxis

London-style black cabs operate at railway stations and city centre ranks and may be hailed in the street. For mini-cabs call: **The Belfast Cab Co**; *tel: (01232) 331551*. **City Cab**; *tel: (01232) 242000*.

Staying in Belfast

Accommodation

Hotel chains in Belfast include *FC, Nv. Hn* is expected to open a deluxe hotel in the city by

---

Tourist Information–Arriving–Getting Around–Staying in Belfast　　**301**

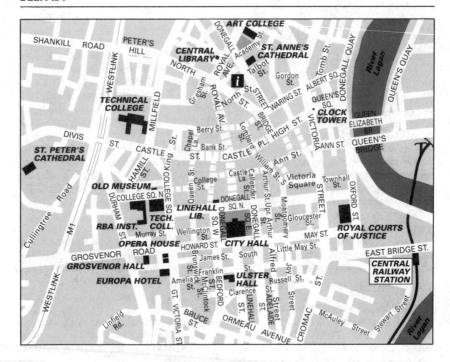

early 1997. Some of the better hotels, including the famous **Europa** on *Great Victoria St, tel: (01232) 327000*, are operated by the locally owned Hastings group.

The greatest concentration of b. & b. accommodation and guesthouses is in the area surrounding **Queen's University**, south of the city centre. **HI**: *Belfast Youth Hostel, 22–32 Donegall Road, Belfast BT12 5JN; tel: (01232) 324733.* The nearest campsites to the city centre are **Belvoir Forest** (3 miles south), *tel: (01232) 524456*, off the A504, take Ulsterbus 13 or 188, and **Jordanstown Lough Shore Park** (5 miles north), *Shore Road, Newtownabbey; tel: (01232) 868751*, take Ulsterbus 167.

Eating and Drinking

No one need go hungry – or thirsty – in Belfast. Cuisine ranges from sandwich bars and pizza parlours to *haute cuisine* and ethnic cooking from many parts of the world. The best area for food and drink is the *Golden Mile* – from the Crown Liquor Saloon on *Great Victoria St* south

towards the university there is a plethora of good eating places and pubs. A green plaque bearing the symbol of a steaming ladle signifies establishments which have attained a **Taste of Ulster** membership and feature dishes created from the finest local ingredients. Start the day with an **Ulster Fry**, a heaped breakfast plate of sausages, egg, bacon, black and white pudding and farls (potato cakes), threateningly rich in cholesterol but guaranteed to get you through until dinner (though Ulster folk will be ready for another gargantuan feast at lunchtime). Some aficionados claim the Guinness in Belfast is even better than it is in Dublin.

Communications

Main post offices are in *Donegall Sq, Castle Pl* and *Shaftesbury Sq*. Each has post restante facilities.

Consulates

USA: *Queens House, 14 Queen St, Belfast BT1; tel: (01232) 328239.*

Entertainment

Details of performances, concerts and exhibitions are available at the tourist information office and are listed in the daily *Belfast Telegraph*. The **Grand Opera House**, *Great Victoria St; tel: (01232) 241919*, offers a varied programme of opera, ballet, drama and music hall. Irish drama and stage classics are presented at the **Lyric Players Theatre**, *Ridgeway St; tel: (01232) 381081*. **The Arts Theatre**, *Ave; tel: (01232) 324936*, specialises in musicals and modern Ulster and English drama.

Ulster Hall, *Bedford St; tel: (01232) 323900*, is where classical music is performed by the Ulster Orchestra and where major rock and pop concerts are staged. Superstar events take place in **King's Hall**, *Lisburn Road; tel: (01232) 665225*. Pubs and clubs where you can hear live music – folk, jazz, blues, rock and traditional – are mainly located in the *Royal Ave* area. Film classics and foreign productions are shown at the **Queen's Film Theatre**, *University Square Mews, off Botanic Ave; tel: (01232) 667687*, and there are several major cinemas showing current releases in the city centre.

Events

The city's major cultural event, the **Belfast Festival**, staged at Queen's University in November, is one of the largest in the British Isles and covers a wide spectrum of the arts. The **Lord Mayor's Show**, in May, is a noisy, colourful parade.

Shopping

Major stores are located in **Donegall Pl** and **Royal Ave** in the heart of the city. **Castle Court** shopping mall is a modern complex on *Royal Ave*. Irish linen, hand-made woollens, pottery and Tyrone Crystal can be found in several of the city centre arcades and pedestrianised shopping areas. A variety market is held in **May St** on Friday mornings.

Sightseeing

During the summer months **Citybus Tours** *(tel: (01232) 246485)* runs a series of tours of Belfast and surrounding areas. A good introduction to the city is a 3½-hour tour with multilingual commentary (adult fare £4.50). Departures from *Castle Pl*. Another option is the **Cityhopper**, offering unlimited travel between 1000 and 1700 for £1.50.

Donegall Sq, a good orientation centre, is dominated by the huge, ornate **City Hall**, domed in the manner of St Paul's Cathedral, London, and opened in 1906. On the east side of City Hall a sculptured group commemorates those who died when the Belfast-built *Titanic* sank after striking an iceberg in 1912. The **Linenhall Library**, *17 Donegall Sq North*, was founded in 1788.

Botanic Gardens, *Stranmillis Road; tel: (01232) 776277*. Open daily 1000–dusk; **Palm House and Tropical Ravine** open Mon–Fri 1000–1700, weekends 1400–1700. Admission: free. Take bus 69 or 71. **Arts Council Sculpture Park**, *185 Stranmillis Road*, has works in bronze, steel, wood, iron and ceramics on show in pleasant gardens. **The Entries**, mainly between *Ann St* and *High St*, are a maze of narrow alleys where many of Belfast's grandest pubs are hidden, including the city's oldest, **White's Tavern**, in *Winecellar Entry*. **Albert Memorial Clock Tower**, at the junction of *High St* and *Victoria St*, was built in 1865 and tilts some 4 ft from the vertical because of poor foundations. From here there is a good view across the River Lagan to the **Harland and Wolff shipyard**.

Lagan Lookout Centre, *Donegall Quay; tel: (01232) 328507*, illustrates the industrial and folk history of Belfast docks, with views over the new Lagan weir. Open Mon–Sat 1000–1800, Sun 1400–1800 (1600 in winter). Admission: £1.50. **Belfast Zoological Gardens**, *Antrim Road; tel: (01232) 776277*, overlooks the city from the slopes of Cave Hill. Open daily 1000–1700 (Apr–Sept); 1000–1530 (Oct–Mar). Closes 1430 Friday. Admission £4. Take buses 2, 3, 4, 5, 6 or 45. **Dixon Park**, *Upper Malone Road; tel: (01232) 320702*, is the venue each July for the City of Belfast International Rose Trials. The park has a beautiful Japanese garden. Freely accessible. Take bus 70 or 71.

Churches and Cathedrals

The Protestant **St Anne's Cathedral**, at the junction of *Donegall St* and *York St*, is a neo-Romanesque basilica which took 80 years to complete after building commenced in 1899. Entombed beneath the nave floor is the body of Lord Edward Carson (1854–1935), the opposer of Home Rule.

St George's Church, *High St*, also Protestant, was completed in 1816. Its fine, classical portico came from the palatial home of Frederick Hervey, Earl Bishop of Derry, which was dismantled when he died. The Catholic **St Malachy's Church**, *Alfred St*, is regarded as the city's finest late Georgian building. It has a fan-vaulted ceiling modelled on that of the Henry VII Chapel in Westminster Abbey and contains some fine interior stucco work.

St Patrick's, another Catholic church, in *Upper Donegall St*, has a chapel which was decorated by the painter, Sir John Lavery, who was born nearby and baptised in the church. On St Patrick's Day and other special occasions the Shrine of St Patrick's Hand, a 15th-century reliquary containing a relic of the saint, is exposed for veneration. **Sinclair Seamen's Church**, *Corporation Sq*, has a pulpit built in the shape of a ship's prow, with port and starboard navigation lights on each side of the organ. Seamen have worshipped here for more than 140 years.

Museums

Royal Ulster Rifles Regimental Museum, 5 *Waring St; tel: (01232) 232086*. Open: Mon–Fri 1000–1600. Admission: free. **Ulster Folk and Transport Museum**, *Cultra, Holywood; tel: (01232) 428428*, straddles the A2, Belfast–Bangor road. The Folk Museum re-creates Ulster life at the turn of the century in a reconstructed village. Exhibits in the Transport Museum range from donkey creels to vertical take-off aircraft, and there is an impressive railway section. Open Mon–Fri 0930–1700, Sat 1030–1800, Sun 1200–1800 (Apr–June, Sept); Mon–Sat 1030–1800, Sun 1200–1800 (July and Aug); Mon–Fri 0930–1600, Sat and Sun 1230–1630 (Oct–Mar). Admission £3. Take bus 1 or 2,

five miles east. **Ulster Museum**, *Botanic Gardens, Stranmillis Rd; tel: 381251*. Treasure from a Spanish Armada ship wrecked off the Giant's Causeway in 1588 is among exhibits covering 9,000 years. Open Mon–Fri 1000–1645, Sat 1300–1645, Sun 1400–1645. Admission: free.

 Side Tracks from Belfast

LARNE

Tourist Offices: *Narrow Gauge Road; tel: (01574) 260088*. Open Mon–Sat 1000–1600 year-round; Mon–Wed 0900–1700, Thur–Sat 0900–1930 (July and August). Services offered: local accommodation reservations, BABA, GULLIVER. Larne Harbour, *Ferry Terminal; tel: (01574) 270517*. Open Mon–Sat 0900–1200, 1300–1730. Services offered: local accommodation reservations.

Station: *Circular Road; tel: (01574) 260604*. Larne Town is reached in 30–42 minutes from Belfast Central Station. The journey to Larne Harbour, the ferry terminal, takes another three minutes. The service is roughly half-hourly but a few services turn back at the Town station instead of the Harbour. Ulsterbus service 252 from Belfast (see above) takes about one hour.

Sightseeing

Larne marks the southern end of the spectacular **Antrim Coast Road**. The town's major landmarks are the ruined 16th-century **Olderfleet Castle** and the **Chaine Memorial Tower**, a modern replica of a round tower built to commemorate James Chaine, MP, who was buried in an upright position overlooking the entrance to Lough Larne. **Larne Interpretive Centre**, in the *Narrow Gauge Road TIC*, tells the story of the Antrim Coast Road.

 Connection: Dublin

Dublin is served by six trains on weekdays, three on Suns. Improvements to the frequency are scheduled for 1996. The fastest journey is two hours; most take 2 hrs 20 mins.

BELFAST to LONDONDERRY

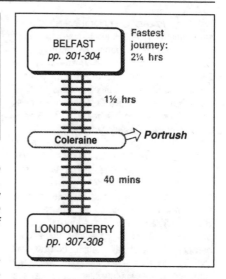

This route snakes south-west from Belfast to Lisburn and north to Antrim, on Lough Neagh, and Ballymena, an important linen industry centre. At Coleraine, on the River Bann, the line splits, travelling east to the resort of Portrush and west to ancient Londonderry.

TRAINS

ETT tables: 631, 633

 On Track

Belfast–Coleraine–Londonderry

Seven trains Mons-Fris, six on Sats and three on Suns make the journey from Belfast Central to Londonderry in 2 hrs 15 – 2 hrs 30 mins. All trains call at Coleraine 1 hr 40 mins from Belfast.

- - - - - - - - - - - - - - - - - -

 Side Tracks from Coleraine

PORTRUSH

Tourist Office: *Dunluce Centre, Sandhill Drive; tel: (01265) 823333; (01265) 44623* out of season. Open daily 0900–2100 (Easter Week); 0900–1700 (Easter–May); 0900–1800 (June); 0900–2100 (July–Aug); weekends 1200–1700 (Oct–Easter). Services offered: local accommodation reservations, BABA, GULLIVER, bureau de change.
Station: *Eglinton Street; tel: (01265) 822395.* A shuttle train service (taking 13 minutes) connecting with Belfast and Londonderry trains at Coleraine provides the majority of rail services from Portrush. There is an occasional through train to Belfast.

A lively seaside resort with good beaches, Portrush is on the Ramore Peninsula, about five miles north of Coleraine. Ulsterbus service 172 connects Coleraine with Portrush, Bushmills and the Giants Causeway. The **Antrim Coaster**, Ulsterbus long-distance service 252, also covers part of the route.

Sightseeing

The town has all the usual resort amenities, including two 18-hole golf courses – one being the **Royal Portrush championship course** – tennis courts and bowling greens. Boating and sea angling are popular, and salmon and trout fishing is to be had nearby. The stretch of coast below the Recreation Grounds, off *Lansdowne Crescent*, is a geological nature reserve noted for fossil ammonites. The **White Rocks**, to the east, is an area of limestone cliffs which have been carved into strange shapes by the weather. **Cathedral Cave**, the largest phenomenon, is 180 ft long.

Waterworld; *tel: (01265) 822001)*, has water slides, saunas, jacuzzis, whirlpools, steambaths and a sub-tropical wet area, as well as a children's section. Open Mon–Sat 1000–2045, Sun 1200–2045 (Easter–Sept). Admission: £3.75.

Dunluce Centre; *tel: (01265) 824444,* has

high-tech presentations of local legends and the environment, a white-knuckle ride and a high tower presenting a panorama of the coast. Open Mon–Thur 1000–1800, Fri–Sat 1000–2100 (June); daily 1000–2100 (July–Aug); inquire about opening times in other months. Admission: £4. **Dunluce Castle**, about 3 miles east of Portrush, on the road to the **Giant's Causeway**, was abandoned after the kitchen (and staff) fell into the sea during a storm in 1639. Open Tues–Sat 1000–1900 (–1600 Oct–Mar). Admission: £1.50. Ulsterbus 172 passes the castle.

Three miles or so east of Dunluce Castle is the **Giant's Causeway**, also reached by Ulsterbus 172 (in July and August this is an open-top bus) which runs four times daily between Coleraine rail station, Portrush rail station, Bushmills and the causeway. The causeway is freely accessible, but there is a charge for the car park and for an audio-visual show and static exhibition. The Visitor Centre is open daily 1000–1600 (–1900 July–Aug).

A World Heritage Site administered by the National Trust, the Giant's Causeway consists of 38,000 polygonal basalt columns that march into the sea on the west side of Benbane Head. The causeway was formed as molten basalt cooled after a massive underground explosion millions of years ago. Information panels set up along four marked walks tell the story of the formations.

During July and August a mini-bus shuttles between the Visitor Centre and the head of the causeway, about half a mile away. There is also a circular walk which takes visitors to the Grand Causeway, passing amphitheatres of stone columns and formations with such names as the Honeycomb, the Giant's Granny and the King and His Nobles and taking in *Port na Spaniagh* where the Spanish treasure ship *Girona* foundered in 1588.

Boat trips take visitors from the causeway to caves to the west. These include Portcoon Cave, 450 ft long and 40 ft high, and the spectacular Runkerry Cave, 700 ft long and 60 ft high.

The **Old Bushmills Distillery**; *Distillery Road, Bushmills, tel: (01265) 731521*, about a mile and a half inland from the causeway, has been distilling whiskey since 1608, and is the world's oldest licensed distillery. Visitors can take a one-hour guided tour. Open Mon–Thur 0900–1200, 1330–1530, Fri 0900–1145. Admission: £2.

LONDONDERRY

TIC: *8 Bishop St; tel: (01504) 267284*. Open Mon–Thur 0900–1715, Fri 0900–1700; Mon–Sat 0900–2000, Sun 1000–1800 (July–Sept). Services offered: local accommodation reservations, GULLIVER.

Station: *Duke St, Waterside, Londonderry; tel: (01504) 42228*. The station is on the eastern side of the River Foyle, about a mile from the city centre.

Bus Station: Ulsterbus and Bus Éireann operate services throughout the North and the Republic from the main bus station in *Foyle St; tel: (01504) 262261*. Services into north Donegal, across the border, are operated by Lough Swilly Bus Services, *tel: (01504) 262017*.

Getting Around

Most of Londonderry's major attractions are in and around the 17th-century walls and can easily be reached on foot. You can walk along the walls themselves, which are at least 18 ft thick and about a mile round. There is a comprehensive local bus service.

Staying in Londonderry

Accommodation

Accommodation in the city ranges from three-star hotels to guesthouses. Most b. & b. accommodation is to be found some distance from the centre. **HI**: Derry City Hostel, *4–6 Magazine St, Londonderry BT48 6HH; tel: (01504) 372409*. There is a new purpose-built hostel within the city's famous walls; 150 yards from the bus station (1 mile from the railway station). There are no campsites.

Eating and Drinking

Regional specialities are Lough Foyle salmon, Donegal lobster and locally-cured Londonderry ham and bacon. The widest range of restaurants is to be found in *Shipquay St, William St* and *The Strand*. Many pubs also serve food and provide evening entertainment in the form of traditional Irish music and dancing.

Communications

Post Office: *3 Custom House St; tel: (01504) 362274).* Post restante facilities.

Entertainment and Events

Arts and entertainment thrive in the city. The **Londonderry Arts Association** stages a number of concerts throughout the year in the Great Hall of Magee University College and the **Ulster Orchestra** performs from time to time in the Great Hall of the Guildhall, with a season of concerts in October. The Guildhall is also the venue for performances by **Field Day**, a progressive theatre company noted for *avant-garde* productions by contemporary Irish dramatists. Londonderry's **musical pubs** are a great source of entertainment. Some of the best places to hear Irish music are in *Waterloo St*, just beyond the northern walls. There are cinemas in *Orchard St* and *Strand Road*. Entertainment listings may be obtained from the TIC and are also published in the local newspapers, the *Derry Journal* and the *Londonderry Sentinel*.

The **Londonderry Feis**, staged in February or March, is a festival of traditional Irish music and dancing. The **City of Derry Drama Festival** and the **Light Opera Festival** take place in March or April. A **Mini Jazz Festival** is held in July and the **Swilly Open Regatta** is in August. November sees the **Foyle Film Festival**. **Halloween** is a lively event with lots of fireworks and street activities.

Shopping

The most sought-after local products in this part of Ireland are ceramics, shirts, hand-crocheted garments, Donegal tweeds and traditional hand-knitted Aran sweaters. The **Derry Craft Village**, open Mon–Sat 0930–1730, is in *Magazine Street*, in the heart of the old walled city. Souvenirs and craft goods may be purchased in a number of boutiques and workshops. Another shopping area within the walls is the modern **Richmond Centre**, located on the corner where *Shipquay St* and *Ferryquay St* meet *The Diamond*. *Orchard St* is the scene of an **open-air market** on Saturdays.

Sightseeing

Derry was prefixed by 'London' in 1613 when areas of land were given to the Companies of the Corporation of London. Today, Nationalists call the city 'Derry' while Unionists insist it is Londonderry.

A walk along the top of Londonderry's **Old Walls**, is a worthwhile orientation exercise for newcomers to the city. The walls are pierced by seven gates, including the four originals – Bishop's Gate, which was refurbished as a triumphal arch in 1789, Shipquay Gate, Ferryquay Gate and Butchers Gate.

The easiest access for walkers is from *Bank Place*, just inside Shipquay Gate. The walls have withstood many attacks, including the Great Siege of 1689 when the garrison and inhabitants held out for 105 days against the forces of James II. 'Roaring Meg', which played a significant role in the siege, is the largest of a number of ancient cannon laid-out along the top of the walls. Also displayed along the walls are a number of modern, lifesize figures in cast-iron, the work of the sculptor, Anthony Gormley.

Londonderry has two cathedrals. The Protestant **St Columb's**, in *Bishop St Within*, was built in 1633 and heroic scenes from the great siege are depicted in stained glass. The 17th-century locks and keys of the four original gates to the city and a number of siege relics are among treasures on view in the chapterhouse. An audio-visual presentation tells the story of the siege and outlines the cathedral's history. The Catholic **St Eugene's Cathedral** is a short distance from the north-west corner of the walls, along *William Street*, beyond *Waterloo Place*. It was completed in 1873, but it was 1903 before the spire was in place.

Just outside the walls, the **Guildhall** on *Foyle St* has dozens of stained-glass windows illustrating the city's history. From **Derry Quay**, behind the Guildhall, thousands of Irish emigrants sailed to America. Next to the Guildhall, the **Harbour Museum** features

Londonderry's maritime history and includes a replica of the craft in which St Columba sailed to Iona in 563, as well as displays describing the port's strategic role in World War II.

Long Tower Church, off *Bishop St Without*, was built in 1784 and has a magnificent interior. The stained glass was the work of Meyer of Munich. The city's oldest Catholic church, it stands on the site of the great medieval cathedral of Templemore, built in 1164 and flattened in 1567 when an English arsenal installed in the building accidentally exploded.

Back inside the walls, the 1813 **Courthouse**, *Bishop St*, is said to be one of the best examples of Greek revival architecture in Ireland. The **Heritage Library**, at *12 Bishop St*, is a reference library and reading room in which exhibitions and lectures are staged. It has an excellent genealogy centre.

Another look at the Londonderry story from pre-historic times to the present day is taken in the **Tower Museum** (admission: £1.50), and in **O'Doherty's Tower** (above the museum, near Shipquay Gate) there are artefacts from ships of the Spanish Armada wrecked off the coast of Ireland in 1588. Admission: £2.50

The **Orchard Gallery**, on the corner of *Orchard St* and *Foyle St*, is a centre for the visual arts, popular music and other activities.

The **Foyle Valley Railway Centre**, in *Foyle Road*, near Craigavon Bridge, *tel: (01504) 265234)*, features the narrow gauge systems of the County Donegall Railway and the Londonderry and Lough Swilly Railway. Open Tue–Sat 1000–1700, Sun 1400–1800 (May–Sept); train rides Sat and Sun afternoons. Admission: £2.

Three miles north of Londonderry, off the A2, the **Ballyarnett Wildlife Sanctuary and Community Farm** and the **Earhart Centre**, are located in Ballyarnett Country Park *tel: (01504) 354040*. Amelia Earhart, the first woman to fly solo across the Atlantic, landed here in 1932. Open Mon–Fri 0900–1630, Sat–Sun 0900–1800 (summer only). Donations. From Londonderry take the Shantal Estate bus to within a mile of the park.

Politics and History

In few places are these two subjects more closely entwined than in Ireland. It is difficult for an outsider to understand the troubled present of Ireland without a knowledge of its past. Whilst the political situation, in all its intricacy, is a constant topic in both the Republic and Northern Ireland, it is not a subject the visitor should embark lightly upon in conversation. Religion, so closely bound up with politics here, is also a topic best avoided.

After centuries of British rule, the division of the island into the Republic of Ireland, a self-governing, independent member state of the European Community, and Northern Ireland, part of the United Kingdom of Great Britain and Northern Ireland, began in the 1920s, when 26 of the 32 Irish counties secured their independence. The 6 remaining counties which today make up Northern Ireland are often referred to loosely as Ulster, although a substantial part of the ancient province of Ulster lies in the Republic. The separation of the Republic and the United Kingdom was formalised in 1949. Northern Ireland originally had some autonomy within the United Kingdom, including its own parliament, but an increase in sectarian violence led the British government to resume direct rule of the province in 1972.

At the time of writing, with the IRA cease-fire still in operation, a real prospect of peace in Northern Ireland seems in view, but even the most optimistic observer would agree that there is a long way to go yet before a lasting and peaceful settlement can be achieved. However, the new situation has led to a well-merited increase in the numbers of visitors, from all parts of the world, who are discovering one of the most beautiful and least-spoiled parts of Britain.

DUBLIN

Like a duchess in an urchin's cap, Dublin is likely to plunge those meeting her for the first time into confusion. Unarguably a capital city, it is at the same time stately and vulgar. The elegance of its Georgian buildings is tempered by crumbling streets of working-class dwellings and acres of bleak suburbs. But the heart of Dublin is a joy: lively, interesting and reasonably compact. Some of its best-known sights – Custom House, the Four Courts, the General Post Office on O'Connell St – are instantly recognisable, but others will need to be sought out.

Tourist Information

Dublin Tourism's main office is at *14 Upper O'Connell St; tel: (01) 284 4768*. Information and an accommodation booking service cover the whole island; open Mon–Fri 0900–1700, Sat 0900–1530 (Jan and Feb, mid-Sept–end Dec); Mon–Sat 0900–1700 (Mar–June); Mon–Sat 0830–2000, Sun 1030–1400 (July and Aug); Mon–Sat 0830–1800 (first half Sept). There is another information office for personal callers at *Baggott St Bridge*; open Mon–Fri 0915–1715. **An Oige**, the Irish Youth Hostels Association, is at *39 Mountjoy Square; tel: (01) 830 4555*.

Arriving and Departing

Airport

Dublin Airport, *tel: (01) 874 6301*, is six miles north of the city. For an international airport serving major destinations, it is a little old-fashioned and rather small. At busy times catering facilities tend to be overworked, and the shops area cramped. There is a post office, a bureau de change and a Bord Fáilte (Irish Tourist Board) information office in the ground floor arrivals area. The airside duty-free stores are well-stocked, but again space is limited. An

Airlink express coach service operated by Dublin Bus, *tel: 873 4222*, runs from the airport to the city centre and Heuston railway station every 20–30 mins Mon–Sat 0640–2300, Sun 0710–2300. The journey to Dublin's Central Bus Station takes about 25 mins. Coaches run from the bus station to the airport Mon–Sat 0705–2225, Sun 0735–2230; from Heuston Station Mon–Sat 0820–2030, Sun 0805–2215. Fares: £2.50 (city centre), £3 (Heuston Station). See also Airport Connections on p. 11.

Stations

Connolly Station, *Amiens St; tel: (01) 836 6222*, is a 15-min walk from *O'Connell St*, but well served by a number of bus routes and DART trains (see p. 312). It serves Wexford, Sligo and the North. There are left luggage facilities.

Heuston Station, *Stevens Lane; tel: (01) 836 6222*, is at the end of Victoria Quay on the south side of the River Liffey, a long way from the city centre. It is served by several bus routes, including no. 90, a shuttle service between Connolly and Heuston stations. This runs every ten mins and the journey takes about 15 mins. Fare: £0.90. Heuston Station is the starting point for trains to the west, south and south-west. Left luggage facilities.

Ferries

Dublin is served by two Irish-Sea ferry terminals. *Dublin Port* (about 20 mins from the city centre by Dublin Bus 53) is the terminus for **B & I Line**, *tel: (01) 660 6666*, which serves Holyhead, Wales. *Dun Laoghaire*, 20 mins from Connolly Station by DART, is the port used by **Stena Sealink**, *tel: (01) 280 8844*, which also connects with Holyhead. Dublin Tourism maintains an information office at the ferry pier, *St Michael's Wharf; tel: (01) 280 6984*. Open daily 0800–2000. For more details on ferries, see Ferry Crossings on p. 12.

Buses

Bus Éireann, Ireland's national bus company, operates a comprehensive network of services throughout the country from *Busaras*, the central bus station in *Store St*, off *Amiens St; tel: (01) 836 6111*. Dublin Connolly rail station is

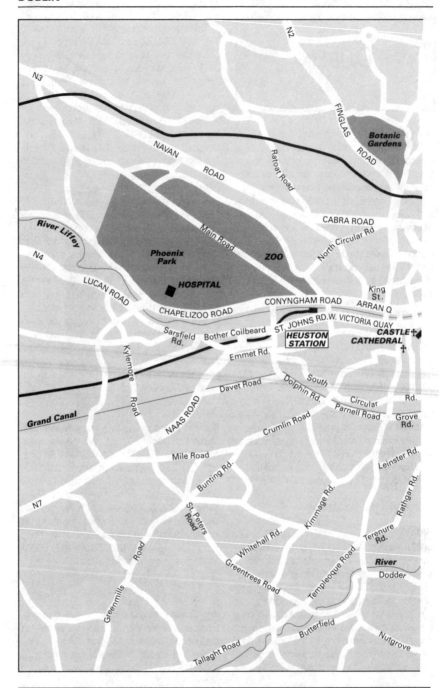

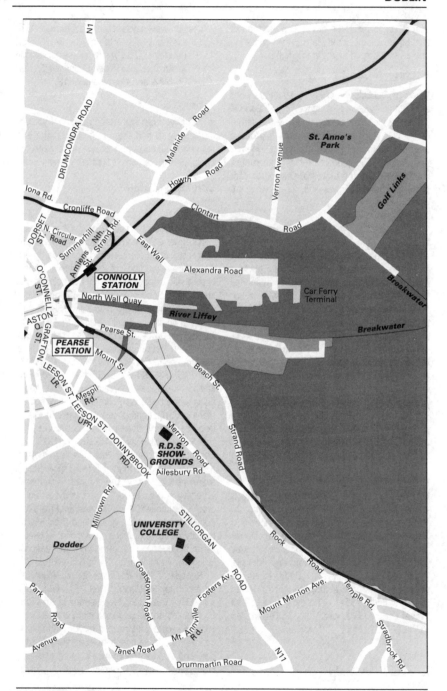

very close; to reach the bus station use the exit leading down the ramp, rather than the stairs and cross the road at the traffic lights.

Getting Around

Many of Dublin's major sights and attractions are within walking distance of **O'Connell Bridge**, which can be regarded as the centre of the city. An excellent large-scale map of the city, with details of places of interest, cinemas and theatres, shopping centres and bus routes, is available from the offices of Dublin Tourism, price £1. Suburban bus and rail services are good.

Tickets

There are a number of ticket options covering the city's transport systems. For example, the **Dublin Explorer** costs £10 and is valid for four days on Dublin Bus and DART/Suburban Rail services within the city commuter area. It cannot be used before 0945 Mon–Fri, but there is no restriction over the weekend. Suburban transport services are divided into four zones, or 'hops' radiating from the city centre. The Short Hop zone radiates north to *Balbriggan*, west to *Maynooth* and south to *Kilcoole*. Giant Hop, the farthest zone, goes north to *Dundalk*, west to *Mullingar* and south to *Gorey*. A weekly Giant Hop ticket, which must be accompanied by a photo identity card, covers all services, including InterCity and Bus Éireann services, and costs £26.

Metro

DART – the Dublin Area Rapid Transit system - is an electric suburban rail service covering 25 stations. It extends from *Howth* in the north to *Bray* in the south and connects at Dublin Connolly with all main line services and at Bray with trains to and from Wexford and Rosslare. Trains are fast, clean and comfortable. The service runs Mon–Sat from about 0530 to midnight and 0735–2330 Sun. Inquiries: **Rail Travel Centre**, *35 Lower Abbey St, Dublin; tel: (01) 836 6222*.

Buses

Dublin Bus serves the city with about 100 routes. On weekdays services start around 0630 and the last buses leave the city centre at about 2330. Timetables (£0.50) and maps are available from Dublin Bus, *59 Upper O'Connell St, tel: (01) 873 4222*, and from newsagents.

Taxis

In theory you can hail cruising cabs but you are more likely to find them in groups at the two major rail stations and at the rank near the Shelbourne Hotel, on *St Stephen's Green*.

Staying in Dublin

Accommodation

Surprisingly, only a couple of the big international hotel chain names appear in Dublin. But that is not say there is a dearth of good hotels. There are a number of home-grown groups with quality properties throughout Ireland. It is advisable to book accommodation in advance if you are visiting the city in July and August.

Hotel chains in Dublin include *BW, DH, FC, HI, Ju, Mn, MO, RH*. The city's most famous hotel – an institution in its own right – is **The Shelbourne**, *27 St Stephen's Green, Dublin 2; tel: (01) 676 6471*. Opened in 1824, The Shelbourne is still accepted as the most distinguished address in Ireland. It has hosted many celebrities and played an important role in Ireland's history. Bullets hummed around it in the Easter Rising of 1916 and in 1922 the Constitution of the Irish Free State was drafted here. Accommodation at all levels is spread fairly evenly across the city. The cheapest – and least attractive – area for b.&b. accommodation is around Connolly Station. The best area from the point of view of price, quality and proximity to the city centre is probably Ballsbridge, between *Lansdowne Rd* and *Sandymount* DART stations, less than ten mins from Connolly Station.

Hostels: *Dublin International Youth Hostel, 61 Mountjoy St, Dublin 7; tel: (01) 830 1766/ 830 1396*. This is also headquarters of An Oige, the Irish Youth Hostel Association, and facilities include secure parking for bicycles and cars, bicycle hire, touring and reservations information and special train fares to other hostels. From Dublin Airport, Dublin Bus no. 41A goes to

Dorset St, three mins from the hostel, which is on the no. 10 North and South City bus route. Campers will need to travel some distance from the city. **North Beach Caravan and Camping Park**, *Rush, Co. Dublin; tel: (01) 843 7131*, bus no. 33 from *Eden Quay*, or Suburban Rail from Connolly Station to *Rush/Lusk*, about 25 mins. **Shankhill Caravan and Camping Park**, *Shankhill, Co. Dublin; tel: (01) 282 0011*, bus no. 46 from *College St*, Suburban Rail from Connolly Station to *Shankhill*, about 35 mins.

Eating and Drinking

Unless you are going well upmarket for dinner, you would be advised to eat early in Dublin. By 1800 most middle-range restaurants in the city centre are full and by 2000 are lowering the shutters. Nevertheless, there is a good choice of restaurants with modestly priced menus. Pubs are a good choice for soup and sandwiches at lunchtime. **Temple Bar** is the place for lively bistro-type establishments. The **Grafton St** area offers a wide choice of menus and prices. Two Dublin establishments have achieved the status of institution. **Beshoff**, renowned for fish and chips, has restaurants at *7 Upper O'Connell St*, and *14 Westmoreland St*. **Bewley's**, on *Grafton St, South Great George St* and *Westmoreland St*, is the place for noisy get-togethers over coffee, cream cakes and sticky buns (the upstairs restaurant at *Grafton St*, potted plants and all, is rather more genteel and there is a museum into the bargain).

Traditional Dublin dishes are Irish stew, bacon and cabbage, soda bread and potato cakes. *Champ* is chopped scallions (spring onions) stirred into creamy mashed potatoes. On the seafood side, Dublin Bay prawns and oysters served with Guinness are renowned delicacies. And the sad demise of Molly Malone, heroine of one of Ireland's most famous popular songs, failed to discourage the Dubliners' penchant for cockles and mussels. In fact, Molly is such a local heroine that a striking statue has been erected in her memory in *Grafton St*.

Communications

Dublin's imposing **General Post Office**, *O'Con-* *nell St*, is open Mon–Sat 0800–2000, Sun 1000–1830 (poste restante facilities are available). The building was shelled and set alight during the Easter Rising of 1916 when it served as headquarters of the Irish Volunteers.

Money

Banking hours are Mon–Fri 1000–1530; major branches remain open to 1700 on Thur. Branches of major banks abound in the city centre.

Consulates

Australia: *Fitzwilliam House, Wilton Terrace, Dublin 2; tel: (01) 676 1517* (bus no. 10 to *Baggot St Bridge*).
Canada: *65 St Stephen's Green, Dublin 2; tel (01) 478 1988* (numerous bus services converge on *St Stephen's Green*).
UK: *31 Merrion Rd, Ballsbridge, Dublin 4; tel: (01) 269 5211* (DART to Lansdowne Rd station; numerous bus services).
USA: *42 Elgin Rd, Ballsbridge, Dublin 4; tel: (01) 668 8777* (DART to Lansdowne Rd station; numerous bus services).

Entertainment

Daily newspapers are a good source of information about entertainment in the city. Listings are also published in *Events of the Week* and *Dublin Tourism News*, both freely available at tourist information offices. *In Dublin* is a city entertainments magazine published every two weeks.

Performances of classical music by the National Symphony Orchestra, the RTE Concert Orchestra and international artists are presented in the **National Concert Hall**, *Earlsfort Terrace, Dublin 2; tel: (01) 671 1888.* **Dublin Grand Operatic Society** performs in the *Gaiety Theatre, South King St; tel: (01) 677 1717.* Free **open air concerts** are organised by Dublin Tourism on *St Stephen's Green* in the summer months.

The theatre has always been one of Dublin's great strengths and the eccentric traditions of Wilde, Yeats, Shaw, Synge, O'Casey and Brendan Behan continue to flourish. The **Abbey Theatre**, *Lower Abbey St; tel: (01) 878 7222*, is home of the National Theatre and is noted for presenting classical Irish drama as well as the work of more recent writers. Another landmark, the **Gate Theatre**, *Cavendish Row, Parnell Sq; tel (01) 874 4045*, has a deserved reputation for productions of contemporary plays. The Gaiety, Dublin's oldest theatre, stages a mixed bag of entertainment – comedy, dance, drama – as does the **Olympia Theatre** on *Dame Street; tel: (01) 677 7744.*

Nightclubs are best forgotten – expensive and mundane. Cabaret, however, thrives in isolated pockets, notably in the Irish Cabaret staged from May to mid-Oct at **Jury's Hotel**, *Pembroke Road, Ballsbridge; tel: (01) 660 5000*, and at the **Burlington Hotel**, *Leeson St, Dublin 4; tel: (01) 660 5222*. The **Abbey Tavern**, *Howth; tel: (01) 839 0307*, at the northern end of the DART line, stages an evening of traditional music and song Mon–Sat year round and Sun Mar–Oct. **Clontarf Castle**, *Castle Ave, Clontarf, Dublin 3; tel: (01) 833 2321*, stages international entertainment and dinner Mon–Sat year round. **Pink Elephant**, *South Frederick St, Dublin; tel: (01) 677 5876*, features promising and established rock singers.

As so often in Ireland, the pubs are the greatest source of entertainment. Rock fans will probably head for the **International Bar**, *23 Wicklow St; tel (01) 677 9250*, while those with a more eclectic musical taste will prefer **Slattery's**, on *Capel Street; tel: (01) 872 7971*, noted for blues, trad, folk and rock. A number of pubs have literary associations. Brendan Behan used to booze at **McDaid's**, *3, Harry St; tel: (01) 667 9395*. Over the years, **The Bailey** at *2 Duke St*, off *Grafton St; tel: (01) 677 0600*, has attracted a galaxy of literary stars, including Behan, Oliver St John Gogarty and Patrick Kavanagh. Directly opposite, at *21 Duke St; tel (01) 677 5217*, **Davy Byrne's** is where Leopold Bloom in James Joyce's *Ulysses* snacked on a gorgonzola sandwich and a glass of burgundy, enough to bring the devotees back year after year on **Bloomsday**, 16 June.

Most of Dublin's central cinemas are in *O'Connell St* and the surrounding area, and there are a number of multi-screen houses in the suburbs. No cinema specialises in art films.

Information on sporting fixtures and events can be obtained from the tourist information offices and the sports pages of the daily press. Major matches in **Gaelic football** and **hurling** – two uniquely Irish games – take place at *Croke Park* where the all-Ireland finals of the Gaelic Games inter-county championships are played each September. **Greyhound racing**, one of the country's most popular spectator sports, is held in *Shelbourne Park Stadium, Ringsend* bus nos 1, 2, 3), on Mon, Wed and Sat at 2000, and at *Harold's Cross Stadium* (bus nos 49, 49A, 65) on Tues, Thur and Fri at 2000 Feb–Dec. During late Dec and Jan racing starts at 2000 at Shelbourne Park (Mon and Sat) and at Harold's Cross at the same time Tues and Thur. **Horse racing** takes place at six courses within an hour's drive of Dublin. The nearest – *Leopardstown* – is only six miles from the city centre at *Foxrock, Dublin 18; tel: (01) 289 7277*. During the summer **polo** is played at 1730 Wed and 1500 Sat and Sun in *Phoenix Park* (bus nos 23, 25, 26). Some of the world's finest **show jumping** can be seen at the *Royal Dublin Society Showgrounds, Anglesey Rd, Ballsbridge, Dublin 4; tel: (01) 660 1700*. National and international **rugby** matches are played at the *Lansdowne Rd Ground, Ballsbridge*.

Events

There is always something going on in Dublin but key events start when the Royal Dublin Society kicks off the New Year with its **Irish Crafts Fair** in January, followed in February by the **Dublin Film Festival** and the **International Arts Festival**. March sees the city gearing up before and winding down after **St Patrick's Day**, 17 March, when there's a huge parade through the city. The **Dublin International Piano Competition** takes place in April and May sees the city's **Spring Show** and **Industries Fair**. James Joyce is celebrated on 16 June, **Bloomsday**, when *aficionados* do their best to follow in the footsteps of Leopold Bloom in *Ulysses*.

Shopping

Dublin's major shopping arteries are **O'Connell**

St and **Grafton St**. *O'Connell St* and its adjoining thoroughfares are the area for more down-to-earth shopping: booksellers, travel agents, general department stores and the like. **Moore St** is a colourful market place with vendors selling from barrows. Pedestrianised *Grafton St* is rather more upmarket, with stores selling Donegal tweed, Aran knitwear, Waterford crystal glassware and jewellery. It leads to three modern shopping malls: **Powerscourt Town House Centre** and **Westbury Mall**, on *Clarendon St*, and **St Stephen's Green Centre**. **Temple Bar**, reached through Merchant's Arch on the south side of Ha'penny Bridge, is the place for trendy boutiques and shops selling jeans, colourful clothing, fashion jewellery and records.

Sightseeing

Dublin Bus runs a three-hour sightseeing tour of the city by open-top bus twice daily Apr–Oct. Departures 1015 and 1415 from Dublin Bus, *59 Upper O'Connell St; tel: (01) 873 4222*. Adult fare: £6. The Dublin Heritage Trail is a continuous tour with hourly departures from Dublin Bus head office and nine other specially located stops. Passengers may hop on and off the bus as often as they wish. Tours daily 1000–1600, May–Sept. Fare: £5.

DART and Suburban Rail provide excellent opportunities for sightseeing along the coast and inland from the city. A weekly *Runabout* ticket covering services between *Balbriggan* in the north, *Kilcoole* in the south and *Maynooth* to the west costs £12.50. A one-day *Family Rambler* ticket covers two adults and up to four children under the age of 16 for £5.

The **Dublin Literary Pub Crawl** is a congenial way to gain an insight into the city's literature, history and architecture. The tours, which take place year-round, are led by actors who play the part of Dublin's famous and infamous characters from the past as groups progress from pub to pub, starting at The Bailey in *Duke St*. Tours start Mon–Sat 1500, June–Aug; daily 1930, May–Sept; Fri–Sat 1930 (Oct–Apr); Sun noon, year round. Reservations from the Dublin Tourist offices in *O'Connell St* and at the airport or *tel: (01) 454 0228*. Admission: £6.

A more sober view of the city is taken on **Bewley's Walks** which start daily at 1430 in the museum at Bewley's Café on *Grafton St*. The Medieval Walk takes groups through the oldest parts of the city. The Literary Walk traces the lives of some of Ireland's greatest writers in a stroll through the city's Georgian squares and streets. Each tour lasts about two hours and costs £4. Inquiries, *tel: (01) 496 0641*.

Bank of Ireland, *College Green; tel: (01) 677 6801*. Built in 1729, this striking building housed the Irish Parliament until 1800 when the British and Irish Parliaments were united in London. The chamber in which the Irish House of Lords sat contains 18th-century tapestries, the golden mace and a crystal chandelier of 1,233 pieces dating from 1765. Open Mon–Fri 1000–1600 (Thursday to 1700). Guided tours Tues 1030, 1130 and 1345. Admission: free.

Chester Beatty Library and Gallery of Oriental Art, *20 Shrewsbury Rd; tel: (01) 269 2386*. Bequeathed to the nation in 1956 by Sir Alfred Chester Beatty, the library contains some 22,000 manuscripts, rare books, miniature paintings and objects from the West, the Middle East and the Far East. Open Tues–Fri 1000–1700, Sat 1400–1700. Guided tours Wed and Sat 1430. Closed Tues after a Bank Holiday Mon. Admission: free. Take DART to Sandymount Station or buses 5, 6, 6A, 7A, 8 (from *Eden Quay*); 46A, 10 (from *College St* and *O'Connell St*).

Custom House, *Custom House Quay*, is one of Ireland's finest 18th-century buildings. In a commanding position beside the River Liffey, it was designed by James Gandon and opened in 1792. Set on fire by nationalist forces in 1921 and severely damaged, it was restored in the 1980s. Custom House is not open to the public. **Dublin Castle**, *Dame St; tel: (01) 677 7129*. Standing on the site of a Viking fortress, the castle dates from the 13th century. Its State Apartments are used for Presidential inaugurations and state functions. Open Mon–Fri 1000–1215, 1400–1700, Sat–Sun 1400–1700. Admission: £1.75.

Dublin Experience, *Thomas Davis Theatre, Trinity College Campus; tel: (01) 677 2941*. An entertaining multi-media presentation of the city's history from the 10th century to today. Open daily 1000–1700. Admission: £2.75. **Dublinia**, *Christ Church Pl; tel: (01) 679 4611*. A recreation of Dublin's development between 1170 and 1540, with a scale model of the city, life-size reconstructions and genuine artefacts from the National Museum of Ireland. Open daily 1000–1700. Admission: £3.95. Dublinia adjoins Christ Church Cathedral. Take buses 21A, 78, 78A, 78B (from *Fleet St*); 50, 50A (from *Aston Quay*). **Dublin Zoo**, *Phoenix Park; tel: (01) 677 1425*, is the world's third oldest public zoo, founded in 1830. It is set in 30 acres of gardens and has a large collection of animals and birds, including some endangered species. There is a pets corner for children and visitors can ride a train round the zoo. Open Mon–Sat 0930–1800, Sun 1030–1800. Admission: £5.50. Take buses 10 (from *O'Connell St*); 25, 26 (from *Middle Abbey St*).

Four Courts, *Inns Quay*. Another James Gandon masterpiece, completed in 1802, this splendid building houses the Irish Law Courts. It was badly damaged at the start of the civil war in 1922. Open Mon–Fri 1100–1300, 1400–1600. Admission: free. **Guinness Hop Store Visitor Centre**, *James's Gate, Crane St; tel: (01) 453 6700 ext 5155*. A four-storey 19th-century building in the heart of The Liberties district houses the World of Guinness exhibition, a model cooperage, transport museum and of course a bar where visitors can taste 'the black stuff'. Open Mon–Fri 1000–1600 (closed Bank Holidays). Admission: £2. Take buses 21A, 78, 78A (from *Fleet St*).

Irish Whiskey Corner, *Bow St; tel: (01) 672 5566*. A museum and audio-visual presentation of the story of Irish whiskey housed in a former distillery built in 1791. Tastings in the Ball o' Malt Bar. **Kilmainham Gaol**, *Inchicore Rd; tel: (01) 453 5984*. A bastion of punishment and correction from 1795 to 1924, the gaol has held many famous figures associated with Ireland's turbulent past. Here, the leaders of the 1916 Easter Rising were executed. It was opened as a museum in 1966 by President Eamonn de Valera who had himself been a prisoner in Kilmainham. Open daily 1100–1800 (May–Sept); Mon–Fri 1300–1600, Sun 1300–1800, closed Sat (Oct–Apr). Admission: £2. Take buses 51, 51A, 78, 79 (from city centre).

Marsh's Library, *St Patrick's Close; tel: (01) 454 3511*. Built in 1701 by Archbishop Narcissus Marsh, this is Ireland's oldest public library. It contains 25,000 volumes including manuscripts and early printed books. It has beautiful dark-oak bookcases and three elegant cages in which readers studying rare books are locked. The Delmas Conservation Bindery restores and repairs rare books and manuscripts. Open Mon and Wed–Fri 1000–1245, 1400–1700, Sat 1030–1245. Admission: donation. The library is next to St Patrick's Cathedral. Take buses 50, 50A, 56A (from *Aston Quay*); 54, 54A (from *Burgh Quay*).

National Botanic Gardens, *Glasnevin; tel: (01) 837 7596*. Ireland's premier botanical and horticultural establishment was founded in 1795 and now has some 20,000 different plant species in 45 acres of rock, herb and rose gardens and in the elegant curvilinear glasshouses built in the mid-19th century. Open Mon–Sat 0900–1800, Sun 1100–1800 (summer); Mon–Sat 1000–1630, Sun 1100–1630 (winter). Admission: free. Take buses 13 or 19 (from *O'Connell St*); 34, 34A (from *Middle Abbey St*). **National Wax Museum**, *Granby Row, Parnell Sq; tel: (01) 872 6340*. Life-size figures of leaders in Irish politics and literature are featured with Irish and international stars in sport and entertainment. Exhibitions include a Chamber of Horrors, Children's World of Fairy-tale and Fantasy, Hall of Megastars and a replica of Leonardo da Vinci's *Last Supper*. Open Mon–Sat 1000–1730, Sun 1200–1730. Admission: £3.50. Take buses 11, 13, 16, 22, 22A (from *Westmoreland St*).

Newman House, *85–86 St Stephen's Green; tel: (01) 475 7255*. The historic seat of University College Dublin, the building comprises two 18th-century houses decorated with superb Palladian and Rococo plasterwork. Gerard Manley Hopkins, James Joyce and Flann O'Brien are among authors who have worked here. Open Tues–Fri 1000–1600, Sat 1400–1630, Sun 1100–1400 (June–Sept). Admission: £1. **Number Twentynine**, *29 Lower Fitzwilliam St; tel: (01) 702 6165*. A completely restored middle-class house of the late-18th century housing a unique collection of artefacts and works of art. Open Tues–Sat 1000–1700, Sun 1400–1700. Admission: free. Take DART to Pearse Station or buses 6, 7, 8, 10, 45 (from city centre).

Shaw Birthplace, *33 Synge St; tel: (01) 475 0854*. Opened to the public in 1993, the famous Irish writer's first home authentically reflects domestic life in Victorian Dublin. Open Mon–Sat 1000–1300, 1400–1700, Sun and public holidays 1000–1300, 1400–1800 (May–Oct). Admission: £3.80. Take buses 16, 19, 22; 15-min walk from *St Stephen's Green*. **Trinity College**, *College Green; tel: (01) 677 2941*. Founded by Queen Elizabeth I in 1592, Trinity is Ireland's oldest university and today caters for some 8000 students. Beyond its great arched gate, flanked by statues of graduates Oliver Goldsmith and Edmund Burke, are 40 acres of grounds with cobbled squares and gardens and buildings dating from the 17th to the 20th centuries. The grounds are freely accessible. The *Book of Kells* is displayed with other illuminated manuscripts and an early Irish harp in **The Colonnades** exhibition gallery and the **Long Room**, which house more than 200,000 of Trinity's oldest books. Open Mon–Sat 0930–1730, Sun 1200–1700. Admission: £2.50.

Waterways Visitor Centre, *Grand Canal Basin, Ringsend; tel: (01) 661 3111*. A modern building constructed over the water of the canal basin, the centre houses an exhibition designed to introduce visitors to the historical role of Ireland's inland waterways and to the range of activities and experiences they offer today. Open daily 0930–1800. Admission: £1.50. Take DART to Pearse Station then walk east along *Pearse St* to Pearse St Bridge (about 10 mins) or take buses 1, 2, 3 (from city centre).

Art Galleries

Hugh Lane Municipal Gallery, *Parnell Sq; tel: (01) 874 1903*. The second largest public art collection in Ireland includes works ranging from the impressionists to contemporary Irish artists. Open Tues–Fri 0930–1800, Sat 0930–1700, Sun 1100–1700. Admission: free. Numerous bus services pass through *Parnell Sq*.

Irish Museum of Modern Art, *The Royal Hospital, Kilmainham; tel: (01) 671 8666*. A permanent collection and temporary exhibitions of international and Irish art of the 20th century are staged in what is said to be Ireland's finest 17th-century building. Open Tues–Sat 1000–1730, Sun 1200–1730. Admission: free. Take buses 24, 79, 90. **National Gallery**, *Merrion Sq West; tel: (01) 661 5133*. Every major European school of painting is extensively represented and there is a major collection of Irish paintings, many of which are on permanent display. Open Mon–Sat 1000–1730, Thur 1000–2030, Sun 1400–1700. Admission: free. Take DART to Pearse Station then walk south along *Westland Row* (about five mins) or take buses 44, 47, 48A, 62.

Cathedrals and Churches

Christ Church Cathedral, *Christ Church Pl; tel: (01) 677 8099*. This historic Church of Ireland cathedral originated as a simple wooden church built in 1038 by Sitric Silkenbeard, King of the Dublin Norsemen. In 1169 it was rebuilt in stone by Richard de Clare, Earl of Pembroke, also known as Strongbow. Open daily (except 26 Dec) 1000–1700. Admission: donation. Take buses 21A, 78, 78A (from *Fleet St*); 50, 50A (from *Aston Quay*). **St Patrick's Cathedral**, *Patrick's Close; tel: (01) 475 4817*. The saint himself is said to have baptised converts in a nearby well, and a church has stood on the site since 450. The present building dates from 1191. Jonathan Swift, Dean of St Patrick's for more than 30 years, is buried in the nave. Open Mon–Sat 0900–1800, Sat 0900–1600 (Nov–Mar), 0900–1700 (Apr–Oct), Sun 1000–1630. Admission: £1. Take buses 50, 50A, 56A (from *Aston Quay*); 54, 54A (from *Burgh Quay*).

St Michan's Church, *Lower Church St; tel: (01) 872 4154*. The composer Handel is said to have played the finely carved 18th-century organ, but the church's chief attraction for visitors lies in the mummified corpses exposed in the vaults. Open Mon–Fri 1000–1245, 1400–1645, Sat 1000–1245. Admission: donation. **Whitefriar Street Carmelite Church**, *57 Aungier St; tel: (01) 475 8821*. The church contains the remains of St Valentine, presented by Pope

Gregory XVI in 1835, after being exhumed from the cemetery at St Hippolytus, Rome.

Museums

Dublin Writers Museum, *18 Parnell Sq; tel: (01) 872 2077*. Memorabilia of Ireland's most famous writers, together with rare books and manuscripts, are exhibited in an elegantly restored 18th-century mansion. The museum also accommodates the Irish Writers' Centre where contemporary writers can meet, talk and work. Open daily 1000–1700. Admission: £2.50. Numerous buses pass through *Parnell Sq*.

National Museum of Ireland, *Kildare St and Merrion Row; tel: (01) 661 8811*. Opened in 1890, the museum contains artefacts and masterpieces dating from 2000 BC to the present day. The National treasury features Ardagh Chalice, Tara Brooch, Cross of Cong and the finest collection of prehistoric gold artefacts in Europe. Other departments feature Irish history 1916–1921, decorative arts and scientific instruments. Open Tues–Sat 1000–1700, Sun 1400–1700. Admission: free. Take DART to Pearse Station or buses 7, 7A (from *Eden Quay*); 10, 11, 13 (from *O'Connell St*). **Natural History Museum**, *Merrion St; tel: (01) 661 8811*. Collections illustrate the wildlife of Ireland and other parts of the world. Open Tues–Sat 1000–1700, Sun 1400–1700. Admission: free. Take DART to Pearse Station or buses 7, 7A, 8 (from *Eden Quay*).

Out of Town

Howth Transport Museum, *Howth Castle; tel: (01) 847 5623*. A small but interesting collection of early fire engines, tractors and other vehicles, including a Giant's Causeway tram. Open Sat, Sun and public holidays 1400–1800. Admission: £1.50. Take DART to Howth Station.

James Joyce Tower, *Sandycove; tel: (01) 280 9265*. One of a series of Martello towers built in 1804 against a threatened French invasion, this was where James Joyce stayed briefly with Oliver St John Gogarty in 1904, later using it as the setting for the first chapter of *Ulysses*. Now owned and run by Dublin Tourism, it contains a collection of Joyce memorabilia, including letters, documents and first and rare editions. Open Mon–Sat 1000–1300, 1400–1700, Sun and public holidays 1400–1800 (Apr–Oct). Admission: £1.90. Take DART to *Sandycove* or bus 8 (from *Eden Quay*).

Malahide Castle, *Malahide, Co. Dublin; tel: (01) 845 2655*. The Talbot family lived here from 1185–1973, except for a short period of exile. It now houses portraits from the National Gallery. Open Mon–Fri 1000–1700 (year round); Sat, Sun, public holidays 1400–1700 (Nov–Mar); Sat 1100–1800, Sun, public holidays 1130–1800 (Apr–Oct). Admission: £2.65. The **Fry Model Railway Museum** is in the castle grounds. Admission: £2.25. Combined castle/model railway: £4.25. Take a Suburban Rail train from Connolly Station to *Malahide* or bus no. 42 from *Busaras*. **National Maritime Museum**, *High Terrace, Dun Laoghaire; tel: (01) 280 0969*. A noted collection of model ships and many other exhibits displayed in the 1837 Mariners' Church. Open Tues–Sun 1430–1730 (May–Sept). Admission: £1.50. Take DART to *Dun Laoghaire*.

Drogheda is 25 miles north of Dublin and can be reached by Dublin Suburban rail service. Heavily fortified by the 14th century, only one of the its original ten town gates survives. **St. Laurence's Gate**, on *Laurence St*, is one of Ireland's best-preserved medieval town gates. **Newgrange**, one of the most spectacular prehistoric tombs in Europe, is 5 miles west of Drogheda; *tel: (041) 24488*. Open: Tues–Sat 1000–1300, 1400–1700, Sun 1400–1700; daily 1000–1900 (mid-June–mid-Sept); Mon–Sat 1000–1700, Sun 1400–1700 (Apr–mid–June, mid-Sept–mid-Oct). Admission: £2.

Further north on the Northern Suburban line, and also served by Dublin–Belfast InterCity train (see below), is **Dundalk**. The town's history goes back to the 7th century, but few traces of its past remain. Its oldest structure, a ruin known as **The Castle**, on *Castle St*, is actually the bell tower of a 13th-century Franciscan friary.

⬇ Connection: Belfast

There are six trains on weekdays (four on Sun) from Connolly Station to Belfast (see p. 301), the journey taking around 2 hrs 20 mins.

DUBLIN to CORK

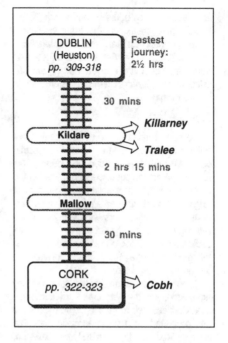

DUBLIN
(Heuston)
pp. 309-318

Fastest
journey:
2½ hrs

30 mins

Kildare → Killarney

→ Tralee

2 hrs 15 mins

Mallow

30 mins

CORK
pp. 322-323 → Cobh

This journey crosses the lush open grasslands of County Kildare and the countryside becomes more rugged as the train progresses through counties Laois and Tipperary. Palm trees on the platforms at Mallow station are an indication of the mellower climate of south-west Ireland.

TRAINS

ETT table: 640

 → Fast Track

Seven weekday trains (five on Sun) run direct from Dublin Heuston to Cork. Two other services require a change of train at Mallow. Journey time vary according to the number of stops en route: 2 hrs 20 mins is the fastest, 3 hrs 15 more usual.

 On Track

Dublin–Kildare

A mixture of InterCity and suburban trains provide a weekday service of 30 trains per day between Dublin Heuston and Kildare. On Sun there are only InterCity trains and the number of services falls to 11 or 12; these are long-distance trains and leave at convenient times for such passengers. Consequently gaps of 3 hrs between services occur, and there is no service from Kildare to Dublin before 1100. The journey time 30 mins by InterCity train or 40 mins by suburban service.

Kildare–Mallow

Four weekday trains, (three on Sun) link Kildare directly with Mallow; two other services are available on weekdays by changing at Portar-

lington. The journey takes about 2 hrs 15 mins.

Mallow–Cork

Around ten trains a day (express and local services) run between Mallow and Cork. The journey takes 30 mins.

KILDARE

Tourist Office: Kildare has no permanent tourist office. A temporary information office operates from a caravan in the town's main car park during summer months. Otherwise, contact **Midlands-East Tourism**: *Dublin Rd, Mullingar, Co Westmeath; tel: (044) 48650*.
Station: Kildare Station, *Kildare; tel: (045) 21224*, ¼ mile from the town centre; *tel: (045) 21224*. The town has a good **Bus Éireann** service to and from Dublin.

Staying in Kildare

Accommodation is sparse in Kildare. The town has only one hotel – the **Curragh Lodge**, *Dublin St; tel: (045) 22144* – and half a dozen b. & b.

---

establishments registered with the Irish Tourist Board. There are no youth hostels or holiday hostels. **Carasli Caravan and Camping Park**, *tel: (045) 24331*, is at *Rathangan*, about 5 miles north-west of Kildare on R336. A one-star establishment, it has six tent pitches and mobile homes for hire.

Sightseeing

The centre of Ireland's racehorse breeding and training industry, Kildare is a pleasant, prosperous town with a population of around 4500. Just off the market square, and dominating the town, is the Church of Ireland **Cathedral of St Brigid**. The saint founded a religious order here in 490. The stained-glass west window of the cathedral, a restored 13th-century structure, depicts saints Patrick, Columba and Brigid. In the graveyard is a 108 ft **round tower**, the second highest in Ireland.

About a mile south of the town, clearly signposted, are the **National Stud** and **Japanese Gardens**, *tel: (045) 21617*, both of which may be visited for a single admission fee. The National Stud includes the **Irish Horse Museum**, in which the skeleton of Arkle, the famous racehorse of the 1960s, is displayed. The superb Japanese Gardens are considered to be the finest in Europe, with miniature lakes and many Oriental trees and flowers. They were laid out between 1906 and 1910. Open daily 0930–1800 (Easter Sunday–Oct). Admission: £4.

 Side Tracks from Mallow

KILLARNEY

Tourist Office: *Town Hall, Main St; tel: (064) 31633.* Open Mon–Sat 0900–2000, Sun 1000–1800 (July–Aug); Mon–Sat 0900–1900 (June and Sept); Mon–Fri 0915–1730, Sat 0915–1300 (Oct–May).
Station: Killarney Station, *East Avenue Rd, tel: (064) 31067.* The station is just a few minutes' walk from the town centre. A bicycle rental centre adjoins the station building. About nine services run daily from Mallow to Killarney, taking around 1 hr.

Bus Station: the **Bus Éireann** terminus is in *East Avenue Rd; tel: (064) 34777*.

Getting Around

Killarney owes its popularity to the surrounding lakes and mountains, so its best sights are some distance away – but not so far that they can't be reached in a gentle hike or by jaunting car (the traditional Irish pony and trap). These operate from *Main St*, near *East Avenue Rd*, and cost about £12 for up to four people. The trip to **Ross Castle** (see below) and back takes about 45 mins, including a 15-min stop at the castle.

Killarney is pleasant, compact and very busy in July and Aug, but easy to stroll in. Excursions to outlying attractions and around the **Ring of Kerry** (a spectacular route encircling the Iveragh Peninsula and traversing Killarney National Park) can be taken from the town (details from the tourist office).

Staying in Killarney

Thanks to the discovery of its lakes and fells by travellers of the calibre of Sir Walter Scott and William Thackeray, Killarney is a well-established inland resort rich in accommodation options. There are more than 30 hotels, ranging from moderate to de luxe, and a huge choice of b. & bs. Hotel chains in Killarney include *BW, Ch, GS, HH, Mn, RH*. Hotels of all grades are dispersed throughout the town, as are b. & b. establishments. Cheaper lodgings are on the outskirts.

Youth Hostel: *Aghadoe House, Killorglin Rd; tel: (064) 31240.* This year-round *An Oige* hostel is about three miles west of the town, but there is a free mini-bus service between the station and hostel. There are tours of the Ring of Kerry and other attractions from the hostel. Advance booking is essential in July and Aug. There are four holiday hostels registered with the Irish Tourist Board and about half a dozen registered campgrounds within three miles of the town. The nearest are the two-star **Flesk Caravan and Camping Park**, about a mile south on *Kenmare Rd; tel: (064) 31704*, and the four-star **Flemings Whitebridge C & C Park**, a mile east on the banks of the River Flesk, off *Cork Rd; tel: (064) 31590*.

Shopping

Souvenir shops abound, some piled with trash but many offering quality goods ranging from Celtic jewellery to excellent knitwear and tweeds. A good place for bargain garments and craft goods is the **Blarney Woollen Mills** shop, *10 Main St; tel: (064) 33222.*

Sightseeing

Fourteenth-century **Ross Castle**, south of the town centre, about 15 mins by jaunting car, commands a wonderful view over Lough Leane. The castle and lake are in Killarney National Park. Admission: free.

Muckross House, a mile or so beyond Ross Castle, is a 19th-century manor housing the Kerry Folklife Centre, where ancient crafts are demonstrated. Open daily 0900–1900 (July–Aug); daily 0900–1800 (Mar–June and Sept–Oct); Tues–Sun 1100–1700 (Nov–Feb). Admission: £2.50.

TRALEE

Tourist Office: *Ashe Memorial Hall, Denny St; tel: (066) 21288.* Open Mon–Sat 0900–2000, Sun 1100–1500 (July–Aug); Mon–Sat 0900–1800 (May–June and Sept); Mon–Fri 0930–1300, 1400–1730, Sat 0930–1300 (Oct–Apr). Services offered: local and all-Ireland accommodation.

Station: Tralee Station, *John Joe Sheehy Rd, Tralee; tel: (066) 23566.* A 10-min walk (¼ mile) to town. The station has a reservations service and a bureau de change. About nine services run daily from Killarney to Tralee, taking around 40 mins.

Bus Station: the terminal for **Bus Éireann** services is *Casement Station; tel: (066) 23566.* There are five buses a day from Dublin (four on Sun) and four buses a day (one on Sun) travel to the Dingle Peninsula.

Staying in Tralee

The town has eight hotels rated from one to three stars and five guesthouses in the two- and three-star categories. There is a profusion of b. & b. establishments. Hotel chains in Killarney

include *Ch.* The only registered holiday hostel is **Lisnagree**, *Clash East; tel: (066) 27133.* **Bayview Caravan Park**, *tel: (066) 26140,* a mile north of the town on the *Ballybunion road,* is a three-star establishment with 16 tent pitches and mobile homes to rent. Open April–Oct.

Entertainment and Events

Siamsa Tíre, the National Folk Theatre of Ireland, presents drama, song and dance in a theatre designed along the lines of a 2000-year-old Irish stone fort in *Godfrey Pl; tel: (066) 23055.* Shows start at 2030 Mon–Sat (July–Aug) and Tues and Thurs (May, June and Sept).

The biggest event of the year is the **Rose of Tralee International Festival**, a week of pageantry in late July or early Aug. **Geraldine Tralee**, a 'time car' trip through medieval streets, is in *Ashe Memorial Hall; tel: (066) 27777.* Open Mon–Sat 1000–2000, Sun 1400–1800. Admission: £3.

Sightseeing

Although it is Co Kerry's largest town, with a population of around 17,000, Tralee is easy to negotiate on foot. The oldest parts date from the 18th century and there are some attractive Georgian terraces in *Denny St* and *Day Pl.*

CORK

Tourist Office: Cork-Kerry Tourism, *Tourist House, Grand Parade; tel: (021) 273251.* Open Mon–Fri 0900–1800, Sat 0900–1300. Services: bureau de change; computerised local and all-Ireland accommodation reservations service; good selection of information, leaflets and maps. Guide books are available for purchase.

Station: Kent Station, *Lower Glanmire Road; tel: (021) 506766;* on the north side of the River Lee, ¼-mile from the city centre.

Ferries: Ferry services operate from *Ringaskiddy,* about 10 miles south east of Cork. There is a connecting bus service between the harbour and the city. Sailings to the UK are operated by **Swansea–Cork Ferries**, *55 Grand Parade, Cork; tel: (021) 271166.* **Brittany Ferries**, *42 Grand*

Parade; tel: (021) 277081, sail to Roscoff. For further details, see Ferry Crossings on p. 12.

Buses: Bus Éireann and **Provincial Bus** services arrive and depart from the bus station in Parnell Pl, off Merchants' Quay; tel: (021) 508188. Bus Éireann also operates city bus tours and excursions to Bantry Bay, Killarney, Limerick and Tipperary; for information tel: (021) 503399 ext 318.

Getting Around

Cork's major attractions are either on or close to 'the flat', so walking is the best way to get around. In any event, it's an interesting muddle of a place and pedestrians have the edge on vehicular traffic, which is frequently brought to a halt in the narrow, twisty streets.

Local bus services operate from the bus station in Parnell Pl; tel: (021) 508188. A standard fare operates within the city area.

There are taxi stands adjacent to the rail and bus stations, near major hotels and opposite the Savoy Centre, Patrick St. **Cork Taxi Co-op**, tel: (021) 272222; **Shandon Cabs**, tel: (021) 502255; **Tele-Cabs**, tel: (021) 505050.

Staying in Cork

Cork gets very busy during the summer, so it's wise to book ahead (though Cork-Kerry Tourism will do its best to accommodate you on the spot). However, the spectrum of choice is broad, with a good selection of guesthouses and many b.&b. establishments. Hotel chains in Cork include BW, TI, HH, Ju, MO.

As much a part of Cork as the River Lee itself, the three-star **Imperial Hotel** on South Mall; tel: (021) 274040, was designed in the classical style by Cork architect Thomas Deane and opened in 1816. Some of its 101 rooms – each with private bath – still have the old mahogany furniture and velvet upholstery and others have been renovated in Art Deco style.

Youth Hostel: Cork International Youth Hostel, 1/2 Redclyffe, Western Rd; tel: (021) 543289. This year-round An Oige hostel is just over a mile from the city centre, and can be reached by bus no. 8. Four registered holiday hostels are within easy reach of the centre: **Campus House**, 3 Woodland View, Western

Rd; tel: (021) 343531; **ISAAC's**, 48 Mac Curtain St; tel: (021) 500011; **Kinlay House**, Shandon; tel: (021) 508966; **Sheila's Hostel**, Belgrave Pl, Wellington Rd; tel: (021) 505562. **Cork City Caravan and Camping Park**, Togher Rd; tel: (021) 312711. City bus service no.14 stops at the gate. Open May–Oct.

Corkonians love eating out and the city has lots of options. One of the best-value places to eat is the café at the **Triskel Arts Centre**, Tobin St, off South Main St, which serves home-made bread, soups and hot dishes for vegetarians and meat-eaters. As you might expect, there's no shortage of pubs in the city – and the brew here is Murphy's, rather than Guinness.

Post Office: Oliver Plunkett St. Open Mon–Sat 0900–1730. Poste restante, bureau de change. Tel area code: (021).

Entertainment

Despite its no-nonsense, workaday appearance, Cork offers a wide range of cultural experiences. At one end of the scale, there's Gaelic football and hurling in **Páirc Ui Chaomh Stadium**, tel: (021) 963311; at the other, lunchtime and evening concerts of classical music – details from Cork-Kerry Tourism, or check listings in the daily Cork Examiner or Evening Echo. Drama, musical comedy, ballet and opera are staged at the **Cork Opera House**, Emmet Pl; tel: (021) 270022. Musical productions, poetry and prose readings, plays and films are presented at the **Triskel Arts Centre**, Tobin St, South Main St; tel: (021) 272022. Cork has musical pubs in abundance and plenty of discos.

Cork keeps the cultural pressure up with a number of world-class festivals. The **International Jazz Festival** takes place at the end of Oct, preceded at the start of the month by the **Cork Film Festival**, of short and feature-length movies. The **Cork International Choral and Folk Dance Festival** draws choirs and folk dance teams from all over the world at the beginning of May.

Shopping

Lots of shops sell crystal glass, china, linen, knitware, tweeds and craftware of all kinds. **Coal Quay Market**, off Cornmarket St, is the place for antiques, and the **English Market**, off *Grand Parade*, has stalls selling fish, meat, fruit and vegetables.

Sightseeing

Always busy, with a jumble of narrow streets and a river at its heart, Cork wears the jauntiness of a sailor and the quick-wittedness of a market trader. Ireland's second city began as a monastic island settlement in the 6th century and developed as a fortified trading post under the Vikings and Normans. Today it has crossed both channels of the River Lee, climbing slopes to the north and south, but its centre is still that old island site known as 'the flat of the city'.

Cork has a signposted walking trail, which visitors can follow with the aid of a booklet from the tourist office. Guided walking tours are organised by **Discover Cork**, *Belmont, Douglas Rd; tel: (021) 293873*. Afternoon and evening cruises around Cork Harbour and trips to **Fota Island** (Wildlife Park) take place July–Sept. Details from the tourist office or **Marine Transport**, *Atlantic Quay, Cobh; tel: (021) 811485*.

Nineteenth-century life on the wrong side of the law is illustrated in **Cork City Gaol**, *Sunday's Well, tel: (021) 305022*. Open daily 0930–1800 (May–Sept); Mon–Fri tours at 1030 and 1430, Sat–Sun 1000–1600 (Oct–April). Admission: £3. **Crawford Municipal Art Gallery**, *Emmet Pl; tel: (021) 276573*. Open Mon–Sat 1000–1700. Admission: free. **St Finbarre's Cathedral**, *Bishop St; tel: (021) 964742*. Open daily 0900–1800 Admission: free. **St Anne's Church**, *Church St, Shandon; tel: (021) 501672*. Climb the distinctive pepperpot steeple and choose a tune to be played on the carillon. Open daily 0900–1800. Admission: donation.

 Side Tracks from Cork

COBH

Tourist Office: *Cobh Heritage Centre; tel: (021)* *813591*. Open Mon–Fri 0900–1800, Sat 0900–1300 (Easter–Sept). Information, local accommodation reservations.

Station: *Westbourne Pl; tel: (021) 611655*. The restored Victorian station houses **Cobh Heritage Centre**. Ten trains on weekdays, 5 on Suns connect Cork with Cobh, a journey of 24 mins.

Staying in Cobh

Cobh has some two-star hotels, a guesthouse and half a dozen b. & b. places registered with the Irish Tourist Board. There are no hostels and no camping facilities. A signposted Heritage Trail guides visitors around the town.

Sightseeing

Because of its position in the sheltered harbour, Cobh (pronounced 'cove'), a small resort town and port, has always had close maritime associations. The Royal Cork Yacht Club, said to be the oldest of its kind in the world, was founded here in 1720.

From 1750 the town was the embarkation point for thousands of emigrants seeking a new life in Australia, New Zealand, Canada and the United States. Today, it is an important point of call for cruise liners.

Cobh's involvement with ships and emigration is highlighted in **The Queenstown Story**, a multi-media exhibition in the Heritage Centre. Open daily 1000–1800 (last admission 1700). Admission £3.50. From 1849 to 1922 Cobh was called Queenstown to mark a visit by Queen Victoria. The exhibition illustrates life aboard the convict ships to Australia and the emigrant ships bound for the New World. Exhibits tell the stories of the *Titanic* – Cobh was her last port of call – and the *Lusitania*, sunk by a German submarine off Kinsale in 1915 with a loss of nearly 1200 lives.

The town is dominated by the Gothic Revival splendour of **St Colman's Cathedral**. Designed by the 19th-century architects Ashlin and Pugin, it has a 47-bell carillon.

DUBLIN
to
LIMERICK

This journey skirts between the Wicklow Mountains and the Irish Sea before reaching the low-lying countryside of Co Wexford. It then traverses the ancient province of Munster, striking westwards across the Golden Plain of Tipperary to the tidal reaches of the River Shannon.

TRAINS

ETT tables: 637, 638, 640, 641, 643

 Fast Track

Two through trains run daily from Dublin Heuston to Limerick, taking about 2 hrs. A more regular service is provided by express trains from Dublin Heuston to Limerick Junction with connecting trains from there to Limerick with total journey times of about 2 hrs 20 mins. The 'On Track' route below is a much more roundabout route and it is not possible to complete it in one day.

On Track

Dublin–Wicklow–Arklow–Wexford
Three trains daily (two on Suns) operate from Dublin Connolly to Wexford, calling at Wicklow and Arklow en route. Dublin to Wicklow takes just under an hour; Wicklow to Arklow takes 35 mins and Arklow to Wexford takes about 1 hr.

Wexford–Waterford
This service is by bus. There are four or five buses daily (three on Suns), taking one hour.

Waterford–Limerick
On weekdays, one train (increased to two in

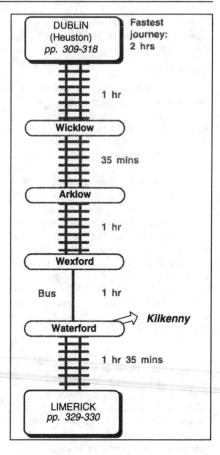

high summer) runs between Waterford and Limerick, taking about 2 hr 35 mins.

WICKLOW

Tourist Office: *Rialto Centre, Fitzwilliam Sq; tel: (0404) 69117*. Open Mon–Fri 0900–1800, Sat 0900–1300. Services offered: local and all-Ireland accommodation reservations, bureau de change.
Station: Wicklow Station, *Station Rd; tel: (0404) 67329* (¼ mile from the centre).
Bus Station: Bus Éireann serves the town with 12 buses on weekdays, 7 on Sundays from Dublin.

Getting Around

Wicklow is compact enough to cover on foot, but major attractions are some distance away. However, most of them can be reached by provincial bus services which run daily (information from the Tourist Office).

Staying in Wicklow

Accommodation

There is a good range of reasonably priced accommodation – small hotels, guesthouses and b. & b.s. **Hostel;** The Lodge, *Glendalough, Co Wicklow; tel: (0404) 45342.* The hostel is next to the Visitor Centre at the Glendalough monastic site, 10 miles from Wicklow on the edge of the Wicklow Mountains. It can be reached daily from Dublin by **St Kevin's Bus Service** *tel: (01) 281 8119.* Buses leave from the Royal College of Surgeons, *St Stephen's Green.* A simpler hostel is at *Tiglin, Ashford; tel: (0404) 40259,* 6 miles north of Wicklow on the N11. Take the Dublin bus to Ashford from Wicklow railway station. From Ashford it's a well signposted 4½-mile walk.

Roundwood Camping and Caravan Park, *tel: (01) 281 8163,* is in the village of Roundwood, off the N11 3 miles north of Wicklow. There is a daily bus service from the park to Dublin.

Eating and Drinking

For eating, there are a few moderate restaurants and cafés in town, but pubs offer the best option.

Sightseeing

Wicklow is a pleasant seaside resort and county town with a population of about 6000. The town's former courthouse, near *Market Sq, tel: (0404) 67324,* is now a **Heritage and Genealogical Centre**. Open Mon–Sat 0900–1700. Admission: free.

The life-size figure of a pikeman in *Market Sq* is the **1798 Memorial**, honouring the Wicklow men who took part in the rising of that year. An obelisk of polished granite in *Fitzwilliam Sq* commemorates Captain Robert Halpin, who commanded the *Great Eastern*, the ship that laid the first transatlantic cable.

The ruins of a 13th-century **Franciscan Friary** stand in the grounds of the parish priest's house at the town entrance on *Main St* (*tel: (0404) 67196* for permission to view the ruins). The ruined **Black Castle**, on a rocky promontory south of the harbour, was built in 1176 by Maurice Fitzgerald. It is freely accessible.

Planted along the banks of the River Vartry at Ashford, on the N11 four miles north of Wicklow, **Mount Usher Gardens,** *tel: (0404) 40116,* are a fine example of a 'wild garden'. More than 5000 species, including rare trees, shrubs and flowers from all over the world and 70 species of eucalyptus, are contained in 20 acres. Craft shops, a book shop and a café are on the site. Open: Mon–Sat 1030–1800, Sun 1100–1800 (17 Mar–31 Oct). Admission: £2.80. Take bus to Ashford from railway station.

Founded by St Kevin in the 6th century, **Glendalough** was Ireland's most important early Christian settlement whose fame as a centre of learning spread throughout Europe. The monastery's development came to an end in 1398 when the place was attacked by English forces. Among the ruins are a well-preserved round tower and a 10th-century cathedral. The history of the site is told in the Visitor Centre. Open daily 1000–1700 (Mar–May and Sept–Oct), daily 1000–1900 (June–Aug). Admission: £1. A private mini-bus departs twice daily to Glendalough from the Bridge Tavern (*tel: (0404) 67718)* in the town centre.

Avondale House, about 6 miles south-west of Wicklow, *tel: (0404) 46111,* is the restored home of the 19th-century nationalist leader, Charles Stewart Parnell. Built in 1779, the house is surrounded by the 520-acre **Avondale Forest Park**. Open daily 1000–1300, 1400–1800 (May–Sept), Sat–Sun 1200–1800 (Oct–Apr). Admission: £2. Take the train (four daily Mon–Fri, fewer at weekends) from Wicklow to Rathdrum (approx. 16 mins), then 1½-mile walk.

ARKLOW

Tourist Office: *The Parade Ground; tel: (0402) 32484.* Open Mon–Fri 0900–1800, Sat 0900–

1300 (June–Aug). Services offered: local and all-Ireland accommodation reservations, bureau de change.

Station: Arklow Station, *Station Rd; tel: (0402) 32519.*

Bus Station: The town is served by six Bus Éireann Expressway services a day from Dublin, *tel: (01) 836 6111,* and is linked with places in Co Wicklow through the Provincial Bus network.

Staying in Arklow

There are privately owned hotels and a wide selection of b. & b. accommodation in town and country houses and, on the outskirts, in farmhouses. The nearest *An Oige* hostel is **Aghavannagh House**, about 8 miles north of *Aughrim, tel: (0402) 36102.* The town has a cinema and most pubs provide entertainment.

Sightseeing

An important seaside resort with excellent beaches stretching to the north and south, Arklow is also a noted centre for fishing and boat-building. *Gypsy Moth III,* the yacht that Sir Francis Chichester sailed round the world, was built here. The **Maritime Museum** is located in the public library building, near the railway station, *tel: (0402) 32868.* Open Mon–Fri 1000–1300, 1400–1700 (June–Sept). Admission: £1.

There are guided tours of the **Arklow Pottery** on the quayside *tel: (0402) 32401.* Open Mon–Fri 0930–1300 and 1400–1645, Sat–Sun 1000–1645. Admission: free. The Gothic Revival **St Saviour's Church**, built in 1900, has a three-light window by Harry Clarke, one of Ireland's best-known 20th century stained-glass artists.

Four miles inland, on R747, the hamlet of Avoca is in a picturesque valley at the confluence of the Avonbeg and Avonmore rivers. Here, in 1807, the poet Thomas Moore was inspired to write his famous work *The Meeting of the Waters.* **Avoca Handweavers**, *tel: (0402) 35105,* produces tweed fabrics in the traditional way. Visitors are welcome. The mill is open Mon–Fri 1000–1630, the shop Mon–Fri 0930–1730; Sat–Sun 1000–1730. There are two buses a day from Arklow and one from Wicklow.

WEXFORD

Tourist Office: *Crescent Quay; tel: (053) 23111.* Open Mon–Fri 0900–1715 (Jan–Mar, Nov); Mon–Sat 0900–1800 (Apr–Sept); Sun 1000–1700 (July–Aug). *Ferry Terminal, Rosslare; tel: (053) 33622.* Open daily 1400–1700, 1800–2030 (Jan–Mar, Oct–Dec); daily for all sailings (Apr–Sept). Services offered: local and all-Ireland accommodation reservations, bureau de change.

Station: *Commercial Quay, tel: (053) 23111.*

Bus Station: The Bus Éireann terminal *(tel: 053) 22522* is at the railway station. There are six to eight Expressway services daily between Dublin and Wexford, depending on time of year.

Ferries: these sail to and from Rosslare Harbour (about 20 mins from Wexford by train and 30 mins by Bus Éireann (6 journeys on weekdays, 4 on Suns). **B & I Line**, *tel: (053) 33311,* operates services to Pembroke Dock, and **Stena Sealink**, *tel: (053) 33115,* sail to Fishguard. For more information see Ferry Crossings on p. 12.

Staying in Wexford

Accommodation

Hotel chains in Wexford include *BW, CC* and *MO.* Accommodation ranges from three-star hotels and guesthouses to town houses, country homes and farmhouses. **Hostel**: *An Oige Hostel, Goulding St, Rosslare Harbour; tel: (053) 33399.* The three-star **Ferrybank Caravan and Camping Park**, *tel: (053) 42611 or 44378* is immediately over the bridge from Commercial Quay, five mins from the town centre.

Eating and Drinking

There are plenty of restaurants and cafés in the town and as always the pubs and bars offer reasonable fare.

Entertainment

Live entertainment, including traditional Irish music, is found in many bars in the evening. Wexford's renowned **Opera Festival** is staged each October in the Theatre Royal, *High St; tel: (053) 22240.*

Sightseeing

Ancient Wexford is a maze of narrow lanes – ideal for walking. Evening **walking tours** are guided by members of Wexford Historical Society during summer months. Details at hotels or tourist offices or *tel: (053) 41081*.

Westgate Heritage Tower; *Spawell Rd; tel: (053) 46506*, traces the town's development. Open daily 1100–1730 (Sept–May), daily 0900–1300, 1400–1700 (July–Aug). Admission: £1.50. **Irish National Heritage Park**, *Ferrycarrig; tel: (053) 41733*, is an open-air museum showing how Irish society developed. Open daily 0900–1900 (17 Mar–30 Oct). Admission: £3.

WATERFORD

Tourist Office: *41 The Quay; tel: (051) 75788*. Open Mon–Sat 0900–1800 (Apr–Oct), Sun 1000–1700 (July–Aug); Mon–Fri 0900–1715 (Jan–Mar, Nov–Dec). Services offered: local and all-Ireland accommodation reservations, bureau de change.

Station: *Plunkett Station, The Bridge; tel: (051) 73401* (centrally located).

Bus Station: Bus Éireann, *tel: (051) 79000*. Local services use the bus station adjoining the railway station on the north side of the River Suir.

Getting Around

With a network of narrow streets and lanes – a legacy of the city's Viking and Norman origins – Waterford is a good place to explore on foot.

Staying in Waterford

Accommodation

There are about half a dozen hotels and a similar number of guesthouses, as well as a good selection of b.&b. accommodation in both town and country houses. Hotel chains in Waterford include *BW, Ch, HH, Ju*. There are cheaper b.&b.s around *The Mall, O'Connell St* and *Parnell St*. **Viking House**, *Coffee House Lane, The Quay; tel: (051) 53827*, is a holiday hostel with accommodation in single, twin and four-bed rooms as well as dormitories.

Eating and Drinking

Waterford has plenty of restaurants, cafés and pubs serving food. There are establishments offering traditional Irish fare, fastfood places, pizza parlours and Chinese restaurants. There's even a reasonably priced but imaginative restaurant in the former Royal Irish Constabulary barracks on *Mary St*. No shortage of good pubs, either, in this city of 41,000 people.

Communications

Post Office: *Keyser St, The Quay*. Open Mon–Sat 0900–1800. Poste restante facilities.

Entertainment

Details of performances, concerts, exhibitions, etc, are listed in the Tourist Office. Discos are held at most of the hotels at weekends, and live music – rock, blues, country and the like – is to be found in a number of pubs, as is traditional Irish music. The city's major theatre is the **Theatre Royal**, *The Mall; tel: (051) 74402*, and drama, concerts of classical music, art shows and exhibitions are staged at the **Garter Lane Arts Centre**, *O'Connell St; tel: (051) 55038*.

Events

Amateur musical societies from all over Ireland and Britain compete each September in the **Waterford International Festival of Light Opera**, staged in the Theatre Royal.

Shopping

Tweeds, knitwear and crystal dominate the windows of stores in arcades along *Broad St* and *George's Court* and shops on *Barronstrand* and *The Quay*. Bargain-hunters will no doubt want to head for **Waterford Auction Galleries**, *O'Connell St* (closed Sun, Mon). A general market takes place in *Applemarket*, Fri and Sat, and the shops stay open until 2100 on Fri.

Sightseeing

Walking tours of the city take place daily at noon and 1400 (Mar–Oct). Starting at the Granville Hotel on *The Quay*, tours last about an hour and include two cathedrals, four national monuments and a wealth of Georgian buildings. The tours are organised by **Waterford Tourist Services**, *Jenkins Lane, Waterford; tel: (051) 50645.*

The city's most dominant landmark is **Reginald's Tower**, *The Quay; tel: (051) 73501.* A massive round Norman tower, it was built in 1003 and now houses Waterford's museum, displaying royal charters, records and artefacts. Open 1000–1300, 1400–1700 Mon–Sat. Admission: £0.75.

A 17-minute audio-visual presentation traces the history of glassmaking during a tour of the **Waterford Glass Factory,** *Cork Rd; tel: (051) 73311.* Visitors are guided through production areas where the world-famous crystal is made. Open Mon–Sat 0830–1700 (Apr–Oct). Admission: £2. Viking and Norman artefacts are displayed in the **Waterford Heritage Centre,** *Greyfriars St; tel: (051) 73501.* Open Mon–Fri 1000–1300, 1400–1800, Sat 1000–1300 (Apr–May); Mon–Fri 1000–2000, Sat 1000–1300, 1400–1700 (June–Sept). Admission: £0.75.

- -

 Side Track from Waterford

KILKENNY

Tourist Office: *Kilkenny Tourism, Rose Inn St; tel: (056) 21755.* Open Tues–Sat 0900–1715 (Jan–Mar, Nov–Dec); Mon–Sat 0900–1800 (Apr–Oct), Sun 1000–1700 (May–Sept). The office is in the 16th-century **Shee Almshouse**. Services offered: local and all-Ireland accommodation reservations, bureau de change.

Station: *MacDonough Station, Carlow Rd; tel: (056) 22024* (5-min walk from the city centre). There are four services daily from Waterford to Kilkenny (three on Sun), taking about 45 mins.

Bus Station: The terminal for **Bus Éireann** services is at *MacDonough Station*. The company has an information desk in the tourist office. Kilkenny is at an intersection of national routes.

Getting Around

Local bus services operate from *The Parade*, near the castle. Most attractions can be visited on foot, however.

Staying in Kilkenny

Accommodation

There are a number of hotels and guesthouses within walking distance of the centre. Hotel chains in Kilkenny include *BL, BW, MO.* There is also a wide selection of town and country house accommodation. **Hostel**: *Foulksrath Castle, Jenkinstown, Co Kilkenny; tel: (056) 67674.* Located in a 16th-century castle, this *An Oige* hostel is 8 miles north of Kilkenny, off the N77. Open Mar–Oct. **Buggy's Buses**, *tel: (056) 41264,* has a twice-daily service Mon–Sat from Kilkenny to Jenkinstown. A bus also runs on Sun (July and Aug). **Kilkenny Tourist Hostel**, *35 Parliament St, Kilkenny; tel: (056) 63541,* and **Mrs Murphy's Campsite**, *25 Upper Patrick St; tel: (056) 62973,* are close to the centre.

Eating and Drinking

Kilkenny has a good range of eating places – restaurants, cafés, pubs – especially along *John St, High St* and *Parliament St.* There are pubs galore – **Langton's**, *69 John St; tel: (056) 65133,* ornate inside and out, has won the National Pub of the Year Award and the National Restaurant Award a number of times.

Communications

Post Office: *73 High St.* Open Mon–Sat 0900–1730. Poste restante facilities.

Entertainment

Many pubs provide live entertainment. **John Cleere's Pub**, *Parliament St,* presents traditional Irish and folk music and has a small theatre where dramatic and comedy productions are staged. **The Watergate** is a newly opened theatre on *Parliament St.* Details of events and times are issued by the tourist office, local press and radio. Some hotels have discos. The city's cinema is **The Regent**, *William St.*

Events

The major event in the city calendar is **Kilkenny Arts Week Festival**, a programme of classical music, jazz, folk, art exhibitions and literary readings staged in August.

Shopping

A number of stores sell craftware, crystal and quality souvenirs. The **Kilkenny Design Centre** at *Kilkenny Castle; tel: (056) 22441*, sells a range of craft goods, including ceramics, textiles and jewellery.

Sightseeing

Said to be the finest example of a medieval settlement in Ireland, the city has many interesting streets and narrow lanes, best seen on foot. **Tynan's Walking Tours**, *10 Maple Drive; tel: 63955*. Guided tours of medieval Kilkenny depart from the tourist office daily Mar–Oct. **Cityscope Exhibition**, *Shee Almshouse, Rose Inn St; tel: (056) 51500*. A miniature scale model of 17th-century Kilkenny, with other scaled-down exhibits. Open Tues–Sat 0900–1700; Mon–Sat 0900–1800, Sun 1100–1700 (May–Sept). Admission: £1.

Kilkenny Castle, *The Parade; tel: (056) 21450*. A magnificently restored 12th-century castle set in extensive parkland. Open daily 1030–1700 (Apr–May); daily 1000–1900 (June–Sept); Tues–Sat 1030–1245, 1400–1700, Sun 1100–1700 (Oct–Mar).

Rothe House, *Parliament St; tel: (056) 22893*. This 16th-century merchant's home houses a museum, period costume collection and a genealogical centre. Open Mon–Sat 1030–1700, Sun 1500–1700 (Apr–Oct); Sat–Sun 1500–1700 (Nov–Mar).

St Canice's Cathedral, *Irishtown; tel: (056) 21516*. Completed in 1285, the cathedral has rich timber carvings, marble monuments and colourful glass. Open Mon–Sat 0900–1800, Sun 1400–1800 (Easter–Oct); Mon–Sat 1000–1300, 1400–1600, Sun 1400–1600 (Oct–Apr).

LIMERICK

Tourist Information: the Irish Tourist Board has a well-organised, well-stocked office at *Arthur's Quay*, off *Patrick St; tel: 317522*. Open Mon–Fri 0900–1830, Sat 0930–1730, Sun 1100–1500 (June–Aug); Mon–Fri 0900–1800, Sat 0930–1730, Sun 1100–1500 (May and Sept); Mon–Fri 0930–1730, Sat 0930–1300, 1400–1730 (Oct–Apr). Services offered: local and all-Ireland accommodation reservations, bureau de change.

Airport: Shannon Airport, *tel: (061) 61444*, is 15 miles west of Limerick and is Ireland's gateway for transatlantic flights. It is also served by airlines from the United Kingdom and other parts of Europe. Its comfortable terminal contains an Irish Tourist Board information office, bars, self-service restaurant, shops and banking services, open seven days a week. It has extensive duty-free facilities. The bus service to Limerick operates at irregular intervals: about 23 services on weekdays, but only 10 on Sundays. The trip takes about half an hour. For further information, see Airport Connections on p. 11.

Station: Colbert Station, *Parnell St; tel: (061) 315555*. There are services from Dublin Heuston, Rosslare Harbour, Waterford, Cork and Tralee.

Buses: Bus Éireann services arrive at the bus station adjoining the Railway Station on *Parnell St; tel: (061) 313333* or *319911* (talking timetable).

Getting Around

Limerick has three distinct centres. **Englishtown**, the oldest part, is located on an island in the River Shannon. **Irishtown**, dating from the 13th century, is on the river's west bank. **Newtown Pery**, now the city centre, has the greatest concentration of Georgian streets. Limerick's attractions can easily be toured on foot. Bicycles may be rented in the city.

Staying in Limerick

Accommodation

Limerick has an extensive choice of accommodation. There are about a dozen hotels, ranging from five- to two-star ratings. Guesthouses are rather sparse, but there are plenty of town and country houses offering bed and breakfast. Hotel chains in Limerick include *BL, BW, Ch, HH, Ju, Mn, MO, RH*. The greatest concentration of accommodation – hotels and b. & b.s – is in the *Ennis Rd* area, across Sarsfield Bridge at the north end of *O'Connell St*. **HI**: *An Oige, 1 Pery Sq; tel: (061) 314672*. Located opposite *People's Park*, the hostel is a 5-min walk from the bus and railway stations and the city centre.

Eating and Drinking

Hotels apart, Limerick has little to offer those seeking sophisticated cuisine and, as elsewhere in Ireland, it is wise to eat early, before places close. There are a number of moderately priced cafés and many pubs serving food. The local specialty is home-cured ham and bacon.

Communications

Post Office: *Henry St*. Open Mon–Sat 0900–1730. Poste restante facilities.

Entertainment

Entertainment and events listings can be found in *Night Times*, a free publication available from the tourist office.

Limerick has a lively reputation as a centre for music – contemporary and rock, as well as traditional Irish. As always, pubs and bars are the best places. For traditional music try **Nancy Blague's**, *19 Upper Denmark St; tel: (061) 46327*, and **Foley's Bar**, *Lower Shannon St; tel: (061) 48783*. **Tait's Tavern**, *54 Parnell St; tel: (061) 418133*, is the venue for both traditional music and jazz sessions. The **Royal George Hotel**, *O'Connell St; tel: (061) 414566*, features traditional music in its **Glory Hole Bar** and a disco in **Tropics** at weekends.

Medieval banquets are featured twice-nightly during the summer at **Bunratty Castle**, seven miles west of Limerick on the N18 – the road to Shannon Airport – and at **Knappogue Castle**, about five miles further along the N18. **Bunratty Folk Park**, in the castle grounds, features a nightly *ceili*, with Irish stew and traditional song and dance. *Tel: (061) 360788* for reservations at the three attractions.

Horse racing, Gaelic football, hurling, soccer and rugby are pursued passionately in Limerick. Irish and other drama is produced at the **Belltable Arts Centre**, *69 O'Connel St; tel: (061) 319866*, while international contemporary art is exhibited at the **City Art Gallery**, *Pery Sq; tel: (061) 310633*.

Sightseeing

The third largest city in the Republic, Limerick stands at the head of the Shannon Estuary. It was first settled by Viking raiders in the 9th century, later developing into a fortified port. Only a few fragments of the city walls survived destruction in the 18th century. Today's Limerick is mainly Georgian, with fine, wide streets. It has no connection whatsoever with its poetic namesake.

King John's Castle, *Castle St; tel: 312344*, was built by the Normans in the 13th century. Open daily 1000–1800 (June–Sept). Built as a palace in the 12th century, **St Mary's Church of Ireland Cathedral**, *Bridge St*, has a number of original architectural features. Fifteenth-century misericords bear grotesque carvings in black oak. Aspects of Limerick's history are featured in a *son et lumière* display performed twice nightly June–Sept. Admission: £2.50.

The Roman Catholic **St John's Cathedral**, in Irishtown, is a 19th-century Gothic revival building with the tallest spire (280 ft) in Ireland. The exquisitely worked mitre and crosier of Cornelius O'Dea, a 15th-century bishop of Limerick, are displayed in the presbytery. The **Hunt Museum**, in the grounds of *Limerick University*, *Plassey*, on the outskirts of Limerick, has a fine collection of Celtic and medieval treasures. Open daily 0930–1700 (May–Sept). Admission: £1.50. **Bunratty Castle and Folk Park**; *tel: (061) 361511*. Built in 1277, the restored castle houses a fine collection of furniture and furnishings from the 14th to the 17th centuries. Open daily 0930–1700 (until 1900 June–Aug). Last admission to castle 1615. Admission: £4.50. Buses to Shannon Airport stop at Bunratty.

Knappogue Castle, *Quinn, Co Clare; tel: (061) 368102*, was built in 1467 and has been fully restored. Open daily 0930–1700 (Apr–Oct). Admission: £2.50. **Craggaunowen Historical Project**, six miles south of Quinn, *tel: 72172*, features a reconstructed *crannog*, a Bronze Age lake dwelling. The replica of St Brendan's leather boat, sailed across the Atlantic by Tim Severin, is also on show. Open daily 1000–1800 (May–Sept). Admission £3.50.

DUBLIN to SLIGO

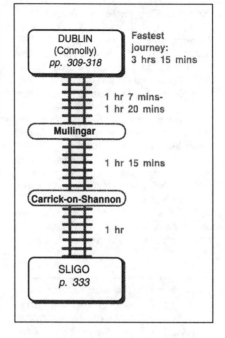

This journey crosses rich farmlands and cattle-rearing country before reaching the River Shannon. From here, the mountains of north-west Ireland come into the frame and the countryside grows more rugged as Sligo nears.

TRAINS

ETT table: 636

 Fast Track

Three trains a day run between Dublin Connolly and Sligo, (four depart Dublin on Fris) taking 3 hrs 10 mins for the journey.

 On Track

Dublin–Mullingar–Carrick-on-Shannon–Sligo

All services between Dublin Connolly and Sligo call at Mullingar and Carrick-on-Shannon. Dublin to Mullingar takes 1 hr 10 mins; Mullingar to Carrick-on-Shannon takes 1 hr 15 mins and Carrick-on-Shannon to Sligo takes 55 mins.

MULLINGAR

Tourist Office: *Midlands-East Tourism, Dublin Rd; tel: (044) 48650.* Open: Mon–Fri 0900–1800, Sat 0900–1300. Information, maps, literature on a wide area as well as Mullingar itself. Local and all-Ireland accommodation reservations; bureau de change.

Station: Mullingar Station; *tel: (044) 48274* (central). There are seven **Bus Éireann** services between Mullingar and Dublin (weekdays), four

on Suns. The nearest Bus Éireann information office is at Athlone; *tel: (0902) 72651.*

Staying in Mullingar

The town has three hotels – two classified as two-star and the other a one-star establishment. Hotel chains include *BW*. There is a wide range of b. & b. establishments but no registered holiday hostels or camping and caravan parks.

Sightseeing

The busy centre of a cattle-raising area, Mullingar is a compact county town. It is dominated by the Roman Catholic **Cathedral of Christ the King**, a Renaissance-style structure completed in 1939. Inside there are mosaics of St Patrick and St Anne by the Russian artist Boris Anrep. Adjoining the cathedral is an **ecclesiastical museum**. Open daily 0900–1730. Admission: free.

The **Market Hall Museum**, *Main St*, is run by volunteers and has an eclectic collection of local artefacts, including weapons and Iron Age implements. Open Mon–Sat 1130–1300, 1400–1700 (May–Sept). Admission: £1. The **Military Museum**, *Columb Barracks; tel: (044) 48391*, houses a collection of weapons from both World Wars and sections featuring the old IRA, with uniforms and weapons from local units. Open Mon–Fri 0900–1630. Admission: free.

Three miles south of Mullingar, on the N52 (no public transport – take a taxi), is **Belvedere House and Gardens**; *tel: (044) 40861*. Built in 1740, the house overlooks Lough Ennel, which is reached by three descending terraces of gardens. The Jealous Wall, Ireland's largest folly, stands in the grounds. Open daily 1200–1800 (Easter–Oct). Admission: £1. (NB Belvedere House is currently under restoration and is closed until 1996; the gardens are open as usual).

CARRICK-ON-SHANNON

Tourist Office: *The Quay; tel: (078) 20170.* Open Mon–Fri 0900–1800, Sat 0900–1300 (May–Sept). Services offered: local and all-Ireland accommodation reservations, bureau de change.

Station: *Station Rd; tel: (078) 20036;* on the Roscommon side of the River Shannon at the junction of the R368 and R370, about half a mile from the town centre.

Buses: Bus Éireann has three services a day in each direction between Carrick-on-Shannon and Dublin. The nearest bus information office is at Longford, *tel: (043) 45208.*

Staying in Carrick-on-Shannon

Accommodation

The county town of Leitrim, Carrick is the leading cruising centre on the River Shannon, so most of its visitors sleep on boats. However, it has a reasonable selection of quality accommodation, including three hotels (two two-star, one three-star), a three-star guesthouse and a good choice of reasonably priced b. & b. accommodation in town houses, country homes and farmhouses.

There are no registered hostels. Free camping is

allowed on the strip of grass beside the river on the Roscommon side of the bridge.

Eating and Drinking

Catering largely for boating holidaymakers, Carrick has plenty of eating places, especially pubs, good provisions stores and delicatessens. If you're shopping to feed yourself, Clancy's Supermarket, on the Roscommon side of the bridge, can meet most demands – and has an especially helpful staff.

Entertainment

It comes down to pubs again, but you won't have to search far to find music, especially traditional Irish.

Sightseeing

Boating apart, Carrick-on-Shannon has one major claim to fame: the second smallest chapel in the world. This is the **Costello Chapel**, *Main St*, erected in 1877 by Edward Costello, a local tycoon, as a memorial for his young wife. The couple are interred in lead coffins, side by side, sunk in the floor and covered by glass.

The Shannon

Longest of the Irish rivers, the Shannon rises in Co. Cavan and flows south for over 200 miles to join the Atlantic past Limerick. On the way it passes through Lough Ree and Lough Derg, embodying a greater area of inland water than any other river in Britain and Ireland. It is naturally a popular highway for boating and cruising, and Carrick-on-Shannon, although a small town, is a major centre for water-borne holidays.

The re-opening of the Ballyconnell Canal in 1995 will connect the Shannon to Lough Erne in Northern Ireland, creating a 500-mile cruising route between the North and the South.

SLIGO

Tourist Office: *Aras Reddan, Temple St; tel: (071) 61201*. Open Mon–Fri 0900–1800, Sat 0900–1300. Services offered: local and all-Ireland accommodation reservations, bureau de change.

Station: *Lord Edward St; tel: (071) 60066*. The station is in the town centre. Sligo is served by three trains a day (four on Fris from Dublin). The Dublin terminal is at Connolly.

Bus Station: **Bus Éireann** services stop at the rail station, *Lord Edward St; tel: (071) 60066*. There are three Expressway services daily in each direction between Sligo and Dublin.

Getting Around

Sligo is the largest and most important town in the Republic's north-west region, and its streets, centred on two bridges across the Garavogue River, are busy, especially in July and Aug. Nevertheless, it's easy to stroll around. The town's chief attractions are its connections with W B Yeats and his brother Jack, the painter.

Staying in Sligo

Accommodation

Sligo's accommodation strength lies in the breadth of its b. & b. choices, many handily located on *Strandhill Rd*, south of the rail station. Hotels in the town range from one to three stars, and the choice is widened slightly if you consider the seaside resort of **Strandhill**, five miles away, and reached by Bus no. 285. Hotel chains include *HH, Mn*.

The only registered holiday hostel in Sligo is **Eden Hill**, *Pearse Rd, Marymount; tel: (071) 44113/43204*. Open Feb to mid-Dec.

here are two campgrounds. **Greenlands Caravan and Camping Park**; *tel: (071) 77113/45618*, is a four-star establishment at Rosses Point, 5 miles north of Sligo – bus no. 286. It has 25 tent pitches and mobile homes for hire. Open Easter weekend and end-May to mid-Sept. **Strandhill Caravan and Camping Park**, off *Airport Rd, Strandhill; tel: (071) 68120*, is three-star and has 40 tent pitches. Open May to mid-Sept.

Eating and Drinking

As befits a busy market town – and tourist centre – Sligo has no shortage of eating places and few will put much of a strain on your pocket. Most pubs serve bar lunches. Sligo's pubs are famous throughout the north west. If you want to do your own catering, there are plenty of food shops and a well-known delicatessen is **Cosgrove's**, *Market Sq*.

Entertainment

The Sligo Champion newspaper is the best source of entertainment information. Many pubs provide entertainment – pop and rock as well as traditional Irish music. The **Leitrim Bar**, *The Mall*, has a good reputation for traditional entertainment. The **Sligo Park Hotel**, *tel: (071) 60291*, and the **Southern Hotel**, *Lord Edward St; tel: (071) 62101* both stage discos, live bands and country and western shows. Amateur and professional productions are presented at the **Hawk's Well Theatre**, *Temple St; tel: (071) 61526*.

Sightseeing

Free walking tours, with students as guides, start from the tourist office at 1100 and 1900 daily in July and Aug.

Works by Jack Yeats and his father John, a well-known portraitist in his day, are displayed in the **Municipal Art Gallery** in the *County Library and Museum, Stephen St; tel: (071) 42212*. Among them are portraits of W B Yeats. The works of other Irish artists are also on show. Yeats memorabilia, such as letters, first editions and the flag in which his coffin was draped, may be seen in the museum. The **Yeats Memorial Building**, near *Douglas Hyde Bridge; tel: (071) 42693*, is the headquarters of the Yeats Society, which stages an annual Yeats Summer School in Aug. Public exhibitions and lectures are staged from time to time.

Drumcliff, where W B Yeats is buried in the Protestant churchyard at the foot of Benbulben mountain, as he wished, is five miles north of Sligo on the N15 (bus nos. 290 and 291).

DUBLIN to WESTPORT

This journey travels right across central Ireland, crossing rich agricultural land and the majestic Shannon. At Athlone the line splits, one section heading northwest to the Georgian elegance of Westport, Co Mayo, the other continuing west to Galway, a vibrant city on a stunning bay.

TRAINS

ETT table: 645

➡ Fast Track

Three trains on weekdays, two on Sun, link Dublin Heuston and Westport with a journey time of between 3 hrs 35 mins and 3 hrs 55 mins.

 ### On Track

Dublin–Athlone

Seven or eight trains on weekdays and five on Sun provide the service between Dublin Heuston and Athlone, with journey times of between 1 hr 24 mins and 1 hr 50 mins.

Athlone–Roscommon–Westport

Three trains on weekdays and two on Sun run from Athlone to Westport. Athlone to Roscommon takes about 30 mins, Roscommon to Westport takes about 1 hr 30 mins.

Note: Manulla Junction is shown on the diagram opposite simply as a starting point for trains to Ballina. See note on p. 336.

ATHLONE

Tourist Office: *The Castle, Market Sq; tel: (0902) 94630.* Open Mon–Fri 0900–1800, Sat

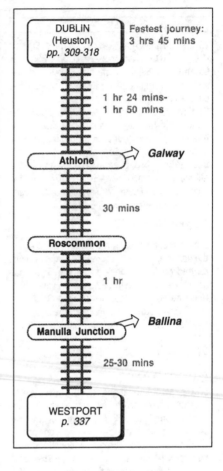

0900–1300 (Apr–Nov). Services offered: local and all-Ireland accommodation reservations; bureau de change.
Station: *Southern Station Rd; tel: (0902) 73311.* The station is an easy 10-min walk from the town centre.
Buses: the stop for **Bus Éireann** services from Dublin (eight a day) is at the railway station on *Southern Station Rd; tel: (0902) 72651.*

Getting Around

With a number of light industries, the town is a marketing and distribution centre. It spills over both banks of the River Shannon, but is nonetheless compact enough to be explored on foot.

Staying in Athlone

Accommodation

Athlone has half a dozen hotels classified from one to three stars and an abundance of b. & b. accommodation, mostly on the Co Westmeath side of the river. Hotel chains include *HH, MO.*

There are no youth hostel or holiday hostel facilities in the Athlone area, but there are two camping and caravan parks in good locations within three miles of the town. **Hodson Bay Caravan and Camping Park**, *Yew Point, Hodson Bay, Kiltoom, Co Roscommon; tel: (0902) 92448*, is on a 100-acre farm on the shores of Lough Ree. It carries a four-star rating, has 15 tent pitches and is open May–Sept. **Lough Ree Caravan and Camping Park** is in *Ballykeeran, Co Westmeath; tel: (0902) 78561.* It has a two-star rating and 30 tent pitches. Open: Apr–Sept.

Eating and Drinking

There are a few reasonably priced eating places, but pubs offer the best choice, some with the bonus of traditional Irish music in the evening.

Communications

Post Office: *Pearse St.* Open Mon–Sat 0900–1730. Poste restante facilities.

Sightseeing

A busy road and rail junction, and a port on the River Shannon, Athlone stands more or less at the geographical heart of Ireland on the border between the provinces of Leinster and Connacht and straddling counties Westmeath and Roscommon. Its greatest attraction is the River Shannon, providing access to Lough Ree upstream and to Clonmacnois near Shannonbridge downstream. Boat trips leave daily in both directions from *The Strand.* MV Avonree, *tel: (0902) 92513,* operates to Lough Ree July–Sept. Fare: £3.50. MV Ross, *Jolly Mariner Marina: tel: (0902) 72892,* operates daily year-round to Shannonbridge. Fare: £3.50.

Athlone Castle, *Market Sq; tel: (0902)* *94630/92912.* Built in the 13th century to command an important Shannon crossing, the castle now contains a museum, tea shop and tourist office. There are audio-visual presentations on the flora, fauna and power resources of the River Shannon and the 1691 siege that followed the Battle of the Boyne. Another presentation features the career of Count John McCormack, the celebrated tenor who was born in Athlone. Open Mon–Sat 1100–1630, Sun 1200–1630 (June–Sept).

Clonmacnois, *Shannonbridge, Co Offaly; tel: (0905) 74195* is a monastic settlement founded in AD 545 by St Ciaran. One of Ireland's most sacred sites and a burial place for the kings of Connacht and Tara, it contains two round towers, the remains of a cathedral, ruined churches, a 13th-century castle, high crosses and more than 200 grave slabs. Open daily 0900–1900 (mid-June to Sept); daily 1000–1800 (Oct–May). Admission: £1.50. **Clonmacnois and West Offaly Railway**, *Blackwater Works, Shannonbridge; tel: (0905) 74114.* A guided tour of the extensive Blackwater Peat Bog aboard a quaint light-railway train gives visitors an insight into the bog's development over a period of 12,000 years. Open daily 1000–1700 (Easter–Sept). Admission: £3.

Side Tracks from Athlone

GALWAY

Tourist Offices: *Aras Failte, Victoria Pl, Eyre Sq; tel: (091) 63081.* Open Mon–Fri 0900–1745, Sat 0900–1245; Mon–Sat 0900–1745 (May–June, Sept); daily 0900–1845 (July–Aug). Services: computerised information and accommodation reservations; bureau de change. **Tourist Information Office**, *Salthill; tel: (091) 63081.* Open daily 0900–2030 (end May–mid-Sept); Mon–Sat 0900–1745 (June and Sept). Services offered: local and all-Ireland accommodation reservations, bureau de change.

Station: *Ceannt Station, Eyre Sq; tel: (091) 64222.* The station is right in the heart of the city. There are four trains daily from Athlone taking 1 hr 10 mins.

Buses: the main terminal for **Bus Éireann** national and local bus services is beside the railway station in *Eyre Sq; tel: (091) 62000.* There are 9 bus services on weekdays, 7 on Suns from Athlone to Galway, taking 1 hr 30 mins.

Getting Around

Galway is the largest city in the west of Ireland, but most of its sights and attractions can be seen in a comfortable two-hour stroll.

Staying in Galway

Accommodation

Galway and its seaside resort suburb Salthill present a wide range of accommodation. The most expensive hotels are in the city centre, with the widest choice of lodgings in *Salthill.*

Hotel chains include *BW, GS, Ju, RH.* The city's grandest hotel is the **Galway Great Southern**, *Eyre Sq; tel: (091) 64041,* which opened when the railway arrived in 1845. Sharing its central position, the **Skeffington Arms**, *28 Eyre Sq; tel: (091) 63173,* is a favourite with budget-minded travellers. **HI:** *Galway International Youth Hostel, St Mary's College, St Mary's Road; tel: (091) 27411.* This temporary hostel (open July-Aug) is on the west side of the River Corrib, a 20-min walk from Eyre Sq. Year-round hostels are **Galway City Hostel**, *25–27 Dominick St; tel: (091) 66367;* **Grand Holiday Hostel**, *The Promenade, Salthill* (buses for *Salthill* depart from *Eyre Sq*); tel: (091) 21150; **Stella Maris Holiday Hostel**, *151 Upper Salthill; tel: (091) 26974.* **Ballyloughane Caravan and Camping Park**, *tel: (091) 75209,* is three miles from the city centre, on the edge of Galway Bay, just off the N6. Open May–Sept.

Communications

Post Office: *Eglinton St.* Open Mon–Sat 0900–1730. Poste restante, bureau de change.

Entertainment

Events are listed in the free publication, *The Word.* Pubs are alive with the sound of music – jazz, rock, country and western, as well as traditional Irish. Discos flourish. New Irish works are included in productions by the **Druid**

Theatre Company, *Chapel Lane, Shop St; tel: (091) 68617.* Dance, drama, music and visual arts exhibitions are staged at the **Galway Arts Centre**, *Nun's Island; tel: (091) 65886.* The city's best-known events are its **Arts Festival** and **Galway Races**, both held in July, and the **Galway Oyster Festival** in Sept.

Shopping

Galway's shops abound with craft goods, tweeds and Aran knitwear, but a popular souvenir is the Claddagh ring depicting two clasped hands and a heart.

Sightseeing

Walking tours of the city may be arranged through the tourist office in *Eyre Sq,* where you can also make reservations to join a cruise into Lough Corrib. **Corrib Tours**, *tel: (091) 68903,* operates daily at 1430 and 1630 (Apr–Oct). Fare: £5. **Nora Barnacle House Museum**, *Bowling Green; tel: (091) 64743.* The former home of James Joyce's wife features the couple's Galway connections. Open Mon–Sat 1000–1700 (May–Sept). Admission: £1. The **Collegiate Church of St Nicholas**, *Lombard St,* was built by the Anglo-Normans in 1320 and enlarged in the 15th and 16th centuries. It contains many fine medieval carvings and relics.

_ _ _ _ _ _ _ _ _ _ _ _ _ _ _ _ _ _ _ _

 Side Track from Roscommon

BALLINA

Tourist Office: *Cathedral Rd; tel: (096) 70848.* Open Mon–Sat 1000–1800 (May–Sept). Services offered: local and all-Ireland accommodation reservations, bureau de change.

Station: *Station Road; tel: (096) 71618.* The station is ¼ mile from the town. Three trains on weekdays, 2 on Suns run from Roscommon to Manulla Junction (see note below) where passengers must change onto a branch line train for Ballina. Total journey time is around 1 hr 30 mins. *Note:* Manulla Junction is not accessible by road and is only of use to passengers changing trains (there are no public facilities there whatsoever).

Bus Station: three (four on Suns) **Bus Éireann** services run between Dublin and Ballina, which is also served by provincial buses.

Staying in Ballina

The largest town in Co Mayo, Ballina has a reasonable selection of accommodation, including four hotels. There is a wide range of b.&b.s. **HI**: The nearest *An Oige* hostel is at Killala, *tel: (096) 32172*, eight miles north of Ballina on R314. Open Easter–Sept. **Belleek Caravan and Camping Park**, *tel: (096) 71533*, is a four-star establishment 300 yards from the R314, less than two miles north of *Ballina*. Open Mar–Oct.

Shopping

Shoppers will find knitwear, tweeds and other craft goods, but Ballina is also a good centre for antiques.

Entertainment

Ballina has a cinema and traditional entertainment in a number of pubs. The **Downhill Hotel** *tel: (096) 21033*, is noted for music.

Sightseeing

Standing on the River Moy, the cathedral town of Ballina is a noted centre for salmon and trout fishing. Largely modern, it still shows some of the planned elegance from its founding by Lord Tyrawley in 1730. There is a pleasant walk beside the river in which salmon trawling takes place. Near the railway station is the **Dolmen of the Four Maols**, said to mark the grave of four foster-brothers who murdered a bishop in the 6th century and were themselves killed by his brother. Ballina marks the start of the **North Mayo Sculpture Trail**, where works by leading sculptors from eight countries and three continents are located in wild and beautiful countryside. Information from *Moy Valley Resource Centre, Ballina; tel: (096) 70905*.

- -

WESTPORT

Tourist Office: *The Mall; tel: (098) 25711*. Open Mon–Fri 0900–1800, Sat 0900–1300.

Services offered: computerised information and accommodation reservations (local and all-Ireland); bureau de change. **Station**: *Altamount St; tel: (098) 25263*. The station is a 15-min walk from the town centre. **Bus Station**: there are three **Bus Éireann** services on weekdays, one on Sun, in each direction between Westport and Dublin and the town is also served by provincial buses.

Staying in Westport

There is a wide choice of accommodation in Westport – half a dozen two- and three-star hotels, a couple of guesthouses and many b.&b.s. Hotel chains include *HH*. **IYHA**: *Club Atlantic, Altamount St; tel: (098) 26644*. This *An Oige* hostel is located opposite the railway station and is close to the town centre. Open Mar–Oct. **The Old Mill Holiday Hostel**, *James St; tel: (098) 27045* is open year-round. **Parkland Caravan and Camping Park**, *tel: (098) 25141*, is two miles from Westport on the Westport House estate. Open mid-May to mid-Sept.

Entertainment

There is no shortage of entertainment in Westport, especially from mid-July, which sees the start of the **Westport Street Festival**, and end-Sept, when the end of summer is marked by the town's **Arts Festival**. The best music pubs and restaurants are to be found around *The Quay* and along *Bridge St* where Matt Molloy of The Chieftains has his bar. The **Wyatt Theatre** in the Town Hall features Irish drama. There are excellent beaches in the area and an 18-hole championship golf course.

Sightseeing

Superbly located on Clew Bay, Westport is a most attractive Georgian town with an unusual octagonal centre. The chief attraction is **Westport House**, *The Quay; tel: (098) 25430*, built in 1788 for the Marquess of Sligo. Open Mon–Sat 1400–1700 (mid- to end-May, end-Aug to mid-Sept); Mon–Sat 1400–1800 (June); Mon–Sat 1030–1800 (July–Aug); Sun 1400–1800 (mid-May to mid-Sept). Admission: £4.50.

BUS ROUTES
in
IRELAND

There are large areas in both Northern Ireland and Eire without rail services. The best way to travel in these regions is by the respective national long-distance bus companies: Ulsterbus 'Goldline' and Bus Éireann 'Expressway'. A selection of routes that complement the rail network is given below – a change of bus may sometimes be necessary (ask the driver).

From . . . To	Frequency of Journeys	Average Journey Time	Operating Company
BELFAST	(tel: (01232) 333000)		
Armagh	7–11 (2–4 on Suns)	1 hour 15 mins	Ulsterbus
Ballina	1 Mons to Sats	5 hours 30 mins	Ulsterbus
Enniskillen	9–11 (7 on Suns)	2 hours 30 mins	Ulsterbus
Galway	2 (3 on Fris, 1 on Suns)	6 hours 45 mins	Ulsterbus/Bus Éireann
Sligo	1 Mons to Sats	3 hours 45 mins	Ulsterbus
Westport	1 Mons to Sats	6 hours 30 mins	Ulsterbus
LONDONDERRY (tel: 01504 262261)			
Dublin	4 (2 on Suns)	4 hours 20 mins	Ulsterbus/Bus Éireann
Letterkenny	3 (2 on Suns)	45 mins	Ulsterbus
Omagh	4 (2 on Suns)	1 hour	Ulsterbus/Bus Éireann
Monaghan	4 (2 on Suns)	2 hours	Ulsterbus/Bus Éireann
DUBLIN (tel: (01) 836 6111 or (01) 703 2433)			
Armagh	4 (3 on Suns)	2 hours 45 mins	Bus Éireann
Cahir	3 (2 on Suns)	3 hours 5 mins	Bus Éireann
Carrick-on-Suir	3 (4 on Fris and Suns)	2 hours 50 mins	Bus Éireann
Clonmel	3 (4 on Fris and Suns)	3 hours 15 mins	Bus Éireann
Donegal	4 (5 on Fris, 3 on Suns)	4 hours 15 mins	Bus Éireann
Ennis	6 (4 on Suns)	4 hours 20 mins	Bus Éireann
Enniskillen	4 (5 on Fris, 3 on Suns)	3 hours 5 mins	Bus Éireann
Letterkenny	4 (5 on Fris, 3 on Suns)	4 hours 5 mins	Bus Éireann
Monaghan	7 (9 Fris, 7 Sats, Suns)	2 hours	Bus Éireann
Omagh	4 (5 on Fris, 3 on Suns)	3 hours 5 mins	Bus Éireann
Shannon Airport	6 (4 on Suns)	4 hours 30 mins	Bus Éireann

CROSS-COUNTRY SERVICES   For journey times and frequencies tel:
Cork: *(021) 508188*; Galway: *(091) 62000*; Limerick: *(061) 313333*; Sligo: *(071) 60066*; Tralee: *(066) 23566*; Waterford: *(051) 79000*; Killarney: *(064) 34777*; Ennis: *(065) 24177*.

Tralee–Killarney–Cork–Waterford–Wexford–Rosslare. Galway–Limerick–Tralee–Killarney.
Westport–Galway–Ennis–Limerick–Mallow–Cork.
Londonderry–Letterkenny–Donegal–Sligo–Knock–Galway–Limerick–Mallow–Cork.
Kilkenny–Carrick-on-Suir–Clonmel–Cahir–Cork.
Limerick–Tipperary–Cahir–Waterford.

PRIVATE RAILWAYS

Britain is rich in privately operated railways, run by enthusiasts to preserve some of the romance of the steam age. The following is a selection; many others are mentioned in the main text of this book. Always check opening times by phone; most open every weekend in summer, and the more popular ones may run daily.

North Yorkshire Moors Railway

Tel: (01751) 472508
Possibly the best of all such lines in Britain, access is by British Rail from Darlington and Middlesbrough along the lovely Esk Valley line towards Whitby. Alight at Grosmont, where BR and the NYMR share stations. The heavy gradients and sheer popularity of this line in summer mean big steam engines working very hard in both directions (the steepest climb though is from Grosmont to the delightful little village of Goathland). At the southern end, Pickering is a touristy, busy town well worth a visit.

West Somerset Railway

Tel: Minehead (01643) 704996
Running from the small station of Bishops Lydeard (limited Saturday bus link from Taunton 5 miles/20 mins away) across the Quantock Hills to the sea at the holiday resort of Minehead, this line (at 20 miles the longest of its kind in the UK) offers both moorland and coastal scenery. Journey time is 80 mins each way.

Severn Valley Railway

Tel: (01299) 403816
A well-run railway, it is close to Birmingham and much of the West Midlands. It runs from Kidderminster (BR station adjacent) to Bridgnorth along the valley of the River Severn, from which it takes its name. Glimpses of the river, and the pleasant countryside around the line make a nice day out. Bridgnorth town itself is worth a look round.

Keighley and Worth Valley Railway

Tel: (01535) 645214
A steeply graded railway running directly from the British Rail station at Keighley up the Worth Valley through Oakworth (where the film *The Railway Children* was largely filmed), Haworth (close to the parsonage where the Brontë sisters lived - frequent bus link on summer Sundays) to Oxenhope. The valley is rich in plant and wildlife and the 25-min ride is very pleasant indeed. Country walks between Oakworth, Haworth and Oxenhope can make up a full day's outing.

Paignton and Dartmouth Steam Railway

Tel: (01803) 555872
Starting from a major West Country seaside resort, this railway can hardly fail to be popular. Seven miles long, it runs along the Torbay Coast, almost on the beach, before turning inland to Churston and over the hill to Kingswear. Take the ferry across the River Dart to the town of Dartmouth.

Ravenglass and Eskdale Railway

Tel: (01229) 717171
The 'Ratty' is a 15-inch narrow-gauge railway in the north of England, running through the beautiful rugged, upland country of Cumbria for 7 miles between Ravenglass and Dalegarth (Eskdale). In summer, some trains convey passengers in open wagons! Dalegarth is the starting point for walks to the nearby village of Boot, Dalegarth waterfalls and mountain climbing on Scafell. Access is from Lancaster, by taking a Carlisle-bound stopping train via Barrow-in-Furness to Ravenglass.

Snowdon Mountain Railway

Tel: (01286) 870223
Britain's only true mountain railway climbs steeply up Snowdon's 3560-ft side, almost reaching the summit. Most trains are steam operated – high maintenance costs make the

trip necessarily expensive but the stunning views from the top across the Snowdonia National Park make it all worthwhile. Go only on a clear day though, and go very early, as long queues can quickly build up after breakfast time. Take a packed meal and beat the rush! It is very nice to ride up and walk down, but be aware that the weather can change dramatically in a short space of time.

Isle of Wight Steam Railway

Tel: (01983) 882204
A lovely little line with plenty of 1930s atmosphere: 100-year-old small tank locomotives haul ancient coaches from Smallbrook Junction (on the 'main' line from Ryde to Shanklin), through Havenstreet to Wootton, 3 miles from Newport – long-term proposals exist to bring the railway here, where there is much more for the tourist to do, and also to extend it to the port of Ryde.

Ffestiniog Railway

Tel: (01766) 512340
A 13½-mile narrow-gauge line, traversing the Snowdonia National Park, the line starts in Porthmadog and runs along along the sea wall before turning inland. The train, clinging defiantly to the mountainside, curves sharply past lakes and waterfalls and through heavily wooded countryside for about an hour to the slate-quarrying town of Blaenau Ffestiniog, where you can visit the highly recommended Llechwedd Slate Caverns. Don't come if it is wet, for the scenery must not be missed and Blaenau in the rain is perhaps the most depressingly drab place in all Wales. To reach this railway, take the BR Cambrian Coast service to Porthmadog or the Conwy Valley line to Blaenau Ffestiniog – both offer varying and dramatic scenery for arriving visitors.

Talyllyn Railway

Tel: (01654) 710472
Opened in 1865 to serve slate quarries, this line was saved in 1951, making it the first to be so treated. A delightful amble from Tywyn Wharf (close to the BR station) through the hedgerows is followed by a climb up the forested mountainside to Dolgoch (break your trip here to visit the waterfalls – allow 2 hours) before continuing to Abergynolwyn. The line continues a short way to Nant Gwernol, where well-signed footpaths penetrate the surrounding area.

Bluebell Railway

Tel: (01825) 723777
The railway, which gets its name from the early spring displays of flowers in the woods, is accessed by bus to Sheffield Park from the nearby railhead at Haywards Heath. The line runs through fields and woods via Horsted Keynes station, a mile from its village, to its terminus at Kingscote. Extension to East Grinstead is a long-term project. An early preservation scheme, this line secured ex-Southern Railway engines, many of which are now unique. Sheffield Park Gardens display excellent collections of plants and trees from around the world.

Kent and East Sussex Railway

Tel: (01580) 765155
Built cheaply by the eccentric railway entrepreneur Colonel Holman Stephens around 1896, this line retains much of its charm: twisting single track through the lovely East Sussex countryside, steep climbs, small trains and delightful country stations. Closed between 1954 and 1973, it has been rebuilt from Tenterden to Northiam (7 miles) and it is aiming for Robertsbridge (13½ miles). Bus services link Tenterden, where there is also a collection of historic vehicles, to Ashford.

Isle of Man

Tel: (01624) 663366
On this island, 4 hours from mainland UK, and well worth a week of the traveller's time, can be found the spectacular beauty of the 18-mile Isle of Man tramway from Douglas through Laxey to Ramsey, the steeply climbing Snaefell Mountain Railway from Laxey, and the quaint Steam Railway, leaving Douglas southwards to Castletown and the quiet fishing village of Port Erin. See also the tiny Groudle Glen Railway: narrow gauge, and running from the wooded glen of its title to the wild headland overlooking the sea.

SPECIAL TRAINS

Several luxury trains operating across the UK have been a success in recent years and details of the train operators appear below. British Rail privatisation at time of going to press means that some of the information given may be subject to change: check with the operator or a specialist rail travel agent.

Venice Simplon-Orient-Express

Operator: **VSOE Ltd**, *Sea Containers House, 20 Upper Ground, London SE1 9PF. Tel: (0171) 620 0003. Fax: (0171) 620 1210.*

The company that resurrected the legendary service across Europe also runs day excursions throughout England, in 1920s and 30s carriages restored to their former glory.

Day excursions for 1995 include Canterbury, Bath, Salisbury, Bristol, Cambridge, Ely, Sandringham, Warwick Castle, Chatsworth House (home of the Duke of Devonshire). Weekend trips are run to Chester and Stratford-upon-Avon. Have a day at the races – Royal Ascot or The Grand National – travelling in style.

The Royal Scotsman

Operator: **Great Scottish and Western Railway Co. Ltd.**, *46a Constitution St, Edinburgh EH6 6RS. Tel: (0131) 555 1344. Fax: (0131) 555 1345*

Three-, five- and seven-day excursions in Scotland are a speciality of this service – passengers liken their trip to a stay as guests at a select country house.

A typical seven-day itinerary might travel from London to Henley-in-Arden for Charlecote House, on to Keighley for Harewood House, across the wilds of the Settle–Carlisle (see p. 294) and the Scottish Highland lines to Mallaig, Boat of Garten, Ballindalloch and back to Edinburgh. The train stops at the end of each day to ensure a good night's sleep.

The Queen of Scots

Operator: **Scottish Highland Railway Co. Ltd.**, *Mills Road, Aylesford, Maidstone, Kent ME20 7NW. Tel: (01622) 716734, fax: (01622) 719140.*

This train has no specific schedule: it is a charter service tailored fully to the requirements of the customer. The Queen of Scots train offers travellers the comfort and period style of a bygone age. The observation car, built in 1891, contains a spacious panelled sitting room with large observation windows. The dining car was transported to France during the World War I for use as part of the private train and mobile HQ for the Commander-in-Chief, Field Marshal Earl Haig. It was built in 1890, making it the oldest dining car in the world. Gourmet cuisine to rival the finest restaurants, hand-cut crystal lighting and luxurious upholstery combine to make an unforgettable journey.

Premier Land Cruises

Operator: **Waterman Railways**, *P O Box 4472, Lichfield, Staffordshire WS13 6RU. Tel: (01543) 419472. Fax: (01543) 250817.* Note: this address/phone number will change in 1995.

Premier Land Cruises are long weekend trips in first-class Pullman coaches with overnight stays in quality hotels. Each passenger is guaranteed a window seat to ensure enjoyment of the scenery. Off-train visits are usually included in the price. Premier Days Out offer a variety of day trips across England and Wales, with seat reservations in First Class coaches, an at seat meal service, transfer to and from points of interest at tour destinations and, in Club Plus class, a guaranteed window seat at tables for two persons. In 1995 there will be regular steam trains from Bristol to Exeter, Torquay and Paignton.

Other Operators

Hertfordshire Railtours, *28 Chestnut Walk, Welwyn Garden City, Hertfordshire, AL6 0SD. Tel: (01438) 715050. Fax: (01438) 714502*

Pathfinder Tours, *Stag House, Gydynap House, Inchbrook, Woodchester, Gloucestershire. GL5 5EZ. Tel (and Fax): (01453) 835414.*

CONVERSION TABLES

INCHES AND CENTIMETRES

Unit	Inches	Feet	Yards
1mm	0.039	0.003	0.001
1cm	0.39	0.03	0.01
1metre	39.40	3.28	1.09

Unit	mm	cm	metres
1 inch	25.4	2.54	0.025
1 foot	304.8	30.48	0.304
1 yard	914.4	91.44	0.914

To convert cms to inches, multiply by 0.3937
To convert inches to cms, multiply by 2.54

24 HOUR CLOCK

Midnight = 0000   12 noon = 1200   6 pm = 1800
6 am = 0600   1 pm = 1300   Midnight = 2400

WEIGHT

Unit	Kg	Pounds
1	0.45	2.205
2	0.90	4.405
3	1.35	6.614
4	1.80	8.818
5	2.25	11.023
10	4.50	22.045
15	6.75	33.068
20	9.00	44.889
25	11.25	55.113
50	22.50	110.225
75	33.75	165.338
100	45.00	220.450

1 kg = 1000 g
100 g = 3.5 oz
1 oz = 28.35 g
1 lb = 453.60 g

FLUID MEASURES

Litres	Imp. gal.	US gal.
5	1.1	1.3
10	2.2	2.6
15	3.3	3.9
20	4.4	5.2
25	5.5	6.5
30	6.6	7.8
35	7.7	9.1
40	8.8	10.4
45	9.9	11.7
50	11.0	13.0

1 litre (l) = 0.88 imp.quarts
1 litre (l) = 1.06 US quarts
1 imp. quart = 1.14 l
1 imp. gallon = 4.55 l
1 US quart = 0.95 l
1 US gallon = 3.81 l

DISTANCE

km	miles	km	miles
1	0.62	30	21.75
2	1.24	40	24.85
3	1.86	45	27.96
4	2.49	50	31.07
5	3.11	55	34.18
6	3.73	60	37.28
7	4.35	65	40.39
8	4.97	70	43.50
9	5.59	75	46.60
10	6.21	80	49.71
15	9.32	90	55.92
20	12.43	100	62.14
25	15.53	125	77.67

1 km = 0.6214 miles
1 mile = 1.609 km

METRES AND FEET

Unit	Metres	Feet
1	0.30	3.281
2	0.61	6.563
3	0.91	9.843
4	1.22	13.124
5	1.52	16.403
6	1.83	19.686
7	2.13	22.967
8	2.44	26.248
9	2.74	29.529
10	3.05	32.810
14	4.27	45.934
18	5.49	59.058
20	6.10	65.520
50	15.24	164.046
75	22.86	246.069
100	30.48	328.092

LADIES' SHOES

UK	Europe	USA
3	36	4.5
4	37	5.5
5	38	6.5
6	39	7.5
7	40	8.5
8	41	9.5

MEN'S SHOES

UK	Europe	USA
6	40	7
7	41	8
8	42	9
9	43	10
10	44	11
11	45	12

LADIES' CLOTHES

UK	France	Italy	Rest of Europe	USA
10	36	38	34	8
12	38	40	36	10
14	40	42	38	12
16	42	44	40	14
18	44	46	42	16
20	46	48	44	18

MEN'S CLOTHES

UK	Europe	USA
36	46	36
38	48	38
40	50	40
42	52	42
44	54	44
46	56	46

MEN'S SHIRTS

UK	Europe	USA
14	36	14
15	38	15
15.5	39	15.5
16	41	16
16.5	42	16.5
17	43	17

TEMPERATURE

°C	°F	°C	°F
-20	-4	10	50
-15	5	15	59
-10	14	20	68
-5	23	25	77
0	32	30	86
5	41	35	95

Conversion Formula
°C x 9 ÷ 5 + 32 = °F
1 Deg. °C = 1.8 Deg. °F
1 Deg. °F = 0.55 Deg. °C

Advertisement

READER SURVEY
Fill in this form and you can win a full-colour guidebook!

If you enjoyed using this book – or if you didn't – please help us to improve future editions, by taking part in our reader survey. Every returned form will be acknowledged, and to show our appreciation for your help we will give you the chance to win a *Thomas Cook Travellers* illustrated guidebook for your travel bookshelf. Just take a few minutes to complete and return this form to us.

When did you buy this book?

Where did you buy it? (Please give town/city and if possible name of retailer)

Did you/do you intend to travel in Britain and Ireland by train in 1995/96?
☐ Have travelled ☐ Will travel 1995 ☐ Will travel 1996

If so, which cities, towns, villages, national parks and other places did you/do you intend to visit?

When did you/do you intend to travel?

For how long (approx.)?

Did you/will you travel on:
☐ point-to-point ticket
☐ Rail Pass (please give name of pass and where you bought it from)

Did you/do you intend to use this book:
☐ For planning your trip? ☐ During the trip itself? ☐ Both?

Did you/do you intend to also purchase any of the following travel publications for your trip?
☐ Thomas Cook European Timetable
☐ Thomas Cook Rail Timetable of Britain, France and Benelux
☐ Thomas Cook Rail Map of Great Britain & Ireland
☐ Other guidebooks/maps. Please specify:

Please rate the following features of On the Rails around Great Britain & Ireland for their value to you (Circle the 1 for 'little or no use,' 2 for 'useful,' 3 for 'very useful'):

Feature	little or no use	useful	very useful
The themed itineraries on pages 36–40	1	2	3
The 'Travel Essentials' section on pages 16–27	1	2	3
The 'Travelling by Train' section on pages 28–35	1	2	3
Information on rail routes and trains	1	2	3
The rail route diagrams	1	2	3
Information on towns, cities, national parks, etc	1	2	3
The city maps	1	2	3
The colour planning map	1	2	3

READER SURVEY

Please use this space to tell us about any features that in your opinion could be changed, improved, or added in future editions of the book, or any other comments you would like to make concerning the book:

Your age category:
☐ Under 30 ☐ 30–50 ☐ over 50

Your name: Mr/Mrs/Ms (First name or initials)
(Last name)

Your full address (please include postal code or zip code):

Your daytime telephone number:

Please detach this page and send it to: The Project Editor, On the Rails around Britain and Ireland, Thomas Cook Publishing, PO Box 227, Peterborough PE3 8BQ, United Kingdom.

North American readers: Please mail replies to: E. Taylor, On the Rails around Britain & Ireland, Passport Books, 4255 West Touhy Avenue, Lincolnwood (Chicago), Illinois 60646-1975, USA.

Ten guidebooks to be won!

*All surveys returned to us before the closing date of 31 October 1995 will be entered for a prize draw on that date. The senders of the first **ten** replies drawn will each be invited to make their personal selection of any book from the Thomas Cook Travellers* range of guidebooks, to be sent to them free of charge. With 36 cities and countries to choose from, this new, full colour series of guides covers the major tourist destinations of the world. Each book, retail price £7.99/$14.95*, offers 192 pages of sightseeing, background information, and travel tips.*

*North American readers please note: in the United States this range is published by Passport Books under the name "Passport's Illustrated Guides from Thomas Cook". North American winners will receive the US edition of their selected book.

Prizewinners will be notified as soon as possible after the closing date and asked to select from the list of titles. Offer is subject to availability of titles at 1 November 1995. A list of winners will be available on receipt of a stamped self-addressed envelope.

INDEX

This index lists place names and topics in one alphabetical sequence. All references are to page numbers. **Bold** *numbers refer to map pages. To find routes between cities, see pp 8–9.*

KEY TO SYMBOLS
ROUTE DIAGRAMS

CITY BEGINNING OR ENDING ROUTE
(Name of station where necessary)
Page reference to description of city

Fastest train time between start and end of route

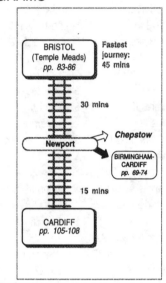

Side-trip destination   Side-trip opportunity (not necessarily by rail) mentioned in route description

Town or city on the route
(NB not all trains will necessarily stop at every city shown: check route description and timetables)

CONNECTING ROUTE
Page reference to route   Connection in this city with another route in the book

Fastest journey time between each pair of cities

CITY MAPS

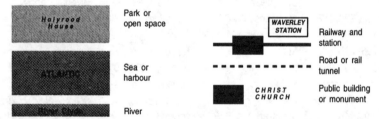

Park or open space

Sea or harbour

River

Railway and station

Road or rail tunnel

Public building or monument

COLOUR MAPS

Black lines show railways.
Red lines show high speed lines.
Lines on a ***green*** background are scenic.
Purple lines show selected bus routes.

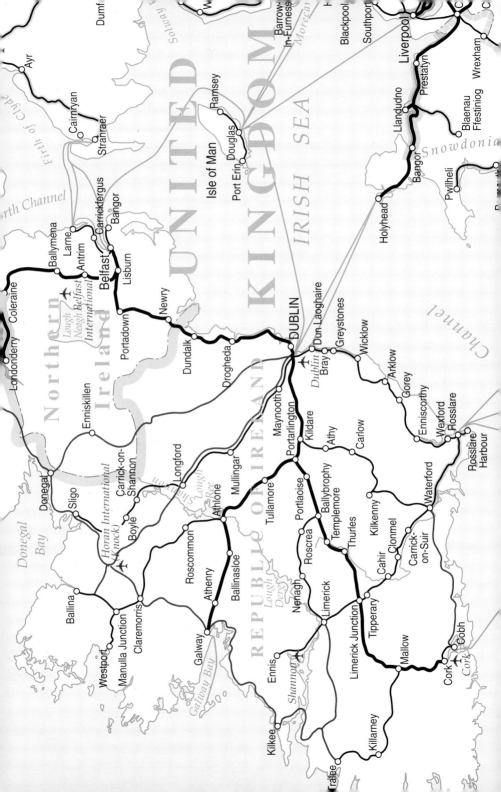

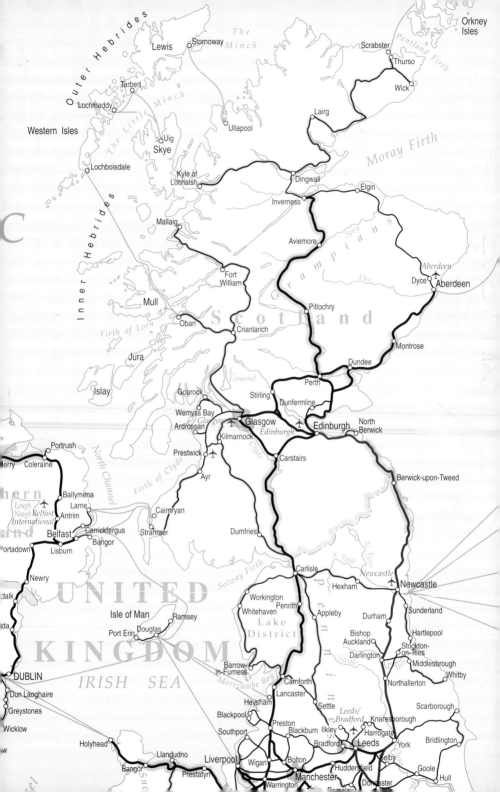

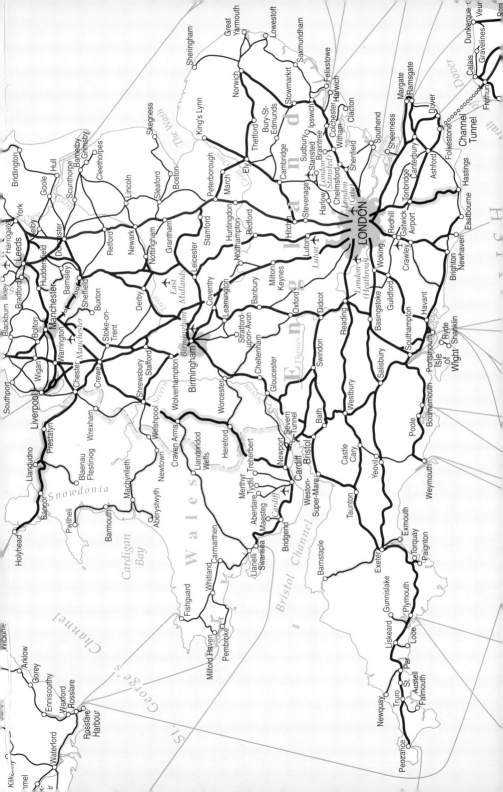

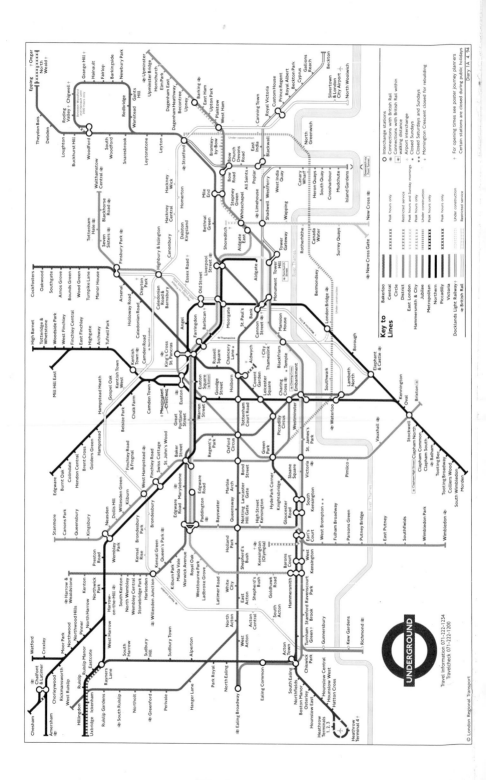